Measuring Global Values

MEASURING GLOBAL VALUES

The Ranking of 162 Countries

Michael J. Sullivan III

Greenwood Press
New York • Westport, Connecticut • London

Library of Congress Cataloging-in-Publication Data

Sullivan, Michael J.
   Measuring global values : the ranking of 162 countries / Michael
J. Sullivan III.
     p.   cm.
   Includes bibliographical references and index.
   ISBN 0-313-27649-8 (alk. paper)
   1. Social indicators. 2. Economic indicators. I. Title.
HN25.S85 1991
301'.072—dc20   90-25209

British Library Cataloguing in Publication Data is available.

Library of Congress Catalog Card Number: 90-25209
ISBN: 0-313-27649-8

First published in 1991

Greenwood Press, 88 Post Road West, Westport, CT 06881
An imprint of Greenwood Publishing Group, Inc.

Printed in the United States of America

The paper used in this book complies with the
Permanent Paper Standard issued by the National
Information Standards Organization (Z39.48-1984).

10 9 8 7 6 5 4 3 2 1

To Marianna

Contents

Illustrations

Preface

Measuring Global Values is the product of eight years' research completed under grants from Drexel University, the World Policy Institute, and the Pew Foundation Glenmede Trust Program for the Implementation of Microcomputer Technology in College Curricula.

The work employs various data-based management software systems to compare 162 countries with respect to more than 100 indicators measuring each of five global values: peace, economic well-being, ecological balance, social justice, and political participation. As such it should be of interest to students in several fields, most notably and respectively world politics, international political economy, global ecology, international law, and comparative government.

The scope and method of this study bridge the gap in orientation between those interested in promoting the five values and those who feel such normative concerns should be supplemented by more experiential data. The combination of covering five subject areas and drawing upon two methodological traditions makes this book a unique contribution to the scholarly literature in several of the fields indicated.

In addition to the institutions mentioned above which provided funds to release me from teaching duties to pursue this research, a few individuals deserve special thanks. Professors J. David Singer of the University of Michigan, Richard A. Falk of Princeton University, and Lynn H. Miller of Temple University read all or parts of this manuscript and offered suggestions and encouragement over the years. Professor Rudolf Borges and the Institut fur Didaktik Mathematik at the Johan Wolfgang Goethe University, Frankfurt, West Germany, were instrumental in providing desperately needed office space and an environment for serious study during a self-financed sabbatical year at a crucial point in the development of this project. Richard A. Binder and his various assistants throughout the decade of the 1980s were unstinting in their support at the Drexel University Library. The Federal Work-Study Program subsidized the efforts of many students who helped me process data over the years, among the most notable of whom were Jim Linn, Brent Kyler, Ho Lee, and Kijune Kim. Last but not least, the students of my Comparative Government and International Politics classes deserve a special thanks for putting up with the experimental nature of these courses as the framework of *Measuring Global Values* was implemented over the period of several semesters.

Introduction

MEASURING GLOBAL VALUES

During the 1970s in a series of books written by scholars on five continents, the World Order Models Project (WOMP) of the Institute for World Order (known since 1982 as the World Policy Institute) proposed a set of values as goals for a "model of a preferred world" (Kothari, 1974; Falk, 1975; Mendlovitz, 1975; Mazrui, 1976; Lagos and Godoy, 1977; Galtung, 1980). The values suggested were at a level of sufficient abstraction and desirability that it was hoped they could be accepted by states from all cultural milieus and political ideologies. They will be referred to in this study as global values.

In the years which followed, many scholars embraced the WOMP framework and produced several works suggesting ways for the global community of nations to achieve the proposed values (Ajami, 1980-81; Alexander and Swinth, 1987; Beer, 1979; Beres, 1981; Falk, 1977 and 1983; Falk, Kim, and Mendlovitz, 1982; Galtung, 1980; Kim, 1983; Mendlovitz, 1977 and 1981; Miller, 1985; and Walker, 1984 and 1987). Most of these works were in the normative tradition, praising (or criticizing) government policies which seemed to advance (or hinder) movement toward the preferred world. However, seldom was any measurement using empirical data proposed as a way of judging state performance in any systematic or comparative way. The precise definition, and even the number, of values to be advanced varied in each of the WOMP publications. (For critiques of WOMP, see Farer, 1977; Michalak, 1980; Oakes and Stunkel, 1981; and Alker and Biersteker, 1984; for replies, see Falk, 1978 and 1980; Kim, 1981; and Sylvester, 1981.)

This study has synthesized for further analysis the following *five* global values: (1) peace; (2) economic well-being; (3) ecological balance; (4) social justice; and (5) political participation. The goal of this work is to develop a set of political and social *indicators* of these five values, as well as a set of *measures* by which national policies regarding these indicators might be analyzed and state performance with respect to these values judged. By applying these measures to states in various geographic regions, evidence of conformance with these global values can be collected, and states can be classified and compared on the basis of their progress toward the preferred world model. The value indicators and measures proposed here represent initial steps in the building of a global model whose final framework must be the product of subsequent testing and experimentation. The goal is not so much to measure and assess specific states as to provide conceptual and methodological tools of analysis for those who wish to do this kind of research.

Although many data sets of social indicators exist (see, e.g., Taylor, 1980; Taylor and Jodice, 1983; OECD, 1982; Miles, 1985; Howell, 1983; World Bank, 1988), there are few statistics which are consciously gathered as bits of "world order data." Therefore, this study "re-packages" much information which is often collected, but which is not normally catalogued under headings which are useful to world order researchers. It uses existing reference material, but displays it in categories relating to global values according to a model whose underlying assumptions will be described below. The elaboration of this conceptual framework, as contrasted with blind faith in the data collected, is the main purpose of this study, which thus should be regarded as a work of political theory.

One objective of this undertaking is to enable individual scholars with an interest in global values to contribute to the development of a more elaborate framework of analysis, even though they might not have the collective expertise or resources of more richly endowed organizations which regularly evaluate the world's states such as the United Nations, the US Department of State, and the World Bank.[1] Nothing as extensive as the Global Monitoring System for appraising the effects of government on human dignity proposed by Snyder, Hermann, and Lasswell (1976) is envisioned. For this project, there is no need for transnational cooperation of governments or wealthy private organizations like Freedom House, Amnesty International, or the Stockholm International Peace Research Institute which produce annual global surveys on areas of their specific concern—civil and political liberties, political prisoners, and military expenditures, respectively. Here, a general framework will be proposed, and data will be taken where data can be found—i.e., in encyclopedias, annual reference books, scholarly journals, and reputable newspapers of record.

Among the sources regularly employed in this study are such newspapers and magazines as the *New York Times*, the *International Herald Tribune*, and *The Economist*; regularly updated series such as *Keesing's Contemporary Archives/Record of World Events, Facts on File*, and *Current World Leaders;* annuals such as *Europa Yearbook, Statesman's Yearbook,* the US Central Intelligence Agency's *World Factbook,* and the *Annual Register of World Events;* and general political encyclopedias and data references such as Banks

(1989 and earlier), Taylor and Jodice (1983), Kurian (1987 and 1984), Crow and Thomas (1984), Current History (1982), and the US Department of State's *Countries of the World and their Leaders: Background Notes* (various dates). Such sources are accessible in most libraries; in the regularity of their appearance they can be counted on to employ the same, or a progressively improving, methodology with respect to the data they publish. The main advantage of using such standard references as sources is the ease of participation and potential for collaboration in research by individuals interested in specific values, countries, or regions.

Such a procedure has certain disadvantages, however, regarding the variability and timeliness of data. Most statistics found in annual reference books are two to three years older than the date of publication of the books themselves. Publications appearing in a given year are apt to have data drawn from a number of different years. Scholars working on a particular value might employ different sources for similar data and thus not be using the same numbers. However, the judgment is made at the outset of this work to opt for availability of sources, comprehensiveness of coverage, and the potential for widespread scholarly collaboration in future research rather than a high degree of accuracy with respect to any single measure. In fact, several sources (variously dated from the late 1980s through December, 1990) often will be suggested for each indicator of the global values to be discussed.

State ranks shown in this study are not meant to be definitive, but rather to provoke discussion and debate with the goal of achieving higher conceptual clarity for the method of value measurement being proposed. With respect to much of the statistical data which appears in Chapters 1 through 3, it has been found not to vary widely from year to year, particularly with respect to *rankings of states* within global value categories and within smaller geographic regions. Due to the qualitative nature of much inquiry associated with world order values, however, some of the information relevant for this research is inherently "soft," and clusterings (not rankings) of states will be more appropriate, especially in Chapters 4 and 5.

One final word about the nation-state, the level of analysis for the proposed research. Although the values being measured are often not the product of phenomena limited to the confines of a single country, the state as a unit of measurement is invariably a necessary point of departure when attempting to collect data on a worldwide basis employing standard reference materials (Singer, 1970-71: 197, 206; Skocpol, 1984). In the analysis which follows, however, state records regarding world order values will be analyzed in the context of specific *geographic divisions* of the world. In this manner, inappropriate comparisons across gross cultural barriers will be avoided and states will be studied only as parts of groups of similar geopolitical heritage.

GEOGRAPHIC ZONES OF ANALYSIS

The geographic divisions to be used in this study employ a framework of analysis which groups 162 states in five *zones* (broadly representative of historic centers of civilization) and 15 *regions* (three in each zone, created on the basis of more recent political history). Figure I.1 is a Peters-projected map on which the five zones are annotated. Table I.1 displays the regional clusters within these zones, with the 162 states being listed according to a roughly contiguous geographic order within each region. From top to bottom and left to right throughout the table, the regions start in the north Atlantic and circumnavigate the globe in a generally eastern and southern direction ending in the Caribbean. The 162 states represent the 160 members of the United Nations (less Byelorussia and the Ukraine) plus Switzerland, Taiwan, North Korea, and South Korea. Although the two Germanys and the two Yemens were in the process of unifying in 1990 as the final draft of this text was being prepared, they will be retained here as individual entities because most data pertaining to them will be from earlier years when they were separate.

Political judgments are inevitably made in creating any such groupings (Russett, 1967; Cantori and Spiegel, 1970; Falk and Mendlovitz, 1973; Cohen, 1982), and the assumptions undergirding the framework of Table I.1 need to be made explicit. One of the objectives of this project is to incorporate the global values perspective into the comparative analysis of government. The division of the world presented here offers many interesting insights for comparing states of various political types within a given region.

Before the political changes in eastern Europe in 1989, Americans were socialized into viewing the world in three "camps" representing, roughly, the Free World of Western democracies, the Soviet Bloc of communist states, and the Third World of developing nations. Even before the changes of 1989, this division was highly Eurocentric and gave undue emphasis to the advanced industrial world and its Cold War rivalries. It disproportionately reduced to about one-third of the total picture *most* of the world's states and peoples, and the various polity types found in the non-white world. The display used here provides more appropriate attention to the many states of Africa, Asia, and Latin America, a perspective that becomes even more relevant now that Europe is becoming one again.

The five *zones* of civilization in Figure I.1 roughly correspond to continental clusters of states, except for the Islamic grouping, which cuts across Africa, Asia, and even southern Europe. The term "Middle East" (a phrase with colonial overtones which made sense in that era when London ruled most of the world) is purposely not used as one of the basic zonal divisions. *Islam* is the driving force which today best describes the politics of the zone stretching from Morocco and Mauritania in northwest Africa to Iran, Afghanistan, and Pakistan in southwest Asia. (Nevertheless, because of the general familiarity of the term, Middle East is occasionally used in this text when the phrase Islamic zone would sound false or inappropriate.)

Two other border areas between zones which should be mentioned at the outset involve the placement of eight states often reported as African in many sources into other zones. The four states of Chad, Sudan, Djibouti, and Somalia are considered to be Islamic here; the last three are members of the Arab League, and Chad's politics in recent years have been increasingly focused upon penetrations from Libya and Sudan. Four other states off the east coast of Africa in the southern Indian Ocean—Comoros, Madagascar, Mauritius, and Seychelles—are considered here to be part of south Asia, within India's sphere of influence, increasingly concerned with a maritime "zone of peace" and more like the island-states of Oceanic Asia in this respect than like the countries of sub-Saharan black Africa. The impact of these judgments is to reduce the number of African states to 38, and to increase the number in the Islamic and Asian zones to 28 and 33, respectively, making for more roughly comparable (in number of states) zones of analysis.

Similar explanations could be made to justify the boundaries drawn to create the 15 regions, a rationale elaborated at greater length in the author's forthcoming comparative government textbook, *Political Participation in 160 Countries*, which expands upon Chapter 5 of this study. At this point, however, it might be pointed out that there are about 200 pages of tables in this book, each of which could be the source of extended commentary. Indeed, they would make for a very lengthy perusal if each one was thoroughly dissected upon the reader's first encountering it. To understand the main thrust of this work, it is recommended rather that a read-through of the 200 pages of narrative be accomplished first, noting the tables in their context, to be followed by an in-depth consideration of data displays of particular interest at a later time.

In any event, the geographic framework of zones and regions draws heavily upon the author's experience over the past several years in teaching comparative government from a global perspective (Sullivan, 1985). For purposes of this study, the zones are the more important unit of analysis, especially in Chapters 1 through 3 where more than 115 displays will present state rankings with respect to various statistical measures in the five zonal columns of Table I.1. In Chapters 4 and 5, regional affinities are often more obvious in accounting for the clustering of certain states in the narrative excerpts which will be drawn from this project's data bank.

It is also true that if the zonal columns of the tables in Chapters 1 through 3 were broken into regional clusters, in many instances geography would be a most significant determinant accounting for the close rank-positions of countries from otherwise different formal political types. Throughout the pages which follow, this point might be kept in mind when noting the rankings of such pairs of states as Greece and Yugoslavia, Iran and Iraq, Syria and Lebanon, Zaire and Congo, North and South Korea, and (before their unifications) East and West Germany, and North and South Yemen.

Figure I.1 – Measuring Global Values – The Five Zones

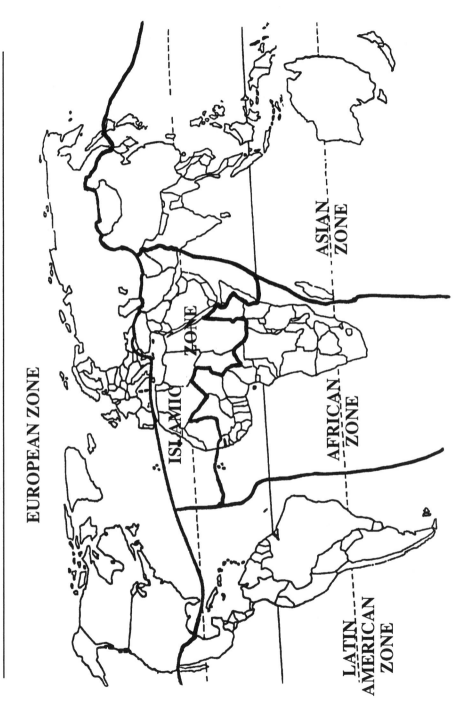

I.1 - Comparative Government: Zones & Regions

Europe	Islamic	Africa	Asia	Latin America
		western (15)		
n. Atlantic (10)	west Asia (9)	Cape Verde	south (10)	south(12)
US	Israel	Guinea Bissau	India	Paraguay
Canada	Lebanon	Senegal	Nepal	Brazil
Iceland	Syria	Gambia	Bhutan	Uruguay
Ireland	Cyprus	Mali	Bangladesh	Argentina
UK	Turkey	Burkina Faso	Sri Lanka	Chile
Norway	Iraq	Niger	Maldive I.	Bolivia
Netherlands	Iran	Nigeria	Seychelles I.	Peru
Belgium	Afghanistan	Benin	Mauritius	Ecuador
Luxembourg	Pakistan	Togo	Madagascar	Colombia
France		Ghana	Comoros I.	Venezuela
		Ivory Coast		Guyana
central (11)	Arab.peninsula(9)	Liberia	east,mainland(10)	Suriname
Austria	Jordan	Sierra Leone	China	
Switzerland	Saudi Arabia	Guinea	Mongolia	central(8)
W.Germany	Kuwait		N.Korea	Panama
Denmark	Bahrain	east-cent.(13)	S.Korea	Costa Rica
Sweden	U.A.Emirates	Ethiopia	Taiwan	Nicaragua
Finland	Qatar	Kenya	Vietnam	Honduras
USSR	Oman	Tanzania	Cambodia	El Salvador
Poland	S.Yemen	Uganda	Laos	Guatemala
E.Germany	N.Yemen	Rwanda	Thailand	Mexico
Czechoslovakia		Burundi	Myanmar	Belize
Hungary		Zaire		
		Congo		
southern(9)	n. Africa(10)	Cent.Af.Rep.	offshore,oceanic(13)	Caribbean(13)
Portugal	Egypt	Cameroon	Japan	Jamaica
Spain	Libya	Gabon	Philippines	Cuba
Malta	Tunisia	Equat.Guinea	Brunei	Bahamas
Italy	Algeria	SaoTome&Pr.	Malaysia	Haiti
Greece	Morocco		Singapore	Dom.Republic
Albania	Mauritania	southern(10)	Indonesia	St.Chris.-Nevis
Yugoslavia	Chad	S. Africa	Papua New Guinea	Antigua-Barbuda
Romania	Sudan	Lesotho	Solomon I.	Dominica
Bulgaria	Djibouti	Swaziland	Vanuatu	St.Lucia
	Somalia	Mozambique	Fiji	St.Vincent & G.
		Malawi	W.Samoa	Barbados
		Zimbabwe	New Zealand	Grenada
		Zambia	Australia	Trinidad-Tobago
		Botswana		
		Namibia		
		Angola		
n=30	n=28	n=38	n=33	n=33 (TOT.162)

n=162: United Nations' 160 (through latest UN member Namibia, 4/90) less Ukraine and
   Byelorussia, plus Switzerland, N.Korea, S.Korea, and Taiwan.
Note: Throughout Chapters 1 through 4, W.Germany and E.Germany, and N.Yemen and S.Yemen,
   will be referred to as separate states for the data applied to them are for years before their
   1990 unifications. Also, Kuwait will not be considered as permanently annexed by Iraq.

DEFINITIONS OF VALUES

Some of the five global values to be analyzed in this book—V1=peace, V2=economic well-being, V3=ecological balance, V4=social justice, and V5=political participation—might appear to be European in origin, and so cultural bias is an issue that must be addressed. The appointment of Directors of the World Order Models Project from Africa (Mazrui), India (Kothari), Japan (Sakamoto), and South America (Lagos), as well as from Europe (Galtung) and North America (Falk) was one way to ensure that much of the original literature in this field reflected broadly based perspectives. The framework of geographic zones for applying measures to value indicators to be employed here represents another effort in this direction. Finally, it is hoped that as these values are defined below and interpreted in their particular regional contexts, the global relevance of this study will be evident.

It is possible that the five values could be accounted for in fewer, or more, or different categories. For example, there is some obvious overlap between values V1 and V2, V2 and V3, V2 and V4, and V4 and V5, and among many of the measures and indicators for particular values. The definitions of values, indicators, and measures to be described next, however, are organized in such a way as to draw attention to and reinforce these points of contact while keeping them analytically distinct.

Value #1 (V1) - peace

Peace, or the minimization of militarism in the pursuit of political objectives, is the value most frequently proclaimed by world order advocates. As used here, this word means not merely the absence of war, but also a minimum of reliance upon organized violence and other manifestations of militarism in the external affairs of state; it also applies to the absence of belligerent activity between contending political factions within countries.

While the extreme of non-violence or pacifism is seldom adopted as policy by states in the international community (despite the existence of a few countries with no standing army for external use), measurements and rankings can be made of the varying dependencies of states upon preparations for and participation in organized military activity vis-a-vis other states. Extended breakdowns of law and order resulting in civil war, insurgency, or militarized governance will also be covered here.

The value indicators and their measures for value **V1 (peace)** are:

.1 - wars: both international and civil; measured in their severity (i.e., by number of deaths) and duration; also, an analysis of current insurgencies and of refugees generated by war; a ranking of states by their experience in warlike activities (frequency and duration).

.2 - domestic impact of war, including military budget items such as armed personnel (the number of persons in each state's military service, plus several measures of soldiers-to-civilian groups in society); and military expenditures (both the absolute dollar value expended, and several relative measures of military spending as a function of population, Gross National Product, Central Government Expenditures, soldiers supported); as well as military coup regimes (frequency and duration of militarized governance of countries since 1945, or year of independence, whichever is more recent).

.3 - external manifestations of war, including force projections (number of troops deployed beyond a state's home borders, and the states where they can be found; reciprocally, the number of foreign troops "hosted," and the states from which they come); weapons transfers (measures over a multi-year period of the volume of arms trade, both exports and imports, in constant-year absolute dollars, and as a percentage of total exports and imports, including dependencies upon Great Power and Third World producers); and armaments issues of global concern (atomic, biological, chemical weapons), as well as treaties signed to control them.

Main Sources (see the bibliography of Chapter 1 for complete citations):

1. Center for Defense Information, 1986 and 1983; 2. Degenhardt, 1988 and 1983; 3. International Institute of Strategic Studies, annual, 1989 and earlier; 4. Sivard, annual, 1989 and earlier; 5. Stockholm International Peace Research Institute, annual, 1990 and earlier; 6. US Arms Control and Disarmament Agency, annual, 1990 and earlier.

Value #2 (V2) - economic well-being

In defining an acceptable level of economic well-being, one must guard against ethnocentrism. In many countries a good deal of economic activity occurs "off the books," and aggregate measures of a society's productivity, savings, and capital flows say little about the distribution of benefits and costs to individuals. Nevertheless, there are certain measures (growth, investment, inflation, consumption, aid, trade, etc.) which reflect broad tendencies over time and, when compared with other states, relative rankings of a society's economic vitality. Such statistics will be used in this study as rough approximations of economic well-being. An attempt is made to measure the relative conditions of autarchy versus dependence in states' economies, as well as the dissemination of economic well-being throughout a society; however, the issue of equitable distribution of power is deferred to Chapters 4 and 5 on social justice and political participation.

Value indicators and measures for V2 (economic well-being):

.1 - inherent economic strength: Gross National Product (or its equivalent), in absolute and per capita terms, and with respect to its recent record of growth; absolute and relative measures of investment and savings; status of a country's financial reserves and current account balance.

.2 - economic weaknesses: inflation and (where possible) unemployment; patterns of consumption and deficit government spending, external debt and the ability to service it.

.3 - international capital flows: net direct investment and workers' remittances from abroad; economic development aid in both absolute and relative terms and with respect to various donors; trading patterns, with particular attention to export concentration indexes and dependencies on particular products and trading partners, as well as price in the context of terms of trade.

.4 - domestic distribution of benefits: amenities, such as electricity, telephones, and automobiles; educational expenditures, resources (teachers) and results (as reflected in literacy); health expenditures, numbers of doctors, nurses, hospital beds; public consumption of welfare and other social services; indexes of private consumption including consumer expenditures and Gross National Income per capita.

Main Sources (see the bibliography of Chapter 2 for complete citations): 1. United Nations Conference on Trade and Development, annual, 1988 and earlier; 2. United States, Agency for International Development, annual, 1990 and earlier; 3. United States, Central Intelligence Agency, annual, 1989 and earlier; 4. World Bank, *World Development Report,* annual, 1990 and earlier; and 5. World Bank, *World Tables,* annual, 1989 and earlier.

Value #3 (V3) - ecological balance

Environmental quality is often a function of economic development, and many of the issues discussed in the V3 category tend to trade off reciprocally with those mentioned in V2. By being considered as a separate category, however, the analytic construct of V3 enables V2 to be limited strictly to economic measurements regardless of their impact on a more widely defined "quality of life," whereas V3 assesses that latter issue irrespective of the fact that economics is undoubtedly a critical factor affecting the ecological quality of a society.

One indicator stressed in this section is population and its inevitable connection to environmental degradation in the process of food, energy, and resource consumption. Certain composite indicators of physical and societal quality of life are also cited. The most difficult factors to account for are actual resource depletions or environmental despoliations which often occur but are seldom recorded in any consistent manner.

Value indicators and measures for **V3 (ecological balance)**:

.1 - population: the absolute number in each state, along with the percentages in key age cohorts, growth rates, and the years for certain stability rates; an analysis of National Family Planning programs, abortion policies, and fertility rates; finally, the relationship between population and world hunger (malnutrition as measured by infant mortality, child deaths, and food consumption in calories and protein per capita).

.2 - environment: various measures of land (area, population density, percent arable, pasture, etc.) and water (rivers, lakes, coastlines, etc.) resources; the impact of urbanization (slum populations, city sizes, growth rates, etc.); pollution, as measured by poisons in the atmosphere (SO_2, CO_2, etc.) and in waters (suspended sediment, dissolved minerals, etc.); percentage of population with safe water and basic sanitation facilities.

.3 - consumption: particularly of energy with respect to use of electricity and nuclear power generation; also, production and consumption of depletable natural resources such as fossil fuels (oil, gas, coal), selected minerals and metals, forests and fisheries.

.4 - international and composite measures: exports of depletable resources; international environmental programs relating to "heritage" sites, wetlands, and biosphere reserves, as well as treaties concerning the oceans, ozone layer, and ten other ecologically significant issues; and "quality of life" indicators created by Sivard (Economic and Social Rank), Morris (Physical Quality of Life Index), Estes (Index of Social Progress) and the United Nations (Human Development Index).

Main Sources (see the bibliography of Chapter 3 for complete citations):

1. Brown et al., annual, 1990 and earlier; 2. Hunger Project, 1985; 3. Population Reference Bureau, annual, 1990 and earlier, and 1986a; 4. United States Department of Commerce, Bureau of the Census, 1986; 5. United States Department of Interior, Bureau of Mines, 1987; 6. World Resources Institute and the International Institute for Environment and Development, annual, 1990 and earlier.

Value #4 (V4) - social justice

Regardless of geographic region, historical culture, or political ideology, there are some standards of justice to which any regime can be held accountable. A majority of the world's states have signed various elements of the International Bill of Human Rights (IBIIR), which espouses such values as equality, the integrity of the person, the rule of law, and some personal freedoms. The latter three will be related, respectively, to human rights, civil rights, and political rights in this study. With respect to equality, analyses will be made of ethnic, linguistic, and religious groups, for it is typically members of such non-governing (not necessarily "numerical") minorities that are most often subjected to unjust or inhumane treatment at the hands of a ruling elite drawn disproportionately from a different constituency. Despite the variability of application of these concepts across diverse cultures and political systems, they provide a standard which can be referred to at least in theory.

Value indicators and measures for **V4 (social justice)**:

.1 - International Bill of Human Rights: a survey of the structure of, and signatories to, the international conventions on Civil and Political Rights, and on Economic, Social, and Cultural Rights; an analysis of "watch groups" (Amnesty International, Freedom House, Humana, US Department of State, etc.) which report on compliance.

.2 - equality: analysis of societal composition by ethnic, religious, and linguistic groups, with attention given to instances of discriminatory policies toward certain such groups. (Much of the data in this section is often found in other world order studies as a separate value under the rubric "positive identity.")

.3 - integrity of the person (human rights): surveys of governmental attitudes toward certain basic human rights, as reflected in legal executions, extrajudicial killings and disappearances, torture, and imprisonment, particularly of politically active persons.

.4 - rule of law (civil rights): government powers of arrest and detention, and more general control over people's movements and privacy; women's rights; analysis of the relevance of the state's constitution (i.e., is it frequently suspended), and the independence of its court system; civil liberties rankings as contrasted with those for political freedoms.

.5 - personal freedoms (potential political rights): the general status of freedom of expression, with particular attention to the role of organized religion, the press (both printed and electronic media), and trade union movements.

Main sources (See the bibliography of Chapter 4 for complete citations):
1. Africa/Americas/Asia/Helsinki/Middle East Watch, periodic reports; 2. Amnesty International, annual, 1990 and earlier; 3. Gastil, annual, 1989 and earlier; 4. Humana, 1986 and 1984; 5. US Department of State, annual, *Country Reports on Human Rights Practices* , 1990 and earlier.

Value #5 (V5) - political participation

Although there could be a tendency to identify this term with Western-style forms of governance, the effort here will be to look at indigenous political institutions and to determine whether they provide evidence of access to, and influence over, the centers of political power. Recognizing that all government is in some respects an instrument of the elite, V5's emphasis will be on the openness of the political process both within and beyond a society's favored groups.

Whereas V4 tends to focus on individual citizens and groups with latent political *potential*, V5 will look at how the agencies of government affect significant political *actors* and institutions. Whereas V4 is concerned with protections for individuals even as they might be members of ethnic associations or interest articulation groups, V5 concentrates on the access of persons to the political arena through explicitly political organizations like political parties, and other centers of power in the government (e.g., representative assemblies and the military).

Value indicators and measures for V5 (political participation):

.1 - governmental systems: a division of the world's states into two gross (civilian vs. military), three major (multi-party, one-party, and no-party) and ten minor polity types, defined in such a way as to focus on the existence, number, and functioning of political parties; the role of elections and other means of regime legitimacy.

.2 - power-sharing: relationship between heads of state, government, and party; the role of a representative assembly including its size, term, and manner of selection; the existence of any other power centers or constitutional weighting formulas which relate to the way power is shared in the government.

.3 - participation in civilian polities: data on the most recent election, referendum, plebiscite, or other means used to legitimate the current ruling administration; detailed analysis of political party strength (percentage of votes, number of seats in representative assembly), depending on whether political system is multiparty (strong or weak) or one-party (dominant, communist, or "other").

.4 - militarized governance: analysis of how governments build political institutions (parties, representative assemblies, elections, etc.) in nascent party-states (multiparty or one party dominant), and in military regimes (moderating and entrenched).

.5 - anachronistic polity types with limited political participation: analysis of monarchies, colonies, states in transition, and divided nations.

Main Sources (see the bibliography of Chapter 5 for complete citations):

1. Banks, annual, 1989 and earlier; 2. *Clements Encyclopedia of World Governments*, annual, 1990 and earlier; 3. Day and Degenhardt, 1988 and 1984; 4. DeLury, 1987 and 1983; 5. Staar, annual, 1989a, 1990b, and earlier; US Department of State, various dates, 1986-1990, *Background Notes.*

A schematic summary of all values, indicators, and measures comprising this book's framework for measuring global values can be found on the last page of this book's concluding chapter as Figure C.1.

METHODOLOGY

The chapters which follow this introduction explain at greater length the general value indicators and the specific statistical and narrative measures for each of these five values. A data bank is maintained on an Apple Macintosh microcomputer in which the indicators and measures referred to in this text are entered and coded for individual states. Support for this research originally came from the Pew Foundation Glenmede Trust Program for the Implementation of Microcomputer Technology in College Curricula at Drexel University. The data bank continues to be maintained and updated regularly by the author and will be employed in his forthcoming globally oriented comparative government text. If this current book were to be used in the classroom, updating the tables (using the latest edition of the annual sources listed at the bottom of each display) would be a good assignment for students. If subsequent editions of this work were to be published, the 200 pages of tables could be readily updated and reproduced.

Data for ranking states according to these measures is drawn from a number of authoritative references and reflects various levels of accuracy and comprehensiveness. Sources are employed from across the ideological spectrum, from the United Nations to the US Central Intelligence Agency, from

Amnesty International to Freedom House, from the Stockholm International Peace Research Institute to the London International Institute for Strategic Studies. Ideological biases of source materials will be discussed, particularly in Chapters 1 and 4 where they have the greatest impact on the data collected (i.e., in the sections on military expenditures and human rights).

For reasons mentioned in the opening section, this study will be eclectic in its use of reference books, opting for comprehensiveness and accessibility of data in an effort to build a framework for further elaboration by others. The reader must make an individual judgment as to the appropriateness of the source for the data being displayed or the region being illustrated. As indicated earlier, different materials could yield different results in the state-rankings for various indicators. The main purpose of this work, however, is to elaborate conceptual categories for defining world order values and to suggest possible indicators for measuring or ranking countries with respect to these categories. The reference literature which produces data to perform these two functions will be reviewed, and examples will be made to show how that data might be put to comparative use. The applications of these indicators and measures to specific states and regions, however interesting, is a secondary objective of this work. The conceptual and methodological tools which are presented, however, will assist anyone who does wish to measure and assess state performance.

Various types of presentations of data are employed throughout this book. In Chapters 1, 2, and 3 most of the displays will be of seemingly "hard" statistical data; in Chapters 4 and 5 narratives drawn from the data bank associated with this project will be more extensively used. Abbreviations such as "90f88" will be used to indicate the publication date (1990) and the date of the information being cited (1988).

For some measures, global displays reflecting the positioning of all the world's states, ranked from highest to lowest in their zones, will be made. Such listings will include data like population (Table I.2), Gross National Product (V2.1a), and Central Government Expenditures (V2.2c) which are often used as denominators for other measures. Other significant measures for which global coverage (n=162 states) is attempted include:

V1.2a-armed personnel; V1.2b-military expenditures;

V2.2a-inflation; V2.2d-debt; V2.3a-overseas investment; V2.3c-trade; V2.4b-literacy;

V3.1a-population growth and fertility rates; V3.1d-child death rates; V3.2a-land area; V3.2c-urbanization; V3.2d-safe water; V3.4c-composite quality of life ranks;

V4.1b-International Bill of Human Rights signatories; V4.2a-ethnic homogeneity percentages; V4.3-human rights rankings; V4.4d-civil liberties and political rights rankings; V4.5b-status of organized religion; V4.5c-freedom of the press; and V4.5d-workers' rights.

V5.1a-polity types; V5.1b-elections; V5.2a-modes of government power-sharing; and V5.2b-size and strength of representative assemblies.

For other measures only the world leaders, illustrated by the top five to ten states in each of the five zones, will be presented, e.g.:

V1.2a-soldier-to-civilian ratios; V1.2b-relative military expenditures; V1.3b-leading weapons exporters and importers;

V2.3b-recipients of economic aid; V2.3d-aid and trade dependencies;

V3.2a-allocations of land use; V3.3cd-fuel and mineral production, consumption, and reserves; V3.3d-forest and fisheries depletion.

As a variation of this approach and for contrast, the bottom five to ten states will sometimes be provided as well; e.g.,

V2.1b-domestic investment and savings; V2.4a-economic amenities (e.g., electricity, telephones, automobiles); V2.4b-education (spending and personnel); V2.4c-inputs to national health policy; V2.4d-private economic consumption;

V3.1d-daily calories and protein consumption per capita, as compared with Recommended Daily Allowances; V3.3a-per capita energy consumption.

Such displays, generally covering about half of all states, will show not only the range of scores within each zone, but also the gaps among geographic areas, especially, for example, how the measures for the lowest states in Europe are often comparable to those of the highest states in the other four zones.

In some categories, the number of relevant states is not equal to all of the world's countries; the data presented in such cases is the most complete available for the phenomena under consideration, e.g.:

V1.1a-wars; V1.1b-current insurgencies; V1.2c-military coup regimes; V1.3a-force projections; V1.3b-Third World arms producers;

V2.1e-Least Developed States; V2.3b-donors of economic aid;

V3.1b-abortion rates; V3.2c-cities; V3.3a-nuclear power, V3.4b-locations of ecologically preserved areas;

V4.2d-ethnically divided states; V4.4d-countries under states of emergency;

V5.2c-federal states; V5.3-civilian polities; V5.4-militarized governments; V5.5a-monarchies; and V5.5b-colonies and possessions.

Finally, where the data is somewhat "softer," as in Chapters 4 and 5, the methodology for comparison must be significantly modified. With respect to social justice, a 1-through-4 rating system is developed to *classify* (as opposed to measure with great accuracy) state policies in the areas of human, civil, and political rights. Concerning political participation, ten types of political systems are proposed, and states are compared along a number of power sharing dimensions within each category. In order to show the format according to which country data is being collected for these indicators, narrative summaries for selected exemplar states will be excerpted from the data bank maintained for this project. Such excerpts will be presented for ongoing insurgencies (V1.1b); state ethnic compositions (V4.2); government violations of human rights (V4.3); power-sharing within governments (V5.2); and political party strengths (V5.3abcd, V5.4abcd, V5.5a).

The point of employing different kinds of presentations and bases of statistical display is to provide a multiplicity of examples of how the proposed analytic categories might be used to measure global values. This practice also reflects the variegated texture of government and politics in the world today, and of the data bases which have been compiled to describe this world.

The scope and method of this work thus should appeal both to those interested in promoting the five values and to those who feel such normative concerns should be supplemented by more experiential data. Drawing upon these two traditions and attempting to address subject areas roughly corresponding to the academic disciplines of world politics, international political economy, global ecology, international law, and comparative government, raises the risk of not satisfying the particular standards of several potential audiences. Nevertheless, the choice has been made for comprehensiveness of coverage and accessibility of confirmatory data. Within such parameters, it is hoped that employing data-based management software to compare 162 countries using more than 200 measures will represent a unique contribution to understanding the many issues raised in this study.

APPLICATION

Throughout the chapters which follow, judgments must be made as to whether to include information on all states, or to focus on a smaller subset of countries. Much of the data used in this work is drawn from sources which exclude states with populations of less than one million from their published analyses, reducing the universe of countries for comparison to about 130. Because population will be such a basic indicator throughout this study, being the denominator for many relative (i.e., per capita) rankings, it seems appropriate at the outset to provide a list of the 162 countries this study will recognize—from Super Powers to ministates—in order of their population. Applying the analytic tools of this study to this first measure will not only provide a sample of the methodology to be employed, but also show once again the potential for controversy in displaying such a seemingly simple listing. Table I.2 introduces a "clustering" method of display which will be used throughout this book. This manner of presentation enables one not only to make comparisons across the five geographic zones, but also to identify similar groups of countries within each zone. The inappropriateness of comparing vast civilizations like China and India with city-states or islands like Singapore and the Seychelles is obvious, and as units of analysis it might make more sense to study only states in the context of their approximate peers in terms of population. Nevertheless, for the sake of completeness, this study will make an effort to display information on as many as possible of the 162 countries listed here. Readers may then extract subsets of states for comparison based upon common size, geography, or other criteria.

When the source being used for tables in this book does not cite certain states--usually due either to their insignificant size (i.e., ministates), the disruptive effects of war (e.g., Iran, Iraq, Lebanon,), or traditions of secrecy (many communist countries)--the total number of countries reported upon will be listed at the end of each geographic column. Where information in the source cited is listed there as "not available," it is reported that way here, i.e., "na"; if the state itself is not found in the source consulted, it may also be reported here as "na" (where there is a need to account for all 162 states) or it may simply not be listed, in which case the number of states cited (out of the highest possible number noted in Table I.2 for each zone (i.e., 30, 28, 38, 33, and 33) will be given at the bottom of each zonal column.

The list of states in the lowest tier in Table I.2 provides a quick reference as to the identities of the 31 ministates often omitted from many global analyses. A quick glance at some of their names (Iceland, Cyprus, Gambia, Brunei, Grenada) makes clear their oftentimes unexpected importance in international politics, and hence the reason for attempting to collect data on them in as many categories as possible.

The clustering method of display also draws attention to some other notable groups: the ten "Super States" with populations of more than 100 million people each, which collectively account for almost 60% of the planet's people; 20 "Significant Powers" with between 30 and 100 million people each; and 42 "Middle-Sized States" with about 9 to 29 million apiece. The use of the designations "super" and "power" in reference to many of the countries in the first two categories can be debated; a large population might be a downright drain upon the economic and ecological quality of life, a point which is emphasized in Chapters 2 and 3. The rankings displayed in this study thus do not necessarily provide definitive answers with respect to the "best" or "worst" states in a particular category. Rather, this table—like many others in this work—provides an opportunity for discussion based upon an extended analysis of the terms and assumptions employed in its creation.

Finally, from page 2 of Table I.2, it can be seen that most of the world's states (n=90) have populations less than that of Greater New York City (˜10 million). But because of the concept of sovereignty, such relatively small political entities as Sweden, Israel, Liberia, Cambodia, and Nicaragua cannot be denied attention despite the modest number of people they represent. Nor will they be ignored in this study in its quest for comprehensiveness of coverage.

I.2 - **Populations** (mid-1990, in millions)

Europe	Islamic	Africa	Asia	Latin Amer.
			China-1,135.5	
USSR-289.0			India-853.4	
US-248.8			Indonesia-180.5	Brazil-150.4
	Pakistan-122.7		Japan-123.5	
		Nigeria-113.0	Bangldsh.-115.6	

---------------------------------100 million (Super States), n=10---------------------------------

				Mexico-88.6
W.Ger.-60.5			Vietnam-67.2	
Italy-57.3	Iran-56.6		Phil. I.-66.1*	
UK-56.9	Turkey-55.6			
France-56.2	Egypt-54.1		Thailand-55.7	
		Ethiopia-46.7	S.Korea-43.6	
Spain-39.3			Myanmar-41.7	
Poland-38.4		Zaire-36.0		Argentina-32.3
		S.Africa-35.2		Colombia-31.8

------------------------------30 million (Significant Powers), n=20------------------------------

Canada-26.5	Algeria-25.3	Tanzania-27.3		
	Sudan-25.2			
Yugo.-23.8	Morocco-25.1	Kenya-25.1	N.Korea-22.9	Peru-22.3
Romania-23.3			Taiwan-20.2*	
	Iraq-18.9	Uganda-18.4	Nepal-19.1	Venez.-19.7
E.Ger.-16.6			Malaysia-17.3	
Czech.-15.7	Afghan.-16.6	Mozambq.-15.7	SriLanka-17.2	
Nethrlds.-14.8	Saudi A.-14.1ˉ	Ghana-15.0	Australia-16.7	
	Syria-12.5	Iv. Coast-12.6		Chile-13.2
Hungary-10.6			Madgscr.-12.0	
Portugal-10.3		Cameroon-11.2		
Greece-10.0		Angola-10.0		Ecuador-10.8
Belgium-9.9		Zimbabwe-9.7		Cuba-10.3
Bulgaria-9.0		Mali-9.4		
		Burkina F.-9.0		

------------------------------9.0 mil. (Middle Sized States), n=42------------------------------

Subtot:

19	11	15	17	10

(n=72 states > ˜9 million population;

n=90 states less than Greater New York City in population on next page.)

Table I.2 (continued)

---9.0 mil.---

Sweden-8.3	Tunisia-8.2	Zambia-8.5		
	N.Yemen-8.0[+]	Malawi-8.4	Cambodia-8.2	
	Somalia-7.6			
Austria-7.5		Senegal-7.4		Bolivia-7.3
		Rwanda-7.2		Dom.Rep.-7.2
Switzrld.-6.5		Niger-7.1		Haiti-6.5
Denmark-5.1	Chad-5.7	Guinea-6.9		
Finland-5.0				El Sal.-5.3
	Israel-4.6	Burundi-5.5		Honduras-5.1
Norway-4.2	Libya-4.5		Laos-4.1	
		Benin-4.7	Papua NG-4.0	Paraguay-4.3
Ireland-3.7	Jordan-3.4º	Sierra L.-4.2		Nicaragua-3.9
	Lebanon-3.0			Uruguay-3.1
Albania-3.2		Togo-3.5	N.Zealand-3.4	CostaRic.-3.0
	S.Yemen-2.5	C.Af.R.-2.9		
	Kuwait-2.1	Liberia-2.6	Singapore-2.7	Jamaica-2.5
	Mauritania-2.0	Congo-2.0		Panama-2.4
		Namibia-1.9	Mongolia-2.2	
		Lesotho-1.8	Bhutan-1.5	
	UAE-1.6			
	Oman-1.5	Botswana-1.3		Trinidad-1.3
		Gabon-1.2	Mauritius-1.1	Guyana-1.0
Subtot: 8	13	17	8	13

--------------------------between 1 & 9 million, n= 59 (most)states --------------------------

≤ 1 million (ministates, n=31, pops. in 1000's)

		GBissau-987	Fiji-748	
	Cyprus-700	Gambia-858		
		Swaziland-789	Comoros-518	Suriname-403
	Bahrain-515		Solomons-273^	Barbados-261
Luxmbrg.-367	Djibouti-406	Eq. Guinea-440	Brunei-221^	Bahamas-232^
Malta-352	Qatar-367	C.Verde-379	Maldives-178^	Belize-161^
Iceland-253			W.Samoa-163^	St.Lucia-122^
			Vanuatu-134^	St.Vincent-102^
				Grenada-88^
		STP-88^		Antigua-80^
			Seychelles-66^	Dominica-74^
				St.Chris.-44^
n=3	n=4	n=6	n=8	n=10

~TOT:				(~5.3 bil.)
1.06 bil.	450 mil.	460 mil.	2.90 bil.	430 mil.
n=30	n=28	n=38	n=33	n=33 (162)

Source: UN Population Fund (1990); supplemented by: *Pop. Reference Bureau (1990);
    ^CIA World Factbook (1987); and º New York Times (1989) for Jordan without West Bank.
[+] and ~ = other sources suggest significantly higher (N.Yemen) or lower (Saudi A.) number.

NOTE

1. The United Nations publishes global yearbooks on human rights, disarmament, trade, food, labor, demographics, and other statistics; the US Department of State annually produces its massive *Country Reports on Human Rights Practices*; the World Bank measures global economic development in its annual *World Development Report*.

BIBLIOGRAPHY

AJAMI, F. (1980-81) "World Order: The Question of Ideology," *Alternatives* 6: 474-485.

ALEXANDER, A. S., and R. L. SWINTH (1987) "A Value Framework for Assessing the Social Impacts of Multinational Corporations," *Essays in International Business* 7: 1-110.

ALKER, H. R., and T. J. BIERSTEKER (1984) "The Dialectics of World Order: Notes for a Future Archaeologist of International Savoir Faire," *International Studies Quarterly* 28:121-42.

ANDRIOLE, S. J., and G. W. HOPPLE (1984) "The Rise and Fall of Event Data: From Basic Research to Applied Use in the U. S. Department of Defense," *International Interactions* 10: 293-309.

ANNUAL REGISTER OF WORLD EVENTS (annual) Detroit: Gale Publishing Co.

BANKS, A. S. (annual) *Political Handbook of the World.* New York: McGraw-Hill.

BEER, F. A. (1979) "World Order and World Futures," *Journal of Conflict Resolution* 23:174-192.

BERES, L. R. (1981) *People, States and World Order.* Itasca, Ill.: F. E. Peacock.

BERTSCH, G. K. (1982) "Comparative Analysis: Economic Well-Being and the Global Human Condition," *Global Policy Studies* 3: 91-145.

BOYD, G. (1984) *Regionalism and Global Security.* Lexington, Mass.: Lexington Books.

CANTORI, L. J., and S. L. SPIEGEL (1970) *The International Politics of Regions: A Comparative Approach.* Englewood Cliffs, N. J.: Prentice-Hall.

CERVENCA, Z. (1976) "Africa as a Case of Regional Contradictions," *International Social Science Journal* 28: 736-753.

COHEN, S. B. (1982) "A New Map of Global Geopolitical Equilibrium: A Developmental Approach," *Political Geography Quarterly* 1: 223-241.

CROW, B., and A. THOMAS (1984) *Third World Atlas.* Philadelphia: Taylor and Francis.

CURRENT HISTORY (1982) *Encyclopedia of Developing Nations.* New York: McGraw-Hill.

CURRENT WORLD LEADERS (regularly updated) Pasadena: International Academy.

ECKHARDT, W. (1975) "Global Imperialism and Global Inequality," *International Interactions* 2: 299-332.

(THE) ECONOMIST London, weekly.

EISENBERG, J. M. (1979) "Planning for Regional Cooperation in the Middle East," *Middle East Review* 11: 5-9.

EUROPA YEARBOOK (annual) London: Europa Publications, 2 vols.

FACTS ON FILE (regularly updated) New York: Facts on File Publications.

FALK, R. A. (1975) *A Study of Future Worlds*. New York: Free Press.

_____. (1977) "Contending Approaches to World Order," *Journal of International Affairs* 31:171-198.

_____. (1978) "The World Order Models Project and Its Critics: A Reply," *International Organization* 32: 531-545.

_____. (1980) "The Shaping of World Order Studies: A Response," *Review of Politics* 42:18-30.

_____. (1983) *The End of World Order*. New York: Holmes and Meier.

_____. (1987) *The Promise of World Order: Essays in Normative International Relations*. Philadelphia: Temple University Press.

FALK, R. A., S. S. KIM, and S. H. MENDLOVITZ (eds.) (1982) *Studies on a Just World Order*. vol. I: *Towards a Just World Order*. Boulder: Westview Press.

FALK, R. A., and S. H. MENDLOVITZ (1973) *Regional Politics and World Order*. San Francisco: W. H. Freeman and Co.

FARER, T. J. (1977) "The Greening of the Globe: A Preliminary Appraisal of the World Order Models Project (WOMP)," *International Organization* 31: 129-147.

FORRESTER, J. W. (April, 1982) "Global Modelling Revisited," *Futures:* 95-110.

GALTUNG, J. (1980) *The True Worlds: A Transnational Perspective*. New York: Free Press.

HALLIDAY, J., and R. MCCORMACK (1973) *Co-Prosperity in Greater East Asia: Japanese Imperialism Today*. New York: Monthly Review Press.

HOWELL, L. D. (1983) "A Comparative Study of the WEIS and COPDAB Data Sets," *International Studies Quarterly* 27:149-159.

HUGHES, B. B. (1985) "World Models: The Bases of Difference," *International Studies Quarterly* 29: 77-101.

"Inequality, Militarization, and Human Rights: Selected Bibliography," (1980) *Bulletin of Peace Proposals* 11: 413-415.

INTERNATIONAL HERALD TRIBUNE Paris, daily.

INTERNATIONAL YEARBOOK AND STATESMAN'S WHO'S WHO (annual) West Sussex, England: Thomas Skinner Directories Ltd.

JOHANSEN, R. C. (1980) *The National Interest and the Human Interest*. Princeton: Princeton University Press.

KEESING'S CONTEMPORARY ARCHIVES/RECORD OF WORLD EVENTS (regularly updated) New York: Keesing's Reference Company.

KIM, S. S. (1981) "The World Order Models Project and its Strange Critics," *Journal of Political and Military Sociology* 9: 109-115.

_____. (1983) *The Quest for a Just World Order*. Boulder: Westview Press.

KOTHARI, R. (1974) *Footsteps into the Future: Diagnosis of the Present World and a Design for an Alternative*. New York: Free Press.

KURIAN, G. (1984) *New Book of World Rankings*. New York: Facts on File Publications.

_____. (1987) *Encyclopedia of the Third World*. New York: Facts on File Publications.

LAGOS, G., and H. H. GODOY (1977) *Revolution of Being: A Latin American View of the Future*. New York: Free Press.

MAZRUI, A. A. (1976) *A World Federation of Cultures: An African Perspective*. New York: Free Press.

————. (1981) "The Moving Cultural Frontier of World Order: From Monotheism to North-South Relations," *Alternatives* 7: 1-20.

MENDLOVITZ, S. (1975) *On the Creation of a Just World Order: Preferred Worlds for the 1990s*. New York: Free Press.

————. (1977) "The Program of the Institute for World Order," *Journal of International Affairs* 31: 259-265.

————. (1981) "A Perspective on the Cutting Edge of World Order Inquiry: The Past, Present, and Future of WOMP," *International Interactions* 8: 151-60.

MERRITT, R. L., and D. A. ZINNES (1987) *Data Development in   International Research*. Boulder: Lynne Rienner Publishers.

MICHALAK, S. J., JR. (1980) "Richard Falk's Future World: A Critique of WOMP-USA," *Review of Politics* 42: 3-17.

MIHAILOVIC, K. (1975) *Regional Development: Experience and Prospects in East Europe*. The Hague: Mouton.

MILES, I. (1985) *Social Indicators for Human Development*. London: Frances Pinter.

MILLER, L. H. (1985) *Global Order: Values and Power in International Politics*. Boulder: Westview Press.

NEW YORK TIMES New York, daily.

OAKES, G., and K. STUNKEL (1981) "In Search of WOMP," *Journal of Political and Military Sociology* 9: 83-99.

ORGANIZATION OF ECONOMIC COOPERATION AND DEVELOPMENT (1982) The OECD List of Social Indicators. Paris: OECD.

PAYNE, A. (1980) *The Politics of the Caribbean Community, 1961-1979: Regional Integration among New States*. New York: St. Martin's Press.

POPULATION REREFERENCE BUREAU (annual)   *World Population Data Sheet*. Washington: Population Reference Bureau.

RICHARDSON, J. M., JR. (April, 1982) "A Decade of Global Modelling," *Futures* 14:136-145.

RONEN, D. (1976) "Alternative Patterns of Integration in African States," *Journal of Modern African Studies* 14: 577-596.

RUMMEL, R. J. (1972, 1977, 1978) *Dimensions of Nations* Series. vol. 1-*Dimensions of Nations;* vol. 2-*Field Theory Evolving;* vol. 3-*National Attributes and Behavior: Data, Dimensions, Linkages, and Groups 1950-1965*. Beverly Hills: Sage Publications.

RUSSETT, B. M. (1967) *International Regions and the International System: A Study in Political Ecology*. Chicago: Rand-McNally and Co.

SAKAMOTO, Y. (1972) "The Rationale of the World Order Models Project," *American Journal of International Law* 66: 245-252.

SHEPHERD, G. W. (1987) *The Trampled Grass: Tributary States and Self-Reliance in the Indian Ocean Zone of Peace*. Westport, Conn.: Greenwood Press.

SINGER, J. D. (1970-71) "Individual Values, National Interests, and Political Development in the International System," *Studies in Comparative International Development* 6: 197-210.

SKOCPOL, T. (1984) "Bringing the State Back In: Strategies of Analysis in Current Research," in EVANS, P. B., et al. (eds.) *Bringing the State Back In.* Cambridge: Cambridge University Press.

SNYDER, R. C., C. F. HERMANN, and H. D. LASSWELL (1976) "A Global Monitoring System: Appraising the Effects of Government on Human Dignity," *International Studies Quarterly* 20: 221-260.

STATESMAN'S YEARBOOK (annual) New York: St. Martin's Press.

SULLIVAN, M. J. (1985) "Regions of the World: Revisions for the 1980s," paper delivered at International Studies Association, annual meeting, Washington, D. C.: 1-28.

SYLVESTER, C. (1981) "In Defense of the World Order Models Project: A Behaviorist's Response," *Journal of Political and Military Sociology* 9: 101-108.

TAYLOR, C. L. (ed.) (1980) *Indicator Systems for Political, Economic, and Social Analysis.* Cambridge, Mass.: Oelgeschlager, Gunn and Hain.

TAYLOR, C. L., and D. B. JODICE (1983) *World Handbook of Political and Social Indicators.* vol. 1-*Cross National Attributes and Rates of Change;* vol. 2-*Political Protest and Government Changes;* vol. 3-*Domestic Political Events Data.* New Haven: Yale University Press.

TAYLOR, P. (1983) *The Limits of European Integration.* New York: Columbia University Press.

UNITED NATIONS (annual) *Statistical Yearbook.* New York: United Nations Publications.

UNITED NATIONS POPULATION FUND (1990) *State of World Population 1990.* New York: United Nations Publications.

UNITED STATES CENTRAL INTELLIGENCE AGENCY (annual) *World Factbook.* Washington: US Government Printing Office.

UNITED STATES DEPARTMENT OF STATE (various) *Countries of the World and their Leaders: Background Notes.* Detroit: Gale Research Co.

WALKER, R. B. J. (ed.) (1984) *Culture, Ideology, and World Order.* Boulder: Westview Press.

————. (1987) *One World, Many Worlds: Struggles for a Just World Peace.* Boulder: Lynne Rienner Publications.

WEBB, K. E. (1972) *Geography of Latin America: A Regional Analysis.* Englewood Cliffs, N. J.: Prentice-Hall.

WEHR, P., and M. WASHBURN (1976) *Peace and World Order Systems: Teaching and Research.* Beverly Hills: Sage Publications.

WESTON, B. H. (1984) "Peace and World Order Education: An Optimal Design," in WIEN: 55-77.

WIEN, B. J. (ed.) (1984) *Peace and World Order Studies: A Curriculum Guide,* 4th edition. New York: World Policy Institute.

WORLD BANK (1988) *Social Indicators of Development 1988.* Baltimore: Johns Hopkins University Press, for the World Bank.

1

Peace

The first value in this model for global values is peace, defined here to mean a state's not resorting to organized institutional violence for the settlement of political disputes. Peace will thus be identified by reference to its reciprocal or negative (war) as well as to the preparations therefor and aftermaths thereof. As will become clear in the sections to follow, what would appear to be a rather obvious, large-scale phenomenon—war—is often surprisingly difficult to identify and certainly hard to measure in any meaningful statistical manner.

Several indicators will be used in this chapter to provide examples of militarized modes of conflict resolution, and their domestic and external manifestations. They will include such measures as the duration and severity of wars and insurgencies, defense budgets, military coup regimes, overseas deployments, and arms trade. Arms control treaties are a final, positive indicator of a commitment to the peaceful resolution of disputes.

V1.1. WAR IN THE "POST-WAR" WORLD

VI.1a. Wars by Type, Severity, and Duration

It is difficult to identify clearly examples of belligerent states in this era of undeclared wars, revolutions without borders, military aid for probes by proxies, and other blurred distinctions between domestic and international conflict. A survey of several respected analyses of war since 1945 (Brogan, 1990; Hartman, 1984; Kidron and Smith, 1983; Carver, 1981; Eckhardt and Azar, 1979; Butterworth, 1976; Donelan and Grieve, 1973) reveals varying totals for the number of wars, the participants involved, and the toll of battle deaths, in any given period. One reason for the divergence in results, in addition to the different time frames covered, is the disagreement over what is recognized as a war (Levy, 1987; Maoz, 1988). This study attempts to clarify this issue by identifying three types of wars—international, anticolonial, and civil—and then further describing some conflicts by use of the terms "periodic" and "insurgency."

It would seem that countries with armed troops on another state's soil would by that fact be in a state of international belligerency. But in many instances the troops of one state are on the territory of another at the "request" of the "hosting" government (e.g., the US in West Germany, the USSR in Mongolia, Syria in Lebanon), and at another extreme there are cases of formal belligerency in which countries have not violated the territory of their enemy in years, but are still technically in a state of war (e.g., North and South Korea, Israel and several Arab League states).

The task of defining war can be made somewhat easier by identifying (in the tradition of Cioffi-Revilla, 1989; Singer, 1979; and Richardson, 1960) the grossest examples of warlike behavior in terms of the scale of death and destruction. Hence this study begins with Table VI.1a, an analysis of wars in the "post-war" world—i.e., since 1945—focusing upon their *severity*, as measured by the number of deaths. A cutoff of 1000 deaths is used as a minimum level for civil wars (as opposed to insurgencies—see section VI.1b). For international wars, however, significant hostile violations of national sovereignty (i.e., troops from one state moving onto another's territory) are defined as war even if the deaths are few (e.g., the Berlin Airlift, the Cuban Missile Crisis, and the 1969 Sino-Soviet border shootings), and even if a "letter of invitation" is subsequently produced by the winning side (e.g., the US in Dominican Republic and Grenada, the USSR in Czechoslovakia and Afghanistan). Even in these cases, it is not always easy to distinguish between wars and "shows of force" (Blechman and Kaplan, 1978).

Table VI.1a draws primarily upon the work of Sivard (1985ff), Laffin (1986ff), the Center for Defense Information (1983 and 1986), and Kende (1978), with appropriate updates via the media of record (*New York Times, Economist*) through 1990. The description provided in the first column of Table VI.1a facilitates determining which years (or phases) of certain protracted wars are being identified. In wars where "allies" operated in distinctly subordinate roles—e.g., the "Warsaw Pact intervention" in Czechoslovakia (1968), the "Organization of Eastern Caribbean States rescue" of Grenada (1983)—only the principal combatants (USSR and USA, respectively) are included in the *state* summaries of years at war which follow in this section's concluding Table VI.1d. Wars involving cross-zonal participants (e.g., the US in Vietnam, the Soviet Union in Afghanistan) are listed in the geographic zone where the wars took place (i.e., Asia, Islamic, respectively). Note also Pakistan and Somalia, most of whose wars are outside their home zones as defined in Table I.1.

Using 1945 as a base year, this survey concludes that as of 1990 there have been about 140 wars and some 25 million deaths during the "post-war" era. The reason for approximate figures is due to the inherent softness of data relating to such a chaotic phenomenon as war. This is certainly true concerning the number of deaths involved in battle, but also with respect to such apparently obvious matters as the starting and ending dates of some conflicts, and even whether a war has occurred. Nevertheless, certain generalizations can be made about the frequency and severity of war across the five main zones. (See summary on p.1 of Table V1.1a.)

The most wars have been fought in Asia (about 45), compared to some 35 in the Islamic world, and about 25 each in Latin America and Africa; there have been only 5 wars in the European zone. Asia has also suffered the most fatalities in war, more than 17 million, compared to the Islamic zone's 5.3 million, Africa's 4.5 million, and less than 1 million in Latin America and Europe combined. These rounded totals confirm the theses of Knorr (1966), Levi (1981), Sivard (1989), and Mueller (1989) that military conflict in the nuclear era has shifted to the Third World. As the detailed analysis of Table V1.1a will reveal, war today (and certainly deaths related to war) is a phenomenon generally limited to the non-European (non-white) peoples of this planet.

International war, even with the somewhat broad definition introduced above, seems to be a disappearing phenomenon; less than 25% of the wars listed below (35 of 141) are identified as such. Similarly, the era of *anti-colonial wars* —after the several in Asia, Africa, and the Islamic zone during the years 1945-1975—has virtually come to an end, except for two "successor-colonial" states still fighting to put down independence movements in the Western Sahara and East Timor.

Most significantly, the great majority of wars in the contemporary era (90 out of 141 identified here) have been more domestic than international in character. These *civil* wars present the most difficult cases for categorization and often continue on at low levels even after their apparent resolution. Therefore, a special section (V1.1b) will analyze the distinction between civil wars, insurgencies (coded ^ in the table), and periodic wars (coded *), as represented in a number of current conflicts. (A final related concept—revolution—is discussed in V1.2c.)

V1.1b. Civil Wars and Insurgencies

A study of 13 *current* civil wars (i.e., those designated by "ff" following last date next to a state in Table V1.1a) will illustrate some of the problems of definition associated with this phenomenon, especially when contrasted with low-level, sporadic "insurgencies" (^) and "periodic wars" (*). William

Eckhardt of the Peace Research Laboratory in Florida suggests as a criterion "more than 1000 total deaths, with at least 250 deaths per year" before a conflict is considered a civil war (Sivard, 1989: 22). A second consideration is added here: the rebellious side should also have controlled some amount of national territory for a sustained period of time.

The first criterion rules out from inclusion as civil wars in Vl.la a few long-standing, but essentially low-level, insurgencies in places like Northern Ireland and Spain. The second condition eliminates from consideration some insurrectionary movements which have suffered significant casualties but which have seldom retained control over territories they claim (Israel's Palestinians, Turkey's Kurds, Sri Lanka's Tamils, and India's tribal and religious minorities).

Also excluded here from the definitions of insurgency or civil war are rapid repressions by governments of *potentially* rebellious groups—e.g., the massacres of thousands of fundamentalist Moslems by Syria, Nigeria, Yugoslavia, Sudan and Indonesia, and of other dissidents in Brazil and China. Similarly, communal strife in places like India, Pakistan, Malaysia, and the Soviet Union and electoral violence in states such as India, Jamaica, and the Philippines—even when the scale of death is high and there is evidence that it might be condoned by government forces—are not considered "wars" but are treated in Chapters 4 and 5 under the rubrics of social justice and political participation. Finally, military coups with less than 1000 deaths are also excluded here; by definition a coup is a *quick* blow against the state, not prolonged enough in time to merit the description of a war.

Terrorism—a less regular and more random use of force, often aimed at innocent members of the population to reveal the inefficacy of current ruling authorities and thereby undermine their legitimacy (Bell, 1977)—is a term which will not be used in this study. So-called terrorist groups in most countries are often outlawed political parties taking up arms against a government which refuses to allow them more acceptable forms of political participation (Chomsky, 1986). Rather than engage in pejorative stereotyping as to whether such insurgent groups are terrorists or legitimate parties in a civil war, this study will employ the objective criteria of land held and intensity of struggle (as measured by deaths over time). Current conflicts which do not meet both of these criteria will be labelled "insurgencies" and coded ˆ in Table Vl.1b.

A mention of a few other conflicts not included in Table Vl.1b will further clarify the definition of civil war. The struggle between Morocco and Western Sahara is considered to be an anachronistic example of a war of independence against the successor to the original colonial power (Spain). Also not included here are conflicts in Chad, Somalia, Liberia, Uganda, South Africa, Laos, and Nicaragua, which seem to have petered out in recent years. Some of these, however, may not be definitively ended, and so one more concept must be addressed before completing this analysis.

A "periodic" war (*) is one which over a long period of time has had occasional periods of activity which fulfill the above definitions of war, but which is more often dormant or at the lower level of insurgency. More than 20 such wars are identified in Table V1.1a, including several which are currently active. Inherent in the concept of a periodic war is the idea that it may be gaining or losing strength at any particular point in time. As a group, however, these periodic wars are not considered as significant as the rather constant civil wars and insurgencies which are identified in Table V1.1b and subjected to further investigation.

Employing these criteria, it can be said that as of 1990 civil wars are occurring in some 13 states as identified in section V1.1a. An additional eight insurgencies (including three in India) in six states are introduced for further analysis here. States engaged in these two types of conflicts are ranked below in Table V1.1b by both (i) the severity of struggle (i.e., war deaths), and (ii) the amount of land controlled by non-governmental forces. (In five cases where fighting involves more than one clearly identifiable adversary, states are annotated with a "º".)

A detailed analysis of the non-governmental forces in several of the 19 states found in Table V1.1b is presented in a special section of excerpts drawn from the data bank associated with this project. Information on these groups is necessarily sketchy with both sides having reasons to inflate or deflate true strength depending on political circumstances (e.g., need for higher counterinsurgency budgets by governments, need to rally supporters' morale by rebels). Estimates presented here are taken from a number of reference books, many of which have varying data owing to the amorphous nature of some of these groups; these sources are then regularly supplemented by the latest information from authoritative current newspapers and magazines. Although this information sometimes becomes outdated (especially with respect to numerical strengths and names of groups coming into and going out of existence or into alliances with one another), it is nevertheless a useful base for clues relating to leadership and ideological orientation, as well as to ethnic affiliation and geographic locations, of insurgent strength.

Levels of government and opposition forces are compared, although an insurgency can often be successfully sustained with relatively few armed fighters, especially if its (non-combatant) supporters (local and external) are significant in size or resources. Another point to note is that often there are several insurgent groups which may sometimes cooperate against the common governmental enemy, but which are just as likely to be rivals for power after their insurgency is successful; the cases of Afghanistan and Cambodia are instructive in this regard. Only the main groups operating in a given state are reprinted below.

Paramilitary forces suspected of being allied with the government are generally not included among the groups cited here. Although such "death squads" have the potential of moving into an anti-government (or insurgent) position (note, for example, the situation in El Salvador, 1984-88), until such orientation becomes explicit they will not be analyzed now, but rather in section V4.3b (illegal government killings). Other connections between insurgents and the rest of this book include information on each group's origins and ideology in sections V5.3-4 (if they become accepted as legal political parties), and data on ethnicity in section V4.2 (where the practice of italicizing the names of *minority ethnic groups* is explained). The information which follows, thus, is presented not only as an indicator of the lack of peace in these states today, but in anticipation of certain measures which will affect these countries' standings in later sections of Chapters 4 (Social Justice) and 5 (Political Participation).

The three pages of EXCERPTS following Table V1.1b are drawn from the narrative data banks associated with the Measuring Global Values project. The following format is employed for insurgent groups:

Data Bank Format for V1.1b-Insurgent Groups

(if a civil war, % land held by rebels in:) **State, size of government forces** v.
    tot. # insurgents under arms, in # of main insurgent groups;
       (+ death tolls preliminary to V1.1a inclusion for insurgencies^);
    for each group, list:
    (a)-group name, founding date and origins, and leader(s); including:
       faction of ?, ideology (includes *ethnicity*);
    (b)-estimated armed strength and support, both local (where found, + % land,
       % population represented there), and foreign (often relates to ideology in
       line (a));
    (c)-ties to: V1.1a (deaths, war progress related to this group),
       V4.3b (pro-government paramilitary groups), Chapter 5 (parties).

The original base for the V1.1b data bank was built from Janke, 1983; Degenhardt, 1983; Schmid, 1984; and the International Institute of Strategic Studies (IISS), *Military Balance 1985/86* . It has been updated since that time through Degenhardt, 1988; Schmid, 1988; IISS (annually through 1989); the US Department of State, *Terrorist Group Profiles* (1988), and *Patterns of Global Terrorism* reports to the Congress (1989 and 1990); the *New York Times* and *The Economist* (regularly); and through the reference books mentioned in the introduction (Banks; the US Department of State, *Background Notes*), and in Chapter 5 (*Clements Encyclopedia*, DeLury).

V1.1c. Refugees from War

One final phenomenon which helps in identifying the existence of war is the presence of refugees swarming out of a country which has become a battle zone. In the 1980s, the total number of such unfortunate persons throughout the world annually exceeded more than 12 million. The number of refugees is also correlated with economic deprivation (V2) and social injustice (V4); but even a casual look at statistics for those countries which are the top "generators" of refugees persuades one that the primary reason why people would leave their families and possessions and flee to another state is war (Ferris, 1985).

Despite a 1951 UN Convention and 1967 UN Protocol on the status of refugees, sources vary in the way they define and report numbers of refugees. The Organization of African Unity's definition is broader than that of the UN Convention, and the UN High Commission for Refugees itself includes in its totals all persons reported by asylum-country governments, whether or not they fall within the official definition and qualify for UN assistance. On the other hand, the United States, because it is such a magnet for refugees, applies the 1951 definition strictly and recognizes only those "with a well-founded fear of political persecution" if they returned to their native land; persons fleeing poverty, famine, or natural disaster are normally excluded from its State Department's yearly *World Refugee Report* .

This study will employ another definitive source for data on refugees: the US Committee on Refugees, a private organization which has been publishing an annual *World Refugee Survey* since 1961. In its most recent report, published in 1990 for the year 1989, it has estimated the total number of refugees at 15,093,900. Its findings, reported in Table VI.1c in three different categories, repeat the identities of some of the familiar countries from the previous sections on current wars and insurgencies.

Table VI.1c.i identifies 24 countries as the principal sources of the world's refugees. The count may understate the total number of refugees from a given country as asylum nations do not always specify countries of refugees' origin. The data also does not include some 4.5 million people in "refugee-like" circumstances covered in Table VI.1c.ii. These are peoples who may fear persecution if returned to their home countries, and so are undocumented, or unregistered, or for some other reason fall outside the legal protection mechanisms of host countries and international agencies. Precise data on these groups is hard to document, and some of the numbers cited here are averages of ranges of estimates reported by the US Committee. Finally, Table VI.1c.iii displays 23 countries in which more than 17 million people have been displaced *within* their homelands as a result of war and civil strife. Although they share many characteristics with refugees who cross international borders, they are generally not eligible for international refugee assistance. Again, the US Committee's ranges of estimates are averaged here for ease in comparing with the previous parts of this table.

V1.1d. State Experience in War

Table V1.1d.i analyzes, within their respective zones, the conflicts listed in Tables V1.1a and .1b from a state-by-state perspective in an effort to identify those countries with the most contemporary experience in war. For most states, the number of years at war is taken directly from those two tables, where significant fighting or deaths at any time during a calendar year is counted as one year.

For those 23 wars which are designated periodic (*) in Table V1.1a, and for the 8 conflicts identified as current insurgencies (^) in V1.1b, the total number of years involved is calculated as *one-half* the number of years listed because it is judged that the state's commitment to such war efforts is less than that in a full-scale civil or external war. The years for these "lesser" forms of war are listed in italics, along with the appropriate * or ^ designation, in Table V1.1d.i. However, a major year of fighting in the midst of a periodic war is not included in the total for computing the periodic "half-years," but rather is added in separately to the state's total.

For example, although the civil strife in Myanmar has been periodic over 42 years since 1948, there have been only 10 years (1948-51, 1980, 1984-90) with significant fighting; hence the total duration is computed as:

$$10 + (42-10)/2 \ = \ 10 + (32/2) \ = \ 10 + 16 \ = \ 26.$$

With respect to total number of years at war, the above calculating methods reveal that the following states have been at war in at least one-half of the 45 years since 1945: Portugal, UK, France, US (but not the USSR) from the European zone; Israel, Iraq, Sudan, N. Yemen in the Islamic world; South Africa, Ethiopia, Angola in Africa; and Vietnam, the Philippines, India, Myanmar, and China in Asia (see column 4 in Table V1.1d.i). Concerning the actual number of different wars (column 2), the leaders are: China (with 12) and India (with 11); followed by the United States and Vietnam, with 10 each; United Kingdom, France, and Israel (8 apiece); Iraq (7); and the USSR, Pakistan, and Indonesia (6 each).

Most of the states mentioned in this summary have been in the vanguard of the "North-South" decolonization struggle of the post-World War II era. As noted earlier, most of these conflicts have been fought in the Asian and Islamic zones. Although India and China have fought the most wars there, their conflicts have generally been limited in time and scope. At the other extreme, Vietnam has been at war almost constantly since it declared independence in 1946; its struggles are broken up here into four different phases during the pre-1975 struggle for independence and unity, plus six involvements since that time with its neighbors.

In the Islamic zone, where the replacement of the British and French imperial presence has been particularly protracted, Israel is identified with eight wars (counting the ongoing insurgency with the PLO, and the occupation of southern

Lebanon), while Iraq, Iran, Egypt, Syria, Lebanon, Jordan, and Turkey have each been in three or more, many involving the submerged nations of Palestinians and Kurds.

Among the "unfinished business" of independence after the era of European imperialism has been the resolving of ethnic conflicts previously suppressed by the European colonial powers. In states like Sudan, Israel, Lebanon, Angola, Uganda, Myanmar, and India, these issues unfortunately have often been worked out in a violent manner.

With respect to the Northern powers trying to hold on to, or replace one another in, imperial positions, the comparison between the United States (with 10 wars over 28 years) and Britain, France, and Portugal (total of 20 wars, 98.5 years among them) on the one hand, and the USSR with active belligerency on only 6 occasions totaling 15 years, is striking.

Finally, the number and total duration of wars are combined (multiplied) to give for each state a summary score with respect to its tendency to have been involved in war since 1945. By this rough standard, the 44 states indicated with scores greater than 20 in Table V1.1d.ii would rank as those least committed to the peaceful resolution of political disputes. A comparison of the states ranking high here with those at the top of the lists in the more traditional measures of militarism developed in the next two sections (V1.2 and V1.3) will reveal many of the same countries.

V1.1a — Summary, Wars since 1945, by Type and Severity

Zone	#wars:	intl.	+ colonial	+ civil	#dead	V1.1b^	periodic*
Europe	5	3	0	2	0.2 mil.	2	0
Islamic	37	10	4	23	5.3 mil.	2	11
Africa	26	2	7	17	4.5 mil.	0	4
Asia	46	14	5	27	17.0 mil.	2	6
Lat.Am.	27	6	0	21	0.6 mil.	0	2
Totals	141	35	16	90	27.6 mil.	6^	23*

^ = *current* (1990) insurgencies only; see V1.1b.

* = applied to years of wars which are only periodically active (n=23).

Other abbreviations used in display which follows:

ff = "and following"; applied to most recent year of continuing wars (n=13 in V1.1b).

+ = added to totals for continuing wars where significant increases are expected in future.

n.k.= number of deaths not known (generally small).

† = occasionally applied to notable number of deaths for particular side (or time) in war.

qv = quis vis = which (referred to war) reader should also see. (N. Yemen, Eritrea, etc.)

V1.1a — Wars, by # of Deaths - European Zone

i. international wars:	Dates	Deaths
USSR v. Hungary	Nov. 1956	10,000-30,000?
USSR(+Warsaw Pact) v. Czechoslovakia	Aug. 1968	low, <10?
Berlin Blockade & Airlift (US,UK,Fr. v. SU)	1948-49	0 (?)

ii. anti-colonial wars of independence - none

iii. civil wars:		
Greece: fascists v. monarchists. v. democrats. v. comms.	1945-49	160,000
Romania: overthrow of Ceausescu regime	Dec. 1989	1-2,000

Totals: 5 wars   < 200,000† deaths

plus see 2 current insurgencies^ (N.Ire., Spain) in V1.1b.

†perhaps another 200,000 European deaths (# not always known, but generally about 1/10 the total given) in wars listed in other zones; see below, mention of European states in the wars of:

Islamic zone: Suez Canal ('56), Algeria (54-62), Morocco (53-56), Tunisia (52-54), Afghanistan (79ff), Cyprus (74), Lebanon (58).

Africa: Angola ('61-75), Mozambique (65-75), Guinea Bissau (63-74), Kenya (52-53ff).

Asia: Korea ('50-53), 2nd Indochina (65-73), China (69), 1st Indochina (46-54), SVN (60-64), Cambodia (70-75), Laos (63-73), Malaya (50-60), Indonesia (45-48), Madagascar (47-48).

Latin America: Dominican Republic ('65), Falklands (82), Panama (89), Grenada (83), Nicaraguan contras (81ff), Guatemala (54), Cuba (61), and Cuba (62).

V1.1a — Wars, by # of Deaths - Islamic Zone

i. international wars:	Dates	Deaths
Iran v. Iraq	1980-88	1.0-1.5 mil. (6:1)
Israel #3: "Six-Day War" v. Egypt,Jordan,Syria	June '67	70,000
Israel #5: incursions of Lebanon, 1978ff* esp.....	1982	20,000
Israel #4: "Yom Kippur War" v. Egypt, Syria	Oct. '73	16,000
Israel #1: Independence v. Syr.,Jord.,Eg.,Leb.,Iraq	May-Dec.'48	9,000
Libya v. Chad (Aouzou strip), periodic*, esp.....	1973,'80,'87	7,000
Israel #3.5: "War of Attrition" v. Egypt	1967-70	5,000
Israel #2: "Suez Canal War" w/ UK, Fr. v. Egypt	Oct. '56	3,000
Iraq v. Kuwait	Aug. '90	700
N. Yemen v. S. Yemen, periodic 1967-89*, esp.	1972,1987	low

ii. anti-colonial wars of independence:		
Algeria, independence v. France† (†=16,000 d.)	1954-62	1.1 mil.
Western Sahara (POLISARIO) v. Morocco/Mauritania (to '78)	1975ff*	16,000 (7000)
Morocco, independence v. France	1953-56	3,000
Tunisia, independence v. France	1952-54	3,000

iii. civil wars:		
Afghanistan (civ.war,SU intervene,12/79-2/89;14,000†)	1978ff	1,300,000+
Sudan civil war-II: black SPLA v. Islamic law	1983ff	506,000+
Sudan civil war-I: black south Anyanya v. north (Arabs)	1955-72	500,000
Lebanon civil war, including:	4/75ff.,incl:	160,000+, incl:
Syr.+Xtns. v. PLO,2 Moslems,Druze	1975-76	100,000
Israel+Xtns. v. PLO v. Druze+Shiites v. Sunni	1982-5	18,000
PLO v. Amal Shiites v. Hezbollah Shiites	1985-8	12,000
Kurds v. #2=Iraq, periodic* since '58 ,esp......	'61-70,74,84,88^	140,000
N.Yemen: repubs.+Egypt v. monarchists+S.Arabia	1962-69	101,000
Somalia v. SNM Isaaks, USC Hawiyes, etc. periodic* since......	1988	50,000
Iran v. ethnic separatists (includ. Kurds #3), NLA dissidents	1979, 1989	25-40,000
Chad civil wars, l965ff* periodic; esp......	1979-82; 90	21,000
Iranian Revolution (Isl. Fundmtlsts. v. Shah)	1978-79	17,000
S. Yemen: change of govt.	Jan. 1986	13,000
Pakistan v. Baluch ('75 esp.) & other separatists	1972-77*	9,000+
Turkey: left v. right "terrorism"....mil. coup	1976-80	5,000-6,000
Cyprus: Gr.coup, Turk.invas., & partition	July 1974	5,000
Jordan v. PLO (esp. w/ Syria v. Black Sept.'70, 3000d)	1969-73*	5,000
N.Yemen: Yahya family v. Govt., coup attempt	1948	4,000
Iraq revolution (+ aftermath v. Shammars, 2000 d.)	1958-59	4,000
Kurds v. #1=Turkey, periodic* since 1920s, esp.	1980ff^	3,500
Algeria: former rebel leaders v. Govt.	1962-63	2,000
Lebanon: Xtn.Gov.+US(1 d.) v. pro-Nasser Moslems	1958	2,000
N.Yemen civil war (1950s prelim. to 1962-69,qv), esp.	1950-52	1,000+
Oman v. Dhofaris, periodic* in	1955-59,64-75	n.a.
N.Yemen (civil war reprise v.left Natl.Dem.Frnt.,'79-82 esp.	1979	n.a.

Total: 37 war   ~5.3 million deaths.

incl current (ff) civil wars, n=3: Afgh.,Leb.,Sudan; and periodic* wars, n=11: Isr.v.Leb., Libya v. Chad, Yemen, W. Sahara, 2 Kurds, Chad, Somalia, Pakistan, Jordan, Oman; plus see 2 current insurgencies (Israel, Turkey) in V1.1b.

V1.1a - Wars, by # of Deaths — African zone

i. international wars:	Dates	Deaths
Ethiopia v. Somalia(W.Som./Ogaden)1962ff*,esp..	7/77-3/78	38,000
Tanzania v. Uganda (overthrow Amin)	11/78-6/79	3,000

ii. anti-colonial wars of independence:		
Angola indep. (MPLA,FNLA,UNITA) v. Portugal	1961-75	50-75,000
Cameroon independence v. France, UK	1955-60	32,000
Mozambique indep. (FRELIMO) v. Portugal	1965-75	30-60,000
Namibia (SWAPO) v. (S&)SWAfrica, periodic*	1966-88	22,500
Zimbabwe indep. (ZAPU,ZANU,ZPA) v. Rhodesia	1972-79	19,500
Guinea Bissau indep. (PAIGC) v. Portugal	1962-74	15,000
Kenya independ. (Mau Mau) v. UK; 1950s,esp....	1952-53	15,000

iii. civil wars:		
Nigeria v. Biafra's Ibos	1967-70	2,000,000
Ethiopia v.Erit.,Tigre,Somali civ.war+famine('84,5,8)	1978ff	600,-1,000,000
Mozambique v. MNR (+ S.Africa intervene, 1978-84)	1978ff	400,-900,000
Uganda-III (anti-Obote/Okello; esp. 1983-5)	1981-86	300,-400,000
Angola(+Cuba'75-91) v. UNITA(+ S.Af.'75-89,CIA '85ff)	1975ff	200,-350,000
Uganda-II: Idi Amin rule & civil war	1971-78	200,-300,000
Burundi: Tutsi govt.(10,000†) v. Hutu 86% pop.	1972	100,-200,000
Rwanda: Hutu govt. v. Tutsi 14% minority pop.	1956-65	105,000
Zaire post-independ.wars(Congo v.Katanga,etc.)	1960-65	100,000
Ethiopia v. Eritrea, 1961-78ff(qv), *periodic, esp....	1976-78	36,000
Liberia: Doe v. Taylor & Johnson; Krahns v. Gios & Manos	1990	20,000
Uganda-IV: Museveni v. Obote,Amin remnants in n.east	1987-88	sevl. 1000s
S.Africa v. ANC, 1960ff, periodic* esp.................	'60,'76,'83-86	4,000+
Tanzania = Tanganyika v. Zanzibar	1963	2,500-5,000
Zimbabwe post-indep.pol.viol.,1980-83,esp....	1983	3,000+
Uganda-I: v. Buganda secession	1966	2,000
Zaire v. Shaba province	1977-78	n.a.

Total: 26 wars   ~4.5 million deaths
incl.: current (ff) civil wars, n=3: Ethiopia, Mozambique, Angola;
   and periodic* wars (n=4) in W. Somalia, Namibia, Eritrea, S.Africa.

Vl.la - Wars, by # of Deaths - Asian Zone

i. international wars:	Dates	Deaths
Korean War: NK & China v. SK & †US(UN)	1950-53	2,900,000 (†US=53,000)
2nd Indochina War (SVN, †US v. NVN,VC)	2/65-1/73	2,058,000 (†US=58,000)
Bangladesh(+India,Dec.'71) v. Pakistan,	Mar.-Dec.1971	1,500,000
India & Pakistan Partition (Muslim v. Hindu)	1947	800,000
VN v. China (border; "lesson"); '79ff periodic* esp.	Feb.'79, '87	45,000 (†5:2=VN:Ch)
India v. Pakistan (Bangla. indep.)	Dec.'71	30,000
India v. Pakistan: Kutch; Kashmir	1965	20,000
VN v. Cambodia (oust Pol Pot; +see Camb.79ff)	Dec.'78	20,000
India v. Pakistan	1947-49	3,200
India v. Sri Lanka Tamils	1987-90	2,500
India v. China (border)	1962	2,000
China v. USSR (border)	1969	1,000
Indonesia-Malaysia "Confrontation"	1962-66	700
India v. Portuguese Goa	1961	n.k.

ii. anti-colonial wars of independence:		
1st Indochina War (Viet Minh v. France)	1946-54	600,000
Indonesia annex. E.Timor, '75ff* esp.	1975-76	150,000 (=23% of pop.!)
Indonesia: indep. v. Netherlands (&UK)	1945-48	5-75,000 (1/3 Dutch)
Malaysia: Communists v. UK/Malaya Govt.	1950-60	13,000
Madagascar v. France	1947-48	5-15,000

iii. civil wars:		
China "Great Leap Forward"	1957-62	2.5-5.0 mil. (incl.Tibet)
Cambodia civil war (Pol Pot "Killing Fields")	1975-78	1.0-1.5 mil. (of 8m. pop.!)
China civil war (KMT v. CCP)	1946-49	1,000,000
China: post-civil war Govt. v. landlords	1950-51	1,000,000
Chinese "Cultural Revolution", 1966-75 esp....	1966-68	500,000+ (incl.Tibet)
Indonesia "Yr. of Living Dangerously"	1965-66	500,000 (esp.Chinese)
S. Vietnam civil (VC-NLF v. SVN,US)	5/59-1/65	300,000
Vietnam civil (VC-NLF,NVN v. SVN)	1/73-4/75	200,000
Cambodia: Lon Nol+US v. Khmer Rouge	1970-75	155,000
Tibet v. China-II (revolt, Dali Lama flees)	1958-59	100,000
Bangladesh v. Chakmas in Chittagong,'72ff* esp.	1985	85,000
Philippines v. Moros (Muslims), 1972ff*, esp.	1972-76	45,-60,000
Cambodia (+VN('79=89†=18,000)) v. 3 guer. armies	1979ff	44,-50,000
Laos (+VN v. anti-comms.,tribes,Thai.), periodic*	1975-87*	40,-50,000
Philippines v. communist NPA	1969ff	30,-40,000
Indonesia, destabilizing Sukarno	1956-61	35,000
Myanmar civil wars, '48ff* periodic, esp.	1948-51,80,84ff	20,000
Laos "Secret War" (CIA,Hmong v. NVN,NLF)	1963-73	19,000
Sri Lanka v. Tamils (w/India(=1000 dead),'87-90)	1983-87;88ff^	14,000+
Philippines: Huks v. Govt., 1945-54 esp.....	1950-52	9,000
Sri Lanka v. anti-India Peop. Lib. Front (JVP)	7/87-12/89	8,500
Laos: Pathet Lao v. neutralist Govt.	1960-62	5,-10,000
Sri Lanka v. Maoist Peop. Lib. Front	1971	2,-10,000
Indonesia v. communists, Moluccans	1950	5,000
Tibet v. China-I (conquest, annexation)	1950-51	2,000
India v. princelies (Hyderabad,Junagadh)	1947-8	2,000
China KMT v. Taiwan/Formosa	Feb-Mar.'47	1,000

Totals: 46 wars   ~17 million deaths

incl. current(ff) civil wars, n=3: Myanmar, Camb., Ph. I.;   and periodic* wars (n=6) in VN/China, Indonesia,
   Bangladesh, Phil. I., Laos, Myanmar; plus see 2 current insurgencies (India, Sri Lanka) in V1.1b.

V1.1a - Wars, by # of Deaths — Latin American Zone

i. international wars:	Dates	Deaths
"Soccer War": El Sal. v. Honduras	6/69-7/69	4,500
US(+OAS) v. Dominican Republic	4/65-8/65	3,000 (26 US†)
Falklands/Malvinas (Arg. v. UK) War	4/82-6/82	1,200 (200 UK†)
US v. Panama (overthrow Noriega Govt.)	Dec. 1989	700 (23 US†)
US(+OCES) "rescue" of Grenada	Oct. 1983	87
Cuban Missile Crisis (US,SU,Cuba)	Oct. 1962	1 US U2 pilot

ii. anti-colonial wars of independence:
  NONE

iii. civil wars:	Years	# of deaths
Colombia civil war-I ("La Violencia": Libls. v. Cons.)	1948-58	200,-300,000
Guatemala: Govt.+right v. Indians+left, periodic*	1958ff*	138,000, incl:
1966-74 (30,000 d.) and 1979ff (60,000+ d.) esp. '82-83		
El Salvador v. FMNLF	1979ff	75,000+
Nicaragua I: revolution: Sandinistas v. Somoza	1975-79	35,000
Nicaragua II: v. contras + US CIA	11/81-2/88	30,000
Chile: Allende overthrow + aftermath	1973-74	25,000
Colombia-II v. left. guers. & right. drug cartels	1978ff	20,000, incl:
v. leftist guers.,'78-84 (12,000 d.), and v. left + rightist drug cartels '85ff (8,000 d.)		
Peru v. Shining Path, etc. guers.	1980ff	18,000
Argentina: Govt.v.left ("disappearances")	1976-82	9,-15,000
Cuban Revolution: Castro v. Batista	1958-9	5,000
Argentina army coup v. Peron	1955	4,000
Costa Rican Revolution	1948	2,000
Bolivia civil war-II: MNR (Paz Estensoro) wins	1952	2,000
Argentina v. left(ERP, Monteneros) & right(Peronists)	1974-76	1,100+
Bolivia civ. war-I (Villarroel Gov. wins)	1946	1,000
Paraguay civil war: libls. v. cons. govt.	1947	1,000
Guatemala: Arbenz Govt. v. CIA,Armas exiles	June '54	1,000
Cuba:"Bay of Pigs": CIA,exiles v. Castro	Apr.'61	272(1US†)
Uruguay v. Tupamaros, periodic* during... ...	1963-72*	111
Suriname (Bouterse Govt. v. Brunswijk blacks)	1985-87	n.k.
Peru v. Mvmt. of Rev. Left (MIR)	1965	n.k.

  Total 27 wars   ~600,000 deaths

incl. current (ff) civil wars, n=4: El Salvador,Guatemala,Peru,Colombia;
        and periodic* wars (n=2) in Guatemala, Uruguay.

Source: V1.1a Data Bank

V1.1b - Major Current (1990) Civil Wars and Insurgencies (=^)

.i - By Severity and Type, within Zone

Europe (n=0+2^):
^Northern Ireland: UK & Prots. v. IRA & Catholics	1969ff	2,800
^Spain: Govt. v. Basques	1968ff	650-700

Islamic (n=3+2^):
Afghanistan civ. war (w/ SU intervention, '79-89)	1978ff	1,300,000
Sudan civ. war II	1983ff	506,000+
Lebanon civil war	1975ff	160,000+
^PLO v. Israel(+others), periodic* since	1965ff	8,000, incl:

@Kramh(Jordan)'68, 400; @Arkubel(Golan)'72, 1000; in s.Leb. 3/78, 400, & 3/81, 1000;
& 12/87ff *intifada*, 800+. (+See PLO under Leb.'75-6,'82-8, and Jordan, '69-'73 in V1.1a.)

^Turkey v. Kurds, periodic*, since 1920s including......	1980ff	3500

Africa (n=3):
Ethiopia v. Eritrea, Tigre, Somali, etc.	1978ff	600,-1,000,000
Mozambique v. MNR(w/ S. Africa intervntn.,'78-'84)	1978ff	400,000-900,000
Angola(+Cuba'75-91)v.UNITA (+S.Af.'75-89,CIA'85ff)	1975ff	200,000-350,000

Asia (n=3+2º):
Cambodia(+VN,'79-89) v. natlst. coalition of 3 armies	1979ff	44-50,000
^India v. Sikhs (Punjab);	1984ff	20-60,000
Phil. I. v. communist NPA	1969ff	30-40,000
Myanmar civil wars; periodic* '48ff esp...	1948-58,80,84ff	20,000
^Sri Lanka v. Tamils (w/ India 8/87-4/90=1000 dead)	1983-87; 88ff^	14,000
^India v.NE rebs.(W.Bng.,Assam,Nag,Man,Trip,Miz,Grkh)	1955ff*	5,000
^India v. Kashmiri Moslems	1987ff	1,000

Latin America (n=4+0^):
El Salvador v. FMNLF/FDN	1979ff	75,000+
Guatemala II: Govt.+right v. Indians & left	1979ff	60,000+
Colombia-III: v. leftist guerillas & rightist druglords	1978ff	20,000+
Peru: Govt. v. Shining Path guerillas	1980ff	18,000+

.ii - By % Territory Controlled by Non-Government Forces

Europe	Islamic	Africa	Asia	Latin America
	ºLebanon-90%			
	Afghan.-80%	Mozambq.-35-80%		Peru-30%
		Angola-30%	Phil.I-20%	El Sal.-25%
	Sudan-30%	ºEthiopia-30%	ºMyanmar-5-30%	Guatemala-10%
			Cambodia-10%	ºColombia-5%
------	------	---- insurgencies = ^	------	------
UK(N.Ire.)	Turkey		SriLanka	
Spain	Israel		ºIndia	
n=2	n=5	n=3	n=5	n=4

Total: 19 states (24+ conflicts), 13 with civil wars, 6 with ^insurgencies.

Legend:
^ (below dotted line) = insurgencies: no land held; &/or deficit intensity (1000 tot.+250/yr.)
º = more than one conflict in same state (Lebanon, Ethiopia, Myanmar, India, Colombia).

Latent or Waning Periodic* Conflicts to watch (1990ff):
W.Sahara,Chad,Somalia; Liberia,Uganda,S. Africa; Laos; Nicaragua

Source: Tables V1.1a ("ff" in col. 2) for civil wars; V1.1b Data Bank for insurgencies(^).
Totals: ≥13 civil wars, ≥8 insurgencies in 19 states (ºsevl. conflicts are separately identified for India; treated on one line for Ethiopia, Lebanon, Myanmar, Colombia).

Europe

(^=0%)—**UK - 330,000** (10,000 on site); 2800 dead, 20,550 injured ('69-90); vs.

1.a) (official) Irish Republican Army - pre-1921 independence movement; now largely legitimate (see Sinn Fein party in V5.3a); b.) n ≤200, no terrorism since 1972.

2. a) Provisional Irish Republican Army - 1969 breakaway faction; has assumed IRA name.

   b) n=400 core, of wh. 60 active; down from 2000 in early 1970s; but still with several thousand (DOS 8/88) active sympathizers. Ldrs: G. Adams, M. McGuinness.

Islamic

(30%)—**Sudan - 65,000** (+some loyal tribal militias); vs.

1.a) SPLA-Southern Peop.Lib. Army - Col. J. GARANG, non-Marxist Christian; started in 3/83 to protest Islamic Law; esp. strong among *Dinkas* (pop. 2 mill.)

   b) n=20,-30,000(MB88/9), esp. in 3 southern provinces (Upper Nile, Equatoria, Bahr el Ghazal); backed by (Marxist, Christian) Ethiopia, and (blacks in) Kenya, Uganda; controls 95% of the south (=30% tot. land & 7/22 mill. of population).

   c) 500,000+ dead, including of starvation, especially in 1988.

(^=0%)—**Turkey - 815,000** (40,000 on site, in south-east); 3500 dead, 1980-89; vs.

1. a) PKK-*Kurdish* Workers Party-Ldr: Abdullah OCALAN in Damascus. Marxist; since mid-'70s.

   b) n=300-1000 in south-east where 9 of 67 provinces under martial law (10/87); claims support of most of 8-10 mil. Kurds in Turkey (pop.56 mill.).

   c) 20 mil. *Kurds* in 5 states (Turkey=47%=9.5 mil.; Iran=27%=5.5 mil.; Iraq=21%=4 mil.; Syria=5%=.6mil.;&SU=<1%=.2mil.). About 6 major insurgs. in 70 yrs. since 1919 League promise of homeland broken after 1920s discovery of oil in Kirkut(UK Iraq). Only Turk's want a separate (Marxist) state; Iraq's two (Ldrs: Talabani of PUK, Barzani of KDP) would settle for "real autonomy"; Iran's (Ldr. Qassemlou, assass. by Govt.,7/89) for "social justice".

2.a) ASALA-*Armenian* Secret Army for Lib. of Armenia-1975ff, to avenge 1.5 mil. WWI deaths; has assassinated 20+ Turkish diplomats. Ldr. H. Hagopian assass. by Govt., 4/88.

   b) n=several hundred (DOS8/88); ties to Syria, Libya, PFLP, PFLP-GC in Lebanon (leftists).

Africa

(30%)—**Ethiopia - 280,000**; vs. two major and several lesser historic ethnic separatist movements; 600-1,000,000 d.; 55,000 Eth. POWs (2/90)

1. a) EPLF-*Eritrean* Peopl.Lib.Front. Marxist. Ldrs: SG Isseyas Afeworki, R. M. Nur, Osman M. Omer. Founded 1970; for secession/independence, end of federalism for ex-Italy colony.

   b) n = 30,000 armed; some Saudi sympathy. Coop. agreement with #2 TPLF, '88ff.

   c) controls all but capital Asmara (=95%) of Eritrea (pop. 3.5mil.= 7.6% of Ethiopian total, after .5 mil. deaths since '61); EPLF has after long struggle absorbed other (more Islamic) Eritrean groups ELF, ELF-PLF, and ELF/RC fighting since '61 annexation.

2.a) TPLF-*Tigrean* Peoples(Popular)Lib.Front; since '74-75.

   b) n=20,-30,000; controls 100% Tigre province (1/89), moving into Wollo prov. (9/89); Saudi sympathy despite more rigid Marx-Leninist than Govt.; for overthrow, not secession.

   c) 4/88 coop. agreement with #1 EPLF despite different goals; and with #4 EPDM

3. Other ethnic-based (currently dormant):

.1.a) WSLF-West.*Somali* Lib.Front. Abdullah Hassan Mahmud; b. n=1000(MB88/9) in Ogaden.

.2.a) ALF-*Afar* Lib.Front - Sultan Ali Mirah Hanfare; b. n=5,000 armed, near Djibouti.

.3.a) OLF-*Oromo-Galla* Natl. Lib. Front; b. n=600 armed of 8000 tot., in south-center.

4. Less-ethnic based - EPDM -Ethiop. Peop. Dem. Mvmt.; in Wolo (100 mi. fm. Addis Ababa) & Gondar (near Sudan) provs.; allied with TPLF in EPRDF (Ethiop.Peop. Rev. Dem. Front).

V1.1b EXCERPTS (continued)

(35-80%)—**Mozambique** - **55,000** vs.:
1. a) RENAMO ('82; = exMNR=Natl. Resistance Mvmt.) - Ldr. Afonso Dlakama; 1976ff.
   b) n=15,000-25,000 armed; 20,000, 10,000 trained (MB88/9);   22,000 (DOS8/88); supported by Rhodesia ('76-79); S. Africa, '79-84(ff? despite Nkomati Agreement); control most of countryside. 400,-900,000 d.; 1/3 pop. displaced; 7% pop. (=1 mil.) refugees.

(30%)—**Angola-64,000**(+=19,000-0^W Cubans(see V1.3a.ii) + SU aid @ $500 mil./yr.); vs:
1. a) UNITA-Natl.Union for Total Indep. of Angola - Ldr: Jonas Savimbi.
   b) n=28,000 + 37,000 support militias = 65,000 (MB88/9); mainly *Ovimbundu;* control 30% of land, 15% of people; 150,000 supporters (CIA Factbook, 1989).
   c) Backed by S.Af.,11/75-12/88(Namibia cf), and by US CIA @ $80 mil./yr. since '85.
2. FNLA-*Bakongo* in northeast; and 3. FLEC-*Cabindans* in northwest - both now defunct.

Asia

(20%)—**Philippines** - **157,000** vs. n=13 (left, ethnic, and right) of which:
A.Left: 1.a)New Peoples Army - since '69, army of (Maoist) Communist Party; which controls Natl. Dem. Front, an umbrella group, with much influence in Bayan (coalition of left parties).
    b)est. n=25,000+10,000 in home militias; about half armed; active in 61/73 provinces; controls 7000/42000 villages (¯16%).
B. Ethnic: *Moslems* = 4/60 mil. (6% pop., esp. in s.(Mindinao & Sulu); inactive 3/89; formerly,
   2. a)Moro Natl.Lib.Front & Bangsa Moro Army-Ldr: Nur Misuari, early '70s. b) n=15,000
   3. a)Moro Islamic Lib. Front - Ldr: Hashem Salama; would accept autonomy. b) n=5000
   4. a)3rd Moro faction - Ldrs: D. Pendato & M. Abbash, for autonomy; b) smallest, n=1500.
C. Army Right: pro-Marcos groups in army responsible for 7 failed coups, 1986-90; including:
   5. a)Reform the Armed Forces, Col. Greg. Honasan et al.(8/87 et al. coups); b) n=2000?
   6. a)Young Officers Union, Capt. D.Valeroso.
D. Other Right: many (n=50?) private landlord & vigilante armies; b) tot. n=12,000 armed.

(10%)—**Cambodia** - **40,000** (+VN=5000 in '90) vs. UN-recognized 6/82 nationalist coalition Govt. of Pres.Sihanouk., VP Samphan, PM Sann); tot. ¯60,000 troops incl. ¯15,000 inside Camb.
   1. a) KR=Khmer Rouge. Ldr. Khieu Samphan since '81; ex-Pol Pot Govt. 1975-78; leftist.
      b) n=40,000 (25:15=fighters:logistics); 100,000 supporters in its camps.
   2. a) Sihanouk Federation of 3 groups(KN,NLMK,NUFINPCK); 1954-70 Govt.; centrist/natlst.
      b) National Sihanoukienne Army, n=10,000(DOSHR88)+6500 reserves (=¯17,000);
      Army Cmdr. = son Norodom Ranariddh. #2 in strength, 52,000 in its refugee camps.
   3. a) KPNLF=Khm.Peop.Natl.Lib.Front. Ldr: Son Sann, since '79; ex-'70-75 Govt.; rightist.
      b) n=12-20,000, incl. 3-5,000 inside, 5000 unarmed reserves. Mil. ldr: Sak Sutsakhan.
      c) least armed, but most supporters (n=174,000 of tot.325,000 in border refugee camps).

Latin America

(10%)—**Guatemala** - **40,000** vs. n=4 main groups with 2200 mbrs.; Waning, for ratio was 18,000 v.9000 in '82, 33,000 v.3000 in '85.   138,000 dead since '58, esp. '66-74, '79ff.
   1. a) EGP=Guerilla Army of the Poor, '75ff, Ldr: Rolando Moran Camel Diaz
      b) n=700 hard-core; most active group (Schmid) before '80s defeats; on Mex. border.
   2. a) FAR=Rebel Armed Forces. Ldr: Pablo Monstanto, Cesar Montes (El Chris)
      b) n=500 (MB88/9), most active group in late '80s.
   3. a)PGT=Party of Guatemalan Workers;   b) n=200 (MB88/9)
   4. a) ORPA=Org. of People in Arms. Ldr. R.Asturias, largest group left in '85 (Laffin'87);
      b) n=350 (MB88/9); ex-MIRA=Indep.Armed Rev.Mvmt., n=4000 once, now defunct.
   5. a) URNG=Guat. Natl. Revol. Unity - Leader: Raul Molina Mejia.
      b) coalition to unify all guerilla armies in the field; n=1500 (*Econ.,* 3/4/89).

V1.1b EXCERPTS (continued)

(30%)—**Peru - 127,000**; vs. n=2+ in 7 emerg. zones with 40-50% pop.=21 mil.
1. a) Shining Path - since '69. Ldr: Manuel A. Guzman; Maoist; indep., xenophob.: accepts no aid.
   b) largest; n=4500(MB88/9)+11,000 supporters; rural *Indians*, esp. Ayacucho province.
2. a) Tupac Amaru Rev. Movement (1984ff); Ldrs: V. Rolay Campos, N. Serpa, E.Montes Aliaga.
   b) smaller, n=200-500; more tradtl.(intl.), urban, pro-Cuban leftist group; in north.

(25%—**El Salvador-54,000** ('88) vs. total guers > 7000, down from 12,000 '83 high, but up from 5000 in '87; in n=30+ of wh: FMNLF=Farabundo Marti Natl. Lib. Front = FDR + DRU:
1. a) FDR=Rev. Dem. Front (coalition of 20+ pop.orgs.). Ldr: Guillermo Ungo.
   b) polit. arm incl. 3 parties: PCES (Sh. Handal,communists), MNR (Ungo,socialists), and (ex-Xtn.Dems R.Zamora, J.Villacorta); above ground supporters of armed DRU units (qv):.....
2. a) DRU=Unified Revolutionary Directorate. Ldr: Cayetano Carpio; of #3-7:
3. a) ERP=Peop. Rev. Army. Ldr: Joaquin Villalobos; most extreme of five rebel groups.
   b) n=2800 (MB88/9), once the largest (pre-FARN split); in n. Morazan.
4. a) FPL=Pop.Forces of Lib. - Ldrs: L.Gonzalez, S.Samayoa, Rojas, Guttierez, Rodriguez;
   b) n=3000 (MB88/9); largest(50% FMNLF forces); best organized(Banks); in Chalatenango.
5. a) FARN=Armed Forces of Natl.Resistance. Ldr:Herman Cienfuegos.
   b) n=900 (MB88/9)-1800(others), breakoff from ERP.
6. a) FAL=Armed Liberation Forces=PCES mil. wing. Ldrs: Jorge Shafik Handal & Mauro Araujo.
   b) small in #s, n=450(MB88/9)-1300(others); ties to Nicaragua.
7. a) PRTC=C.Am.Rev.Workers P. Ldr: Miss Nidea Dias, inter alia. Marxist.
   b) smallest, n=350 (MB88/9)-700(DOS 8/88)-1200? under arms; some in Honduras.
vs. pro-Govt. death squads (see also V4.3b) such as:
8. a) Natl. Dem. Org. (ORDEN); Govt. ally (1968-80).
   b) once n=3,000; dwindling (since post-'79 US aid cutoff threats) into successors such as: Max. Hern. Martinez Anti-Comm.Brig., and R. d'Aubuisson followers (in govt. after 1988-89).

V1.1b Data Bank states not excerpted here due to space limitations, n=8:
Spain - ETA=*Basque* Homeland and Freedom; since 1968; n=⁻200.
Israel - > 15 *Palestinian* groups incl: pro-PLO (Fatah,Shabibeh,ALF); anti-PLO (PFLP,PPSF, PFLP-GC,PLF,Saiqa,FatahUprising,FatahRev.Cmd.); and independs.(PCP,DFLP,Uprising,Hamas).
Lebanon - incl. 10 *Sunni*, 9 *Shiite*, 6 *Christian*, 1 *Druse*, & 4 secular militias.
Afghanistan - incl. 3 *Sunni* traditlist, 4 *Sunni* Fundmtalist, & 4 *Shiite* groups; + indep. cmdrs.
India - incl. several each in Punjab*(Sikhs)*, Kashmir*(Moslems)*, and north east (n=6 tribes).
Sri Lanka - incl. 5 *Tamil* groups, incl. LTTE Tigers, and one *Sinhalese* (JVP).
Myanmar - incl. 9 ethnic tribal groups (incl. 3 *Shan* armies), 1 *Muslim*, and 1 secular (BCP).
Colombia - 2 remain on left (FARC,NLA); + several on right, including 2 drug cartels, in 1990.

V1.1b states to watch, insurgencies growing or waning in 1990ff:
W.Sahara(POLISARIO) v. Morocco - UN mediation, 1989ff; seems headed for resolution.
Chad - 12/90 victory by Deby might finally end 25 years of periodic war supported by Libya.
Somalia - Somali Natl. Movement (northern *Isaaqs*) since '82; major battle(10,000d.),5/88.   Also, United Somali Congress (central zone *Hawiyes*) and 3 other clan groups increasing in strength in late 1990.
Liberia - Fall '90 W. Af. regional force intervention has stopped Doe v. Johnson v. Taylor war.
Uganda - 6/88 ceasefire with Ug. Peop. Dem. Army; one expected soon with Ug. Peop. Army.
S.Africa - #1 insurgent group ANC legalized 2/90; Mandela etc. now contesting in polit. arena.
Laos - war seems to have petered out 1986-87. Vietnam troops withdrawn 2/88.
Nicaragua - 3/88 ceasefire led to 2/90 elections which UNO (contra front) won.

V1.1c - State Generators of Refugees, 1989

Europe	Islamic	Africa	Asia	Latin America

.i - Principal Sources of Refugees

Europe	Islamic	Africa	Asia	Latin America
	Afghan. 5,934,000			
	#Palestine 2,340,000			
		Mozambique 1,354,000		
		Ethiopia 1,035,000		
	Iraq 508,000			
	Sudan 435,100	Angola 438,000		
	Somalia 388,100		Cambodia 334,166	
	Iran 270,100	Rwanda 233,000		
	#W.Sahara 165,000	Burundi 186,000	Vietnam 124,779	
			China(Tibet)112,000	
			Sri Lanka 103,000	
				Nicaragua 89,700
		Liberia 68,000	Laos 69,044	El Sal. 61,100
	S.Yemen 55,000	Zaire 50,400	Bangladesh 50,000	Guatemala 58,700
	n=8	n=7	n=6	n=3 (24)
TOTALS:	10095300	3355400	742989	209500

.ii - Populations in "Refugee-Like" Circumstances

Europe	Islamic	Africa	Asia	Latin America
	Palestinians 1,389,000			Cent. Am. 1,987,00(
				Haiti 1,227,500
	n=1			n=2 (3)

.iii - Internally Displaced People

Europe	Islamic	Africa	Asia	Latin America
	Sudan 2,600,000	S.Africa 3,570,000*		
	Afghan. 2,000,000	Mozambique 1,700,000		
		Ethiopia 1,100,000*		
	Iraq 750,000*	Angola 908,000		
	Lebanon 750,000			
SU 500,000	Iran 500,000		Sri Lanka 500,000	
			Phil. I. 450,000	Nicarag. 390,000
		Uganda 300,000		Guatemal.300,000
	Cyprus 265,000			El Sal. 272,000
	Somalia 235,000			
	Chad 225,000		Myanmar 150,000*	
			India 65,000	Peru 80,000
				Honduras 22,000
n=1	n=8	n=5	n=4	n=5 (23)
TOTALS:	7,325,000	7,578,000	1,165,000	1,064,000

Source: US Committee for Refugees, 1990, Tables 2, 3, and 4.

\# = not one of 162 independent states recognized in this book.

* = includes persons forcibly relocated in govt. resettlement programs.

^ = data does not include 1.5 million refugees from Kuwait, and .5 million from Liberia as result of wars in 1990.

V1.1d.i - States at War, by Total Years Duration

State	# of wars	Dates of Wars	Total Years Europe
Portugal	4	1961,61-75,62-74,65-75	37 yrs.
UK	8	1945-48,48-9,50-52-53,55-60,56,82; *69ff* ^	22 + *10.5+* = 32.5+
France	8	1946-54,47-48,48-9,52-54,53-56,54-62,55-60,56	29
US	10^Δ	1948-9,50-53,58,59-65,62,65,65-73,70-75,83,89	28
USSR	6	1948-9,56,62,68,69,79-89	15
Spain	1	*1968ff* ^	0 + *11+* = 11+
Greece	2	1945-49,74	5
Netherlands	1	1945-48	3
Hungary	1	Nov. 1956	<1
Czechoslovakia	1	Aug. 1968	<1
Romania	1	Dec. 1989	<1

^Δ^Note: US wars do not include interventions with"deniability," listed in V1.1a as "CIA" wars.

State	# wars	Dates	Tot. Yrs. Islamic
Israel	8	1948,56,67,67-70,73,82,*78ff* *; *65ff* ^	9 + *18.5* + = 27.5+
Iraq	7	1948,58,59,61-70,1980-88; 84-88; 90	25
Sudan	2	1955-72, 1983ff	24+
N. Yemen	5	1948,1950-2,1962-69,*67-89* * esp.72 & '87,79	13 + *10+* = 23
!Palestine	9	*1965ff* ^, incl:68,72,78,81,87ff; 75-76,82-88; 69-73	19 + *3+* = 22+
!Kurdistan	5	1961-70,74,79, 84-88; *1980ff* ^	15 + *5+* = 20+
Morocco	2	1953-56, 1975ff	18+
Lebanon	3	1948,58,75ff	17+
Chad	2	*1965ff** esp.1979-82,1990; 1973,1980,1987	8 + *8.5+* = 16.5+
!W. Sahara	1	1975ff	15+
S.Yemen	2	Jan.'86, *1967-89** esp. 1972 & 1987	3 + *10+*= 13
Afghanistan	1	1978ff	12+
Iran	4	1978-9, 1979, 1980-88, 1989	12
Turkey	3	1974,76-80; *80ff* ^	5 + *5+* = 10+
Algeria	3	1945-54,54-62,62-63	10
Pakistan	6	AS:1947,47-49,65,71,71; ISL:*1972-77** esp. 75	7 + *2* = 9
Oman	2	*1955-59*,1964-75**	0 + *7.5* = 7.5
Egypt	5	1948,56,67,67-70,73	7
Syria	5	1948,67,70,73,75-76	6
Jordan	3	1948,67,*69-73**	2 + *2* = 4
Libya	1	1973,1980,1987	3
Tunisia	1	1952-54	2
Somalia	2	1977-78(in AF. zone), *1988ff* *	1 + *1* = 2
Cyprus	1	July 1974	<1
Kuwait	1	August 1990	<1

Legend:
!= not among the 162 recognized states in this study (Palestine, Western Sahara, Kurdistan, Tibet.)
Italics = on-going insurgencies (^) & periodic wars (*) whose yrs. are added on (in half-yr. increments)
    after the totals of more conventional conflicts.
ff = and following; a continuing war, results in a + after tot.# of yrs. at war.

State	# wars	Dates	Tot.Yrs. **Africa**
South Africa	4	*1966-88*;*75-89;78-84; *60ff* esp.60,76,83-6	25 +*23.5+* = 48.5+
Ethiopia	3	*1962*ff,* 77-78;78ff; *61-78*,*76-78	15 +*21+* = 36+
Angola	2	1961-75; 1975ff	29+
Mozambique	2	1965-75; 1978ff	22+
Uganda	4	1966; 71-78; 78-79; 81-86; 87-8	15
Guinea Bissau	1	1962-74	12
Namibia(SW Af.)	1	*1966-88**	0 +*11* = 11
Rwanda	1	1956-65	9
Zimbabwe	2	1972-79,83	8
Zaire	2	1960-65; 77-78	6
Cameroon	1	1955-60	5
Nigeria	1	1967-70	3
Tanzania	2	1963; 1978-79	3
Kenya	1	1952-53	1
Liberia	1	1990	<1
Burundi	1	1972	<1

State	# wars	Dates	Tot.Yrs. **Asia**
Vietnam	10	1946-54,59-65,65-73,73-5; 78,79; *75-87*,* 79-89,87; *79*ff*	37 +*11.5+* = 48.5+
Philippines	3	1950-2, 69ff, *72ff** esp.72-76	27 +*9+* = 36+
India	11	1947,47-8,47-9,61,62,65,D'71; *87ff ; 84ff , 55ff* ,* 87-90	11 +*22+* = 33+
Myanmar	3	*1948ff*,* incl. 1948-51,80,84ff;	10 +*16+* = 26+
China	12	1946-9,50-1,50-1,50-3,57-62,58-9,62,66-8,69,79,87, *79ff**	20 +*5.5+* = 25.5+
Indonesia	6	1945-8,50,56-61,62-66,65-66,*75ff** esp. 1975-76	14 +*7+* = 21+
Laos	3	1960-62,63-73; *75-87**	12 + *6* = 18
Cambodia	4	1970-75,75-78,78; *79ff*	9 +*5.5+* = 14.5+
Malaysia	2	1950-60, 62-66	14
Bangladesh	3	Mar.-Dec.'71,*1972ff**,1985	2 +*9+* = 11+
Sri Lanka	4	1971, 83-87, 87-89, *88ff*	7 +*1+* = 8+
Taiwan	3	1946-49 (as KMT in China); 1954-55; Feb -Mar '47	5
Koreas,N.&S.	1	1950-53	3
!Tibet	2	1950-51,58-59	3
Madagascar	1	1947-48	1

State	# wars	Dates	Tot. Yrs. **Lat. Am.**
Guatemala	3	1954, *1958ff** esp. '66-74, '82-83	11 +*10.5+* = 21.5+
Colombia	3	1948-58,78-84,85ff	21+
Cuba	4	1958-9,Ap.'61,Oct.'62,75-91	19
El Salvador	2	1969,1979ff	12+
Peru	2	1965,1980ff	11+
Nicaragua	2	1975-79, 1981-88	11
Argentina	4	1955, 74-76, 76-82, 82	10
Uruguay	1	*1963-72**	0 +*4.5* = 4.5
Suriname	1	1985-87	2
Bolivia	2	1946,52	<2
Chile	1	1973-4	1
Costa Rica	1	1948	<1
Dom.Rep.	1	1965	<1
Paraguay	1	1947	<1
Honduras	1	1969	<1
Grenada	1	1983	<1
Panama	1	1989	<1

V1.1d.ii -Summary of States with Most Experience in War

(#s = # wars X # total years at war*^)

Europe	Islamic	Africa	Asia	Latin America
			Vietnam 485+	
			India 363+	
US 280			China 306+	
UK 260+				
France 232	Israel 220+			
	!Palestine 198+	S.Africa 194+		
	Iraq 175			
Portugal 148			Indonesia 126+	
	N.Yemen 115	Ethiopia 108+		
	!Kurdistan 100		Phil. I. 108+	
USSR 90				
			Myanmar 78+	Cuba 76
				Guatemala 64.5+
		Uganda 60		Colombia 63+
	Pakistan 54	Angola 58+	Cambodia 58+	
	Lebanon 51+		Laos 54	
	Sudan 48+			
	Iran 48			
		Mozambique 44+		Argentina 40
	Morocco 36+			
	Egypt 35			
	Chad 33+		Bangladesh 33+	
	Turkey 30+		Sri Lanka 32+	
	Syria 30		Malaysia 28	
	Algeria 30			El Salvador 24+
	S.Yemen 26			Peru 22+
				Nicaragua 22
n=5	n=16	n=5	n=11	n=7 (44)

Source: V1.1ab Data Banks

*^ = years of *periodic wars and on-going ^insurgencies are counted in half-year increments and added to totals of more conventional conflicts.

+ = war which is continuing in 1990.

! = not one of 162 independent states recognized in this book.

V1.2. WAR'S DOMESTIC IMPACT

The next two sections will analyze the lingering manifestations of war, in both the domestic (V1.2) and external (V1.3) relations of states.

The measures discussed first, in section V1.2—defense budget line items and military coup regimes—are arguably related to either past or present wars. At a minimum they are evidence of a violent approach to the resolution of political issues, both domestic and foreign. Section V1.3's measures—force projections, weapons transfers, and armaments of global concern—are both present and future threats to peace.

The statistics to be cited in sections V1.2a and V1.2b on armed personnel and military expenditures would seem to lend themselves readily to comparative analyses by state, but the numbers can often be deceptive; data relating to matters of "national security" are often in dispute especially among ideological or regional rivals. Similarly in section V1.2c, identifying personalities and dates associated with military coup regimes can also involve subjective judgments; nevertheless, the information which emerges will provide not only evidence of a lack of commitment to the peaceful settlement of disputes, but also data which will form the basis for Chapter 5's distinction between civilian and militarized polities.

V1.2a. Armed Personnel

The number of persons in the uniformed armed forces of a country is an obvious indicator of that state's commitment to military means as a method of settling political conflict. Such an undertaking of mobilization is relatively difficult to disguise, and data on armed forces are available in many reputable references; see, for example, the annual yearbooks of Sivard, US Arms Control and Disarmament Agency (ACDA), International Institute of Strategic Studies (IISS), and the Stockholm International Peace Research Institute (SIPRI). Depending on the source consulted, however, widely varying sets of figures might result; one must also be aware of how reservists, home militias, and other paramilitary forces are being counted. In addition to minor discrepancies resulting from the different methodologies employed by these data-gathering sources, one distinctive emphasis has historically emerged: an overestimation on the part of the official US sources in the case of Warsaw Pact countries. This pattern becomes even more pronounced, and is explained, in section V1.2b on military expenditures, where the statistics are even softer. This bias will probably change with the dissolution of the eastern European military bloc in the 1990s, but the latest (1989/90) sources employed here (with data for a few years earlier) still reflect this earlier orientation.

Despite examples of conflicting data, however, in most instances the *relative rankings of states within zones* will be similar no matter which source is used. Moreover, once the analysis moves beyond the sensitive European zone, the differences in estimates among reporting agencies are not that great. Accordingly, this study will often cite ACDA data because it is more comprehensive than SIPRI and IISS (which do not report for many small states) and generally one year more recent than Sivard. In this context it should be noted that ACDA's *World Military Expenditures and Arms Transfers 1990*, with data for 1988, was published in October, 1990, and will be referred to here as ACDA90.

Keeping in mind such institutional biases and methodological differences, Table V1.2a.i ranks and clusters states in their zones in order of their number of armed personnel in 1988, the latest year for which data is available. Table V1.2a.i utilizes absolute numbers, and presents world rankings for 149 states (out of this study's universe of 162). It is followed by a table giving country rankings using relative numbers for which only the highest and lowest states in each zone are listed. This pattern of displaying global rankings with absolute numerical data first, followed by shorter state lists for relative measures, will be employed frequently in the first three chapters of this book. It makes for ease in updating as new data becomes available, or in comparing if other sources are used. It also provides the reader the greatest access to the most important numbers, while giving examples as to how analyses of items of more particular interest may be made.

One advantage of displaying these rankings in clusters across the five zones is that geographic differences become readily apparent. For example, Table V1.2a.i highlights the relatively *unarmed* status of states in the African and Latin American zones as compared with those in Europe, Asia, and the Islamic world. There are ten countries in the world with armies in excess of 600,000 people; after the US and USSR, they include five in Asia and three in the Middle East. With respect to Asia, this finding parallels its status as the world's most populous zone; for poor states with large populations it is easier to make a military commitment in personnel than in capital or technology. In order to test whether the size of armies is simply a function of populations, however, some *relative* ratios of armed personnel might be used as measures.

Table V1.2a.ii(a) lists the highest and lowest seven states in each zone in terms of soldiers per 1000 people. Other rankings, comparing soldiers to workers (adult males and females engaged in non-subsistence labor, to age 65), or soldiers to available manpower (fit males, aged 15 to 49, the prime draft-age cohort), would yield similar displays.

More than half of the top (n=7) states in each zone in Table V1.2a.i (absolute numbers) are not present in this new (relative) listing. The 16 of 35 which do repeat as zonal leaders in V1.2a.ii(a) are indicated by a •. The other 19 are judged to have made armed personnel commitments larger than the size of their population might warrant.

At the bottom of the list, the 14 states which are Δ'ed are also among the lowest seven states in their zones in V1.2a.i; the other 21 countries can be interpreted as having made less of a commitment to militarized modes of conflict resolution than might be expected. Notable in this regard are five of the world's most populous countries (Pakistan, India, Indonesia, Brazil, and Mexico), whose apparently big armies are not so large in a relative sense; this is also true of Japan whose score in this measure (2.0) is close to that of the seven lowest states in its zone. The high soldier-civilian ratios of the Islamic and European states in both the leading and lowest categories—especially in comparison with the remaining three zones—are also particularly pronounced in Table V1.2a.ii(a).

Table V1.2a.ii(b) displays the leading and lowest seven states in terms of soldiers per square kilometer of area to be defended. While to some degree this ratio is a function of the size of the state (large countries have lower scores, small countries have higher numbers), this display can be helpful in comparing states in similar geographic circumstances (e.g., North and South Korea, Rwanda and Burundi). It is also interesting in highlighting certain large states with high numbers (e.g., W. Germany, Iraq, Ethiopia), and small states with low numbers (Ireland, Fiji) which run counter to the expected pattern. Most notable are the extremely high numbers for Singapore, Taiwan, Israel, Bahrain, and North and South Korea, and the generally low numbers for all African states.

A final measure related to armed personnel (and the militarization of a society) pertains to mandatory conscription, the requirement that all able-bodied males (generally) commit some period of their lives to the militarized defense of their nation.

Table V1.2a.iii displays states for the year 1985 (the last for which complete comparative information was available), as updated for a few states which have made changes since that time. The table lists, first: 65 countries which require no such military commitment; then, 40 states with some provision for conscientious objection to such service; and finally, 38 countries where the requirement of military service is absolute. Among the latter group of states, which could be called the most militarized by this measure, it might be noted that one of the first acts of many of the newly democratized legislatures in eastern Europe has been to remove or reduce the requirement of mandatory military service.

V1.2b. Military Expenditures

Military expenditures, both in absolute dollar values and with respect to various relative measures, are a second defense budget line item for which data is readily available, and which can be regarded as giving some indication of a country's commitment to militarized modes of conflict resolution. Compared with armed personnel, however, statistics on a country's military spending are more highly suspect. In addition to the methodological problems related to periodic devaluations and conversion of local currencies to a common unit of measurement (current US dollars), estimates made by competing countries of each other's preparations for war are often overinflated. Even reputable scholarly sources have difficulty penetrating the hidden and disguised costs of projects in the defense budgets of many states.

A comparison of data in the standard military references for a common base year will show particularly dubious results in the case of ACDA's statistics for Warsaw Pact states. ACDA's data is drawn from CIA estimates, which have been particularly skewed since the mid-1970s when an alternate method of calculating Soviet bloc expenditures was devised (by the CIA's "Team B"). The result was to increase Warsaw Pact expenditures by some 50% more than the numbers previously used by the US government, and still employed by most of the rest of the world (Holzman, 1989).

Under this methodology, every element of Warsaw Pact military force is valued at the price that it would cost if purchased in the United States. The objective is not to establish a basis for international comparison, but to produce a summary indicator of the value of communist country military effort in US dollar terms. Thus, the very large Soviet army, bought at low cost in rubles, is greatly increased in value when priced at US pay scales, and rises every time US forces receive pay raises. In the six other Warsaw Pact countries, military personnel costs jump from ratios of 12-35% of military expenditures in their domestic currencies to 42-80% of military expenditures in dollars (Sivard, 1987: 54-55). In addition, for those parts of military budgets not devoted to personnel (generally about two-thirds of the total), the CIA's method has built into it an upward bias because of the worst-case assumptions applied to the many unknowns in the estimating process for research and development and, to a lesser extent, for investment (procurement of equipment and construction). (Ibid; see also Holzman, 1982 and 1980; and US Congress, Select Committee on Intelligence, 1980.)

Despite these drawbacks, ACDA is generally the most recent and most complete of the standard sources for this information (coverage for n=144 states in its October, 1990, publication). In addition, ACDA is helpful in making available (in its annual publication before 1988, on mimeograph after that time) 20 pages of "Country Rankings by Variable," from which can be extrapolated estimates of data for countries for which exact statistics are not otherwise provided.

Table V1.2b.i's five-zone geographic display of military spending highlights the predominance of European states (especially the US and USSR), and the relatively small amounts spent in Africa and Latin America. NATO and Warsaw Pact states account for more than three-quarters of the world's military expenditures, with the United States and Soviet Union alone representing about 60%. The 18th largest military spender in Europe (Switzerland) exceeds the totals of such regional "powers" in their respective zones as South Africa and

Brazil. In all the non-European world, only China, Japan, Saudi Arabia, Iran, and Iraq exceed $10 billion a year, a figure which represents less than 3.4% of what the Americans and Soviets spend.

If military expenditure statistics were displayed according to *relative* measures, however, state rankings would be quite different. Table V1.2b.ii presents the leaders in each zone for four such rankings of military spending—a.) per capita; b.) as a percentage of Gross National Product (GNP); c.) as a function of Central Government Expenditures (CGE); and d.) per soldier. These statistics are readily available each year from ACDA, but suffer from the ideological biases which produce some suspect numbers as the numerators in the calculations which need to be made (the denominators are similar in all sources). Hence, where the top seven countries according to ACDA statistics are presented here, the leading states from another source (Sivard or World Bank) are also listed, even though they may be older or cover fewer countries. In all cases cited in Table V1.2b.ii, even though the numbers and base years vary among the different sources, the *relative rankings of the zonal leaders* are again (as with military personnel) often comparable.

As contrasted with Table V1.2b.i, Tables V1.2b.ii (a)-(d) reveal a number of new states as heavy military spenders. In Asia, for example, the relatively high standings of the two Koreas, Singapore, and Taiwan, and the absence of China, would not have been expected from a perusal of only the absolute figures. Other states with modest absolute expenditures which score high in the relative data rankings include (grouped by zone): Oman, United Arab Emirates; Gabon, Congo, Cape Verde, Botswana; Brunei, New Zealand; Trinidad, Guyana, El Salvador, and Peru. Some comments with respect to each of the relative measures follow.

(a) - Military expenditures per capita would seem to be an obvious indicator of a society's commitment to militarism, but this statistic does not take into account the ability to pay and the degree of sacrifice a country might be willing to make. So although this measure is a good place to begin to get an idea of countries least prone to peaceful options in the resolution of political disputes, one must move on to militarism relative to GNP, CGE, and other measures for a better appreciation of this phenomenon.

(b) - Military expenditures as a percentage of Gross National Product would tend to show the ability of states to afford these expenditures. Although this is the most widely available statistic of its type, there are more precise related measures which could be used, such as the annual ACDA composite relating mil.exp./GNP to GNP/capita, to be cited at the end of this section, and the work of James Payne, which relates soldier-to-civilian ratios to a society's "discretionary income," a fraction of the GNP which varies with each country's level of development (ACDA, 1986: 49-52).

(c) - Military spending as a percentage of Central Government Expenditures would show a government's priorities. However, caution should be used in accepting this figure at face value for many states. The 25% figure often cited for the United States, for example, hides many items which might add another 25% to the true federal budget for war, such as nuclear weapons in the Department of Energy account, a separate Veterans Administration, and the paying off of interest on budget deficits caused by earlier military spending in the Department of Treasury. Other states no doubt engage in similar legerdemain to mask the true level of military spending from their enemies as well as their own citizens.

(d) - Military expenditures per soldier would tend to show which armies were most highly paid, as well as expenditures on the technology needed for advanced weaponry, and the inevitable "waste, fraud, and abuse" in the military procurement process. The European states seem to have higher scores by this measure than in the previous categories.

To conclude this section, Table V1.2b.iii reproduces ACDA's "relative burden" display which presents in a 30-cell matrix (5 rows x 6 columns, in the original ACDA publication), groups of states ranked by their military expenditures as a percentage of GNP in the rows, in comparison with their GNP per capita in the columns.

The 18 states in ACDA's six lower-right cells—with mil.exp./GNP < 2% and GNP/capita > $1000—seem not to be taxing their resources in spending for national defense, and hence would be the least committed to militarism as this concept has been employed here. The 23 states in the lower-left corner—with mil.exp./GNP < 2% and GNP/capita < $1000—are spending for defense within their meager means.

States spending between 2 and 5% of GNP on the military, regardless of the level of their GNP/capita, form a large group of 58 states across the middle row of the ACDA matrix, spending an amount on the military which is in line with what the rest of the world seems to judge appropriate.

The 29 countries in the six upper-right cells—with mil.exp./GNP > 5% and GNP/capita > $1000—are extravagant in their expenditures, but either can afford it, or have security threats so pressing that they are willing to make the sacrifice. Finally, the 16 countries in the upper-left corner of the matrix—with mil.exp./GNP > 5% and GNP/capita < $1000—seem ill able to afford such expenditures regardless of the perceived threats to national security, and are deemed here to be the most bellicose group by this measure.

The fact that military spending is a burden, and not a stimulus, to the economy—a thesis which is argued by Leontief (1983), Nincic (1982), and Szentes (1984)—can be seen by comparing the position of those countries which scored highest in this section, with their relatively low rankings in the economic categories relating to productivity, growth, investment, and savings in the following chapter (sections V2.1a and .1b). One way in which some military spending can be recouped—by the development of an arms export capacity—is covered in this chapter in section V1.3b. But before moving on to either of these subjects, one final domestic impact of war and the preparations therefor must be addressed, and that is the phenomenon of military coup regimes.

V1.2c. Revolutions and Coup Regimes

There are two types of governments which are based upon the use of force and violence in their initial creation—revolutionary regimes and military coup administrations. They will be distinguished in this study, with greater attention as regards militarism being given to the latter, more common form of government.

A *revolution* is a successful insurgency and will be defined here as a thorough and coercive overturning of a society's indigenous political institutions (Dunn, 1989; Midlarsky, 1986; Eisenstadt, 1978; Leiden and Schmitt, 1968). Wars of national liberation to remove *foreign* (i.e., colonial) regimes are excluded by this definition, although they undoubtedly have an impact on societal transformation. As compared with a coup, a revolution involves more than a mere change in top government personnel. The armed force employed is not exercised by the institutional military, but rather by oppositional (V1.1b) forces. To be successful in such an undertaking, a revolution generally must be more broadly based than a coup and have more of a policy (i.e., an ideological) dimension to gain this support. After attaining power, revolutionary regimes generally adopt civilian political structures to maintain control over the established military. There have been very few genuine revolutions in contemporary history. Perhaps only these seven would qualify in this century: Mexico (1911-19), USSR (1917), China (1945-49), Cuba (1959), Vietnam (Laos and Cambodia) (1946-75), Iran (1978-79), and Nicaragua (1978-79).

There have also been some instances, generally involving the overthrow of monarchies, in which changes in society's political institutions were carried out not by opposition forces, but "from within" by the traditional military. Among those in the contemporary era, the following might be cited: Syria (1948), Egypt (1952), Iraq (1958), N. Yemen (1962), Libya (1969), Afghanistan (1973), and Ethiopia (1974). Such "modernizing" military regimes will not be considered revolutions here, for they are more like military coup regimes; they typically have not resulted in rapid or thorough societal transformation, and they have generally been followed by subsequent coups.

The regime changes in eastern Europe in 1989 present a special case. Except in the case of Romania (and possibly Bulgaria), military coercion was not used; the degree of societal transformation in these two states is also unclear at the time of this writing. In the other countries, there appears to have been a peaceful evolution between polity types, a phenomenon which is discussed more fully in Chapter 5.

A *military coup*—the overthrow of a government by forces from within the institutional military establishment—generally leaves most of society's basic structures untouched, and effectuates change only in the top administrative strata of government. Military coup regimes often do not have a coherent economic or political belief system as part of their ideology; they intervene for self-aggrandizement, or to preserve "law and order" and to maintain public safety (Andrews and Ra'anan, 1969; Jackman, 1978; David, 1986).

The concept of militarized governance will be covered at length in Chapter 5; at this point, it might be instructive to list the names of 38 current military coup regimes (as of December 20, 1990). They include many of the governments to be designated in section V5.4 as "entrenched military," "moderating military," and "militarized party states" where the original coup leader is still the most significant political actor. Table V1.2c identifies these governments, the dates when they came to power, and the major personalities involved (including the leader's rank at the time of the coup; most have since promoted themselves to general). Countries are counted as coup regimes even though power may have formally been passed on to a civilian figurehead if the determination is made (substantiated in section V5.2c's data bank) that the coup leader is still the most important political actor. The total number of years this government has been in power is listed in the fourth column.

As the examples in Table V1.2c indicate, "electing" military (or "recently retired" military) leaders to head governments they originally helped to establish complicates the issue of determining the length of a military coup regime. In this study, countries will be listed as having coup regimes until the successful passing of power on to personalities *not* involved in the original coup regime (e.g., Mubarak in Egypt, Chattichai in Thailand).

Two ways to measure persistent governmental militarism in a country are to count the number of regime changes by coup, and to total up the number of years the military has ruled before credible returns to civilian institutions were made. Criteria for a coup regime are somewhat lower here than in section V5.4, where transitions to civilian modes in contemporary regimes come under closer scrutiny before a state is moved from the military to civilian polity category. Here, where historic transfers to civilian rule have proved successful, regimes are accepted as civilian from the time of their announcement. (See in the data bank associated with this section, Egypt-1981, Sierra Leone-1968, and Thailand-1988, for examples of successful power transitions from military to civilians through political party institutions; but not Egypt-1970, Algeria-1979, Niger-1987, or Myanmar-1988, where the party machinery did not provide for the voluntary passing of power on to a new leader uninvolved in the original coup regime.)

In the survey which follows, coups refer to coercive transfers of rule by the governing regime's military forces as described above, a definition which includes 1.) "palace" coups (as in Iran-1953, and Qatar-1970); 2.) the outcomes of civil wars between army factions claiming to be the rightful government (Zaire-1965, Chad-1982 and 1990, Uganda-1986); 3.) extended "martial law" coups by constitutionally created governments (as in Taiwan-1949, Haiti-1957, Rwanda-1969, Lesotho-1970, Philippines-1972), a phenomenon covered in section V4.4d; and 4.) coups in which outside forces "assisted" the local military establishment in taking over the reins of government, as in Czechoslovakia-1948 and 1968, Hungary-1956, Dominican Republic-1965, Laos-1975, Cambodia -1978, Uganda-1979, Afghanistan-1979, Grenada-1983, Comoros-1989, and Panama-1989.

In coding coups in the data bank associated with this project, a "one-half" coup unit is assigned to a country in which power is passed peacefully from one group in a junta to another. See Algeria, Iraq, Afghanistan, and Niger with the two successive leaders listed in Table V1.2c, and the historical examples of Brazil (1967, '69, '74, & '79), Argentina (1981, '82, '83), and other (especially Latin American) states with power transfers designated by a • in the data bank.

Not included as coups are cases where the military intervenes to uphold the political process, even if this results in a change of leadership (Philippines -1986); and violent changes in rule brought about by *opposition* forces as explained in the definition of revolution above (China-1949, Cuba-1959, Vietnam (Laos and Cambodia)-1975, Iran-1979, and Nicaragua-1979).

Tables V1.2c.i and .2c.ii assess country experiences with military coup regimes going back to 1945, or a base year of independence if this is later. A state is considered to have had a history of military rule if at the time of a government's passage from power its most important political actors were still those installed by a coup. This usually happens when one coup regime is replaced by another, and not through the medium of any civilian institutions (parties, assemblies, electoral machinery, etc.) it may have created.

Military rule at any time during a calendar year is counted as a full year in the following summaries. The base year indicated is used to determine the denominator when calculating the coup frequency ratio in Table V1.2c.i, and the percentage of coup regime years in Table V1.2c.ii. According to this survey, some 76 countries (including more than half of all states in the four non-European zones) have experienced a total of almost 250 coups leading to changes of regime since 1945.

Following Tables V1.2c.i and ii is a page of excerpts from the data bank associated with this project illustrating how the numbers used to compute the state rankings are substantiated. Selections are from the African zone, which has had more than 55 successful coups in 20 states and where according to one estimate there was a coup or coup attempt every 55 days during one 12-year period (Clark, 1986: 337-44). The Latin American zone has had more coups (about 90), but the base year for most of its countries goes back to 1945, as contrasted with the average 1960-date for Africa. The abbreviations explained at the end of the excerpts illustrate many of the difficulties in measurement mentioned in the preceding paragraphs.

V1.2a.i - Armed Personnel (in 1000s), 1988

Europe	Islamic	Africa	Asia	Latin America
USSR 3900			China 3783	
US 2246	Iraq 1000		India 1362	
	Turkey 847		Vietnam 1100	
France 558	Iran 654		N.Korea 842	
W.Germany 495*			S.Korea 626	
Italy 446	Pakistan 484			Brazil 319
Poland 430	Egypt 452		Taiwan 390	Cuba 297
	Syria 400		Indonesia 284	
UK 324			Thailand 273	Mexico 154
Spain 304		Ethiopia 250	Japan 245	
E.Germany 242*	Morocco 195		Myanmar 186	Peru 111
Yugoslavia 229	Israel 191	Nigeria 107		Chile 96
Romania 220	Jordan 165	Angola 107	Malaysia 108	Argentina 95
Czech. 219	Algeria 126	S.Africa 100	Phil. I. 105	
Greece 199		Mozambique 65	Bangladesh 102	Colombia 76
Bulgaria 160	S.Yemen 88	Zaire 51		Nicaragua 74
Hungary 117	Libya 86	Zimbabwe 45	Australia 71	Venezuela 73
Belgium 110	Saudi A. 84	Tanzania 40	Cambodia 60	
Nethrlds. 107	Sudan 65		Singapore 56	Ecuador 46
Portugal 104	N.Yemen 62	Uganda 25	Laos 56	El Salvador 45
	Afghanistan 55	Cameroon 21	Sri Lanka 47	Guatemala 36
Canada 88	Somalia 47	Kenya 20		
Sweden 65	UAE 43	Zambia 17	Nepal 35	Uruguay 29
	Tunisia 40	Ghana 16	Mongolia 32e	Bolivia 28
Austria 55		Congo,Guinea-15		Dom.Rep. 20
	Chad 33	Senegal 14	Madagascar 21	Honduras 19
Albania 42		Burundi 11		
Norway 40	Oman 27	GBissau 10	N.Zealand 13	Paraguay 16
Finland 36	Lebanon 20+	Burkina Faso 8		
Denmark 30	Kuwait 15	Ivory Coast 8		Panama 11
Switzrld. 23	Mauritania 14	Mali,Gabon-8		Haiti 8
Ireland 13	Cyprus 13	Liberia,Malawi-7	Brunei 4^	Costa Rica 8
		Togo 6	Fiji 4	
	Qatar 7	C.Af.R. 5	Papua NG 3	Suriname 4
		Rwanda 5		Guyana 4
		Benin 5		Jamaica 3
	Bahrain 5	Sierra Leone 4	Seychelles 1^	Trinidad 2
		Niger,Botswana-4	Mauritius 1	Barbados 1
	Djibouti 4^	Swazilnd 3		Bahamas 0.75^
Luxmbrg. 1		C.Verde 3	Maldives-na	Belize 0.70^
Malta 1		Lesotho 2	Comoros-na	Dominica-na
		Eq.Guin. 1	Bhut.,Vanuatu-na	Grenada-na
Iceland 0		STP,Gambia-1	W.Samoa-na	Antigua-na
		Namibia-na	Solomons-na	St.V,St.C.,St.L.-na
n=30	n=28	n=37/38	n=27/33	n=27/33 (149)

Source: ACDA 90f88, n=144, Table I, where e=extrapolations; plus ^IISS89/90f88, n=5.

* = united Germany will have 370,000 by 1993-94.

+ = 15,000 more in dissident Christian Army (Lebanon, 9/88-11/90).

V1.2a.ii - Armed Personnel, Relative Measures, 1988

Europe	Islamic	Africa	Asia	Latin America

(a) Soldiers per 1000 People, 1988

Europe	Islamic	Africa	Asia	Latin America
Greece 19.9	Jordan 57.9	•Angola 13.0	•N.Korea 38.3	•Cuba 28.7
Bulgaria 17.8	•Iraq 56.9	GBissau 10.5	Singapore 21.0	•Nicaragua 21.7
E.Germany 14.6	•Israel 44.5	C.Verde 8.5	•Taiwan 19.5	Suriname 10.1
•USSR 13.6	S.Yemen 36.1	STP 8.5	•Vietnam 16.9	Uruguay 9.7
Czech. 13.5	•Syria 34.6	Gabon 7.4	Mongolia 15.1e	•El Salvador 8.4
Albania 13.3	UAE 21.7	Congo 6.9	•S.Korea 14.6	•Chile 7.6
•Poland 11.3	Libya 21.7	•Ethiopia 5.2	Laos 14.4	•Peru 5.2
....	....	....	....	....
ΔFin.,Aust.-5.2	Saudi A. 5.4	Malawi 0.9	Phil. I. 1.7	Colombia 2.4
ΔIreland 3.7	Algeria 5.2	Kenya 0.9	India 1.7	Brazil 2.1
ΔSwitz. 3.5	Tunisia 5.2	Mali 0.9	Indonesia 1.5	ΔBarbados 2.0
Canada 3.4	Pakistan 4.5	Burkina F. 0.9	ΔMauritius 0.9	Mexico 1.8
ΔMalta 3.3	Afghanistan 3.8	Iv.Coast 0.7	Bangladesh 0.9	ΔTrinidad 1.6
ΔLuxmbrg. 2.7	Sudan 2.7	Rwanda 0.7	ΔPapua NG 0.9	ΔHaiti 1.3
ΔIceland 0.0	ΔDjibouti 0.1^	ΔNiger 0.6	Brunei 0.2^	ΔJamaica 1.2

Source: ACDA 90f88, Table I, Column 12; or ^ = computed (n=2).

• = state also found among top 7 states in zone in V1.2a.i.

Δ = state also found among lowest 7 states in zone in V1.2a.i

undesignated = state ranking is higher or lower than expected given its size.

(b) Soldiers per 1000 sq.km. Area, 1988

Europe	Islamic	Africa	Asia	Latin America
Belgium 3.54	Israel 9.10	STP 1.00	Singapore 93.33	Cuba 2.68
Malta 3.33	Bahrain 8.33	C.Verde 0.75	Taiwan 10.83	Barbados 2.50
Nethrlds 2.89	Iraq 2.29	Burundi 0.38	N.Korea 6.96	El Salvador 2.14
E.Ger. 2.24	Syria 2.16	GBissau 0.28	S.Korea 6.39	Nicaragua 0.57
W.Ger.1.99	Lebanon 2.00	Ethiopia 0.20	Vietnam 3.33	Dom.Rep. 0.41
Czech. 1.71	Jordan 1.68	Rwanda 0.19	Seychelles 2.00	Trinidad 0.40
Greece 1.50	Cyprus 1.44	Swaziland 0.18	Bang.,Sri L.-0.71	Guatemala 0.33
....	....	....	....	....
Ireland 0.19	Somalia 0.07	Ivory Coast 0.02	Fiji 0.22	Paraguay 0.04
USSR 0.17	Algeria 0.05	Zaire 0.02	Indonesia 0.15	Brazil 0.04
Sweden 0.14	Libya 0.05	Zambia 0.02	New Zealand 0.05	Argentina 0.03
Norway 0.12	Saudi A. 0.04	C.Af.R. 0.01	Madagascar 0.04	Belize 0.03
Finland 0.11	Sudan 0.03	Botswana 0.01	Mongolia 0.02	Bolivia 0.03
Canada 0.01	Chad 0.03	Mali 0.01	Australia 0.01	Guyana 0.02
Iceland 0.00	Mauritania 0.01	Niger 0.003	Papua NG 0.01	Suriname 0.02

Source: *calculated* from V1.2a.i, and V3.2a.i (land area).

V1.2a.iii - Conscription vs. Conscientious Objection (CO)

Europe	Islamic	Africa	Asia	Latin Amer.

No Conscription, n=65

Europe	Islamic	Africa	Asia	Latin Amer.
Canada	Bahrain	Bots.,Bur.,Cam.	Australia	Bahamas
Iceland	Chad	CAFR,Congo	Bangla.,Bhutan	Barbados
Ireland	Lebanon	Ethiopia,Gambia	Brunei,Fiji	Costa Rica
Luxembourg	Mauritania	Ghana,Kenya	India, Indon.	Dom. Rep.
Malta	Oman	Lesotho,Liberia	Japan, Malays.	Grenada
UK	Pakistan	Malawi,Nigeria	Maurits.,Mald.	Guyana
US	Qatar	Rwan.,Sen.,SLeo.	Nepal,NZealand	Jamaica
	Somalia	Swazi.,Tanzania	Papua NG	Panama
	Sudan	Togo, Uganda	Sri Lanka	Suriname
	UAE	Zambia,Zimbwe.	W. Samoa	Trinidad

Conscription with some provision for CO (by length of term, where known), n=40

Europe	Islamic	Africa	Asia	Latin Amer.
Switz. 4 mo.				
Austria 6-8 mo.				
Finland 8 mo.				
Denmark 9 mo.				
Italy 12 mo.				
France 12 mo.				
E.Germany 12 mo.				Uruguay
Sweden 9-13 mo.				Paraguay
Nthrlds 12-14 mo.			Mexico	
Norway 12-15 mo.	N.Yemen		Phil. I.	Honduras
W.Germany 15 mo.	Morocco		Mongolia	Haiti
Belgium 8-18 mo.	Kuwait		Madagascar	Guatemala
Spain 15-18 mo.	Iraq	Burkina Faso	Laos	El Salvador
Portugal 18 mo.	Iran	Cape Verde	Cambodia	Brazil
Greece 22-26 mo.	Israel 24-26 mo.			Bolivia
Poland 2-3 yr.		S. Africa 2 yr.	S. Korea 18-36 mo.	

Conscription, with no provision for CO (by length of term, where known), n=38

Europe	Islamic	Africa	Asia	Latin Amer.
	Cyprus 6 mo.			Venezuela
	Turkey 20 mo.	Benin 12-18 mo.		Argentina
Yugo. 18-24 mo.	Jordan 2 yr.	Guinea		Peru
Hungary 18-24mo.	Algeria	Ivory Coast	Thailand	Ecuador
Albania 24 mo.	Afghanistan	Eq.Guinea	N.Korea	Cuba
USSR 24 mo.^	Syria,Saudi A.	Gabon	Myanmar	Colombia
Czech. 24-27 m.	Egypt	Mali,Niger		Chile 2yr.
Romania 30 mo.	Tunisia	Zaire	Singapore 2-3 yr.	
Bulgaria 2-3 yr.	Libya 3-4 yr.	Angola 3 yr.	China 3-5 yr.	
30	26/28	34/38	27/33	26/33 (143)

Source: *SIPRI Yearbook 1985* (or ^later), pp. 622-624.

V1.2b.i - Military Expenditures (US $ mil.), 1988

Europe	Islamic	Africa	Asia	Latin America
US $307,700				
USSR 299,800			Japan $28,870	
	Saudi A. $13,560		China 21,270	
France 35,950	Iraq 12,400e			Argentina $2972
W.Ger. 35,100	Iran 11,200e		India 9458	
UK 34,680			S.Korea 7262	Peru 1505e
Italy 20,430	Egypt 6086		Australia 6170	
Poland 15,660	Israel 6001	S.Africa $3607	Taiwan 6156	
E.Ger. 14,320			N.Korea 5840	
Canada 10,020	Libya 3175e	Angola 828e		
Czech. 9818	Turkey 2664	Ethiopia 514e		Cuba 1326
Romania 7670	Pakistan 2516	Zimbabwe 386	Thailand 1718	
Spain 7171	Qatar 2200e	Kenya 294	Vietnam 1400	
Bulgaria 6842		Cameroon 234e	Indonesia 1400	Brazil 1209
Netherlands 6729	Algeria 1784	Nigeria 223	Singapore 1321	
Sweden 4975	Syria 1604	Ivory Coast 199		Mexico 1016
Hungary 4489	UAE 1587	Gabon 167	Malaysia 908	
Belgium 4097	Oman 1371	Zambia 125e	N.Zealand 889	Venezuela 848
Switzerland 3888	Kuwait 1340	Tanzania 111	Phil.I. 680	Chile 808
Greece 3378	Morocco 1138	Congo 103e		Colombia 656
Norway 2895	Jordan 882	Botswana 99	Myanmar 350	
Denmark 2320	N.Yemen 566	Senegal 97	Sri Lanka 321	El Salvador 212
Yugoslavia 2080	Lebanon 368e	Mozambique 92e	Mongolia 300	Uruguay 168
Finland 1701	Tunisia 255	Uganda 68	Bangladesh 244e	Bolivia 162
Austria 1426	Afghanistan 217e	Burkina F. 55	Brunei 193^	Ecuador 155
Portugal 1347	S.Yemen 205e	Zaire 49	Cambodia 109	Guatemala 129
	Bahrain 187	Togo 46e		Honduras 120
Ireland 462	Sudan 175	Mali 45	Laos 62	Nicaragua 116e
		Liberia 43	Papua NG 49	Panama 105
Albania 157	Cyprus 44	Benin 38	Nepal 35	Trinidad 101e
Luxembrg. 86	Mauritania 41e	Rwanda 37	Madagascar 34	Paraguay 84
	Chad 39	Malawi 34		Bahamas 77^
	Djibouti 36^	Burundi 34e	Fiji 25	Guyana 46
	Somalia 31e	C.Verde 29e		Dom.Rep. 45
		Guinea 27	Seychelles 13^	Suriname 39
		Ghana 23		Haiti 34
Malta 22		Niger 21	Mauritius 4	Jamaica 32
		C.Af.R. 163	Comoros 3^*	Costa Rica 20
		Lesotho 13e	Maldives 2^*	Barbados 10
		Swaziland 8		Belize 10^
		Sierra L. 6		
		Eq.Guinea 5e		
		GBissau 3e	Solomons-na	
		Gambia 2e	W.Samoa-na	St.L.,Dominica-na
Iceland 0		STP 1e	Vanuatu-na	St.V.,Grenada-na
		Namibia-na	Bhutan-na	St.C.,Antigua-na
n=30	n=28	n=37/38	n=29/33	n=27/33 (151)

Source: ACDA90f88 where e=extrapolated from ACDA's mimeographed "Country Rankings by Variable, 1988," n=144; plus IISS89/90f88^ or earlier^*, n=7.

59

V1.2b.ii - Relative Military Expenditures, 1988

Europe	Islamic	Africa	Asia	Latin America

(a)-mil. exp./capita - ACDA90f88

Europe	Islamic	Africa	Asia	Latin America
US-$1250	Qatar-$1500e	Gabon-$159	Singapore-$499e	Cuba-$128
USSR-1047	Israel-1396	S.Africa-103	Australia-379	Suriname-99
E.Germany-863	Oman-1083	Angola-101	Taiwn-308	Argentina-94
Bulgaria-763	Saudi A.-878	Botswana-83	N.Korea-266	Trinidad-86e
Norway-691	Libya-832e	C.Verde 79e	N.Zealand-266	Peru-69e
France-644	UAE-801	Congo-48e	Japan-235	Chile-64
Czech.-629	Iraq-728e	Zimbabwe-40e	S.Korea-168	Guyana-60

(a) - mil. exp./capita - Sivard 89f86, Table III

Europe	Islamic	Africa	Asia	Latin America
US-$1153	Oman-$1515	Angola-$149	Brunei-$1,099	Cuba-$144
USSR-954	Saudi A.-1448	Gabon-119	Singapore-383	Nicaragua-138
Norway 476	UAE-1339	S.Africa-75	Australia-333	Peru-72
UK-447	Israel-1210	Congo-39	Taiwan-203	Guyana-65
E.Germany-432	Kuwait-752	Zimbabwe-31	N.Zealand-148	Trinidad-53
France-431	Iraq-716	Botswana-22	Japan-129	Uruguay-48
Sweden-394	Libya-651	Mozambique-18	S.Korea-124	Chile-47

e=extrapolated from ACDA "Country Rankings by Variable, 1988".

(b) - mil. exp. as % GNP - ACDA90f88

Europe	Islamic	Africa	Asia	Latin America
Bulgaria-12.7%	Qatar-25.0e%	C.Verde-9.4e%	N.Korea 20.0%	Guyana-14.6%
USSR-11.9	Jordan-21.0	Mozambique-9.3e	Mongolia-11.6e	Nicaragua-11.1e
Poland-8.7	S.Yemen-20.5e	Ethiopia-8.5e	Cambodia-11.3	Bolivia-4.0
E.Germany-7.7	Iraq-19.5e	Botswana-8.3	Vietnam-9.6e	Peru-4.0e
Czech.-7.1	Oman-19.1	Angola-7.9	Laos-9.2e	Chile-4.0
Romania-6.5	Saudi A.-16.5	Zimbabwe-6.3	Singapore-5.3	El Salvador-3.8
Greece-6.5	Israel-13.8	Congo-5.3e	Taiwan-5.2	Cuba-3.8

(b) - mil. exp. as % GNP - Sivard 89f86,Table II

Europe	Islamic	Africa	Asia	Latin America
USSR-11.5%	Iraq-32.0%	Angola-12.0%	Mongolia-10.5%	Nicaragua-16.4%
US-6.3	Oman-27.6	Ethiopia-8.6	N.Korea-10.0	Guyana-12.2
Greece-5.7	Saudi A.-22.7	Mozambique-7.0	Brunei-7.1	Cuba-7.4
UK-5.0	S.Yemen-22.0	Zimbabwe-5.0	Malaysia-6.1	Peru-6.5
E.Germany-4.9	Iran-20.0	Congo-4.6	China-6.0	Honduras-5.9
Czech.-4.1	Israel-19.2	Uganda-4.2	Taiwan-5.7	El Salvador-3.7
Albania-4.0	Syria-14.7	S.Africa-3.9	Sri Lanka-5.7	Chile-3.6

e=extrapolated from ACDA "Country Rankings by Variable, 1988".

60

Table V1.2b.ii (continued)

Europe	Islamic	Africa	Asia	Latin America

(c) - mil. exp. as % CGE - ACDA90f88

Europe	Islamic	Africa	Asia	Latin America
Yugoslavia-67.5%	Afghan.-63.0e%	Mozambq.-54.0e%	Vietnam-48.0e%	Argentina-51.0e%
Poland-44.1	Qatar-60.0e	Angola-28.7e	N.Korea-40.7	Peru-37.2e
USSR-43.2	Iraq-57.0e	Ethiopia-22.0e	Cambodia-34.0	El Salvador-34.9
US-27.5	Chad-45.1	Uganda-20.9	Taiwan-31.3	Bolivia-28.1
Bulgaria-26.6	UAE-41.1	C.Verde-19.0e	S.Korea-25.2	Guyana-22.3e
Czech.-22.6	Oman-38.4	Benin-18.0e	Myanmar-24.3	Nicaragua-20.6e
Romania-15.8	Saudi A.-36.0	Liberia-17.5	Singapore-24.2	Paraguay-17.6

(c)-mil. exp as % CGE - World Bank 90f88*

Europe	Islamic	Africa	Asia	Latin America
Yugo.-55.1%	UAE-45.3%^	Uganda-26.3%	S.Korea-27.1%	El Sal.-25.7%
US-24.8	Syria-40.4	Burkina F.-17.9	India-19.3	Peru-20.0
UK-12.6	Oman-38.2	Zimbabwe-16.3	Thailand-18.7	Paraguay-12.1^
Switz.-10.3^^	N.Yemen-31.2	Tanzania-13.8^	Singapore-14.6	Chile-10.4
W.Ger.-8.9	Pakistan-29.5	Botswana-12.1	Myanmar-12.9	Ecuador-11.8^
Norway-8.3	Israel-27.2	Togo-11.1	Phil. I.-11.6	Uruguay-10.2
Canada-7.7	Jordan-26.5	Lesotho-9.6^	Bangladesh-11.2^	Dom.Rep.-8.1

*World Development Report (WDR) 1990, n=62 states only, so this list is not directly comparable
with ACDA where n=144; supplemented by ^WDR89f87 and ^^WDR88f86.
e=extrapolated from ACDA "Country Rankings by Variable, 1988".

(d) - mil. exp./soldier (in nearest hundred US$) - ACDA90f88

Europe	Islamic	Africa	Asia	Latin America
Switz. $169,100	Qatar $175,000e	S.Africa $36,670	Japan $117,900	Trin. $55,000e
US 137,000	Saudi A. 162,500	Iv.Coast 24,850	Australia 87,520	Argentina 31,280
Canada 113,900	Kuwait 89.360	Botswana 24,810	N.Zealand 69,450	Barbados 20,980
UK 107,000	Oman 56,530	Gabon 21,440	Singapore 23,810	Peru 17,710e
Luxmbg. 86,030	Bahrain 37,450	Kenya 14,860	Taiwan 15,790	Guyana 13,200
Denmark 77,350	Libya 37,100e	Cameroon 12,000e	Papua NG 15,390	Venez. 11,620
USSR 76,870	UAE 36,910e	C.Verde 9130	S.Korea 11,510	Jamaica 10,690

(d) - mil. exp./soldier (in nearest hundred US$) - Sivard 89f86**

Europe	Islamic	Africa	Asia	Latin America
US $131,000	Saudi A. $257,100	Gabon $41,300	Australia $76,400	Trin. $32,000
Switz. 107,500	Kuwait 116,800	S.Africa 24,400	Japan 64,600	Jamaica 17,000
Canada 97,700	Oman 84,500	Angola 23,600	Brunei 63,800	Venez. 16,600
UK 78,200	Bahrain 60,700	Cameroon 23,000	N.Zealand 38,900	Argentin.15,000
USSR 74,100	UAE 43,700	Kenya 11,600	Singapore 17,900	Peru 11,800
Norway 53,800	Libya 34,700	Mozambq.16,800	Sri Lanka 16,900	Hond. 10,900
Sweden 51,000	Israel 34,300	Burkina F. 9300	Malaysia 16,300	Mexico 9600

**calculated from Table III

e=extrapolated from ACDA "Country Rankings by Variable, 1988".

V1.2b.iii - Composite on "Relative Burden" of Military Spending

(mil.exp./GNP compared with GNP/capita, 1988)

Europe	Islamic	Africa	Asia	Latin America
Underspending (Most Committed to Peace?), n=18				
Iceld.,Ireld.	Cyprus	Cameroon	Japan	Brazil,Venezuela
Malta				Paraguay
Austria			Mauritius	Colombia,Mexico
Finland				Costa Rica
Luxmbrg.				Barbados,Jamaica
Spend within their Meagre Means, n=23				
	Somalia	Niger,Nigeria	Bangladesh	Haiti
		Sierra L.,Gambia	Nepal	Dom.Rep.
		Ghana,Guinea	Indonesia	Guatemala
		STP,C.Af.R.,Zaire	Papua NG	Ecuador
		Uganda,Rwanda	Phil. I.	
		Lesotho,Swaziland		
Middle Group (Global Norm), n=58				
UK,Canada	Turkey	Iv.Coast,GBissau	India,Myanmar	Argentina,Peru
Denmark,Sweden	Iran	Senegal,Benin	China	Uruguay,Chile
Switz.,W.Germany	Chad	Burkina F.,Mali	Madagascar	Bolivia
Belgium	Mauritania	Eq.Guin.,Togo	Sri Lanka	Suriname
Netherlands	Sudan	Liberia	S.Korea	Honduras
Norway	Algeria	Burundi	Malaysia	El Salvador
France, Italy	Tunisia	Kenya,Tanzania	Thailand	Panama
Yugoslavia		Malawi,Zambia	Fiji	Trinidad
Spain, Portugal		S.Africa	Australia, N.Zealand	Cuba
Somewhat Extravagant in Military Spending, n=29				
US,USSR	Israel,Jordan	Angola	N.Korea	
Greece	Syria,Lebanon	Gabon	Mongolia	
Bulg.,Romania	Iraq,Egypt,Oman	Botswana	Singapore	
E.Germany	Qatar,Bahrain		Taiwan	
Poland	UAE, Saudi A.			
Czech.,Hungary	Kuwait, Libya			
Can Least Afford Current Levels (Most Bellicose?), n=16				
Albania	N.Yemen,S.Yemen	C.Verde,Congo	Vietnam	
	Morocco	Ethiopia	Laos	Nicaragua
	Afghanistan	Zimbabwe	Cambodia	Guyana
	Pakistan	Mozambique		
n=30	n=27/28	n=37/38	n=25/33	n=25/33 (144)

Source: Adapted from ACDA 1990, Figure 16.

62

V1.2c - Military Coup Regimes, Leaders, Dates (n=38; 12/20/90)

State	Date of Coup	Leader	# yrs.
		Islamic (n=11)	
Algeria	June '65/Feb.'79	Col. H.Boumedienne/Col.B.Chadli	25 yrs.
Iraq	July '69/July'79	Gen.A.H.al-Bakr/Saddam Hussein	21 yrs.
Libya	Sept.'69	Col. Muammar Qaddafi	21 yrs.
Somalia	Oct.'69	Gen. Siad Barre	21 yrs.
Syria	Nov.'70	Gen. Hafez al Assad	20 yrs.
ΔN.Yemen	July '78	Lt.Col. ali Abdallah Salih	12 yrs.
Afghanistan	Dec.'79/May'86	SU + Babrak Karmal/Gen. Najibullah	11 yrs.
Mauritania	Dec.'84	Col. M.Ould Taya	6 yrs.
ΔS.Yemen	Jan.'86	ali Salim (Saleh M.) al-Beedh	4 yrs.
Sudan	July '89	Brig. Omar Hassam Ahmed al Bashir	1 yr.
Chad	Dec.'90	Gen. Idris Deby	<1 yr.
		Africa (n=18)	
Zaire	Nov.'65	Col. Jos. Mobutu	25 yrs.
Togo	Apr.'67	Maj. Gnassingbe Eyadema	23 yrs.
Mali	Nov.'68	Lt. Moussa Traore	22 yrs.
Benin	Oct.'72	Maj. Mathieu Kerekou	18 yrs.
Rwanda	July '73	Maj.Gen. Juvenal Habyarimana	17 yrs.
Niger	Apr.'74/Nov.'87	Lt.Col. S. Kountche/Col.ali Seybou	16 yrs.
Ethiopia	Feb.'77	Lt.Col. Mengistu H. Mariam	13 yrs.
Congo	Feb.'79	Col. Denis Sassou Nguesso	11 yrs.
Equat. Guinea	Aug.'79	Lt.Col. Obiang Nguema	11 yrs.
Guinea Bissau	Nov.'80	Maj. Joao Bernardo Vieira	10 yrs.
C.Afr.Republic	Sept.'81	Col. Andre Kolingba	9 yrs.
Ghana	Dec.'81	Flt.Lt. Jerry Rawlings	9 yrs.
Guinea	Apr.'84	Col. Lansana Conte	6 yrs.
Nigeria	Aug.'85	Gen. Ibrahim Babangida	5 yrs.
Lesotho	Jan.'86	Gen. Justin Lekhanya	4 yrs.
Uganda	Jan.'86	Maj. Yoseri Museveni	4 yrs.
Burundi	Sept.'87	Maj. Pierre Buyoya	3 yr.
Burkina Faso	Oct.'87	Capt. Blaise Campaore	3 yr.
		Asia (n=7)	
Indonesia	Mar.'66	Gen. Suharto	24 yrs.
Madagascar	June '75	Adm. Didier Ratsiraka	15 yrs.
Seychelles	June '77	Albert Rene	13 yrs.
Cambodia	Dec.'78	Vietnam + Hun Sen	12 yrs.
Fiji	May '87	Col. Sitivi Rabaka	3 yr.
Myanmar	Sept.'88	Gen. Saw Maung	2 yrs.
Comoros	Dec.'89	France + S. M. Djohar	<1 yr.
		Latin America (n=2)	
Paraguay	Feb.'89	Gen. Andres Rodriguez	1 yr.
Panama	Dec.'89	US + Guillermo Endara	<1 yr.

Source: V1.2c Data Bank.

Δ = 2 Yemeni coup regimes united in May, 1990 (see Chapter 5).

63

V1.2c.i,ii - Military Coup Measures

<table>
<tr><td colspan="4" align="center">.i - Coup Frequency Ratio</td><td colspan="3" align="center">.ii - % Coup-Regime Years</td></tr>
<tr><td colspan="4" align="center">(# since 1945, or indep. yr.)</td><td colspan="3" align="center">(+ = continuing at present)</td></tr>
<tr><td colspan="7" align="center">as of 20 December 1990</td></tr>
<tr><td>State</td><td>ratio</td><td>Data</td><td>Indep./Base Yr.</td><td>State</td><td>% Yrs.</td><td>Data</td></tr>
</table>

Europe (n=6 states*, 10 coups)

State	ratio	Data	Indep./Base Yr.	State	% Yrs.	Data
Portugal	.056	2.5/45	1945	Spain	.667	30/45
Greece	.056	2.5/45	1945	Portugal	.644	29/45
Czech.	.044	2/45	1945	Greece	.156	7/45
Hungary	.022	1/45	1945	Czech.	.156	7/45
Poland	.022	1/45	1945	Hungary	.111	5/45
Spain	.022	1/45	1945	Poland	.089	4/45

*No coups in 10/10 in n. Atl.; 8/11 in c. Eur.; and 6/9 in s. Eur. (n=24 states)

Islamic (n=17 states*, 53.5 coups)

State	ratio	Data	Indep./Base Yr.	State	% Yrs.	Data
S. Yemen	.217	5/23	1967	Oman	1.000	20+/20
Syria	.182	8/44	1946	Syria	.932	41+/44
Sudan	.147	5/34	1956	S.Yemen	.913	21+/23
Chad	.133	4/30	1960	Algeria	.892	25+/28
Mauritania	.117	3.5/30	1960	Sudan	.765	26/34
Afghan.	.100	4.5/45	1945	Iraq	.711	32+/45
Iraq	.100	4.5/45	1945	Somalia	.700	21+/30
N. Yemen	.089	4/45	1945	Pakistan	.581	25/43
Pakistan	.070	3/43	1947	Iran	.556	25/45
Cyprus	.067	2/30	1960	Libya	.538	21+/39
Turkey	.067	3/45	1945	Chad	.500	15+/30
Algeria	.054	1.5/28	1962	N.Yemen	.467	21+/45
Oman	.050	1/20	1970	Egypt	.400	18/45
Somalia	.033	1/30	1960	Mauritania	.400	12+/30
Egypt	.033	1.5/45	1945	Afghanistan	.378	17+/45
Libya	.026	1/39	1951	Turkey	.244	11/45
Iran	.022	1/45	1945	Cyprus	.033	1/30

*No coups in: Israel,Leb.; Saudi A.,Jordan,Kuw.,Bahrain,UAE,Qatar; Djib.,Morocco,Tun.(n=11)

Asia (n=13 states*, 37.5 coups)

State	ratio	Data	Indep./Base Yr.	State	% Yrs.	Data
Comoros	.300	4.5/15	1975	Comoros	1.000	15+/15
Thailand	.200	9/45	1945	Seychelles	.929	13+/14
Bangladesh	.158	3/19	1971	Taiwan	.927	38/41
Madagascar	.117	3.5/30	1960	Thailand	.844	38/45
Fiji	.100	2/20	1970	Bangladesh	.778	14+/19
Myanmar	.095	4/42	1948	Myanmar	.714	30+/42
Laos	.083	3/36	1954	S.Korea	.619	26/42
Seychelles	.071	1/14	1976	Madagascar	.600	18+/30
Cambodia	.056	2/36	1954	Indonesia	.571	24+/42
S.Korea	.048	2/42	1948	Laos	.444	16/36
Taiwan	.037	1.5/41	1949	Cambodia	.444	16+/36
Indonesia	.024	1/42	1948	Philippines	.318	14/44
Philippines	.023	1/44	1946	Fiji	.150	3+/20

*No coups in: India,Nepal,Bhutan,SriLanka,Maldives,Mauritius; China,Mongolia,N.Kor.,VN;
   Japan,Brunei,Malaysia,Singapore,PapuaNG,Solomons,WSam.,Van.,Australia,NZ. (n=20)

For coup regimes starting before 1945 & extending after that year (Portugal, Spain), coup is counted
   in .2c.i, but only the years since 1945 are counted in .2c.ii.

.5 coup weight assigned when power is passed peacefully from one group in a junta to another.

Regardless of how many months in a year a coup regime rules, .2c.ii counts a full year.

Table V1.2c.i,.ii (continued)

.i - Coup Frequency Ratio   .ii - % Coup-Regime Years

Africa (n=20 states*, 55.5 coups)

State	ratio	Data	Indep./Base Yr.	State	% Yrs.	Data
Burkina F.	.200	6/30	1960	Togo	.900	27+/30
Nigeria	.200	6/30	1960	Burundi	.857	24+/28
Benin	.167	5/30	1960	Zaire	.833	25+/30
Ghana	.152	5/33	1957	Lesotho	.833	20+/24
Uganda	.143	4/28	1962	Burkina Faso	.800	24+/30
Burundi	.107	3/28	1962	C.AF.R.	.800	24+/30
Sierra L.	.103	3/29	1961	Benin	.800	24+/30
C. Af. R.	.100	3/30	1960	Rwanda	.750	21+/28
Congo	.100	3/30	1960	Mali	.733	22+/30
Togo	.100	3/30	1960	Congo	.733	22+/30
Lesotho	.083	2/24	1966	Nigeria	.633	19+/30
Rwanda	.071	2/28	1962	Guinea Bissau	.588	10+/17
Ethiopia	.067	3/45	1945	Ghana	.576	19+/33
Guinea Bissau	.059	1/17	1973	Niger	.533	16+/30
Niger	.050	1.5/30	1960	Uganda	.500	14+/28
Eq. Guinea	.045	1/22	1968	Eq.Guinea	.500	11+/22
Zaire	.033	1/30	1960	Ethiopia	.356	16+/45
Mali	.033	1/30	1960	Liberia	.222	10+/45
Guinea	.031	1/32	1958	Guinea	.188	6+/32
Liberia	.022	1/45	1945	Sierra Leone	.069	2/29

*No coups: CV,Gabon,Gambia,IC,Sen.; Camr.,STP,Kenya,Tanz.; and 9 of 10 states in s. Af.(n=18)

Latin America (n=20 states*, 91 coups)

State	ratio	Data	Indep./Base Yr.	State	% Yrs.	Data
Grenada	.214	3/14	1976	Haiti	1.000	45+/45
El Salvador	.200	9/45	1945	Paraguay	1.000	45+/45
Guatemala	.200	9/45	1945	El Salvador	.867	39/45
Bolivia	.178	8/45	1945	Nicaragua	.756	34/45
Argentina	.167	7.5/45	1945	Guatemala	.689	31/45
Haiti	.167	7.5/45	1945	Panama	.622	28+/45
Honduras	.156	7/45	1945	Argentina	.600	27/45
Ecuador	.156	7/45	1945	Bolivia	.556	25/45
Brazil	.111	5/45	1945	Brazil	.511	23/45
Peru	.111	5/45	1945	Honduras	.489	22/45
Panama	.111	5/45	1945	Suriname	.467	7/15
Dom. Rep.	.089	4/45	1945	Peru	.467	21/45
Venezuela	.078	3.5/45	1945	Dom. Rep.	.422	19/45
Suriname	.067	1/15	1975	Grenada	.357	5/14
Paraguay	.067	3/45	1945	Chile	.356	16/45
Uruguay	.056	2.5/45	1945	Ecuador	.333	15/45
Colombia	.044	2/45	1945	Cuba	.311	14/45
Nicaragua	.044	2/45	1945	Uruguay	.266	12/45
Cuba	.033	1.5/45	1945	Venezuela	.244	11/45
Chile	.022	1/45	1945	Colombia	.089	4/45

*No coups in: Mexico, CR post-'48, & Belize in c. Am.; 10 of 11 in Brit. Caribbean; (n=13)

For LA states whose indep. goes back to 19th century and mil.rule is a tradition, coup regimes are listed beginning with those succeeding the first period of civilian rule after 1945.

For coup regimes starting before 1945 & extending after that year (Dom.Rep.,Arg.,Nic.,Cuba), coup is counted in .2c.i but only the years since 1945 are counted in .2c.ii

.5 coup weight assigned when power is passed peacefully from one group in a junta to another.

Regardless of how many months in a year a coup regime rules, .2c.ii counts a full year.

State & Years # coups=.i	Leader	Years	Duration=.ii

Burkina Faso - 1960 (Upper Volta) indep. ldr. until .....

1/3/66-1971	Lt. Col. Sangoule Lamizana		5
1971-2/8/74	•Maj. Jean Baptiste Oeudreogo		3
2/8/74-11/25/80	•Lt. Col. Sangoule Lamizana (again)		6
11/25/80-11/7/82	Col. Saye Zerbo		2
11/7/82-8/4/83	Maj. Jean Baptiste Oeudreogo (again)		1
8/4/83-10/16/87	Capt. Thomas Sankara		4
10/16/87ff	Capt. Blaise Campaore		3+
# coups = 6		tot. # yrs. =	24+

Ghana - 1957-1966 indep. ldr. (Nkrumah) until ......

2/24/66-8/29/69	Gen. J. A. Ankrah		3
1/17/72-7/5/78	Gen. Ignatius Kutu Acheampong		6
7/5/78-6/4/79	Frederick Akuffo junta		1
6/4/79-9/24/79	Flt. Lt. Jerry Rawlings		<1
12/31/81ff	Flt. Lt. Jerry Rawlings again		9+
# coups = 5		tot. # yrs. =	19+

Nigeria - 1960-66 indep. ldrs. Tafawa Balewa Mohammed et al. until.........

1/15/66-7/29/66	Gen. Johnson Aguiyi Ironsi		<1
7/29/66-7/29/75	Gen. Yakubu Gowon		9
7/29/75-2/13/76	Brig. Murtala Ramut Muhammed		1
2/13/76-1979	Lt.Gen.Olusegun Obasango (to civilian Xition)		3
1/1/84-8/30/85	Maj. Gen. Mohammed Buhari		1
8/30/85ff	Gen. Badamasi Babangida		5+
# coups = 6 (3 assassinations)		tot. # yrs. =	19+

Niger - 1960 indep. ldrs. incl. PM Diori until......

4/15/74-11/87	Lt. Col. Seyni Kountche´		13
11/87ff	•Col. ali Seybou		3+
# coups = 1.5		tot. # yrs. =	16+

<u>Legend</u>:
ff = after date in 2nd col., "+"after tot. yrs. in last col. = states with current coup regime;
    corresponds to the mil^ and mil^{o} regimes in V5.4cd.
• = peaceful transfer of leadership *within* same junta; .5 coup freq. weight; all yrs. added to
    original coup duration.
<u>Other Indicators used in V1.2c Data Bank</u>:
^ = civilian figurehead installed by military, years added to original coup.
Δ = martial law (extended duration) coup by otherwise constitutional civilian regime.
! = coup with external forces instrumental in transfer of power.

VI.3. EXTERNAL MANIFESTATIONS OF WAR

Among the external manifestations of wars (past, present, and perhaps to come) are the deployment of troops from one country onto the territory of another, and international traffic in weapons (the arms trade). This section will also address two issues of general concern to the global community: weapons of mass destruction whose effects cannot be reliably contained within national boundaries, and efforts towards international arms control.

VI.3a - Force Projections

The projection of the armed forces of one country onto the territory of another is a blatant manifestation of militarism. This obviously happens during war, and it sometimes occurs *instead* of war, in the form of alliance commitments in which stronger states station their troops on the soil of weaker countries in need of "protection." Another example of military deployment involves teams of "advisors" which accompany the sale of armaments and other forms of military aid (Harkavy, 1989).

The assumption of the survey presented next is that the total number of troops deployed beyond a state's home borders, and the number of countries in which they might be found, can be taken as *some* indication of reliance upon military might to settle political disputes (and thus absence of peaceful intent). At the least, distinctions can be drawn between those extreme cases of states which seldom experience foreign military activity on their territory or the deployment of their own troops beyond home borders (e.g., Sweden, Tunisia, Botswana, Malaysia, Brazil), and those countries which perennially are the site of some external military presence (e.g., Germany, Lebanon, Ethiopia, Cambodia, Cuba) or the source of deployed troops (e.g., US, UK, France, USSR, Cuba). Tables VI.3a list (i) those countries with the most forces deployed onto foreign soil, and (ii) those states accommodating or "hosting" the most alien troops on their territory.

There were approximately 1.7 million troops in some 150 different deployments stationed abroad in 1990 before the establishment of multinational forces in response to crises in Saudi Arabia and Liberia. Most deployed forces are the result of victory in war. After belligerency, there is often a prolonged period of occupation during which troops from the winning country remain on the territory of the loser. Initially this presence is under conditions of duress; later, it sometimes evolves into a period of sufferance, acceptance, or even "alliance partnership" (e.g., the US in West Germany and Japan, the USSR in East Germany and Poland, since World War II).

Most of the world's deployed forces are found in Europe as a result of the outcome of World War II and the subsequent Cold War between the US and

USSR as each attempted to replace the political influence of Germany in the central European region. Even though the USSR has announced a schedule for withdrawal of its soldiers from Czechoslovakia and Hungary by 1991, and from (East) Germany by 1995, the US seems intent on maintaining significant forces on the continent outside the central European region. The outcomes of the multilateral deployments in Liberia and Saudi Arabia remain unclear at this time and are not reflected in the text or tables which follow.

For other contemporary examples of force projections, attention should be paid to troops deployed overseas intervening in ongoing wars (e.g., France in Chad, Syria in Lebanon), and to "military assistance" teams accompanying the transfer of weapons (e.g., the US and USSR in more than 40 developing countries—see section V1.3b for more details). The data in Tables V1.3a sometimes includes numbers of large contingents of such military advisory groups, but not the handful of military attaches found in the embassies of all significant powers. Numbers associated with deployed military forces will also not include civilian advisors or settlers accompanying troops, although they may sometimes be noted in the narrative excerpts for "hosted" troops. Naval forces, even those permanently on station such as the US Sixth Fleet in the Mediterranean, are not included in the following survey.

Some care should be taken in interpreting the data in Tables V1.3a. Virtually all of the numbers are approximations, rounded off to the nearest 50 or 100 or 1000 soldiers, depending on the size of the deployment. Other explanations of difficult choices for inclusion in this survey (relating to disputed territories or political actors) can be found in the notes accompanying the excerpts. As with so much of the data in this study, precise statistics will vary from year to year (though probably not by more than 10%), but the names and rank order of states deploying and hosting troops remain fairly constant.

The US and the USSR are the unchallenged leaders in deploying forces beyond their borders, with the Soviets having the most soldiers stationed abroad (about 570,000), and the Americans being found in the most other countries (some 36). The other major troop-deploying states are declining imperialist countries like United Kingdom, France, and Spain, and rising regional or ideological leaders like Syria, Morocco, India, Indonesia, and Cuba. Even with the reductions accompanying the thaw in the European Cold War, that continent remains the source of most of the world's deployed troops. Three-quarters of all forces found beyond their home borders come out of the European zone, with the US and USSR accounting for 60 percent of all armed personnel deployed abroad and almost half of all major deployments listed in Table V1.3a.i, though the Soviet numbers can be expected to decline.

With respect to Table V1.3a.ii's "hosting" of foreign military forces, Europe has about 1 million of the 1.7 million deployed troops, with Germany (East and West) accounting for about 75% of these for the post-World War II reasons mentioned above. Elsewhere, Asia has the most foreign troops (some 330,000 in 25 locales) with the Islamic zone third (about 290,000 troops in 25 sites). Lesser numbers are found in Africa (some 55,000 in 16 places) and in Latin America (about 40,000 in 11 locations).

Note the distinction between deployments and sites. In the data bank excerpts which follow, 151 deployments are identified, coming from some 34 sources including such non-state entities as the United Nations, NATO, and the Palestinians.

Deployed troops are found "hosted" in some 98 different locations, 24 of which are in territories whose sovereignty is in some dispute (coded #), including some 17 colonies whose status is covered in this text at the end of Chapter 5. The remaining seven include four states mentioned among section V1.1b's insurgencies and three ethnic sub-nations covered in Chapter 4.2. Undoubtedly other cases of national troops regarded as "foreign presences" could be found, but only the most extreme examples mentioned in the main sources cited below are presented here.

Statistics supporting these summaries are maintained in the data bank associated with this project, six pages of which are excerpted at the end of this section. In the first part of these excerpts (Table V1.3a.i, deployed troops), data is presented as firm; in the second part (Table V1.3a.ii, hosted troops), questionable estimates are sometimes included. See the notes at the end of each table for explanations of codes: !, #, ^{W}, ?, ^{PP}, and $^{\sim}$.

Sivard's annual *World Military and Social Expenditures* and the London International Institute for Strategic Studies' *Military Balance* are the best regular sources for this information. These works are supplemented and updated (through mid-1990) with estimates from other sources such as the *New York Times*, *The Economist*, and the *International Herald Tribune* .

V1.3b. Weapons Transfers

Any analysis of the international impact of war beyond the immediate belligerents should address the growing phenomenon of international traffic in armaments—weapons imported and exported between states (Pierre, 1982; Brzoska and Ohlson, 1987). Imports are significant for countries without their own armaments industry and whose official levels of annual military expenditures might be deceptively low, for the weapons they receive might be given freely (grants) or financed by long-term credits or barter arrangements (Looney, 1988; Ross, 1989). Exports are important for they relate to support for proxy belligerencies (Kaldor et al., 1979).

Military "trade" is chosen as an indicator rather than military "aid," for data relating to aid is not reported in any systematic way, and in any case much of the aid is associated with how to use transferred armaments (Louscher and Salomone, 1987). In this context, SIPRI, IISS, and ACDA are all quite comprehensive in keeping track of the traffic in military hardware, although this entire area is fraught with methodological problems (Fei, 1979). For example, a distinction is often made between the agreement to transfer arms and the actual delivery of the weapons, which often takes place in a subsequent year (US DOD DSAA, annual). There is also the problem of assessing the value of the hardware transferred, particularly in the case of grants or barter agreements. Estimates measured in constant dollars over some multi-year period, however, go a long way in smoothing out some of these problems, and the state rankings displayed in this section fill a gap in the measurement of global militarism.

The IISS's *Military Balance* is best for getting the most-recent-year statistics, and the *SIPRI Yearbook* is good for regional totals for a recent "rolling five-year" cycle. The most complete source, however, is ACDA's *World Military Expenditures and Arms Transfers*, which has data for the previous ten years and provides an excellent history for all states, including not only the total value of their weapons imports, but detailed information on the various sources of their armaments. ACDA (1990 edition) will be used extensively in this section because the historical record is more important here than in section V1.2ab (defense budget line items) since arms transfers are not steady over time. It is common for a state to make a large purchase agreement in one year, and then none at all for several years. The longer time frame also tends to spread out the difference in numbers for specific years as concerns agreements and deliveries.

World arms trade for the most recent five-year period reported on (1984-88) has totaled about $248.3 billion (in deliveries), with most of it (about 85%) coming from nine European states, and about 79% of it going to the developing nations of the Islamic world, Africa, Asia, and Latin America (ACDA 1990: 115). (About 17% of global arms traffic is intra-European and some 4% is among developing nations). Throughout the 1980s, slightly more than 60% of all weapons exports came from the US and USSR. When China is added to the list of major NATO and the Warsaw Pact exporters, about 88% of world trade in armaments can be accounted for by just ten states.

Two final factors should be mentioned when considering the global arms trade—money and race. Of the $195.4 billion worth of arms imported by developing nations in 1984-88, about 39% ($75.3 billion) went to states belonging to the Organization of Petroleum Exporting Countries (OPEC). States in the non-European zones generally do not have the technological expertise to build a formidable military establishment, but if they have money, they can buy whatever is needed from the more advanced states. What this means is that the European zone is the arsenal of militarism for the rest of the world; the white countries are arming the colored peoples of the planet for the wars which are being fought in their parts of the world today (Klare, 1984 and 1987; also recall section V1.1).

i. Exports. To highlight the role of the European zone in this deadly trade, the normal display of five geographic columns will be collapsed in Table V1.3b.i(a) to two—European exporters (n=20) and "other" (n=6). The 26 main weapons-exporting nations during the five-year period 1984-88 include the United States and three NATO allies (France, West Germany, and UK), the USSR and two Warsaw Pact allies (Poland and Czechoslovakia), and China—all with more than $1 billion in average annual transfers; plus a second tier of 18 states all of which have exported more than $150 million a year in arms over this same period.

Table V1.3b.i(b), arms exports for 1988—the most recent year for which data is available—reveals a total of 45 states at the supply end of the arms trade, including 16 developing nations (those in the non-European column, less Japan, Australia, New Zealand, Israel, and South Africa). Some of these states specialize in selling a low-level weapons technology more suitable for the capacities of other developing nations (Katz, 1986; Brzoska and Ohlson, 1986; SIPRI, 1985a; Neuman, 1984); others are passing on old military materiel to more backward states while "trading up" for new models of equipment imported from Europe.

For North Korea and the Soviet Union, arms sales represent more than 19% of their total export trade. Numbers in parentheses are boldfaced for seven states (including the US) for which the weapons percentage of total exports is greater than 4%, and without emphasis for 12 other states where arms are more than 1% of exports. (The percentage is not mentioned at all for the 26 states where it is less than 1%.) Although there are wide annual variations in arms export totals at the lower end of this chart (for this is a competitive business), Table V1.3b.i(b) gives a rough idea of zonal leaders in absolute terms, and (where the percentages are provided) of the importance of the "merchant-of-death sector" in each country's economy.

ii. Imports. Even with the recent Third World additions to the weapons supplier business, arms exporters are still a small subset (about one-quarter) of the world community. Virtually every state, however, *imports* arms, including the European countries who buy extremely costly latest weapons technology from one another. Table V1.3b.ii(a) lists the leading arms importers in each zone (91 states, each with more than $150 million in imports) during the five-year period 1984-88. The data reveal significant differences in the various regional arms races. The Islamic zone—with weapons imports fueled by petrodollars—is easily the region with the most warlike tendencies as measured by this indicator, with 25 of its 28 states represented including 8 of the 12 states in the world totalling more than $6 billion each in arms imports during this period.

The predominance of the Islamic zone would be further confirmed if arms imports *as a percentage of total imports* were considered. Table V1.3b.ii(b), using the latest 1988 statistics, shows 30 states for which weapons comprised more than 8% of their imports, and (in parentheses on the last line) the next highest state under this threshold. (In a few cases, percentages are deceptively high, even more than 100%, because their accounting methods do not include weapons sales in total trade statistics.) The Islamic states predominate with almost half of the states listed. At the other extreme, the economies of European states are so diversified that for only one country in this zone are arms imports in excess of 4% of total imports.

iii. Dependency. The matter of arms imports again raises the issue of dependency suggested in the previous section V1.3a. While not as blatant as having the troops of another nation on one's territory, dependence upon a single external source of weapons for national security creates the potential for an undesirable patron-client relationship (Baek et al., 1989; Catrina, 1988). This situation is not too worrisome for states with small amounts of arms purchases, for these could probably be replaced from another source. But for the 68 states listed in Table V1.3b.ii(a) with arms imports of more than $400 million over the five-year period 1984-88, the degree of dependency on the leading supplier should be noted. Such countries generally have a large and integrated military establishment to maintain, and cannot easily switch suppliers or technologies.

Table V1.3b.iii summarizes these dependency relationships, using superscripts and abbreviations to indicate the major suppliers. The dominant positions of the US and USSR (the leading suppliers in 78% of the cases, particularly within their respective military alliances) are especially notable. Most key allies are more than 85% dependent on one or the other Super Power. Interesting in their efforts for independence in the European zone are Greece, Norway, and Hungary within the alliances, as well as neutral Switzerland. Potential regional powers with diverse suppliers include Saudi Arabia, Morocco, Egypt, Iraq, Nigeria, Indonesia, China, and Brazil.

In an effort to avoid weapons dependency, many Third World states are now developing their own arms industries. The names of such states, and estimates of their levels of self-sufficiency, vary according to the source cited, but there are about three dozen such actors as of 1990.

SIPRI (1985: Chapter 10) identifies 27 Third World arms producers, divided into five groups based upon ten categories of weapons produced (including 1. fighter planes, jet trainers; 2. light planes, transport planes; 3. helicopters; 4. guided missiles; 5. major fighting ships; 6. small fighting ships; 7. main battle tanks; 8. artillery; 9. light tanks, APCs; 10. small arms); and five stages of indigenous production (including 1. overhaul and refurbishment capacity; 2. assembly; 3. licensed production of components; 4. licensed production of weapons systems/import of sophisticated parts; 5. indigenous design and production). See Table V1.3b.iv(a).

ACDA (1987: 14-15) analyzes some 36 developing countries according to their abilities to produce nine categories of ground, air, and naval armaments. The capabilities range from providing local munitions (M) for systems made elsewhere, to licensed production (L), ability to copy (C), partner in co-production (P), and indigenous capacity for independent design and production (I). Applying a 1-to-5 point system for these five stages of production for each of the nine weapons categories (maximum of 45 points) would yield the ranking of states according to indigenous capacity to produce significant weapons systems, presented in Table V1.3b.iv(b).

V1.3c. Armaments Issues of Global Concern

Although many of the arms discussed in the previous section have a formidable capacity for rendering death and devastation, atomic, biological, and chemical weapons carry with them a particularly lethal potential to destroy those at whom they are not specifically targeted. Not only are they likely to obliterate innocent bystanders near the sites of military objectives, their lingering aftereffects also raise the possibility of unintended poisons spreading over territorial boundaries to neighboring countries and, depending on winds and climate conditions, even drifting back upon the users of such weapons.

The number of countries engaged in the production and stockpiling of such weapons of mass destruction is, thankfully, limited. There are five generally acknowledged nuclear-weapons states: the United States, the Soviet Union, Great Britain, France, and China; and four others with probable nuclear-weapons capabilities: Israel, South Africa, India, and Pakistan. In addition there are about seven states suspected of seeking nuclear weapons capacities either at this time or in the recent past: Iran, Iraq, Libya; South Korea, Taiwan; Argentina, and Brazil (SIPRI,1988: 54-59, 358-364). Table V1.3c.i(a) displays these states in their zones and in rough order of their approximate nuclear-weapons destructive power, the states with suspected nuclear capacity listed below the dotted line. When all 16 countries are considered, every zone and major religion of the world is represented.

Chemical weapons are sometimes termed the "poor man's" atomic bombs, and in addition to three Great Powers (US, USSR, France), among the states often reported to possess such an arsenal are Iraq (which actually used them against disloyal Kurdish villages during its war with Iran), and about 14 other developing nations. See Table V1.3c.i(b).

Any state with a modestly developed pharmaceutical industry can also produce biological warfare agents, and US intelligence agencies suspect as many as 10 nations are developing weapons based upon living agents such as viruses and bacteria which can reproduce and spread among humans. Only the Soviet Union (which denies the charge) was specifically identified by US officials in this respect (New York Times, February 10, 1989: 8), while SIPRI

(1989: 115) has mentioned the possibility of Iran and Iraq.

The specter of chemical and biological warfare looms larger when one considers the proliferation of ballistic missile delivery capability against which there is no defense. Using as a broad definition any unmanned self-propelled delivery vehicle which can sustain a ballistic trajectory through most of its flight without relying on aerodynamic lift, SIPRI (1989: Chapter 7) identifies more than 30 states, including 24 in the developing world, which have such a capacity today. See Table VI.3c.i(c).

International treaties have been drafted outlawing the use of some chemical weapons (the 1925 Geneva Protocol prohibiting gas warfare, accepted by 115 countries as of 1989), the possession of biological weapons (the 1972 Biological Weapons Convention, endorsed by 111 states), and the possession of nuclear weapons by states beyond the original five (the 1968 Nuclear-Weapons Non-Proliferation Treaty, accepted by 139) (SIPRI 1989: 478).

Six other treaties have been drafted by the global community, one relating to inhumane conventional weapons (the 1981 treaty against weapons deemed excessively injurious or with indiscriminate effects, signed by 30 states), and five relating to environments from which certain weapons or military activities have been banned: 1. the 1959 treaty banning military activities in the Antarctic, 38 state adherents as of 1989; 2. the 1963 partial test ban treaty banning nuclear weapons tests in the atmosphere, outer space, and underwater (but not underground), 118 states; 3. the 1967 treaty banning weapons from outer space, 91 states; 4. the 1971 treaty prohibiting weapons of mass destruction from the seabed, 82 states; 5. the 1977 convention on the hostile use of environmental modification techniques, 55 states.

As a final indicator of states' commitment to peace—and the only one that measures positive behavior rather than its opposite, the manifestations of militarism—Table VI.3c.ii summarizes the number of these nine multilateral arms control agreements accepted (i.e., signed and ratified) by each country. A single number indicates both signature and ratification (i.e., complete acceptance); if two numbers are given, the second number refers to treaties signed but not yet ratified. Only 13 states, mostly in Europe, have fully endorsed all nine agreements.

VI.4. SUMMARY AND TRANSITION

Chapter 1 will conclude with a look ahead to the next four chapters, for there are many points of contact between some of the measures used to elucidate indicators of the first value (peace) and this book's many other sections.

For example, when analyzing economic growth in Chapter 2, the data from section VI.2a (defense budget line items) and VI.3b (arms imports) can be used to test whether heavy military spending is correlated with stagnant development.

Chapter 3's concern with urbanization and environmental health can be studied in connection with section V1.1's sites of wars and their refugees. Chapter 4's coverage of ethnic minority groups and human rights violations corresponds highly with section V1.1b's lists of current civil wars and insurgencies. Chapter 5's categories of military governance have obvious ties to section V1.2c's work on military coup regimes.

These sorts of connections are mentioned in passing throughout the rest of the text, which is used primarily to promulgate each of the five values' social indicators and some selected measures associated with them. The composite figure in this book's conclusion summarizes on a single page all the measures in a way which makes integration between the chapters' various subsections easier to comprehend.

V1.3a.i - Major Foreign Deployments of Troops, circa 1990

(Rounded summary for 97% of ~1.7 m. troops in approx.150 deployments)

Europe - 10 states, with some 1.3 million deployed troops in 95 sites

USSR	570,000 (in 23 sites)	Belgium	25,000 (1)
US	470,000 (in 36)	Canada	6,000 (1)
UK	100,000 (10)	Netherlands	5,000 (1)
France	85,000 (11)	E.Germany (pre-11/89)	2,000 (9)
Spain	25,000 (2)	Greece	2,000 (1)

Others: - n=13, with some 390,000 deployed troops in (32) sites

Islamic	Africa	Asia	Latin America
Morocco 125,000(3)			
Syria 40,000 (1)		India 50,000(2)	Cuba 20,000(7)
Turkey 30,000 (1)		China 50,000(1)	
!Palestine 19,000 (9)		Indonesia 20,000(1)	
Israel 12,000 (2)	Zimbabwe 10,000(1)		
Libya 3500(2)	Tanzania 4000(1)	Vietnam 5000(1)	

V1.3a.i(a)-Summary: Troops Deployed Beyond Home Borders, ~1990

State	Troops Deployed	Number of "Host" States (incl.#)
USSR	570,400^w	23
USA	472,600	36 (incl.8 Pacific O. sites counted as one, and 7#)
Morocco	125,850	3 (incl. 1#)
UK	99,200	10 (incl. 5#)
France	83,950	11 (incl. 3 Indian O. sites counted as one, and 4#)
India	50,250	2 (incl. 1#)
China	50,000	1#
Syria	40,000	1
Turkey	30,000	1#
Belgium	27,000	1
Spain	24,000	2#
Cuba	22,020^w	7
Indonesia	20,000	1#
!Palestinians	19,200	9
!UN peacekeeping	13,030	10
Israel	12,000	2 (incl. 1#)
Zimbabwe	10,000	1
Canada	6,500	1
Netherlands	5,500	1
Vietnam	5,000	1
Tanzania	4,000	1
Libya	3,600	2
Iran	2,500	1
Greece	2,400	1
E.Germany (pre-11/89)	2,300?	9
Senegal	1,400	1
!Other NATO	1,000	1
New Zealand	750	1
Malawi	700	1
N.Korea	700	6 (incl 1#)
Singapore	500	1
Angola	500	1
Australia	120	1
Iraq	100	1
Totals	1,707,070 in 151 different deployments (incl. 25#)	

Table V1.3a.i (continued)

(1,595,270 troops from 13 states)

State	Number of Troops, Names of States in which Deployed, (by Zone)
USSR	E.Ger.350,000^W, Czech.70,000^W, Hungary 50,000^W,Poland 38,000;
	Syria 3000, Libya 2000, S.Yemen 1000, Algeria 900, Iraq 600, Afghan. 350;
570,400^W	Ethiopia 1000, Angola 1000, Mozambique 500, Mali 200, Congo 100;
in 23	Mongolia 40,000-0^W, Vietnam 2500, Laos 500, Cambodia 200; India 200;
sites	Cuba 8000, Nicaragua 200, Peru 150.
US	W.Germany 245,000, Britain 29,000, Italy 15,000, Spain 11,000
	Greece 3500, Iceld. 3200, Belg. 3000, Nethrlds. 2800, Portugal(#Azores) 1800,
	#Bermuda 1500, Canada 500?, Denmark (#Greenland) 300, Norway 200^{PP};
472,600+	Turkey 4700, Egypt 1200?, Saudi Arabia 500?, Somalia 200^{PP}
in 36+	Persian Gulf States 100^{PP}, Morocco ?^{PP}; Kenya ?^{PP};
sites	Japan(incl.Okinawa)62,000, S.Kor.38,000, Phil.I.17,000, #Guam 9200,
	#DiegoGarcia 1,500, Austral. 800, Pacific islands ~700, incl.:
	Johnston At. 200, Midway 140, + 6 other: Wake I.,Gilbert I.,Canton I
	& ex-Pac.Trust Territories(=Endebury,Eniwetok,Kwajalein) @<75 ea.= ~360;
	Panama 12,000, #Puerto Rico 3500, Cuba 2400, Honduras 1500,
	Andes drug areas 300, El Salvador 100, Grenada/Antigua 100.
Morocco	125,850 in: #Western Sahara ~125,000, UAE 500?, Eq.Guinea 350.
UK	W.Germany 70,000, #N.Ireland 10,000, #Gibraltar 1200, Canada 400;
99,200	Cyprus 4500; #Ascension I. 500; #Hong Kong 8300, Brunei 900;
10 sites	#Falkland I. 1900, Belize 1500.
France	W.Germany 50,000;
83,950	Djibouti 3900, Chad 1300; C.Af.R. 1400, Senegal 1200, Gabon 650, Iv.Coast 500;
11 sites	#N.Caledonia 9000, #Fr.Polynesia 5000, #Indian O.sites 3300; #Fr.Guiana 7700.
India	50,250 in: #Kashmir 50,000, Maldives 250; Sri Lanka 0 (3/90ff).
China	50,000 in: #Tibet.
Syria	40,000 in: Lebanon (17,000 in Bekaa, 15,000 in Beirut, 8000 in Tripoli).
Turkey	30,000 in: (#North) Cyprus (+ 35,000+? settlers).
Belgium	27,000 in: W.Germany.
Spain	24,000 in: #Moroccan enclaves 14,000; #Canary I. 10,000.
Cuba	S.Yemen 450, Libya 100?;
22,020^W	Angola 19,000-0^W, Mozambq. 900, Congo 500, STP 70?;
7 sites	Nicaragua 1000 (pre 2/90 Govt. change).
Indonesia	20,000 in: #East Timor.

Table V1.3a.i (continued)

V1.3a.i(c) - Other Troop Deploying States, circa 1990
(111,800 troops from 21 sources)

State	Number of Troops, Names of States where Deployed, (by Zone)
!Palestine	19,200 in: Lebanon 8000; Syria 4500, Iraq 3700; + V1.1b for ~3,000 troops in Sudan,Algeria,Tunisia; + some in 3 other Islamic.
!UN	13,030 in: Lebanon 5900, Egypt 2500, Cyp. 2100, Syria 1400; Iran/Iraq 400, Israel 100; Afghanistan 50; Angola 70; #Kashmir 40; Central America 400; Nicaragua 70.
Israel	12,000 in: #W.Bank,Gaza 11,000(+ 80,000 settlers); Lebanon 1000.
Zimbabwe	10,000 in: Mozambique
Canada	6500 in: West Germany
Netherlands	5500 in: West Germany
Vietnam	5000 in: Cambodia
Tanzania	4000 in: Mozambique
Libya	3600 in: Chad (Aouzou strip) 2800, Sudan 800 (Pan-African Legion)
Iran	2500 in: Lebanon (Revolutionary Guard, not regular, troops)
Greece	2400 in: Cyprus
E.Germany (pre-11/89)	?2300 in: Libya 400, Algeria 250, Syria 200, Iraq 150, S.Yem.100; Ethiopia 500, Angola 500, Guinea 100, Mozambique 100.
Senegal	1400 in: Gambia (since '82)
!other NATO	1000 in: Belgium (HQ)
N. Zealand	750 in: Singapore
Malawi	700 in: Mozambique
N.Korea	700 in: Iran 300, Madagascar 100, Angola 100?, Mozambique100, Seychelles 50, #WSahara 50.
Singapore	500 in: Brunei
Angola	500 in: STP
Australia	120 in: Papua New Guinea
Iraq	100 in: Lebanon (3/89ff)

Source: Adapted from Sivard 87/88, and IISS 88/89, updated to 8/90; but not including
Iraq in Kuwait, or multilateral forces being deployed in Liberia and in Saudi Arabia/
Persian Gulf area in Fall '90.

Notes for V1.3a.i:
! = not among the 162 states recognized in this study (UN, NATO, Palestinians).
= disputed lands, colonies, etc. from V1.1b., V4.2a, V5.5b; n=24; include (by zone):
  EUR: N. Ireland (V1.1b); Greenland, Bermuda, Gibraltar, Azores (V5.5b);
  ISL: N.Cyprus, W. Sahara, Occupied Territories (V1.1b); Moroccan enclaves (V5.5b);
  AF: Ascension Island, Canary Islands (V5.5b);
  AS: Kashmir, Tibet, E.Timor (V4.2a);
      Reunion, DiegoGarcia, HongKong, Guam, Pacific I.Terr., N.Caledonia, Fr.Polynesia (V5.5b);
  LA: Puerto Rico, French Guiana, Falklands (V5.5b).
w = withdrawals (by SU,Cuba) scheduled for 1990ff; totals unclear at time of printing.
? = data in col.3 not firm; troops are present, but number is not known; often relates to large
      military aid program, change of govt. (e.g., E.Ger., 11/89ff), or to......
pp = estimated small number of advanced forces maintaining prepositioned (US) equipment.

<u>Summary: V1.3a.ii - Foreign Troops "Hosted"</u>

Zone	# Troops "Hosted"
Europe	996,400 in 19 sites, incl. 5#
Islamic	288,000 in 25 sites, incl. 4#
Africa	55,940 in 16 sites, incl. 2#
Asia:	325,910 in 25 sites, incl. 10#
Latin America	40,820 in 13 sites, incl. 3#
*Total	1,707,070 in 98 sites, incl. 24#

*Not including multilateral forces being deployed in Liberia and Saudi Arabia in Fall 1990.

Europe: 996,400 in 19 sites, incl. 5#

State	Number	From
W.Germany	404,000	US 245,000, UK 70,000, France 50,000, Belgium 27,000, Canada 6500, Netherlands 5500.
E.Germany	350,000^w	USSR

(Subtotal in 2 Germanys, including 2 Berlins before 10/90 unification — 754,000)

State	Number	From
Czechoslov.	70,000-0^w	USSR
Hungary	50,000-0^w	USSR
Poland	38,000	USSR
Britain	29,000	US
Italy	15,000	US
Spain	11,000	US
#N.Ireland	10,000	UK
Belgium	4,000	US 3000, incl.400 NATO HQ staff; other NATO, 1000.
Greece	3,500	US
Iceland	3,200	US
Netherlands	2,800	US
Portugal	1,800	US (mostly in #Azores)
#Bermuda	1,500	US
#Gibraltar	1,200	UK
Canada	900	US 500?, UK 400.
Denmark	300	US (mostly in #Greenland)
Norway	200PP	US

Notes:

= disputed lands, colonies, or possessions (N.Ireland,Gibraltar,Azores,Bermuda,Greenland)

w = scheduled withdrawals 1990ff, by USSR from Czech. & Hung. (0 in ea. by 6/91) and from E.Germany (0 by 1995); withdrawal also anticipated from Poland .

? = data in col.3 not firm; small troop presence; often related to large military aid programs or...

pp = estimated number of advanced forces maintaining prepositioned (US) equipment.

~ = estimated number in col. 2; where ? or + (suspected additional troops) in col. 3.

Table V1.3a.ii (continued)

State	Number	From:
		Islamic: 288,000 in 25 sites, incl. 4#
#W.Sahara	125,050	Morocco 125,000; N. Korea 50
Lebanon	57,500	Syria 40,000, Palestinians 8000; UN 5900 (UNIFIL+UNTSO),
		Iran 2500, Israel 1000, Iraq 100
Cyprus (&#N.Cyp.)	39,000	Turkey 30,000, UK 4500, Greece 2400, UN (FICYP) 2100 (+35,000 settlers)
Morocco(#enclaves)	~14,000	Spain #14,000, US-?PP
#Occup. Territories	~11,000	Israel (+80,000 settlers)
Syria	~9,100	anti-PLO Pals.4500, USSR 3000, UN 1400(UNDOF+UNTSO),E.Ger.200
Turkey	4,700	US
Iraq	~4,450	PLO 3700 (after 5/90), USSR 600, E.Ger.150?
Chad	4,100	Libya 2800 (w/o Pan-Islamic militia in Sudan), France 1300.
Djibouti	3,900	France
Egypt	~3,700	UN(TSO) 2500, incl. US 1200?
Libya	~2,500	USSR 2000, E.Ger. 400?, Cuba 100?
Algeria	~2,150	PLO 1000?; USSR 900, E.Ger. 250?
Sudan	1,800	PLO 1000; Libya (Pan-African Legion) 800.
S.Yemen	~1,550	USSR 1000, Cuba 450; E.Ger. 100?
Tunisia	~1,000	PLO
Saudi A.	~500	US 500?
UAE	~500	Morocco?
Iran/Iraq border	400	UN(IIMOG)
Afghanistan	400	USSR 350 (advisors after 2/89 withdrawal), UN(GOMAP) 50
Iran	300	N. Korea
Somalia	200PP	US
Persian Gulf states	~100PP	US (in Bahrain 40, Oman 30 , Kuwait 30)
Israel	~100	UN(TSO ; also in Egypt, Leb. & Syr. since 1948)
Other Islamic	??	PLO remnants in Jordan and 2 Yemens (after 5/90 transfers)
		Africa: 55,940 in 16 sites, incl. 2#
Angola	~20,670W	Cuba 19,000-0W, USSR 1000,EGer.500?,N.Kor.100,UN(TAG) 70
Mozambique	~16,300	Zimbabwe 10,000, Tanzania 4000, Cuba 900, Malawi 700,
		USSR 500, E.Ger.100?, N.Korea 100, +mercenaries.
#Canary Is.	10,000	Spain
Ethiopia	1,500	USSR 1000, E.Ger.500?
C.Af.Rep.	1,400	France
Gambia	1,400	Senegal (since 1982 confederation)
Senegal	1,200	France
Gabon	650	France (incl. 110 officers in Gabon army)
Congo	600	Cuba 500, USSR 100.
STP	~570	Angola 500, Cuba 70?.
#Ascension I.	500	UK
Ivory Coast	500	France
Eq. Guinea	350	Morocco
Mali	200	USSR
Guinea	100	E.Ger.?
Kenya	??	USPP

Notes:

= disputed territories, colonies, or possessions:
   ISL: W.Sahara, N.Cyprus, Morocc.enclaves, Israeli Occup.Territories; AF: Canary I., Ascension I.
w = withdrawals scheduled in 1990-91 from Angola.
? = data in col.3 not firm; small troop presence related to: large mil. aid program, pre-11/89 E.Ger. Govt., or
   (pp) = forces maintaining prepositioned (US) equipment.
~ = estimated number in column 2; where ? or + (suspected additional troops) in column 3.

Table V1.3a.ii (continued)

State	Number	From
		Asia: 325,910 in 25 sites, incl. 10#(w/ 8 Pac.O., 3 Ind.O. counted as one each)
Japan	62,000	US (incl. 19,000 on Okinawa)
#Tibet	50,000	China
#Kashmir	50,040	India 50,000, UN(OG IP) 40
Mongolia	40,000-0^w	USSR (combat troops out by '91, all by '92)
S.Korea	38,000	US
#E.Timor	20,000	Indonesia
Philippines	17,000	US
#Guam	9,200	US
#New Caledonia	9,000	France
#Hong Kong	8,300	UK
Cambodia	5,200	Vietnam 5,000, USSR 200
#Fr. Polynesia	5,000	France
#Indian Ocean	3,300	France (in #Reunion & #Mayotte, & (12/89) Comoros)
Vietnam	2,500	USSR
#Diego Garcia	1,500	US
Brunei	1,400	UK 900, Singapore 500.
Australia	800	US
Singapore	750	New Zealand
#Pacific O. islands (n=8)	˜700	US (incl: Johnston Atoll 200, Midway 140, + <75 each
		in Gilbert, Canton, & Wake I.'s and ex-Pac.Trust Territories, (˜360 Tot.)
Laos	500	USSR
Maldives	250	India
India	200	USSR
Papua New Guinea	120	Australia
Madagascar	100	N.Korea
Seychelles	50	N. Korea

State	Number	From
		Latin America: 40,820 in 13 sites, incl. 3#
Panama	12,000	US
Cuba	10,400	USSR 8000, US 2400.
#Fr.Guiana	7,700	France
#Puerto Rico	3,500	US
#Falklands I.	1,900	UK
Honduras	1,500	US (+sevl. hundred regularly rotated in on "temp. duty")
Belize	1,500	UK
Nicaragua	1,270	Cuba 1000, SU 200 (pre-2/90 Govt.); UN(OMVEN) 70
Central America	400	UN(OGCA)
Andes drug areas	300	US (mobile; in & out of Colombia, Bolivia, Peru @ ˜100 ea.)
Peru	150	USSR
Grenada/Antigua	100	US
El Salvador	100	US

Notes:

= disputed territories, colonies, or possessions:

  AS: Tibet, Kashmir, E.Timor, Hong Kong, Guam, N.Caledonia, French Polynesia,
      Reunion, Mayotte, Diego Garcia, Pacific Ocean Island states.

  LA: French Guiana, Puerto Rico, Falklands.

w = withdrawals scheduled in 1989ff from Mongolia.

˜ = estimated number in col. 2; where ? or + (suspected additional troops) in col. 3.

V1.3b.i(a) - Top 26 Arms Exporters, 1984-88

(5-yr. annual avg., millions of current US $s)

European exporters (n=20)		Other Exporters (n=6)	
USSR	$20.248 bil./yr.		
USA	$11.900 "		
France	$3.621 "		
W.Germany	$1.451 "	China	$1.867 bil./yr
UK	$1.345 "		
Czechoslovakia	$1.144 "		
Poland	$1.120 "		
Italy	$657 mil./yr		
Bulgaria	$495 "	Brazil	$452 mil./yr
Spain	$448 "	Israel	$427 "
E.Germany	$394 "	N.Korea	$407 "
Yugoslavia	$378 "		
Netherlands	$290 "		
Romania	$282 "		
Switzerland	$280 "		
Hungary	$222 "		
Sweden	$194 "		
Belgium	$182 "		
Canada	$172 "	S.Korea	$170 "
Austria	$162 "	Japan	$154 "

Source: ADCA 1990 for 1984-88, Tables II and III.

V1.3b.i(b) - Arms Exports, $ Value (& as % of Total Exports), 1988

(in millions of current US $s)

European Exporters	Other Exporters			
	Islamic	Africa	Asia	Latin America
USSR $21,400 **(19.3%)**				
US 14,300 **(4.5%)**			China $3100 **(6.5%)**	
France 1,890 (1.1%)				
Czech. 850 (3.2%)				
UK 725				
Poland 675 (2.2%)				
Netherlands 525				
E. Germany 430 (1.3%)			N. Korea 470 **(19.6%)**	
Italy 390				Brazil 380 (1.1%)
Bulgaria 380 (1.9%)				
W.Germany 360				Chile 280 **(4.0%)**
Sweden 210				Cuba 230 **(4.2%)**
Yugoslavia 200 (1.6%)				
Canada 180				
Hungary 160	Egypt 170 (2.9%)			
Romania 150 (1.2%e)	Israel 140 (1.5%)			
Spain 150				
Switzerland 110	Iraq 80		Vietnam 70 **(7.5%)**	
Portugal 110 (1.0%)			Japan 70	
Austria 40	Libya 50	S.Afr.60	Australia 60	
Greece 30	Jordan 40 (3.9%)		S.Korea 50	Argentina 30
Belgium 20			Singapore 10	
Finland 10	Pakistan 10		Taiwan 10	
Norway 10	Saudi A. 5		N.Zealand 5	
n=24	-----n=21-----			

Source: ACDA 1990 for 1988 Table II, and "Country Rankings by Variable" (mimeo), n=45.

82

VI.3b.ii(a) - Arms Imported (in current US $ mil.),1984-88

Europe	Islamic	Africa	Asia	Latin America
	Iraq $29,650		India $13,120	
SU $5780	Saudi A.19,530		Vietnam 8580	Cuba $8830
E.Ger. 4600	Iran 10,520			
Poland 4600	Syria 8255		Japan 4940	
Bulgaria 4040	Afghan. 6540	Angola $6865		
Czech. 3880	Egypt 6425		Australia 4370	
UK 3320	Libya 6315		Taiwan 3885	
W.Ger. 3020	Israel 6100	Ethiopia 4100	S.Korea 2570	
US 2855			China 2485	
Nethrlds. 2540	Algeria 3270	Nigeria 1325	N. Korea 2370	
Spain 2430	Turkey 3230			
Switz. 2215	Pakistan 2010			Nicaragua 2275
	Jordan 1730		Thailand 1490	
Belgium 1610	S.Yemen 1510	Mozambique 1130	Cambodia 1280	
Greece 1565	N.Yemen 1420		Singapore 1140	Venezuela 1180
Norway 1045	Kuwait 1325		Malaysia 1040	
Italy 1120			Indonesia 715	Peru 860
Hungary 960				Colombia 820
Canada 910	Morocco 890			Argentina 750
France 890	Oman 670		Laos 585	Brazil 730
Romania 815	UAE 620	Tanzania 300		
Yugoslavia 815	Tunisia 570	Zimbabwe 270		Mexico 440
Denmark 550	Bahrain 505	Guinea 265	New Zealand 320	
Sweden 480	Qatar 360	Congo 175		Ecuador 370
Finland 395	Sudan 350	Kenya 180	Bangladesh 230	El Salvador 350
Portugal 350	Lebanon 295	Gabon 165	Philippines 220	Chile 340
	Chad 230	Uganda 165		Honduras 260
	Somalia 200	Mali 160	Myanmar 160	
n=24/30	n=25/27	n=12/37	n=18/25	n=12/25 (91)

Source: ACDA 1990 for 1984-88, Table III, for n=91 of 144 states surveyed.

VI.3b.ii(b) - Arms M/Total M, 1988, Top 30 States > 8%

	Afghan.100+%	Angola 100+%	Cambodia 100+%	
none>8%	S.Yemen 77.0e	Ethiopia 80.6	Laos 70.0e	
	Syria 58.5		Vietnam 69.0e	
	Iraq 37.1	GBissau 62.0e		Nicaragua 65.6%
	N.Yemen 28.6			
	Somalia 24.0e	Mozambique 26.0e		Cuba 22.4
	Iran 18.2	Uganda 14.7	N.Korea 32.3	
	Saudi Arabia 14.9	Mali 13.7	India 16.7	
	Israel 12.6			
	Jordan 11.6		Myanmar 12.3	Peru 12.5
	Libya 11.5	Tanzania 8.6		
	Algeria 10.6	Gambia 8.3e		
	Chad 9.6	Kenya 8.0		
(Greece 4.7	Sudan 5.7	C.Verde 7.2e	Australia 3.6	El Salvador 6.3e)
n=0	n=13	n=9	n=6	n=2 (30)

Source: ACDA 1990 for 1988, Table II; countries >100% exclude arms from trade statistics.

e = extrapolated estimates from "Country Rankings by Variable" (ACDA 1990, mimeo).

83

V1.3b.iii - Arms Import Dependencies, 1984-88

(% dependent on single major supplier (identified in superscript))

Europe	Islamic	Africa	Asia	Latin America
UK 99%^{U}	Israel 100%^{U}		Japan 99%^{U}	
Belgium 99^U	Afghan. 99^S		Vietnam 99^S	
Italy 98^U	S.Yemen 99^S		Laos 98^S	
Czech. 95^S		Mozmbq.97%^{S}	S.Korea 97^U	
Canada 93^U		Ethiopia 95^S		
Poland 93^S			N.Korea 93^S	
Romania 90^S	N.Yemen 92^S		Australia 92^U	Nicarag. 92%^{S}
Sweden 90^U				
France 90^U				
Bulgaria 87^S		Angola 89^S		
Spain 86^U			Cambodia 86^S	
W.Ger. 83^U	Syria 84^S			
Nethrlds. 83^U				Cuba 84^S
Yugoslav.83^S				
Denmark 82^U	Algeria 76^S		Singapore 79^U	
E.Ger. 78^S			Taiwan 77^U	Colombia 79^G
	Tunisia 70^U		India 73^S	Argentina 77^G
Norway 65^U	Iran 64º		Thailand 67^U	Mexico 73^U
Hungary 63^S	Turkey 62^U			
	Pakistan 60^U			
	Libya 57^S			
	UAE 56^U		China 53º	
	Iraq 52^S		Indonesia 52º	
	Bahrain 50^U			Venezuela 49^U
	Jordan 51^S			
Greece 45^U	Oman 49^K			
SU 43^P	Egypt 44^U			
	Kuwait 40^F			Peru 40^F
US 39^K	Saudi A.38^F			
Switz. 36^G	Morocco 38º	Nigeria 29^I	Malaysia 35º	Brazil 33^U
n=22	n=20	n=4	n=14	n=8 (68)

Source: *Adapted* from ACDA 1990 for 1984-88, Table III.

Legend for Superscripts:
^{U}=dependent on US, n=28; ^{S}= on Soviet Union, n=25;
^{F}=on France, n=3; ^{G}=on W. Germany, n=3; ^{K}=on UK, n=2;
^{P}=on Poland, n=1; ^{I}=on Italy, n=1; ^{º}=on "others", n=5.

V1.3b.iv - Third World Arms Producers

Europe	Islamic	Africa	Asia	Latin America

(a) - SIPRI's n=27, by Group

A=diversified and sizeable

Europe	Islamic	Africa	Asia	Latin America
n.a.	Israel		India	Argentina
				Brazil

B=production in most categories

	Egypt	So. Africa	N.Korea	
			S.Korea	
			Taiwan	

C=production in several categories

	Pakistan		Indonesia	Chile
			Philippines	Peru
			Singapore	

D=limited production

	Iran	Nigeria	Myanmar	Colombia
			Malaysia	Mexico
			Thailand	

E=marginal beginnings

	Algeria	Zimbabwe	Hong Kong#	Venezuela
				Uruguay
	n=5	n=3	n=11	n=8 (27)

Source: *SIPRI Yearbook* 1985, Tables 10.1 through 10.5, citing Archive of Institute for Peace Research & Security Policy, U. of Hamburg, and SIPRI (1985a).

\# = not one of this study's 162 states.

(b) - ACDA's n=36

Europe	Islamic	Africa	Asia	Latin America
	Israel 42			Brazil 43
n. a.			India 29	Argentina 30
			Taiwan 28	
	Egypt 21	S.Africa 25	S.Korea 24	
				Chile 18
			Singapore 12	Mexico 11
	Turkey 8		Indonesia 11	
	Pakistan 7		Phil. I. 10	
			Thailand 10	
	Iran 4	Nigeria 5	Myanmar 6	Peru 6
	Saudi A. 3		Sri Lanka 5	Venezuela 6
	Algeria 2		#Hong Kong 5	
	Libya 2		Malaysia 3	
	Iraq 1			Colombia 1
	Syria 1	Cameroon 1		Paraguay 1
	Sudan 1	Burkina F. 1		Dom.Rep. 1
	Morocco 1			
	n=12	n=4	n=10+1#	n=9 (36)

Source: ACDA 1987, pp. 14-15; as adapted for nine categories and five stages of manufacture.

\# = not one of this study's 162 states.

V1.3c.i - Weapons of Global Concern, 1990

Europe	Islamic	Africa	Asia	Latin America

V1.3c.i(a) - Nuclear Weapons States

Europe	Islamic	Africa	Asia	Latin America	
US					
USSR					
France			China		
UK	Israel	S. Africa	India		
	Pakistan				
	Iran		Taiwan	Brazil	
	Iraq		S. Korea	Argentina	
	Libya				
n=4	n=5	n=1	n=4	n=2	(16)

V1.3c.i(b) - Chemical Weapons States

Europe	Islamic	Africa	Asia	Latin America	
US	Israel	Ethiopia	China		
USSR	Iraq		Taiwan		
France	Syria		N. Korea		
	Egypt		Vietnam		
	Libya		Myanmar		
	Iran		Thailand		
			S. Korea		
n=3	n=6	n=1	n=7		(17)

V1.3c.i(c) - States with Ballistic Missile Capability

Europe	Islamic	Africa	Asia	Latin America	
US	Turkey	S. Africa	India	Argentina	
UK	Iraq		China	Brazil	
France	Iran		Taiwan	Chile	
W. Germany	Afghanistan		S. Korea		
other NATO+	Pakistan		N. Korea		
USSR	Syria		Japan		
Czech.	Israel		Indonesia		
E. Germany	Saudi Arabia		Australia		
	Kuwait				
	N. Yemen				
	S. Yemen				
	Egypt				
	Libya				
	Algeria				
n=7+	n=14	n=1	n=8	n=3	(33+)

Source: *SIPRI Yearbook 1989*, Chapters 1, 4, and 7.

V1.3c.ii - Arms Control Treaties Accepted

Europe	Islamic	Africa	Asia	Latin America
Norway 9			Japan 9	
Sweden 9	Tunisia 8	Benin 7	Australia 9	Argentina 7+1
Bulgaria 9	Cyprus 8	Ghana 6+1	N.Zealand 8+1	
Denmark 9	S.Yemen 7	S.Africa 6	India 8	
Finland 9	Turkey 6+2		Mongolia 8	Ecuador 7
Nethrlds 9	Afghan.6+1	Sierra L. 5+3	S.Korea 8	Brazil 7
USSR 9	Pakistan 6	Togo 5+2		Mexico 7
Czechosl. 9			Papua NG 7	Cuba 7
Poland 9	Morocco 5+3	Nigeria 5+1	Laos 7	
E.Germany 9		Rwanda 5+1		
Hungary 9			Vietnam 6+1	Uruguay 6+1
Romania 8+1	Iraq 5+2	GBissau 5	Mauritius 6	Guatemala 6+1
US 8+1	Egypt 5+2	Kenya 5	Sri Lanka 6	
Greece 8+1	Lebanon 5+2	Niger 5		
W.Germany 8+1	Iran 5+2	CapeVerde 5		Dom.Rep. 6
Canada 8+1				Peru 6
Spain 8+1	Jordan 5+1	Ethiopia 4+3		
Italy 8+1	Kuwait 5+1		Nepal 5+1	Jamaica 5+1
UK 8+1		C.Af.R. 4+2		Panama 5+1
Belgium 8+1			N.Korea 5	Antigua 5
Switzerland 8	Libya 5		Solomons 5	Chile 5
Austria 8	Saudi A. 5	Malawi 4+1	China 5	Venezuela 5
		Ivory Coast 4+1	Taiwan 5	Nicaragua 4+4
Ireland 7+1		Uganda 4+1	Thailand 5	Bolivia 4+3
Iceland 6+2	Syria 4+2	Senegal 4+1	Singapore 5	Barbados 4
Yugoslavia 6+1		Lesotho 4+1	Fiji 5	Bahamas 4
Luxmbrg. 5+3	N. Yemen 3+3		Seychelles 5	
France 5	Sudan 3+2	STP 4	Bangladesh 5	Honduras 3+2
Malta 5				Colombia 3+2
Portugal 4+3	Israel 3	Gambia 3+3	Malaysia 4+2	El Salvador 3+2
	Qatar 3	Liberia 3+3	Philpines 4+2	Paraguay 3+2
	Bahrain 3	Botswana 3+2	Madagscar4+2	Costa Rica 3+1
		Zaire 3+2		Trinidad 3+1
	Chad 2	Burkina F. 3+1		St.Lucia 3
		Zambia 3	Bhutan 4	Grenada 2
	Somalia 1+3	Swaziland 3	Indonesia 3+2	Belize 2
		Congo 3	Cambodia 3+1	Haiti 1+3
	Mauritania 1	Mali 2+3	Myanmar 2+2	
		Tanzania 2+2	W.Samoa 2	
		Gabon 2+1	Maldives 2	Suriname 1
	Algeria 0+1	Burundi 1+4		St. Vincent 1
	UAE 0+1	Cameroon 1+3	Brunei 1	Dominica 1
		Guinea 1+1		Guyana 0+2
		Eq. Guinea 1+1		
		Namibia-na		
Albania-na	Oman-na	Zimbabwe-na	Vanuatu-na	St.Chris.-na
	Djibouti-na	Angola-na	Comoros-na	
		Mozambique-na		
n=29/30	n=26/28	n=34/38	n=31/33	n=32/33 (152)

Source: *SIPRI Yearbook 1989*, Annex A, pp. 475-503.

BIBLIOGRAPHY

AGUERO, F. (1984) "Social Effects: Military Autonomy in Developing Countries," *Alternatives* 10: 75-92.

ANDREWS, W. G., and U. RA'ANAN (1969) *Coup d' Etat.* New York: Van Nostrand Reinhold Co.

AYA, R. (1979) "Theories of Revolution Reconsidered: Contrasting Models of Collective Violence," *Theory and Society* 8: 39-99.

AZAR, E. E. (1980) "The Conflict and Peace Data Bank (COPDAB) Project," *Journal of Conflict Resolution* 24:143-152.

BAEK, K., R. D. MCLAURIN, and C. MOON (eds.) (1989) *The Dilemma of Third World Defense Industries: Supplier Control or Recipient Autonomy.* Boulder: Westview Press.

BELL, J. B. (1977) "The Men with Guns: The Legitimacy of Violent Dissent," in DENITCH, B. (ed.) *Legitimacy of Regimes,* Beverly Hills: Sage Publications.

BLACKABY, F., and T. OHLSON (1982) "Military Expenditures and Arms Trade: Problems of Data," *Bulletin of Peace Proposals* 13: 291-308.

BLECHMAN, B., and S. B. KAPLAN (1978) *Force without War.* Washington: Brookings Institution.

BROGAN, P. (1990) *The Fighting Never Stopped: A Comprehensive Guide to World Conflicts since 1945.* New York: Vintage Books.

BRZOSKA, M., and T. OHLSON (1986) *Arms Production in the Third World.* Philadelphia: Taylor and Francis.

_____. (1987) *Arms Transfers to the Third World, 1971-1985.* New York: Oxford University Press.

BUTTERWORTH, R. L. (1976) *Managing Interstate Conflict: 310 Cases 1945-1974.* Pittsburgh: University of Pittsburgh Press.

CARVER, M. (1981) *War since 1945.* New York: G. P. Putnam's Sons.

CATRINA, C. (1988) *Arms Transfers and Dependence.* New York: Taylor and Francis, for the United Nations Institute for Disarmament Research.

CENTER FOR DEFENSE INFORMATION (1986 and 1983 eds.) *A World at War.* Washington: Center for Defense Information.

CHOMSKY, N. (1986) *Pirates and Emperors: International Terrorism in the Real World.* New York: Claremont Research and Publications.

CIOFFI-REVILLA, C. (1989) *The Scientific Measurement of International Conflict: Handbook of Data Sets on Crises and Wars 1495-1988, A. D.* Boulder: Lynne Rienner.

CLARK, R. P. (1986) *Power and Policy in the Third World.* New York: John Wiley and Sons.

COLE, S. (1980) "The War System and the New International Economic Order: Directions for Disarmament," *Alternatives* 6: 247-286.

COPPER, J. F., and D. S. PAPP (eds.) (1983) *Communist Nations Military Assistance.* Boulder: Westview Press.

DAVID, S. R. (1986) *Third World Coups d'Etat and International Security.* Baltimore: Johns Hopkins University Press.

DEGENHARDT, H. W.   (1983) *Political Dissent: An International Guide to Extra-Parliamentary, Guerilla, and Illegal Movements.* Detroit: Gale Research Co.
_____. (1988) *Revolutionary and Dissident Movements: An International Guide.* Detroit: Gale Research Co., for Keesings Reference Publications.
DOMKE, W. K.   (1988) *War and the Changing Global System.* New Haven: Yale University Press.
DONELAN, M. D., and M. J. GRIEVE (1973) *International Disputes: 50 Case Histories, 1945-70.* London: Europa Publications.
DUNN, J.   (1989) *Modern Revolutions: An Introduction to the Analysis of a Political Phenomenon,* 2nd ed.   Cambridge: Cambridge University Press.
ECKHARDT, W., and E. AZAR (1979)   "Major World Conflicts and Interventions, 1945 to 1975," *International Interactions* 5: 75-110.
EISENSTADT, S. N.   (1978) *Revolution and the Transformation of Societies.* New York: Free Press.
FALK, R. A., and S. S. KIM (eds.) (1983) *The War System: An Interdisciplinary Approach.* Boulder: Westview Press.
FEI, E. T.   (1979) "Understanding Arms Transfers and Military Expenditures: Data Problems," pp. 37-46 in NEUMAN, S. G., and R. HARKAVY (eds.) *Arms Transfers in the Modern World.* New York: Praeger.
FERRIS, E. G.   (1985) *Refugees and World Politics.* New York: Praeger.
GABRIEL, R. A.   (1985) *Fighting Armies.* Westport, Conn.: Greenwood Press, 3 vols.
GREEN, T. H.   (1990) *Comparative Revolutionary Movements: Search for Theory and Justice.* Englewood Cliffs, N. J.: Prentice-Hall Co.
HARKAVY, R. E.   (1989) *Bases Abroad: The Global Foreign Military Presence.* New York: Oxford University Press.
HARKAVY, R. E., and S. G. NEUMAN (1985) *The Lessons of Recent Wars in the Third World.* Lexington, Mass.: Lexington Books.
HARTMAN, T.   (1984) *A World Atlas of Military History, 1945-84.*   London: Leo Cooper, in association with Secker and Warburg.
HOLZMAN, F. D.   (Spring, 1980) "Are the Soviets Really Outspending the United States on Defense?" *International Security* 4(4): 86-104.
_____. (Spring,1982) "Soviet Military Spending: Assessing the Numbers Game," *International Security* 6(4): 78-101.
_____. (Fall, 1989)   "Politics and Guesswork: CIA and DIA Estimates of Soviet Military Spending," *International Security* 14(2):101-131.
HOWELL, L. D.   (1983) "A Comparative Study of the WEIS and COPDAB Data Sets," *International Studies Quarterly* 27, 2(June): 149-159.
INTERNATIONAL INSTITUTE OF STRATEGIC STUDIES (IISS) (annual) *Military Balance, 19xx/xx.* London: IISS.
JACKMAN, R. W.   (1978) "The Predictability of Coups d'Etat: A Model with African Data," *American Political Science Review* 72: 1262-1275.
JACKMAN, R. W., and W. A. BOYD (1979)   "Multiple Sources in the Collection of Data on Political Conflict," *American Journal of Political Science* 23: 434-458.
JANKE, P.   (1983) *Guerrilla and Terrorist Organizations: A World Directory and Bibliography.*   New York: Macmillan Publishing Co.
JOHANSEN, R. C.   (1982/83)   "Toward an Alternative Security System: Moving

Beyond the Balance of Power in the Search for World Security," *Alternatives* 8: 293-349.

JOHANSEN, R. C., and S. LEONARD (1984) "Militarization and Society: Introduction to Special Issue: Appraising the Growth of Military Power," *Alternatives* 10: i-viii.

JONGMAN, B., and H. TROMP (1982) "War, Conflict, and Political Violence: A Description of Five Data Collection Projects," in *UNESCO Yearbook on Peace and Conflict Studies 1982,* Chapter 3.2: 164-191.

KALDOR, M., A. EIDE, and S. MERRITT (1979) *World Military Order: The Impact of Military Technology in the Third World.* London: Macmillan.

KARP, A. (1989) "Ballistic Missile Proliferation in the Third World," in SIPRI (1989): Chapter 7, 287-318.

KATZ, J. E. (ed.) (1986) *The Implications of Third World Military Industrialization: Sowing the Serpent's Teeth.* Lexington, Mass.: Lexington Books.

KEEGAN, J., and A. WHEATCROFT (1986) *Zones of Conflict: An Atlas of Future Wars.* New York: Simon and Schuster.

KENDE, I. (1978) "Local Wars 1945-1976," *Journal of Peace Research* 15: 260-285.

KIDRON, M., and D. SMITH (1983) *The War Atlas: Armed Conflict, Armed Peace.* New York: Simon and Schuster.

KLARE, M. (1984) *American Arms Supermarket.* Austin: University of Texas Press.

_____. (1987) "The State of the Trade: Global Arms Transfer Patterns in the 1980s," *Journal of International Affairs* 40(1): 1-21.

KNORR, K. (1966) *On the Uses of Military Power in the Nuclear Age.* Princeton: Princeton University Press.

LAFFIN, J. (1986ff) *War Annual.* London: Brassey's Defense Publications.

LEIDEN, C., and K. M. SCHMITT (1968) *The Politics of Violence: Revolution in the Modern World.* Englewood Cliffs, N.J.: Prentice-Hall Co.

LEONTIEF, W. W. (1983) *Military Spending: Facts and Figures, World Wide Implications, and Future Outlook.* New York: Oxford University Press.

LEVI, W. (1981) *The Coming End of War.* Beverly Hills: Sage Publications, Library of Social Research, vol. 117.

LEVY, J. S. (1983) *War in the Modern Great Power System, 1495-1975.* Lexington: University of Kentucky Press.

_____. (1987) "Analytic Problems in the Identification of Wars," *International Interactions* 14(2): 181-186.

LOONEY, R. E. (1988) *Third World Military Expenditures and Arms Production.* New York: St. Martin's Press.

LOUSCHER, D. J., and M. D. SALOMONE (eds.) (1987) *Marketing Security Assistance: New Perspectives on Arms Sales.* Lexington, Mass.: D. C. Heath.

MAOZ, Z. (1988) "Conflict Datasets: Definitions and Measurement," *International Interactions* 14(2): 165-171.

MERKL, P. H. (ed.) (1986) *Political Violence and Terror: Motifs and Motivations.* Berkeley: University of California Press.

MICKOLUS, E. F. (1980) *Transnational Terrorism: A Chronology of Events, 1968-1979.* Westport, Conn.: Greenwood Press.

MIDLARSKY, M. I. (1986) *The Disintegration of Political Systems: War and Revolution in Comparative Perspective.* Columbia: University of South Carolina Press.

MISCHE, G. and P. (1977) *Toward a Human World Order: Beyond the National Security Straitjacket.* New York: Paulist Press.

MUELLER, J. (1989) *Retreat from Doomsday: The Obsolescence of Major War.* New York: Basic Books.

NEUMAN, S. G. (1984) "International Stratification and Third World Military Industries," *International Organization* 38: 167-197.

NINCIC, M. (1982) *The Arms Race: The Political Economy of Military Growth.* New York: Praeger.

PIERRE, A. (1982) *The Global Politics of Arms Sales.* Princeton: Princeton University Press.

PORTER, R., and M. TEICH (1986) *Revolution in History.* Cambridge: Cambridge University Press.

RICHARDSON, L. F. (1949) "Variation of the Frequency of Fatal Quarrels with Magnitude," *Journal of the American Statistical Association* 43: 523-546.

_____. (1960) *Statistics of Deadly Quarrels.* Pittsburgh, Pa.: Boxwood Publishing Co.

ROSS, A. L. (1989) "On Arms Acquisitions and Transfers," pp. 97-120 in KOLODZIEJ, E. A. and P. M. MORGAN (eds.) *Security and Arms Control.* vol. 1: *A Guide to National Policy Making.* Westport, Conn.: Greenwood Press.

SCHMID, A. P. (1988 and 1984) *Political Terrorism: A Research Guide to Concepts, Theories, Data Bases, and Literature.* New Brunswick, N. J.: Transaction Books.

SINGER, J. D. (1979) *The Correlates of War.* New York: Free Press.

SINGER, J. D., and M. SMALL (1972) *Wages of War 1816-1965: A Statistical Handbook.* New York: Wiley.

SIVARD, R. (annual) *World Military and Social Expenditures, 19xx.* Washington: World Priorities.

SKOCPOL, T. (1979) *States and Social Revolutions.* Cambridge: Cambridge University Press.

SMALL, M., and J. D. SINGER (1982) *Wages of War 1816-1980: Resort to Arms: International and Civil War.* Beverly Hills: Sage Publications.

SMALL, M., and J. D. SINGER (eds.) (1989) *International War: An Anthology,* 2nd ed. New York: Brooks/Cole Publishing Co.

SMITH, R., A. HUMM, and J. FONTANEL (1985) "The Economics of Exporting Arms," *Journal of Peace Research* 22 (3): 239-247.

STOCKHOLM INTERNATIONAL PEACE RESEARCH INSTITUTE (SIPRI) (1985a) *Arms Production in the Third World.* Philadelphia: Taylor and Francis.

_____. (annual) *SIPRI Yearbook: World Armaments and Disarmament, 19xx/xx.* Stockholm: SIPRI.

SZENTES, T. (1984) "The Economic Impact of Global Militarization," *Alternatives* 10: 45-73.

TILLEY, C. (1978) *From Mobilization to Revolution.* New York: Random House.

UNITED NATIONS (annual) *The United Nations Disarmament Yearbook.* New York: United Nations Publications.

UNITED NATIONS. EDUCATIONAL, SCIENTIFIC, AND CULTURAL ORGANIZATION (annual). *UNESCO Yearbook on Peace and Conflict Studies.* Westport, Conn.: Greenwood Press.

UNITED STATES. ARMS CONTROL AND DISARMAMENT AGENCY (ACDA) (annual, for most recent 10-year period) *World Military Expenditures and Arms Transfers.* Washington: US Government Printing Office.

UNITED STATES. CONGRESS. CONGRESSIONAL RESEARCH SERVICE (annual, for most recent eight-year period) *Trends in Conventional Arms Transfers to the Third World by Major Suppliers.* Washington: Library of Congress.

UNITED STATES. CONGRESS. JOINT ECONOMIC COMMITTEE (annual) *Allocation of Resources in the Soviet Union and China.* Washington: US Government Printing Office.

UNITED STATES. CONGRESS. SELECT COMMITTEE ON INTELLIGENCE (1980) *Hearings: CIA Estimates of Soviet Defense Spending.* Washington: US Government Printing Office.

UNITED STATES. DEPARTMENT OF DEFENSE (DOD). DEFENSE SUPPORT ASSISTANCE AGENCY (DSAA) (annual) *Foreign Military Sales, Foreign Military Construction Sales, and Military Assistance Facts.* Washington: DSAA Data Management Division.

UNITED STATES. DEPARTMENT OF STATE (1988) *Terrorist Group Profiles.* Washington: US Government Printing Office.

_____. (annual) *Patterns of Global Terrorism.* Washington: Department of State Publication.

_____. (annual) *Warsaw Pact Aid to Non-Communist Developing Countries.* Washington: Department of State Publication.

_____. (annual) *World Refugee Report.* Washington: Department of State Publication.

U. S. COMMITTEE ON REFUGEES (annual) *World Refugee Survey.* Washington: American Council for Nationalities Service.

WALLENSTEIN, P., J. GALTUNG, and C. PORTALES (eds.) (1985) *Global Militarization.* Boulder: Westview Press.

WOLPIN, M. D. (1981) *Militarism and Social Revolution in the Third World.* Totowa: Allanheld, Osmun.

2

Economic Well-Being

The next value to be analyzed will be economic well-being for, to paraphrase the author of the European Recovery Plan after World War II, without normal economic health in the world, there can be no assured peace (Robinson, citing George C. Marshall, 1986). In the years since World War II the world capitalist economy was rebuilt with the help of a number of international institutions and agreements; today, despite the impact of decolonization and the creation of some 100 new countries, this system encompasses the overwhelming majority of the world's states. Even those few remaining socialist states supposedly committed to building an alternative world economic structure have many dealings with the states of the capitalist world.

This global economic system is managed by the major capitalist states who through their weighted voting rights control most of the major international financial institutions. At the core of this system are the Group of Seven (G7) largest capitalist powers—the United States, Japan, (West) Germany, United Kingdom, France, Italy, and Canada—whose leaders meet annually in "economic summits" to coordinate policies and set goals for the following year (Putnam, 1984; Williamson and Miller, 1987). (An "inner core" of US, Japan, and Germany sometimes act in concert to influence the others.)

Four non-state bulwarks of the world capitalist system are the World Bank, the International Monetary Fund (IMF), the Organization for Economic Cooperation and Development (OECD), and the General Agreement on Tariffs and Trade (GATT).

The Bank and the Fund each have 153 member-states, including such communist countries as China and (from eastern Europe even before the political changes of 1989) Yugoslavia, Romania, Hungary, and Poland. In keeping with the "ideology of development" (discussed below, in section V2.1e), the announced purpose of the Bank is to improve living standards in less developed countries through long-term project loans for the building of economic infrastructure. The Fund makes loans for "changes in economic policy" which guarantee "stability" in the global capitalist system. Through voting rights based upon amounts of capitalization contributed to the Bank and the Fund, these two organizations are effectively controlled by the seven leading capitalist states, with some proportional representation occasionally expanded to certain nouveau riche nations like Saudi Arabia.

The OECD, a group of the world's wealthiest states—21 from Europe, plus Japan, Australia, and New Zealand—traces its origins to 1948 when the Organization for European Economic Cooperation was set up to coordinate the distribution of Marshall Plan aid. Throughout the subsequent era of decolonization this body was used as a vehicle to guide the development of many former European colonies in the Islamic, African, Asian, and Latin American zones. Before the Group of Seven was formed in 1974, this was the main organization in which the leading capitalist states at the core of the world capitalist system met to coordinate policy among themselves and to standardize measures for national accounting systems.

The GATT consists of 97 countries, plus 28 others who adhere to its rules, and is not an organization like the other three but rather a continuing (more or less permanent) forum for negotiations relating to trade, and a code of rules which guides such discussions. Its main principles are that all trade should be non-discriminatory, that national protection for domestic industries be limited to the customs tariff, and that all quantitative measures of protection (i.e., quotas) should eventually be eliminated.

These four multilateral citadels of world capitalism maintain statistics on the daily workings of the system which yield much information relevant to this study. Aggregate data on productivity, savings, consumption, debt, investment, trade, aid, and distribution of benefits are found in the annual publications of these institutions. To be sure, there is some variation in the availability and reliability of these statistics, and information on communist countries and small states is sometimes hard to find. In the data to be displayed in this chapter, however, no attempt is made to get coverage for all of this study's 162 states, particularly the 31 ministates, the nine non-member states of the Bank and the Fund (USSR, E. Germany, Czechoslovakia, Bulgaria, Albania; Taiwan, North Korea, Mongolia; and Cuba), and certain countries which have been at war and whose economies have been in turmoil in recent years (e.g., Romania; Iran, Iraq, Afghanistan, Lebanon; Angola, Liberia; Myanmar, Vietnam, and Cambodia). With these exceptions, however, there are probably more statistics available with respect to economic activity than any of the other four values being analyzed in this book; more than 60 measures are presented for discussion in this chapter (see Moore, 1985, for more indicators), about half from World Bank sources. Where data is available for some of the problematic states from earlier periods of time or from other sources, it may be integrated with the measures from the standard sources so that the approximate rankings for as many states as possible might be provided.

V2.1. INHERENT ECONOMIC STRENGTH

The first indicator of economic well-being to be analyzed concerns each state's inherent economic strength. Four measures will be used: productivity, investment and savings, international reserves, and current account balances.

V2.la - Productivity

The Gross National Product (GNP) represents the total market value of all goods and services produced by a state's economy. It is adjusted for income its residents receive from abroad for their labor and capital, less similar payments made to nonresidents who contributed to the domestic economy. A related figure, Gross Domestic Product (GDP), measures total final output regardless of the allocation to domestic and foreign claims; for most states its amount is within 5% of that for GNP. Taken together these two statistics—along with the per capita and annual growth rates associated with each—represent good estimates of the basic economic strength of a country and both will be used in this section.

These numbers are generally available not only from the financial institutions undergirding the capitalist system, but also from the United Nations and many independent sources. This does not mean, however, that these measures are always a precise reflection of economic reality. In many countries considerable economic activity goes on "off the books," especially in heavily controlled "command economies" and, at the other extreme, in states where illegal drug traffic is a major enterprise (Afghanistan, Pakistan, Iran; Myanmar, Laos; Bolivia, Colombia, Peru, Mexico, Belize, Jamaica; see US Department of State, 1987: 1-2).

Even when there is record-keeping for most sectors of the economy, differences in the methodologies of national accounting systems and in the manner of converting to a common currency (the US $) will result in different productivity numbers being cited by different sources. A comparison of 1985 GNP statistics as calculated by the World Bank and the United Nations' International Comparison Project shows variations by a factor of three or more in the data presented for such states as Bolivia, Botswana, Chile, Colombia, Costa Rica, Dominican Republic, Ecuador, Hungary, India, Indonesia, Malawi, Pakistan, Peru, Philippines, Poland, and Sri Lanka (World Bank, *World Development Report 1987:* 270, Box A.2; see also Kravis et al., 1982). However, unlike with Chapter 1's military spending, there is no pattern of ideological bias in these differences. Therefore, this study will generally rely upon a few standard sources (especially the World Bank's annual *World Development Report* , hereafter WDR), and note that as in Chapter 1 the state rankings over time within geographic zones do not vary much.

In the tables which follow in this section, both GNP and GDP will be employed, depending upon the comprehensiveness and timeliness of the sources being used. The World Bank annually produces statistics on GDP, and GNP per capita; but information is often not available for communist countries or those with less than 1 million in population, removing about 35 states from this study's desired universe of 162.   ACDA and Sivard give information directly on GNP and GNP per capita, and for more states (n=144 and 142 respectively), but the data in their publications are usually one year later than from the World Bank, and so they will not be used as often in this chapter.

In recent years the United States has accounted for about 20% of the world's productivity, down from a high of 40% in the years after World War II. The European Economic Community produces about 24% of the total world output, Japan about 12%, the USSR 10%, and China 5%.   All the rest of the world put together—146 states, 90% of the sovereign political actors—accounts for less than 30% of the world's economic production. This is true whether GNP or GDP is being considered.

Table V2.1a.i ranks states within their zones in order of Gross National Product as of 1988. This figure has been calculated from GNP per capita and population statistics given in the latest (1990) *World Development Report* for 140 countries. It has then been supplemented by other sources for earlier years in order to provide coverage for all 162 states because this statistic (like population) is one of the most basic socio-economic indicators and is often used as the denominator in computing many other measures.

The relatively high standings of the USSR, China, and India in GNP, however, indicate that this first measure is in many respects a function of a country's size. On the other hand, the data in Table V2.1a.ii for GNP per capita—often taken as a rough indicator of level of development and standard of living—yield significantly different results in state rankings. The presence of such relatively small states as Switzerland, Norway, Luxembourg, Gabon, Brunei, Singapore, Bahamas, Trinidad, Barbados, and five Persian Gulf sheikdoms among zonal leaders in this second measure is notable, as are the lowly positions (~$335 per capita) of China and India.

Economic growth is the lifeblood of the capitalist system. Without growth there is no generation of excess capital which can be invested back into economic enterprise to maintain the system. But statistics on economic growth vary considerably from year to year, so a longer perspective is needed when analyzing this measure.

Table V2.1a.iii(a) lists the leading and lowest states in each zone with respect to the growth of Gross Domestic Product for the most recent years (1980-88) available according to a survey of 105 states by the World Bank. Table V2.1a.iii(b) presents country rankings for growth in Gross National Product per capita for a longer period of time, 1965-88, for 120 states. The second statistic is more meaningful for not only does it encompass three times as many years, it also takes into account population growth, a figure which for most developing states can wipe out the first 2 to 3% of GNP growth each year.

Table V2.1a.iii reveals significant variation in economic growth between the zones, with the widest fluctuations—both high growth in excess of 5% a year, and negative contractions of the economy—taking place in the four columns containing the states of the capitalist world periphery. The core states of Europe generally grow steadily, if modestly, at about 2% per annum on average, but building upon a higher base generate higher absolute dollars than the others, resulting in a growing gap between them ("Patterns of Economic Growth," 1985: 525; see also Garrett and Lange, 1986).

V2.1b. Investment and Savings

After the ability to produce, the next measure of a state's economic strength is its willingness to invest and save, and not totally consume, some of the fruits of its productivity. This section will concentrate on two such measures: Gross Domestic Investment and Gross Domestic Savings, each expressed as a percentage of Gross Domestic Product.

Gross Domestic Investment (GDI) is defined by the World Bank (WDR88: 292) as "outlays for additions to fixed assets of economy, plus net changes in values of inventories." It includes the production of all those goods which are to replace machinery, equipment, and buildings used up in the current year's production, plus any net additions to the economy's stock of capital.

Gross Domestic Savings (GDS) is defined by the World Bank as Gross Domestic Product less total consumption, i.e., productivity less general government consumption (including defense) and private consumption (by households and nonprofit institutions). This can be a negative number, but if positive can (when used in conjunction with the investment figure noted above and consumption data in section V2.2c) give some approximation of national expenditures going into long-term economic infrastructure as opposed to military expenditures (V1.2) and social welfare payments (V2.4).

In both investment and savings, a relative figure (as a percentage of GDP) is more significant than the absolute dollar amount. Tables V2.1b.i and ii rank more than 105 states in their zones for these measures as reported for 1988 by the World Bank. Note in particular the high standings of states with an oil base to their economy, either at the producing or refining stage, as well as of those countries of offshore East Asia (currently the fastest growing industrial area in the world (Harris, 1987)), and those with "command economies."

The bottom halves of these tables show that even the last states of the European zone, which rated strongest in V2.1a, also are high in investment and, especially, savings when compared with the states in the other four zones; it is easier for the rich to get richer than for the poor to become wealthy. Within the European zone, note the relatively low position of the United States when it comes to these measures of deferred economic pleasure; on the other hand, given the size of its GDP (twice that of any other country in the world), it does not need to save or invest a large percentage of its output in order to have significant funds going into these areas of banking for the future.

Finally, a related figure, Gross Fixed Capital Formation, defined as inventories less increase in stocks, is annually reported by the IMF in its *International Financial Statistics Yearbook*, but it is given in terms of local currency, and so will not be used in this study.

V2.1c. Gross International Reserves

Another measure of a state's basic strength is Gross International Reserves, all holdings of monetary gold, special drawing rights (SDRs), and foreign exchange. The total value of this measure for the entire world is more than $500 billion. In 1950, the United States had 49% of the world's reserves; today it still has the largest holdings in absolute terms, but only 6% of the world total. The 12 countries of the European Economic Community (Common Market)— (W.)Germany, France, Italy, Belgium, Netherlands, Luxembourg, UK, Ireland, Denmark, Spain, Portugal, and Greece—have about 40%; and the 13 OPEC members (Organization of Petroleum Exporting Countries)—Saudi Arabia, Kuwait, UAE, Qatar, Iraq, Iran, Libya, Algeria, Nigeria, Gabon, Indonesia, Venezuela, and Ecuador—about 20%. One surprising leader in this measure—fourth highest in the world—is Taiwan.

For a capitalist state, Gross International Reserves is a measure of its reserve position in the International Monetary Fund and is a figure which is fairly stable over time. It is essentially a measure of a country's liquid assets, or usable wealth. Table V2.1c.i displays the absolute dollar amounts for 112 states reporting to the World Bank in 1988 (plus two other states from earlier years). The dominant position of Europe, plus a few newly rich oil-producing countries and the newly industrializing "tigers" of eastern Asia, in the global economic system is once again manifest in this listing, as is the lowly status of most African states.

Reserves can also be expressed in terms of the number of months of imports they can buy. By this measure, large countries with considerable GNP but also heavy import demands are placed on the same footing as smaller states with lesser needs. Because it depends upon variations in a country's trading situation, this number varies somewhat from year to year and in any event is rather hypothetical in that before a country would spend down to its last day of imports, it would have to be assumed that all other productivity in that state had ceased. On the other hand, because it is a relative measure, it gives a truer picture of the country rankings. Table V2.1c.ii displays this statistic for 110 states in 1988.

V2.1d. Positive Account Balances

Some final measures of the strength of countries' economies would be positive balances in their current accounts and trading situations. The balance of trade is the difference between the value of a country's exports and its imports in goods and merchandise. The current account balance is a more encompassing statistic which includes trade in "non-factor services" (i.e., "invisibles" such as tourism, investment income, and workers' remittances); it measures the difference between exports and imports of goods and services "plus flows of unrequited official and private transfers," i.e., foreign aid in the form of grants, technical assistance, and food aid (World Bank, WDR89: 240).

The World Bank provides the current account balance both before and after official transfers. The earlier figure, showing balances before foreign aid reduces the deficits of developing countries, will be reproduced here for this gives a truer picture of the plight of those poor states. Fewer than one-fourth of the states have positive account balances, and three-quarters are in a deficit situation, with about 20% of states shifting between the plus and minus side of the ledger in a given year. Table V2.1d shows the strength of West Germany and the EEC core plus Japan and east Asia's industrializing states in 1988. It also reveals the newly low position of the United States, although as a percentage of its GNP the number is not quite as bad as the lower absolute scores for some of the African countries.

V2.1e. The Ideology of Development

The lists of states consistently scoring high in the measures of economic strength presented in this section reveal a world divided into a handful of strong and an overwhelming number of weak states. In the global economic system of international capitalism, there are the advanced industrial states of the Northern core (n=~25) which have great influence over the dependent national economies of some 125 developing states in the Southern periphery of the rest of the world. The words "North" and "South" are more metaphorical than strictly geographic, with the former including in addition to most European states Australia, New Zealand, and Japan, and by some calculations South Africa and Israel. The South encompasses most of the rest of this study's Islamic, African, Asian, and Latin American zones. Also, historically, there have been another ten or so communist countries (a number declining in 1990) which are either not part of the global capitalist system or only tangentially involved with it.

Politically, the more advanced industrial states attempt to influence the poorer countries to develop in the direction of their respective economic systems. The general rubric under which all international transfers are made is often described by its goal of "development" (OECD, *Development Cooperation*, annually; see also Hunt, 1989; Spero, 1988; Nossiter, 1987; Wallerstein, 1979). It is labeled an *ideology* here, however, because the stability of the system of international economic exchange is undergirded by the *belief* that by playing according to the rules, the less developed countries of the South will eventually grow to the level of economic modernization and well-being of the states of the North, an assumption which is not necessarily true.

According to the ideology of development, there is a continuum between the "less" developed (euphemistically, *developing*) and "more" developed nations, and economic modernization is a process which all states will eventually undergo (Brandt, et al., 1980; Baum and Tolbert, 1985; Harris, 1987; Kohli, 1986). As Chapter 3 will indicate, however, this planet may not have the resource base to sustain two billion Chinese and Indians (not to mention the rest of humanity) at the level of electricity, oil, and steel consumed by the average European today. In this light, one author has dubbed the rich and poor states, respectively, as "overly developed countries" (ODCs), and "less developed countries" (LDCs) (Pirages, 1978).

Within the capitalist world, international transfers of capital take the form of the rich states of the core (and their multilateral banks and lending institutions) giving loans and grants to poor states in the periphery (Watanabe, 1986; Hoogvelt, 1982). The idea is that with such infusions of capital, the poorer states might be able to make investments in economic infrastructure, pay back interest on previous loans, make purchases of goods produced in the advanced countries, and in general remain functioning members of the world capitalist system. (Before the changes of 1989 in eastern Europe, a similar phenomenon, though on a far more modest scale, occurred among the states with command economies through the medium of the Council for Mutual Economic Assistance (CMEA).)

Pursuant to the ideology of development, and the general goal of keeping even the most hapless of developing nations economically functioning, the United Nations has designated certain states as "least developed" countries (LLDCs), and other states as "most seriously affected" (MSAs) by the oil price rises of the 1970s (United Nations, 1984; Weiss and Jennings, 1983), and therefore in need of special assistance from the more advanced countries. A fuller definition of these two terms, and a complete list of the LLDC and MSA countries deemed worthy of special help from the nations of the world community, follows as Table V2.1e.i. (For the historic record, and to round out this section's introduction to the major international economic actors, Table V2.1e.ii gives the names of states associated with the CMEA, an organization which will probably become moribund in the near future.)

V2.1a.i - Gross National Product (US $ billions), 1988

Europe	Islamic	Africa	Asia	Latin America
US $4886.6				
SU 2460.0^			Japan $2577.1	
W.Germany 1132.8				
France 899.4			China 359.2	Brazil $311.9
Italy 765.1			India 277.3	
UK 731.5	Iran $257.8^			
	Saudi A. 86.8	S.Africa $77.9	Australia 203.6	
Canada 441.0				Mexico 147.3
Spain 301.9	Turkey 68.9	Nigeria 31.9	S.Korea 151.2	
Nethrlds. 214.9	Iraq 56.5^	Cameroon 11.3	Taiwan 101.3^	Argentina 79.4
E.Germany 196.9^	Algeria 56.2	Angola 11.2e^		Venezuela 61.1
Switzerland 181.5	Israel 38.1		Indonesia 76.9	
Sweden 162.1	Pakistan 37.2	Ivory Coast 8.6		Colombia 37.4
Czech. 151.3^	Egypt 33.1	Kenya 8.3	Thailand 54.5	Peru 26.9
Romania 146.0^		Zimbabwe 6.0		Cuba 26.4^
Belgium 143.5	Kuwait 26.8	Ethiopia 5.7	Philippines 37.7	Chile 19.3
Austria 117.6		Zaire 5.7	N.Zealand 35.0	Ecuador 11.3
Denmark 94.1	UAE 23.7	Ghana 5.6	Malaysia 32.8	
Finland 93.0	Libya 22.8	Senegal 4.6		Guatemala 7.8
Norway 84.0	Morocco 19.9	Uganda 4.5	N.Korea 25.9^	Uruguay 7.7
	Syria 19.5	Tanzania 4.0	Singapore 23.6	
Poland 70.4	Sudan 11.4	Gabon 3.3		Dom.Rep. 5.0
Bulgaria 64.8^	Tunisia 9.0		Bangladesh 18.5	Panama 4.9
Yugoslavia 59.5		Guinea 2.3		El Salvador 4.7
Greece 48.0	Oman 7.0	Niger 2.2	Vietnam 12.7^	Paraguay 4.7
Portugal 37.6		Zambia 2.2		CostaRica 4.6
Ireland 27.1	Jordan 5.9	Rwanda 2.1	Myanmar 9.3^	Honduras 4.1
Hungary 26.1		Congo 1.9	Sri Lanka 7.0	Trinidad 4.0
	N. Yemen 5.4	Mali 1.8		Bolivia 3.9
Luxmbrg 8.4	Cyprus 4.3	Burkina F 1.8	Brunei 3.6*	
	Qatar 4.1	Benin 1.7	Nepal 3.2	Nicaragua 2.9*
Iceland 5.0		Namibia 1.6º	Papua NG 3.0	Bahamas 2.6
		Mozambique 1.5	Mongolia 2.5e^	Jamaica 2.6
Albania 2.9^	Afghanistan 3.1^	Malawi 1.4	Madagascar 2.1	Haiti 2.4
Malta 1.8	Bahrain 3.1	Botswana 1.2	Mauritius 2.0	
	Lebanon 3.0^	Burundi 1.2		
		Sierra L. 1.1*	Fiji 1.1	Barbados 1.5
	Somalia 1.0	Liberia 1.0*		Suriname 1.1
	S.Yemen 1.0	Togo 1.3	Cambodia 0.9e^	
	Mauritania 0.9	C.Af.R. 1.1	Laos 0.7	Antigua 0.3
	Chad 0.9	Lesotho 0.7	Seychelles 0.3	Guyana 0.3
		Swaziland 0.6	Bhutan 0.3	Belize 0.3
	Djibouti 0.3º	Gambia 0.2	Solomons 0.2	St.Lucia 0.2
		C.Verde 0.2	Comoros 0.2	Grenada 0.2
		GBissau 0.2	Vanuatu 0.1	St. Vincent 0.1
		Eq.Guinea 0.1	W.Samoa 0.1	St.Chris. 0.1
		STP 0.1	Maldives 0.1	Dominica 0.1
n=30	n=28	n=38	n=33	n=33 (162)

Source: *calculated* from WDR90f88, Table 1 & Box A1, n=140 (or *WDR89f87, n=4);
supplemented by ^ACDA89f87 (where e=extrapolated estimate) for n=16, and º other for n=2.

V2.1a.ii - Gross National Product per Capita (US $), 1988

Europe	Islamic	Africa	Asia	Latin America
Switzrld. $27,500			Japan $21,020	
Luxmbrg. 22,400	UAE $15,770			Bahamas $10,700
Iceland 20,190	Kuwait 13,400		Brunei 15,390*	
Norway 19,990			Australia 12,340	Barbados 6010
US 19,840	Qatar 9930			
Sweden 19,300	Israel 8650		N.Zealand 10,000	Antigua 3690
Finland 18,590			Singapore 9070	Trinidad 3350
W.Ger.18,480	Bahrain 6340			Venezuela 3250
Denmark 18,450	Cyprus 6260		Taiwan 5126^	
Canada 16,960	Saudi A. 6200	Gabon $2970		St. Chris. 2630
France 16,090	Libya 5420	S.Africa 2290		Cuba 2576^
Austria 15,470	Iran 5129^	Angola 1300e^	Seychels 3800	Argentina 2520
Nethrlds.14,520	Oman 5000	Botswana 1010	S.Korea 3600	Uruguay 2470
Belgium 14,490		Cameroon 1010		Suriname 2460
Italy 13,320	Iraq 3331e^	Namibia 970º		Brazil 2160
UK 12,810		Congo 910	Malaysia 1940	Panama 2120
E.Ger. 11,860^	Algeria 2360	Swaziland 810	Mauritius 1800	
		Iv.Coast 770	Fiji 1520	Mexico 1760
Czech. 9709^	Lebanon 1900e^	C.Verde 680		Grenada 1720
USSR 8602^		Senegal 650	Mongolia 1245^	Costa Rica 1690
Ireland 7750	Syria 1680	Zimbabwe 650	N.Korea 1208^	Dominica 1680
Spain 7740	Jordan 1500		Thailand 1000	St. Lucia 1540
Bulgaria 7229^		STP 490	Vanuatu 840	Chile 1510
Romania 6365^		Liberia 450*	Papua NG 810	Belize 1500
Malta 5190	Turkey 1280	Guinea 430		
Greece 4800	Tunisia 1230	Lesotho 420		Peru 1300
Portugal 3650	Djibouti 1140º	Eq.Guinea 410	W.Samoa 640	St.Vincent 1200
Yugoslavia 2520		Ghana 400	Philippines 630	Colombia 1180
Hungary 2460	Morocco 830	Benin 390	Solomons 630	Paraguay 1180
Poland 1860	N.Yemen 690	C.Af.R. 380	Indonesia 440	Ecuador 1120
Albania 955^	Egypt 660	Kenya 370	Comoros 440	Jamaica 1070
		Togo 370	SriLanka 420	
	Mauritania 480	Rwanda 320	Maldives 410	Guatemala 960
	Sudan 480	Sierra L. 300*		El Salvador 940
		Niger 300	India 340	
	S.Yemen 430	Nigeria 290	China 330	Honduras 860
		Zambia 290		Nicaragua 830*
		Uganda 280		
	Pakistan 350	Burundi 240	Myanmar 241^	Dom.Rep. 720
		Mali 230	Vietnam 200^	
	Afghanstan 217^	Burkina F. 210	Madagscr. 190	Bolivia 570
		Gambia 200	Laos 180	
		GBissau 190	Nepal 180	Guyana 420
		Malawi 170	Bhutan 180	
	Somalia 170	Zaire 170	Bangladesh 170	Haiti 380
		Tanzania 160		
	Chad 160	Ethiopia 120	Cambodia 140e^	
		Mozambique 100		
n=30	n=28	n=38	n=33	n=33 (162)

Source: WDR90f88, Table 1 and Box A.1 (n=139); supplemented by: *WDR89f87 (n=4), ^ACDA
WMEAT89f87 (n=17).; and ºOther for 1986 (n=2).

102

V2.1a.iii(a) - GDP Average Annual Growth Rate(%),1980-88

Europe	Islamic	Africa	Asia	Latin America
Norway 3.8%	Oman 12.7%	Botswana 11.4%	China 10.3%	Colombia 3.4%
US 3.3	Pakistan 6.6	Burkina F. 5.5	S.Korea 9.9	Brazil 2.9
Canada 3.3	N.Yemen 6.5	Cameroon 5.4	Thailand 6.0	Panama 2.6
Finland 2.8	Egypt 5.7	Burundi 4.3	Singapore 5.7	Costa Rica 2.4
UK 2.8	Turkey 5.3	Kenya 4.2	Mauritius 5.7	Dom.Rep. 2.2
Spain 2.5	Morocco 4.2	Congo 4.0	India 5.2	Ecuador 2.0
Denmark 2.2	Jordan 4.2	Senegal 3.3	Indonesia 5.1	Chile 1.9
Italy 2.2	Chad 3.9	Mali 3.2	Nepal 4.7	Par.,Hond.-1.7
....	....	....	....	....
Austria 1.7	Israel 3.2	Zambia 0.7	Malaysia 4.6	El Salvador 0.0
Ire.,Swed.-1.7	Somalia 3.2	Togo 0.5	Sri Lanka 4.3	Haiti (-0.2)
Nethrlds. 1.6	Sudan 2.5	Sierra L. 0.2	Japan 3.9	Guatemala (-0.2)
Hungary 1.6	Mauritania 1.6	Gabon (-0.2)	Australia 3.3	Argentina (-0.2)
Yugoslavia 1.4	Syria 0.5	Nigeria (-1.1)	Papua NG 3.2	Nicaragua (-0.3)
Greece 1.4	Kuwait (-1.1)	Niger (-1.2)	N.Zealand 2.2	Uruguay (-0.4)
Belgium 1.4	Saudi A. (-3.3)	Liberia (-1.3)	Madagascar 0.6	Bolivia (-1.6)
Portugal 0.8	UAE (-4.5)	Mozambq.(-2.8)	Phil.I. 0.1	Trinidad (-6.1)
n=22/30	n=17/28	n=28/38	n=16/33	n=22/33 (105)

Source: WDR90f1980-88, Table 2, n=105.

V2.1a.iii(b)-GNP per Capita Avg. Annual Growth Rate(%),1965-88

Europe	Islamic	Africa	Asia	Latin America
Malta 7.4%	Oman 6.4%^	Botswana 8.6%	Singapore 7.2%	Brazil 3.6%
Hungary 5.1	Saudi A. 3.8	Lesotho 5.2	S.Korea 6.8	St. Chris. 3.6
Luxmbrg. 4.1	Egypt 3.6	Cameroon 3.7	China 5.4	Paraguay 3.1
Norway 3.5	Tunisia 3.4	Congo 3.5	Indonesia 4.3	Ecuador 3.1
Yugoslavia 3.4	Syria 2.9	Burundi 3.0	Japan 4.3	Dom. Rep. 2.7
Iceland 3.3	Algeria 2.7	Swaziland 2.2	Malaysia 4.0	St. Lucia 2.7
Finland 3.2	Israel 2.7	Kenya 1.9	Thailand 4.0	Colombia 2.4
Portugal 3.1	Turkey 2.6	Mali 1.6	Seychelles 3.2	Belize 2.4
....	....	....	....	....
Spain 2.3	Pakistan 2.5	CAfR,Tanz.(-0.8)	India 1.8	Peru,Chile-0.1
Ireland 2.0	Morocco 2.3	Senegal (-0.8)	Australia 1.7	Argentina 0.0
Nethrlds. 1.9	Somalia 0.5	Ghana (-1.6)	Phil. I. 1.6	El Salvador (-0.5)
Denmark 1.8	Sudan 0.0	GBissau (-1.9)	N. Zealand 0.8	Bolivia (-0.6)
Sweden 1.8	Chad (-0.2)	Zambia (-2.1)	Clomoros 0.6	Venezuela (-0.9)
UK 1.8	Mauritania (-0.4)	Zaire (-2.1)	Papua NG 0.5	Jamaica (-1.5)
US 1.6	Libya (-2.7)	Niger (-2.3)	Bangladesh 0.4	Nicaragua (-2.5)
Switzerland 1.5	Kuwait (-4.3)	Uganda (-3.1)	Madagascar(-1.8)	Guyana (-4.4)
n=23/30	n=16/28	n=30/38	n=20/33	n=31/33 (120)

Source: WDR90f1965-88, Table 1 and Box A1, n=120.

103

V2.1b.i - Gross Domestic Investment as % of GDP, 1988

Europe	Islamic	Africa	Asia	Latin America
		Lesotho 47%		
Yugoslavia 39%			China 38%	
			Singapore 37	
Poland 33	Somalia 34%	Mozambique 33		
Switzerland 31			Japan 31	
	Algeria 31		Laos 31	Venezuela 30%
Portugal 30	Oman 30**		S.Korea 30	Peru 29
Norway 28			Thailand 28	
Austria 27		Gabon 27		Jamaica 27
Finland 27	Saudi A. 27	Botswana 26*	Malaysia 26	Costa Rica 26
	UAE 26		Papua NG 26	
	Jordan 26	Kenya 25	Mauritius 25	Paraguay 24
Hungary 25		Burkina F. 25	Australia 24	Dom.Rep. 24
	Morocco 24		India 24	
Spain 23	Turkey 24		Sri Lanka 23	Ecuador 23
Italy 23				Brazil 23
		Congo 22	N.Zealand 22	
Canada 22		Guinea 22	Indonesia 22	
W.Germany 21		Zimbabwe 21		
UK 21		Tanzania 21		Colombia 21
France 21	Kuwait 20	Togo 21		
	Egypt 20	S. Africa 20	Nepal 20	Mexico 20
Netherlands 19				
Sweden 19	Tunisia 19			
Denmark 18				
Ireland 18	Mauritania 18			
Belgium 18	Pakistan 18			Trinidad 18
Greece 18		Burundi 18		
	Syria 17	Cameroon 17	Phil. I. 17	Chile 17
	Israel 17	Malawi 16		
		Ethiopia 16	Madagascar 16	Honduras 16
		Rwanda 16		
		Senegal 15	Myanmar 15^	
US 15		Mali 15		Argentina 14
		Ivory Coast 14		Guatemala 14
	N.Yemen 13	Nigeria 13		
		Uganda 13		El Salvador 13
	Chad 12	C. Af. R. 12		
		Ghana 12	Bangladesh 12	
		Benin 12		
		Zaire 11		Bolivia 11
		Zambia 11		
		Sierra L. 11		
	Sudan 10	Liberia 10^		Uruguay 10
		Niger 10		Haiti 10
n=21/30	n=18/28	n=30/38	n=19/33	n=19/33 (107)

Source: WDR90f88, Table 9, n=103;
 supplemented by: ^WDR89f87, n=2; *WDR88f86, n=1; **WDR87f85, n=1.

V2.1b.ii - Gross Domestic Savings as % of GDP, 1988

Europe	Islamic	Africa	Asia	Latin America
Yugoslavia 40%	Oman 43%**		Singapore 41%	
			S.Korea 38	
	UAE 36		China 37	
Poland 35			Malaysia 36	
		Gabon 33%	Japan 33	
Switzrld. 31	Algeria 31			
Hungary 28				Brazil 28%
Norway 28			New Zealand 26	Costa Rica 26
Ireland 27			Thailand 26	
Austria 27		Botswana 26*		
Finland 27	Turkey 26	S. Africa 25	Indonesia 25	Venezuela 25
W.Germany 26			Mauritius 25	Peru 24
		Zimbabwe 24		Chile 24
Canada 23	Morocco 23		Australia 23	Paraguay 23
Italy 23		Kenya 22		Mexico 23
Netherlands 23		Ivory Coast 22	India 21	Colombia 22
Spain 22			Laos 21	Ecuador 21
Portugal 21			Papua NG 21	Trinidad 21
Belgium 21				Panama 21*
France 21				
Denmark 21	Saudi A. 20	Congo 20		
Sweden 21	Tunisia 19	Guinea 19		Jamaica 19
		Sierra L. 17	Phil. I. 18	Argentina 18
UK 17	Kuwait 15	Nigeria 15		Dom.Rep.16
	Pakistan 13	Zambia 14		Uruguay 14
US 13	Syria 13	Togo 14	Sri Lanka 13	
		Cameroon 14	Myanmar 12*	
Greece 11	Israel 10		Nepal 10	Honduras 11
	Mauritania 10	Senegal 9		
		Malawi 8		
	Egypt 8	Zaire 8	Madagascar 8	Guatemala 8
	Sudan 7	Rwanda 6		
		Ghana 6		Bolivia 6
		Burundi 5		El Salvador 6
		Uganda 5		
		Ethiopia 4		Haiti 4
	Somalia 3	Niger 4	Bangladesh 3	
	N.Yemen 0	Benin 0		
		C.Af.R. (-1)		Nicaragua (-2)*
	Jordan (-3)	Mali (-4)		
		Burkina F. (-4)		
		Tanzania (-5)		
	Chad (-12)	Mozambique (-15)		
		Lesotho (-73)		
n=21/30	n=18/28	n=29/38	n=19/33	n=21/33 (108)

Source: WDR90f88, Table 9, n= 103;
   supplemented by: *WDR88f86, n=4; and **WDR87f85, n=1.

V2.1c.i - Gross International Reserves (US $), 1988

Europe	Islamic	Africa	Asia	Latin America
US $144.2 bil.				
W.Germany 97.6			Japan $106.7 bil.	
			Taiwan 79.4	
Italy 62.1				
France 58.9				
Switzrld. 58.4	Saudi A. $22.4 bil.		China 23.7	
UK 51.9				
Spain 42.8			Singapore 17.1	
Nethrlds. 34.1	Libya 5.8		Australia16.9	Venezuela $7.8 bil.
Belgium 23.3			S.Korea 12.5	
Canada 22.4	Lebanon 4.8		India 9.2	Mexico 6.3
	UAE 4.8			
Austria 16.0	Israel 4.4		Malaysia 7.5	Argentina 5.2
Norway 13.8	Turkey 3.9		Thailand 7.1	
Portugal 11.7	Algeria 3.2		Indonesia 6.3	Chile 3.8
Denmark 11.4	Kuwait 3.0			Colombia 3.7
Sweden 11.0				
	Egypt 2.3		N.Zealand 2.8	
Finland 7.2		Botswana $2.3 bil.	Phil. Is. 2.2	Uruguay 1.6
Ireland 5.2	Oman 1.2	S.Africa 2.2		Peru 1.2
Greece 5.0	Pakistan 1.2			Brazil 1.1
Yugoslavia 3.1	Tunisia 976 mil.	Nigeria 433 mil.	Bangldsh.829 mil.	Costa Rica 677 mil.
Hungary 2.5	Morocco 836	Zaire 372		Ecuador 568
Poland 2.2	Afghanistan 657	Zimbabwe 341	Mauritius 463	Bolivia 473
Romania 1.9^		Burkina F. 325	Papua NG 419	Guatemala 416
	Jordan 414	Ghana 310		
	Syria 342	Kenya 296	Nepal 283	El Salvador 354
	N.Yemen 285	Togo 237	Sri Lanka 248	Paraguay 338
		Niger 237	Madagascar 224	Dom.Rep. 261
		Ethiopia 171		Nicaragua 220**
		Cameroon 163	Myanmar 180	
		Malawi 151		Trinidad 148
		Zambia 139		Jamaica 147
	Sudan 107	Rwanda 118		
	S.Yemen 97	C.Af.R. 113		Panama 72
		Tanzania 78		
	Mauritania 77	Burundi 76		
	Chad 66	Gabon 71		
		Lesotho 56		Honduras 57
		Uganda 49	Bhutan 47	
		Mali 44		
		Ivory Coast 29		
	Somalia 23	Senegal 22		Haiti 20
		Benin 9	Laos 16	
		Congo 8		
		Sierra L. 7		
		Liberia 0		
n=22/30	n=22/28	n=28/38	n=21/33	n=21/33 (114)

Source: World Bank WDR90f88, Table 18, n=112; plus ^WDR89f87, n=1; **WDR87f85, n=1.

V2.1c.ii - Gross International Reserves (in months imports), 1988

Europe	Islamic	Africa	Asia	Latin America
		Botswana 1.7.7	Taiwan 16.0	
	Afghanistan 9.1			Uruguay 10.3
	Libya 9.0			
Switz. 7.9	Saudi A. 7.9			
Portugal 7.1				
Spain 6.9	Oman 6.6			
	UAE 5.8		China 5.0	Colombia 5.4
				Venezuela 5.4
				Chile 5.2
				Bolivia 5.0
		Niger 4.7		Argentina 4.7
		Burkina F. 4.6	Nepal 4.5	
Norway 4.3		Togo 4.5	Japan 4.4	
Italy 4.3			Singapore 4.2	
	Algeria 4.0		Malaysia 4.0	
Greece 3.8		C.Af. R. 3.9	India 3.8	Costa Rica 3.9
Austria 3.7		Malawi 3.7	Madagascar 3.7	
W.Germany 3.6	Kuwait 3.6		Thailand 3.6	
			Mauritius 3.6	
Denmark 3.3			Australia 3.6	
Nethrlds. 3.2		Rwanda 3.2	Indonesia 3.3	El Salvador 3.0
France 2.9			Bangladesh 2.9	Paraguay 3.0
Finland 2.8	Israel 2.6	Burundi 2.9	Myanmar 2.7	Peru 2.9
Ireland 2.8	Turkey 2.5	Ghana 2.7	N.Zealand 2.7	Guatemala 2.6
US 2.7	Tunisia 2.5	Zimbabwe 2.2	Papua NG 2.6	
Hungary 2.3			S. Korea 2.6	Ecuador 2.1
Yugoslavia 2.2			Phil. I. 2.2	Mexico 2.1
Sweden 2.1	Egypt 1.8	Ethiopia 1.5		
Belgium 2.1	Chad 1.7			
UK 2.0	N. Yemen 1.7	Zaire 1.4		Dom. Rep. 1.4
Canada 1.8	Syria 1.6	Nigeria 1.3		
	Pakistan 1.5	Kenya 1.3		
Poland 1.5	Morocco 1.5	Zambia 1.2	Sri Lanka 1.1	
	Mauritania 1.4	Lesotho 1.2		Trinidad 1.0
	S. Yemen 1.3	S.Africa 1.1		
	Jordan 1.2	Uganda 0.8	Laos 0.9	Jamaica 0.8
		Cameroon 0.7		
	Somalia 0.6	Mali 0.7		Haiti 0.5
	Sudan 0.6	Tanzania 0.6		Honduras 0.5
		Sierra L. 0.4		Brazil 0.4
		Gabon 0.4		
		Benin 0.2		Panama 0.2
		Senegal 0.2		
		Ivory Coast 0.1		
		Congo 0.1		
		Liberia 0.0		
n=21/30	n=21/28	n=28/38	n=20/33	n=20/33 (110)

Source: World Bank, *World Development Report 1990*, Table 18.

V2.1d - Current Account Balance (US $ millions), 1988

Europe	Islamic	Africa	Asia	Latin America
W.Ger.$60,320			Japan $82,610	
			S.Korea 14,117	
Switz. 8311			Taiwan 10,174	
Nethrlds. 5785	Kuwait $4853			
Belgium 5085				Brazil $4448
Yugoslavia 2487	UAE 2800	S. Africa $1207	Singapore 1683	
	Turkey 1139		Malaysia 1618	
France 875	Oman 844	Angola 367		Panama 625
		Botswana 309		
	Morocco 164			Uruguay 13
	Tunisia 13	Congo 7		Jamaica 4
--0--
		Zimbabwe -56	Mauritius -65	
		Sierra L. -86	Bhutan -68	
Poland -107		Togo -122	Laos -118	Paraguay -173
	Mauritania -179	Lesotho -130		Haiti -183
		Malawi -134		Trinidad -184
	Afghanistan -243	Burundi -163		
		Liberia -163		Dom.Rep. -218
		Benin -177	Nepal -251	El Salvador -242
	Chad -252	C. Af. R. -181		
		Ghana -232		Chile -282
		Zambia -234		
	Jordan -281	Niger -248	Madagascar -261	
		Rwanda -258		Colombia -355
		Guinea -279		Costa Rica -356
	Somalia -349	Uganda -289	Myanmar -307	Bolivia -429
Hungary -389		Burkina F. -310		Honduras -431
	S.Yemen -436	Mali -350	Papua NG -380	
		Senegal -467		Guatemala -506
Austria -569	Syria -604	Ethiopia -510	Sri Lanka -611	
		Gabon -627	Phil. I. -694	Ecuador -657
	N.Yemen -784	Kenya -711	N.Zealand -704	
		Mozambique -733		
Ireland -1034	Sudan -1144	Tanzania -743	Vietnam -1099	
Portugal -1320		Cameroon -881	Bangladesh -1112	Peru -1285
Sweden -1434	Pakistan -1685	Zaire -888		
Denmark -1686	Algeria -2040	Nigeria -1045	Indonesia -1500	Argentina -1615
Finland -2578	Libya -2222	Ivory Coast -1335	Thailand -1859	
Italy -2614				
Norway -2858	Egypt -2848			Mexico -3068
Greece -2894			China -3802	
Spain -5220	Israel -4097			Venezuela -4661
Canada -7905				
UK -20,763	Saudi A. -6283		India -7220	
US -113,740			Australia -11,100	
n=21/33	n=21/28	n=31/38	n=22/33	n=20/33 (115)

Source: World Bank, *World Development Report 1990*, Table 18.

108

V2.1e.i - List of LLDC and MSA Countries, 1990

Islamic	Africa	Asia	Latin America
	Least Developed Countries (LLDCs, n=40)		
Chad	Benin	Lesotho	Bangladesh	Haiti
Mauritania	-Botswana	-Malawi	Myanmar	
Somalia	Burundi	Mali	-Bhutan	
Sudan	Cape Verde	Niger	-Comoros	
N.Yemen	C.Af.Repub.	Rwanda	-Maldives	
S.Yemen	Ethiopia	Tanzania	Nepal	
-Djibouti	Gambia	Uganda	W.Samoa	
Afghanistan	Guinea	Burkina Faso	Laos	
	-Eq. Guinea	Guinea Bissau	-Vanuatu	
	-STP	Sierra Leone		
	-Togo	Mozambique		
n=8	n=22	n=9	n=1	
	Most Seriously Affected (MSAs, n=45)		
Chad	Benin	Lesotho	Bangladesh	+El Salvador
S.Yemen	Burundi	Mali	Myanmar	+Guatemala
+Egypt	Cape Verde	Mozambique	+Cambodia	+Guyana
Mauritania	+Cameroon	Niger	+India	Haiti
+Pakistan	C.Af.Rep.	Rwanda	Laos	+Honduras
Somalia	Ethiopia	+Senegal	+Madagascar	
Sudan	Gambia	SierraLeone	Nepal	
N.Yemen	+Ghana	Tanzania	W.Samoa	
Afghanistan	Guinea	Uganda	+SriLanka	
	GBissau	Burkina Faso		
	+Ivory Coast	+Kenya		
n=9	n=22	n=9	n=5	

Source: US Department of State. *Atlas of US Foreign Relations*, Dec. 1985, as updated.

LLDCs were defined in 1971 as states with a per capita GDP of less than $US100; an adult literacy rate
of less than 20%; and a share of manufacturing in total GDP of less than 10%. The GDP figure is
updated periodically to adjust for inflation (1986=$423).

MSAs were defined in 1974 as states with, among other criteria: a balance of payments deficit greater
than 5% of the value of its imports; a per capita income of less than $400 ; a high debt service ratio; a
low level of foreign exchange reserves; and a relatively high importance of foreign trade in the
development process.

+ = 15 states added to the n=40 LLDC list ; but....

- = 10 LLDCs were not "seriously affected." Result: n=40+15-10=45 MSAs.

V2.1e.ii - Council for Mutual Economic Assistance

Europe	Islamic	Africa	Asia	Latin America
		Members (n=10)		
Bulg.,Czech.			Vietnam	Cuba
E.Ger.,Hung.			Mongolia	
Pol.,Rom.,SU				
		Associate Member (n=1)		
Yugoslavia				
		Cooperation Agreements (n=3)		
Finland	Iraq			Mexico
		Observers (n=7)		
	Afghanistan	Angola,Ethiopia	Laos	Nicaragua
	S.Yemen	Mozambique		

109

V2.2. ECONOMIC WEAKNESSES

While data relating to productivity, investment, savings, reserves, and balances are indicative of inherent national economic strength, other measures can be cited which represent drains on a country's economy and weakness in the long term. Four indicators—inflation, unemployment, consumption, and debt—will be analyzed in this section.

The measures to be employed here will again draw attention to the global economic system of international capitalism and of the unequal relationship between the few advanced and the many developing states. Decisions relating to growth, savings, and investment made by major powers and the international financial institutions which they control, can virtually "export" to the periphery of the system some of the ills to be described next.

V2.2a. Inflation

The ravages of rampant inflation can wipe away the wealth generated by a nation's productivity and its hard-earned savings. Yet, more than half the states in the world typically have an inflation rate of more than 10% each year. Some appreciation of the political impact of this indicator might be gained by remembering that two recent American presidents (Ford and Carter) were ousted from office in large measure owing to the "double-digit" inflation (i.e., about 10-11% in each instance) that affected their country during the final years of their terms. Such an "inconvenience" would hardly have been noticed in many of the world's states, especially those in the African and Latin American zones where, Table V2.2a indicates, inflation even over an extended eight-year period is typically considerably greater.

In many developing countries an inflation rate of more than 100% in a given year is not unusual. Some recent (circa 1988-90) examples of high single-year inflation include, by zone, Yugoslavia 250%; Turkey 70%, Iraq 40%, Iran 30%; Zambia 100%, Nigeria 53%; Vietnam 700%, Sri Lanka 30%; Nicaragua 30,000%, Peru 2500%, Brazil 1700%, Argentina 1000%, Venezuela 85%, Uruguay 80%, Paraguay 30%, and Colombia 24%. Such times are often followed by periods of austerity involving devaluations of currency and other restrictive policies imposed by international lending institutions (and resulting in lowering many V2.1 measures of strength and of local government popularity and legitimacy) (Remmer, 1986; Mikesell, 1983; Killeck, 1984). Thus, it is important to take a multi-year perspective when analyzing this measure.

Table V2.2a presents statistics for the years 1980-88, based upon the World Bank's average annual rate of inflation measured by the growth rate of the GDP implicit deflator, the "most broadly based deflator showing annual price movements for all goods and services produced in an economy" (WDR89: 232).

V2.2b. Unemployment

Unemployment is a definite deficiency in the economic well-being of many countries. Unfortunately, accurate statistics for such a politically sensitive measure are often almost impossible to obtain. National definitions of unemployment vary from one country to another as regards age limits (at both upper and lower ranges), reference periods, criteria for seeking work, and treatment of persons temporarily laid off and those seeking work for the first time (especially women). There is also the problem of underemployment involving millions of people who work only on a part-time or seasonal basis (Bean, 1988).

Because of the nature of this book's inquiry, unemployment will be defined here as the failure of a state to provide some regular, full-time contribution to the economic enterprise of that society for all of its able-bodied citizens wishing to work. The OECD publishes monthly detailed data which conforms to this standard for its 24 members; in recent years unemployment has generally ranged from about 3% of the "economically active population" in Japan to just under 20% in southern Europe and Ireland.

Many other countries, however, grossly understate the jobless situation in their states when reporting to agencies such as the UN's International Labour Office. In its annual publication of statistics for about 70 countries in the developing world, the numbers reported are so unrealistically low (generally between 0.1 and 10%) that specific citations do not even merit a mention here; and in another 60-odd states in the world, no unemployment data is released at all. In communist countries, the official rate is zero.

In reality, the figure probably ranges from 25 to 50% for most countries in the developing world. Some statistics from newspaper accounts of states with political unrest due to unemployment in 1989-90 are Iran 50%; South African blacks 40-50%; Mozambique and Philippines, 40% each; Namibia and Dominican Republic 30%; Bolivia 25%; and Turkey, Vietnam, Nicaragua, and Venezuela, 20% each. One source has reported that in Africa only 10% of all adult males were engaged in regular labor for wages (*World Development Forum*, August 15, 1983: 4). Whatever the exact number, it has been estimated that some 750 million new jobs must be created in the developing world within the next generation just to maintain today's depressing employment levels (*Popline*, November, 1985: 3). The number of job seekers continues to increase because approximately 40% of the people living in these countries are under the age of 15 (see section V3.1) and will soon be entering the labor force.

Data is available on the percentage of the workforce in each sector of the economy (agricultural, industrial, service-related) for many countries, and on the growth rate of the labor force (which is nothing more than the growth rate of the 15-to-18-year-old age cohort). But because of the unreliability of the essential first statistic—the percentage of unemployed—nothing more will be said here other than to note this as a measure for which data goes a-begging.

V2.2c. Consumption

Consumption is the next topic to be analyzed under the category of economic weaknesses. The converse of this concept was covered above in section V2.1b when savings was calculated by subtracting total societal consumption (i.e., both government and private) from Gross Domestic Product. However, governmental consumption, depending on how it is targeted, need not be a drain upon a country's economic resources, and could even be a stimulus to greater productivity (Groth and Wade, 1984:19-40). It is at this point, thus, that the ideologies of capitalism and communism and the role of government in the economy must be discussed.

In theory, the economy in capitalist states is in private hands, whereas in communist countries all means of economic production and distribution are supposed to be under the control of the government. In reality, these theories are nowhere totally put into practice. Even in the most frontier capitalist of societies there is government regulation and promotion of certain parts of the economy (e.g., railroads, utilities, atomic energy); whereas in communist states, particularly since the accession of Mikhail Gorbachev and Deng Tsiao Ping in the USSR and China, respectively, there are many sectors of the economy open to capitalist penetration, particularly in the areas of investment and credit.

The role of the government, thus, can be used in either of the two prototypical economic models to advance the particular system. For domestic political reasons, most administrations do not like to admit they are going against the prevailing ideology. Thus, many developing states which proclaim themselves socialist actually have a very small role for the government in their economy, which is still primarily in private corporate (and, generally, foreign) hands. Similarly, many unabashed capitalist countries have a high degree of government spending, but for the purpose of stimulating and advancing (or protecting) domestic capitalist enterprise. Thus, although statistics on the size of the government in the economy must be interpreted with care (Clark, 1986: 123), some measures related to public expenditures and consumption will be discussed here.

Few sources present a complete global listing of states' Central Government Expenditures (CGE), perhaps because of the multiplicity of national accounting systems and the resulting lack of true comparability. In substantiation of its concern over military expenditures "as a percentage of Central Government Expenditures" (V1.2b), the Arms Control and Disarmament Agency's *World Military Expenditures and Arms Transfers 1989*, published in 1990 (referred to here as ACDA90), provides CGE statistics for some 124 states in 1988. Using the extrapolated data from the mimeographed "Country Rankings by Variable" yields information for an additional 20 states. The results are presented below in Table V2.2c.i.

Relative measures of comparative government expenditures are somewhat more accessible, being provided by two regularly appearing sources. ACDA provides data on CGE/GNP and CGE per capita for 144 countries. The results for the leading and lowest states in 1988 are reproduced in Table V2.2c.ii.

The World Bank also provides recent CGE/GNP statistics (WDR90: Table 11), but only for about half of the world's states (see Table V2.2c.iii(a)). Useful among this smaller sample, however, are estimates of the proportion of CGE devoted to five functional categories: defense; education; health; housing, social security, and welfare; and economic services. Section V1.2b above analyzed the percentage of government spending that went to the military; in section V2.4, analyses will be made as to whether government expenditures are being used to redistribute society's economic benefits in the form of education, health, and other social services. These numbers, however, must be used with caution not only because of the differences in national accounting systems, but because they often understate the amount of spending in large states where lower levels of government have autonomy and deliver many social services. There is, moreover, in WDR's Table 11 a sixth category of "other" spending which can account for 35% or more of total spending for as many as one-third of the states under consideration.

Finally, the World Bank has data on General Government Consumption (GGC) as a percentage of Gross Domestic Product for 103 countries. GGC includes current expenditures for goods and services by *all* levels of government, including capital expenditures on national defense and security. When this percentage is added to the percentage of private consumption (i.e., the market value of all goods and services purchased by households and nonprofit institutions), the total generally comes to within 10-15% of total GDP. Table V2.2c.iii(b) ranks the top and bottom states in order of GGC/GDP for 1988.

A perusal of the states appearing in Tables V2.2c.ii and .iii raises some questions with respect to the consideration of government consumption as an economic weakness and reveals some limits regarding ideological labels often applied to national economies. Many country placements in the tables are what one might expect if states were to be classified along a "socialist to capitalist" continuum. For example, to find such capitalist outposts as Spain, Turkey, Morocco, Pakistan, Uganda, Madagascar, Japan, South Korea, Guatemala, Ecuador, Peru, Bolivia, and Paraguay among the bottom tier of states (i.e., with the least governmental involvement in the economy) in at least three out of the four listings is not surprising. However, at the top of the tables where one might expect to find states of a more socialist orientation, the multiple appearances of states like Gabon, New Zealand, Australia, Malaysia, and Panama are somewhat unexpected.

At this point, it should be noted again that Table 11 in the World Bank's *World Development Report* also shows that Central Government Expenditures can go toward "economic services," a phrase which refers to spending associated with "the regulation, support, and more efficient operation of business, economic development, redress of regional imbalances, and creation of employment opportunities" (WDR88: 299). Included in such expenditures could be items of economic infrastructure similar to those mentioned earlier under savings and investment.

Such government aid to the economy is found in both socialist and capitalist countries, showing that the government expenditures alone are not a simple indicator of ideological orientation, and that public consumption could be regarded as either an economic strength or an economic weakness depending on the uses to which it is put, and whether it is spent efficiently or in a wasteful manner.

V2.2d. Deficits and Debt

Regardless of whether the government is spending moneys to help the the public or private sector, or to redistribute wealth, such consumption will represent a net drain on the economy in the long term if the government spends more than it has.

Table V2.2d.i presents deficits as a percentage of Gross National Product for 1988, and shows that relatively few government budgets (15 of 88) showed a surplus, and that the much-maligned $160 billion US deficit was not that large (only 3.2% of GNP) in a relative sense. In fact, it was below the weighted average of 3.6% for all states reporting to the World Bank in 1988 (WDR90: 199).

More important than government deficits which lead to domestic debt (which a country owes to itself) is external debt to parties in other states which can result in dependency in economics and a loss of autonomy in the political arena. In the 1980s a "debt crisis," fueled by private banks' feverish recycling of petrodollars, threatened the global capitalist system. By the end of the decade, nations on the periphery of the system owed more than a trillion dollars to lending institutions in the core of the capitalist world. The figure for public, or publicly guaranteed, debt was approximately $800 billion; if the external obligations of private debtors not guaranteed for repayment by a public entity were added, the figure was more than $1.266 trillion.

Regional shares of this debt were not evenly distributed, with Latin American debtors owing about 32% of the total amount. The approximate percentages for other zones in 1989 were Asia 21%, Africa 16%, and the Islamic world 7% (Bouchet, 1987). (Some nations of the wealthy European zone (led by the United States) are also in a net debtor category, but because of the resources upon which they can fall back (see V2.1), their economic situation is one of *interdependence*, and their political autonomy is not affected. Debt data is not even published on them by international lending institutions interested in development, and as a result their status will not be shown in the charts which follow in this section.)

For most countries on the Southern periphery of the global economic system, including those eastern European states tentatively integrating themselves into the world capitalist economy, the debt statistics which will be displayed next translate into dependence upon the wealthy nations in the core of the capitalist world (George, 1988). The amounts owed to lending institutions in the North represent huge obligations—more than $17 billion each for some 28 countries (above the dotted line in Table V2.2d.ii) led by Brazil and Mexico, each of whose debt is more than $100 billion.

There is often some confusion in the popular media between the total external debt figure (which includes IMF credits, short-term debt, and private debt not guaranteed by governments) presented in Table V2.2d.ii, and that external debt which is owed or guaranteed by governments, sovereign entities which are not about to go out of business or into international receivership (OECD, 1988). The latter figure (external *public* debt) represents about 70% of the total (some $911 billion in 1988, WDR90: Table 24), and about two-thirds of both these amounts are owed to private banks in western Europe, North America, and Japan. It is the unguaranteed private debt which represents a problem for entrepreneurs who overextended themselves by loaning too aggressively and raises some question as to just which parties in the global economic system are experiencing the most discomfort from the "debt crisis" (Kettell, 1986; Kahler, 1986; Schaten, 1987).

The banks may be worried about the absolute amount of money they have loaned; more relevant for individual governments, the focus of this study, is the percentage of external public (or publicly guaranteed) debt with respect to GNP, and the ability to pay back the interest on loans out of current external earnings. As the next two tables show, it would be nearly impossible for much of the debt of the countries at the top of these charts to be paid back. For 17 states in Table V2.2d.iii, the amount of the external public debt is greater than their annual Gross National Product; for another 30 states it is more than 50% of GNP.

From the perspective of the political managers of the global economy, repayment of the total loan in many cases is not the main issue. Many loans were made in the first place to keep the weaker members of the periphery functioning within the system, a kind of pump-priming measure by states at the core to produce "development" at the fringes. With the loans comes control over the nature of economic growth and, indirectly, over political systems as well. Total payback is not expected, and loans can be rescheduled and drawn out over longer periods of time for states in the South which "behave" (i.e., adopt economic policies desired by the lenders in the North).

In the best of circumstances, many of these states can barely afford annual debt *service* (the interest plus a small bit of the loan's principal) out of current external earnings. Table V2.2d.iv's "debt service ratio" (debt service as a percentage of exports) is greater than 25% of such earnings for 26 states, and greater than the 10% cap suggested by many LDC leaders for more than three-quarters of the 92 states on which data is shown.

The average debt service ratio for 81 low and middle income countries reporting to the World Bank in 1988 was 20.5%. In tracking this measure over a number of years, countries can be seen to slowly inch up in percentages owed until their debt is rescheduled (generally spread out over a longer period of time) at which point they drop down to a lower position on the list.

The call for a cap on debt service ratio is tolerable to lenders for it does not challenge the functioning of the system in principle; but demands for unilateral moratoriums, or total abandonment, of debt repayment are not acceptable for these challenge directly the control of the powers at the core (Debt Crisis Network, 1985; Lombardi, 1985). Earlier, in Table V2.2d.ii, the states of Latin America and east Asia led in total amounts owed; here, in Table V2.2d.iv, many countries of Africa and the Islamic world are also seen to be in precarious financial situations. It is these states which have a perennial public debt crisis which, when combined with the aid and trade relationships to be discussed in the next section, results in a permanent state of dependency (Wood and Mmuya, 1986).

V2.2a - Inflation, 1980-88

Europe	Islamic	Africa	Asia	Latin Am.
				Bolivia 482.8%
	Israel 136.6%	Uganda 100.7%		Argentina 290.5
Yugoslavia 66.7%		Zaire 56.1		Brazil 188.7
Iceland 38.0		Sierra L. 50.0^		Peru 119.1
Poland 30.5	Turkey 39.3	GBissau 49.0	Laos 46.5%^	Nicaragua 86.6
	Somalia 38.4	Ghana 46.1		Mexico 73.8
Portugal 20.1	Sudan 33.5	Mozzmbique 33.6		Uruguay 57.0
Greece 18.9		Zambia 33.5		Ecuador 31.2
		Tanzania 25.7		CostaRica 26.9
		STP 18.1	Madagascar 17.3	Colombia 24.1
		Gambia 13.9	Philippines 15.6	Paraguay 22.1
		S.Africa 13.9	Solomons 13.1	Chile 20.8
			N.Zealand 11.4	Jamaica 18.7
		Malawi 12.6	Bangladesh 11.1	El Salvador 16.8
Italy 11.0	Syria 12.7	Lesotho 12.2	Sri Lanka 11.0	DomRep 16.8
	N.Yemen 11.6	Zimbabwe 12.2	W. Samoa 10.5	Guyana 15.1
Spain 10.1	Egypt 10.6	Nigeria 11.6	Bhutan 8.9	Guatemala 13.3
		Swaziland 11.4	Nepal 8.7	Venezuela 13.0
Ireland 8.0		Botswana 10.0	Indonesia 8.5	
Sweden 7.5		Kenya 9.6	Mauritius 7.8	Haiti 7.9
France 7.1	Morocco 7.7	Cape Verde 8.9	Australia 7.8	Grenada 7.4
Finland 7.1	Tunisia 7.7	Guinea 8.3**		Bahamas 6.2
Hungary 6.4		Senegal 8.1	India 7.4	St. Chris 6.2
Denmark 6.3	Pakistan 6.5	Benin 8.0	Maldives 7.1	Barbados 6.1
UK 5.7	Cyprus 6.4	Cameroon 7.0		Antigua 6.1^
Norway 5.6		C.Af.R. 6.7		Dominica 5.8
			Comoros 5.8	Suriname 5.8
	Algeria 4.4	Togo 6.1	Fiji 5.7	
Belgium 4.8	S.Yemen 4.3		S.Korea 5.0	Trinidad 5.3
Canada 4.6		Rwanda 4.1		
Luxmbrg. 4.2		Burundi 4.0		
Austria 4.0		Ivory Coast 3.8	China 4.9	Honduras 4.7
US 4.0		Mali 3.7	Papua NG 4.7	
Switzerland 3.8			Vanuatu 4.3	St.Vincent 4.3
	Chad 3.2	Niger 3.6	Seychelles 3.9	
W.Germany 2.8		Burkina F. 3.2	Thailand 3.1	St.Lucia 3.9
Nethrlds. 2.0	Jordan 2.2	Ethiopia 2.1	Myanmar 2.1*	Panama 3.3
Malta 1.9		Liberia 1.5^	Japan 1.3	Belize 2.2
	Libya 0.1	Gabon 0.9	Malaysia 1.3	
	UAE 0.1	Congo 0.8	Singapore 1.2	
Alb.,Rom.-na	Qatar,Djib.-na	Eq.Guin.-na	Taiwan-na	Cuba-na
SU,Bulg.-na	Iran,Iraq-na	Angola-na	Mong.,NK-na	
Czech.,EGer.-na	Leb.,Afghan.-na	Namibia-na	VN,Cambodia-na	
	Bahrain (-1.3)			
	Kuwait (-3.0)			
	Saudi A. (-4.2)		Brunei (-4.4)	
	Oman (-6.5)			
n=24/30	n=22/28	n=35/38	n=28/33	n=32/33 (141)

Sources: WDR90f80-88, Table 1 and Box A.1, n=135;
plus: ^WDR89f80-87, n=4; *WDR88f80-86, n=1; **WDR87f80-85, n=1.

V2.2c.i - Central Government Expenditures (US $), 1988

Europe	Islamic	Africa	Asia	Latin America
US $1,118.0 bil.			Japan $480.7 bil.	
SU 694.0				
Italy 428.2			China 106.6	Brazil $67.0 bil.
France 408.9	Iran $55.1 bil.		Australia 61.9	Mexico 47.0
W.Ger. 364.0			India 61.3	
UK 280.0	Saudi A. 37.7			Venezuela 13.2
			S.Korea 28.5	
Netherlds.125.6	Egypt 28.0		Taiwan 19.6	Cuba 12.3
Canada 111.3	Israel 25.6		Indonesia 16.7	
E.Ger. 110.0		S.Africa $24.0 bil.	N.Zealand 15.3	
Sweden 72.4	Iraq 21.9e		N.Korea 14.4	Argentina 5.2e
Belgium 58.6	Algeria 19.8	Nigeria 8.7		Chile 5.0
Spain 53.2	Turkey 15.1		Malaysia 10.3	
Austria 51.5	Libya 11.2e	Zaire 3.1		Colombia 4.6
Romania 48.5		Cameroon 3.0e	Thailand 9.5	Peru 4.2
Czech. 43.5	Kuwait 9.8	Angola 2.9	Phil. I. 6.7	
Denmark 42.5	Pakistan 9.3	Zimbabwe 2.6		
Norway 41.8		Ivory Coast 2.2		Trinidad 2.1
Switzrld. 36.5	Morocco 4.8	Ethiopia 2.2	Singapore 3.5	Panama 1.5
Poland 35.5	Syria 4.6	Kenya 2.1		Urug.,Ec.-1.4
Finland 32.5		Senegal 1.6		Jamaica 1.4
Greece 29.3	UAE 3.9	Gabon 1.1	Vietnam 2.5	
Hungary 28.6		Zambia 1.0	SriLanka 2.4	Guat. 958 mil.
Bulgaria 25.7	Oman 3.6	Botswana 961 mil.	Mongolia 2.3e	Honduras 826
	Tunisia 3.5	Congo 833	Bangldsh 2.2	Dom.Rep. 754
Ireland 15.4	Qatar 3.4	Tanzania 758	Myanmar 1.4	Costa Rica 657
Portugal 14.6	Jordan 2.7	Ghana 741	Papua NG 997 mil.	El Salvador 608
		Mali 500e	Nepal 612	
Yugoslavia 3.1	N. Yemen 1.9	Niger 444		
Luxmbrg. 3.1e	Sudan 1.5	Guinea 396	Mauritius 490	Bolivia 576
Iceland 1.5e	Cyprus 1.3	Rwanda 365		Nicaragua 575
Albania 1.4	Lebanon 1.2e	Uganda 325	Cambodia 321	Suriname 543
	Bahrain 945 mil.	Burkina F. 318		Barbados 510
Malta 708mil.		Togo 293	Laos 300	
	S.Yemen 883	C.Af.R. 282		Paraguay 479
		Malawi 278	Fiji 285	Haiti 380e
	Afghan. 333	Liberia 245		
		Benin 230e		Guyana 220e
	Mauritania 190e	Burundi 207	Madagascar 174	
		Moz.,Swazi.-163		
	Somalia 150e	Lesotho 139		
		C.Verde 110e		
		Sierra L. 84		
	Chad 86	GBissau 76		
		Gambia 53e		
		Eq.Guinea 30		
		STP 7		
n= 30	n=27/28	n=37/38	n=25/33	n=25/33 (144)

Source: ACDA 1990 for 1988, Table I, n=144 , with e=extrapolated estimate for n=20.

118

V2.2c.ii(a) - CGE/GNP, 1988

Europe	Islamic	Africa	Asia	Latin America
E.Germany 59.0%	S.Yemen 89.4%	Botswana 79.7 %	Mongolia 85.5e%	Guyana 72.3e%
Greece 55.9	Qatar 82.5	GBissau 53.3	N.Korea 49.2	Nicaragua 54.3
Nethrlds. 55.7	Jordan 65.1	C.Verde 53.0e	Laos 48.0	Trinidad 52.8
Ireland 53.8	Israel 58.7	Zaire 52.0	N.Zealand 37.2	Jamaica 51.5
Italy 53.8	Libya 50.4e	Gabon 33.7	Sri Lanka 34.8	Suriname 46.7
Bulgaria 47.8	Oman 49.7	Zimbabwe 42.2	Cambodia 33.3	Cuba 35.5
Norway 46.1	Saudi A. 45.9	Congo 41.7	Malaysia 31.7	Barbados 32.6
Albania 44.6	Algeria 37.8	Ethiopia 39.4	Papua NG 30.3	Panama 32.5
....	....	....	....	....
USSR 27.5	Mauritania 21.4e	Rwanda 16.4	S.Korea 16.9	Ecuador 14.4
Iceland 26.5	Sudan 20.4	Mozambique 16.1	Thailand 16.8	Bolivia 14.3
Canada 23.6	Lebanon 20.2e	Burkina F. 15.6	Japan 16.8	Guatemala 12.5
US 22.9	Iran 17.3	Ghana 14.8	Phil. I. 16.5	Colombia 12.5
Switzerland 19.9	UAE 16.5	Benin 13.7	Taiwan 16.5	El Salvador 10.8
Poland 19.8	Afghanistan 10.8	STP 13.2	Myanmar 13.1	Peru 10.6
Spain 16.1	Chad 9.6	Sierra L. 9.7	Bangladesh 11.7	Paraguay 8.2
Yugoslavia 5.0	Somalia 8.9e	Uganda 7.3	Madagascar 10.1	Argentina 6.1e
n=30/30	n=27/28	n=37/38	n=25/33	n=25/33 (144)

Source: ACDA90f88, n=144, with e=extrapolated estimate for n=20.

V2.2c.ii(b) - CGE/capita (US $), 1988

Europe	Islamic	Africa	Asia	Latin America
Norway $9775	Qatar $10,364	Gabon $1038	N.Zealand $4570	Barbados $1984
Sweden 8629	Israel 5953	Botswana 808	Japan 3920	Trinidad 1722
Nethrlds. 8538	Kuwait 5082	S.Africa 684	Australia 3086	Suriname 1374
Luxmbrg. 8410	Libya 3325e	C.Verde 395e	Singapore 2062	Cuba 1189
Denmark 8290	Oman 2821	Congo 387	Mongolia 1120e	Venezuela 701
Italy 7452	Saudi A. 2439	Angola 351	Taiwan 982	Panama 624
France 7329	Bahrain 1968	Cameroon 315e	S.Korea 667	Jamaica 586
Austria 6803	UAE 1951	Zimbabwe 265	N.Korea 653	Mexico 563
....	....	....	....	....
USSR 2423	Turkey 278	Ethiopia 45	Laos 78	Colombia 146
Romania 2164	Morocco 205e	Burundi 40	India 75	Ecuador 135
Malta 1917	Mauritania 105e	Burkina F. 38	Cambodia 48	El Salvador 113
Portugal 1407	Pakistan 86	Malawi 36	Vietnam 38	Paraguay 109
Spain 1357	Sudan 62	Tanzania 31	Myanmar 36	Guatemala 108
Poland 936	Afghanistan 23	Sierra L. 21	Nepal 34	Dom.Rep. 106
Albania 438	Somalia 19e	Uganda 20	Bangladesh 20e	Bolivia 89
Yugoslavia 131	Chad 18	Mozambique 11	Madagascar 16	Haiti 61e
n=30/30	n=27/28	n=37/38	n=25/33	n=25/33 (144)

Source: ACDA90f88, n=144, with e=extrapolated estimate for n=20.

V2.2c.iii(a) - CGE/GNP, 1988

Europe	Islamic	Africa	Asia	Latin America
Hungary 58.3%	Israel 50.6%	Botswana 50.9%	N.Zealand 49.1%	Nicaragua 58.0%^
Ireland 58.1	Jordan 49.9	Gabon 45.9	Singapore 35.0	Panama 34.4
Nethrlds. 55.7	Oman 49.3	Zimbabwe 38.7	Papua NG 31.7	Chile 33.4
Belgium 52.4	Egypt 45.5^	Mali 35.5	Sri Lanka 31.4	Costa Rica 28.0
Italy 51.3	Tunisia 37.1	Ethiopia 35.2	Malaysia 31.3	Mexico 27.9
Greece 50.9^	Kuwait 35.7	S.Africa 33.1	Australia 28.7	Brazil 25.1
Portugal 45.3	N.Yemen 31.8	Togo 32.5	Mauritius 24.8	Uruguay 23.7
France 43.1		Malawi 32.0	Indonesia 22.7	Venezuela 21.8
....	....	....	....	....
Austria 40.1		Liberia 27.1	India 17.8	Ecuador 17.1
UK 37.6		Zambia 26.0	Japan 17.0	Bolivia 15.8
Spain 34.1	Morocco 29.2	C.Af.R. 25.7	Madagascar 16.8	Dom.Rep. 15.3^
Finland 30.2	Syria 28.3	Cameroon 23.4^	Thailand 16.4	Colombia 14.7
W.Germany 29.9	Iran 23.5	Tanzania 20.9^	Myanmar 16.3^	Peru 14.6
Canada 23.4	Turkey 22.0	Ghana 14.0	S.Korea 15.7	Guatemala 12.1
US 22.9	Pakistan 21.7	Sierra L. 13.7^	Phil. I. 15.6	El Salvador 11.3
Yugoslavia 7.5	Chad 9.0^	Uganda 10.3	Bangladesh 12.2^	Paraguay 7.2^
n=20/30	n=13/28	n=19/38	n=17/33	n=17/33 (86)

Source: WDR90f88, Table 11, n=73; plus ^WDR89f87, n=13.

V2.2c.iii(b) - GGC/GDP, 1988

Europe	Islamic	Africa	Asia	Latin America
Sweden 26%	Saudi A. 33%	Lesotho 28%	Papua NG 21%	Trinidad 22%
Denmark 25	Israel 31	Burkina F. 26	Australia 19	Bolivia 20
Greece 21	Jordan 27	Ethiopia 24	N.Zealand 15	Honduras 17
US 20	Kuwait 25	Zaire 24	Malaysia 14	Jamaica 15
Norway 20	Chad 22	Mozambique 22	Laos 12	Costa Rica 15
W.Germany 19	UAE 21	Congo 22	India 12	El Salvador 13
UK,Canada-19	N.Yemen 20	Gabon 22	Madagascar 12	Uruguay 13
France,Finld.-19	3 @ 16	3 @ 19	3 @ 11	Brazil 12
....	....	....	....	....
Ireld.,Belg.-16	3 @ 16	Niger 11	S.Korea 10	
Spain 15	Morocco 15	Mali 10	Nepal 10	5 @ 11
Italy 15	Pakistan 14	C.Af.R. 10	Sri Lanka 10	Mexico 10
Yugoslavia 14	Egypt 14	Guinea 10	Bangladesh 9	Venezuela 10
Portugal 14	Mauritania 14	Cameroon 10	Phil. I. 9	Guatemala 8
Switzerland 12	Somalia 10	Ghana 9	Indonesia 9	Peru 8
Hungary 11	Sudan 9	Uganda 8	Japan 9	Dom.Rep. 6
Poland 8	Turkey 9	Sierra L. 6	China 7	Paraguay 6
n=21/30	n=17/28	n=28/38	n=18/33	n=19/33 (103)

Source: WDR90f88, Table 9, n=103.

V2.2d.i - Government Deficit as a Percentage of GNP, 1988

(all %s are negative except those 15 above dotted line)

Europe	Islamic	Africa	Asia	Latin America
	Kuwait 23.5%	Botswana 21.9%		
Denmark 4.7%				
Sweden 2.2			S.Korea 1.6%	
Finland 0.3		Burkina F. 0.4	Thailand 1.0	Paraguay 1.5%^
Norway 0.2		Ghana 0.4	N.Zealand 0.7	
Yugoslavia 0.0		Gabon 0.1^	Mauritius 0.3	

Europe	Islamic	Africa	Asia	Latin America
Switzrld. 0.1*				Bolivia 0.1
Hungary 0.2				Chile 0.2
				El Salvador 0.3
				Colombia 0.7
UK 0.8			Myanmar 0.8^	Uruguay 0.7
W.Germany 1.5	Chad 1.3^		Australia 1.3	Guatemala 1.1
			Bangladesh 1.4^	
			Papua NG 1.9	Dom.Rep. 2.0^
France 2.3				Venezuela 2.1
Poland 2.4		Zaire 2.4**		Ecuador 2.4
		Togo 2.6		
	Syria 2.7	Lesotho 2.6^	Singapore 2.7	
Canada 3.0		Uganda 3.0	Phil. I. 2.8	
		Ivory Coast 3.1*		
US 3.2			Indonesia 3.3	
	Iran 3.9^	Cameroon 3.5^	Japan 3.5	
	Turkey 4.0			Argentina 4.1
Nethrlds. 4.3				Panama 4.4
Spain 4.5				
Austria 4.5	Morocco 4.6	Tanzania 4.7^		Costa Rica 4.7
	Tunisia 4.8			
		Mali 5.5		
		S.Africa 5.7	Nepal 6.2	Peru 5.7
	Egypt 6.6^	Kenya 6.6		
	Pakistan 7.0	Ethiopia 6.8		
		Liberia 7.9^	India 7.9	
			Malaysia 8.0	
Belgium 8.3		Malawi 8.7		
		Sierra L. 8.9^		
		Zimbabwe 9.1		
	Israel 9.9	Zambia 9.8		Mexico 10.0
Ireland 10.7		Nigeria 10.3		
Portugal 11.0				Brazil 12.2
	Oman 12.6		Sri Lanka 12.8	
	N.Yemen 13.1			
Italy 14.2				
Greece 14.4^	Jordan 15.7			Nicaragua 16.3
n=21/30	n=13/28	n=21/38	n=16/33	n=17/33 (88)

Source: WDR90f88, Table 11, n=71; ^WDR89f87,n=14, *WDR88f86,n=2; **WDR87f85,n=1.

121

V2.2d.ii - Total External Debt (US $ billions), 1988

Europe	Islamic	Africa	Asia	Latin America
				Brazil $114.6
				Mexico 101.6
			India $57.5	
	Egypt $50.0		Indonesia 52.6	
Poland $42.1	Turkey 39.6		China 42.0	Argentina 58.9
USSR 38.0Δ			S.Korea 37.2	
Greece 23.5	Israel 26.3^			Venezuela 34.7
Yugoslav. 21.7	Algeria 24.9	Nigeria 30.7	Phil. I. 30.0	
E.Germ. 20.0Δ			Malaysia 21.7^	Chile 19.6
Hungary 17.6	Morocco 19.9		Thailand 20.7	Peru 18.6
Portugal 17.2	Pakistan 17.0			Colombia 17.0
		Ivory Coast 14.1		
	Sudan 11.9		Bangladesh 10.0	Ecuador 10.9
Bulgaria 7.0Δ		Zaire 8.5		Nicaragua 8.1
	Tunisia 6.7	Zambia 6.5		Panama 5.6
Czechoslov. 6.0Δ		Kenya 5.9		Bolivia 5.5
	Jordan 5.5	Congo 4.8	Sri Lanka 5.2	
		Tanzania 4.7		Costa Rica 4.5
		Mozambq. 4.4		Jamaica 4.3
	Syria 4.9	Cameroon 4.2	Singapore 4.5^	
			Myanmar 4.3	DomRep 3.9
		Senegal 3.6		Uruguay 3.8
				Honduras 3.3
	N.Yemen 2.9	Ghana 3.1	Madagascar 3.6	
	Oman 2.9	Ethiopia 3.0		
		Zimbabwe 2.7	Papua NG 2.3	Guatemala 2.6
	S.Yemen 2.1	Gabon 2.7		Paraguay 2.5
Romania 2.8	Mauritania 2.1	Guinea 2.6		
	Somalia 2.0	Mali 2.1		Trinidad 2.0
		Uganda 1.9		El Salvador 1.8
		Niger 1.7		
		Liberia 1.6		
		Malawi 1.3		
		Togo 1.2	Nepal 1.2	
		Benin 1.1		
		Burkina 866 mil.		Haiti 823 mil.
		Burundi 794	Mauritius 861 mil.	
		Sierra L. 727	Laos 824	
	Lebanon 489 mil.	C.Af.R. 673		
		Rwanda 632		
	Chad 346	Botswana 499		
		Lesotho 281	Bhutan 68	
n=10/30	n=17/28	n=29/38	n=17/33	n=21/33 (94)

Source: WDR90f88, Table 21, n=88; plus ^WDR89f87, n=2;

supplemented by: ΔThe Economist, Nov. 18, 1989 for n=4 eastern European states.

V2.2d.iii - External Public Debt as % of GNP, 1988

Europe	Islamic	Africa	Asia	Latin America
		Mozambq.376.1%		
	S.Yemen 199.4%	Congo 205.0		Nicaragua 207.8%^
	Mauritania 196.2	Tanzania 139.8	Madagascar 192.7%	
	Somalia 185.2	Zaire 118.0	Laos 153.5	Jamaica 125.7
		Zambia 116.7		
	Egypt 123.4	Liberia 108.4^		Bolivia 109.9
		Nigeria 101.3		
		Mali 100.8		
....100%...				
	Jordan 94.0	Guinea 94.7		
		Ivory Coast 92.7		Ecuador 93.9
	Morocco 88.8	Malawi 85.7		
		Togo 81.6		CostaRica 81.8
				Panama 81.2
	Sudan 71.3	Burundi 69.8		Dom.Rep. 74.5
		Gabon 65.6		Chile 67.7
	Tunisia 61.7	Senegal 62.9	Phil. I. 60.1	Honduras 65.9
			Sri Lanka 59.9	
		Niger 55.1	Indonesia 55.7	Argentina 57.0
Hungary 54.9%		Sierra L. 54.6		
		C.Af.R. 53.3		
Poland 51.1		Kenya 51.0		
	Israel 50.1^	Ethiopia 50.6		Peru 50.3
....50%...				
		Benin 49.3	Malaysia 49.1	Trinidad 49.2
	Algeria 46.6		Bangladesh 48.5	Mexico 48.0
	Turkey 45.3			
		Ghana 43.9	Myanmar 45.3*	Venezuela 41.1
	N.Yemen 41.7	BurkinaF 43.4		
			Papua NG 38.3	Uruguay 38.7
Portugal 34.1		Botswana 37.9		Colombia 37.9
Greece 33.4	Pakistan 37.4	Zimbabwe 36.5	Nepal 34.6	Paraguay 35.9
		Lesotho 36.5	Mauritius 34.1	
	Oman 34.7			
Yugoslav 28.0	Chad 33.2	Uganda34.3	Bhutan 27.9	
			Thailand 23.5	El Salvador 30.4
		Rwanda 25.5		Guatemala 26.9
	Syria 25.0	Cameroon 23.6		Haiti 27.7
				Brazil 26.3
			India 18.7	
Bulgaria 10.8Δ			S.Korea 12.6	
E..Ger. 10.2Δ			Singapore 12.4^	
Czech. 4.0Δ				
Romania 1.9Δ			China 8.7	
USSR 1.5Δ				
n=10/33	n=16/33	n=29/38	n=17/33	n=21/33 (93)

Sources: WDR90f88, Table 24, n=82; supplemented by: ^WDR89f87, n=5;
*WDR88f86, n=1; and Δcalculated from Figures V2.2d.ii and V2.1a.i, n=5.

V2.2d.iv-Debt Service as % Exports (="Debt Service Ratio"), 1988

Europe	Islamic	Africa	Asia	Latin America
			Laos 143.5%	
E.Ger. 60.0Δ	Algeria 77.0%		Myanmar 59.3^	
Bulgaria 40.0Δ	S.Yemen 46.5	Ethiopia 37.4%	Madagascar 39.0	Colombia 39.8%
	Turkey 34.1	Angola 35.9	Indonesia 34.1	Bolivia 32.9
	Jordan 31.9			Argentina 32.6
Greece 29.8				Mexico 30.3
Portugal 29.3		Congo 28.7		Uruguay 27.3
				Guatemala 26.5
				Honduras 25.5
USSR 25.0Δ		Burundi 25.1	Phil. I. 25.8	Venezuela 25.5
....25%.......................................				
	Morocco 24.8	Zimbabwe 24.8		Paraguay 24.5
	Tunisia 24.2	Nigeria 24.2		Jamaica 24.2
Hungary 23.3	Pakistan 23.5			
	Mauritania 21.6	Guinea 21.9	India 21.8	
	Syria 21.1	Niger 21.1	Bangladesh 20.5	Ecuador 21.1
Czech. 20.0Δ		Ghana 19.7		
		Kenya 19.4		
		Senegal 18.4		
		Togo 18.3		
		Malawi 17.2	Malaysia 17.5	Costa Rica 17.4
	Israel 17.0^	Tanzania 17.1	Sri Lanka 17.2	
	N.Yemen 16.0		Papua NG 16.5	El Salvador 16.6
	Egypt 13.9	Mali 14.2		Chile 14.9
		Zambia 14.2		
		Uganda 14.0		
		Ivory Coast 13.0		Dom.Rep. 13.4
Romania 11.9*		Burkina F. 11.9		Nicaragua 12.9*
		Cameroon 11.9	Thailand 11.3	
Poland 10.0	Oman 11.3^		Mauritius 10.1	
....suggested 10% cap..				
Yugoslavia 9.7	Sudan 9.5	Rwanda 9.6	S.Korea 9.1	Trinidad 9.2
			Nepal 8.5	Haiti 8.8
		Mozambique 7.8		Peru 8.1
		Zaire 6.9	China 6.9	
		Gabon 6.2		
		C.Af.R. 5.9		
		Sierra L. 5.9		
		Benin 5.4		
	Somalia 4.9	Lesotho 5.2		
		Botswana 4.0		
	Chad 2.7	Liberia 2.5^		
			Singapore 1.4^	Panama 0.2
n=10/30	n=16/28	n=30/38	n=16/33	n=20/33 (92)

Source: WDR90f88, Table 24, n=81;

plus: ^WDR89f97, n=4; *WDR88f86, n=3; and ΔThe Economist 1989 for 1988, n=4.

V2.3. INTERNATIONAL CAPITAL TRANSFERS

In addition to lending, there are four main ways in which capital is exchanged between rich nations and poor nations—aid, trade, investment, and remittances. Much data can be found on aid and trade because of the centrality of governments in both processes. Statistics are somewhat less available regarding private investments and remittances which are made by transnational corporations and individuals not beholden to sovereign governments (Bornschier and Chase-Dunn, 1985; Moran, 1985; Jenkins, 1987; Paul and Barbato, 1985).

In the late 1980s, more than $100 billion in capital earmarked for "development" was transferred annually from rich nations to poor. This amount consisted of about $50 billion in Official Development Assistance (ODA); $15 billion in loans at market rates by states and multilateral development banks; $3 billion in export credits given or guaranteed by governments; and $35 billion in private flows consisting of direct investment and bank lending. The debt discussed in the previous section V2.2d included transfers from the last three categories. ODA, or aid, will be discussed in section V2.3b. The main focus next will be on two less predictable measures: private investment and worker remittances.

V2.3a. Investments and Remittances

Private Net Direct Investment is the amount invested in a country by nonresidents in enterprises in which they exercise significant managerial control; the net figure subtracts out the value of direct investment abroad by residents of the state noted. The annual amount has varied during the 1980s between $10 and $20 billion annually.

Recipient-state statistics on investment in the developing world experience wide swings from year to year, and are difficult to interpret for they might reflect a favorable environment for profit-taking which might not translate into "well-being" for the host country. Nevertheless, even in the grossest cases of exploitation there is some trickle-down effect. Table V2.3a.i displays investment statistics for 1988, arranged in order of the largest recipient states in each zone. The dotted line across the center of the table delineates the money flow—from the cash-rich countries of Japan, Saudi Arabia, and western Europe to the areas of profitable investment in southern Europe, east Asia, Latin America, and the United States.

Workers' remittances are important in about 50 (generally southern European and Islamic) states where the moneys that migrant workers (in northern Europe and in oil fields) send back home represent a significant contribution to economic well-being. In about half of these states this amount is higher than the amount of Net Direct Investment received. Data for 1988 is summarized in Table V2.3a.ii. Again, states below the dotted line are those from which the funds are being sent, and generally represent where the jobs are.

V2.3b. Aid

International transfers in the form of Official Development Assistance in recent years have totaled approximately $55 billion per year, of which more than 85% ($48.1 billion in 1988) comes from 18 states in the Organization for Economic Cooperation and Development (Poats, 1985). The total reflects both direct bilateral aid (about three-quarters of the total) and politically buffered contributions to international organizations and multilateral lending agencies such as the United Nations, the World Bank, and various regional development banks (Hancock, 1989).

The remaining aid comes from two dwindling sources of LDC income: OPEC countries ($4.7 billion in 1988, down from $9.6 billion in 1980) and communist states (less than $5 billion per year before the Gorbachev revolution in Soviet foreign policy began phasing out most programs in the late 1980s). The OPEC percentage of the total global aid package is about half what it was during its peak giving years of 1976-81.

In keeping with the ideology of development, most advanced states have endorsed in principle the United Nations target of 1% of GNP as the amount that should be transferred each year to the Less Developed Countries as Official Development Assistance. In reality, few wealthy states ever meet the 1% target, and the givers and receivers of aid are usually motivated by political ties not necessarily reflective of the respective states' levels of economic well-being (Brandt, 1980; Cunliffe and Laver, 1985).

Statistics on foreign aid transfers are difficult to interpret, requiring the consultation of several sources, distinguishing between commitments of aid and its actual delivery or distribution, and the separation of economic from military data. Although almost every developing country receives some form of external financial help, Table V2.3b.i lists only the major recipients in three summary categories: total assistance received, aid per capita, and aid as a percentage of Gross National Product.

With respect to the leading recipients of aid (those in excess of $300 million per year), part (a) of Table V2.3b.i shows the predominant positions of Israel and Egypt, each of whom is annually paid (mainly by the US, since the 1979 Camp David Peace Agreement) in excess of $1.2 billion. India, China, Indonesia, Bangladesh, and Pakistan also receive more than $1 billion each year, but this is not much on a per capita basis as evidenced by the disappearance of these states from part (b) of the table, which displays the top seven states in each zone or all those receiving more than $50 per year per capita. The centrality of economic assistance as a component of state income is seen in the comparatively high "aid as a percentage of GNP" statistics for the LLDCs of the African zone (all over 12% as compared to other zonal "leaders" as low as 2.8%) in part (c). Finally, the relatively high rankings in all three measures of Israel, Jordan, Somalia, Mozambique, Niger, Sri Lanka, Papua New Guinea, Nepal, El Salvador, and Honduras are noteworthy.

Table V2.3b.ii displays the official development aid given in 1988 by the 21 largest donors—the 18 nations of the Development Assistance Committee (DAC) of the OECD plus the 3 OPEC states still financially buoyant enough to make meaningful contributions. Out of a total GNP of more than $13 trillion, this amount of aid represented only about one-third of the UN target of 1% of GNP; since the country average was .61% of GNP, the discrepancy is accounted for by some of the wealthiest states not giving their fair share. The leading aid donor in absolute terms, the United States, gives about 21% of the OECD DAC total; as a percentage of GNP (ability to give), however, the US is next to the worst in the world.

With respect to the recipients of OECD DAC aid, the United States Agency for International Development (AID) annually publishes *US Overseas Loans and Grants and Aid from International Organizations,* a cumulative analysis of the beneficiaries of US economic aid going back to the start of the American foreign assistance program in 1949. The OECD's annual *Geographical Distribution of Financial Flows to Developing Countries* gives totals by receiving state for the most recent four-year period of commitments made by all members of its DAC. These references are helpful in analyzing relationships between givers and receivers of aid which are relatively consistent over the years, a subject more properly deferred to the V2.3d section on specific bilateral economic dependencies in both aid and trade.

Before the Soviet Union put a virtual end to its foreign aid program in 1988, statistics on communist state aid were maintained in the data bank associated with this project. In addition to the normal secrecy associated with these closed societies, methodological problems in gathering this data included the question of which communist state donors (e.g., USSR, eastern Europe, China) should be included, and whether to account for the concessionary trade arrangements made within the CMEA trading organization which integrated the socialist economies of about ten states (recall Table V2.1e.ii).

Employing a variety of methodologies and a multiplicity of sources (OECD, CIA, US State Department), it was discovered that total communist aid was somewhere between $3.5 and $7.0 billion a year, and that the ratio of Soviet to East European aid was about 4 to 1 (OECD, *Development Cooperation* 1986: 81-82; Bach, 1988). After a relatively vigorous foreign aid program in the 1960s and 1970s, China's assistance over the past decade has been negligible.

V2.3c. Trade

The final major category of international transfers—trade—yields additional insights into the workings of the global capitalist system. Balance of trade is in some respects as important an indicator of status as balance of power, and was covered earlier as part of the current account balance in section V2.1d. The trade deficit is directly related to the national deficit and debt (V2.2d). As a result an effort is made to get data on this measure for as many of the 162 states as possible. Fortunately, world trade figures, totaling some $5.3 trillion per year (in 1988) and reflecting most states' merchandise imports and exports, are published annually by several sources.

Table V2.3c lists the total volume of merchandise trade for the leading states in each zone, in both (i) absolute terms and (ii) as a function of GNP. The first list is frequently a function of a country's size. The second is a more interesting measure which shows how dependent a country is upon the outside world for its economic well-being; its leaders include some small island states or transit points (such as Belgium, Netherlands, Luxembourg, Bahrain, Qatar, Botswana, Taiwan, Singapore, Guyana, and Panama), which have total trade in excess of goods and services produced in their lands. At the other extreme are countries at war or which have turned inward and tried to be self-sufficient, and large countries with huge internal markets and (historically) not as great a need to trade with the rest of the world (e.g., US, USSR, India, China, Japan, Brazil, and Argentina).

The data in this section are based upon merchandise trade only and not trade in services, a growing category of many states' GNP. Hence, the familiar balance of trade (i.e., exports minus imports) measure is not employed here because it does not include services or other "invisibles" such as tourism, investment income, and workers' remittances (recall section V2.1d).

A measure related to trade which is significant, however, is "terms of trade," the ratio of a country's export prices to its import prices. This number, presented in Table V2.3c.iii, measures the purchasing power of exports in terms of the imports they buy and reflects problems with specific commodities which have wide fluctuations in value. A country's ranking on this scale shows the profitability of its international trade if it were conducted under barter arrangements. If the terms improve (i.e., export prices rise relative to import prices with respect to some base year) a given quantity of exports will buy more imports than before. The precise ratio for a state fluctuates widely from year to year, being affected by currency devaluations and exchange rates. The general pattern is for advanced industrial states with diversified economies to have positive ratios close to 100 (i.e., between 95 and 110), while developing nations (especially those dependent on exporting a single primary product) have wider fluctuations on the negative side of the ledger (between 65 and 95). Oil-exporting developing countries have seen the biggest swings in their prices in recent years: up by a total of 81% in 1979, down by more than 50% in the late 1980s.

V2.3d. Dependencies

This final section on international transfers will concentrate on identifying specific state dependency relationships with respect to aid and trade (Evans, 1979; Cardoso and Faletto, 1979).

Table V2.3d.i(a) through (d) shows leading recipients of aid from the four main sources of Official Development Assistance (ODA)—United States, other OECD DAC countries, OPEC, and multilateral agencies. There are two main sources for this data: the US Agency for International Development and the Organization for Economic Cooperation and Development. The AID data published in 1989-90 is more current, but only covers the United States and eleven international organizations. OECD statistics, which will be used here, are generally one year behind, but cover more sources (including bilateral data for all 18 OECD donors and 23 multilateral agencies such as three World Bank Group sources, five regional development banks and funds, two European Community granting agencies, six UN programs (UNDP, UNICEF, UNTA, UNHCR, UNRWA, World Food Program), six Arab OPEC agencies, and the International Fund for Agricultural Development). Because of fluctuations in annual donor commitments in a given year, it is not essential to present the latest information to get an appreciation of general patterns of dependence.

Table V2.3d.i(e) displays these dependencies for most of the 117 states reported on by OECD; the nine least dependent states are omitted for reasons of space. The prominence of strategic allies and client states such as Israel, Egypt, Pakistan, Philippines, and several Central American states among the top US aid recipients is notable. A similar pattern appears in the case of OPEC aid to largely Islamic recipients (Hunter, 1985; Benamara and Ifcagwu, 1987). Even among the OECD DAC there is some international "division of labor"—Japan in Asia, France among its former African and Islamic colonies, etc.—as donors concentrate their efforts in areas where they continue to seek markets, raw materials, and political influence (Brown, 1974; Galtung, 1971). A few recipient states—generally found at the bottom of Table V2.3d.i(e)—have succeeded in shifting their dependence from specific bilateral donors to multilateral agencies controlled only indirectly by their former patrons.

The paucity of European zone recipients of official development assistance will probably change (and to the detriment of many current Third World recipients) after 1990, as former communist countries move from the socialist camp to the periphery of the capitalist world. The prominence of (West) Germany as an actor in this area is already evident.

Trade dependencies relate to state reliance upon a few export commodities or upon a few buyers for these products (Johns, 1985; Emmanuel, 1972). Excessive concentration in any one group of commodities makes a country's economy extremely vulnerable to price fluctuations as well as crop failures due to weather conditions. Dependence upon one or two main trading partners leaves a state vulnerable to boycotts and political pressures.

With respect to *products,* three export commodity concentration indexes (XCIs)—of increasing methodological sophistication, and tending to identify the same states as having high dependence upon a few exports—will be analyzed in Table V2.3d.ii. The first measure (#1-CI) simply lists the percentage of exports accounted for by the top export product of each state, and the name of this commodity. The second measure (#3-CI) expresses the current US dollar value of the three most important exports of a country as a percentage of the total current dollar value of all merchandise exports. The third index (H-CI) is based upon the pioneering work of Alfred O. Hirschman (1945) and involves an extremely complex set of calculations which takes into account the concentration of a state's exports among a universe of 182 product categories identified by Standard Industrial Trade Classification (SITC) codes. The eight to ten most dependent states by these measures, presented in Table V2.3d.ii, are drawn from the 1988 *UNCTAD Handbook* published in 1989. (Although UN statistics in this area are somewhat dated by the time they are published, there is not much variation in state rankings from year to year.)

The relative strength of states in the European zone as compared with the other four zones (where the dependency of few of the top states is below 50% in any measure) is impressive. Countries in the Islamic and African zones are the most dependent, but in the former region the dependency is at least upon an export (oil) which is relatively scarce and for which there is some substantial demand and price. Many African states are highly dependent upon more expendable items (e.g., coffee and cocoa) which are also subject to wider price fluctuations and bad weather.

Trading *partner* concentration indexes can also be defined by calculating the percentage of exports purchased by the leading and top three buyers of a country's exports from the annual IMF *Direction of Trade Statistics Yearbook.* Table V2.3d.iii displays the results (a) of the 10 states most dependent upon a small number of purchasers of their exports, and (b) of the 15 states most dependent upon a single buyer of their products, along with the name of that partner. The bottom 5 states in part (a) have the greatest diversification among export partners and are least vulnerable.

The most dependent states are those scoring highest in Tables V2.3d.ii(a) (one main product) and .3d.iii(b) (one main buyer). There are 25 such states: Canada, Poland, Malta, Ireland, Norway, Iceland; Oman, Somalia, Libya, UAE, Qatar; Niger, Rwanda, Burundi, Congo, Nigeria; Brunei, Comoros, Indonesia, Maldives, Mauritius; Bahamas, St. Vincent, Mexico, and Bolivia.

V2.3a.i - Net Direct Private Investment (US $ millions), 1988

Europe	Islamic	Africa	Asia	Latin America
US $40,920				
Spain 5788			China $2344	Brazil $2681
				Mexico 2594
Belgium 1365			Thailand 1093	Argentina 1147
Italy 1337			Singapore 1066	
Greece 907	Egypt $973		Phil. I. 986	
Portugal 820		Nigeria $876	S.Korea 720	
			Malaysia 649	
			Indonesia 542	
Austria 294	Turkey 352	Angola 360	India 280	Colombia 186
	Israel 183			Chile 109
	Pakistan 145	Gabon 121	N.Zealand 119	Dom.Rep. 106
Ireland 91			Papua NG 89	Guatemala 96
	Morocco 85			Venezuela 89
				Ecuador 80
				Costa Rica 76
		Congo 43	Sri Lanka 43	Honduras 47
		Botswana 40		Peru 44
	Tunisia 59	Liberia 39		
	Libya 43	Sierra L. 39		
	Oman 33	Cameroon 34	Mauritius 31	Bolivia 30
		Rwanda 21		Trinidad 26
		Lesotho 21		
		Togo 12		
		Zaire 11		Paraguay 11
		Kenya,Guinea-7		Haiti 10
		Ghana 5		
		Zimbabwe 4		
Nethrlds. 2	Mauritania 2	S.Africa 1		
		Mali,Benin-1		
		Bur.,Uganda-1		
Yugoslavia 0	Jordan,Syria-0	BF,C.Af.R.-0	Nepal 0	
	N.Yemen 0	Malawi,Zambia-0	Madagascar 0	
	Chad,Sudan-0	Mozambique 0	Bangladesh 0	
----	----	----	----	----
Poland (-7)	Somalia (-11)			Uruguay (-2)
Norway (-23)	Algeria (-48)			Jamaica (-16)
				Panama (-36)
		Senegal (-73)		El Sal. (-55)
	Kuwait (-262)		Australia (-460)	
	Saudi A. (-1175)			
Finland (1752)				
Canada (-3306)			Taiwan (-3161)	
Sweden (-4406)				
France (-5986)				
Switzrld. (-6913)				
W.Ger. (-8722)				
UK (-13,078)			Japan (-34,710)	
n=19/33	n=18/28	n=27/38	n=18/33	n=20//33 (102)

Source: WDR90f88, Table 18, n=102.

V2.3a.ii - Workers' Remittances (US $ millions), 1988

Europe	Islamic	Africa	Asia	Latin America
Yugoslavia $4839				
Portugal 3381	Egypt $3386			
	Pakistan 2010		India $2850	
	Turkey 1755			
Greece 1675				
Spain 1413				
Italy 1229	Morocco 1289			
	Jordan 813		Bangladesh 737	
	Tunisia 539			
	Sudan 300		Phil. I. 388	Colombia $384
			Sri Lanka 357	
Austria 284	Algeria 279		N.Zealand 312	Dom.Rep. 328
	S.Yemen 253			Mexico 264
	Syria 210	Burkina F. $215		
	N.Yemen 190		China 129	El Salvador 126*
			Indonesia 99	
		Benin 87		
		Senegal 78		Jamaica 65
		Mali 49	Papua NG 42	Haiti 64
		Mozambique 33^		
		C.Af.R. 29		
		Togo 13		
		Tanzania 5*	Madagascar 8**	
		Cameroon 3		Nicaragua 3^
				Bolivia 1
			Mauritius 0	Guat.,Costa Rica-0
		Zaire 0	Nepal 0	Brazil,Trinidad-0
Poland 0	Chad 0	Sierra L. 0	Malaysia 0	Paraguay 0*
		Ghana (-2)		
		Kenya (-3)		
Sweden (-10)		Rwanda (-17)		
Belgium (-30)	Mauritania(-26)	Zambia (-21)		
		Botswana (-29)^		
		Nigeria (-34)		
		Niger (-45)		
Norway (-50)		Congo (-46)		
		Liberia (-51)		
Nethrlds. (-204)		Gabon (-151)		Venezuela (-203)
	Libya (-496)	Iv. Coast (-480)		
	Oman (-681)			
US (-820)				
Switzrld.(-1549)	Kuwait (-1179)			
France (-1950)				
W.Ger. (-4188)				
	Saudi A. (-4935)			
n=15/30	n=17/28	n=22/38	n=12/33	n=14/33 (80)

Source: WDR90f88, Table 18, n=73; supplemented by:
  ^WDR89f87, n=3; *WDR88f86, n=3; **WDR87f85, n=1.

132

V2.3b.i - Recipients of Economic Aid, Summary, 1988

Islamic	Africa	Asia	Latin America

(a) - Total Economic Aid Received (US $ millions)

Islamic	Africa	Asia	Latin America
Egypt $1537	Tanzania $978	India $2098	
Pakistan 1408	Ethiopia 970	China 1990	
Israel 1241	Mozambique 886	Indonesia 1632	
Sudan 918	Kenya 808	Bangladesh 1592	
	Zaire 580	Phil. I. 854	
	Senegal 568	Sri Lanka 599	
Morocco 482	Zambia 478	Thailand 563	
Somalia 433	Ghana 474	Myanmar 451	
Jordan 425	Ivory Coast 439		El Salvador $420
	Mali 427	Nepal 399	Bolivia 392
	Niger 371	Papua NG 379	
Tunisia 316	Malawi 366		Honduras 321
Turkey 307	Uganda 359	Madagascar 305	

(b) - Economic Aid Received per Capita (US $)

Islamic	Africa	Asia	Latin America
Israel $279.30	Botswana $127.70	Papua NG $101.90	
Jordan 108.80	Gabon 98.30		El Salvador $83.40
Mauritania 96.60	Senegal 81.20		Jamaica 80.30
Somalia 73.40	C.Af.R. 68.40	Mauritius 56.40	Costa Rica 69.90
	Lesotho 64.40		Honduras 66.40
	Zambia 63.30	Bhutan 30.30	Nicaragua 58.80
	Mozambique 59.30	Sri Lanka 30.10	Bolivia 56.70
Chad 48.90	Togo 58.90	Madagascar 28.00	
Tunisia 40.50	Mali 53.50	Nepal 22.20	
S.Yemen 32.30	Niger 51.10	Laos 19.60	Guatemala 27.00

(c) - Economic Aid as % of GNP

Islamic	Africa	Asia	Latin America
Somalia 42.9%	Mozambique 70.6%		
Chad 28.8	Tanzania 31.2		
Mauritania 18.4	Malawi 30.6	Madagascar 16.2%	
	Lesotho 26.3	Laos 14.4	
Jordan 9.3	Mali 22.0	Bhutan 14.0	Bolivia 9.1%
Sudan 7.8	C.Af.R. 17.5	Nepal 13.0	El Salvador 7.7
S.Yemen 7.2	Ethiopia 17.4	Papua NG 10.8	Honduras 7.3
Egypt 4.3	Burundi 17.1	Sri Lanka 8.5	Jamaica 6.0
N.Yemen 3.8	Burkina F. 16.0	Bangladesh 8.2	Haiti 5.9
Pakistan 3.7	Niger 15.5	Myanmar 5.1*	Nicaragua 4.4^
Tunisia 3.2	Togo 14.7		Costa Rica 4.0
Israel 2.8	Zambia 12.0	Mauritius 3.0	Guatemala 2.9

Source: WDR90f88, Table 20, n=97;
   supplemented by: ^WDR89f87, n=2; *WDR88f86, n=1.

Net Disbursements ($ mil.)		as % of GNP (UN Target)	
US	10104	#Saudi Arabia	2.70%
Japan	9134	Norway	1.10
France	6865	Netherlands	0.98
W.Germany	4731	Sweden	0.89
Italy	3193	Denmark	0.88
UK	2645	France	0.72
Canada	2347	Finland	0.59
Netherlands	2231	#Libya	0.52
#Saudi Arabia	2098	Canada	0.50
Sweden	1590	Australia	0.46
Australia	1101	#Kuwait	0.41
Norway	985	Belgium	0.40
Denmark	922	W.Germany	0.39
Switzerland	617	Italy	0.39
Finland	608	Japan	0.32
Belgium	597	Switzerland	0.32
Austria	301	UK	0.32
#Libya	129	New Zealand	0.27
#Kuwait	108	Austria	0.24
New Zealand	104	US	0.21
Ireland	57	Ireland	0.20
TOTAL	$50.47 bil.	AVERAGE	0.61

Source: WDR90f88, Table 19. (6 of the 24 OECD states are not in its DAC: Greece, Turkey, Iceland, Luxembourg, Portugal, and Spain.)

= OPEC states (3 of 13 which are significant aid givers).

V2.3c.i - Top Trading Nations (Total X+M, US $ billions), 1988

Europe	Islamic	Africa	Asia	Latin America
US $774.6			Japan $448.0	
W.Ger. 571.6			#Hong Kong 127.1	Brazil $48.4
France 338.4			S.Korea 112.5	Mexico 39.6
UK 334.5			Taiwan 105.0	
Italy 264.0	Saudi A. $43.6		China 102.8	Venezuela 21.8
Canada 223.5	Turkey 26.0		Singapore 83.0	Cuba 15.6^^
Nethrlds. 202.9	Iran 25.1*		Australia 54.6	Argentina 14.5
USSR 186.2*	Israel 24.6		Malaysia 37.4	
Belg.-Lux.180.1		S.Africa 36.4	India 37.1	
	Iraq 19.3		Indonesia 35.4	Chile 11.9
Switz. 107.0	UAE 19.2	Nigeria 13.7	Thailand 33.7	Colombia 9.8
Spain 100.9	Egypt 15.3			
Sweden 95.7	Algeria 15.1	Zaire 4.2		Peru 5.4
Austria 64.7	Kuwait 12.5	Iv. Coast 3.9		Panama 5.2
E.Germany 55.1*	Libya 12.0	Cameron 3.1	N.Zealand 16.8	Ecuador 3.9
Denmark 54.3	Pakistan 11.9	Kenya 3.0	Phil.I. 15.2	
Norway 45.7		Zimbabwe 2.9		Costa Rica 2.7
Finland 42.6	Morocco 8.4	Botswana 2.5	Brunei 7.8^	Guatemala 2.6
Czech. 41.4*	Tunisia 6.1	Gabon 2.2	Bangladesh 4.2	Uruguay 2.6
Ireland 34.3	Oman 5.8	Ghana 2.0		Dom.Rep. 2.5
	Bahrain 5.5^	Zambia 2.0		Bahamas 2.4^
Bulgaria 27.0*		Senegal 1.9	SriLanka 3.7	Trinidad 2.4
Portugal 26.3	Qatar 3.7^	Angola 1.8*	N.Korea 3.7^^	Jamaica 2.3
Yugoslavia 26.1	Jordan 3.6	Tanzania 1.6	Papua NG 3.1	
Poland 25.3	Syria 3.6	Congo 1.5	Vietnam 2.9º	Honduras 1.9
Romania 24.0º		Ethiopia 1.5	Mauritius 2.2	Paraguay 1.8
Hungary 19.2	Lebanon 2.5º			El Salvador 1.6
Greece 17.4	N.Yemen 2.2	Guinea 1.1	Myanmar 910 mil.	Bolivia 1.2
	Afghan. 2.0º	Burkina F. 946m.	Mongolia 884^	Nicaragua 1.0
	Sudan 1.7	Uganda 816	Nepal 814	
Iceland 3.1^		Mozambique 810		
	Mauritan.786mil.	Niger 799	Madagascar 664	Surinam.613^mil.
	Togo 745	Mali 768		
		Laos 246	Haiti 507	
	S.Yemen 678	Malawi 713	Bhutan 113º	
	Chad 514	Liberia 690		
	Somalia 412	Benin 638		
		Lesotho 589	Solomons 104^	Belize 218^
		Rwanda 483		
		C.Af.R. 368	Seychelles 95^	St.Lucia 178^
		Burundi 288	Maldives 89^	Antigua 157^
		Sierra L. 262	Vanuatu 80^	St.Chris. 105^
		Gambia 139^	W.Samoa 62^	St.Vincent 105^
	Djibouti 85^	GBissau 74^	Cambodia 31^^	Grenada 85^
		C.Verde 70^	Comoros 30^	
Albania-na		Namib.,Swazi.-na		Barbados-na
Malta-na	Cyprus-na	STP,Eq.G.-na	Fiji-na	Dominica-na
n=28/30	n=27/28	n=34/38	n=32/33	n=31/33 (152)

Source: WDR90f88, *calculated* from Table 14, n=114; supplemented by: ºWDR89f97, n=5;
  *WDR88f86, n=6; ^Clements 88f86, n=23; ^^CIA88f86, n=4.
#Hong Kong, 2nd in Asia, not one of 162 states studied here.

V2.3c.ii - Top Trading Nations, X+M as % GNP, 1988

Europe	Islamic	Africa	Asia	Latin America
			Singapore 351.7%	
		Botswan.204.1%^	Brunei 219.4^	Guyana 141.0%^
	Bahrain 177.4%^		Malaysia 114.0	
Ireland 126.6%			Mauritius 110.0	Panama 106.1
Belg.-Lux.-118.6			Taiwan 103.6^	St. Vincent 105.0^
			Papua NG 101.7	St.Chris 105.0^

Europe	Islamic	Africa	Asia	Latin America
Nethrlds. 94.4	Qatar 90.2^	Zambia 90.9	Maldives 89.0^	Bahamas 92.3^
	Mauritania 87.3	Lesotho 84.1		
Hungary 73.6	Lebanon 83.3^	Congo 78.9	Vanuatu 80.0^	St. Lucia 89.0^
Portugal 69.9	Oman 82.9	Zaire 73.7		Jamaica 86.9
	UAE 81.0	Gambia 69.5^	S. Korea 74.4	
Iceland 62.0^		Liberia 69.0^		Belize 72.7
	S.Yemen 67.8	Gabon 66.7		
Sweden 59.0	Tunisia 67.8		W. Samoa 62.0^	Chile 61.7
Switz. 58.9	Israel 64.6	Togo 57.3	Thailand 61.8	Trinidad 60.0
Denmark 57.7	Afghan. 64.5^	Mozambq. 54.0		Cuba 59.1^
	Jordan 61.0	Burkina F. 52.5	Sri Lanka 52.9	Costa Rica 58.6
Austria 55.0	Chad 57.1	Malawi 50.9	Solomons 52.0^	Suriname 55.7^
Norway 54.4	Libya 52.6	Zimbabwe 48.3		Antigua 52.3^
	Saudi A. 50.2	S.Africa 46.7	N.Zealand 48.0	Dom.Rep. 50.0
Canada 50.7		Iv. Coast 45.3	Indonesia 46.0	Honduras 46.3
W.Germany 50.5	Kuwait 46.6	Guinea 45.7		Grenada 42.5^
Finland 45.8	Egypt 46.2	Nigeria 42.9		
UK 45.7	Morocco 42.2	Mali 42.7		Paraguay 38.3
Yugoslavia 43.9	Somalia 41.2	Senegal 41.3		Venezuela 35.7
Bulgaria 41.7^	N.Yemen 40.7	Tanzania 40.0	Phil.I. 40.3	Ecuador 34.5
	Turkey 37.7		Bhutan 37.7^	Nicaragua 34.4
France 37.6		Benin 37.5	Mongolia 35.4^	Uruguay 33.8
Greece 36.3	Iraq 34.2^	GBissau 37.0^	Laos 35.1	Guatemala 33.3
Poland 35.9		Niger 36.3		El Salvador 31.9
		Kenya 36.1		
Italy 34.5		Ghana 35.7		Bolivia 30.8
		C.Verde 35.0^	Seychelles 31.7^	
Spain 33.4		C.Af.R. 33.5	Madagascar31.6	Mexico 26.9
	Pakistan 32.0		China 28.6	Colombia 26.3
E.Germany 28.0^		Cameroon 27.4	Australia 26.8	
Czech. 27.4^	Djibouti 28.3^	Ethiopia 25.6	Nepal 25.4	
	Algeria 26.9		Vietnam 22.8^	Haiti 21.1
		Burundi 24.0	Bangladesh 22.7	Peru 20.1
		Sierra L. 23.8^		
		Rwanda 23.0	Japan 17.4	Argentina 18.3
			Comoros 15.0^	
	Syria 18.5	Uganda 18.1		Brazil 15.5
Romania 16.4^		Angola 16.1^	N.Korea 14.2^	
US 15.9	Sudan 14.9		India 13.4	
	Iran 9.7^		Myanmar 9.8^	
SU 7.6^			Cambodia 3.4^	
n=28/30	n=27/28	n=34/38	n=32/33	n=31/33 (152)

Source: *Calculated* from Tables V2.3c.i and V2.1a.i, for 1988 or ^other.

136

V2.3c.iii - Terms of Trade, 1988 (1980 = 100)

Europe	Islamic	Africa	Asia	Latin America
			Japan 157	
Yugoslavia 120				
Canada 119			India 119	
US 118				Brazil 117
Poland 116	Turkey 115		Mauritius 117	
Finland 114				
Ireland 112			Bangladesh 111	
			Phil. I. 110	
Italy 108		Rwanda 108	N.Zealand 110	
Portugal 107		Zambia 107	S.Korea 108	
Denmark 107	Pakistan 106			
W.Germany 106	Mauritania 104	Ethiopia 104	Taiwan 105	Panama 104
Spain 103	Morocco 103	Liberia 103		Honduras 102
Switzrld. 103	Jordan 102		Sri Lanka 102	Paraguay 102
France 101			Singapore 101	Haiti 101
Austria 98				Uruguay 99
Sweden 95		Zaire 96		Costa Rica 98
		Senegal 96	Madagascar 95	Jamaica 97
		Sierra L. 94		
		Tanzania 94		Chile 94
		C.Af.R. 94	Nepal 93	
		Benin 94		
UK 93	Israel 92	Ivory Coast 92		
Nethrlds. 91	Somalia 91	Kenya 91		
Greece 89			Papua NG 89	Guatemala 87
Belgium 89	Sudan 86	Mali 88		El Salvador 86
		Niger 83		Argentina 86
		Zimbabwe 83	China 84	Nicaragua 84
		Burundi 81	Thailand 82	
		Togo 80		Peru 80
	Tunisia 77	Uganda 78		
Hungary 75	S.Yemen 76	Ghana 78		Dom.Rep. 76
		S.Africa 73	Malaysia 74	
		Malawi 72	Australia 74	
			Myanmar 72	
Norway 67	Egypt 62	Burkina F. 69	Indonesia 70	Colombia 68
	Syria 56	Cameroon 64		Mexico 67
	UAE 54			
	Saudi A. 54	Gabon 54		Bolivia 57
	Kuwait 54			Trinidad 55
	Libya 47	Congo 49		Ecuador 50
	Algeria 41			
	N.Yemen 40	Nigeria 40		Venezuela 41
n=21/30	n=18/28	n=26/38	n=19/33	n=21/33　(105)

Source: WDR90f88, Table 14, n=105.

V2.3d.i - Measures of Official Development Aid (US $ mil.), 1987

Europe	Islamic	Africa	Asia	Latin America

(a) - Commitments from United States

Europe	Islamic	Africa	Asia	Latin America
	Israel $1,225.3			El Salvador $407.1
	Egypt 848.6	Mozambique $60.5	Phil. I. $329.7	Honduras 201.4
	Pakistan 332.5	Tanzania 58.1	Bangladesh 189.5	Guatemala 184.8
	Jordan 110.8	Zaire 52.7	India 168.1	Costa Rica 178.2
		Senegal 47.2	Indonesia 124.2	Jamaica 108.1
	Morocco 91.1	Kenya 47.0		Haiti 101.8
	Sudan 88.2	Liberia 38.1	Sri Lanka 52.6	Bolivia 83.8
	Tunisia 46.9	Cameroon 32.2		Peru 63.7
	Somalia 46.5	Niger 28.5		Dom.Rep. 52.7
	N. Yemen 25.6	Ghana 24.9	Thailand 29.3	Mexico 52.6
	Turkey 21.3	Zambia 22.3		Ecuador 44.4
n=0	n=10/17	n=10/38	n=6/17	n=11/22 (37/98)

(b) - Commitments from 17 Other* OECD DAC States

Europe	Islamic	Africa	Asia	Latin America
	Pakistan $809.9	Tanzania $768.4	India $1919.4	
	Turkey 772.1	Mozambique 466.9	Indonesia 1774.7	
	Egypt 559.3	Kenya 451.8	China 1287.3	
	Somalia 414.9	Ethiopia 421.5	Bangladesh 728.5	
	Morocco 348.8	Senegal 406.7	Phil. I. 689.9	
	Sudan 339.2	Zaire 360.8	Thailand 579.9	
	Tunisia 279.8	Zambia 328.6	Myanmar 390.9	
	Syria 278.9	Ghana 286.5	S.Korea 382.6	Brazil $202.3
		Cameroon 266.5	Papua NG 336.6	Peru 192.4
		Burkina F. 252.9	Nepal 276.0	Bolivia 174.6
		Niger 229.6	Sri Lanka 267.8	
	Israel 143.1	Mali 218.1	Madagascar 167.7	Argentina 143.1
	Chad 141.9	Zimbabwe 218.0		Paraguay 134.0
	N.Yemen 121.4	Ivory Coast 215.8	Malaysia 112.1	Ecuador 92.0
n=0	n=11/20	n=14/31	n=13/20	n=6/23 (44/94)

*other than US; see names in Table V2.3b.ii. (US amount subtracted from DAC total in OECD data.)

(c) - Commitments from Arab OPEC Countries

Europe	Islamic	Africa	Asia	Latin America
	Syria $538.6			
	Jordan 459.6			
None	Sudan 267.8			None
	N.Yemen 149.2			
	Egypt 125.1	Sierra L. $23.0	Indonesia $42.4	
	Turkey 29.5	Mozambique 10.8	India 37.7	
	Tunisia 22.6	Rwanda 10.8	China 22.3	
	S. Yemen 16.4	Ghana 8.7	Vietnam 14.7	
	Mauritania 15.2		Bangladesh 11.9	
	Pakistan 10.9	Mali 5.9		
	Bahrain 10.6	Guinea 5.6	Nepal 8.0	
	Iraq 10.0	Zambia 5.0	Papua NG 7.2	
n=0	n=12/15	n=7/15	n=7/9	n=0 (26/39)

Source: *Calculated* from OECD, *Geographical Distribution*, 1989 for 1987.

Table V2.3d.i (continued)

Europe	Islamic	Africa	Asia	Latin America

(d) - Commitments from 26 Multilateral Agencies*

Europe	Islamic	Africa	Asia	Latin America
	Pakistan $500.6		India $1083.5	
		Senegal $438.4	Bangladesh 945.2	
	Sudan 322.8	Zaire 410.2	China 743.0	
	Somalia 223.1	Ghana 404.6		
		Ethiopia 351.5	Nepal 278.5	
		Tanzania 334.3	Sri Lanka 260.9	
		Uganda 299.2	Indonesia 247.2	El Sal. $205.2
	Chad 178.0	Mozambique 295.5	Madagascar 245.1	
	Egypt 138.1	Guinea 237.2		Bolivia 155.1
	Mauritania 133.2	Niger 205.8	Laos 114.2	
	N.Yemen 102.2	Kenya 160.4	Myanmar 110.9	Ecuador 90.1
n=0	n=7/20	n=10/31	n=9/22	n=3/23 (33/96)

*=includes World Bank Group (IBRD, IDA, IFA); regional development banks and funds; EEC's
EDF and EIB); six UN programs; six Arab OPEC agencies, and the IFAD.

(e) - Dependence upon Leading Source of ODA, 1987

Europe	Islamic	Africa	Asia	Latin America
	Israel 89% US	Congo 81% Fr.	Vietnam 96%CMEA	Cuba 94%CMEA
	Afghan. 85 CMEA	Iv.Coast 70 Fr.	S.Korea 86 Jap.	Paraguay 75 Jap.
Port.82%WGer.	Bahrain 84 OPEC	Gabon 67 Fr.	Taiwan 73 WGer.	Belize 75 US
	Jordan 66 OPEC	Liberia 58 EEC	Thailand 67 Jap.	Costa Rica 75 US
Greece 71WGer.	Oman 64 US		Indonesia 61 Jap.	Antigua 73 UK
	Syria 64 OPEC	Angola 43 EEC	Singapore 59 Jap.	Honduras 63 US
	Egypt 51 US	Togo 41 IDA	Myanmar 56 Jap.	Guatemala 62 US
	Turkey 49 WGer.	Ghana 40 IDA	Papua NG 55 Austrl.	El Sal. 61 US
	Iran 48 WGer.		Phil. I. 54 Jap.	Bahamas 57 UN
	Somalia 47 It.	Eq.Guinea 34 Fr.		Dom.Rep. 57 US
	Djibouti 45 Fr.	Ethiopia 33 It.	Solomons 42 EEC	Suriname 56 EEC
	Algeria 44 Fr.	Swaziland 32 EEC	Malaysia 42 Jap.	St.L. 56 CarDB
	Cyprus 44 US		Seychelles 41 Fr.	Nic. 53 CMEA
	Morocco 43 Fr.	Cameroon 28 W.Ger	Comoros 50 Fr.	St.Chris. 50 US
	Iraq 40 OPEC	Zaire 28 IDA	Fiji 39 Austrl.	
Yugo.37WGer.	N.Yemen 38 OPEC	Uganda 28 IDA	Cambodia 37 UN	Haiti 43 US
	Tunisia 30 It.	Guinea 27 EEC	Mauritius 35 EEC	Argentina 43 It.
		Botswana 27 AfDF	China 35 Jap.	Trinidad 43 UN
	Sudan 26 OPEC	Nigeria 24 US	Laos 33 AsDB	Gren. 43 CarDB
	Lebanon 26 OPEC	Sierra L. 24 EEC	Nepal 31 Jap.	Guyana 40 US
	Chad 24 EEC	Kenya 23 EEC	Madagascar 31 IDA	St.Vincent 37 UK
	S.Yemen 23 UN	Tanzania 23 It.	Sri Lanka 30 Jap.	Chile 36 WGer.
	Pakistan 23 AsDB	Burundi 22 EEC	Vanuatu 28 EEC	Uruguay 34 US
	Mauritania 21 IDA	Senegal 22 EEC	India 26 IDA	Brazil 33 WGer.
		Burkina F. 22 Fr.	W.Samoa 26 Jap.	Mexico 32 US
		Benin 21 EEC	Bangladesh 23 AsDB	Panama 29 UK
		Rwanda 20 EEC		Ecuador 28 IDA
		GBissau 20 AfDF		Peru 23 WGer.
		Malawi 20 EEC		Bolivia 22 IDA
		Lesotho 19 UN		Colombia 20 Fr.
n=3/3	n=23/23	n=27/34	n=25/35	n=30/32 (108)

Source: *Calculated* from OECD, *Geographical Distribution*, 1989 for 1987.

V2.3d.ii - Export Commodity Concentration Indexes

Europe	Islamic	Africa	Asia	Latin America

(a) - #1-CI, Top Export Only, Coded by Name

Europe	Islamic	Africa	Asia	Latin America
Iceland 60.0 fish	Iraq 95.5 oil	Uganda 94.8^coffee	Seychell.80.6petrp.	Baham.77.5 petrp.
Malta 34.9 clothg.	Iran 94.7 oil	Guinea 90.6^ ore	Comoro 78.2^ spices	Cuba 75.1 sugar
Norway 33.3 oil	Oman 91.4 oil	Nigeria 90.1 oil	Fiji 67.8 sugar	Suriname 64.5 ore
Canada 26.2 auto	Libya 87.9 oil	Congo 88.5 oil	Brunei 56.1 oil	Ecuador 64.3 oil
Finland 22.1paper	Qatar 87.9 oil	Zamb.87.7 copper	W.Samoa 54.9copra	El Sal. 62.7 coffee
Ire. 18.0 mach.	Saudi A. 83.0 oil	Brndi.84.0 coffee	Vanuatu 54.3 nuts	Barbad.58.9 mach.
Czech. 17.3 mach.	S.Yem.82.4^petrp.	Gabon 83.9 oil	Maldives 47.6 fish	Mexico 55.5 oil
UK 17.0 oil	Somalia79.4 anim.	Rwand.80.8coffee	Indonesia 47.6 oil	St.Lucia 54.1 fruit
Portug.17.0clothg.	UAE 78.2 oil	Niger 80.8 Uran.	Maurits. 46.7sugar	St.V. 52.4^fruit
Poland 14.5 coal	Bahrain 68.7petrp.	Angola 76.2 oil	Sri Lanka 39.2 tea	Bolivia 51.9 gas
n=24/30	n=27/28	n=33/38	n-26/33	n=32/33 (142)

Abbreviations: auto-automobiles, motor vehicles; clothg=clothing; ore=iron or non-ferrous base
   metal ores; oil=crude oil; petrp=petroleum products; seeds=oil seeds, nuts, and kernels;
   Uran.=uranium and other radioactive materials; anim.=live animals; mach.=machines.

(b) - #3-CI, Sum of %s of Exports of Top Three Commodities

Iceland 78.6	Somalia 99.2	Niger 100.0	Brunei 99.94	Bahamas 94.8
Norway 56.1	Algeria 97.4	Uganda 97.9^	Comoros 94.8^	Bolivia 91.3
Malta 53.6	Saudi A. 96.7	Gabon 95.8	Maldives 91.4^	Cuba 90.5
Canada 36.3	Iraq 96.3	Guinea 94.4^	Seychelles 90.4	Trinidad 87.6
Finland 35.7	Iran 96.2	Congo 94.2	Fiji 82.7	Suriname 85.4
Ireland 31.0	Libya 95.9	Burundi 94.1	Solomons 79.9	Guyana 82.3^
Sweden 29.8	Oman 95.4	Nigeria 93.1	Mauritius 79.1	Barbados 81.4
Czech. 28.4	Mauritan. 94.8	Zambia 91.2	Vanuatu 77.7	Paraguay 79.4
n=24/30	n=27/28	n=33/38	n=27/33	n=33 (144)

(c) - H-CI, Concentrations Within 182 SITC Categories

Iceland 62.0	S.Yemen 97.0	Guinea 95.2	Seychelles 81.1	Cuba 73.3
Malta 38.1^	Iraq 96.8	Nigeria 94.3	Comoros 78.0	Bahamas 67.1
Norway 33.8	Iran 96.5	Uganda 93.2	Vanuatu 72.6	Venezuela 65.2
Canada 24.3	Libya 92.4	Congo 89.4	Fiji 68.3	St.Lucia 65.0
Finland 21.0	Oman 91.3^	Angola 87.4	Brunei 67.7	Barbardos 62.2
Ireland 17.5	Saudi A. 88.7	Zambia 84.4	Mauritius 65.6	Ecuador 61.6
Portugal 16.2	Qatar 85.2	Rwanda 81.1	Maldives 61.8	Dominica 59.8
UK 15.0	Bahrain 80.2	Gabon 79.0	Papua NG 49.5	Bolivia 58.4
n=21/30	n=27/28	n=35/38	n=27/33	n=32/33 (142)

Source: UN Conference on Trade and Development, *UNCTAD Handbook* 1988 for 1985,
   Tables 4.3 and 4.5; or ^UNCTAD 86f83.

V2.3d.iii - Trading Partner Concentration Indexes

Europe	Islamic	Africa	Asia	Latin America

(a) % to Top 3 Export Partners

Europe	Islamic	Africa	Asia	Latin America
Canada 78.6%	Oman 81.3%	Niger 90.4%	Comoros 88.2%	Haiti 91.1%
Poland 62.2	Afghanistan 79.4	Rwanda 87.0	Nepal 82.0	St.Vincent 85.2
Malta 57.3	Somalia 77.6	STP 83.5	Laos 81.8	Dom.Rep. 84.7
Ireland 55.6	Djibouti 73.6	Burundi 77.1	Brunei 78.5	Mexico 81.6
Belg.-Lux. 54.1	Libya 64.7	C.Verde 75.0	Mauritius 71.6	Bahamas 81.6
Nethrlds. 51.1	Qatar 61.9	Burkina F. 74.7	Maldives 69.2	Belize 79.8
Norway 51.1	Mauritania 60.5	C.Af.R. 73.4	Papua NG 67.3	Bolivia 76.3
Yugoslavia 47.6	N.Yemen 60.0	Zaire 73.4	Indonesia 65.5	Jamaica 73.4
Iceland 46.8	Tunisia 58.3	Gambia 72.6	Solomons 65.4	El Salvador 72.9
USSR 44.7	Syria 57.4	2 @ 67.7	W.Samoa 64.0	Dominica 70.5
....	....	....	....	....
Romania 36.0	Bahrain 35.1	Tanzania 35.0	Malaysia 42.2	2 @ 43.7
Czech. 35.4	Iran 32.5	Iv.Coast 34.4	Bangladesh 41.5	Brazil 39.9
UK 34.7	Pakistan 28.9	Mozambique 32.3	Sri Lanka 37.4	Cuba 39.0
Sweden 32.9	Lebanon 25.7	Zimbabwe 31.3	Myanmar 37.1	Uruguay 37.1
W.Germany 31.0	Chad 10.6	S.Africa 22.2	Fiji 32.1	Argentina 29.0

(b) "% to" and "Name of" Top Export Purchaser

Europe	Islamic	Africa	Asia	Latin America
Canada 70%US	Afghan.69%SU	Rwanda 82%Kenya	Brunei 52%Jap.	Haiti 85%US
Poland 43SU	Oman 53Jap.	Niger 80France	Laos 47Turkey	Dom.Rep. 79US
Ireland 35UK	Qatar 48Jap.	STP 54WGer.	Comoros 45US	Mexico 73US
Hungary 28SU	Somalia 44Saud.	C.Af.R. 45Belg.	Indonesia 41US	Bahamas 63US
Malta 27WGer.	UAE 38Jap.	Congo 45US	Papua NG 40Jap.	Trinidad 57US
Norway 27UK	Mauritan.37Jap.	Zaire 43Belg.	Maldives 39Thai.	Dominica 56UK
Romania 26SU	Djibouti 36NYem.	Eq.Guinea 42Spain	China 38HongKong	St. Vincent 55UK
Nethrlds.26WGer.	Libya 34Italy	Gambia 42Jap.	Solomons 37Jap.	Jamaica 53US
Iceland 23UK	Israel 29US	C.Verde 40Angola	Phil. I. 36US	Bolivia 52Arg.
Greece 22WGer.	Syria 29SU	Nigeria 36US	S.Korea 35US	Venezuela 51US
USSR 22Poland	Morocco 25Fr.	Liberia 36Norway	Mauritius 35UK	Panama 51US
US 21Canada	Tunisia 25Fr.	Burundi 36W.Ger.	Japan 34US	Honduras 49US
Yugoslavia 21SU	Algeria 22US	Gabon 36Fr.	Vietnam 34Jap.	Ecuador 46US
Switz. 21WGer.	Egypt 21It.	Burkina F. 34Fr.	Madagascar 33Fr.	Costa Rica 41US
Belgium 20Fr.	N.Yemen 21WGer.	Zambia 30Jap.	N.Korea 32Jap.	Belize 41US
n = 28/30	n=28	n=34/38	n=29/33	n=29/33 (148)

Source: IMF, *Direction of Trade Statistics 1989* for year 1988, calculated.

V2.4. DISTRIBUTION OF ECONOMIC BENEFITS

To this point Chapter 2 has presented macro-level statistics relating to states' inherent economic strengths and weaknesses, and their positions with respect to international transfers and dependencies. The final section of this chapter focuses on how the benefits of a state's economy are being distributed *within* a given society, a rather difficult task considering the state level of analysis of this study. Nevertheless, four indicators are helpful: amenities, education, health, and social welfare and other consumption. An obvious addition to this list, food, is deferred to Chapter 3 where it is considered so basic a human need as to be part of ecological well-being, not economic quality (Stewart, 1985; Ghai et al., 1977).

V2.4a. Amenities

Three measures which correlate with most manifestations of modernization also reflect distribution of some modest amenities among the mass population; they concern electricity, telephones, and automobiles.

With respect to electricity, the United Nations Conference on Trade and Development's survey of per capita consumption has more complete coverage (157/162 states) but could indicate concentrations in industrial plants. A second measure, Kurian's percentage of dwellings with access to electricity, is more related to equitable distribution among ordinary people, but statistics are dated and available for only 85 states (see Tables V2.4a.i(a) and (b)). Because this data is not directly comparable, only the leading and lowest states in each zone are presented.

The International Telecommunications Union has cited many studies which prove that the total number of telephones installed in a country provides a better barometer of economic development than even per capita income (*Development Forum*, November-December, 1986: 7). As with electricity, the data displayed in Table V2.4a.ii shows a tremendous gap between the European zone and the other four in numbers of telephones per 1000 people. In the developing world, Latin American states are generally better off by this measure than all but the leading states in Asia and the Islamic world. There is also a possible connection between relatively closed societies and low numbers for this measure of openness of communications; notice the surprising scores—lower than those of the leaders in three of the four developing zones—of the otherwise developed USSR and eastern European states.

Finally, owning an automobile is an economic luxury giving the individual a freedom and independence that money cannot otherwise buy. The state rankings in Table V2.4a.iii for passenger car ownership per 1000 people complete this section on economic amenities and repeat many familiar state-names and patterns in both the upper and lower categories.

V2.4b. Education

One of the most effective ways of distributing the benefits of a country's economic well-being over the long term is to increase the educational level of the people. In this section statistics on literacy will be cited as evidence of past governmental investment in this area, and moneys expended upon education as well as student-teacher ratios will be cited as evidence of current commitment.

Literacy is defined as the percentage of the adult population over the age of 15 which can read and write. It is one of the few statistics for which data is available for all 162 countries. However, the numbers found in Table V2.4b.i perhaps overstate each country's claims to a literate population; the US figure of 99%, for example, ignores the millions of functional illiterates unable to fill out forms and otherwise operate effectively in a technologically advanced society. As with unemployment data, it is often politically embarrassing for a government to admit to a high illiteracy rate. Nevertheless, for a state to "fudge" such figures would only be self-deceiving and the display presented here is probably correct in the generally low position of African and Islamic states as opposed to those of the other zones.

Concerning a society's spending on education, there are methodological problems involved in making strict comparisons. Education in many countries, particularly large states, is a local responsibility; in other places it is a role often assumed by religious groups. Thus, concentrating on Central Government Expenditures alone would not give the correct picture of national effort. See, for example, in Table V2.4b.ii(a) the low scores for large federal states like US, West Germany, Yugoslavia, India, Argentina, and Brazil. This World Bank data also suffers from the problems related to its WDR Table 11 on CGE categories cited above in section V2.2c.

UNESCO provides more complete information (i.e., statistics on 138 states) on educational expenditures per capita, and its data does reflect spending at all levels of public education (see Table V2.4b.ii(b)). Here, it appears that the greatest effort is expended in Europe, the advanced states of Asia, and in the Islamic oil-producing states. Africa and non-industrialized Asia are the worst zones, although in the case of Asian states, low per capita figures are often a function of their large populations.

Perhaps a better measure of current commitment to education than moneys spent is population per teacher (Table V2.4b.ii(c)). Once again the states of the African and the Islamic zones—at the bottom of so many other indicators of current economic well-being—are in the lowest ranks of this measure of investment in the future. Asia, with its huge populations, can hire teachers at comparatively low costs and so scores better in this ranking than in the other relative measures of education.

V2.4c. Health Care Policy

The systematic delivery of health care services to even the lowliest members of a society is a function which can be used to measure a country's commitment to the equitable distribution of some tangible benefits to its citizens. Statistics which are gathered in this regard generally reflect two functions: a.) the amount of public moneys spent on health care; and b.) the number of health care professionals available to the population. Together, this data will give a picture of both the inputs and outputs of a state's national health policy. (Additional health policy results relating to infant mortality and life expectancy are found in Chapter 3.)

Tables V2.4c.i and ii summarize state rankings for the leading and lowest states in six measures relating to government health policies. The first displays—Tables V2.4c.i—relate to policy input, or the effort states make as measured by expenditures on health care (a) as a percentage of Central Government Expenditures, (b) on a per capita basis, and (c) as a percentage of Gross National Product. Because health is a function carried out in many (especially the more capitalist) countries by private corporations, these statistics are not strictly translatable into average citizen benefits, and caution must be used in comparing "national efforts" (Raffel, 1985). The relatively low standing (within its zone) for the United States, whose data is annotated in italics, in two of these three measures illustrates this problem. With respect to part (a), the cautions mentioned above concerning WDR Table 11 must be repeated here; note especially the low ranks of several states supposedly strong in social welfare policies like Sweden, Denmark, Israel, India, and Mexico.

Table V2.4c.ii, which measures health policy output as reflected in the number of doctors, nurses, and hospital beds as related to population, is a somewhat better measure to indicate the seriousness with which states consider public health a national priority. The "nursing persons" category is relevant in the four non-European zones where the delivery of primary health care is often able to be accomplished by professionals lacking the highly specialized credentials required for health care in the more technologically advanced world.

Again, US figures, inserted or highlighted in each display for comparative reference, reveal that in only one of the three categories is the US among the leaders in its zone. Because these are relative measures of output (and not simply comparisons of governmental input), this low standing cannot be explained away by the fact that health care in this country is a local or a private function. It means that the local private method of delivery does not provide as many of these facilities to citizens as in countries with more "socialized" health care systems. In this regard the rating of 10 per 1000 in infant mortality for the United States, again not among the leaders in its zone, should be noted both here and in connection with the annotations made below in Chapter 3 (Table V3.1d.i).

V2.4d. Social Welfare and Other Consumption

Just as the amounts of resources devoted to the military, education and health were helpful earlier, so too the percentage of a country's Central Government Expenditures devoted to social welfare services can be used to indicate equitable distribution of economic benefits. As defined here, this measure will include public expenditures on housing and slum clearance, community development, and sanitary services; on compensation for the loss of income to the sick, the temporarily disabled, and the elderly (i.e., social security); on unemployment, family, maternity, and child allowances; and on the cost of welfare services such as care for the aged, the disabled, and children (WDR89: 239).

These expenditures, many of which are investments in human capital which will pay off for the state in the future, inevitably represent moneys spent for the benefit of specific individuals in the present. To the extent that it is difficult to skew such person-intensive expenditures too heavily in favor of a few rich and powerful members of society, this measure seems to be a good estimate of the fairness of a country's economic well-being.

The World Bank reports the percentage of government spending going to such social welfare services for 61 states in 1988 (and 21 more in earlier years), and these findings, supplemented by the IMF's *Government Finance Statistics Yearbook* for other years in order to get the widest possible coverage, are reported in Table V2.4d.i. The caveats concerning the breakdown of Central Government Expenditures in WDR Table 11 are noted again; only 82 states are covered in the World Bank's analyses, and about a third of these have more than 35% of their CGE accounted for by spending other than in the five major budgetary categories found there. (Other sources sometimes give a larger percentage for "welfare," but these generally include education and health expenditures, items treated separately in this study, in V2.4b and .4c, respectively).

Nevertheless, for the states surveyed, the distributions presented in Table V2.4d.i are interesting. The countries of the European zone have been committed to the welfare state for many generations and spend a considerably higher percentage of their government budgets on such services (Flora, 1987) than the rest of the world. Even the lowest states in this region—including the United States—spend a higher percentage of their national budgets on social welfare services than most governments in the developing world.   South America is the region with the next largest commitment, whereas the newly independent states of Africa have barely begun to contemplate this role as a function for government, despite many of their protestations of being "socialist" states with a supposed commitment to their citizens' social welfare.

Social welfare services were part of the public consumption statistics reported in section V2.2c, where it was noted that governmental expenditures may or may not be used for the redistribution of society's economic benefits. Private consumption includes the market values of goods and services purchased or received as income in kind by households and nonprofit institutions. As mentioned earlier, the percentage of Gross Domestic Product going into private consumption is not simply the reciprocal of General Government Consumption for there are other factors in total demand such as savings, investment, and trade balance. Thus, a high percentage of private consumption is not necessarily beneficial to society as a whole.

More to the point, however, and presented for 108 states surveyed in Table V2.4d.ii, would be the *ratio* of private to government consumption as a percentage of GDP. The states at the top of such a listing should be the most "capitalist" and have the least equitable distribution of wealth. Most of the highest-ranking states by this measure are on the periphery of the global capitalist system, in the four non-European zones, with the fewest governmental protections against its swings and distortions. Those scoring lowest in this figure have the greatest government involvement in the economy and are the "mature" states of the capitalist core with a more balanced mixture of capitalism and social welfare measures in the economy.

With respect to explicit measures of equitable distribution of economic benefits, scholars have made efforts at developing indexes which measure the percentage of national income for some top strata (10%, 20%, etc.) of society and for comparably sized groups on the bottom (WDR90: Table 30). Because such information is often politically controversial, however, it is not systematically collected or organized by most states and what data is obtained by international organizations is often out of date and inaccurate (Mahler, 1989; Smith, 1982). Rather than cite such statistics, three final consumption measures indirectly related to income distribution will be presented to conclude this chapter.

Consumer expenditures per capita are a measure of consumption generally found in sources concerned with selling products, such as Euromonitor's two annual volumes, *International Marketing Data and Statistics* and *European Marketing Data and Statistics*. The data, displayed for the leading and lowest states in each zone in Table V2.4d.iii, reflect varying years in the mid-1980s.

Gross National Income per capita results in a rank order listing of states similar to the GNP per capita statistics with which this chapter began (see section V2.1a). The two measures are often confused by many observers, and sometimes sources listing GNI per capita are actually citing GNP per capita. It is true that the absolute values of the two numbers are sometimes close for a given state. However, GNI per capita is generally lower, and it relates more to how much each citizen on average receives from the economy rather than how much he or she has produced. Table V2.4d.iv presents statistics drawn from *The Economist*'s 1988 study *The World in Figures*.

Finally, Table V2.4d.v presents data from the UN Development Program (1990) for *Real* Gross Domestic Product per capita, a number which purports to give "true purchasing power" after adjusting for exchange rates and the varying availability and prices of goods in different countries. With this number the chapter on economic well-being concludes.

V2.4a.i - Electricity, Measures of Distribution

(a) - Electricity Per Capita
(kilowatts of installed capacity per 1000 people)

Europe	Islamic	Africa	Asia	Latin America
Norway 5610	Qatar 3190	S.Africa 664	Australia 1983	Bahamas 1594
Sweden 3972	Kuwait 2888	Zambia 259	N.Zealand 1923	Suriname 1107
Canada 3905	UAE 1869	Zimbwe. 175	Japan 1403	Venezuela 722
Iceland 3897	Bahrain 1678	Gabon 174	Singapore 1235	Trinidad 646
Luxmbrg. 3410	Saudi A. 1188	Liberia 148	W.Samoa 1000^	Argentina 525
US 2949	Israel 973	Mozambq.129	S.Korea 428	Uruguay 432
....	....	....	....	....
Greece 720	Mauritania 29	Ethiopia 8	Bhutan 12	Dominica 90
Yugo. 659	Afghan. 25	GBissau 8	Maldives 11	El Salvador 90
Portugal 595	Sudan 15	Mali 7	Madagscr. 10	Bolivia 89
Hungary 544	N.Yemen 14	Burkina F. 6	Nepal 10	Grenada 70
Malta 535	Somalia 11	Benin 4	Comoros 9	Honduras 65
Albania 243	Chad 8	Burundi 2	Cambodia 6	Haiti 24
n=30	n=28	n=34/38	n=32/33	n=33 (157)

Source: UNCTAD87f85, n=156; and ^UNCTAD85f83.

(b) - % of Dwellings with Access to Electricity

Europe	Islamic	Africa	Asia	Latin America
E.Ger. 99.9%^	Cyprus 99.0%	Senegal 95.9%	Australia 99.8%	Uruguay 80.7%
W.Ger. 99.9	Israel 96.5	Zimbwe. 91.6	N.Zealand 99.5	Venezuela 78.4
Luxmbrg. 99.9	Bahrain 94.0	Nigeria 81.3	Taiwan 94.0	Costa Rica 71.1
Belgium 99.7	Morocco 79.6	Ethiopia 58.7	Brunei 90.1	Cuba 70.8
Czech. 99.7	Turkey 75.4		Singapore 87.0	Chile 69.6
....	....	....	....	....
Spain 89.3	UAE 24.2		Seychelles 27.4	Honduras 25.0
Greece 88.3	Tunisia 24.1	Zambia 27.5	Phil. I. 23.2	St.Chris. 24.1
Yugo. 88.1	Jordan 18.9	Malawi 16.3	Thailand 18.9	Dom.Rep. 20.0
Portugal 64.2	Pakistan 17.8	Congo 4.0	W.Samoa 18.8	Paraguay 17.5
Romania 48.6	Iraq 17.1	Iv.Coast 0.7	Sri Lanka 10.5	Haiti 4.0
n=19/30	n=14/28	n=8/38	n=17/33	n=27/33 (85)

Source: Kurian 1984 for 1980, citing UN Compendium of Housing Statistics;
supplemented by ^World Bank, *World Tables*, 1980 for 1976.

V2.4a.ii - Telephones per 1000 People

Europe	Islamic	Africa	Asia	Latin America
Sweden 889	Israel 381	S.Africa 138	N.Zealand 645	Bahamas 402
Switz. 818	Qatar 328	Zimbabwe 30	Japan 533	Barbados 299
US 755	Cyprus 296	Swaziland 26	Austrl. 532	Antigua 140
Denmark 749	Bahrain 266	STP 24	Singapore 399	Costa Rica 118
Canada 664	UAE 241	Botswana 17	Taiwan 293	Uruguay 113
Norway 662	Kuwait 160	Gabon 12	S.Korea 171	Panama 105
W.Ger. 621	Saudi A. 152	Ken.,Zamb.-12	Seych. 165	Argentina 104
....	....	....	....	....
Bulgaria 200	N.Yemen 6.4	Burkina F. 2.2	India 4.7	El Salvador 26
Portugal 174	Pakistan 5.4	Guinea 1.8	Bhutan 4.3	Bolivia 24
Hungary 134	Sudan 3.3	Niger 1.7	Madagscr. 3.7	Paraguay 23
Yugo.132	Mauritan.2.7	Burundi 1.3	Vietnam 1.8	Nicaragua 16
Poland 105	Afghan. 2.0	Zaire 1.3	Myanmar 1.4	Guatemala 12
USSR 98	Chad 1.4	Mali 1.2	Bangldsh. 1.3	Honduras 11
Romania 67	Somalia 1.1	Rwanda 1.1	Nepal 1.2	Haiti 4.8
n=29/30	n=28	n=37/38	n=33	n=33 (160)

Source: The Economist, *The World in Figures 1988*, for 1984.

V2.4a.iii - Passenger Cars per 1000 People

Europe	Islamic	Africa	Asia	Latin America
US 537	Qatar 240	S.Africa 90	Australia 500	Bahamas 234
W.Germany 428	Kuwait 226	Zimbabwe 30	N.Zealand 453	Trinidad 203
Canada 427	Cyprus 188	Swaziland 26	Brunei 320	Venzeuela 130
Iceland 426	Saudi A. 184	Congo 22	Japan 230	Argentina 123
Luxmbrg. 414	Lebanon 170	STP 22	Singapore 87	Barbados 123
Switzrld. 404	UAE 164	Iv. Coast 19	Malaysia 72	Uruguay 98
Italy 392	Bahrain 160	C.Af.R. 16	Seychelles 52	Antigua 91
....	....	....	....	....
Greece 127	S.Yemen 8.7	Malawi 2.2	Myanmar 1.4	Dom.Rep. 19
Yugo.125	Mauritan. 7.8	Uganda 2.0	Bhutan 1.0	Peru 19
Bulgaria 115	Sudan 4.5	Guinea 1.7	Nepal 1.0	Jamaica 18
Poland 98	Somalia 4.2	Burundi 1.6	N.Korea 1.0	Bolivia 17
USSR 40	Pakistan 2.5	Rwanda 1.1	Bangldsh. 0.5	Nicaragua 9.9
Romania 11	Afghan 1.9	Ethiopia 0.9	China 0.3	Honduras 8.6
Albania 1.6	Chad 1.5	Togo 0.8	Cambodia 0.1	Haiti 6.6
n=30	n=28	n=37/38	n=32/33	n=33 (160)

Source: The Economist, *The World in Figures 1988*, for 1983-5.

V2.4b.i - % of Literate Adults

Europe	Islamic	Africa	Asia	Latin America
Norway-100%			Japan-99%	Barbados-99%
Luxmbrg.-100	Israel-95%		N.Zealand-98	St.Chris.-98º
Finland-100			Australia-98	Grenada-98º
Iceland-100	Cyprus-91		W.Samoa-98º	Uruguay-97
				Argentina-96
US-99			N.Korea-95	Cuba-96
W.Germany-99	Lebanon-77		S.Korea-94	St.Vincent-96º
Canada-99	Jordan-75	S.Africa-85%	Mongolia-93	Trinidad-96
Switzrld.-99	Bahrain-73	Tanzania-85	Thailand-91	Guyana-96
Denmark-99			Taiwan-90	Dominica-94º
UK-99	Kuwait-70	Zambia-76		CostaRica-94
Sweden-99	Turkey-69	Zimbabwe-74		Jamaica-94
Nethrlds.-99	UAE-68^	Lesotho-74	Sri Lanka-87	Chle-94
Belgium-99	Libya-67	Namibia-72	Singapore-86	Bahamas-93º
USSR-99		Botswana-71	Phil. I.-86	Belize-91º
France-99	Syria-60	Swaziland-68	Fiji-86	Mexico-90
Ireland-99	Iraq-58			Nicaragua-88
Poland-99	Tunisia-54	Congo-63	Vietnam-84	Paraguay-88
Hungary-99	Qatar-51	Gabon-62	Mauritius-83	Antigua-88º
Czech.-99	Iran-51	Zaire-61	Maldives-82º	Panama-88
E.Germany-99	Oman-50	Kenya-59	Brunei-78	Colombia-88
	Algeria-50	Rwanda-57	Indonesia-74	Venezuela-87
		Uganda-57	Malaysia-73	Peru-85
Austria-98	Egypt-44	Cameroon-56	Myanmar-70	Ecuador-82
	S.Yemen-41	Ghana-53	China-69	St.Lucia-82º
Italy-97		STP-50º	Madagascar-68	Brazil-78
Romania-97				Dom.Rep.-77
		Iv.Coast-43	Solomons-60º	
Bulgaria-95		Nigeria-42	Seychelles-58º	Bolivia-74
Spain-94		Togo-41	Laos-51	El Salvador-72
	Saudi A.-34	Malawi-41	Cambodia-50	Suriname-65º
	Morocco-33	C.Af.R.-40		Honduras-60
Greece-92		Eq.Guinea-40	Papua NG-46	
Yugoslavia-91	Sudan-31	Angola-39	India-44	
	Pakistan-30	Mozambique-38		Guatemala-55
Malta-84		Cape Verde-37º	Bangladesh-33	
Portugal-84	Chad-25	Liberia-35	Nepal-26	Haiti-38
	Afghanistan-24	Burundi-29		
		Sierra L.-29		
Albania-75	Djibouti-20º	Benin-28		
	Mauritania-17	Senegal-28		
		Guinea-28	Comoros-15º	
	N.Yemen-14	Gambia-25	Vanuatu-15º	
		GBissau-19º		
	Somalia-12	Mali-17		
		Ethiopia-15		
		Niger-14		
		Burkina F.-3	Bhutan-5º	
n=30	n=28	n=38	n=33	n=33 (162)

Source: Sivard87/88f84, and ^86f83, n=142; supplemented by ºODC *Agenda* 85-86, n=20.

V2.4b.ii - Relative Measures of Education

Europe	Islamic	Africa	Asia	Latin America

(a) - % CGE on Education

Europe	Islamic	Africa	Asia	Latin America
Finland 13.9%	Iran 19.6%	Ghana 25.7%	Thailand 19.3%	Ecuador 24.5%^
Belgium 12.2	N.Yemen 17.6	Zimbabwe 22.0	S.Korea 19.0	Venez. 19.6
Nethrlds 11.9	Morocco 17.0	Kenya 21.5	Papua NG 15.9	Bolivia 18.4
Ireland 11.8	Tunisia 14.6	Iv.Coast 20.5*	Phil. I. 15.7	El Salvador 17.1
Portugal 9.5	Kuwait 14.2	Togo 19.9	Singapore 14.4	Costa Rica 16.2
....	....	....	....	....
Hungary 2.1	Oman 10.7	Mali 9.8	Bangladesh 10.6^	Mexico 7.4
Romania 1.8^	Syria 10.4	Tanzania 8.3^	Indonesia 10.0	Uruguay 7.1
US 1.7	UAE 9.7*	Zambia 8.3	Sri Lanka 7.8	Argentina 6.9
W.Germany 0.6	Israel 9.6	Nigeria 2.8	Australia 7.0	Haiti 6.0**
Yugoslavia 0.0	Pakistan 2.6	Zaire 0.8*	India 2.9	Brazil 4.8
n=17/30	n=12/28	n=15/38	n=14/33	n=13/33 (71)

Source: WDR90f88, Table 11, n=63; plus ^WDR89f87, *WDR88f86, and **WDR87f85, n=8.

(b) - Educational Expenditures per Capita (US $)

Europe	Islamic	Africa	Asia	Latin America
Canada $1051	Qatar $694	Gabon $152	Japan $640	Trinidad $296
Sweden 1045	Saudi A. 674	S.Africa 95	Australia 638	Barbados 290
Norway 1031	Kuwait 626	Botswana 89	Brunei 522	Venezuela 194
Denmark 962	Libya 534	Zimbabwe 54	Singapore 370	Cuba 124
US 928	Israel 451	Congo 49	N.Zealand 342	Panama 119
....	....	....	....	....
Malta 118	Sudan 16	Uganda 5	China,India,Mad.-9	Peru 18
Greece 115	Somalia 14	Mali 5	Nepal 5	Paraguay 13
Portugal 114	Pakistan 7	Ethiopia 5	Myanmar 4	Dom.Rep. 13
Romania 73	Afghanistan 6^	Burkina F. 4	Bangladesh 4	Bolivia 13
Albania 50^	Chad 3	Zaire 1	Laos 3	Haiti 4
n=30	n=27/28	n=34/38	n=23/33	n=24/33 (138)

Source: Sivard 89f86, Table III or ^Sivard88f84, citing UNESCO for all levels of public education.

(c) - School Age Population per Teacher

Europe	Islamic	Africa	Asia	Latin America
Canada 13	Qatar 15	S.Africa 42	Brunei 19	Cuba 21
Denmark 14	Israel 17	Swaziland 43	Australia 21	Barbados 23
Austria 18	Libya 20	Zimbabwe 44	N.Zealand 24	Argentina 25
Norway 18	Lebanon 21	Ghana 49	Japan 28	Uruguay 28
E.Germany 19	Kuwait 23	Gabon 50	Fiji 33	Trinidad 32
Luxembourg 19	UAE 27	Botswana 53	Mauritius 33	Venezuela 37
Ital.,Fin.,Fr.-21	Cyprus 32	Namibia 65	Singapore 34	Panama,Parag.-38
....	....	....	....	....
Yugoslavia 31	Sudan 112	Guinea 193	Madagascar 64	Guyana 55
Spain 32	N.Yemen 119	Burundi 213	India 65	Dom.Rep. 63
Poland 33	Pakistan 119	Mozambique 219	Cambodia 85	Nicaragua 66
Albania 34	Mauritania 169	Mali 227	Myanmar 87	Guatemala 70
Czech. 34	Somalia 191	Ethiopia 237	Nepal 92	Honduras 73
Romania 38	Afghanistan 239	Niger 245	Papua NG 94	El Salvador 76
Switzerland 40	Chad 268	Burkina F.353	Bangladesh 129	Haiti 78
n=30	n=27/28	n=32/38	n=26/33	n=24/33 (141)

Source: Sivard89f86, Table III.

150

V2.4c.i - Relative Measures of Health (Policy Inputs)

Europe	Islamic	Africa	Asia	Latin America

(a) - % CGE in Health

Europe	Islamic	Africa	Asia	Latin America
France 20.8%^	Kuwait 7.7%	Ghana 9.0%	N.Zealand 12.4%	CostaRica 19.3%
W.Germany 18.2	UAE 6.2*	Zimbabwe 7.5	Papua NG 9.6	Panama 16.7
UK 13.6	Iran 6.0	Botswana 7.4	Australia 9.6	Dom.Rep.10.0*
Switzerland 13.1*	Tunisia 5.9	Liberia 7.1^	Mauritius 7.6	Venezuela 10.0
Austria 12.8	Oman 4.8	Lesotho 6.9^	Thailand 7.2	Brazil 9.5
....(US 12.5)....	....	....	....	....
Hungary 1.7	Morocco 3.0	Ethiopia 3.6	Nepal 4.3	Uruguay 4.8
Denmark 1.3	Egypt 2.5^	Cameroon 3.5^	Singapore 3.6	Paraguay 3.1^
Sweden 1.1	Turkey 2.4	Mali 2.6	S. Korea 2.2	Argentina 2.1
Romania 0.8^	Syria 1.5	Uganda 2.4	India 1.8	Bolivia 1.9
Yugoslavia 0.0	Pakistan 0.9	Nigeria 0.8^	Indonesia 1.8	Mexico 1.1
n=20/30	n=13/28	n=16/38	n=14/33	n=14/33 (77)

Source: WDR90f88, Table 11, n=63; plus ^WDR89f87, n=10, and *WDR88f86, n=4.

(b) -Public Health Expenditures per Capita (US $)

Europe	Islamic	Africa	Asia	Latin America
Switzerld. $1211	Kuwait $398	Gabon $63	Australia $638	Barbados $184
Sweden 1099	Saudi A. 257	Botswana 28	Japan 624	Trinidad 153
Canada 935	Bahrain 214	Congo 20	N.Zealand 398	Panama 115
Norway 833	Oman 173	Zimbabwe 15	Brunei 108	Costa Rica 79
US 783	Libya 159	Swaziland 13	Taiwan 90	Venezuela 79
....	....	....	....	....
Yugoslavia 157	Afghanistan 2^	Ghana,Mali-1	India 3	Guatemala 9
Portugal 149	Somalia-2	Burkina F. 1	Indonesia 3	El Salvador 8
Malta 119	Afghan.-2	Ethiopia 1	Myanmar 2	Paraguay 3
Romania 75	Sudan-1	Zaire 1	Nepal 2	Haiti 3
Albania 32	Chad-1	Uganda 1	Bangladesh 1	Bolivia 2
n=30	n=25/28	n=34/38	n=23/33	n=24/33 (136)

Source: Sivard 89f86, Table III, or ^Sivard 87/88f84, citing WHO & UN.

(c) % GNP in Public Health Expenditures

Europe	Islamic	Africa	Asia	Latin America
Sweden 8.0%	Saudi A. 4.0%	Botswana 2.9%	N.Zealand 5.6%	Nicaragua 6.6%
Ireland 7.8	Oman 3.3	Swaziland 2.4	Australia 5.1	Costa Rica 5.4
Netherlands 7.5	Libya 3.0	Malawi 2.4	Japan 4.9	Panama 5.4
Switzerland 6.8	Kuwait 2.9	Zimbabwe 2.3	Papua NG 3.3	Guyana 4.6
Can.,France-6.6	Tunisia 2.7	Gambia 2.3	Taiwan 2.5	Barbados 3.6
...(US=4.5)	....	....	....	....
USSR,Bulg.-3.2	Chad 0.6	S.Africa 0.6	Indonesia 0.7	Haiti 0.9
Hungary 3.2	Turkey 0.5	Rwanda 0.6	Brunei 0.7	Colombia 0.8
E.Germany 2.6	Sudan 0.2	Nigeria 0.4	Phil. I. 0.7	Guatemala 0.7
Albania 2.3	Somalia 0.2	Ghana 0.3	Bangladesh 0.6	Paraguay 0.4
Romania 1.9	Pakistan 0.2	Uganda 0.2	S.Korea 0.3	Bolivia 0.4
n=30	n=24/28	n=33/38	n=23/33	n=24/33 (134)

Source: Sivard 89f86, Table II.

V2.4c.ii - Relative Measures of Health (Policy Outputs)

Europe	Islamic	Africa	Asia	Latin America

(a) - Population per Physician

Europe	Islamic	Africa	Asia	Latin America
USSR 235	Israel 410	S.Africa 1434	Mongolia 401	Argentina 379
Hungary 304	Qatar 485	Gabon 3094	Australia 436	Cuba 455
Spain 318	Kuwait 636	Zimbabwe 6590	N.Zealand 537	Uruguay 523
Czech. 327	Saudi A. 688	Namibia 6604	Japan 652	Venezuela 712
Belgium 333	Egypt 698	Ghana 6987	Singapore 930	Ecuador 804
...(USA 462)...	....	....	....	....
Albania 671	Afghanistan 9686	Malawi 43,406	Indonesia 9155	Jamaica 2099
Ireland 689	Sudan 9770	Mozambq. 43,997	Madagascar 9171	Guatemala 2289
UK 691	Mauritania 12,093	Guinea 51,875	Papua NG 12,739	El Salvador 2830
Italy 706	Somalia 14,727	Burkina F. 53,933	Cambodia 14,404	Guyana 7193
Malta 829	Chad 39,546	Ethiopia 78,249	Nepal 23,635	Haiti 7447
n=30/30	n=27/28	n=35/38	n=25/33	n=24/33 (141)

Source: Sivard89f86, Table III.

(b) - Population per Nursing Person

Europe	Islamic	Africa	Asia	Latin America
Norway 60	Israel 110	Gabon 270	N.Zealand 80	Uruguay 190**
Denmark 60	Kuwait 200	Niger 450	Australia 110	Trinidad 260
Finland 60	Saudi A. 320	Congo 570	Japan 180	Chile 370
US 70	Algeria 330	Ghana 640	Mongolia 240*	Cuba 370**
SU,Sweden-100	Libya 350	Botswana 700	Laos 530	Venezuela 380**
....	....	....	....	....
Spain 260	Iraq 1660	Malawi 3130	China,India-1700	Paraguay 1000
Yugoslav. 260	N.Yemen 2680	Rwanda 3650	Phil. I. 2740	Dom.Rep.1210
Romania 280	Chad 3390	Ethiopia 5290	Bhutan 2990	Brazil 1210
Greece 450	Pakistan 4900	Mozambique 5760	Nepal 4680	Haiti 2290
Portugal 660**	Afghan. 26,000**	Guinea 6380	Bangladesh 8980	Bolivia 2480
n=25/30	n=24/28	n=23 /37	n=21/33	n=19/33 (112)

Source:WDR89f84, Table 28, n=102; plus *WDR87f81, n=4; and **WDR85f80, n=6.

(c) - Population per Hospital Bed

Europe	Islamic	Africa	Asia	Latin America
Sweden 50	Israel 160	Eq.Guinea 60	Japan 80	Barbados 140
Norway 60	Cyprus 180	Gabon 170	Mongolia 90	Guyana 180
Finland 70	Libya 190	Namibia 230	N.Zealand 100	Cuba 190
Neth.,Lux.-80	Bahrain 260	Congo 250	Australia 170	Uruguay 200
USSR,Czech.-80	Kuwait 280	Zambia 280	Taiwan 240	Argentina 200
....	....	....	....	....
Greece 170	S.Yemen 1270	Nigeria 1140	India 1230	El Salvador 810
Poland 180	Somalia 1420	Niger 1800	Myanmar 1430	Paraguay 840
US 190	Pakistan 1860	Burkina F. 1840	Indonesia 1540	Honduras 840
Spain 200	Mauritania 2610	Mali 2180	Bangladesh 3660	Mexico 1080
Portugal 260	Afghanistan 3330	Ethiopia 3710	Nepal 4600	Haiti 1140
n=30	n=27/28	n=35/38	n=25/33	n=24/33 (141)

Source: Sivard 89f86, Table III.

152

V2.4d.i - Social Welfare Services as % CGE

Europe	Islamic	Africa	Asia	Latin America
Sweden 54.2%				Uruguay 49.5%
Switzerland 50.6*				
Luxembourg 49.8^				Chile 39.2
W.Germany 49.4				Paraguay 32.3º
Austria 47.5				Argentina 32.0
Belgium 43.3			N.Zealand 29.7%	
Denmark 41.1			Australia 28.6	C.Rica 26.7
Spain 40.4º				Bolivia 25.6
Netherlands 39.6			Maldives 19.3^	Brazil 24.2
France 38.5º				
Canada 37.3			Mauritius 16.6	Panama 16.0
Finland 36.1				Barbados 14.3^
Norway 36.1				Dom.Rep. 13.3*
Italy 35.4			Myanmar 13.2	
Malta 34.4^				Venezuela 11.7
	Tunisia 22.0%			Mexico 9.3
US 31.5	Israel 21.2		Sri Lanka 11.7	
UK 30.9	Kuwait 20.1		Singapore 11.0	Bahamas 7.4^
Ireland 30.3				Suriname 6.7^
Hungary 28.7	Iran 17.4			Trinidad 6.0^
Portugal 25.7	Cyprus 16.2^			Guyana 5.5^
Romania 21.9º	Egypt 16.0º			
Iceland 15.9^		Cameroon 11.9%º		Grenada 5.0^
Yugoslavia 11.2	Jordan 9.5	Ghana 11.9	Bangladesh 9.8º	
	Pakistan 8.7	Botswana 11.0		
	Oman 8.3	Ethiopia 9.3	S.Korea 8.5	
	Morocco 7.3	Togo 8.5		Honduras 4.7^
	UAE 5.0*	Senegal 5.6^	Seychelles 6.8^	
	Syria 4.5		India 5.4	El Salvador 4.4
		Zimbabwe 3.8	Thailand 5.4	Nicaragua 4.4^
		Kenya 3.5		
		Burkina F. 3.4º		
	Mauritan. 3.9^	Mali 3.3	Nepal 3.3	Jamaica 3.3^
		Uganda 2.9		
	Turkey 3.1	Zambia 2.3		
		Rwanda 2.3^	Fiji 2.6^	
		Malawi 2.0	Phil. I. 2.2	
	Sudan 2.2^	Gambia 2.0^		
	Bahrain 2.1^	Sierra Leone 2.0*		
		Liberia 1.9º		Belize 1.7^
		Ivory Coast 1.8*		Haiti 1.7**
	Somalia 1.7^	Niger 1.7*	Papua NG 1.7	
		Tanzania 1.7º	Indonesia 1.7	Dominica 1.5^
		Lesotho 1.5º		
		Nigeria 1.5		Ecuador 0.9º
		Zaire 0.6**		
	N.Yemen 0.0	Swaziland 0.0^	Malaysia 0.0*	St.Vincent 0.0^
n=23/30	n=18/28	n=24/38	n=18/33	n=26/33 (109)

Source: WDR90f88, Table 11, n=61; supplemented by ºWDR89f87, n=12; * WDR88f86, n=7;
  **WDR87f85, n=2; ^IMF *Government Finance Statistics Yearbook* 1983, n=27.

153

V2.4d.ii - Ratio: Private to Government Consumption, as % GDP

Europe	Islamic	Africa	Asia	Latin America
		Sierra L. 12.8		Dom.Rep. 13.0
		Uganda 10.9		Paraguay 12.0
	Sudan 9.4		Bangladesh 9.8	
		Mali 9.3		Guatemala 10.5
		Ghana 9.3		
		C.Af.R. 9.0	Phil. I. 8.1	Peru 8.5
		Tanzania 7.8	China 8.0	Haiti 7.8
	Somalia 8.6	Niger 7.7	Nepal 8.0	
		Cameroon 7.6	Sri Lanka 7.8	
		Benin 7.4		
		Guinea 7.1		Mexico 6.7
	Turkey 7.2	Rwanda 6.8	Indonesia 7.2	Venezuela 6.6
Poland 7.0		Nigeria 6.1		Argentina 6.5
	Egypt 5.6		Madagascar 6.7	El Salvador 6.2
Hungary 5.5	Mauritania 5.4		Japan 6.3	Ecuador 6.2
	Pakistan 5.2	Malawi 5.6		Colombia 6.1
		Lesotho 5.1		
		Burundi 4.6	Mauritius 5.8	
Switzerland 4.8		Senegal 4.6	Thailand 5.7	
Portugal 4.7	Syria 4.5		India 5.6	Chile 5.9
			Laos 5.5	
		Mozambique 4.2	Myanmar 5.3*	Uruguay 5.6
		Togo 4.1		
	Tunisia 4.1	Zambia 4.1	S.Korea 5.1	Brazil 5.0
Spain 4.2	Morocco 4.1			
Italy 4.1	Chad 4.0	Liberia 3.8^	Singapore 4.4	Jamaica 4.4
Belgium 3.9	N.Yemen 4.0		N.Zealand 4.0	Honduras 4.2
		Ivory Coast 3.1		
		S.Africa 3.1		Costa Rica 3.9
USA 3.4		Kenya 3.1	Malaysia 3.5	Bolivia 3.7
Yugoslavia 3.4	Algeria 3.3	Zimbabwe 3.0		
UK 3.4		Burkina F. 3.0	Australia 3.1	
Ireland 3.4	Jordan 2.8	Ethiopia 3.0		
Austria 3.3				
Netherlands 3.3		Zaire 2.8	Papua NG 2.8	
France 3.2	Kuwait 2.4	Congo 2.6		
Greece 3.2				Trinidad 2.6
Canada 3.1				Panama 2.6*
W.Germany 2.9	UAE 2.1			
Finland 2.8				
Norway 2.6	Israel 1.9	Gabon 2.0		
Denmark 2.2				
Sweden 2.0		Botswana 1.7*		Nicaragua 1.3*
	Saudi Arabia 1.4			
n=21/30	n=17/28	n=30/38	n=19/33	n=21/33 (108)

Source: *calculated* from WDR90f88, Table 9, n=103; ^WDR89f87, n=1, and *WDR88f86, n=4.

V2.4d.iii - Consumer Expenditures per Capita (US $)

Europe	Islamic	Africa	Asia	Latin America
Switz. $12,632	Bahrain $12,228	Botswana $1017	Japan $7706	Bahamas $5293
US 10,926	Kuwait 7847	Gabon 996	Australia 5806	Trinidad 3807
Iceland 9809	Qatar 7548	Swaziland 752	Singpore 3326	Barbados 2955
Norway 9076	UAE 5041	Zimbabwe 587	Taiwan 1613	Suriname 2671
Denmark 8821	Saudi A. 3489	Cameroon 561	N.Zealand 1459	Argentina 1858
....	....	....	....	....
Hungary 1428	Pakistan 252	GBissau 132	Nepal 118	Honduras 567
Albania 1401	Sudan 213	Malawi 116	Laos 115	Dom.Rep. 550
Romania 1362	Somalia 185	Ethiopia 90	Vietnam 102	Peru 389
Poland 1206	Chad 114	Zaire 85	Cambodia 93	Haiti 335
Yugoslavia 694	Afghanistan 73	Benin 81	Bhutan 85	Guyana 258
n=30	n=26/28	n=34/38	n=29/33	n=27/33 (146)

Source: *International Marketing Data Statistics* 1987/88f82/85, pp.296-99;
supplemented by *European Marketing Data Statistics* 1988/89f86, pp. 234-235.

V2.4d.iv - Gross National Income per Capita (US $)

Europe	Islamic	Africa	Asia	Latin America
US $14,565	UAE $16,100	Gabon $2500	Brunei $13,600	Trinidad $5556
Switzrld. 13720	Kuwait 13,980	S.Africa 1282	Japan 9452	Bahamas 5000
Luxmbrg.11,960	Qatar 9600	Congo 1100	Australia 9196	Barbados 4400
Norway 11,784	Bahrain 7500	Botswana 850	N.Zealand 6100	Suriname 2700
Canada 11,778	Saudi A. 6900	Cameroon 710	Singapore 6100	Venezuela 2519
....	....	....	....	....
Poland 1900	Pakistan 330	Burkina F. 120	Nepal 127	Honduras 696
Yugoslavia 1850	Sudan 310	Mali 120	Vietnam 130	Dom.Rep. 684
Portugal 1820	Somalia 250	Mozambique 120	Bhutan 105	Peru 669
Hungary 1722	Afghan. 180	Ethiopia 110	Laos 100	Guyana 515
Albania 860	Chad 90	Zaire 100	Cambodia 50	Haiti 360
n=30	n=28	n=37/38	n=33	n=32/33 (160)

Source: The Economist, *The World in Figures 1988*, for 1985.

V2.4d.v -Real GDP per Capita (US $)

Europe	Islamic	Africa	Asia	Latin America
US $17,615	Kuwait $13,843	S.Africa $4981	Japan $13,135	Uruguay $5063
Canada 16,375	UAE 12,191	Botswana 2496	Singapore 12,790	Chile 4862
Norway 15,940	Israel 9182	Gabon 2068	Australia 11,782	Argentina 4647
Switzrld. 15,403	Saudi A. 8320	Lesotho 1585	N.Zealand 10,541	Mexico 4624
Denmark 15,119	Oman 7750	Namibia 1500	S.Korea 4832	Brazil 4307
....	....	....	....	....
Bulgaria 4750	Afghanistan 1000	Ethiopia 454	Bangladesh 883	Dom.Rep. 1750
Hungary 4500	Som.,S.Yem.-1000	Niger 452	Myanmar 752	El Sal.1733
Poland 4000	Mauritania 840	Burundi 450	Nepal 722	Bolivia 1380
Romania 3000	Sudan 750	Tanzania 405	Bhutan 700	Honduras 1119
Albania 2000	Chad 400	Zaire 220	Madagascar 634	Haiti 775
n=27/30	n=24/28	n=32/38	n=23/33	n=22/33 (128)

Source: UN Development Program, *Human Development Report 1990*, cited in *The Economist*
(May 26, 1990: 81).

BIBLIOGRAPHY

ARRIGHI, G., and J. DRANGEL (1986) "The Stratification of the World Economy: An
Exploration of the Semiperipheral Zone," paper presented at the Annual Meeting of
the International Studies Association, Anaheim, Calif.:1-64.

BACH, Q. V. S. (1988) *Soviet Economic Assistance to the Less Developed Countries: A
Statistical Analysis.* New York: Oxford University Press.

BAUM, W. C., and S. M. TOLBERT (1985) *Investing in Development: Lessons of
World Bank Experience.* Washington: World Bank Publications.

BEAN, R. (ed.) (1988) *International Labor Statistics: A Handbook, Guide, and Recent
Trends.* New York: Routledge.

BENAMARA, A., and S. IFCAGWU (1987) *OPEC Aid and the Challenge of Third
World Development.* London: Croom and Helm.

BORNSCHIER, V., and C. CHASE-DUNN (1985) *Transnational Corporations and
Development.* New York: Praeger.

BOUCHET, M. H. (1987) *The Political Economy of International Debt: Who, What,
How Much, and Why.* New York: Quorum Books.

BRANDT, W., et al. (1980) *North-South: A Program for Survival: Report of the
Independent Commission on International Development Issues.* Cambridge:
Massachusetts Institute of Technology Press.

BROWN, M. B. (1974) *The Economics of Imperialism.* Baltimore: Penguin.

CARDOSO, F. H., and E. FALETTO (1979) *Dependency and Development in Latin
America.* Berkeley: University of California Press.

CARVOUNIS, C. C. (1984) *The Debt Dilemma of Developing Nations: Issues and
Cases.* New York: Quorum Books.

CLARK, R. P. (1986) *Policy-Making in the Third World.* New York: John Wiley and
Sons.

CLINE, W. R. (1984) *International Debt: Systemic Risk and Policy Response.*
Washington: Institute for International Economics.

(THE) CONFERENCE BOARD (1983ff) *Centrally Planned Economies: Economic
Overviews* (of selected states; series). New York: Conference Board.

CUNLIFFE, A., and M. LAVER (1985) "African Aid Links and UN Voting: A
Research Note," *International Interactions* 12: 95-107.

DEBT CRISIS NETWORK (1985) *From Debt to Development: Alternatives to the
International Debt Crisis.* Washington: Institute for Policy Studies.

DELAMAIDE, D. (1984) *Debt Shock: The Full Story of the World Credit Crisis.* New
York: Doubleday.

DEVELOPMENT FORUM (monthly). New York: United Nations, Division for
Economic and Social Information and the United Nations University.

DEWITT, R. P., and A. S. BANKS (1981) *Economic Handbook of the World.* New
York: McGraw-Hill.

(THE) ECONOMIST (1988) *The World in Figures.* Boston: G. K. Hall and Co.

EMMANUEL, A. (1972) *Unequal Exchange: A Study of the Imperialism of Trade.* New

York: Monthly Review Press.

EUROMONITOR   (annual) *European Marketing Data and Statistics*.   London: Euromonitor Publications.

_____. (annual) *International Marketing Data and Statistics*. London: Euromonitor Publications.

EVANS, P. (1979) *Dependent Development*. Princeton: Princeton University Press.

FIREBAUGH, G., and B. P. BULLOCK (1986) "Level of Processing of Exports: New Estimates for 73 Less-Developed Countries in 1970 and 1980," *International Studies Quarterly* 30: 333-350.

FLORA, P. (ed.) (1987) *Growth to Limits: The Western European Welfare States since World War II*. Hawthorne: Aldine de Gruyter, 2 vols.

FOOD AND AGRICULTURE ORGANIZATION OF THE UNITED NATIONS (annual) *Trade Yearbook*. Rome: Food and Agricultural Organization.

GALTUNG, J. (1971) "A Structural Theory of Imperialism," *Journal of Peace Research* 13: 81-118.

GALTUNG, J., et al. (1975) "Measuring World Development," *Alternatives* 1: 131-158.

GARRETT, G., and P. LANGE (1986) "Performance in a Hostile World: Economic Growth in Capitalist Democracies, 1974-1982," *World Politics* 38: 517-545.

GEORGE, S. (1988) *A Fate Worse Than Debt: The World Financial Crisis and the Poor*. Washington: Institute for Policy Studies.

GHAI, D. P., et al. (1977) *The Basic-Needs Approach to Development*. Geneva: International Labour Office.

GIERSCH, H. (ed.) (1987) *The International Debt Problem*. Boulder: Frederick A. Praeger.

GODFREY, M. (1986) *Global Unemployment: The New Challenge to Economic Theory*. New York: St. Martin's Press.

GOLDTHORPE, J. H. (ed.) (1984) *Order and Conflict in Contemporary Capitalism*. Oxford: Clarendon Press.

GROTH, A. J., and L. L. WADE (1984) *Comparative Resource Allocation: Politics, Performance, and Policy Priorities*. Beverly Hills: Sage Publications.

HANCOCK, G. (1989) *Lords of Poverty: The Power, Prestige and Corruption of the International Aid Business*. New York: Atlantic Monthly Press.

HARRIS, N. (1987) *The End of the Third World: Newly Industrialized Countries and the Decline of an Ideology*. New York: Penguin Books.

HIRSCHMAN, A. O. (1945) *National Power and the Structure of Foreign Trade*. Berkeley: University of California Press.

HOOGVELT, A. M. (1982) *The Third World in Global Development*. London: Macmillan.

HUNT, D. (1989) *Economic Theories of Development: An Analysis of Competing Paradigms*. Lanham, MD: Barnes and Noble Books.

HUNTER, S. (1985) *OPEC and the Third World: The Politics of Aid*. Bloomington: Indiana University Press.

INTERNATIONAL LABOUR OFFICE (annual) *Yearbook of Labour Statistics*. Geneva:

International Labour Office.

INTERNATIONAL MONETARY FUND (annual) *Balance of Payments Yearbook.* Washington: International Monetary Fund (IMF).

_____. (annual) *Direction of Trade Statistics.* Washington: IMF.

_____. (annual) *Government Finance Statistics Yearbook.* Washington: IMF.

JENKINS, R. (1987) *Trans-National Corporations and Uneven Development: The Internationalization of Capital and the Third World.* New York: Methuen.

JOHNS, R. A. (1985) *International Trade Theories and the Evolving International Economy.* New York: St. Martin's Press.

KAHLER, M. (ed.) (1986) *The Politics of International Debt.* Ithaca, N.Y.: Cornell University Press.

KETTELL, B. (1986) *The International Debt Game.* Cambridge, Mass.: Ballinger Publishing Co.

KILLECK, T. (ed.) (1984) *The IMF and Stabilization: Developing Country Experiences.* New York: St. Martin's Press.

KOHLI, A. (ed.) (1986) *The State and Development in the Third World.* Princeton: Princeton University Press.

KRAVIS, I. B., A. HESTON, and R. SUMMERS (1982) *World Product and Income: International Comparisons of Real Gross Product.* Baltimore: Johns Hopkins University Press.

LOMBARDI, R. W. (1985) *Debt Trap: Rethinking the Logic of Development.* New York: Praeger.

MAHLER, V. A. (1989) "Income Distribution within Nations: Problems of Cross-National Comparison," *Comparative Political Studies* 22(1, April): 3-32.

MIKESELL, R. F. (1983) "Appraising IMF Conditionality: Too Loose, Too Tight or Just Right?," pp. 47-62 in WILLIAMSON, J. (ed.) (1983) *IMF Conditionality.* Washington: Institute for International Economics.

MITTELMAN, J. F. (1983-84) "World Order Studies and International Political Economy," *Alternatives* 9: 325-349.

MOORE, G.H. (1985) *International Economic Indicators: A Sourcebook.* Westport, Conn.: Greenwood Press.

MORAN, T. H. (ed.) (1985) *Multinational Corporations: The Political Economy of Foreign Direct Investment.* Lexington, Mass.: Lexington Books.

NOSSITER, B. D. (1987) *The Global Struggle for More: Third World Conflicts with Rich Nations.* New York: Harper and Row.

ORGANIZATION OF ECONOMIC COOPERATION AND DEVELOPMENT (OECD) (1983) *Aid from OPEC Countries.* Paris: OECD Publications.

_____. (1988) *External Debt: Definition, Statistical Coverage, and Methodology.* Paris: OECD Publications.

_____. (annual) *Development Cooperation.* Paris: OECD Publications.

_____. (annual) *Geographical Distribution of Financial Flows to Developing Countries, 19xx-xx* (3-years rolling dates). Paris: OECD Publications.

OVERSEAS DEVELOPMENT COUNCIL (annual). *US Foreign Policy and the Third*

World: Agenda 198x/8x series.   New York: Overseas Development Council.

PAUL, K., and R. BARBATO (1985) "The Multinational Corporation in the Less Developed Country: The Economic Development Model versus the North-South Model," *Academy of Management Review* 10: 8-14.

"Patterns of Economic Growth in Developing Countries, 1960-1984," in *United Nations Report on the World Social Situation* (1985). New York: United Nations Publications No. ST/ESA/165.

PIRAGES, D. (1978) *Global Ecopolitics: The New Context of International Relations.* North Scituate, Conn.: Duxbury Press.

POATS, R. M. (1985) *Twenty-Five Years of Development Cooperation: A Review: Efforts and Politics of the Members of the DAC.* Paris: Organization of Economic Cooperation and Development.

POPLINE (monthly) Washington: The Population Institute.

PUTNAM, R. D., and N. BAYNE (1984) *Hanging Together: The Seven-Power Summits.* Cambridge: Harvard University Press.

RAFFEL, M. W. (1985) *Comparative Health Systems: Descriptive Analyses of Fourteen Health Systems.* University Park: Pennsylvania State University Press.

REMMER, K. L. (1986) "The Politics of Economic Stabilization: IMF Standby Programs in Latin America, 1954-1984," *Comparative Politics* 19 (1, October): 1-24.

ROBINSON, J. D., 3d (May 3, 1986) "For a Japanese Equivalent of the Marshall Plan," *New York Times*, Op-Ed page.

SCHATEN, J. and G. (1987) *World Debt: Who Is To Pay?* London: Zed Books.

SELIGSON, M. A. (1984) *The Gap Between Rich and Poor: Contending Perspectives on the Political Economy of Development.* Boulder: Westview Press.

SMITH, D. M. (1982) *Where the Grass Is Greener: Living in an Unequal World.* Baltimore: Johns Hopkins University Press.

SPERO, J. (1988) *The Politics of International Economic Relations.* Englewood Cliffs, N. J.: Prentice-Hall.

STEWART, F. (1985) *Basic Needs in Developing Countries.* Baltimore: Johns Hopkins University Press.

SYLVESTER, C. (1983-84) "World Order and International Political Economy: Issues of World System Change," *Alternatives* 9: 373-392.

UNITED NATIONS (1984) *The Least Developed Countries: A Report.* New York: United Nations Publications.

———. (annual) *Yearbook of International Trade Statistics* . New York: United Nations Publications.

UNITED NATIONS. CONFERENCE ON TRADE AND DEVELOPMENT (UNCTAD) (annual) *Handbook of International Trade and Development Statistics.* Geneva: United Nations Publications.

UNITED NATIONS. EDUCATIONAL, SCIENTIFIC, AND CULTURAL ORGANIZATION (UNESCO) (annual) *Statistical Yearbook.* Paris: United Nations Publications.

UNITED STATES. AGENCY FOR INTERNATIONAL DEVELOPMENT (annual) *US*

Overseas Loans and Grants, and Aid from International Organizations. Washington: US Agency for International Development.

————. CENTRAL INTELLIGENCE AGENCY (annual) *Handbook of Economic Statistics.* Washington: US Government Printing Office.

————. DEPARTMENT OF STATE. BUREAU OF PUBLIC AFFAIRS (May, 1987) "International Narcotics Control," *gist:* 1-2.

WALLERSTEIN, I. (1979) *The Capitalist World Economy.* Cambridge: Cambridge University Press.

WATANABE, T. (1986) *Facilitating Development in a Changing Third World: Trade, Finance, Aid.* New York: The Trilateral Commission.

WEISS, T. G., and A. JENNINGS (1983) *More for the Least? Prospects for the Poorest Countries in the Eighties.* Lexington, Mass.: D. C. Heath.

WILLIAMSON, J., and M. MILLER (1987) *Targets and Indicators: A Blueprint for the International Coordination of Economic Policy.* Washington: Institute of International Economics.

WOOD, R. E., and M. MMUYA (1986) "The Debt Crisis in the Fourth World: Implications for North-South Relations," *Alternatives* 11: 107-131.

WORLD BANK (annual) *Social Indicators of Development.* Washington: World Bank Publications.

————. (annual) *World Development Report* (WDR). Washington: World Bank Publications.

————. (annual) *World Tables.* Washington: World Bank Publications.

WORLD DEVELOPMENT FORUM (bimonthly). San Francisco: The Hunger Project.

3

Ecological Balance

The third global value—ecological balance— is one of the most difficult for which to find data, for annual reference books of the sort used in Chapters 1 and 2 generally do not present information relating to the quality of a state's natural environment. Nevertheless, there are certain manifestations of sound ecological policies which can be measured to gain an implicit indication of the condition of a country's ecosystem, and the annual publications of the World Resources Institute, the Worldwatch Institute, the Population Reference Bureau, the World Health Organization, and the Food and Agriculture Organization are helpful in gathering such data.

V3.1 POPULATION

Ecology is defined here to mean the relationship between human beings and their environment. The most significant factor relating to the status of the world's ecosystem is global population—the number of people making demands upon the resources of this planet. Thus, before studying the interaction between population and environment certain demographic statistics must be mastered.

V3.1a. Population: Size and Growth Rates

Population data relates directly to economic well-being and social justice (Values V2 and V4). In Chapter 2, it was noted that the economies of most developing states grow at 3 to 4% a year; now it will be shown that most Third World countries' populations also increase by at least this much, meaning that on a per capita basis most of these states find it impossible to improve their average economic standing. A growing population making demands upon a static-sized economic pie leads to disputes over the justness with which its pieces will be distributed. With nine out of every ten new babies being born today coming in developing countries, the demands for justice which will be made upon their political systems, as well as upon the natural resources of this planet, will be formidable.

Certain statistics relating to population size, growth rate, and age cohort structure are readily available for most states. The populations for each state were listed in the introductory chapter (Table I.2); a closer analysis of the most populous states in that table is in order here. The top 30 states, with approximately 4 billion of the planet's 5.3 billion persons, are reproduced again as part of Table V3.1a.i(a). Almost 40% of the world's population can be found in just two states—China and India; if the ten "Super States" with more than 100 million persons each are considered, then more than 60% of the planet's people are accounted for; if the 20 "Significant Powers" with between 30 and 100 million apiece are added, then fully 80% of humankind is covered.

Obviously, these 30 states make the greatest demands upon the ecosystem, and among these those with the highest standards of living consume the most. The remaining 132 states combined include less than 20% of the people in the world, but it is in many of these countries that most of the highest *rates* of population growth occur.

Table V1.3a.i(b) presents for all 162 countries the rate of natural population increase, a figure which adjusts population growth rate (a more common statistic) for the net impact of emigration and immigration. The 30 most populous states from the top half of the table are boldfaced; of the 22 of these in the developing zones, 17 of them still have growth in excess of 1.8% per year. Future calls upon the resources of the globe (Value V3)—and for redistributive economic and social justice as between the rich nations and the poor (Values V2 and V4)—are going to come from those countries which are *both* large *and* have the fastest growing populations. For many of these countries, the next few generations will be a time of severe cultural adjustment—the period of the largest absolute population increases in history, and of massive movements of people from countryside to city in search of jobs and social services (Marden, et al., 1982; Fornos, 1988).

Population growth rates are important because they relate to the per capita growth rates of other indicators and measures. They are particularly interesting if analyzed from the perspective of specific age cohorts, such as those over the age of 65 entering into years of dependency upon the rest of society, and those reaching the age of 18 for whom jobs must be found. Many analysts warn that the main demographic bomb ticking over the next 20 years will not be overall population growth, but the widening gap between the age cohorts in different parts of the world (Salas, 1984).

The age cohort of most concern here is the 0-through-15 year-old group and the anticipated population growth which can be expected when this group moves into its child bearing years. In the advanced industrial world, this generation represents only about 21% of the population; in the developing countries, the number is closer to 40%.

Table V3.1a.ii lists states in order of the percentage of their population in the 0-to-15 age cohort. Future population growth rate rankings will roughly parallel the data in this table, whose leading states, except for a few with vigorous family planning programs, roughly replicate those of the previous table of current population growth.

Finally, a country's "population stability" can be represented by either the year of zero population growth (i.e., ZPG = a stationary population = one birth for one death), or the year when each woman averages one birth in her lifetime (i.e., a Net Reproduction Rate of 1 = one birth for one woman). There is generally a gap of about 50 years between the NRR=1 Year and the ZPG Year.

The World Bank publishes annually the NRR=1 Year for some 124 states. Kurian gives the later ZPG Year for 117 states; this table is more realistic in pinpointing a time when increased demands upon the world's resources will at least in theory stabilize.

Neither will be reproduced here, however, because tracking over the past several years has revealed that these estimated years are subject to significant variation as state behavior changes in response to technology, government programs, and changing societal mores relating to marriage and the family.

V3.1b. Population: Methods of Control

Three policies to address the global population problem—relating to National Family Planning, contraception, and abortion—will be analyzed next. The first is associated with most developing countries, the last with states in the European zone; contraception is a global phenomenon, with the method of choice varying across cultures. Naturally, a National Family Planning program could include elements of both techniques.

i. National Family Planning. More than 90 countries have some sort of official National Family Planning programs, and about a dozen of these have even amended their constitutions to establish a cabinet-level ministry for population. About 50 states provide some lesser forms of indirect support (UN Population Fund, 1990).

For the reasons discussed above relating to economics and resource consumption, it is generally in the developing zones that the population growth is considered a problem serious enough to require an official program to address it. The commitment is often not very firm, however, in countries with an Islamic or Roman Catholic religious tradition. According to the 1990 UN

Population Fund survey, however, only 16 states have absolutely no governmental support provided. They are, by zone, Ireland, Romania, Norway, Albania, Switzerland; Libya, Iraq, Kuwait, Oman, Saudi Arabia, UAE; Gabon; Mongolia, Cambodia, Laos; and Bolivia.

A National Family Program is meaningless, however, unless it is effective, and unless states recognize that they have a fertility rate problem. The Population Reference Bureau divides countries into three broad categories depending on whether the government perceives of its fertility level as too high, too low, or satisfactory. Of 162 states surveyed in 1990, 69 thought their fertility level was satisfactory and 18 thought it was too low. The fact that only 72 states judged their fertility level too high is disquieting in light of the statistics presented elsewhere in this chapter.

The World Bank has developed an index to measure states' commitments to family planning (Birdsall, 1985: 21-22). One hundred twenty points were allocated: 32 for policy and stage setting activities, 52 for service and service-related activities; 12 for record-keeping and evaluation; and 24 for availability and access. Ninety-two developing states were surveyed and the results yielded the numbers reproduced below: states scoring higher than 95 were rated A or very strong in their commitment; those between 70 and 95, B=strong; between 50 and 70, C=moderate; 25 to 50, D=weak; and less than 50, E=very weak. The superior effort of Asian states is notable in the display of these findings in Table V3.1b.i.

ii. Contraception. Whether related to some official National Family Planning program or not, by the mid-1980s more than 250 million couples in the developing world were using some form of contraception. UN projections anticipate a decline in Total Fertility Rate in these states from 4.3 children per woman in 1980 to 3.1 by 2000 and 2.4 in 2025. To achieve this decline, contraceptive use would have to grow from the current 46% of reproductive age couples to 56% in 2000 and 68% in 2025. This latter percentage is about the level of use now in the advanced industrial countries. Because the population will continue to grow through this period, the absolute number of contraceptive users in the less developed countries would have to increase by nearly 200%, to more than 736 million in 2025, to reach the 2.4 fertility rate (Population Reference Bureau, 1986a).

In any event, Table V3.1b.ii presents the latest statistics on the users of contraceptives, measured as the percentage of married women of childbearing age who are practicing any form of contraception. This display is a comprehensive composite of data drawn from three authoritative sources (United Nations, World Bank, Population Reference Bureau) yielding information on a total of 121 states.

iii. Abortion. Legal abortions are permitted only in 26 states, most of them in the European zone. Where such "freedom of choice" is permitted, there is seldom a need for any official government program to limit population growth. However, because of the controversial nature of this practice, even where it is legal, statistics on its extent are somewhat difficult to get. Two measures will be presented here.

Kurian, drawing upon figures from the Population Council, has published the rate of abortions per 1000 women ages 15-44, in the 26 states where this practice was legal in 1984. Because abortion is most common in the European zone, Table V3.1b.iii(a) expands this zone's normal single column display into two, and collapses the rest of the world (where data exists for only six states) into a single "other" column. It appears that abortion was *not legal* (and not just that the data was unavailable) in the following ten (generally Catholic) European states: Ireland, Malta, Portugal, Spain (legalized in 1986), Switzerland, Austria, Belgium, Luxembourg, Greece, and Albania.

While generally not legal (and therefore without official data to substantiate its scope), abortion is often available in developing countries. Tietze (1981) divides state policies on abortions into six categories, each with progressively fewer restrictions. Numerical correlations have been assigned to these practices here, and a final state order ranking computed on the basis of summing up the numbers associated with each policy; the maximum possible score for a state permitting abortions for all five reasons would be 15 (5+4+3+2+1).

Tietze's six categories, along with the numeric characterizations assigned for the computations of state rankings, are listed next.

5 = abortions permitted on socio-economic grounds (woman's age, marital and economic status, size of family. etc.);

4 = abortions permitted on juridical grounds (pregnancies resulting from rape or incest);

3 = abortions permitted on eugenic grounds (fetal birth defects);

2 = abortions permitted if pregnancy would endanger woman's health;

1 = abortions permitted if pregnancy would endanger woman's life;

0 = abortions outlawed (no exceptions, although abortions to save woman's life may be authorized under general principles of criminal law).

Although there is some overlapping of categories and obvious variation in each state's implementation of these guidelines, the country rankings of Table V3.1b.iii(b) are nevertheless a good approximation of state attitudes with respect to public policy on abortion.

V3.1c. Fertility and the Role of Women

A final measure related to population growth is "fertility rate" expressed either as the number of births per 100 women (Kurian, 1984 for 135 states), or the number of births the average woman has in her lifetime (Population Reference Bureau, 1990 for 162 states). The latter statistic, which is easier for the layperson to comprehend, is presented in Table V3.1c. Again, the regional and cultural differences are striking. The average for advanced industrial states is 1.7 children per woman, for upper-middle income states (World Bank definition) 3.5, for lower-middle income countries 4.1, for those in the lowest income group 5.6, and for sub-Saharan Africa 6.6 (World Bank, *World Development Report*, 1989: 216-17).

A fertility rate range of 2.1-2.5 indicates the level at which a country's population would eventually stop growing. This number has been reached by 29 out of 30 states in Europe, but by only 18 states in the rest of the world. According to Brown and Jacobson (1986), because these 47 states account for nearly half the world's population (including the industrial states and China), a demographic transition has been completed for they have or soon will achieve a fertility rate at or below the replacement level. However, in the other half of the world, where birth rates remain high, rapid population growth is beginning to overwhelm local life-support systems in many countries, leading to ecological deterioration and declining living standards.

In the early 1980s the World Bank and the International Monetary Fund, two agencies not known for their sympathies to women, published studies reporting an inverse relationship between the number of children a woman has and the extent of her formal education. Writing in the September, 1984, issue of *Finance and Development*, the financial institutions noted that in all countries women who had completed primary school had fewer children than women with no education, and that the number of children declined regularly as the education of mothers increased above primary-school level. These differences persisted regardless of family income, occupation, religion, or any other factors. These studies also showed that educating women made a greater difference in reducing family size than educating men.

It is clear that women have a central role in solving the world's population problem. As section V4.4c will show, however, women have far from equal status in the world today, and everywhere face barriers to their empowerment. This discrimination, to be discussed at greater length in Chapter 4's analysis of social justice, will thus greatly affect humankind's efforts to control the global problems related to resource use and environmental abuse covered in this chapter.

V3.1d. Hunger

In many minds, the most immediate issue associated with an excess of global population is hunger—will there be enough food to feed the world's peoples?

This Malthusian problem is indeed a very real one in more than half the 162 states, chiefly in the developing world, where more people have died of hunger in the past six years than have been killed in all the wars of the past 150 (Hunger Project, 1985).   About 15 million people each year die of hunger, and malnutrition is an affliction that affects the lives of almost 24% of the global population, a billion people, each day.

The causes of hunger, why it persists in a world of sufficiency, and the solutions and ways of ending it are issues upon which there is little or no agreement among the experts. The reason is that hunger is not a problem of scarcity of food resources, but of the economic systems under which they are distributed. As compared to the fossil fuel and mineral resources to be covered in section V3.3, the land and technology (seeds, fertilizer, irrigation methods) needed to feed the world are available to humankind today. The problem is that under current organizational patterns many countries use all their land to grow crops only for export, and the cash they receive for these exports is insufficient to purchase foods grown (or manufactured and packaged) elsewhere in a fashion that results in an adequate diet for their own people (Warnock, 1987; Grigg, 1986; George, 1984; Hopkins et al., 1982; Murdock, 1981; Lappe and Collins, 1977).

Nevertheless, according to the Hunger Project (1985), 75 countries have ended hunger within their borders as a basic, society-wide issue. According to this report, there is no single prescribed way to achieve the end of the persistence of hunger in a society; what is needed is the political will to come to grips with the distributional arrangements. Some countries have focused on land reform; others have emphasized food subsidies, collectivized agriculture, or privately owned family farms. But, for every country that cited a specific action as crucial to ending hunger, there is another country that ended hunger without it.

Hunger is considered to be chronic when the infant mortality rate (IMR) is above 50 per 1000. Table V3.1d.i's global survey shows that Africa is the zone with the most severe hunger problems, with every one of its states having an IMR greater than 50; approximately one-half of its population experiences severe food shortages daily. Numbers for the top few states in each zone are provided at the bottom of the display for comparative reference.

A perhaps more relevant measure—the *child* death rate—has been developed to highlight the problem of children in developing nations. Based upon the model life tables developed by Coale and Demeny (1966), it lists the number of deaths per thousand of children under the age of five. Its results, presented in Table V3.1d.ii, reflect especially the impact of unhealthy environmental conditions; again, the African zone is the worst by this measure, closely followed by the Islamic and Asian areas.

Other relevant measures pertaining to basic levels of food consumption and whether a society is being adequately fed include (a) protein supply per capita;

and (b) calories consumed per capita, as compared with the World Health Organization's respective Recommended Daily Allowances (RDA).

The protein figure is not cited as frequently, but is important because it relates to human intelligence. Table V3.1d.iii(a) compares it with the WHO recommendation of 65 grams per capita (subject to variations because of age, climate, occupation, and other factors). Table V3.1d.iii(b) displays the average daily food supply in calories per capita available at the retail level after allowance for animal feed, seeds, storage and marketing losses, and waste, as estimated by the Food and Agriculture Organization.

In both cases, the RDA requirements are based upon intake required to maintain moderate activity, taking account of the age/sex structure of the population and climate. The highest and lowest five states in each zone for these two measures are presented. With respect to both calories and protein, all European states achieve the Recommended Daily Allowance. In the other four zones, although the top five states meet the RDA standard, the bottom five never do, nor do many of their other states.

V3.1a.i(a) - World's Most Populous States (> 30 mill. ea.)

Europe	Islamic	Africa	Asia	Latin America
			China-1,135.5	
USSR-288.0			India-853.4	
US-249.2			Indonesia-180.5	Brazil-150.4
	Pakistan-122.7		Japan-123.5	
W.Germany-60.5		Nigeria-111.9	Bangladesh-115.6	
Italy-57.3			Vietnam-67.2	Mexico-88.6
UK-56.9			Phil. I.-64.2	
France-56.2	Iran-56.6	Ethiopia-46.7	Thailand-55.7	
Spain-39.3	Turkey-55.6	Zaire-36.0	S.Korea-43.6	Argentina-32.3
Poland-38.4	Egypt-54.1	So.Africa-35.2	Myanmar-41.7	Colombia-31.8
n=8	n=4	n=4	n=10	n=4 (30)

V3.1a.i(b) - Rate of Natural Population Increase, 1990

	Iraq 3.9%	Kenya,Zamb.-3.8%		
	Syria 3.8	IC,Tanz.-3.7	Maldives 3.7%	
	Iran 3.6	Ug.,Togo-3.6		
	Jord.,N.Yem.-3.5	Rwan.,Malawi-3.4	Solomons 3.5	
	Saudi A.,S.Yem.-3.4	**Zaire 3.3**	Comoros 3.4	Nicaragua 3.3%
	Oman 3.3	Ben.,Liber.-3.2	Madagascar 3.2	Guat.,Hond.-3.1
	Libya,Algeria-3.1	BF,Burundi-3.2	Vanuatu 3.2	Belize 3.1
	Somalia 3.1	Zimbwe.,Nam.-3.2		Grenada 3.0
	Pakistan 3.0	Ghana,Swazi.-3.1		
	Djibouti 3.0	Mali,Niger-3.0		Paraguay 2.8
	Sudan 2.9	Congo 3.0		El Salvador 2.7
	Egypt 2.9	Bots.,**Nigeria-2.9**		Bolivia 2.6
	Mauritania 2.7	CV,Lesotho-2.8	Mong.,WSam.-2.8	Dom.Rep. 2.5
	Morocco 2.6	**S.Africa 2.7**	Papua NG 2.7	Ecua.,CRica-2.5
	Afghanistan 2.6	Moz.,Angola-2.7	**Phil. I. 2.6**	**Mexico 2.4**
	Chad 2.5	STP,Senegal-2.7	**Bangl. 2.5**	Peru 2.4
Albania 2.0%	Kuwait 2.5	Eq.Guin.,Gambia-2.6	**Vietnam 2.5**	Venezuela 2.3
	Bahrain 2.3	Cameroon 2.6	Laos,Brun.-2.5	Panama 2.2
Iceland 1.1	Qatar 2.3	C.Af.R.,Guinea-2.5	Nep.,Malay.-2.5	St. Lucia 2.2
USSR 0.9	**Turkey 2.1**	Sierra L. 2.5	Camb.,Fiji-2.2	Haiti 2.2
US,Malta-0.8	Lebanon 2.1	Gabon 2.2	**India 2.1**	Dominica 2.1
Canada 0.7	Tunisia 2.0	GBissau 2.1	NKor.,Bhut.-2.1	**Colombia 2.0**
Yugo.,Greece-0.6	UAE 1.9	**Ethiopia 2.0**	**Myanmar 2.0**	Trin.,Sur.-2.0
Poland-0.6			**Indonesia 1.8**	**Brazil 1.9**
Romania 0.5	Israel 1.6		Seychelles 1.7	St. V.,Guy.-1.9
France,Neth.-0.4			**Thailand 1.5**	Chile,Jam.-1.7
Spain,Switz.-0.3			Sing.,Sri L.-1.5	Bahamas 1.5
Finld.,Nor.-0.3			**China 1.4**	**Argentin.1.3**
UK,Swed.,Cz.-0.2	Cyprus 1.0		Mauritius 1.3	St. Chris. 1.3
Belg.,Lux.-0.2			Taiwan 1.2	Cuba 1.2
Greece,Port.-0.2			**S.Korea 1.0**	Antigua 1.0
Italy,Bulg.-0.1			Australia 0.8	Uruguay 0.8
Austria 0.1			N. Zealand 0.8	Barbados 0.7
W.Ger. 0.0			**Japan 0.4**	
Den.,E.Ger.-0.0				
Hungary (-0.2)				
n=30	n=28	n=38	n=33	n=33 (162)

Source: Population Reference Bureau, *1990 World Population Data Sheet*.

V3.1a.ii - % Population in Age Cohort 0-15

Europe	Islamic	Africa	Asia	Latin America
	N.Yemen 50%	Kenya 50%		
	Syria 49	Rwanda 49		
	S.Yemen 48	Tanzania 49	Comoros 48%	Honduras 47%
	Somalia 47	Zambia 49		Nicaragua 47
		Uganda 49	Solomons 47	Guatemala 46
	Algeria 46	IC,Togo-49		El Salvador 45
	Afghanistan 46	Burkina F. 48		Belize 44
	Djibouti 46	Malawi 48	Vanuatu45	St. Lucia 44
	Oman 46	Benin 47	Madagascar 45	St. Vincent 44
	Jordan 46	Mali,Niger-47	Maldives 45	Bolivia 43
	Iraq 45	Swaziland 47		Mexico 42
	Sudan 45	Liberia 46	Laos 43	Ecuador 42
	Saudi A. 45	Botswana 46	Bangladesh 43	Paraguay 41
	Iran 45	Ethiopia 46	Nepal 42	Haiti 40
	Mauritania 44	Zaire 46	Vietnam 42	
	Libya 44	Congo,Ghana-45	Mongolia 41	Grenada 39
	Pakistan 44	Burundi 45	Papua NG 41	Venezuela 39
Albania 35%	Chad 43	Zimbabwe 45	W.Samoa 40	Dom.Rep. 39
	Morocco 42	Namibia 45	Philippines 39	Peru 38
Ireland 28		Nigeria 45	India 39	Jamaica 37
	Egypt 41	Burundi 45	Bhutan 38	Guyana 37
Poland 26		Angola 45	Indonesia 38	
USSR 25	Lebanon 40	Gamb.,Camr.-44	Fiji 38	Brazil 36
Romania 25		Sierra L. 44	Malaysia 38	Costa Rica 36
Iceland 25		Senegal 44	Myanmar 37	Panama 36
Czech. 24		Mozambique 44	Brunei 37	Colombia 36
Malta 24	Tunisia 39	Eq.Guinea 43	Seychelles 36	Argentina 34
Yugoslavia 23		Les.,Guinea-43	Cambodia 36	Bahamas 34
Portugal 22		C.Af. R. 42	Sri Lanka 35	Suriname 34
Spain 22		Cape Verde 42	Thailand 35	St.Chris. 34
US 22	Kuwait 37	GBissau 41	N.Korea 34	Trinidad 34
Hungary 21		S.Africa 40	Mauritius 30	Dominica 34
Canada 21	Turkey 36			Chile 31
Bulgaria 21	Bahrain 33	Gabon 33	Taiwan 28	
Greece 20	Israel 32		S.Korea 27	Barbados 28
France 20			China 27	Antigua 27
UK 19	UAE 31		N.Zealand 24	Uruguay 26
Norway 19	Qatar 29			Cuba 25
Finland 19			Singapore 23	
E.Ger. 19	Cyprus 26			
Italy 18				
Austria 18			Australia 22	
Nethrlds. 18				
Denmark 18				
Belgium 18				
Sweden 18				
Luxmbrg. 17				
Switz. 17			Japan 20	
W.Ger. 15				
n=30	n=28	n=38	n=33	n=33 (162)

Source: Population Reference Bureau, *1990 World Population Data Sheet.*

V3.1b.i - Family Planning Programs Effort (120 points max.)

	Europe	Islamic	Africa	Asia	Latin America
	n.a.			China-100.9	
				S.Korea-96.9	
A				Singapore-95.3	
				Taiwan-92.6	
				Indonesia-87.1	Colombia-85.3
				Mauritius-85.3	Mexico-78.6
				SriLanka-81.6	El Salvador-75.4
B				India-74.7	Dom.Rep.-64.3
				Thailand-70.5	Jamaica-64.1
		Tunisia-69.8		Bangladesh-68.7	Cuba-61.5
				Phil.I.-63.6	Panama-59.2
				Malaysia-61.1	Trinidad-55.0
				Vietnam-57.6	Chile-52.1
C				Fiji-55.4	Brazil-50.1
		Pakistan-49.4	Botswana-34.5	Nepal-46.3	Ecuador-49.4
		Egypt-45.7	Kenya-33.7		Haiti-43.8
		Morocco-45.4	Zimbabwe-32.9		Costa Rica-39.8
		Lebanon-42.4	Gambia-31.2		Venezuela-37.5
		Cyprus-39.0	Liberia-27.9	W.Samoa-33.8	Guatemala-34.1
		Turkey-35.0	Rwanda-27.6	Papua NG-30.6	Guyana-29.9
		Algeria-30.0	Tanzania-26.2		Peru-26.4
D					Honduras-26.2
			Senegal-22.9		Nicaragua-22.1
		S.Yemen-20.2	Uganda-21.9		
		Jordan-19.0	Congo-21.5		
		Afghan.-16.7	Ghana-20.5		
			Sierra Leone-17.8		
			Nigeria-17.4		
			Mozambique-17.4		
			Zaire-16.3		
			Lesotho-15.5		
			Zambia-14.7		
			Togo-13.1		
			Burundi-12.3		
			Mali-11.6		Paraguay-10.7
		Somalia-8.5	Cameroon-8.1	Madagascar-8.9	Bolivia-8.7
		Chad-8.3	Niger-7.4		
		N.Yemen-8.2	Ethiopia-7.4		
		Sudan-7.3	Malawi-6.5		
		Syria-7.3	Ivory Coast-3.7		
		Kuwait-6.1	Burkina-3.6	Myanmar-3.4	
		Mauritania-4.2	C. Af. R.-2.8	Cambodia-0	
		Iraq-3.7	Guinea-3.2	Laos-0	
E		Libya-0	Eq.G.-0.5	Mongolia-0	
TOT:		n=20/28	n=29/37	n=22/33	n=21/33 (92)

Source: "Measuring Family Planning Program Effort in Developing Countries, 1972-1982," by W. Parker Mauldin and Robert J. Lapham, in Birdsall (1984: 21-22).

171

V3.1b.ii - Users of Contraceptives, % of Married Women

Europe	Islamic	Africa	Asia	Latin America
Czech. 95%				
UK 83				
Belgium 81			Mauritius 75%	
Finland 80			China 74	
France 78			Singapore 74	Argentina 74%*
Sweden 78			Taiwan 74^	
Italy 78			SKorea 70*	Costa Rica 69
W.Germany 77			N.Zealand 69	
Bulgaria 76			Australia 67^	Brazil 65
Poland 75			Thailand 67	Colombia 64
			Japan 64	Dominica 62^
Hungary 73			Sri Lanka 62	Cuba 60*
Canada 73				Panama 58
Nethrlds. 72				St. Vincent 56^
Switzrld. 71	Lebanon 53%^			Mexico 53
Austria 71	Turkey 51		Malaysia 51	Trinidad 52
Norway 71		S.Africa 48%	Indonesia 47	St.Lucia 52^
	Tunisia 41		Phil. I. 44*	Jamaica 51
US 68	Morocco 35	Zimbabwe 38		Dom Rep 50
Portugal 66		Botswana 27		Venezuela 49*
Denmark 63	Egypt 29			Antigua 48^
Ireland 60^	Jordan 26		Fiji 38^	Barbados 48^
Spain 59	Iran 23*	Kenya 17	India 34	El Salvador 47
Romania 58				Peru 45
Yugoslavia 55		Senegal 11		Paraguay 44
		Rwanda 10		Ecuador 44
		Ghana 9		Chile 43*
	Syria 19	Benin 9	Bangladesh 25	St. Chris. 41Δ
	Iraq 14^	Burundi 8	Solomons 23Δ	Belize 37Δ
		Malawi 6	Vietnam 20*	Honduras 34
		Liberia 6	W.Samoa 18^	Guyana 31
	Pakistan 7	Lesotho 5		Grenada 31Δ
	Algeria 7*	Nigeria 4	Nepal 13	Nicaragua 27
		Mali 4	Vanuatu 13Δ	Bolivia 26
		S.Leone 4		
		Ivory Coast 2		Guatemala 23
	Sudan 4	Cameroon 2		
		Ethiopia 2	Myanmar 5*	
		GBissau 1^	Papua NG 4*	Haiti 6
	Afghanistan 2^	Gambia 1^		
	N.Yemen 1	Niger,Zambia-1*		
	Chad 1^	BF,Guinea-1*		
	Mauritania 0	Zaire,Uganda 1		
	Somalia 0*	Angola, Tanzania 1*		
na=7	na=11	na=10	na-10	na=3
Ice.,Lux.,Malta	Isr,Cyp,Kuw,Bahr.	CV,STP,Eq.G.,Namb.	Mad,Mald,Como,NK	Bahamas
Albania,Greece	Oman,Q,UAE,SaudiA.	Congo,Togo,Gab.,	Seych,Bhut,Mong.	Suriname
SU, E.Ger.	Djib.,SYem.,Libya	CAfR,Moz.,Swazi.	Laos,Camb.,Brun.	Uruguay
n=23	n=17	n=28	n=23	n=30 (121)

Source: UN Population Fund 1990, n=79; plus * WDR88f85 and 87f84, n=21; ΔPop.Ref.Bu.
1988 Data Sheet, n=5; and ^US Dept. of Commerce 1984, Table 5, for various years, n=16.

V3.1b.iii - Abortions
(a) - Legal Abortions per 1000 Women

Eastern Europe	West. Europe/N.Am.	Other(As=4,ME=1,LA=1,Af=0)	
USSR - 180.0	US - 30.2	Japan - 84.2	
Romania - 88.1	Denmark - 21.6		Cuba - 52.1
Bulgaria - 68.3	Sweden - 20.9		
Yugoslavia-43.9	Norway - 17.7	Singapore - 27.7	
Hungary - 35.9	Italy - 15.8		
Czech. - 29.4	Finland - 14.7	Tunisia - 14.6	
E.Germany -22.5	France - 13.9		
Poland - 18.3	UK - 12.0		
	Canada - 11.6		
	W.Germany - 8.8		
	Iceland - 8.6	New Zealand - 5.7	
	Netherlands - 5.3	India - 2.3	
n=8	n=12	n=6	

Source: Kurian, *New Book of World Rankings 1984*, from The Population Council.

(b)-Abortion Policies, State Rankings

Europe	Islamic	Africa	Asia	Latin America
		On Request		
US,USSR			China	Cuba
W.Ger.,E.Ger.			Singapore	
Norway,Sweden			Vietnam	
Austria,Italy,Yugo.				
		Relatively Liberal		
Czech.,Hung.-14			N.Korea-14	
Bulg.,Rom.-14			Japan,India-14	
France-14				
Poland-11		Zambia-10	Australia-10	Uruguay-10
UK-10	Israel-9	S.Af.,Zimbwe.-9	New Zealand-9	
Greece-9	Turkey-8	Liberia-9	S.Kor.,Malay.-9	El Salvador-8
		Somewhat Restrictive		
	Jordan-6	Cameroon-6	Thailand-6	Braz.,Mex.,Ec.-5
				Arg.,Bolivia-3
		2		
Canada, Finland	Algeria	Ghan.,Guin.,Sierra L	Nepal	Nic.,C.Rica,Hond.
Nethrlds.,Switz.	Morocco	Tanz.,Kenya,Uganda	Papua NG	Jamaica,Trinidad
Albania		Ethiopia,Congo		
		Most Restrictive		
		1		
Ireland	Syr,Leb,Iran,Iq,	Benin,IC,Nigeria	Madagascar	Colombia
Belgium	Aghan,Pak,N.Yem.	Senegal,Togo	Bangladesh	Parag.,Chile,Peru
	Saudi,Kuwait	Mozmbq.,Malawi	Laos,Myanmar	Guat.,Panama
	Libya,Chad,Sudan	Lesotho	Sri Lanka	Venezuela
		0		
Portugal	Egypt	Mali,Niger,BF	Phil.I.,Indonesia	Dom.Rep.
Spain(pre-'86)	Somalia	Rwanda,Burundi	Taiwan	Haiti
	Mauritania	C.Af.R.,Zaire	Mongolia	
n=26	n=20	n=28	n=22	n=22 (118)

Source: Tietze (1981), n=136 states surveyed; no data on 18.

173

V3.1c - Fertility Rate (# of Births in a Woman's Lifetime)

Europe	Islamic	Africa	Asia	Latin America
		Rwanda 8.3		
	N.Yemen 7.6	Malawi 7.7		
	Iraq 7.3	Ivory Coast 7.4	Comoros 7.1	
	Saudi A. 7.2	Uganda 7.4		
	Oman 7.2	BF,Mali-7.2		
	Afghanistan 7.1	Togo,Zamb.-7.2	Madagascar 6.6	
	S.Yemen 7.0	Niger 7.1	Maldives 6.6	
		Tanzania 7.1		
	Syria 6.8	Benin,Bur.-7.0	Solomons 6.3	
	Pakistan 6.7	Kenya 6.7		
	Djibouti 6.6	Nigeria 6.5	Nepal 6.1	
	Somalia 6.6	Sierra L. 6.5		
	Mauritania 6.5	Sen.,Gambia-6.4		
	Sudan 6.4	Liberia 6.4		
	Iran 6.3	Ang.,Moz.-6.4	Papua NG 5.7	
		Ghana 6.3		Guatemala 5.6
		Guinea 6.2		Nicaragua 5.5
	Algeria 6.1	Ethiopia 6.2	Laos 5.5	Honduras 5.3
		Zaire 6.2	Vanuatu 5.5	Bolivia 5.1
	Chad 5.9	Namibia 6.1	Bhutan 5.5	Haiti 5.1
	Jordan 5.9	Swaziland 6.1		Belize 5.0
		Congo 6.0		Grenada 4.9
		Zimbabwe 5.8	Bangladesh 4.9	Paraguay 4.6
	Libya 5.5	Cameroon 5.8	Mongolia 4.8	El Salvador 4.4
		Lesotho 5.8	W.Samoa 4.6	Ecuador 4.3
		C.Af.R. 5.6	Cambodia 4.5	Peru 4.1
		Eq. Guinea 5.5	Phil. I. 4.3	St. Lucia 3.8
Albania 3.2		GBissau 5.4	Myanmar 4.2	Dom. Rep. 3.8
	Morocco 4.8	STP 5.4	India 4.2	Mexico 3.8
USSR 2.5	UAE 4.8	Botswana 5.3	Vietnam 4.2	Venezuela 3.5
Ice.,Rom.-2.3	Egypt 4.7	Cape Verde 5.2		Colombia 3.4
Ireland 2.2	Qatar 4.5	Gabon 5.0	Brunei 3.6	Brazil 3.3
Cz.,Pol.-2.1		S. Africa 4.5	Malaysia 3.6	Costa Rica 3.3
Malta 2.0	Bahrain 4.2`		Indonesia 3.3	Trinidad 3.1
Swed.,US-2.0	Tunisia 4.1		Fiji 3.3	Panama 3.1
Yugo.,Bulg.-2.0				Argentina 3.0
Nor.,Hung.-1.8	Kuwait 3.7		Seychelles 2.7	Suriname 3.0
UK,France-1.8	Lebanon 3.7		Thailand 2.6	Guyana 2.8
E.Germany 1.7	Turkey 3.5		N.Korea 2.5	St. Vincent 2.8
Can.,Fin.-1.7			Sri Lanka 2.3	Dominica 2.7
Portugal 1.6	Israel 3.1		China 2.3	St. Chris. 2.6
Switzrld. 1.6			Singapore 2.0	Chile 2.5
Belg.,Den.-1.6	Cyprus 2.4		Mauritius 2.0	Uruguay 2.4
Spain 1.5			N.Zealand 2.0	Jamaica 2.4
Greece 1.5			Taiwan 1.8	Bahamas 2.3
Nethrlds. 1.5			Australia 1.8	Cuba 1.9
Luxmbrg. 1.4			S.Korea 1.6	Barbados 1.8
W.Germany 1.4			Japan 1.6	Antigua 1.7
Austria 1.4				
Italy 1.3				
n=30	n=28	n=38	n=33	n=33 (162)

Source: Population Reference Bureau. *1990 World Population Data Sheet.*

174

V3.1d.i - States with Chronic Hunger (IMR>50), 1985-90

Europe	Islamic	Africa	Asia	Latin America
	Afghanistan 183	Mali 169		
		Sierra Leone 169		
	Djibouti 152º	Gambia 164		
	Somalia 149	Malawi 150		
		Ethiopia 149	Cambodia 130	
	Chad 132	Guinea 147		
		Mozambique 141	Bhutan 128	
		Burkina F. 139	Nepal 128	
	Mauritania 127	Angola 137		
	N.Yemen 120	Niger 135		
	S.Yemen 120	C. Af. R. 132	Bangladesh 119	Haiti 117
		GBissau 132		Bolivia 110
	Pakistan 109	Senegal 131		
	Iran 107	Eq.Guinea 127	Laos 110	
	Sudan 106	Liberia 122		
	Oman 100	Rwanda 122	Vanuatu 101º	
		Swaziland 118		
		Namibia 116º	India 99	
	Egypt 85	Burundi 114		Peru 88
		Benin 110		
		Tanzania 106		
	Morocco 82	Nigeria 105	Comoros 80	
	Libya82	Gabon 103		
		Uganda 103	Indonesia 74	
		Ivory Coast 100		
		Lesotho 100	Maldives 68º	Honduras 69
	Turkey 76	Zaire 98	Vietnam 67	
	Algeria 74	Cameroon 94		Dom.Rep. 65
		Togo 93		
	Tunisia 71	Ghana 90		
	Saudi A. 71	Zambia 80		Brazil 63
	Iraq 69	STP 74º	Myanmar 63	Ecuador 63
		Congo 73	Papua NG 62	
		S. Africa 72*		Nicaragua 62
		Kenya 72		
		Zimbabwe 72		Guatemala 59
		Botswana 67		El Salvador 59
		Cape Verde 63	Madagascar 59	
	n=19	n=38	n=14	n=10 (81)

Europe	Islamic	Africa	Asia	Latin America
4 @ 10*	Qatar 32		Mauritius 23	Chile 20
4 @ 9	UAE 32		N.Zealand 11	Jamaica 19
Can.,Lux.,Fr.-8	Bahrain 27	N	Singapore 9	Costa Rica 18
Neth.,Switz.-7	Kuwait 20	O	Australia 8	Grenada 15º
Nor.,Denmk.-7	Cyprus 15	N	Taiwan 7º	Cuba 14
Ice,Fin,Swed.-6	Israel 14	E	Japan 6	Dominica 13º
n=30	n=28	n=38	n=33	n=33

Source: World Resources Institute 1988-89, Table 15.3; supplemented by ºODC *Agenda* 88f85.
*S. Af. IMR is 12 for whites, 69 for urban non-whites, 282 for rural blacks (*World Development Forum*, August 15, 1984). US IMR is 10.4, 8.9 for whites, 18.0 for blacks.

V3.1d.ii - Child (ages 0 to 5) Death Rate, (per 1000), 1985-90

Europe	Islamic	Africa	Asia	Latin America
	Afghanistan 318	Mali,Sierra L.-291		
		Gambia 281		
		Malawi 263		
	Somalia 252	Ethiopia 252		
		Guinea 249		
	Chad 223	Mozambique 241		
		Burkina F. 235		
		Angola 232		
		Niger 228		
		C.Af.R. 223	Bhutan 196	
	Mauritania 214	GBissau 223	Nepal 196	
		Senegal 222	Cambodia 192	
		Eq.Guinea 214	Bangladesh 188	
	N.Yemen 196	Liberia 206		
	S. Yemen 196	Rwanda 205		
	Sudan 175	Burundi 191		Bolivia 171
	Pakistan 165	Benin 184		Haiti 170
	Oman 157	Tanzania 174	Laos 160	
	Iran 155	Nigeria,Swazi.-173	India 148	
	Egypt 124	Gabon 169	Comoros 127	Peru 122
	Morocco 118	Uganda 169		
	Libya 118	Zaire 161	Indonesia 117	Honduras 106
	Algeria 105	Cameroon 153		
	Tunisia 99	Togo 152		Guatemala 99
	Saudi A. 98	Ivory Coast 148	Vietnam 91	Nicaragua 93
Albania 48	Iraq 94	Ghana 145	Madagascar 91	Ecuador 87
	Turkey 92	Lesotho 135	Myanmar 85	Brazil 86
Romania 28	Syria 63	Zambia 127	Papua NG 84	El Salvador 84
Yugoslavia 28	Jordan 57	Congo 115	Philippines 72	Dom.Rep. 82
USSR 27	Lebanon 49	Zimbabwe 113	Mongolia 58	Mexico 68
Portugal 20	UAE 38	Kenya 113	Thailand 49	Colombia 68
Poland 19	Qatar 38	S. Africa 96	China 44	Paraguay 61
Bulgaria 19	Bahrain 32	Botswana 92	Sri Lanka 43	Venezuela 43
Hungary 19	Kuwait 23	C. Verde 86	Malaysia 35	Argentina 38
Greece 16			S.Korea 31	Guyana 37
Czech. 16	Cyprus 16		N.Korea 31	Suriname 37
Malta 13	Israel 16		Fiji 31	Panama 33
US,W.Ger.-12			Mauritius 28	Uruguay 30
Austria 12				Chile 24
Belg.,Italy-12				Trinidad 23
Irelnd,Spain-11			N. Zealand 12	Jamaica 23
UK,E.Ger.-11				Costa Rica 22
France,Lux.-10			Singapore 11	Cuba 18
Denmk.,Norway-9			Australia 10	Barbados 14
Canada,Neth.-9				
Switzerland 8			Japan 8	
Finland,Sweden-7				
Iceland 7				
n=30	n=27/28	n=36/37	n=26/33	n=25/33 (144)

Source: WRI, *World Resources 1988-89*, Table 15.3, n=144.

176

V3.1d.iii - Food Consumption

Europe	Islamic	Africa	Asia	Latin America

(a)-Protein Supply per Capita vs. 65 RDA

Europe	Islamic	Africa	Asia	Latin America
Iceland 130	Cyprus 108	Gabon 79	N.Zealand 115	Argentina 113
Poland 108	Israel 105	Botswana 76	Mongolia 99	Uruguay 87
France 108	Kuwait 102	S.Africa 76	Australia 90	Barbados 87
Greece 108	Libya 98	Lesotho 73	Japan 89	Paraguay 80
Ire.,US-106	UAE 93	Ethiopia 73	S.Korea 85	Chile 76
....	....	....	....	....
UK 90	Som.,Sud.,Jor.-65	Tanzania 41	Thailand 47	Bol.,Col.-55
Sweden 89	Afghan. 64	Ghana 41	Nepal 46	Honduras 52
Malta 87	N.Yemen 61	Guinea 40	Sri Lanka 45	Ecuador 50
Albania 86	Chad 58	Zaire 33	Papua NG 41	Dom.Rep. 47
Portugal 85	Pakistan 56	Mozambq. 32	Bangldsh. 40	Haiti 45
n=30	n=24/28	n=33/38	n=23/33	n=24/33

Source: Sivard 1985 for 1982.

(b)-Calorie Supply per Capita vs. 2300 RDA

Europe	Islamic	Africa	Asia	Latin America
E.Ger. 3791^	UAE 3733	S.Africa 2924	N.Zealand 3464	Argentin.3210
Greece 3688	Libya 3601	Congo 2619	Australia 3326	Mexico 3132
Belgium 3679^	Egypt 3342	Iv.Coast 2562	N.Korea 3151^	Cuba 3122^
Bulgaria 3663^	Iran 3313	Gabon 2521	S.Korea 2907	Trinidad 3082
US 3645	Syria 3260	Swazi. 2499*	Japan 2864	Barbad. 3054*
Denmark 3633	Turkey 3229	Niger 2432	Singapore 2840	Paraguay 2853
....	....	....	....	....
UK 3256	Pakistan 2315	Sierra L. 1854	Thailand 2331	Peru 2246
Finland 3122	S.Yemen 2298	Rwanda 1830	Vietnam 2297	El Sal. 2160
Malta 3103*	Sudan 2208	Guinea 1776	India 2230	Bolivia 2143
Sweden 3064	Somalia 2138	Ghana 1759	Papua NG 2205	Honduras 2068
Iceland 3013*	Afghan. 1833*	Ethiopia 1749	Nepal 2052	Ecuador 2058
Albania 2726^	Chad 1717	Mozambq.1595	Bangldsh.1927	Haiti 1902
n=29/30	n=22/28	n=32/38	n=23/33	n=24/33 (130)

Source: WDR90f86, Table 28, n=113; plus ^WDR87f85, *Kurian84f80, n=17.

V3.2. ENVIRONMENT

In counterpoint to V3.1's study of the world's growing population, this section will investigate the comparatively static environment upon which humankind is making its growing demands (Caldwell, 1985; Dahlberg, et al., 1985; Holdgate, et al., 1982; Falk, 1972). First, an analysis will be made of the stock of basic land and water resources available to each country, and of the relationship of population to available land and water. This will be followed by coverage of the growing phenomena of urbanization and environmental pollution, and a general survey of access to healthy living conditions around the world.

V3.2a. Land

Those countries with the largest land areas are generally blessed with many natural resources and the potential for great wealth and power (V2 and V1) in the international system. Their ecological potential is also favorable as the discussion of fuels, metals, minerals, forests, and fisheries in the upcoming section on depletable natural resources (V3.3) will show. First, however, restrictions on states' environments will be analyzed. Countries with limited land area are hurt not only by their lack of potential, but also in certain unfavorable dimensions relating to population density. Table V3.2a.i ranks all states in order of their physical size, followed by two listings of the population densities of each zone's ten most "compacted" countries (Table V3.2a.ii(a) and (b)).

Population density as related to agricultural land is important for there are many countries which are vast in total territory, but where most of the people are concentrated within a single fertile area (such as along the banks of the Nile in Egypt). The growing population's consumption of food certainly results in demands upon this land, but not nearly as much as the call for resources by the energy needed for industrialization and modernization which will be covered later in this chapter (FAO, 1984).

Reference books regularly report for most of the world's states either the percentage of land which is arable (i.e., permanent cropland, land under temporary crops, and land temporarily fallow), or under cultivation (the above plus meadows and permanent pastures). The annual study of land use by the World Resources Institute and the International Institute for Environment and Development (WRI) includes both these measures, plus an inventory of forests and woodland, and land put to other uses. The leading states in the first two categories, presented in Table V3.2a.iii, provide a good listing of those countries which use most of their lands for agricultural purposes. Some of these states, despite devoting a significant percentage of their territory to farming, are still not self-sufficient in food because the crops they grow are exported on the world market for hard currency. As mentioned in the previous sections, only about half the world's states have solved the problems of famine and malnutrition.

V3.2b. Water

Water is a critical input to a state's environmental quality. Table V3.2b.i—a listing of 26 landlocked countries cut off from easy access to the sea, and of 25 small island states totally surrounded by water—shows the extremes of countries with too little or too much water as part of their environment. (Small island states refer to those of less than 30 square kilometers in area, and do not include large and potentially resourceful islands or any islands shared by more than one state.) Not coincidentally, most of these 51 water-denied and water-isolated states are among the poorest and least developed countries (LLDCs) identified in Chapter 2.

Among those states with access to the sea, the length of their maritime coastlines is a measure which gives some indication of the opportunities available for developing this natural resource. Table V3.2b.ii presents state rankings according to this measure, and it is not surprising that the countries at the top of this list here correlate highly with the major fishing states covered below in section V3.3d.

Inland water is made up of lakes and rivers and is an important resource denied to more than 50 states and in very short supply in many others. There are two ways in which inland water can be measured: total area, and internal renewable water resources per capita (referring to the average annual flow of rivers and aquifers generated from endogenous precipitation).

Table V3.2b.iii displays (a) the 36 countries with more than 10,000 square kilometers of inland water, and (b) the 28 states with more than 10,000 cubic meters per capita per year of inland renewable water resources. It also includes (c) those 52 states without any significant inland water at all.

Table V3.2b.iv presents (a) the world's 43 largest rivers, the total areas of the basins which they irrigate, and the number of states through which they flow; and (b) the 18 largest lakes (in terms of their surface area).

The Soviet Union and the North American continent's two main states dominate these two listings. Where rivers or lakes span two zones, their names are either spread across both columns, or mentioned twice and annotated with an asterisk.

V3.2c. Urbanization

The development of cities can indicate both an opportunity for economic development (V2) and a threat to the environment (V3) (Oberai, 1987;

Timberlake, 1985). Although there are various definitions as to exactly what a city is and how many people constitute one (Kurian, 1984: Table 16), there are according to the International Labour Office two important population thresholds for growing cities—one-half million people and 2 million people. Up to 500,000 people, job prospects improve as the city grows and living conditions stay much the same. Between 500,000 and 2,000,000 people, job prospects continue to improve, but living conditions deteriorate. Beyond 2 million people, living conditions continue to deteriorate and employment prospects do not improve.

There are almost 500 cities in the world with populations greater than one-half million, and 85 with more than 2 million (US Department of Commerce, 1986; Marlin et al., 1986). More than 40% of the world's cities are in the European zone where urbanization generally represents a high stage of economic development, and governments have the expertise to cope with any environmental threats accompanying such manifestations of modernization. In the developing world, however, the phenomenon of urbanization is increasing at the fastest rates and has more baneful effects.

In 1950 only 17% of the people in the Third World lived in cities; today about 33% do, and by 2000 it will be 44% (McAusland, 1985). In these developing countries, each year millions of people migrate in search of jobs from rural areas into central cities unequipped to provide the basic elements of housing and sanitation. The result is often squalid slums and high rates of disease and ill health. McAusland reports that more than 1 billion people (25% of global population) have no homes in the commonly accepted sense; they live on the streets or other public property, or as squatters in shacks on land they don't own. The UN has estimated that perhaps 2 billion or 40% of the world's people lack adequate sanitation.

Table V3.2c.i(a) reproduces data compiled by the UN Center for Housing, Building, and Planning, which identifies the percentage of people living in squatter settlements in 76 selected cities. Even these statistics grossly understate the size of the problem, because many states did not respond to the UN survey. Nevertheless, this table provides some indication of the dimensions of the problem. When combined with data pertaining to population density in the largest 25 urban agglomerations (Table V3.2c.i(b)), the relationship between urbanization and environmental quality can be put into perspective. In both tables, Asian countries predominate, as might be expected since this zone accounts for more than half of the world's people.

Table V3.2c.ii is a global survey of cities which indicates (a) the states with the 498 cities with more than one-half million people each, and (b) the names and population of those 74 cities with in excess of 2.8 million people. For the latter list, "city" is defined as any continuously built-up population cluster with a density of more than 5000 people per square mile (i.e.,"urban area"), and two sources were used to get the highest possible estimates. Finally, Table V3.2c.iii, percentage of population which is urban, gives a good general picture of the phenomenon, but it accommodates differing estimates of what is meant by the word "urban."

While Europe by these measures is the most urbanized zone in terms of having the most cities (208) and the highest percentage of its population living in metropolitan areas (26 of its 30 states with more than 50% urban population), Asia actually has more people living in cities and larger cities. Africa is the least urbanized continent.

Two other measures, regularly available in the same source as Table V3.2c.iii's measure, do not result in significantly different state rankings and so will not be reproduced here. The first rates all states according to a single standard—urban population in cities of more than one-half million—but is based upon a relatively old 1980 UN study. The second measure—percentage of population in a country's largest city—will not be used for it is not relevant to states where there is more than a single magnet city attracting people off the countryside.

A third measure, urban population growth, will also not be used because the definition of what is meant by urban is not made clear. Regarding growth rates, however, it should be noted that until recently, the world had been urbanizing slowly. In 1950, only 29% of the world population lived in urban areas; but by 1985, that figure had risen to 42%; and by the year 2000, 50% of the world's population is expected to live in urban areas.

Urban growth occurs at the fastest pace in the developing world. The contrast between the African and the Islamic zones (where the urban population is growing in the leading states at 6 to 8% per year), and Europe (where the average increase is less than one-third such rates) is stark. It is in the developing countries, moreover, that the greatest environmental dangers are faced as rural populations flood into urban areas and are unable to find the barest minimum of shelter and sanitation. If the ILO guidelines regarding the 2-million-people threshold are used, then most of these newly arriving people do not have satisfactory job prospects either, making for a potentially explosive social and political situation.

V3.2d. Pollution

Only a few measures of environmental pollution have been developed for use on a global scale (UN Statistical Office, 1984; UN Environment Program and World Health Organization, 1988). The most prominent are those of the United Nations Environmental Program's (UNEP) Global Environmental Monitoring System (GEMS), which has some 30 international projects dealing with climate, land, oceans, health, the preservation of essential natural resources, and the long-range transportation of pollutants. Its air monitoring project has more than

175 sites in 75 cities; its water quality network has some 340 sampling stations.

Some preliminary measures of clean air and water will be presented next for selected cities and rivers around the world, as drawn from UNEP and presented in various annual WRI reports. They will be followed by measures indicating the percentage of population with access to safe water and sanitation.

i. Air Pollution. The release of carbon and sulfur dioxide from fossil fuel combustion is the cause of most of the world's air pollution. The World Resources Institute regularly reports on two UNEP GEMS measures: (a) the amount of sulfur dioxide (SO_2), in average annual concentrations of micrograms per cubic meter; and (b) concentrations of suspended particulate matter (SPM), also in average annual micrograms per cubic meter.

WHO recommends that average annual SO_2 levels not exceed 40 micrograms per cubic meter, and that SPM levels not exceed 60 (as measured by high volume gravimetric samplings) or 50 (as measured by smoke shade samples). The most recent studies, for 1982-85 (or earlier), report on 64 urban areas for SO_2 concentrations, and 61 cities for concentrations of suspended particulate matter. Tables V3.2d.i(a) and (b) reproduce the average results for all GEMS sites in each city, and with a dotted line annotated to separate the countries above and below the recommended average annual levels.

The world's 400 million cars emit some 547 million tons of carbon into the atmosphere each year (Brown et al., 1989). The United States is responsible for almost one-fourth of these emissions (Postel, 1988). When other states in the European zone are added, they account for some 60% of the carbon dioxide emissions into the atmosphere each year.

Table V3.2d.i(c) lists the 20 leading countries responsible for about 80% of global carbon dioxide emissions in order of their percentage of the world total; the tons of carbon generated per person in each state are given in parentheses.

World Resources 1990-91 has developed a new measure of each country's net additions to atmospheric pollution which combines not only carbon dioxide emissions (which are responsible for 62.7% of the total), but also gases generated by chlorofluorocarbons (23.7%) and methane (13.6%). The net annual increases of the latter two items are converted into the equivalent amount of carbon which, if released as carbon dioxide, would have the same "greenhouse heating" effect which might lead to the rising of ocean levels and other unanticipated climate changes. They are added to the carbon produced directly in CO_2 emissions, yielding a figure in thousands of tons of carbons produced for each state.

By adding the last two items, the destruction of forests, use of air conditioning and a host of other human activities are reflected. A more complete global picture emerges than that yielded if only the CO_2 produced by the burning of fossil fuels in the industrialized countries is considered. Although 26 of the 30 states in the European zone are still among the top 70 states with more than 7 million tons of carbon generated in the years 1986-87, Table V3.2d.i(d) also reveals that three developing nations (Brazil, China, and India) are among the top six contributors to the phenomenon of global warming.

ii. Water Pollution. The UNEP/WRI reports do not have as extensive data on water pollution, but GEMS notes that Europe's rivers have 45 times their natural levels of nitrogen and phosphorus. Because of the high amount of chemicals in rivers, the cost of producing safe, palatable drinking water has risen dramatically (*Development Forum,* March, 1988:15). Table V3.2d.ii presents data on water pollution for 29 major rivers in 1986 and 1988: the first measure (a) is for average suspended sediment in million metric tons per year, for 14 rivers; the second (b) for concentration of dissolved minerals in milligrams per liter, on 23 rivers. (Eight rivers are represented in both studies.)

iii. Access Measures. The United Nations estimates that 1.2 billion people in the world have no safe drinking water. Unclean water is the major cause of disease in the developing world today, and is responsible for 80% of all childhood deaths there (Mathews, 1988: 4). It is also estimated that 1.9 billion people lack adequate sanitation facilities for the disposal of human waste. "Adequate" is defined here to mean simple latrines and safe disposal methods for personal waste and household garbage (Sivard, 1989: 54).

Tables V3.2d.iii(a) and (b) rank the countries in each zone in order of the percentage of their population with access to safe water and sanitation facilities. Most European states, and about a half-dozen countries each in the Islamic world, Asia, and Latin America seem to have solved these problems for their people, while the African states still have some distance to go.

V3.2a.i - Land Area of States (in 1000 sq. kms.)

Europe	Islamic	Africa	Asia	Latin America
USSR 22,402				
Canada 9976	Sudan 2506		China 9597	Brazil 8512
US 9363	Algeria 2382	Zaire 2345	Australia 7687	
	Saudi A. 2150		India 3288	Argentina 2767
		Niger 1267		Mexico 1973
	Libya 1760	Angola 1247	Indonesia 1905	
	Iran 1648	Mali 1240	Mongolia 1565	Peru 1285
		Ethiopia 1222		Colombia 1139
	Chad 1284	S.Africa 1221		Bolivia 1099
	Mauritania 1031	Tanzania 945		
	Egypt 1001	Nigeria 924		Venezuela 912
		Namibia 824		
	Pakistan 804	Mozamb. 802		
	Turkey 781	Zambia 753		Chile 757
France 547	Afghanistan 648		Myanmar 676	
Spain 505	Somalia 638	C.Af.R. 623	Madagascar 587	
Sweden 450		Botswana 600	Thailand 514	
Finland 337	Morocco 447	Kenya 583		
Norway 324	Iraq 437	Cameroon 475	Papua NG 462	Paraguay 407
Poland 313			Japan 372	
Italy 301		Zimbabwe 391	Malaysia 330	
Yugoslavia 256	S.Yemen 333	Congo 342	Vietnam 330	
W.Germany 249		Iv.Coast 322	Phil. I. 300	
UK 245		Burkina 274		Ecuador 284
Romania 238		Gabon 268	N.Zealand 269	
	Oman 212	Guinea 246		Guyana 215
Greece 132	N.Yemen 195	Ghana 238	Laos 237	Uruguay 176
Czech. 128	Syria 185	Uganda 236	Cambodia 181	Suriname 163
Bulgaria 111	Tunisia 164	Senegal 196	Bangladesh 144	Nicaragua 130
E. Germany 108			Nepal 141	Honduras 112
Iceland 103		Malawi 118		Cuba 111
Hungary 93		Benin 113	N.Korea 121	Guatemala 109
Portugal 92	Jordan 98	Liberia 111	S.Korea 98	Panama 77
Austria 84	UAE 84			Costa Rica 51
Ireland 70			Sri Lanka 66	Dom.Rep. 49
Denmark 43		SLeone 72	Bhutan 47	Haiti 28
Switzrld. 41		Togo 57	Taiwan 36^	Belize 23
Nethrlds. 37		GBissau 36		El Salvador 21
Belgium 31	Djibout 22	Lesotho 30	Solomons 28	Bahamas 14
Albania 29	Israel 21	Burundi 29	Fiji 18	Jamaica 11
	Kuwait 18	Eq.Guinea 28	Vanuatu 15	
	Qatar 11	Rwanda 26		Trinidad 5
	Lebanon 10	Swaziland 17	Brunei 6	St.Lucia 1
	Cyprus 9	Gambia 11	W.Samoa 3	Grenada <1
			Mauritius 2	Dominica 0.8
Luxembourg 3		C.Verde 4	Comoros 2	St.Vincent 0.4
			Singapore 0.6	Antigua 0.4
		STP 1	Seychelles 0.5	Barbados 0.4
Malta 0.3	Bahrain 0.6		Maldives 0.3	St.Chris. 0.2
n=30	n=28	n=38	n=33	n=33

Source: Sivard 1986 Table II, supplemented by ^*Information Please Almanac 1987.*

184

V3.2a.ii(a) - Population Density (pop./sq.km.)

Europe	Islamic	Africa	Asia	Latin America
Malta-1097	Bahrain-469	Rwanda-223	Singapore-4067	Barbados-625
Nethrlds.-344	Lebanon-267	Burundi-158	Bangladesh-666	Grenada-285
Belgium-322	Israel-182	Nigeria-106	Taiwan-587	St.Vincnt-250
W.Germany-247	Pakistan-99	STP-87	Maldives-487	Trinidad-234*
UK-229	Kuwait-71	Cape Verde-79	Mauritius-460	ElSalvador-222
Italy-189	Cyprus-67	Gambia-64	S.Korea-382	Jamaica-197
E.Germany-155	Turkey-57	Uganda-59	Japan-311	St.Chris.-188
Switzrld.-153	Syria-45	Malawi-56	Sri Lanka-238	St.Lucia-183
Luxmbrg.-140	Morocco-44	Ghana-50	Seychelles-225	Haiti-179
Czech.-119	Tunisia-42	SierraL-50	India-198	Antigua-170
Denmark-119		Togo-50		

Source: Kur84f80c*UN Demographic Yearbook*, plus *Siv86f83 for updates. See also WRI
88-89, Table 16.1 for this measure per 1000 hectares.

V3.2a.ii(b)-Density/Agricultural Land (pop./sq.km.)

Europe	Islamic	Africa	Asia	Latin America
Malta-2486	Bahrain-6383	C.Verde-526	Singapore-30250	Bahamas-1488
Nethrlds.-694	Egypt-1553	Benin-372	Maldives-3800	Suriname-753
Belgium-682	Kuwait-1061	Rwanda-361	Japan-2145	Trinidad-702
Luxmbrg.-566*	Lebanon-904	Liberia-315	Taiwan-2125*	Grenada-700
W.Germany-465	UAE-465	Kenya-273	S.Korea-1719	Barbados-692
Norway-455	Qatar-442	Senegal-268*	Seychelles-1320	St.Vincent-626
Italy-326	Pakistan-356	Burundi-245	Brunei-1258	St.Lucia-610
Switzrld.-314	Israel-321	STP-230	Bangladesh-954	Jamaica-463
UK-304	Jordan-223	Nigeria-178	Mauritius-829	Haiti-425
E.Germany-267	Djibouti-185	Togo-162	N.Korea-808	Dominica-416

Source: Kur84f80c*UN Demographic Yearbook*,
plus*=*Information Please Almanac 1985* for 1981-83.

185

V3.2a.iii - Land Use

Europe	Islamic	Africa	Asia	Latin America

(a) - % Arable Land and Permanent Cropland

Europe	Islamic	Africa	Asia	Latin America
Denmark 62%	Cyprus 47%	Burundi 51%	Bangladesh 68%	Barbados 77%
Hungary 57	Turkey 36	Rwanda 41	Mauritius 58	St. Vincent 50^
Poland 49	Syria 31	Nigeria 33	India 57	Grenada 44
E.Germany 47	Tunisia 31	Uganda 30	Comoros 42	St.Chris. 40
Romania 46	Lebanon 29	Senegal 27	Phil. I. 38	El Salvador 35
Malta 44	Pakistan 26	Togo 26	Thailand 37	Haiti 33
Italy 42	Israel 21	Sierra L. 25	Sri Lanka 34	Trinidad 31
Malta 41	Morocco 19	Malawi 25	W.Samoa 24	Dom. Rep. 30
Czech. 41	N.Yemen 14	Benin 16	S.Korea 22	Cuba 29^
Portugal 39	Iraq 13	Gambia 16	Vietnam 21	St. Lucia 27^
n=30	n=28	n=36/38	n=31/33	n=33

(b) - % Meadows and Permanent Pasture

Europe	Islamic	Africa	Asia	Latin America
Ireland 70	Somalia 46	Botswana 75	Mongolia 79	Uruguay 79
UK 48	Afghan. 46	Swaziland 67	Australia 59	Argentina 52
Greece 40	Syria 45	Lesotho 66	Madagascar 58	Dom.Rep. 43
Switz. 40	Israel 40	S.Africa 66	Mozambique 56	Costa Rica 42
Nethrlds. 34	Saudi A. 40	GBissau 48	N.Zealand 54	Nicaragua 42
US 26	Mauritania 38	Zambia 47	China 31	Mexico 39
Austria 25	Chad 36	Ethiopia 41	Nepal 13	Paraguay 39
Yugoslavia 25	N.Yemen 36	Tanzania 40	Comoros 7	Honduras 30
France 23	Morocco 28	Burkina F. 37	Indonesia 7	El Salvador 29
Belgium 21	Iran 27	Burundi 36	Sri Lanka 7	Colombia 29
Spain 21	S.Yemen 27			
n=29/30	n=27/28	n=35/38	n=28/33	n=25/33

Source: World Resources Institute, *World Resources 1986*, for 1981-1983, Table 4.1; supplemented by ^Population Reference Bureau, *1987 World Population Data Sheet.*

186

V3.2b.i - Water-Denied and Water-Isolated States

(a) Landlocked States (n=26)

Switzerland	Afghanistan	Mali	Bhutan	Bolivia
Austria	Chad	Niger	Nepal	Paraguay
Hungary		Burkina F.	Mongolia	
Czechoslovakia		C.Af.R.	Laos	
Luxembourg		Rwanda		
		Burundi		
		Uganda		
		Zambia		
		Malawi		
		Zimbabwe		
		Botswana		
		Swaziland		
		Lesotho		
n=5	n=2	n=13	n=4	n=2

(b) Small* Island States (n=25)

Malta	Cyprus	Cape Verde	Seychelles	Bahamas
	Bahrain	Eq. Guinea	Mauritius	St.Chris.
		STP	Comoros	Antigua
			Maldives	Dominica
			Singapore	St. Lucia
			Fiji	St. Vincent
			Vanuatu	Barbados
			W.Samoa	Grenada
			Solomons	Trinidad
				Jamaica
n=1	n=2	n=3	n=9	n=10

Source: V3.2b Data Bank.

* = "small" means island states of less than 30 square kilometers in area.

List does not include such *large* islands as:

Iceland, Madagascar, Sri Lanka, Indonesia, Philippines, Australia, New Zealand, and Cuba; or, any islands shared by more than one state such as:

Ireland/UK, Indonesia/Malaysia/Brunei, Indonesia/Papua, or Haiti/Dominican Republic.

V3.2b.ii - Length of Maritime Coastline (kms.)

Europe	Islamic	Africa	Asia	Latin America
Canada 90,908				
SU 46,670			Indonesia 54,716	
			Australia 25,760	
			Phil. I. 22,540	
US 19,924			N.Zealand 15,134	
Greece 13,676			China 14,500	
UK 12,429			Japan 13,685	
				Mexico 9330
	Turkey 7200		India 7000	Brazil 7491
				Chile 6435
Italy 4996			Solomons 5313	
Spain 4964			Papua NG 5152	Argentina 4989
France 3427			Madagasacar 4828	Cuba 3735
Norway 3419			Vietnam 3444	
Denmark 3379	Iran 3180		Thailand 3219	
Sweden 3218	Somalia 3025	S.Africa 2881	Myanmar 3060	Venezuela 2800
	Saudi A. 2510			Panama 2490
	Egypt 2450	Mozambq.2470	N. Korea 2495	Colombia 2414
	Oman 2092		S.Korea 2413	Panama 2414
	Morocco 1835		Malaysia 2068	Ecuador 2237
Yugoslavia 1521	Libya 1770	Angola 1600		Haiti 1771
W.Ger. 1488	UAE 1448	Tanzania 1424		
Ireland 1448	S.Yemen 1383		SriLanka 1340	
	Algeria 1183			CostaRica 1290
Finland 1126	Tunisia 1143	Ethiopia 1094	Fiji 1129	DomRep 1288
	Pakistan 1046	C.Verde 965		Jamaica 1022
E.Germany 901		Gabon 885		Nicaragua 910
Portugal 860	Mauritania 754	Nigeria 853		Honduras 820
	Cyprus 648	Liberia 574	Bangladesh 580	Uruguay 660
	Qatar 563	Ghana 539		
		Kenya 536		
	N.Yemen 523	Senegal 531		
Poland 491	Kuwait 499	Iv.Coast 515		Guyana 459
Nethrlds. 451		Cameroon 402	Cambodia 443	Guatemala 400
Albania 418		Sierra L. 402		Suriname 386
Bulgaria 354	Djibouti 314	Guinea 346	Comoros 340	Trinidad 362
	Israel 273	Eq.Guinea 296		El Salvador 307
Romania 225	Lebanon 225	GBissau 274		
Malta 140	Syria 193	Congo 169	Singapore 193	
	Bahrain 161	Benin 121	Mauritius 177	
		Gambia 80		Barbados 97
Belgium 64	Iraq 58	Togo 56		
	Jordan 26	Zaire 37		
		(+ 26 landlocked states, see V3.2b.i)		
n=24	n=25	n=23	n=23	n=23

Source: WRI, *World Resources 1986*, Table 10.1, n=118.

V3.2b.iii - Inland Water

Europe	Islamic	Africa	Asia	Latin America

(a) - Inland Water (in 1000s sq.km. of Area)

Europe	Islamic	Africa	Asia	Latin America	
Canada 755			India 314		
US 236			China 271	Colombia 100	
SU 130	Sudan 130	Ethiopia 121	Indonesia 93	Brazil 55	
Sweden 38		Zaire 78	Australia 69	Mexico 50	
Finland 32	Chad 25	Tanzania 59		Argentina 30	
	Pakistan 25	Uganda 36		Venezuela 30	
		Malawi 24	Myanmar 19	Guyana 18	
Norway 16	Iran 12	Mali 20		Bolivia 14	
		Mozambique 18			
	Somalia 10	Liberia 15	Bangladesh 10	Nicaragua 11	
	Turkey 10	Botswana 15	Papua NG 10		
n=6	n=6	n=9	n=7	n=8	(36)

Source: WRI, *World Resources 1986*, Table 4.1, n=140.

(b) - Inland Renewable Water Resources per Cap.(1000 cu.meters)

Europe	Islamic	Africa	Asia	Latin America	
Iceland 674.6					
Canada 109.5			N.Zealand 115.6		
Norway 97.1			Laos 59.5	Panama 60.8	
				Nicaragua 46.7	
				Venezuela 44.5	
				Brazil 35.2	
				Colombia 34.3	
Finland 22.2			Myanmar 27.0	Costa Rica 33.1	
Sweden 21.2			Malaysia 26.9	Ecuador 29.9	
		Cameroon 18.8	Australia 20.8	Argentina 21.4	
USSR 15.2			Indonesia 14.2	Honduras 20.6	
Ireland 13.2			Bangladesh 12.0	Guatemala 13.0	
			Mongolia 11.6		
US 10.0			Cambodia 10.9		
n=8	n=0	n=1	n=9	n=10	(28)

Source: WRI, *World Resources 1988-89*, Table 21.1, n=109.

(c) - NO Significant Inland Water Resources

Europe	Islamic	Africa	Asia	Latin America	
Belgium	Algeria,Libya	Burkina Faso	Comoros	Barbados	
	Morocco	Eq.Guinea	Mauritius	Trinidad	
Bulgaria	Mauritania	Cape Verde	Bhutan	Jamaica	
	Djibouti	C.Af.R.	Mongolia	Haiti	
Malta	Kuwait,Qatar	Niger	S.Korea	Dom. Rep.	
	Lebanon	Guinea	N.Korea	Cuba	
Portugal	Oman,UAE	Sierra Leone	Singapore	Costa Rica	
	Bahrain	Angola	Fiji	El Salvador	
Yugoslavia	Israel,Cyprus	S.Africa	N.Zealand	Honduras	
	Afghanistan	Lesotho		Guatemala	
	Saudi Arabia	Swaziland			
	N.Yemen,S.Yemen				
n=5	n=17	n=11	n=9	n=10	(52)

Source: WRI, *World Resources 1986*, Table 4.1, n=140.

189

V3.2b.iv - Major Rivers and Lakes

Europe	Islamic	Africa	Asia	Latin America

(a) - River Basins in 1000 sq.kms. (and # of States Affected)

Europe	Islamic	Africa	Asia	Latin America
				Amazon 6300 (2)
Mississippi 3267(1)		Congo 4000 (4)		
Yenesi 2600 (1)		Nile 3000 (5)		
Ob 2500 (1)				Parana 2800(3)
Lena 2430 (1)				
			Yangtze 1950(1)	
Amur 1850(2)*			Amur 1850(2)*	
Mackenzie 1800(1)				
Volga 1350(1)		Zambezi 1340(5)	Hsi 1350(1)	Madeira 1380(2)
Nelson 1150(1)				
St.Lawrence 1025(2)		Niger 1125(4)	Murray 1070(1)	
			Ganges 975(3)	Orinoco 950(2)
Danube 805(7)			Indus 950(3)	Tocantins 900 (1)
Yukon 770 (2)		Orange 800(2)	Mekong 795(6)	
			Huang Ho 745(1)	Negro 755(3)
Rio Grande 670(2)*				Rio Grande 670(2)*
Columbia 670(2)				
Kolyma 645(1)		Chari 600(3)		
Colorado 635(2)*				Colorado 635(2)*
			Brahmaputra 580(3)	Xingu 540(1)
Dnieper 500(1)	Amu-Darya 450(2)			Tapajos 500(1)
Don 420(1)	Shatt al-Arab 410(4)		Irrawaddy 430(1)	S.Francisco 470(1)
n=15.5	n=3	n=5	n=9.5	n=10 (43)

Source: WRI, *World Resources 1988-89*, Table 21.3

(b) Lakes, Surface Areas in sq.kms. (and # of States Affected)

Europe	Islamic	Africa	Asia	Latin America
Caspian S. 394,299(2)				
Superior 82,444(2)				
Aral 66,457(1)		Victoria 69,485(3)		
Huron 59,596(2)				
Michigan 58,016(1)				
Baikal 31,500(1)		Tanganyika 32,893(4)		
Great Bear 31,080(1)				
Great Slave 28,930(1)		Nyasa 30,044(3)		
Erie 25,719(2)		Chad 25,760(4)		
Winnipeg 23,553(1)				
Ontario 19,477(2)				
Balkash 18,428(1)				
Ladoga 18,130(1)				Maracaibo 13,010^(1)
n=12.5	n=1	n=3.5	n=0	n=1 (18)

Source: Information Please Almanac 1989, pp. 470-471,
   supplemented by ^WRI, *World Resources 1988-89*, Table 21.4.

V3.2c.i(a) - % of Population in Squatter Settlements

Islamic	Africa	Asia	Latin America
	Addis Ababa,Eth.-90%		Buenvent.,Col.-80%
	Yaounde,Cam.-90		S.Dmngo,DmRp.-72
Mogdshu.,Som.-77%	Douala,Cam.- 87	Calcutta,India-67%	Chimbote,Peru-67
Casblnca,Mor.-70	Ibadan, Nig. - 75	Agra,India-60	Bogota,Colom.-60
	Lome,Togo-75	Pnompenh,Camb.-46	Maracaibo,Ven.-50
Izmir,Turkey-65		Bombay,India-45	Recife,Brazil-50
	Nairobi,Kenya-70	Colombo,Sri L.-44	Guayaquil,Ec.-49
Ankara,Turkey-60	Mombasa,Ken.-67	Kuala Lmpr.,Malay.-37	Mex.City,Mex.-46
Rabat,Mor.-60	Accra,Gh.-61	Delhi,India-36	
Pt.Sudan,Sud.-55	Kinshasa,Zaire-60	Manila,Ph.I-35	Caracas,Ven.-42
Tunis,Tunisia-43	Dakar,Sen.-60	Antanarive,Mad.-33	Brasilia,Brazil-41
Istanbul,Turkey-40	Abidjan,IC-60	Makasara,Indon.-33	Barqismeto,Ven.-41
	Blantyre,Malawi-56	Pusan,SK-31	Arequipa,Peru-40
	Ouagadugu,BF-52	Seoul,SK-29	Lima,Peru-40
	Monrovia,Liberia-50	Ahmedabad,India-27	Ciudad Guyana,G.-40
	Dar'Salaam,Tnz.-50	Bandung,Indon.-27	Guat.City,Guat.-30
Baghdad,Iraq-29	Lusaka,Zambia-50	Jakarta,Indon.-26	Cali,Col.-30
		Madras,India-25	Rio de Janeiro,Brz.-30
Karachi,Pak.-23			Santiago,Chile-25
Kabul,Afghan.-22		Katmandu,Nepal-22	Tegucigalpa,Hond.-25
Tripoli,Libya-20		Baroda,India-19	Cartagena,Col.-23
Amman,Jord.-17		Dacca,Bngldsh.-18	Panama City,Pan.-17
		Bangkok,Thai.-15	Bel Horizonte,Brz.-14
		Singapore-15	Porto Alegro,Brz.-13
Beirut,Leb.-2		Banglaore,India-13	Buenos Aires,Arg.-5
n=14	n=16	n=22	n=24

Source: Kur 1984 for 1980 from UN Center for Housing, Building, and Planning, n=76.

V3.2c.i(b) - Densest Cities (population per sq. mi.)

Europe	Islamic	Africa	Asia	Latin America
			Hong Kong 270,750	
		Lagos 108,100	Jakarta 106,860	
			Bombay 106,700	
			HoChiMinh C. 104,839	
			Shengyang 104,769	
	Cairo 82,640		Dhaka 102,594	
	Alexandria 76,000		Ahmedabad 94,906	
	Casablanca 71,286		Tianjin 94,327	
			Chengdu 90,400	
			Shanghai 85,870	
			Harbin 83,953	
	Teheran 65,660		Pusan 74,000	
	Lahore 63,211		Bangalore 73,700	
Madrid 62,682			Surajaya 68,884	Bogota 59,633
		Kinshasa 49,018	Calcutta 50,050	Caracas 55,426
n=1	n=5	n=2	n=15	n=2 (25)

Source: US Department of Commerce, *World Population Profile 1985*, Table 12.

191

V3.2c.ii(a) - # Cities with > 1/2 Million Population, by State

Europe	Islamic	Africa	Asia	Latin America
US 65	Pakistan 7	Nigeria 9	China 78	Brazil 14
USSR 50	Iran 6	S.Africa 7	India 36	Mexico 7
UK 17	Morocco 4	Zaire 2	Indonesia 9	Argentina 5
W.Germany 11	Turkey 4	Ghana 2	Japan 9	Colombia 4
Italy 9	Iraq 3		S.Korea 7	Venezuela 4
Canada 9	Egypt 2	Tanzania 1	Australia 5	Peru 2
Poland 8	Syria 2	Benin,Guinea 1	Vietnam 4	Ecuador 2
Spain 6	Saudi A. 2	Kenya,Uganda 1	Taiwan 4	Chile 1
France 6	Sudan 1	Mozambique 1	Bangladesh 3	Cuba 1
Yugoslavia 3	Afghanistan 1	Cameroon 1	Phil.I. 2	Nicaragua 1
Nethrlds. 3	Tunisia 1	Ivory Coast 1	Myanmar 2	Guatemala 1
Sweden 3	Lebanon 1	Angola 1	N.Korea 2	Dom.Rep. 1
E.Germany 3	Jordan 1	Zimbabwe 1	Thailand,Camb. 1	Haiti,Jamaica 1
Greece 2	Algeria 1	Zambia 1	Madag.,SriLanka 1	Pan.,Hond.,CRic.1
Belgium 2	Israel 1	Senegal 1	Malaysia 1	Urug.,Paraguay 1
11 @ 1	Libya 1	Ethiopia 1	Sing.,N.Zealand 1	Bolivia 1
4 @ 0	12 @ 0	21 @ 0	14 @ 0	16 @ 0
n=208	n=38	n=33	n=168	n=51 (498)

Source: WDR90f80, Table 31.

V3.2c.ii(b) - Urban Areas with more than 2 million Population

			Tokyo/Yokohama 25.4m.	
			Seoul 13.7	Mexico C. 19.4^m.
New York 14.6 m.			Osaka/Kyoto 13.6	Sao Paolo 18.4^
			Shanghai 11.9^	
London 10.6^			Calcutta 11.8^	Buenos Aires 11.6^
			Bombay 11.1^	Rio de Janeiro 11.1^
Moscow 9.9			Beijing 9.7^	
Los Angeles 9.6	Tehran 9.2m.^		Jakarta 9.4^	
Paris 8.6	Cairo 9.1^		Delhi 8.6^	
Milan 7.9^			Manila 8.5	
Essen,WGer.7.6	Karachi 8.0^		Tianjin 8.4^	
Chicago 6.5		Lagos 7.6m.^	Bangkok 7.2^	
	Istanbul 5.4		Taipei 5.5	Lima 6.5^
Leningrad 5.4^	Baghdad 5.4^		Hong Kong 5.4	
Madrid 5.1^			Madras 5.0	Bogota 4.7
Naples 4.3^			Bangalore 4.9^	Santiago 4.7
Manchester,UK 4.2			Pusan 4.8^	
Philadelphia 4.0			Shengyang 4.5^	
Barcelona 3.8	Lahore 4.1^		Nagoya 4.5	Caracas 4.0^
San Francisco 3.8			Wuhan 3.7^	
Rome 3.7^			Ahmedabad 3.6^	BelHorizon.,Brz.3.8^
Katowice 3.6			Hyderabad 3.5^	
Athens 3.3			Sydney 3.4	
Houston 3.2^	Ankara 3.6^		Ho Chi Minh C.3.3	
Miami 3.1	Algiers 3.4^		Dhaka 3.3	
Detroit 3.1	Alexandria 3.3^		Guangzhou 3.2	
Toronto 3.0	Casablanca 3.3^		Rangoon 3.2^	
Berlin 3.0			Melbourne 2.9	Pt.Allegre,Brz.3.1^
Montreal 2.8		Kinshasa 2.8	Surabaya,Indon.2.8	
n−23	n=10	n=2	n=29	n=10 (74)

Source: US Dept. of Commerce, *World Population Profile 1985* ; ^*US Statistical Abstract 1989*.

Europe	Islamic	Africa	Asia	Latin America
Belgium 97%	Kuwait 95%		Singapore 100%	Argentina 86%
UK 92	Israel 91		Australia 86	Uruguay 85
Iceland 89^	Qatar 88^		N.Zealand 84	Chile 85
Nethrlds 88			Japan 77	Venezuela 83
W.Germany 86	Bahrain 81^			Bahamas 75^
Denmark 86	Lebanon 80^		Taiwan 71^	Brazil 75
Malta 85^	UAE 78		S.Korea 69	Cuba 72^
Sweden 84	Djibouti 78^		N.Korea 64^	Mexico 71
Luxembourg 79^	Saudi A. 76		Brunei 59^	Peru 69
Spain 77	Iraq 73			Colombia 69
E.Germany 77^			Seychelles 52^	Trinidad 67
Canada 76	Libya 68	Eq. Guinea 60%^	Mongolia 52^	Suriname 66^
Czech. 75^	Jordan 67	S.Africa 58	China 50	Nicaragua 59
Norway 74	Cyprus 62^	Zambia 54		DomRep 59
France 74	Tunisia 56	Namibia 51^		Antigua 58^
US 74	Iran 54	Cameroon 47		Ecuador 55
Italy 68	Syria 51	Ivory Coast 45	Mauritius 42	Panama 54
Bulgaria 67^		C. Af. R. 45		Jamaica 51
USSR 66^	Egypt 48	Gabon 44	Phil. I. 41	Belize 50^
	Turkey 47	Liberia 43	Malaysia 41	Bolivia 50
Greece 62	Morocco 47	Congo 41		Paraguay 46
Poland 61	Algeria 44	Benin 40	Fiji 39^	St. Lucia 46^
Switzerland 61	S.Yemen 42	Zaire 39		St. Chris. 45^
Finland 60	Mauritania 40	Senegal 38		Costa Rica 45
Hungary 60	Somalia 37	STP 38^	India 27	El Salvador 44
Ireland 58		Nigeria 34	Indonesia 27	
Austria 57		Ghana 33	Maldives 26^	Honduras42
Romania 49	Chad 31	Tanzania 30		
Yugoslavia 49		Angola 27	Myanmar 24	Guyana 33^
		Zimbabwe 27	Madagascar 24	Guatemala 33
Albania 35^		GBissau 27^	Comoros 23^	Barbados 32^
Portugal 32		Cape Verde 27^		
		Swaziland 26^	Sri Lanka 21	
		Sierra L. 26	W.Samoa 21^	
		Togo 25	Thailand 21	
	N.Yemen 23	Guinea 24		Haiti 29
	Pakistan 21	Mozambique 24	Vietnam 20^	
	Sudan 21	Kenya 22		St. Vincent 21^
		Botswana 22		
		Gambia 21^	Vanuatu 18^	
		Lesotho 19	Laos 18	
	Afghanistan 18^	Mali 19	Papua NG 15	
		Niger 18	Bangladesh 13	
		Malawi 14	Cambodia 11^	
		Ethiopia 13	Nepal 9	
		Uganda 10	Solomons 9^	
		Burkina F. 9		Grenada-na
	Oman 10	Rwanda 7		Dominica-na
		Burundi 7	Bhutan 5	
n=30	n=28	n=38	n=33	n=31/33 (160)

Source: WDR90f88, Table 31, n=116; supplemented by ^Pop.Ref.Bur.*Data Sheet* 90f88, n=44.

V3.2d.i - Measures of Air Pollution in Selected Urban Areas

Europe	Islamic	Asia	Latin America

(a)-Sulfur Dioxide in 64 Cities (avg.ann.microgms/cu.meter),1982-85

Europe	Islamic	Asia	Latin America
		Shenyang 156.8	
Milan 137		Beijing 131	
		Seoul 121.5	
Prague 110.3^	Tehran 108.7	Xian 77.8	Rio de Janeiro 93
Gourdon 84.5^		Guangzhou 76.5	Sao Paulo 80
Zagreb 71			Santiago 76
Madrid 62		Manila 61.7	
Brussels 50		Calcutta 59	
Frankfurt 49.5		Shanghai 55.3	
New York 49		Delhi 51.3	
Glasgow 48			
Wroclaw 44			
London 41.5		Hong Kong 41.3	
Fairfield 40	Cairo 41^		Medellin 40.3
....(recommended maximum level)...			
Warsaw 39.3			
Dublin 37			
Athens 37			
Stockholm 35.8^			Bogota 35
St. Louis 34^			Havana 34.6^
Hamilton 33.5			
Chicago 30		Tokyo 30	Caracas 31
Helsinki 28.3		Osaka 28.7	
Copenhagen 28			
Lisbon 27			
Harris County 25^		Christchurch 25.7	
Amsterdam 24.7			
Montreal 24			
Houston 23			
Munich 22		Bombay 19.8	
		Sydney 19.3	
	Baghdad 18^	Bangkok 18	
Vancouver 14	Tel Aviv 13.5		
Toronto 9.7		Melbourne 10	Cali 11
Toulouse 4.5^		Davao 7.5	
		Aukland 5	
		Kuala Lumpur 4	Lima 4.3^
		Jakarta 0.5	
n=30	n=4	n=21	n=9 (64)

Source: WRI, *World Resources 1988-89*, Table 23.4, for 1982-85 (^or earlier).

(b)-Particulate Matter in 61 Cities (avg.ann.microgms./cu.meter)

Europe	Islamic/Africa	Asia	Latin America	
		High Volume Gravimeter Samplings		
	Baghdad 518^	Shenyang 426		
		Xian 414		
		Calcutta 380		
		Beijing 376		
	Tehran 264	Delhi 372		
Athens 183.5		Bangkok 220.5		
		Shanghai 220.3		
Prague 134^		Guangzhou 207		
Zagreb 127.7		Bombay 179.5		
St. Louis 109^		Davao 172		
Lisbon 101		Manila 139.3	Rio de Janeiro 110.3	
Chicago 100		Jakarta 130.5		
Hamilton 94.5		Kuala Lumpur 103		
Helsinki 86.7	Accra 95			
Birmingham 82		Sydney 86.5		
Houston 77				
Harris County 71				
Toronto 65		Melbourne 63		
Montreal 61.5				
..................................(recommended maximum level)...................................				
Chattanooga 58				
New York 54				
Fairfield 53				
Copenhagen 52				
Vancouver 48			Cali 40	
Frankfurt 36			Medellin 39	
Brussels 21				
n=20	n=3	n=15	n=3	(41º)
		Smoke Shade Samplings		
	Tehran 128		Santiago 117	
	Cairo 92	Manila 95	Sao Paulo 89	
Madrid 75			Bogota 78^	
Wroclaw 72.7				
Warsaw 61.3		Tokyo 51.7	Havana 64.3^	
..................................(recommended maximum level)...................................				
Gourdon 39.3		Osaka 46.3		
Dublin 38.7		Hong Kong 37.3		
Copenhagen 29			Caracas 30	
Brussels 23.3		Melbourne 21^	Cali 18.5^	
London 22.5		Christchurch 20	Medellin 18^	
Toulouse 22^			Lima 15^	
Glasgow 17		Aukland 5.3		
n=10	n=2	n=7	n=8	(27º)

Source: WRI, *World Resources 1988-89*, Table 23.5, for 1982-85 (^ or earlier).

º = 7 cities on both lists: Copenhagen, Brussels, Tehran, Manila, Melbourne, Cali, and Medellin.

Table V3.2d.i (continued)

(c) - % World Total CO2 Emissions (and Tons per Person),1986

Europe	Islamic/Africa	Asia	Latin America
US 22%(5.0T)			
SU 17%(3.5)		China 10%(0.5T)	
W.Ger. 4%(3.0)		Japan 5%(2.0)	
UK 3% (2.9)			
Poland 2.5%(3.0)		India 3%(0.2)	
Canada 2%(4.2)			
France 2%(1.8)			
Italy 1.5%(1.8)			
E.Ger.1%(5.5)	S.Africa 1%(3.0T)		
Czech. .5%(4.2)		Australia .5%(4.0T)	Mexico .7%(0.2)
Romania .5%(2.5)			Brazil .5%(0.5)
Spain .5%(1.5)		S.Korea .3%(1.1)	
n=12	n=1	n=5	n=2 (20)

Source: International Atomic Energy Agency, *IAEA Bulletin 1989*, vol. 31, No. 2: 17.

(d)-Net Additions to Greenhouse Effect (in 1000 Tons Carbon)

Europe	Islamic	Africa	Asia	Latin America
US 1,000,000				
USSR 690,000			China 380,000	Brazil 610,000
W.Ger. 160,000			India 230,000	
UK 150,000			Japan 220,000	
France 120,000			Indonesia 140,000	
Italy 120,000				
Canada 120,000				
Poland 76,000			Myanmar 77,000	Mexico 78,000
Spain 73,000			Thailand 67,000	Colomb.69,000
E.Ger. 62,000		Nigeria 53,000	Australia 63,000	
Nethrlds. 43,000	Saudi A. 42,000	S. Africa 47,000		
Czech. 33,000	Iran 33,000	Ivory Coast 47,000		
Romania 28,00	Turkey 29,000		Phil. I. 40,000	
Yugoslavia 26,000			Vietnam 38,000	Argentin.31,000
Belgium 25,000	Algeria 25,000		Laos 38,000	
Greece 20,000				Venez. 27,000
Austria 17,000			S.Korea 29,000	
Portugal 17,000			Malaysia 26,000	
Bulgaria 17,000	Egypt 17,000			Peru 23,000
Switzerland 16,000	Sudan 15,000	Zaire 16,000	Bangladesh 22,000	
Denmark 15,000	Pakistan 15,000	Cameroon 16,000	N.Korea 20,000	Ecuador 21,000
Sweden 14,000				
Finland 13,000	Iraq 9300		Madagascar 13,000	
Hungary 13,000	Israel 9300		N.Zealand 10,000	
Ireland 9200	UAE 8400	Ethiopia 7800		Nicaragua 8400
Norway 8700	Kuwait 7600	Malawi 7300	Singapore 7100	Costa Rica 7800
n=26/30	n=11/28	n=7/38	n=17/33	n=9/33 (70)

Source: WRI, *World Resources 1990-91* for 1986-87, Table 24.2; n = 1st 70 of 145 states.

V3.2d.ii - Measures of Pollution in 29 Selected Rivers

Europe	Islamic	Africa	Asia	Latin America

(a)-Avg.Suspended Sediment (mill.metric tons/year), 14 Rivers, 1986

Europe	Islamic	Africa	Asia	Latin America	
			Huang He 1600		
			Ganges 1455		
			Brahmaputra 726		
			Yangtze 501		
Miss./Mo. 365			Indus 436	Amazon 363	
			Irrawaddy 299		
		Nile 111	Mekong 170		
		Zaire 65		Orinoco 87	
		Niger 5		Parana 82	
n=1	n=.5	n=2.5	n=7	n=3	(14º)

Source: WRI, *World Resources 1986*, Table 9.3.

(b) - Dissolved Minerals (milligrams/liter), 23 Rivers, 1988

Europe	Islamic	Africa	Asia	Latin America	
	Amu Darya 600				
Don 495			Huang He 450		
Danube 300	Shatt al-Arab 320				
Volga 290			Indus 295		
Dnieper 219			Irrawaddy 215		
		Nile 208	Ganges 208		
		Orange 182	Yangtze 185	Ucayali 180	
		Zambezi 70		Magdalena 120	
				Maranon 105	
	Chari 64			Parana 100	
		Niger 53		Madeira 60	
		Congo 38		Amazon 52	
n=4	n=3	n=5	n=5	n=6	(23º)

Source: WRI, *World Resources 1988-89*, Table 21.3.

º = 8 rivers are in both lists:
   Nile, Niger, Huang He (Yellow), Indus, Irrawaddy, Yangtze, Amazon, and Parana.

197

V3.2d.iii(a) - % of Population with Safe Water

Europe	Islamic	Africa	Asia	Latin America
US 100	Bahrain 100		Singapore 100	Bahamas 100*
Denmark 100	Cyprus 100		N.Zealand 100	Trinidad 99
Nethrlds 100	Kuwait 100		N.Korea 100	Barbados 99
W.Germany 100	Israel 98		Mongolia 100	Chile 94
UK 100	Libya 96			Costa Rica 91
Austria 100	Qatar 95		Australia 99	
Luxmbrg 100	Jordan 93	Gabon 92	Japan 98	Jamaica 86
Sweden 100	UAE 93		Seychelles 95*	Venezuela 83
Malta 100	Lebanon 92		Mauritius 95	Suriname 83*
Iceland 100	Saudi A. 91		Brunei 90	Cuba 82
USSR 100				Panama 82
Italy 99	Iraq 89		S.Korea 83	Uruguay 80
Switzerland 99	Algeria 88	Rwanda 59	Fiji 83	
France 99		Botswana 57		Brazil 77
Norway 99	Turkey 78	Zimbabwe 52		Mexico 75
Ireland 97	Egypt 76	Cape Verde 52*	W.Samoa 69*	Guyana 73
Canada 97	Tunisia 75	Malawi 51	Malaysia 69	
Bulgaria 96	Syria 75	Tanzania 50	Thailand 66	
Spain 95	Iran 75	Ghana 50	Phil. I. 66	Colombia 70
Greece 95		Zambia 48	Vanuatu 64*	Honduras 69
Belgium 95		STP 45*		
Portugal 92		Gambia 45	India 56	Argentina 64
Albania 92		Senegal 42		Belize 64*
E.Germany 90	Pakistan 53	Burundi 39		
	S.Yemen 46	Swaziland 38	Vietnam 41	Dom.Rep. 62
Hungary 84	Djibouti 43*	Togo 35	Bangladesh 40	
Finland 79		Niger 34	Indonesia 36	
Romania 77	Mauritania 37	Nigeria 33	Sri Lanka 36	Nicaragua 56
Czech. 74	Somalia 36	Angola 32	Nepal 34	Peru 55
		Kenya 28	Myanmar 29	Guatemala 52
Yugoslavia 68	N.Yemen 31	Cameroon 26	Maldives 21*	Bolivia 49
Poland 67	Morocco 27	Sierra Leone 22	Laos 21	Ecuador 47
	Chad 26	Congo 21	Madagascar 18	El Salvador 40
		Burkina Faso 20	Bhutan 17†	
	Sudan 21	Liberia 20	Papua NG 16	Haiti 35
	Afghanistan 19	Ivory Coast 19		
		Benin 18		Paraguay 26
		Uganda 16		
		C.Af.R.16		
		Guinea 15	Cambodia 3	
	Chad 14	Lesotho 14		
		Mozambique 13		
		Mali 12		
		Zaire 9	Comoros-na	Antigua-na
		Ethiopia 6	Solomons-na	Grenada-na
		Eq.G.,S.Af.-na	Taiwan-na	Dominica-na
		Namibia-na	China-na	St.C.,St.L.,St.V.-na
n=30/30	n=28/28	n=35/38	n=29/33	n=27/33 (149)

Source: Sivard '89f86, supplemented by *WRI '88-89f85, and †Pop.Ref.Bureau '87.

V3.2d.iii(b) - % of Population with Access to Sanitation

Europe	Islamic	Africa	Asia	Latin America
UK 100				
Iceland 100	Kuwait 100			
Denmark 100	Bahrain 100		N.Korea 100	Barbados 100
Luxembourg 100	Cyprus 100			
Nethrlds 100			Australia 99	Trinidad 98
Malta 100	Jordan 98		Mauritius 97	
Belgium 99				Costa Rica 95
Italy 99				
US 98				Jamaica 90
	Israel 95		N.Zealand 88	Guyana 90
Ireland 94			Singapore 85	
Spain 90				Paraguay 85
W.Germany 88			Brunei 80	Chile 84
France 85		Tanzania 78		Panama 80
Austria 85		Gambia 77	Malaysia 75	
Norway 85	UAE 86	Rwanda 60		
Switzrld. 85	Saudi A. 86	Malawi 55		
Sweden 85		Burundi 52		Argentina 69
Finland 72		Gabon 50		Colombia 68
E.Germany 70	Lebanon 75	Zambia 47	Sri Lanka 66	Ecuador 65
		Kenya 44		El Salvador 62
Czechoslov.60	Egypt 70	Congo 40		Uruguay 59
Hungary 60	Libya 70	Botswana 36		Mexico 57
Canada 60	Iraq 69	Cameroon 36		
Yugoslavia 58	Iran 65	Ghana 26	Phil. I. 56	
Poland 50		Zimbabwe 26		
Romania 50	Morocco 46	Sierra L. 21	Mongolia 50	Peru 47
USSR 50	Tunisia 46	Liberia 21		Venezuela 45
Portugal 41	S.Yemen 45	Mali 21	Thailand 45	
		C.Af.R. 19	Indonesia 30	Cuba 31
	Qatar 35	Angola 18	Vietnam 30	Honduras 29
		Iv.Coast 17		Nicaragua 27
	Pakistan 19	Togo 14		Dom.Rep. 27
	Somalia 17	Uganda 13		Brazil 24
	Chad 14	Lesotho 12		Guatemala 23
	N.Yemen 12	Guinea 12	Myanmar 20	Bolivia 21
	Turkey 10	Mozambq. 10		Haiti 21
		Benin 10	India 8	
	Sudan 5	Burkina F. 9	Bangladesh 4	
	Afghanistan 2	Niger 8	Nepal 2	
na=3	na=5	na=11	na=16	na=9
	Algeria	CV,GB,STP	Maldiv.,Seychell.	
	Mauritania	S.Africa,Swaziland	Madagas.,Comoro	Antigua,Dominica
Albania	Djibouti	Namibia	S.Korea,Japan	Bahamas,Grenada
Greece	Oman	Ethiopia,Zaire	China, Taiwan	St.Chris.,St.Lucia
Bulgaria	Syria	Nigeria,Senegal	Camb.,Laos,Bhut.	St. Vincent
		Eq.Guinea	Fiji,Papua NG	Belize,Suriname
			W.Sam.,Sol.,Van.	
n=27/30	n=23/28	n=27/38	n=17/33	n=24/33 (118)

Source: Sivard 1989 for 1986, Table III, n=118.

V3.3. RESOURCE CONSUMPTION

The relevance of the "population-to-environment" equation for most countries does not relate primarily to hunger, urbanization, or pollution, but rather to the consumptive demands of a growing population upon the natural resources needed for economic development. This section will analyze the call for resources to provide the energy needed for the world's growth toward greater industrialization and modernization, and hence is more connected to Chapter 2 (Economic Well-Being) than the previous two sections on ecological balance have been.

Starting with the report of the Club of Rome (Meadows et al.,1972), there has been increasing concern whether the resources of the globe are sufficient to sustain the continued growth of all the world's nations to the level of development currently enjoyed in the European zone (see also Meadows et al., 1974, 1982; Laszlo, 1977; US Council of Environmental Quality, 1980). There is a genuine question, for example, as to whether there is enough iron ore and crude oil to allow the 1 billion people of China to develop a mobile, transcontinental society with as much per capita resource use as that consumed by Americans today (Sadik, 1988).

The "tragedy of the commons" is a fable about farmers taking their sheep to the village commons because that was where the best grass grew. From the perspective of the individual shepherd, it made sense to have his sheep eat as much as they could in order to keep them fattened and wooly. But if this behavior were repeated every year by every shepherd, eventually the village commons would become depleted and there would come a time when grass ceased to grow and all would suffer.

The concept of the "global commons" has been adopted by many analysts of international relations over the past two decades (Hardin and Baden, 1977; Pirages, 1977; Ophuls, 1977; Ghosh, 1984; Repetto, 1985a; Harf and Trout, 1986; Tolba, 1987; Blackburn, 1988). In 1987, the United Nations' Brundtland Report concluded that the global commons could not be managed from any national center and that threats to environmental security could only be dealt with by "joint management and multilateral procedures and mechanisms" (World Commission on Environment and Development, 1987b). Even the World Bank admitted, in its 1984 development report, that economic development alone could not solve the world's "population-versus-resources" problem, and that the developing nations are simply in far different circumstances from those of the developed states when they went through their periods of rapid industrialization.

V3.3a. Energy

The resources analyzed in this section (fossil fuels, selected strategic minerals and metals, forests and fisheries) all exist in finite capacities and will be exhausted some day if measures of conservation or substitution are not developed (Mesarovic and Pestel, 1974; Brown, 1978). All relate to the generation of energy needed for the promotion of industry associated with the concept of development. As with urbanization, the economic gains associated with high energy consumption must be weighed against the resultant environmental pollution associated with practically all power generation (Hughes et. al, 1985).

The measures in this section will deal with the amount of energy consumed each year, as well as with the spread of nuclear power as an alternate energy source to the fossil fuel pollutants. At the outset of this analysis, it should be pointed out that many of the resources consumed to generate energy in the rich states of the North are found in the poor states of the South, a form of exploitation more literal than that extolled in theories of purely economic imperialism.

Table V3.3a.i displays (a) the highest and lowest eight states in each zone in terms of total commercial energy consumption in petajoules (where a petajoule is the equivalent of 163,400 barrels of oil or 34,140 metric tons of coal); and (b) the first and last ten states in each zone in the more significant consumption-per-capita figure. Presenting this data in a format which highlights the top and bottom countries in each zone enables one to see the tremendous difference in energy use (both absolute and per capita) between Europe and the other four zones. The pitiable state of the African countries (apart from South Africa) is especially evident.

Until the 1986 explosion of the Soviet reactor at Chernobyl, many states considered atomic energy as an attractive alternative to reliance upon the heavily polluting fossil fuels of oil and coal. Since that time four states have abandoned their nuclear power programs, and orders for new nuclear plants in many others have been severely cut back. However much money is saved by resorting to nuclear technology, the long-term environmental risks probably outweigh any economic benefits derived. When the relationship of nuclear power generation to weapons proliferation is considered—especially with respect to nuclear-weapons "threshold states"—the danger to the world community becomes even greater.

Data on nuclear power plants are complicated by the long lead-time between the start of construction and the actual firing of a plant. As of 1989, there were 429 operating in 26 states, with another 105 under construction (Table V3.3a.ii (a)). The impact of this dubious technology is greatest in the European zone, where almost 90% of the world's installed capacity is generated. However, it is there that the reaction against nuclear power has been the greatest; in the US, utilities have not placed any new orders for nuclear power plants since 1978, and in Sweden, Austria, and Italy voters have decided in referendums to prohibit any new constructions. Table V3.3a.ii(b) gives the total installed capacity and percentage of reliance upon nuclear power for generation of electricity in the 26 states which have made the Faustian bargain for the nuclear option.

V3.3b. Fossil Fuels

Fossil fuels—petroleum (oil), natural gas, and coal— are the world's main sources of energy. In 1978, they supplied 90% of the world's needs, but because of increasing awareness of the dangers of pollution, this figure is expected to decline to about 75% of global needs by the year 2000.

Among the three fossil fuels, the ratio of use in the mid-1980s was 38.3% oil, 31.9% coal, and 29.8% natural gas (*World Eagle*, May, 1987: 29). The demand for coal and gas (at the expense of oil, which at one point satisfied 54% of world energy needs) has risen steadily since the oil price rises of the 1970s. Depletion, however, is the main consideration here; at present consumption rates, known oil and gas reserves are expected to last for 30 to 50 years, and coal reserves for at least 300 (US Department of State, 1985: 42), but the situation varies widely for specific countries.

The data in this section, when combined with the energy consumption statistics in section V3.3a, describe a pattern of the wealthy industrial nations of the North exploiting resources which are generally found in the South. With respect to oil, for example, in 1985 the 24 OECD states consumed 33.5 million barrels of oil per day, an average of 3.4 barrels per person per year, whereas the poorer 138 nations consumed only one-third of this amount at only one-half the rate, 11.8 million barrels of oil per day, or 1.7 barrels per person per year (*World Eagle*, May, 1987: 30).

This section's three tables will each have two columns with states arranged, within their zones, with respect to the percentage of global totals associated with the leading country in each category. The right-hand column displays the locations of the largest known *reserves* of oil, natural gas, and coal (the major focus of this section) circa 1989-90; the left-hand column will note the major *producers* of each for purposes of reference.

In the case of oil (Table V3.3b.i), an extra column notes the estimated number of years remaining before the reserves will be depleted given current production level and assuming no new discoveries. Twenty-three states accounting for 96.8% of world reserves are presented, and the dominance of countries in the Islamic zone is manifest.

Table V3.3b.ii displays natural gas reserves for 24 states accounting for 94.7% of world reserves. Less than half that many countries are involved in most of the current production.

The distribution of coal is more highly concentrated than that of oil and gas, with virtually all the world's reserves found in the ten countries listed in Table V3.3b.iii. Among these, just three continent-sized states—the United States, Soviet Union, and China—account for more than half of all production and reserves.

V3.3c. Minerals and Metals

In addition to fossil fuels, there are a number of other mineral resources which are considered necessary for modern industrial development. The US Department of State (1985: 43) says flatly that iron, copper, and bauxite are the three "most useful" nonfuel minerals, but there is some disagreement in the literature as to just which of some three dozen other materials are the most necessary. The definition of which minerals are "strategic" or "critical" is obviously a subjective one which varies from country to country. Five sources consulted for this report identified some 37 different minerals as important to a nation's economy or security.

The United States Bureau of Mines (US Congress, OTA, 1985) lists 13 minerals as "essential to the national economy and whose supply is relatively limited and vulnerable to interruption"; among these are a "first tier" of four "strategic" materials (for which the "quantity required for essential uses exceeds a reasonably secure supply and for which timely substitutes are not available"). The US Defense Department (US GAO, 1983) has identified 11 "critical" minerals "vital to defense production with limited substitution possibilities and for which US is highly dependent on imports."

D. Hargreaves and S. Fromson (1983) created a "strategic risk index" for 25 minerals on the basis of the security of supply and the costs of disruption of that supply. Each of these two factors is a combination of four components of risk relating to production, transportation, consumption, and trade; the minerals are ranked on a scale from 4.3 to 41.5 (out of a possible 100). Ruth W. Arad and Uze B. Arad (1979) developed a formula to rank 14 minerals in a priority order on the basis of their "essentiality." Finally, Rex Bosson and Bension Varon (1977) ranked 27 important minerals on the basis of the size of their world reserves: a.) "ample" reserves (90 years or more); b.) minerals whose reserves present "no serious problems" (i.e., 30-90 years); and c.) reserves which are "tight, critical" (0-25 years). (See also Crowson, 1987; US Department of Interior, Bureau of Mines, 1987; and Weston, 1984.)

The findings of these five sources regarding the minerals they respectively found to be the most important are summarized in Table V3.3c.i, where the 37 minerals are listed in alphabetical order.

This section will next concentrate on what it considers to be the ten most important minerals—bauxite, chromium, cobalt, copper, iron ore, manganese, nickel, platinum, tin, and titanium. These metals are used as intermediate inputs in such important industries as chemicals, electronics, energy, machinery, steel, and transportation. Their areas of use include catalysts, semiconductors, superconductors, batteries, magnets, steel, and heat-resistant alloys. The level of their use is significantly correlated with a country's GNP and state of modernization. The minerals selected appear in at least four of the above lists and are analyzed by Crowson (1987) with respect to two measures of their level of reserves: "Static Reserve Life," which assumes production continues at mid-1980s levels; and "Ratio of Identified Reserves to Cumulative Primary Demand, 1985-2000," which takes into account new discoveries and rising demand based on projections by the US Bureau of Mines.

Table V3.3c.ii(a) lists these two measures for each of these minerals, along with the percentages of global reserves held by the leading states in the mid-1980s. Table V3.3c.ii(b) gives similar percentages for the leading producers of each mineral as drawn from three studies reflecting activity during the 1980s. The favored positions of the large continent-sized states in both these lists is noteworthy; the USSR is associated with all 10 minerals, Australia with 7, South Africa 7, China 6, Canada 6, Brazil 5, and India 5. Surprisingly, the US has or produces only 2 of these minerals.

V3.3d. Forests and Fisheries

In addition to coverage of the more obvious fuels and minerals, (statistics for which are often available in other sources), the regular reports of the Worldwatch Institute (Brown et al.) and the World Resources Institute (WRI) also cover such unglamorous natural resources as topsoil, trees, and fisheries.

As the demand for food has increased, the world has begun to mine its soils, virtually converting them into a nonrenewable resource. According to Brown et al. (1984: 9) erosion of cropland is exceeding new soil formation by 23 billion tons per year. At this rate topsoil reserves will disappear in about 150 years, and encroaching deserts now pose a greater threat to national survival than do invading armies (Brown et al., cited in *World Development Forum*, August 31, 1986: 2). Overgrazing and cropping of already poor land is turning some 6 million hectares annually into desert and rendering 21 million more to zero economic productivity. State-by-state data on this phenomenon is not available, but it is on forests where the extent of the world's growth has declined steadily as agriculture has expanded around the world, and on fisheries where there is evidence of overexploitation as technology comes up with ever-more efficient ways of making huge catches.

i. Forests. In the industrialized world today, forests are suffering from air pollution and acid rain. In the tropics, ten trees are being cut for every one planted; in Africa, the ratio is 29-to-one. The world's tropical forests are disappearing at a rate of 2% per year, faster in west Africa and southeast Asia, where they will probably be totally destroyed by the end of this century (Brown et al., 1986:10). This situation prompted the formation in 1986 of the International Tropical Timber Organization of 42 states comprised of the owners of the world's rain forests and the rich nations which consume their precious but dwindling hardwood.

Table V3.3d.i(a)—a survey of forests and woodlands as a percentage of total land—shows that the African, Asian, and Latin American zones are the most heavily thicketed, and the Islamic zone the least. Table V3.3d.i(b) reports the average annual removal of forest products including all fuelwood, charcoal, and industrial wood. In some respects, the leading states in this category are simply the largest countries with the most wood resources. Thus, only the top states in each zone are ranked. Table V3.3d.i(c), which analyzes the *rate* of deforestation in 83 tropical countries whose wooded lands are most endangered, is more relevant to the concerns of this chapter. The rate of global deforestation is an indicator of how fast the world is extinguishing species, destroying watersheds, manipulating microclimates, and affecting carbon and nutrient cycles. The nine states with *'s have only small areas of their national forests remaining. Data is based upon the *Tropical Forest Assessment* of the United Nations' FAO and UNEP for the early 1980s as updated and revised through 1990 in *World Resources 1990-91*.

ii. Fisheries. A recent United Nations analysis of the global fishing industry reports a 2% annual growth in demand for fish as compared to a 1% growth in supply. This trend translates into a possible shortfall of some 20 million tons of fish within the next 15 years, two-thirds of which will be in the developing countries (UN, *Development Forum*, November-December, 1987: 8).

Like most resources discussed in this section, many of the fish are taken from environments (i.e., offshore waters) of developing nations, but consumed in the advanced industrial world. In Latin America, for example, production figures would indicate an annual per capita consumption of 28 kilograms, but actual consumption is only 8 kilograms. The "missing" 20 kilograms are exported or processed into industrial products such as fish meal, fish oil, or animal feed.

Table V3.3d.ii(a) lists the average annual marine fish catch, in thousands of metric tons, for the 54 leading fish-producing states in 1985-87, the most recent years for which data is available. Only nine countries in all of Africa and the Islamic zone catch more than 100,000 metric tons of fish per year. The major countries in this pursuit are from Asia and Europe, with Japan and the Soviet Union being the top two by a significant margin, accounting for about 25% of the global total of some 78.9 million metric tons each year. The dominance of these states indicates that this resource, like the others cited in this section, though often found in the "global commons" off the coasts of many developing nations, is chiefly exploited by more advanced states from further afield.

Table V3.3d.ii(b) completes the global fisheries picture by citing data on the average annual freshwater catch, a lesser activity accounting for about 14% of the total marine catch.

V3.3a.i - Energy Consumption

Europe	Islamic	Africa	Asia	Latin America

(a)-Total Commercial Energy Consumption, 1987 (petajoules)

Europe	Islamic	Africa	Asia	Latin America
US 68,079	Saudi A. 2328	S.Africa 3154	China 23,469	Mexico 4130
USSR 54,724	Iran 1932	Nigeria 495	Japan 13,367	Brazil 3178
W.Ger. 10,023	Turkey 1536	Zimbabwe 189	India 6462	Argentina 1745
UK 8522	Egypt 991	Cameroon 85	Australia 3243	Venezuela 1616
Canada 7518	Algeria 975	Ivory Coast 70	S.Korea 2173	Colombia 717
France 6064	Pakistan 814	Kenya 66	N.Korea 1648	Cuba 426
Italy 5991	UAE 803	Zaire 61	Indonesia 1382	Chile 345
Poland 5320	Kuwait 501	Ghana,Zambia-55	Thailand 770	Peru 343
....	....	....	....	....
Switzld. 726	S.Yemen 61	4 @ 6	Madagascar 12	Paraguay 32
Greece 718	Afghanistan 60	Togo 5	Nepal 12	Nicaragua 30
Portugal 398	Cyprus 49	C.Af.R. 4	Fiji 8	El Salvador 27
Ireland 367	Mauritania 42	Burundi 3	Cambodia 6	Honduras 26
Luxmbrg. 120	N.Yemen 40	Gambia 3	Laos 4	Suriname 14
Albania 116	Somalia 12	GBissau 2	Solomons 2	Guyana 14
Iceland 39	Djibouti 4	Eq.Guinea 1	Comoros 1	Barbados 11
Malta 18	Chad 3	Cape Verde 0	Bhutan 1	Haiti 9
n=30/30	n=27/28	n=37/38	n=27/33	n=25/33

(b)-Commercial Energy Consumption per Capita, 1987 (gigajoules)

Europe	Islamic	Africa	Asia	Latin America
Luxmbrg. 326	Qatar 642	S. Africa 83	Australia 201	Trinidad 169
Canada 291	UAE 552	Gabon 34	Singapore 140	Venezuela 88
US 280	Bahrain 430	Zimbabwe 21	N.Zealand 113	Argentina 56
E.Ger. 231	Kuwait 269	Congo 12	Japan 110	Mexico 50
Nethrlds. 213	Oman 245	Cameroon 8	N.Korea 79	Barbados 43
Norway 199	Saudi A. 185	Zambia 7	Mongolia 53	Cuba 43
USSR 194	Libya 83	Ivory Coast 6	S.Korea 52	Suriname 36
Czech. 185	Israel 82	Nigeria 5	Malaysia 38	Jamaica 31
Bulgaria 173	Cyprus 72	Ghana,Gambia-4	China 22	Chile 28
Finland 167	Algeria 42	Senegal,Liberia-4	Mauritius 16	Colombia 24
....	....	....	....	....
Switzrld.111	Egypt 20	Benin,Guinea-1	Sri Lanka 4	Costa Rica 15
France 109	Tunisia 19	GBissau 1	Vietnam 3	Guyana 14
Italy 105	Djibouti 11	BF,C.Af.R.-1	Myanmar 2	Dom.Rep. 12
Ireland 101	Morocco 10	Uganda 1	Comoros 2	Nicaragua 9
Greece 72	Pakistan 7	Mozambique 1	Bangladesh 2	Bolivia 9
Yugoslavia 71	N.Yemen 5	Ethiopia 1	Nepal 1	Paraguay 8
Spain 62	Afghanistan 4	Rwan.,Bur.-1	Bhutan 1	Honduras 6
Malta 52	Sudan 2	Tanzania 1	Madagascar 1	Guatemala 5
Portugal 39	Somalia 2	Mali,Malawi-1	Laos 1	El Salvador 5
Albania 38	Chad 1	Cape Verde 0	Cambodia 1	Haiti 1
n=30/30	n=27/28	n=37/38	n=27/33	n=25/33

Source: WRI, *World Resources 1990-91*, Table 21.1

Europe		Other Zones		
Western	Eastern	Isl./Afr.	Asia	Lat.Am.

(a)-Nuclear Power Plants: Operating and Under Construction, 1989

Western	Eastern	Isl./Afr.	Asia	Lat.Am.
US 108+7 = 115	USSR 56+26 = 82			
France 55+9 = 64				
UK 40+2 = 42			Japan 38+12=50	
W.Ger. 23+2 = 25				
Canada 18+4 = 22	Czech. 8+8 = 16		India 6+8 = 14	
Sweden 12+0=12	E.Germany 5+6 = 11			
Spain 10+0 = 10			S.Korea 8+1 = 9	
Belgium 7+0 = 7	Bulgaria 5+2 = 7			
Switz. 5+0 = 5	Romania 0+5 = 5		Taiwan 6+0 = 6	
Finland 4+0 = 4	Hungary 4+0 = 4			Argentina 2+1 = 3
			China 0+3 = 3	
Italy 2+0 = 2		S.Africa 2+0 = 2		
Nethrlds. 2+0=2				Brazil 1+1 = 2
	Poland 0+2 = 2	Iran 0+2 = 2		Mexico 0+2 = 2
				Cuba 0+2 = 2
	Yugoslavia 1+0 = 1	Pakistan 1+0 = 1		
n=310 in 12	n=128 in 8	--------------------n=96 in 12--------------------		

(TOTAL n= 534 in 32 states, 6 of whose plants are still being constructed.)

Source: WRI, *World Resources 1990-91*, Table 21.5

(b)-Nuclear Power: Installed Capacity (and % of Total Electricity)

Western	Eastern	Isl./Afr.	Asia	Lat.Am.
US 77,084(17%)	USSR 27,756(11%)			
France 37,533(69%)			Japan 23,665(29%)	
W.Ger. 16,413(32%)				
UK 10,120(17%)				
Canada 9776(15%)				
Sweden 9000(45%)				
Spain 5577(32%)				
Belgium 5486(65%)			Taiwan 4918(48%)	
Switz. 2882(38%)			S.Korea 2720(53%)	
Finland 2310(36%)	Czech. 1980(25%)	S.Africa 1840(4%)		
	E.Ger. 1694(10%)			
Italy 1273(1%)	Bulgaria 1632(28%)		India 1140(3%)	
				Argentina 935(13%)
	Hungary 825(39%)			
	Yugoslavia 632(5%)			Brazil 626(1%)
Nethrlds. 508(5%)		Pakistan 125(2%)		
n=12	n=6	--------------------n=8---------------------		

Source: "World Overview of Nuclear Power Programs", *World Eagle*, Jan.
1989, p. 30, citing IAEA.

i- PETROLEUM

Production - % of world		**Reserves**, % world, mil. brls., yrs. left			
1989 Tot.=59,380,800 brls/day		(World Tot. = 1,001,571 mil. brls.; 1/90)			

Europe

USSR	20.5%	USSR	5.8%	58,400	13 yrs.
US	12.9	US	2.6%	25,860	10 yr.
UK	2.9	Norway	1.2%	11,546	25 yr.
Canada	2.7	Canada	0.6%	6,133	14 yr.
Norway	1.5	UK	0.4%	4,256	5 yr.

Islamic

Saudi Arab.	8.3%	Saudi A.	25.5%	254,959	95 yr.
Iran	4.9	Iraq	10.0%	100,000	^131 yr.
Iraq	4.8	UAE	9.7%	98,105	^188 yr.
UAE	3.1	Kuwait	9.4%	94,525	^200 yr.
Kuwait	2.6	Iran	9.3%	92,860	^109 yr.
Libya	1.9	Libya	2.3%	22,800	59 yr.
Algeria	1.2	Algeria	0.9%	9,200	36 yr.
Qatar	0.7	Neutral Zone	0.5%	5,200	45 yr.
Neutral Zone	n.a	Egypt	0.4%	4,500	13 yr.
Oman	n.a.	Qatar	0.5%	4,500	n.a.
Egypt	n.a.	Oman	0.4%	4,250	n.a.
S. Yemen	n.a.	S. Yemen	0.3%	3,000	n.a.

Africa

Nigeria	2.7%	Nigeria	1.6%	16,000	32 yr.

Asia

China	4.7%	China	2.4%	24,000	23 yr.
Indonesia	2.0	Indonesia	0.8%	8,200	20 yr.
India	n.a.	India	0.8%	7,516	27 yr.

Latin America

Mexico	4.4%	Venezuela	5.8%	58,504	97 yr.
Venezuela	2.9	Mexico	5.6%	56,640	54 yr.
Ecuador	0.5	Ecuador	n.a.		

Source:"The Worldwide Report," *Oil and Gas Journal*, Dec.25,1989, cited in *World Eagle* ,
March 1990: 30-31; years from *The Economist*, July 15, 1989: 99 and ^February 13, 1988:107.

Table V3.3b (continued)

ii - NATURAL GAS

Production, % of world (% of bil. cu. ft., 1986)		Reserves (% world & bils. cu.ft., 1/90) (World Total: 3,989,119 bil. cu. ft.)		
		Europe		
US	32.7%	USSR	37.6%	1,500,000
USSR	30.8	US	4.1%	165,000
Canada	20.5	Canada	2.4%	94,300
Norway	3.2	Norway	2.1%	82,160
Netherlands	3.1	Netherlands	1.5%	61,100
UK	2.0	UK	0.5%	20,820
		Islamic		
Iran	n.a.	Iran	12.5%	500,000
UAE	n.a.	UAE	5.2%	208,000
Saudi A.	n.a.	Saudi Arabia	4.5%	181,347
Qatar	n.a.	Qatar	4.1%	163,100
Algeria	1.6%	Algeria	2.9%	114,000
Iraq	n.a.	Iraq	2.4%	95,000
Kuwait	n.a.	Kuwait	1.2%	48,600
Iraq	n.a.	Libya	0.6%	25,500
Libya	n.a.	Pakistan	0.5%	18,000
		Africa		
Nigeria	n.a.	Nigeria	2.2%	87,400
		Asia		
Indonesia	1.6%	Indonesia	2.2%	87,015
Malaysia	n.a.	Malaysia	1.3%	51,900
China	0.6%	China	0.9%	35,300
India	n.a.	India	0.6%	22,973
Australia	n.a.	Australia	0.4%	16,467
		Latin America		
Venezuela	0.7%	Venezuela	2.5%	100,846
Mexico	0.6	Mexico	1.8%	73,380
Argentina	n.a.	Argentina	0.7%	27,299

Source: "The Worldwide Report," *Oil and Gas Journal*, Dec.25,1989, cited in *World Eagle*, Mar. 1990: 32; production percentages computed from CIA, *Handbook of Economic Statistics 1989*.

iii - COAL

	Production		Reserves		
	% world			% world	mil.met.T.
China	21.2%		USSR	40.5%	173,000
US	18.1		US	23.9%	102,000
USSR	16.4		China	8.8%^	n.a.
Poland	6.3		Poland	8.7%	37,000
W.Germany	4.9		S.Africa	7.0%	30,000
Australia	4.2		W. Germany	6.0%	25,500
India	4.2		India	3.9%	16,650
S.Africa	4.2^^		UK	3.3%	14,000
Czechoslovakia	3.1		N. Korea	2.3%	10,000
UK	2.6		Yugoslavia	2.0%	8,700

Source: CIA, *Handbook of Economic Statistics 1989*, Tables 99, 107, 108; plus ^^*World Eagle*, Dec. 1986: 3, and ^Kurian 1984.

V3.3c.i - Lists of Important Minerals

	OTA/BuMines 1985	GAO/JCS 1983	Hargreaves &Fromson 1983	Arad & Arad 1979	Bosson &Varon 1977
alumin/bauxite*	x	x	#7	#3	no probs.
antinomy					no probs.
asbestos					no probs.
barite					critical
beryllium	x		#14		
bismuth					critical
cadmium			#24		
chromium	1st tier	x	#1	#8	ample
cobalt	1st tier	x	#3	#7	no probs.
columbium	x	x	#8		ample
copper			#4	#2	critical
diamonds, indust.	x		#10		
feldspar					ample
flourspar					critical
germanium			#16		
gold			#6		
graphite	x				
iron ore			#22	#1	ample
lead			#23	#10	critical
magnesium					ample
manganese	1st tier	x	#2	#4	no probs.
mercury				#12	critical
molybdenum			#15		no probs.
nickel		x	#11	#5	no probs.
phosphates					ample
platinum group	1st tier	x	#5	#9	
potash					ample
silicon			#25		
silver			#21	#6	critical
sulfur					no probs.
tantulum	x	x	#20		
tin	x	x	#9	#13	critical
titanium ores**	x	x	#12		no probs.
tungsten		x	#19		critical
uranium			#18	#11	
vanadium	x		#13		ample
zinc			#17	#14	critical
Total	n=13	n=11	n=25	n=14	n=27

Sources: US Congress, Office of Technology Assessment, *Strategic Materials* (1985); US General Accounting Office, *Report on Defense Spending* (1983: Chart 34); Hargreaves and Fromson, *World Index of Strategic Minerals* (1983); Arad and Arad, *Sharing Global Resources* (1979); and Bosson and Varon, *The Mining Industry and the Developing Countries* (1977).

*alumina, and aluminum and bauxite are combined; **titanium includes both rutile and ilmenite.

(a)-% Share of World *Reserves* (with Static Life & Demand Ratios)

1. bauxite (250 yrs., ratio 12:1) — Australia 20-35%, Guinea 16-34%, Brazil 11-15%, Suriname 7-11%, Jamaica 5-15%, Guyana 5%, Cameroon 4%, SU 3%.

2. chromium (123 yrs., ratio 21:1) — S. Africa 63-68%, Zimbabwe 22-33%; + Finland, USSR, Turkey, Philippine Islands

3. cobalt (130 yrs., ratio 7:1) — Zaire 28-49%, Zambia 14-16%, Australia 2-27%, N. Caledonia 4-18%, SU 9-13%, Cuba 8-14%, Phil. I. 8%, Morocco 2%.

4. copper (41 yrs., ratio: 2:1) — US 20-22%, Chile 16-20%, USSR 9-13%, "other communist" 11%, Zambia 8-10%, Canada 9%, Peru 6-8%, Zaire 5%.

5. iron ore (149 yrs., ratio 8:1) — USSR 31-32%, Brazil 10-17%, Canada 12-14%, Australia 10%, #New Caledonia 6%, US 4%,; + Liberia, Mauritania.

6. manganese (116 yrs., ratio 6:1) — USSR 25-45%, S. Africa 8-45%, Gabon 3-15%, Australia 6-8%, + France, Japan.

7. nickel (75 yrs., ratio 3.5:1) — #New Caledonia 22-44%, Cuba 9-24%, Canada 14-16%, USSR 10-14%, Indonesia 8-13%, Phil. I. 10%: + Norway, Dom. Rep.

8. platinum metals group (146 yrs., ratio 8:1) — S. Africa 64-81%, USSR 17%.

9. tin (15 yrs., ratio 1:1) — Thailand 12-34%, China 15-24%, Malaysia 12-14%, Indonesia 8-16%, USSR 10%, Bolivia 9-10%, Zaire 3%, Nigeria 2%, Australia/#New Caledonia 2%.

10. titanium (43 yrs., ratio 6:1) — Norway 20%, Canada 17%, US 17%, USSR 17%.
    incl: ilmenite — India 23%, Canada 22%, Norway 18%, S. Africa 15%, Australia 8%, US 8%.
    incl: rutile — Brazil 74%, Australia 7%, India 6%, S. Africa 4%, Italy 2%, Sierra Leone 2%, USSR 2%.

Sources: Bosson & Varon (1977), Arad & Arad (1979), US Bureau of Mines (1985), US General Accounting Office (1983); supplemented by US Department of Commerce report in *New York Times*, August 25, 1985: 19.
Leading states only; %s range due to multiplicity of sources cited.
= colony of France, not one of 162 states recognized in this study.

Table V3.3c.ii (continued)

(b) - % Share of World *Production*

1. bauxite (89% world production, 1988) — Australia 36.0%, Guinea 16.1, Brazil 9.0, Jamaica 7.6, USSR 4.0, Suriname 3.5, China 3.3, Yugoslavia 3.1, India 3.1, Hungary 3.0.

2. chromite (95% world production, 1983*) — USSR 30.3%, S. Africa 27.6, Albania 11.1, Brazil 8.3, Zimbabwe 5.3, Turkey 4.9, India 4.4, Finland 4.2, Phil. I. 4.1, #New Caledonia 1.1, Iran 0.6, Greece 0.5, Madagascar 0.5.

3. cobalt (94% world production, 1980^) — Zaire 50%, USSR 15, Zambia 11, Canada 5, Australia 5, Phil. I. 4, Finland 4.

4. copper (77% world production, 1988) — Chile 17.4%, US 16.8, Canada 9.0, USSR 7.6, Zaire 6.2, Poland 5.2, Zambia 4.7, China 3.5, Peru 3.5, Mexico 3.3.

5. iron ore (88% world production, 1988) — USSR 27.4%, Brazil 15.8, China 11.5, Australia 10.5, US 6.3, India 5.7, Canada 4.2, S. Africa 2.8, Sweden 2.2, Venezuela 2.1.

6. manganese (99% world production, 1983*) — USSR 46.3%, S. Africa 12.8, Brazil 9.4, Gabon 8.2, China 7.1, Australia 6.0, India 5.9, Mexico 1.6, Ghana 0.8, Hungary 0.4, Morocco 0.3.

7. nickel (88% world production, 1988) — Canada 23.8%, USSR 22.8, #New Caledonia 8.1, Australia 7.5, Indonesia 6.3, Cuba 5.3, S. Africa 4.2, Dom. Rep. 3.5, China 3.2, Botswana 3.2.

8. platinum (98% world production, 1983^) — USSR 48%, S. Africa 45, Canada 5.

9. tin (92% world production, 1988) — Brazil 19.6%, Indonesia 15.2, Malaysia 14.3, China 12.4, USSR 8.0, Thailand 7.0, Bolivia 5.3, Australia 3.6, UK 2.2, Peru 2.2.

10. titanium ores, including:
   a. ilmenite (88% world production, 1980^) — Australia 27%, Canada 18, Norway 17, USSR 9, S. Africa 7, India 4, Malaysia 3, Finland 3.
   b. rutile (97% world production, 1980^) — Australia 69%, Sierra Leone 12, S. Africa 11, Sri Lanka 3, USSR 2.

Source: WRI, *World Resources 1990-91*, and *1986* ; plus ^US Joint Chiefs of Staff, *US Military Posture 1984*.
= colony of France, not one of 162 states recognized in this study.

(a)-Forest Land as Percentage of Total Land

Europe	Islamic	Africa	Asia	Latin America
Finland 76%		Zaire 78%	Solomons 93%	Suriname 96%
		Gabon 78	Cambodia 76	Guyana 83
Sweden 64			Brunei 75	
			N.Korea 74	
Albania 45		C.Af.R. 64	Papua NG 71	Brazil 67
Canada 44		Congo 62	Bhutan 70	
USSR 41		Zimbwe 62		Peru 55
Portugal 40		Eq.Guinea 61	Japan 68	Panama 54
Austria 39		Cameroon 54	S.Korea 67	Paraguay 52
Czechosl. 37		Tanzania 47	Malaysia 67	Bolivia 52
Yugoslav. 37		Malawi 45	W.Samoa 65	Ecuador 52
Bulgaria 35		Guinea 43	Fiji 65	Colombia 50
Luxmbrg 33^		Angola 43	W.Samoa 65	Belize 44^
Spain 31		Liberia 39	Taiwan 55^	Trinidad 44
US 30		Ghana 38	Laos 55	St.Vincent 41^
W.Germany 30		GBissau 38	Myanmar 49	Dominica 41^
		Benin 35		Guatemala 40
Poland 29				Venezuela 39
E.Germny 28		Senegal 30	Phil.I. 41	Nicaragua 36
Romania 28		Uganda 30	Vietnam 38	Honduras 35
Norway 27		Togo 29	SriLanka 37	Costa Rica 33
France 27	Turkey 26	Sierra Leone 29	N.Zealand 37	Jamaica 28
Switzrld. 26		Zambia 27	Nepal 33	Mexico 25
	Sudan 20	Burkina Faso 26	Thailand 31	Bahamas 23^
	Cyprus 18^	Ethiopia 24	Mauritius 31	Argentina 22
Italy 22	Chad 16	Gambia 20	India 23	Chile 21
Belgium 21	Mauritania 15	Mozambique 19	Madagascar 23	
Greece 20	Somalia 14	Nigeria 16		
	Morocco 12		Seychelles 18^	
Hungary 18	Iran 11		Bangladesh 16	
	N.Yemen 8	Rwanda 11	Comoros 16	St.Chris. 17^
	S.Yemen 7		China 14	Cuba 17
Denmark 12	Lebanon 7	Mali 7	Australia 14	Antigua 16^
Nethrlds. 9	Israel 6	Swaziland 6	Mongolia 10	St.Lucia 13^
UK 9	Tunisia 4			Dom. Rep. 13
	Pakistan 4	S. Africa 4		
Ireland 5	Afghanistan 3	Kenya 4	Singapore 5	Grenada 9^
	Iraq 3			
	Syria 3	Niger 2		El Salvador 6
	Algeria 2	Botswana 2		
	Saudi A 1	Burundi 2	Maldives 3^	Haiti 4
	Egypt,Djib.-0	Lesotho 0		Uruguay 4
Iceland 1	Oman,Qatar-0	C.Verde 0	Vanuatu 1^	
Malta 0	UAE,Bahr.,Kuw.-0	STP 0^		Barbados 0^
	Jord.,Libya-0	Namibia-na		
n=30	n=28	n=38	n=33	n=33 (162)

Source: WRI, *World Resources 1986* for 1981-83, Table 4.1, n=146;
     plus ^Population Reference Bureau, *Data Sheet 1987*, n=16.

Table V3.3d.i (continued)

Europe	Islamic	Africa	Asia	Latin America

(b)-Avg. Ann. Removal of Forest Products, 1985-87 (000 cu.mtrs.)

Europe	Islamic	Africa	Asia	Latin America
US 485.6			China 269.1	Brazil 237.8
SU 374.9			India 250.3	
Canada 179.5			Indonesia 158.1	
		Nigeria 98.6		
Sweden 52.5		Ethiopia 38.9	Malaysia 40.2	Mexico 21.5
Finland 41.4		Kenya 33.8	Thailand 36.9	Colombia 17.5
France 39.9		Zaire 31.4	Phil. I. 35.8	Chile 16.2
W.Ger. 31.6		Tanzania 23.9	Japan 32.6	
Romania 24.5	Pakistan 21.4	S.Africa 18.8	Bangladesh 27.8	Argentina 11.2
Poland 23.7	Sudan 20.1	Mozambique 15.2	Vietnam 25.4	
Czech. 18.9	Turkey 16.2	Uganda 12.9	Australia 19.9	Ecuador 8.7
Spain 16.6	Iran 6.8	Cameroon 12.1	Myanmar 19.1	Paraguay 8.1
Yugoslavia 16.0	Afghanistan 6.7	Ivory Coast 11.9		Peru 7.7
n=12/30	n=5/28	n=10/38	n=11/33	n=8/33 (47)

Source: WRI, *World Resources 1990-91*, Table 19.2, n=146.

(c)-Rates of Tropical Deforestation, % per year, 1980s

Europe	Islamic	Africa	Asia	Latin America
		Ivory Coast 5.2	Nepal 4.0	Costa Rica 6.9
		Malawi 3.5	Sri Lanka 3.5	*Haiti 3.8
		*GBissau 2.7		Argentina 3.5
		Nigeria 2.7		*El Salvador 3.2
		Burundi 2.7		*Jamaica 3.0
		Niger 2.6		Nicaragua 2.7
	Mauritania 2.4	Gambia 2.4	Thailand 2.5	Ecuador 2.3
	Algeria 2.3	*Rwanda 2.3	India 2.3	Honduras 2.3
		Liberia 2.3	Myanmar 2.1	Guatemala 2.0
		Burkina F. 1.7	Vietnam 1.7	
	Tunisia 1.7	*Benin 1.7	Phil. I. 1.5	Colombia 1.7
		*Kenya 1.7	Malaysia 1.2	Mexico 1.3
		*Mozambique 0.8	Madagascar 1.2	Paraguay 1.1
		*Uganda 0.8	Laos 1.0	
		Ghana 0.8	Bangladesh 0.9	Panama 0.9
		Guinea 0.8	Indonesia 0.8	
		Cameroon 0.8		Chile 0.7
	Chad 0.6	Togo 0.7		Venezuela 0.7
	Iran 0.5	Mali 0.5		Dom.Rep. 0.6
		Senegal 0.5		Brazil 0.5
	Pakistan 0.4			Peru 0.4
	Morocco 0.4	Zimbabwe 0.4		Trinidad 0.4
		Sierra L.,Zamb.-0.3	Cambodia 0.2	
		Tanz.,Ethiopia-0.3	Fiji 0.2	Bolivia 0.2
	Sudan 0.2	Eq.G.,C.AF.R.-0.2	Papua NG 0.1	
		Zaire,Angola-0.2	Bhutan 0.1	Cuba 0.1
	Somalia 0.1	Congo,Gabon-0.1	Solomons 0.0	Guyana 0.0
		Botswana 0.1	Australia,NZ-0.0	Suriname 0.0
n=0	n=9	n=32	n=19	n=23 (83)

Source: WRI, *World Resources 1990-91*, Table 19.1, n=83; * = states with only small areas of national forest remaining.

V3.3d.ii - Fisheries

Europe	Islamic	Africa	Asia	Latin America

(a) - Average Annual Marine Catch, 1985-87 (000 metric tons)

Europe	Islamic	Africa	Asia	Latin America	
			Japan 11,532		
USSR 10,041					
US 5075				Chile 5063	
			China 4627	Peru 4746	
Norway 1982			S.Korea 2821		
Denmark 1747			Thailand 2135		
Iceland 1656			Indonesia 1861		
Canada 1416			India 1711		
Spain 1410			N.Korea 1597		
			Phil. I. 1378	Mexico 1181	
UK 895				Ecuador 922	
France 820		S.Africa 710	Malaysia 609		
Poland 637				Brazil 607	
Italy 515	Turkey 551		Vietnam 593		
Nethrlds. 460	Morocco 520		Myanmar 524	Argentina 453	
Portugal 364			N. Zealand 360		
Ireland 235	Pakistan 334	Ghana 273		Venezuela 273	
Sweden 220		Senegal 265	Bangladesh 209	Cuba 209	
Romania 194				Panama 193	
W.Germany 186					
E.Germany 180			Australia 177		
Finland 125	Iran 113	Nigeria 154	Sri Lanka 148	Uruguay 138	
Greece 115	Oman 104				
n=20	n=5	n=4	n=15	n=10	(54)

Source: WRI *World Resources 1990-91*, Table 23.2, n=146.

(b) - Average Annual Freshwater Catch, 1985-87 (000 metric tons)

Europe	Islamic	Africa	Asia	Latin America	
			China 3415		
			India 1169		
			Indonesia 610		
			Bangladesh 585		
			Phil. I. 545		
			Vietnam 242		
		Tanzania 263	Japan 210	Brazil 213	
	Egypt 190	Uganda 186	Thailand 173		
		Zaire 158	Myanmar 147	Mexico 135	
	Chad 112	Kenya 113	N. Korea 103		
n=0	n=2	n=4	n=10	n=2	(18)

Source: WRI *World Resources 1990-91*, Table 23.2, n=146.

215

V3.4. INTERNATIONAL AND COMPOSITE MEASURES

The final section of this chapter on ecological balance will consider certain international and composite measures which relate to "quality of life" and recognition by states of the need to work cooperatively to solve some of the "problems of the commons."

V3.4a. Exploiting for Exports

Natural resources are not normally exploited and used within the country where they are found, but rather are traded on the world market in exchange for other scarce commodities. The "depletable-resource-for-hard-currency" exchange is the price many developing countries pay in order to participate in the global capitalist economy.

Table V3.4a.i lists the percentage of exports accounted for by depletable fuels, minerals, and metals for 122 states in 1988. It is followed by an analysis, in Table V3.4a.ii, of just which resources are being exploited from the 43 states (above the dotted line in the first table) which gain more than 30% of their export income from this depletion of their natural heritage. About half of these states are exporting oil and its byproducts, and for 13 OPEC countries the second table also gives a "vulnerability index," with a 0 (best) to 200 (worst) point range, based upon foreign exchange reserves, ability to raise output when prices fall, and proportion of export receipts based on this depletable resource (*The Economist*, March 19, 1988).

V3.4b. Global Cooperation

The exploitation of the natural resources of the less developed countries for consumption by the advanced industrial states is only one of the problems relating to ecological balance mentioned in this chapter. Transnational pressures generated by pollution and population growth are among the others. International cooperation and an integrated interdisciplinary approach will be needed if the goals of ecological quality and sustainable growth and development are to be reconciled.

In addition to the Worldwatch Institute and the World Resources Institute, a number of scholars have addressed these issues and offered some blueprints for "planet management" (Myers, 1987; Repetto,1985b; Ghosh, 1984; Heilbroner, 1986; Pirages, 1978; Ophuls, 1977). The five volumes in the Duke University Press policy-study series dealing with population (Marden et al., 1982), food (Hopkins et al., 1986), environment (Dahlberg et al., 1985), energy (Hughes et al., 1985), and resources (Harf and Trout, 1986) represent an especially fine integrated approach to these matters.

This section analyzes some of the very limited first steps that the world's *policy-makers* have made in this direction. It will be divided into two parts: i. international programs for the designation of specially protected ecological areas; and ii. international treaties for the protection of the environment.

i. Protected Areas. The United Nations Environmental Program, especially UNESCO's Man and the Biosphere Program, in cooperation with the International Union for Conservation of Nature and Natural Resources, have endeavored to get states to designate certain percentages of their national territory as natural world heritage sites, wetlands of international importance, and biosphere reserves.

World heritage sites are natural areas which contain examples of a major stage of the earth's evolutionary history, a significant ongoing geological process, a unique natural phenomenon, formation, or feat; or a habitat for endangered or rare species of plants and animals required for the survival of the species. Wetlands of international importance are specifically designated by any of the 45 countries that have ratified the International Wetlands Convention. Central to the concept of biosphere reserves is the conservation of large units of landscape containing both "natural" ecosystems (in which people have little impact), and "managed" ecosystems (in which people substantially influence the processes). Surrounding the core area, protected from human disruption to conserve a representative example of ecosystems, are areas managed for agriculture, grazing, forest production, fisheries, recreation or other economic uses of renewable resources.

Table V3.4b.i surveys state participation in these programs.

ii. International Treaties. The following 12 international treaties pertaining to the environment—completed by the global community between 1963 and 1989—have been surveyed for state endorsement and ratification as of 1991. The place and date indicate the circumstances of original signing; the numbers refer, respectively, to states which have ratified these conventions and states which have signed but whose ratifications are pending.

1. Treaty Banning Nuclear Weapon Tests in the Atmosphere, in Outer Space, and Under Water - Moscow, 1963; n=105 + 12 pending.

2. Convention on Wetlands of International Importance Especially as Waterfowl Habitat - Ramsar, 1971; now ratified by 49 states.

3. Convention on the Prohibition of the Development, Production, and Stockpiling of Bacteriological (Biological) and Toxin Weapons, and on their Destruction - London, Moscow, Washington, 1972; n=101 + 24 pending.

4. Convention Concerning the Protection of the World Cultural and Natural Heritage - Paris, 1972; n=100.

5. Convention on the Prevention of Marine Pollution by Dumping of Wastes and Other Matter - London, Mexico, Moscow, Washington, 1972; n=56 + 4 pending.

6. Convention on International Trade in Endangered Species of Wild Fauna and Flora - Washington, 1973; n=94 + 6 pending.

7. International Convention for the Prevention of Pollution from Ships - London, 1978; n=50 + 6 pending.

8. Convention on the Conservation of Migratory Species of Wild Animals - Bonn, 1979; n=30 + 11 pending.

9. United Nations Convention on the Law of the Sea - Montego Bay, 1982; n=36 + 99 pending.

10. Convention for the Protection of the Ozone Layer - Vienna, 1985; n=54 + 3 pending.

11. Protocol on (Chlorofluorocarbon) Substances that Deplete the Ozone Layer - Montreal, 1987; n=49 + 9 pending.

12. Convention on the Control of Transboundary Movements of Hazardous Wastes and their Disposal - Basel, 1989; n=1 + 40 pending.

Individually, the impact of these treaties may be limited as concerns the behavior of individual countries. Taken as a whole, however, they reflect a growing commitment of governments to building an international legal regime to protect the environment.

Table V3.4b.ii summarizes state ratifications of these treaties, out of a maximum possible of 12; again the first number refers to completed ratifications, the second to treaties which have only been signed. As with most aspects of international law, the commitment is greatest among states in the European and Latin American zones.

V3.4c. Composite "Quality of Life" Rankings

To conclude this chapter, data from four composite indicators which attempt to measure the quality of life are presented. One common element in all of them—life expectancy at birth—is given first in Table V3.4c.i. The four composites will then be displayed in the order in which they were developed.

Ruth Sivard has been reporting each year since 1978 in her *World Military and Social Expenditures* publication an "Economic and Social (ECOSOC) Rank" which lists states (from first to 142nd in the world in the latest ranking) in an order based upon eleven variables—five relating to health, five to education, and GNP per capita. The method of averaging gives equal importance to each of the three elements. The latest scores (from Sivard's 1989 edition) appear in Table V3.4c.ii.

Morris D. Morris (1979) developed for the Overseas Development Council a

"Physical Quality of Life Index" (PQLI) which rates countries on a scale of 1 to 100 in accordance with their infant mortality, life expectancy, and level of literacy. The figure is updated regularly for that organization's *Agenda* series on US and the Developing Countries. The latest figures available appeared in its 1988 edition (Sewell et. al.), and are reproduced here as Table V3.4c.iii.

Richard Estes (1984) created an "Index of Social Progress" (ISP) which combines 44 indicators across 11 categories (education, health, status of women, defense, economics, demography, geography, political stability, political participation, cultural diversity, welfare). The measure was introduced in his 1984 *The Social Progress of Nations,* and is updated according to a three-to-five-year schedule. Data presented here in Table V3.4c.iv is from his 1987 book, and covers 124 countries.

Finally, the United Nations Development Program (UNDP) in 1990 presented a "Human Development Index" which purports to measure the "process of enlarging people's choice." It combines life expectancy, literacy, and purchasing power. For each measure a "minimum" (42 years, 12% literacy, $220 per year) and a "desirable" (78 years, 100% literacy, $4861 per year (the official poverty line for nine industrial countries adjusted for purchasing power parity)) value are specified and arrayed in intervals of 0 to 1. The placements for 129 states are adjusted on the basis of 1000 for the display in Table V3.4c.v.

The health and demographic components of these composites (6/11 of Sivard's, 2/3 of Morris', 12/44 of Estes', and 2/3 of the UNDP's) relate to ecological quality as it has been defined in this chapter. Such aggregate measurements, indicative of general tendencies, should be used only when correlated with other more specific data. They are included here for the sake of conceptual completeness and general reference. They also each, in their individual ways, represent arguable links between this chapter's ecological concerns and the issues raised earlier in Chapter 2 (Economic Well-Being) and later in Chapter 4 (Social Justice).

V3.4a.i - % Exports in Fuels, Minerals, and Metals, 1988

Europe	Islamic	Africa	Asia	Latin America
	Iraq 99%Δ		Brunei 100%ºº	
	Libya 99	Angola 97%Δ		
	Iran 98Δ	Zambia 95		
	Bahrain 98ºº	Guinea 95º		
	Algeria 96			
	Qatar 95ºº			Venezuela 90%
	Oman 91	Nigeria 88		Bolivia 89
	S.Yemen 90			
	Saudi A. 90			
	Kuwait 90	Niger 76		
	N.Yemen 88	Congo 72		Chile 67
	UAE 79	Togo 69		Suriname 61º
	Egypt 64	Zaire 64	Papua NG 63	Trinidad 61
Norway 51%		Gabon 59		Peru 58
	Syria 50	Liberia 54		
	Afghan. 47^	Cameroon 53	Indonesia 49	Ecuador 45
	Jordan 43	Benin 36		Guyana 41º
	Mauritania 32	Ghana 32	Australia 37	Mexico 38
....	....	....	....	....
		Senegal 25	Laos 25	
Poland 19			Cambodia 25º	Colombia 26
Canada 18	Morocco 21	Sierra L. 21	Malaysia 18	Brazil 21
Greece 15		Kenya 20	Singapore 15	Dom.Rep. 21
Nethrlds. 12	Tunisia 19	Zimbabwe 13	Madagascar 14	
UK 10		+S.Africa 11	Phil. I. 12	Jamaica 15
Yugoslavia 9		Rwanda 9	China 10	
Hungary 8			India 9	
Belg.+Lux. 8	Sudan 13		N.Zealand 8	Panama 13
Spain 7			Sri Lanka 7	
US 6		Tanzania 6		
Sweden 6		Uganda 4		Honduras 10
Finland 5		Ethiopia 3	Nepal 4	
Czech.5*		Ivory Coast 3	Thailand 3	Argentina 5
Austria 5		Mozambique 3	Myanmar 3	Haiti 4
France 5		Burkina F. 0	S.Korea 2	Guatemala 3
Portugal 4	Turkey 6	C.Af.R. 0	Bangladesh 2	El Salvador 3
Switzerland 4		Burundi 0	Taiwan 1	Costa Rica 1
W.Germany 4	Lebanon 3^	Mali 0	Japan 1	Nicaragua 1^
Denmark 4	Israel 2	Malawi 0	Mauritius 0	Uruguay 1
Italy 3	Pakistan 1	na	na	Paraguay 0
Ireland 2	Somalia 0	+Bots.,Les.,Swazi.	Bhutan,Maldives	na
Ice.,Malta-na	Chad-na	GB,CV,STP	Como.,Seych.,Van.	St.C.,St.L.,St.V.
SU,EGer.,Rom.-na	Cyprus-na	Eq.G.,Gambia	Mong.,N.Korea,Sol.	Belize,Dom.,Gren.
Alb.,Bulg.-na	Djibouti-na	Namibia	VN, Fiji,W.Sam.	Antigua,Bahamas
				Cuba,Barbados
n=23/30	n=25/28	n=29/38	n=22/33	n=23/33 (122)

Source: WDR90f88, Table 16, n=108; plus ^WDR88f86, ΔWDR87f85, *WDR86f84, and ºV2.3d=#1XCI, ººV2.3d=#3CI; n=14.

+ = states in customs union with larger state noted in zone.

V3.4a.ii - States with Depletable Resources > 30% of Exports
(with name of chief fuel, mineral, & metal exports; & "vulnerability index")

State	FMM%X	Name of Chief Fuel, Mineral, or Metal	Vulnerability Index
Brunei	100%	crude oil, natural gas, petroleum products	
Iraq	99	crude oil, petroleum products, natural gas	(125)
Libya	99	crude oil, petroleum products, natural gas	(99)
Iran	98	crude oil, coal, petroelum products, natural gas	(85)
Bahrain	98	petroleum products, crude oil, coal, aluminum	
Angola	97	crude oil, petroleum products, diamonds, manganese, gold, uranium, natural gas	
Algeria	96	crude oil, petroleum products, natural gas	(99)
Zambia	95	copper, ore, silver, platinum, zinc, lead, cobalt, coal	
Qatar	95	crude oil, natural gas, iron	(106)
Guinea	95	iron ore, bauxite, diamonds, gold	
Oman	91	crude oil	
S.Yemen	90	petroleum products, crude oil	
Saudi Arabia	90	crude oil, natural gas, petroleum products	(92)
Venezuela	90	crude oil,petrol.prods.,natl.gas,iron ore,gold,bauxite,aluminum	(80)
Kuwait	90	crude oil, petroleum products, natural gas, coal	best=(66)
Bolivia	89	tin, natl. gas, petrol., lead, zinc, tungsten, antinomy, gold, copper	
Nigeria	88	crude oil, petroleum products, natural gas, tantalum	worst=(164)
UAE	79	crude oil, natural gas, silver, platinum	(97)
Niger	76	radioact. matl., crude oil, petrol. products, coal, iron, tin, phosphates	
Togo	69	petroleum products, phosphates, limestone	
Chile	67	copper,nitrates,oil,iron ore(coal),gold,silver,natl. gas,mlybdnm.	
Egypt	64	crude oil, petroleum products	
Zaire	64	copper; cobalt, zinc, tin, gold, diamonds, iron, coal, oil, tantalum	
Papua NG	63	copper, silver, gold, gas, iron ore	
Congo	72	crude oil; potash, natural gas, diamonds	
Trinidad	61	petroleum products, crude oil, inorganic elements	
Suriname	61	bauxite (aluminum), iron ore	
Gabon	59	crude oil, iron ore, manganese, uranium, natural gas	(124)
Peru	58	crude oil, copper, lead, silver, iron ore, gold, zinc, natural gas	
Liberia	54	iron ore, diamonds, manganese	
Cameroon	53	crude oil, bauxite, iron ore, rubber	
Norway	51	oil; natural gas; titanium: ilmenite	
Syria	50	crude oil, petroleum products	
Indonesia	49	crude oil, tin, copper, silver, gold, iron ore, coal, natural gas, nickel, petroleum products	(81)
Afghanistan	47	natural gas	
Ecuador	45	crude oil	(82)
Jordan	43	phospates	
Guyana	41	non-ferrous base metals and ores	
Mexico	38	oil, silver, platinum, copper, gold, lead, zinc, natural gas, coal	
Australia	37	coal, coke, iron ore	
Benin	36	non-ferrous metals & other crude minerals	
Mauritania	32	iron ore	
Ghana	32	gold, manganese	

Source: Table V3.4a.i and V2.3d data bank using UNCTAD85f82, Europa 84f82, and Kurian 84f80
for names of FMMs; "Vulnerability Index" from *The Economist*, March 19, 1988.

V3.4b.i - Protected Areas

Europe	Islamic	Africa	Asia	Latin America

(a) - Percentage of National Land Area Protected, 1990

Europe	Islamic	Africa	Asia	Latin America
Luxembourg 25.1%				Ecuador 38.4%
Austria 19.3		Botswana 17.7%	Bhutan 18.6%	Panama 17.3
Czech. 15.8		Tanzania 13.4		Chile 16.0
Norway 15.5		Malawi 11.3		
W.Germany 11.3	Israel 11.6%	Senegal 11.3	Sri Lanka 11.4	Costa Rica 12.0
UK 10.6	Pakistan 9.8	Rwanda 10.5	N.Zealand 10.5	Dom.Rep. 11.4
US 8.6		Zambia 8.6		Venezuela 9.8
France 8.2		Togo 8.5	Thailand 9.1	
Iceland 7.9		Benin 7.6	Indonesia 7.8	Cuba 7.8
		Zimbabwe 7.1	Nepal 7.0	
Poland 7.2		Gabon 6.8		
Portugal 6.8	Sudan 3.4	Uganda 6.7	Japan 6.4	Barbados 5.8
Denmark 6.7		C.Af.R. 6.3		
		Ivory Coast 6.2	S.Korea 5.7	Colombia 5.4
Hungary 5.5		Ethiopia 6.2		Honduras 5.2
Spain 5.1		Kenya 5.4	Singapore 4.8	Suriname 4.6
Nethrlds. 4.4	Iran 2.2	Ghana 5.1	Australia 4.8	Bolivia 4.5
Italy 4.3		S.Africa 4.8	India 4.4	Peru 4.3
Yugoslavia 4.1		Congo 4.0		Argentina 4.0
Sweden 4.1	Mauritania 1.4	Zaire 3.9	Malaysia 3.4	
Greece 4.1		Cameroon 3.6		Trinidad 3.1
Canada 3.7	Jordan 1.0	Burkina F. 2.7	Vietnam 2.6	Mexico 2.9
Switzrld. 3.0	Cyprus-0.8	Swaziland 2.3	Mauritius 2.0	Paraguay 2.8
Belgium 2.6	Morocco 0.7		Madagascar 1.8	Brazil 2.4
Finland 2.6	Egypt 0.7	Liberia 1.4	Phil. I. 1.7	
Albania 2.0	Djibouti 0.5	Sierra Leone 1.4	China 0.8	
Bulgaria 1.2	Tunisia-0.4	Niger 1.3	Bangladesh 0.7	El Salvador 1.1
USSR 0.9	Saudi A. 0.4	Nigeria 1.1	N.Korea 0.5	Guatemala 0.9
E.Germany 0.7	Lebanon 0.3	Mali 0.7	Myanmar 0.3	Nicaragua 0.4
Romania 0.7	Oman,Turk.-0.3	Angola 0.7	Fiji 0.3	Haiti 0.3
Ireland 0.4	Alg.,Afghan.-0.2	Lesotho 0.2	Mongolia 0.2	Uruguay 0.2
Malta 0.0	Chad,Libya-0.1	Guinea 0.1		Guyana 0.1
n=30	n=19/28	n=30/38	n=22/33	n=24/33 (125)

Source: WRI, *World Resources 1990-91*, Table 20.1.

(b) - World Heritage Sites (n=86) in 37 states, 1990

Europe	Islamic	Africa	Asia	Latin America
US 11				
Canada 6		Zaire 4	Australia 8	
Yugoslavia 4		Tanzania 4		Peru 3
UK 3		Iv.Coast 3	India 5	Ecuador 2
Bulgaria 2		Senegal 2		Argentina 2
Greece 2	Turkey 2	Cameroon 1	N.Zealand 2	Brazil 1
France 1	Algeria 1	Ethiopia 1	Nepal 2	Costa Rica 1
Poland 1	Tunisia 1	C.Af.R.,Guinea-1	China 1	Guat.,Hond.-1
Spain 1		Malawi,Zimbwe.-1	Sri Lanka 1	Pan.,Mex.-1
n=9 w/ 31	n=3 w/ 4	n=10 w/ 19	n=6 w/ 19	n=9 w/ 13

Source: WRI, *World Resources 1990-91*, Table 20.1, n=37 states with 86 sites.

Table V3.4b.i (continued)

(c)-Important International Wetlands 1990 (thousands of hectares)

Canada 12,937				
SU 2,987	Iran 1,298			Australia 3,305
US 970	Mauritania 1,173	Gabon 1,080		
Denmark 734				
W.Ger. 314				
Netherlands 306				
Sweden 271		Niger 220		Uruguay 200
UK 169		S. Africa 208		
Hungary 111		Mali 162	India 119	
Greece 107	Egypt 106	Eq. Guinea 106		
Austria 102		Senegal 100		
Finland 101				
France 85				
Italy 54				Mexico 47
Spain 52				
E.Germany 46	Pakistan 21			
Portugal 31			Nepal 18	
Iceland 20	Tunisia 13		N.Zealand 15	
Yugoslavia 18	Morocco 11		Vietnam 12	Suriname 12
Norway 16		Uganda 15		
Belgium 9.6				Venezuela 10
Ireland 9.1	Algeria 8.4	Ghana 7.3	Cambodia 7.4	
Poland 7.1	Jordan 7.4			
Bulgaria 2.1			Japan 5.6	Chile 4.9
Switzrld. 1.8				
n=25	n=8	n=8	n=7	n=5 (53)

Source: WRI, *World Resources 1990-91*, Table 20.1; n=53 states with 432 wetlands.

(d) - Biosphere Reserves, 1990 (in hectares of coverage)

Dnmk(Grnld)70,000				
US 19,046				Colombia 2,514
SU 9,331	Algeria 7,200		Australia 4,743	Peru 2,507
Norway 1,555	Iran 2,610	Tanzania 2,338		Chile 2,407
Canada 843	Sudan 1,901	C.Af.R. 1,640	China 1,602	Argentina 2,005
Spain 615		Iv.Coast 1,480	Indonesia 1,482	Ecuador 1,466
France 486		Senegal 1,093		Mexico 1,288
Yugoslavia 350		Benin 880		
Netherlands 260		Kenya 851		
Czechoslovakia 177		Cameroon 850		Costa Rica 729
Hungary 129		Mali 771		Panama 597
Sweden 97		Zaire 298		Honduras 500
UK 44		Uganda 220	N.Korea 132	Bolivia 435
Romania 41		Congo 172	Japan 116	Cuba 324
Austria 28		Guinea 133		Uruguay 200
Poland 26	Tunisia 32		S.Korea 37	
Bulgaria 25	Pakistan 31		Thailand 26	
E. Germany 25			Phil. I. 24	
Switzerland 17		Burkina F. 16		
W. Germany 13		Rwanda 15		
Greece,Ireld.-8.8		Gabon 15	Sri Lanka 9.4	
Italy 3.8	Egypt 1.0	Ghana 7.8	Mauritius 3.6	
n=23	n=6	n=16	n=10	n=12 (67)

Source: WRI, *World Resources 1990-91*, Table 20.1.

223

V3.4b.ii - International Environmental Treaties Accepted, 1990

Europe	Islamic	Africa	Asia	Latin America
Italy 10+2	Tunisia 11			
Spain 10+2				Panama 9+2
Norway 10+2			Australia 9+1	
Denmark 10+2				Mexico 8+2
Sweden 10+2				Chile 7+3
Finland 10+2		Nigeria 9	N.Zealand 8+2	Guatemala 7+2
Hungary 10+2			Japan 8+1	
W.Ger. 10+1		S.Africa 8+1		Brazil 7
UK 10+1	Egypt 9+1		India 7+1	
Portugal 9+3		Ghana 8	China 7+1	Uruguay 6+2
Switzrld. 9+2				
Nethrlds. 9+2		Senegal 7+2	Phil. I. 6+3	Peru 6
USSR 9+1			Sri Lanka 6+2	
E.Ger. 9+1	Jordan 9		Thailand 6+1	Argentina 5+4
US 9		Kenya 7		Colombia 5+3
France 8+3		Gabon 6+2		Venezuela 5+2
Greece 8+3		Niger 6+1	Malaysia 5+2	
Canada 8+2	Pakistan 6+1	Cameroon 6+1	Singapore 5+1	Suriname 5+1
Belgium 8+2	Cyprus 6+1	Zaire 6	Fiji 5	Dom.Rep. 5+1
Luxmbrg. 7+3	Morocco 5+5	Ivory Coast 5+2		Paraguay 5+1
Ireland 7+3		Uganda 5+2		Costa Rica 5+1
Austria 7+1	Afghanistan 5+2	Benin 5+1	Nepal 4+3	Honduras 5+1
Malta 7+1	Iran 5+1	CapeVerde 5		
Iceland 7	Lebanon 4+3	Togo 4+3	Indonesia 4+2	Trinidad 5
Yugoslavia 7	Israel 4+2	Mali 4+2		
Poland 6+2	Syria 4+2	Gambia 4+1	Papua NG 4+1	
Bulgaria 5+1	Algeria 4+2	Tanzania 4+1	S.Korea 4+1	
	Libya 4+1	Zambia 4	Bangladesh 4+1	
	S.Yemen 4	Liberia 3+3		
	Sudan 4	C.Af.R. 3+3		Bolivia 4+2
	Oman 4	Burkina 3+2	Madagascar 3+3	Nicaragua 4+1
		Malawi 3+2		Ecuador 4
Czech. 3+1	UAE 3+3	Congo 3+2		Cuba 4
	Kuwait 3+3	Ethiopia 3+2	Laos 3+1	
	Chad 3+3	Rwanda 3+1	Mauritius 3+1	
Romania 2+1	Somalia 3+3	Guinea 3		Jamaica 3+2
		GBissau 3		
	Iraq 3+1	Burundi 2+3		
	Mauritania 3+1	Botswana 2+2	Myanmar 2+2	Haiti 2+4
	Turkey 3+1	Mozambique 2+1	Vietnam 2+2	Guyana 2+1
		Sierra L. 2+1	N.Korea 2+1	
	Saudi A. 2+2	Zimbabwe 2+1	Bhutan 2+1	El Salvador 1+2
	N.Yemen 2+2	Lesotho 1+3	Solomons 2+1	Barbados 1+1
	Bahrain 2+1	Swaziland 1+1	Mongolia 2+1	
	Qatar 2+1	Eq. Guinea 1+1		
Albania 0		Angola 0+1	Cambodia 1+2	
	Djibouti 0+1	STP,Namibia-na	Comoros 0+1	
n=30	n=28	n=38	n=27/33	n=25/33 (148)

Source: WRI, *World Resources 1990-91*, Table 25.1. First number indicates treaties ratified, second number indicates treaties signed but awaiting ratification as of June 1990.

V3.4c.i - Life Expectancy at Birth (years)

Europe	Islamic	Africa	Asia	Latin America
Switzerland 77				Dominica 75*
Sweden 77	Israel 75		Japan 77	Cuba 74
Iceland 77	Cyprus 75		Australia 76	CostaRica 74
Netherlands 77	Kuwait 73		N.Zealand 75	Barbados 74
Canada 76	Bahrain 71		Brunei 74*	Jamaica 74
Norway 76	UAE 69		Taiwan 73**	Antigua 73*
Finland 75	Qatar 69		Singapore 73	Panama 72
UK 75	Lebanon 67		Fiji 70	St.Lucia 72*
Spain 75	Jordan 66		Seychelles 70*	Uruguay 71
Greece 75	Syria 65		Sri Lanka 70	Chile 71
France 75	Turkey 64	STP 65*	China 69	Argentina71
US 75	Saudi A. 64	C.Verde 62	S.Korea 69	Bahamas 70*
Denmark 75	Iraq 64		Malaysia 69	St.Chris 70*
W.Germany 75	Tunisia 63	Zimbabwe 58	N.Korea 69	Suriname 70
Italy 75	Algeria 63	Botswana 57	Mauritius 68	Venezuela 70
Belgium 74		S.Africa 56		Trinidad 70
Austria 74	Morocco 61	Kenya 55	W.Samoa 65	Guyana 70
Ireland 74	Egypt 61	Ghana 54	Mongolia 65	St.Vincent 69*
E.Germany 73	Libya 61	Ivory Coast 53	Thailand 64	Grenada 68*
Portugal 73		Tanzania 53	Phil. I. 64	Mexico 67
Bulgaria 73	Iran 59	Zambia 53	Vanuatu 63*	El Salvador 67
Malta 73		Togo 53		Paraguay 66
Yugoslavia 72		Cameroon 53	Vietnam 61	Belize 66*
Czech. 72	Oman 55	Zaire 52	Myanmar 60	Brazil 65
Poland 72		Nigeria 51		Colombia 65
USSR 72		Gabon 51		Ecuador 65
Albania 72	Pakistan 52	Lesotho 51	India 58	Dom.Rep. 65
Luxmbrg. 72	S.Yemen 51	Uganda 51	Solomons 58*	
Hungary 71	N.Yemen 51	Swaziland 51		Nicaragua 63
Romania 71	Sudan 50	Liberia 51	Indonesia 56	Honduras 63
		Rwanda 49	Papua NG 54	
	Djibouti 47	Congo 49	Maldives 54*	Guatemala 62
	Mauritania 46	Burundi 49	Madagascar 52	Peru 61
	Chad 45	Malawi 47	Comoros 52	
		Mozambique 47	Laos 52	
		Burkina F. 47		Haiti 55
		Benin 46	Bangladesh 50	
		Eq.Guinea 46		Bolivia 53
	Somalia 42	C.Af.R. 45	Bhutan 48	
		Niger 45	Nepal 48	
		Senegal 45	Cambodia 48	
		GBissau 45		
		Angola 44		
	Afghanistan 39	Mali 44		
		Guinea 42		
		Ethiopia 42		
		Gambia 37		
		Sierra L. 36		
		Namibia-na		
n=30	n=28	n=38	n=33	n=33 (162)

Source: WRI90-91 for '85-90, n=145; plus *WDR88f86 (n=15), **Sivard87f84 (n=2).

V3.4c.ii - Sivard's ECOSOC Ranks (1 to 142)

Europe	Islamic	Africa	Asia	Latin America
Canada-1				
Norway-2T			Australia-10T	
Iceland-2T	Israel-23		Japan-10T	Barbados-29
US-4	Qatar-20		Brunei-18	Trinidad-35
Denmark-5	Kuwait-27		N.Zealand-20	Cuba-40
Sweden-6				
Finland-7T	UAE-33		Singapore-32	Argentina-44
Luxembourg-7T	Cyprus-38			Panama-46T
Switzerland-9		Gabon-63	Taiwan-45	Uruguay-46T
France-10T		S.Africa-69		
		Zimbabwe-77		Venezuela-49
W.Germany-13	Libya-40	Botswana-78	Fiji-52	Mexico-50
Netherlands-14	Bahrain-42	Congo-87T	S.Korea-53	Chile-53
UK-15		Swaziland-87T	N.Korea-55T	CostaRica-55T
Austria-16T	Saudi A.-51	Namibia 91	Malaysia-55T	Jamaica-55T
E.Germany-16T		Cameroon-96	Mauritius-60	
Belgium-18		Lesotho-98	Mongolia-67	Brazil-66
	Oman-60T	Kenya-100		Ecuador-67
Italy-22	Syria-60T	Zambia-102	Sri Lanka-75	
Ireland-23		Ghana-103	Thailand-80	Colombia-71T
Spain-25T	Algeria-63T	Angola-104T		Peru-73
USSR-25T	Iraq-63T	Iv. Coast-104T	Indonesia-91	
Hungary-28	Jordan-69	Liberia-104T	Philippines-93	Nicaragua-76
Czech.-29	Iran-71T	Nigeria-107	China-94	
Greece-31	Tunisia-74			
Bulgaria-33	Turkey-78	Tanzania-114		Dom.Rep.-80T
Malta-35		Uganda-114	Papua NG-98	Paraguay-80T
Poland-37	Lebanon-83	Togo 117	Vietnam-101	Guyana-83
Portugal-38	Egypt-87	Senegal-119	India-110	Guatemala-85
	Morocco-97		Madagascar-111	Honduras-86
Yugoslavia-43		Zaire-122	Myanmar-112	ElSalvador-90
Romania-46	N.Yemen-107	C.Af.R.-123		
	S.Yemen-109	Benin-124T	Laos-120	
Albania-55		Gambia-124T		Bolivia-94
		Sierra L.-124T		
	Mauritan-116	Eq.Guinea-127		Haiti-112
	Pakistan-117	Rwanda-128		
	Sudan-120	Burundi-130T	Bangladesh-129	
		Mozambique-130T	Cambodia-130T	
		Guinea-133T	Nepal-133T	
		Malawi-133T		
		Niger-136T	Solomons-na	St.C.,St.L.,St.V.-na
	Somalia-136T	Mali-138T	W.Sam.,Van.-na	Suriname-na
	Chad-138T	Burkina F.-138T	Bhutan-na	Belize-na
	Afghanistan-141	Ethiopia-142	Maldives-na	Antigua,Baham.-na
	Djibouti-na	GB,CV,STP-na	Seych.,Comoros-na	Dominica,Gren.-na
n=30	n=27/28	n=35/38	n=26/33	n=24/33 (142)

Source: Sivard 1989 for 1986.

T=Tied for this position; na=not accounted for by Sivard.

V3.4c.iii - Morris' PQLI (100 to 0)

Europe	Islamic	Africa	Asia	Latin America
Iceland 100			Australia 100	
France 100			Japan 99	Cuba 98
Sweden 99				Barbados 95
Norway 99			N.Zealand 96	Costa Rica 94
Finland 99	Israel 96		Taiwan 94	Jamaica 92
Nethrlds. 99	Cyprus 93		Singapore 91	Chile 91
Switzerland 99			Brunei 90	Uruguay 91
Denmark 98			Seychelles 88	Trinidad 90
Canada 98	Kuwait 84		S.Korea 88	Panama 90
US 98	Bahrain 81	STP 69	Sri Lanka 87	Argentina 90
Italy 98	Lebanon 79	Zimbabwe 67	W.Samoa 86	Bahamas 89
Spain 98	Jordan 77	Botswana 66	N.Korea 85	Antigua 88
Belgium 97		S. Africa 66		Dominica 88
Greece 97	UAE 74	C.Verde 65	Mauritius 83	Venezuela 87
Luxmbrg. 97	Turkey 73	Congo 64	Fiji 83	Grenada 86
W.Germany 97	Qatar 73	Tanzania 63	Thailand 82	Guyana 86
UK 97	Syria 71	Zambia 62	Malaysia 81	Belize 86
Austria 96		Lesotho 61	Mongolia 80	St. Lucia 85
Ireland 96	Tunisia 66		China 80	St. Chris. 85
	Libya 66	Kenya 58	Vietnam 80	Suriname 84
Poland 94	Iraq 62	Cameroon 58	Phil. I. 79	St. Vincent 84
E.Germany 94	Algeria 62	Swaziland 58		Mexico 84
Malta 94	Egypt 60	Zaire 55	Myanmar 71	Paraguay 83
Czechoslovakia 93	Iran 59	Ghana 55	Maldives 67	Colombia 82
Hungary 93	Saudi A. 56	Gabon 54	Indonesia 63	
	Morocco 54	Uganda 51		Ecuador 79
Bulgaria 92		Ivory Coast 49	Madagascar 57	Brazil 77
USSR 91	Oman 46	Togo 48	Comoros 57	Dom.Rep. 75
Romania 91	Pakistan 43	Namibia 47	India 55	El Salvador 74
Yugoslavia 91		Nigeria 47	Papua NG 54	Nicaragua 74
Portugal 91	Sudan 41	Rwanda 45	Laos 52	Peru 71
		C.Af.R. 43	Solomons 51	Honduras 67
Albania 82	S.Yemen 39	Liberia 43	Cambodia 50	Guatemala 64
		Mozambique 41		Bolivia 59
	Chad 34	Burundi 41	Bangladesh 43	
	Mauritania 33	Benin 40	Vanuatu 42	Haiti 48
	Djibouti 31	Eq. Guinea 38		
	Somalia 29	Angola 37	Nepal 36	
	N.Yemen 28	Malawi 37		
		Senegal 36	Bhutan 26	
	Afghanistan 21	GBissau 29		
		Burkina F. 29		
		Mali 28		
		Niger 28		
		Gambia 28		
		Guinea 28		
		Sierra L. 26		
		Ethiopia 25		
n=30	n=28	n=38	n=33	n=33 (162)

Source: ODC, *Agenda 88* for 1985, Table D1.

227

(1983 weighted rankings)

Europe	Islamic	Africa	Asia	Latin America
Italy 1.5				
W.Germany 1.5			Japan 6.25	
Denmark 3			N.Zealand 13.5	
Austria 4.5	Israel 31.25		Australia 15	
Sweden 4.5		Liberia 29		Uruguay 28
France 6	Tunisia 55		Singapore 38.3	Costa Rica 30
Norway 7	Jordan 56	S.Africa 62.25	Maurits. 41.3	Venez. 31.25
Ireland 8.25	Turkey 57.5	Zimbabwe 70.3		
Nethrlds. 8.25		Lesotho 76.5	Taiwan 45.25	Argentina 31.25
Belgium 8.25	Syria 60.5	Congo 81	Sri Lanka 45.25	Cuba 35
	Iran 60.5		S.Korea 51	Jamaica 36.5
UK 12	Egypt 66.5	Kenya 86.5	Malaysia 52.5	Trinidad 38.3
Switzrld. 13.5	Iraq 70.3	Nigeria 88	Thailand 52.5	Colombia 38.3
	Algeria 73.3	Zambia 89.5		
Canada 16.5	Morocco 73.3		Indonesia 59	Chile 41.3
Finland 16.5	Libya 76.5	Iv.Coast 91		Panama 41.3
Spain 18.5	Saudi A. 86.5	Zaire 92.5	Phil.I. 62.25	
US 18.5	N.Yemen 94.3	Rwanda 92.5	N.Korea 62.25	
Greece 20		Tanzania 94.3		Brazil 44
Hungary 21		Cameroon 94.3	Mongolia 68.5	Dom.Rep.45.25
	Pakistan 98.2	Senegal 97	China 70.3	Ecuador 49.5
	Sudan 98.2	Togo 98.2	Vietnam 73.3	Paraguay 49.5
Portugal 22.5	Lebanon 98.2	Benin-103.3	Madagascar 78.5	Mexico 54
E.Germany 22.5	S.Yemen 98.2	Ghana 106.3	Myanmar 82.5	Honduras 62.25
Bulgaria 24.5		C.Af.R. 106.3	Papua NG 82.5	Peru 66.5
Czech. 24.5		Uganda 109.5	India 84	El Salvador 68.5
	Mauritan.106.3	Burkina F. 111.5		Bolivia 78.5
Poland 26		Burundi 113.5	Nepal 103.3	Nicaragua 80.0
Romania 27		Niger 113.5	Bangaldesh 103.3	
Yugoslavia 31.25		Mozambq.115		Guatemala 85
Albania 42.25		Sierra L. 116	Laos 109.5	Haiti 89.5
USSR 52.5		Mali 117	Cambodia 111.5	
	Somalia 118.5	Malawi 118.5		
		Guinea 120		
	Afghanistan 121	Angola 122		
	Chad 123	Ethiopia 124		
na=3	na=7	na=9	na=9	na=11
Malta	Kuwait,Bahrain	STP,CV,GB	Bhutan,Seychelles	Belize,Sur.,Guyana
Iceland	UAE,Qatar,Oman	Gambia,Gabon	Comoros,Maldives	St.C.,St.L.,St.V.
Luxmbrg.	Cyprus	Eq.Guinea,Namibia	Fiji,Sols.,Brunei	Bahamas,Barbados
	Djibouti	Bots.,Swazi.	Vanuatu,WSamoa	Antig.,Dom.,Grenada
n=27/30	n=21/28	n=29/38	n=24/33	n=22/33 (124)

Source: Estes, "Trends in Global Social Development 1970-1986," mimeographed update of *The Social Progress of Nations*, for use in *Trends in World Development* (NY: Praeger, 1984 and 1987, respectively); n=124 (with Hong Kong = 36.5).

Estes Legend: .5=two states tied at this rank; .3=three states tied, .25=four states tied, etc.

V3.4c.v - UNDP's Human Development Index, 1990

Europe	Islamic	Africa	Asia	Latin America
Sweden 987			Japan 996	
Switzerland 986				
Nethrlds. 984			Australia 978	
Canada 983				
Norway 983			N. Zealand 966	Chile 931
France 974	Israel 957			Costa Rica 916
Denmark 971			S. Korea 903	Uruguay 916
UK 970			Singapore 899	Argentina 910
Finland 967				Trinidad 885
W.Germany 967				Panama 883
Italy 966	Kuwait 839			Cuba 877
Belgium 966			Malaysia 800	Mexico 876
Spain 965				Venezuela 861
Ireland 961	UAE 782		Sri Lanka 789	
Austria 961			N.Korea 789	Jamaica 824
US 961			Mauritius 788	Colombia 801
E.Germany 953	Iraq 759	S. Africa 731	Thailand 783	Brazil 784
Greece 949	Jordan 752	Botswana 646		Paraguay 784
Czech. 931	Turkey 751	Lesotho 580		Ecuador 758
USSR 920	Lebanon 735	Zimbabwe 576		Peru 753
Bulgaria 918	Libya 719	Gabon 525	Mongolia 737	Nicaragua 743
Hungary 915	Saudi A. 702	Zambia 481		
Yugoslavia 913	Syria 691	Kenya 481	China 716	Dom.Rep. 699
Poland 910	Iran 660	Cameroon 474	Phil. I. 714	
Portugal 899	Tunisia 657	Tanzania 413		El Salvador 651
Romania 863	Algeria 609	Namibia 404		
Albania 790		Congo 395	Vietnam 608	Guatemala 592
	Oman 535	Ivory Coast 393		Honduras 563
	Egypt 501	Ghana 360	Indonesia 591	Bolivia 548
	Morocco 489	Uganda 354	Myanmar 561	
	Pakistan 423	Togo 337	Laos 506	
		Liberia 333	Cambodia 471	
	S. Yemen 369	Nigeria 322	Papua NG 471	
		Angola 304	Madagascar 440	Haiti 356
	N.Yemen 328	Rwanda 304	India 439	
		Zaire 294		
		Ethiopia 282		
		Senegal 274		
	Sudan 255	C. Af. R. 258		
		Malawi 250	Bangladesh 318	
	Afghanistan 212	Mozambique 239		
	Mauritania 208	Burundi 235	Nepal 273	
	Somalia 200	Benin 224		
		Guinea 162	Bhutan 236	
	Chad 157	Burkina Faso 150		
		Sierra Leone 150		
		Mali 143		
		Niger 116		
n=27/30	n=24/28	n=32/38	n=24/33	n=22/33 (129)

Source: Adapted from UN Development Program, *Human Development Report 1990*, cited in *The Economist* (May 26, 1990: 81).

229

BIBLIOGRAPHY

ARAD, R. W. and U. B., et al. (1979) *Sharing Global Resources* New York: McGraw-Hill Book Co., for the Council on Foreign Relations.

BERARDI, G. (ed.) (1986) *World Food, Population, and Development.* Totowa, N. J.: Rowman and Littlefield.

BIRDSALL, N., et al. (eds.) (1985) *The Effects of Family Planning Programs on Fertility in the Developing World.* Washington: World Bank Publications.

BLACKBURN, A. M. (1988) *Pieces of the Global Puzzle: International Approaches to Environmental Concerns.* Golden, Colo.: Fulcrum.

BLAKE, G. (ed.) (1987) *Maritime Boundaries and Ocean Resources.* Totowa, N.J.: Rowman and Littlefield.

BOSSON, R., and B. VARON (1977) *The Mining Industry and the Developing Countries.* New York: Oxford University Press, for the World Bank.

BROWN, L. R. (1978) *The Twenty-Ninth Day.* New York: W. W. Norton Co.

_____. (1981) *Building a Sustainable Society.* New York: W. W. Norton Co.

BROWN, L. R., and J. L. JACOBSON (1986) *Our Demographically Divided World.* Washington: Worldwatch Institute.

BROWN, L. R., et al. (annual) *State of the World 198x: A Worldwatch Report on Progress toward a Sustainable Society.* New York: W. W. Norton Co. and Worldwatch Institute.

CALDWELL, L. K. (1985) *International Environmental Policy: Emergence and Dimensions.* Durham, N. C.: Duke University Press.

CARRYING CAPACITY, INC. (1986) *Beyond Oil: The Threat to Food and Fuel in the Coming Decades.* New York: Ballinger.

COALE, A., and P. DEMENY (1966) *Regional Model Life Tables and Stable Populations.* Princeton: Princeton University Press.

COMMONER, B. (1982) *The Closing Circle.* London: Jonathan Cape.

CROWSON, P. (1987) *Minerals Handbook, 1986-87: Statistical Analyses of the World's Minerals Industry.* New York: Stockton Press.

DAHLBERG, K., et al. (1985) *Environment and the Global Arena: Actors, Values, Policies, and Futures.* Durham, N. C.: Duke University Press.

DALEY, H. A. (ed.) (1973) *Steady-State Economy.* San Francisco: W. H. Freeman.

DALY, H. E., and J. B. COBB, JR. (1990) *For the Common Good: Redirecting the Economy toward Community, the Environment and a Sustainable Future.* Boston: Beacon Press.

DE LA COURT, T. (1990) *Beyond Brundtland: Our Common Future Re-Examined.* London: Zed Books.

DEVELOPMENT FORUM (monthly) "Ecowatch" column. New York: United Nations Publications.

DRAKAKIS-SMITH, D. (1987) *The Third World City.* New York: Methuen.

ESTES, R. J. (1984) *The Social Progress of Nations.* New York: Praeger.

_____. (1987) *Trends in World Development.* New York: Praeger.

FALK, R. A. (1972) *This Endangered Planet: Prospects and Proposals for Human Survival.* New York: Random House.

FOOD AND AGRICULTURE ORGANIZATION OF THE UNITED NATIONS (1983a) *Potential Population Supporting Capacities of Lands in the Developing World.* Rome: Food and Agriculture Organization (FAO).

_____. (1984a) *Land, Food, and People.* Rome: FAO.

_____. (annual) *Production Yearbook.* Rome: FAO.

FORNOS, W. (1988) *Gaining People, Losing Ground.* Washington: The Population Institute.

FRANCOME, C. (1984) *Abortion Freedom: A Worldwide Movement.* Boston: Allen and Unwin.

FURLONG, W., J. JOSHI, and B. E. WENNERGREN (1986) *Solving World Hunger: The US Stake.* Bethesda, MD.: Seven Locks Press.

GEORGE, S. (1984) *Ill Fares the Land: Essays on Food, Hunger, and Power.* Washington: Institute for Policy Studies.

GHOSH, P. K. (1984) *Population, Environment and Resources and Third World Development.* Westport, Conn.: Greenwood Press.

GRIFFIN, K. (1987) *World Hunger and the World Economy, and Other Essays in Developing Economics,* New York: Holmes and Meier.

GRIGG, D. (1986) *The World Food Problem, 1950-1980.* Cambridge, Mass.: Basil Blackwell Publishers.

HARDIN, G., and J. BADEN (eds.) (1977) *Managing the Commons.* San Francisco: W. H. Freeman.

HARF, J. E., and T. B. TROUT (1986) *The Politics of Global Resources: Population, Food, Energy, and Environment.* Durham, N. C.: Duke University Press.

HARGREAVES, D., and S. FROMSON (1983) *World Index of Strategic Minerals: Production, Exploitation, and Risk.* New York: Facts on File.

HEILBRONER, R. (1986) *An Inquiry into the Human Prospect: Updated and Reconsidered for the 1980s.* New York: W. W. Norton.

HOLDGATE, M. W., M. KASSAS, and G. F. WHITE (eds.) (1982) *The World Environment 1972-1982: A Report by the United Nations Environment Programme.* New York: United Nations Publications.

HOPKINS, R. F., R. L. PAARLBERG, and M. B. WALLERSTEIN (1982; 1986) *Food in the Global Arena.* New York: Holt, Rinehart and Winston; and Durham, N. C.: Duke University Press.

HUGHES, B. B., et al. (1985) *Energy in the Global Arena: Actors, Values, Policies, and Futures.* Durham, N. C.: Duke University Press.

(THE) HUNGER PROJECT (1985) *Ending Hunger: An Idea Whose Time Has Come.* New York: Praeger.

(THE) INDEPENDENT COMMISSION ON INTERNATIONAL HUMANITARIAN ISSUES (1986) *The Vanishing Forests: The Human Consequences of Deforestation: A Report.* London: Zed Books.

INTERNATIONAL PLANNED PARENTHOOD FEDERATION (1983) *Family Planning in 5 Continents.* London: International Planned Parenthood Federation.

KURIAN, G. (1984) *New Book of World Rankings.* New York: Facts on File Publications.

LAPPE, F. M., and J. COLLINS (1977) *Food First: Beyond the Myth of Food Scarcity.* Boston: Houghton-Mifflin Co.

LASZLO, E., et al. (1977) *Goals for Mankind: A Report to the Club of Rome on New Horizons of Global Community*. New York: E. P. Dutton.

LEONARD, J. H. (ed.) (1985) *Divesting Nature's Capital: The Political Economy of Environmental Abuse in the Third World*. New York: Holmes and Meier.

MCAUSLAND, P. (1985) *Urban Land and Shelter for the Poor*. Washington: Earthscan, for the International Institute for Environment and Development.

MARDEN, P. G., D. G. HODGSON, and T. L. MCCOY (1982) *Population in the Global Arena*. New York: Holt, Rinehart and Winston.

MARLIN, J. T., I. NESS, and S. T. COLLINS (1986) *Book of World City Rankings*. New York: The Free Press.

MATHEWS, J. T. (1988) "Redefining National Security: The Environmental Dimension," paper delivered at International Studies Association annual meeting, St. Louis, Mo.

MEADOWS, D. L., et al. (1972) *The Limits to Growth*. New York: Universe Books.

———. (1974) *Dynamics of Growth in a Finite World*. Cambridge, Mass.: Wright-Allen.

———. (1982) *Groping in the Dark*. New York: Wiley.

MESAROVIC, M. D., and E. PESTEL (1974) *Mankind at the Turning Point*. New York: Dutton.

MILBRAITH, L. W. (1989) *Envisioning a Sustainable Society: Learning Our Way Out*. New York: State University of New York Press.

MINDICK, B., and R. TAYLOR (eds.) (quarterly) *Population and Environment: Behavioral and Social Issues*. New York: Human Sciences Press.

MORRIS, M. D. (1979) *Measuring the Condition of the World's Poor*. New York: Pergamon Press.

MURDOCK, W. (1981) *The Poverty of Nations: The Political Economy of Hunger and Population*. Baltimore: Johns Hopkins University Press.

MYERS, N. (ed.) (1987) *GAIA: An Atlas of Planet Management*. New York: Anchor Press/Doubleday.

OBERAI, A. S. (1987) *Migration, Urbanization, and Development*. Washington: World Bank Publications.

OGUNBADIJO, O. (1985) *The International Politics of Africa's Strategic Minerals*. Westport, Conn.: Greenwood Press.

OPHULS, W. (1977) *Ecology and the Politics of Scarcity*. San Francisco: W. H. Freeman and Co.

ORGANIZATION FOR ECONOMIC COOPERATION AND DEVELOPMENT (1986) *Living Conditions in OECD Countries: A Compendium of Social Indicators*. Paris: OECD Publications.

PIRAGES, D. (1978) *Global Ecopolitics: The New Context for International Relations*. North Scituate, Mass.: Duxbury Press.

———. (ed.) (1977) *The Sustainable Society: Implications for Limited Growth*. New York: Praeger.

POPULATION REFERENCE BUREAU (annual) *World Population Data Sheet* Washington: Population Reference Bureau.

———. (1986a) *World Population: Toward the Next Century*. Washington: Population Reference Bureau.

POSTEL, S. (1988) *Altering the Earth's Chemistry.*   Washington: Worldwatch Publications.

RA'ANAN, U. and C. M. PERRY (eds.) (1985) *Strategic Minerals and International Security.* New York: Pergamon-Brassey's.

REPETTO, R. (ed.) (1985a) *The Global Possible: Resources, Development and the New Century.* New Haven: Yale University Press.

_____. (1985b) *World Enough and Time: Successful Strategies for Resource Management.* New Haven: Yale University Press.

RICHARDS, J. F., and R. P. TUCKER (eds.) (1988) *World Deforestation in the Twentieth Century.* Durham, N. C.: Duke University Press.

SADIK, N. (1988) "Development Is Mandatory and Has to Be Different," *International Herald Tribune,* May 7-8: 5.

SALAS, R. M. (1984) *Reflections on Population.* New York: Pergamon Press.

SEWELL, J. W., S. K. TUCKER, et al. (1988) *U. S. Policy and the Developing Countries: Growth, Exports, and Jobs in a Changing World Economy: Agenda 1988.* New Brunswick, N. J.: Transaction Books.

SIVARD, R. L. (annual) *World Military and Social Expenditures.* Washington: World Priorities Inc.

TANZER, M. (1980) *The Race for Resources: Continuing Struggle over Minerals and Fuels.* New York: Monthly Review Press.

TIETZE, C. (1981) *Induced Abortion: A World View.* New York: Population Council.

TILTON, J. E., R. G. EGGERT, and H. H. LANDSBERG (eds.) (1988) *World Mineral Exploration.* Baltimore: Johns Hopkins University Press.

TIMBERLAKE, M. (ed.) (1985) *Urbanization of the World Economy.* Orlando, Fla. Academic Press.

TOLBA, M. (1987) *Sustainable Development: Constraints and Opportunities.* London and Boston: Butterworth.

TULCHIN, J. S. (1986) *Habitat, Health, and Development: A New Way of Looking at Cities in the Third World.* Boulder: Lynne Rienner Publications.

TULLIS, F. L., and W. L. HOLLIST (eds.) (1985) *Food, the State, and International Political Economy: Dilemmas of Developing Countries.* Lincoln: University of Nebraska Press.

UNITED NATIONS (1985) *Compendium of Human Settlements Statistics.* New York: United Nations Publications.

UNITED NATIONS. DEVELOPMENT PROGRAM (1990) *Human Development Report 1990.* New York: United Nations Publications.

_____. ENVIRONMENT PROGRAM AND WORLD HEALTH ORGANIZATION (1988) *Global Pollution and Health.* New York: United Nations Publications.

_____. POPULATION FUND (1990) *The State of the World Population 1990.* New York: United Nations Publications.

_____. STATISTICAL OFFICE (1984) *A Framework for the Development of Environmental Statistics.* New York: United Nations Statistical Papers, Series M, No. 78.

UNITED STATES. CONGRESS. OFFICE OF TECHNOLOGY ASSESSMENT (1985) *Strategic Materials: Technologies to Reduce US Import Vulnerability.* Washington: US Government Printing Office.

_____. COUNCIL OF ENVIRONMENTAL QUALITY AND DEPARTMENT OF STATE (1980; 1982) *The Global 2000 Report to the President of the United States.* Washington: US Government Printing Office; and New York: Penguin Books.

_____. DEPARTMENT OF COMMERCE. BUREAU OF THE CENSUS (1986) *World Population Profile: 1985.* Washington: US Government Printing Office.

_____. DEPARTMENT OF ENERGY. ENERGY INFORMATION ADMINISTRATION (1986) *International Energy Outlook.* Washington: US Government Printing Office.

_____. DEPARTMENT OF INTERIOR, BUREAU OF MINES (1987) *Minerals Commodities Survey.* Washington: US Government Printing Office.

_____. DEPARTMENT OF STATE (1985) *Atlas of US Foreign Relations.* Washington: Department of State Publication 9350.

_____. GENERAL ACCOUNTING OFFICE (June, 1983) *Report on Defense Spending.* Washington: US Government Printing Office.

_____. SENATE. COMMITTEE ON ENERGY AND NATURAL RESOURCES (1983) *Hearings: Geopolitics of Strategic and Critical Materials.* 98th Congress, 1st Session, May 19, June 20, and July 22, 1983.

WARNOCK, J. W. (1987) *The Politics of Hunger: The Global Food System.* New York: Methuen.

WESTING, A. (ed.) (1986) *Global Resources and International Conflict: Environmental Factors in Strategic Policy and Action.* New York: Oxford University Press.

WESTON, R. (1984) *Strategic Materials: A World Survey.* Totowa, N J.: Rowman and Allenheld.

WORLD COMMISSION ON ENVIRONMENT AND DEVELOPMENT (1987a) *Food 2000: Global Policies for Sustainable Agriculture.* New Jersey: Humanities Press International Inc.

_____. (1987b) *Our Common Future.* New York: Oxford University Press.

WORLD EAGLE (monthly) Wellesley, Mass.: World Eagle Publications.

WORLD HEALTH ORGANIZATION OF THE UNITED NATIONS (annual) *World Health Statistics Annual.* Geneva: World Health Organization.

WORLD RESOURCES INSTITUTE AND THE INTERNATIONAL INSTITUTE FOR ENVIRONMENT AND DEVELOPMENT (annual) *World Resources 19xx/19xx: An Assessment of the Resource Base that Supports the Global Economy.* New York: Basic Books.

YOUNG, O. (1989) *International Cooperation: Building Regimes for Natural Resources and the Environment.* Ithaca, N. Y.: Cornell University Press.

4

Social Justice

Statistics and aggregate data are less helpful when values such as justice and participation are analyzed. As a result, a different methodology will be employed in the last two chapters of this book, using narrative summaries, excerpted from the data bank associated with this project, for exemplar states to illustrate broad categories of behavior.

In the case of social justice, such summaries will be combined with the results of some elementary numerical data rankings with respect to human rights which social scientists began to collect in the 1970s (Nanda et al., 1981). This data often comes in two categories: a.) events-based, which relies upon counts of specific violations, which can be disaggregated and converted to population-based rates to facilitate comparative analysis; and b.) standards-based, where one or more "judges" use available information to assign scale values to countries for comparative purposes.

Despite the difficulty of measuring a concept like justice, some impressive attempts have been made. A recent two-year study by the American Association for the Advancement of Science (AAAS) and the American Statistical Association (ASA) reports that a beginning has been made toward developing a social accounting scheme for human rights indicators, and concludes that the "prospects for reliable and credible standards-based human rights data systems are favorable" (Claude and Jabine, 1986: 564). A parallel is seen between the use of statistics in human rights reports, and the earlier development of indicators such as the unemployment rate and the consumer price index, which gained general acceptance and became influential only after decades of debate over policy and definitions. The general sense is that "there is sufficient reliability in human rights scoring to disarm accusations that the subject is intrinsically incapable of measurement" (Humana, 1986: 4, citing David L. Banks' report to the AAAS/ASA project). Despite strong cultural and individual differences in working concepts of human freedom, "for practical purposes different people find substantial agreement in their ratings" (ibid.; see also Renteln, 1985). In short, there is considerable information in the public domain, much of it in the form of narrative surveys in annual reference books, which might help to develop the beginnings of a standards-based assessment process for the last two values in this study.

V4.1. INTERNATIONAL BILL OF HUMAN RIGHTS

The organizational framework for this chapter on social justice will be based upon the structure of the International Bill of Human Rights, made up of the 1948 Universal Declaration of Human Rights (hereafter, UD), the 1966 International Covenant on Civil and Political Rights (hereafter, CP), and the 1966 International Covenant on Economic, Social, and Cultural Rights (hereafter, ESC). One or more of these documents have been signed by more than 100 of the world's states and, as such, they provide a universal standard to which a large majority of the world community can be held regardless of political ideology or regional culture (Henkin, 1981; Donnelly, 1984 and 1989).

To be sure, the western European (and by extension, Latin American) roots in international law of many of the rights that will be discussed in this chapter must be acknowledged. In particular, when the Universal Declaration was signed by all the United Nations' members in 1948, more than two-thirds of its countries were from the European and Latin American zones. Nevertheless, all states which have entered the world organization since that time have at least accepted the UN Charter's Article 55c, which calls for "universal respect for and observance of human rights and fundamental freedoms" (Humphrey, 1984). In addition the two later conventions, particularly the ESC document, incorporate many values of nations of Africa, Asia, and the Islamic world as well as of the communist eastern European states (Eide, 1986; Onuf and Peterson, 1984; Franck,1982).

V4.1a. Structural Analysis

Utilizing the structure of the International Bill of Human Rights as a framework, Table V4.1a summarizes those human rights practices which will be analyzed in this chapter. An indication is also given, in column 5, of the section in this chapter in which they will be covered, an ordering which roughly parallels that of the UN documents.

The following paragraphs elaborate upon the organization of this chapter. The numbers in parentheses at the end of each paragraph refer, respectively, to the relevant articles in UD, CP, and ESC being cited.

a.) governmental respect for *equality* of treatment of individual human beings, especially as concerns discrimination with respect to race, color, religion, national origin, cultural heritage, political opinion, property ownership, etc. (UD 1-2,15, 27; CP 2-3, 26-27; ESC 15). — See section V4.2.

b.) governmental policies pertaining to the *integrity of the person,* especially as relates to the death penalty, torture, cruel and degrading punishment, as such practices might be applied to prisoners (especially political prisoners) and others in government custody (UD 3-5; CP 6-8). — See section V4.3.

c.) evidence of government respect for the *rule of law,* especially regarding arbitrary arrest and detention, due process, fair and public trials by independent judiciaries, states of emergency (UD 6-11,28; CP 9-11); and related civil rights pertaining to privacy, freedom of movement, and the rights of women (UD 1-2, 13-14; CP 2-5,12-13). — See section V4.4.

d.) government attitude towards such individual *personal freedoms* as thought, expression, and association, especially as they might be applied to situations relating to religion, the press, and workers' unions (UD 18-20, CP 18-21). — See section V4.5.

As Table V4.1a indicates, there are also in the International Bill of Human Rights articles relating to some explicitly "economic" and "political" rights. The former include the right to own property, to work (in safe conditions, with fair remuneration and opportunities) reasonable hours and, implicitly, the right to not work (i.e., to strike) (UD 17, ESC 6-7); also, the right to have social security in the workplace (including unions, unemployment compensation, and special protections for women and children) (UD 22-24, CP 22, ESC 8-10); as well as the right to "economic justice" as reflected in access to adequate food, shelter, clothing, education, medical care, and social services (UD 25-26, ESC 11-14). Except for the rights relating to unions (considered in this study as relating to freedom of association), these economic matters are discussed in this text in Chapters V2.4 (distribution of the benefits of economic well-being), and V3.1 and .4 (sections on hunger and quality of life).

Similarly, the rights relating to politics and government listed in UD 21 and CP 25—free elections, secret and universal suffrage, opportunity to serve, etc.—are more related to what is covered in Chapter 5 on political participation. Value-indicators relating to legitimacy and accountability in government are also treated there, and as a whole that chapter analyzes states with an eye to how individuals might affect (participate in) their government.

The remainder of this chapter relates most essentially to how governments treat the individual, and will focus upon those matters in the International Bill of Human Rights relating to equality, the integrity of the person, the rule of law, and personal freedoms.

From the perspective of legal theory, these topics could be said to relate, respectively, to equal rights, human rights, civil rights, and political rights. The matters covered under government respect for the integrity of the person (freedom from illegal executions, torture, and imprisonments) are owed to everyone by virtue of their basic humanity. Issues under the rule of law (due process, fair trials, freedom of movement, and privacy) ought to be enjoyed in normal times by all citizens in their states. The personal freedoms of thought, expression, and association, if respected by one's government, are potentially powerful political instruments. The way a society defines these concepts and whether they are implemented equitably upon all individuals and groups (especially upon minority group members) significantly determine the quality of justice that society will experience.

V4.1b. Signatories

In addition to the implicit acceptance of the UD by all members of the United Nations, as of 1 January 1990 some 96 states had signed the ESC, and 91 the CP (Amnesty International, 1990: Appendix VI). Moreover, a minority of states (47) had signed an optional protocol to the CP which allows individuals' complaints relating to that document to be heard by the UN Human Rights Committee. Finally, as of 1988, some 50 countries had accepted the jurisdiction of the International Court of Justice whose authority (in theory) can be invoked with respect to these covenants.

Table V4.1b indicates how many of the four international legal instruments mentioned above to which accession is explicit and voluntary—i.e., the ESC, CP, Optional Protocol, and ICJ—have been accepted (i.e., signed *or* ratified) by the states of the world community. Fifty-five countries have accepted none at all; these include a number of very small states whose foreign ministries may not have adequate resources in their legal departments to address such issues, as well as a number of Asian, African, and Arabian peninsula states still wary of "Westernized" international law. About 50% of the states in these regions accept none of these documents as compared with only 1% non-acceptors in Europe and Spanish Latin America. Nevertheless, that still leaves some 107 of the states surveyed endorsing one or more critical aspects of the International Bill of Human Rights and its putative enforcement machinery.

V4.1c. Reporting Agencies and Methodologies

Signatures on human rights documents are obviously not the definitive measure of their acceptance by countries. The record of some states that have signed none of the documents (like Antigua or Dominica) is often better in actuality than that of some signatories of all four (e.g., Panama, El Salvador). To bridge the gap between signatures on legal documents and actual state practices, one must peruse the annual narratives of various human rights watch groups monitoring affairs in states and regions of their concern.

This study will rely heavily upon the global surveys regularly published by the US State Department, Amnesty International, Freedom House's Raymond F. Gastil, and Charles Humana (referred to hereafter as **DOS, AI, FH, and HUM**, respectively; see bibliography for complete citations). If these four surveys are supplemented by reports from groups with specific regional expertise, they provide an adequate base on which to make some comparative judgments with respect to social justice around the world.

The three annuals, listed in chronological order of their typical time of publication of information for the previous year, and with the number of states last covered, are DOS, which appears each February and surveys 170 countries (including 9 not recognized here); FH, which is published in June and covers 218 political actors (including many colonies and "related territories"); and AI, which comes out in October and surveys 133 states. Humana takes a longer view (1983, 1986; future editions are expected in the 1990s) while analyzing 120 states, 88 in depth.

Although these four studies are the most regular and exhaustive in scope, they each come with their particular political and ideological biases and specific areas of interest (Howard, 1990). The State Department, originally interested only in recipients of US aid, is notably tolerant of the human rights abuses of certain strategic American allies and friends (such as the UK in N. Ireland, Israel in the Occupied Territories, South Korea, the Philippines, and the states of Central America other than pre-1990 Nicaragua), and intolerant of similar practices in communist countries or by "radical enemies" like Libya and Iran. It is also uninterested in the death penalty as a violation of human rights and in economic and social rights in general. Freedom House has a similar bias and is particularly concerned with such "bourgeois freedoms" as private enterprise, freedom of the press, and relief from too much taxation and government bureaucracy. Amnesty International provides a good corrective to the first two, but is rather narrowly focused on prison situations, the judicial system, and the death penalty. Humana is the broadest in perspective, basing its 40 areas of concern upon specific articles in the International Bill of Human Rights; unfortunately, it has only been published twice in eight years.

FH and HUM are the most daring in a methodological sense in that they actually assign numbers to the rights or freedoms they attempt to measure. Although FH covers more countries, assigning to each state scores of 1-through-7 for both "political rights" and "civil liberties," Humana is more useful for the 88 of its 120 states for which it gives substantiation for its ratings in a disaggregated and weighted fashion which can easily be translated into a 1-through-4 scale for each of 40 measures. AI refuses to make such numerical distinctions between degrees of torture and death. DOS cross-references its findings with FH and AI and since 1985 has been quite explicit in the definitions it applies, but for reasons of diplomacy shrinks from numerical scorings.

A special rating system has been developed for this chapter wherein various rights violations by states will be ranked according to a 1-through-4 scale where:

1 = **few** accounts; occurs rarely or not at all; clean recent record.

2 = random or sporadic accounts, **sometimes**, occasionally; worse record in recent past (last 10 years) than in most current year.

3 = occurs frequently or **often**, continuing at present time; though often denied as official policy.

4 = a **regular**, consistent pattern (tantamount to policy) of gross abuses.

This is a general guide which will be adapted for specific indicators in later sections of this chapter. The time frame to which these scores will be applied is the most recent three-year period with flexibility being retained to produce a cumulative multi-year score for countries which experience abrupt changes in social justice practices as a result of extreme changes of governments in the most recent year.

One interesting result which comes from disaggregating state violations of rights into their component parts is the discovery that the worst offenders are not inevitably bad in all categories; that is, a state does not necessarily get all "4s" or "3s." Some kill their political opponents before there is any chance of torturing or jailing them; others imprison many, but kill and torture few. Some countries arrest and detain many marchers and demonstrators, but retain few in jail over the long term; others have imprisoned so many key political actors, there is no need to arrest and detain great masses of their followers. Some states tolerate freedom of religion but not of the press; others allow unions, but not public demonstrations.

Claude and Jabine caution that such numerical ratings should only be used "in combination with non-statistical information and by those who have sufficient understanding of the issues to put the data in context" (1986: 560). Accordingly, this study supplements its use of the four major global surveys by drawing upon more complete analyses of state behavior from a number of other organizations with specific regional or functional expertise. Among those which publish such reports are:

a. UN committees associated with oversight of the two 1966 conventions – e.g., the UN Commission on Human Rights (which publishes an annual yearbook), the Working Group on Enforced or Involuntary Disappearances, the Special Rapporteur on Summary and Arbitrary Executions, and the Economic and Social Council (Tolley, 1987);

b. official regional human rights organizations – e.g., the Human Rights Courts and Commissions of the Council of Europe and of the Organization of American States, and the Commission of Human and Peoples Rights of the Organization of African Unity. As of 1990, there is no such organization of governments in the Asian zone, and the UN Human Rights Center is helping to establish an Arab Institute for Human Rights.

c. governments – in addition to the United States, the Netherlands and Norway also prepare reports on human rights for countries to which they give aid or have other interests.

d. other non-governmental organizations (NGOs), including:

i. those with global sweep, such as Cultural Survival, the Minority Rights Group, the International Commission of Jurists, the International League for Human Rights (New York), the International Human Rights Law Group (Washington), and the Lawyers Committee for International Human Rights (New York).

ii. those with specific regional expertise, like the five Human Rights "watch groups" (Helsinki Watch, Middle East Watch, Africa Watch, Asia Watch, and Americas Watch), the Commission on Security and Cooperation in Europe, the Helsinki Federation (Vienna), the Organization for Protection of Human Rights in the Arab World (Cyprus), the Washington Office on Africa, the Society for the Protection of East Asian Human Rights, the Asian Coalition of Human Rights Organizations, the Washington Office on Latin America, the Council on Hemispheric Affairs, and the Ecumenical Committee on the Andes.

There are many organizations and reports with a specific *state* focus, and readers with such particular interests are urged to consult them to provide greater detail (or corrections) to the findings drawn here from organizations with wider and comparative scope. One might also consult such publications as the scholarly journal *Human Rights Quarterly* and the more topical *Human Rights Internet Reporter*, which appears five times a year and contains extensive updates on troublesome states across all zones. Human Rights Internet also regularly publishes directories of human rights organizations in specific regions.

To be sure, as Claude and Jabine (1986: 566) remind, "each of these institutions (and reports) has its own strengths and weaknesses: some lack adequate resources; some, by their very nature, lack wide credibility; and the UN agencies are constrained in their ability to learn and disseminate unpalatable facts about member nations." Of the above list, the NGOs are generally more helpful than the official governmental organizations. In all cases, some of the worst state-violators (e.g., Albania, North Korea, etc.) refuse to allow any outside groups in for a first-hand look at conditions within their countries, and information about such states is often speculative. Nevertheless, if such caveats are kept in mind, one can make informed judgments as to the status of human rights and social justice in specific countries if a comprehensive use is made of what is available in the public domain. Such a standard is sought in the reports which follow.

V4.1a - IBHR Articles: Location of their Coverage in this Work

Human "Right"	1948 UD Art.	1966 CPArt.	1966 ESC Art.	Text Coverage
equality	1-2,15,27	2-3,26,27	15	**V4.2**
integrity of person	3-5	6-8		**V4.3**
rule of law, civil rights	6-11,28 1-2,13-14	9-11 2-5,12-13		**V4.4**
personal freedoms	18-20	18-21		**V4.5**
economic rights	17,22-24	22	6-10	V2 & V3
economic justice	25-26		11-14	V2 & V3
participation in government	21	25		V5

V4.1b - IBHR-Analysis of Component Acceptors

Europe	Islamic	Africa	Asia	Latin America

Have accepted *four* instruments (ESC,CP, Optl.Protocol, ICJ^)

Europe	Islamic	Africa	Asia	Latin America
Austria	Egypt	Gambia	Mauritius	Barbados
Canada		Togo	Philippines	Panama
Denmark				Colombia
Finland				Venezuela
Luxembourg				Uruguay
Nethrlds.				El Salvador
Norway				Honduras
Portugal				Nicaragua
Sweden				Costa Rica
UK				Dom. Rep.
n=10	1	2	2	10 (25)

Have accepted *three* instruments

Europe	Islamic	Africa	Asia	Latin America
Belgium^	Cyprus	Kenya^	Australia^	Mexico^
US^	Sudan^	Liberia^	New Zealand^	Argentina
Bulgaria	Israel^	Cameroon	Japan^	Bolivia
France		C.Af.R.	India^	Ecuador
Iceland		Congo	Cambodia^	Peru
Italy		Eq.Guinea	Madagascar	St. Vincent
Spain		Guinea		Jamaica
Hungary		Niger		Trinidad
		Senegal		Suriname
		Zaire		
		Zambia		
n=8	3	11	6	9 (37)

Have accepted *two* documents (generally* CP & ESC)

Europe	Islamic	Africa	Asia	Latin America
Ireland	Afghanistan	Uganda*	N.Korea	
W.Germany	Iran, Iraq	Mali	Mongolia	
Malta*	S.Yemen	Gabon		Chile
	Jordan	Rwanda	Sri Lanka	
Czech.	Lebanon	Tanzania		
E.Germany	Libya		Vietnam	
Yugoslavia	Morocco			Guyana
Romania	Syria			
Poland	Tunisia			
USSR	Algeria			
n=9	11	5	4	2 (31)

* = accept ESC & ICJ.

Table V4.1b (continued)

Europe	Islamic	Africa	Asia	Latin America
		Have accepted _one_ document only		
		ICJ only (11)		
Switzerland	Turkey Pakistan Somalia	Nigeria S.Africa Swaziland Botswana Malawi	Taiwan	Haiti
		ESC only (3)		
Greece n=2	3	5	Solomons 2	Guatemala 2 (14)
		States accepting _NO_ instruments		
Albania	Saudi A. Kuwait Bahrain UAE Qatar Oman N. Yemen Mauritania Djibouti Chad	Cape Verde Burkina F. GBissau Benin Sierra L. Ghana Ivory Coast STP Ethiopia Burundi Zimbabwe Lesotho Mozambique Angola Namibia-na	Nepal Bhutan Bangladesh Maldives Seychelles Comoros China S.Korea Laos Myanmar Thailand Brunei Malaysia Singapore Indonesia Papua NG Fiji W.Samoa Vanuatu	Brazil Paraguay Belize Cuba St. Chris. Antigua Dominica St. Lucia Grenada Bahamas
n=1	10	15	19	10 (55)
TOTS. 30	28	38	33	33 (162)

Source: compiled from Amnesty International, _1990 Report_, Appendix VI;
^supplemented by United Nations _Yearbooks_ and Ozmanczyk, 1985, for ICJ signatures (n=50).

V4.2 EQUALITY

The first articles of the Universal Declaration of Human Rights assert that "all people are born *equal* in dignity and rights," implying that the rights to be surveyed in this chapter should be applied to all citizens of a state without regard to race, ethnicity, religion, or any other basic category of birth. Unfortunately, in virtually all countries this theoretical equality of opportunity ceases seconds after birth. Poor people and women everywhere are treated with less respect for their rights; and in most countries, there are members of ethnic, religious, or linguistic minorities who experience discrimination on the basis of their group affiliation.

The inequitable distribution of economic benefits was covered in section V2.4 (see also Thompson and Ronen, 1986). With respect to equal rights for members of minority groups, there is a dispute among scholars and theorists of international law as to whether the rights of such persons should be protected only in their status as individuals, or as members of groups (Capotorti, 1979; Rothchild, 1981). After reviewing the constitutional practices of many states, Van Dyke (1985) concludes that it is desirable and even necessary that groups should be the repositories of some human rights if the interests of their members are to be protected effectively.

Being a member of a minority group is a relative and flexible concept. Generally, the definition includes as divisive factors separating one group from another, elements of race, religion, and language, but not necessarily all three in all cases. This study will employ the term "ethnicity" to stress the most *politically significant* social identifications operating in different countries today, a characteristic which will vary from state to state (Said and Simmons, 1976; Snyder, 1982; Stack, 1986).

V4.2a. Ethnicity

A list of states in their order of ethnic homogeneity has been developed, with an eye to asking whether the divisions within each society are so great as to provoke institutionalized discrimination on the part of the ruling group, and/or desires for separation on the part of any subjugated peoples (Shiels, 1984). Table V4.2a presents the results of this survey in four classes whose boundaries draw upon the work and terminology of Nielsson and Jones (1988): a.) the most homogeneous "nation-states" where 90% or more of the population belongs to the same ethnic group (n=50); b.) "state-nations," relatively homogeneous countries with between 65 and 89% of the population belonging to the main ethnic group (n=51); c.) states with relatively mixed ethnicity and where the largest group comprises between 41 and 65% of the population (n=33); and extremely heterogeneous states where no ethnic group comprises more than

40% of the population (n=28).

Explanations to substantiate the percentages found in Table V4.2a will be provided in section V4.2d, after a brief explanation here of some of the factors involved in identifying the most relevant ethnic elements, and a more in depth discussion in sections V4.2b and .2c of the issues of religion and language.

In the United States with its "melting pot" ideology, the operationally relevant ethnic percentage is racial (white) and linguistic (English speaking). The combination of race (Arab v. black) and religion (Islam v. Christian/ animist) is the main issue dividing the Sudan. In Canada, the most significant issue is the number who speak English (rather than French) as their primary language; linguistic differences are also significant in Belgium. In Lebanon the major divisions are between Christian and Moslem, and in Sri Lanka between Buddhist (Sinhalese) and Hindu (Tamils); in other places, the divisions may relate to arcane differences within a common religious tradition: e.g., the percentage of Sunni v. Shiite Moslems in Iraq, and Catholic v. Protestant Christians in Northern Ireland (UK).

In many states it is difficult to decide just which of several increasingly embracing ethnic classifications is most significant. In India, a larger overarching group ("Hindus" or "Indo-Aryans") is regarded as more significant than smaller ethnic-linguistic divisions like "Punjabis" or "Bengalis." In South Africa it is four main racial divisions (rather than the smaller tribal lines which undergird its "homelands" policy) which are controlling. In south and central America, it is wiser to recognize the larger mestizo (Spanish mixed with American Indian) group than to emphasize either of its component parts.

In Uganda, on the other hand, smaller tribes from within the larger Nilotic-Sudanese population have traditionally ruled over the largest (Bugandan) tribe, which in turn is part of a relatively smaller Bantu ethnic type; a similar situation exists in Togo (with respect to the Ewe) and in Gabon (vis-a-vis the Fang). For these states, the smaller tribal category is reflected in Table V4.2a. If reverse selections for the most politically significant ethnic characteristic were made, these states (and a few others like Mali, Sierra Leone, Tanzania, Botswana, and Zambia where larger tribal groupings were chosen over smaller) would have different positions in the above homogeneity scale.

Table V4.2a reveals that countries in the European zone most closely approximate *nation-states* built around core ethnic groups (i.e., 26 of 30 states in the highest two categories). However, most of these countries had to fight several wars over many years to attain such levels of national homogeneity. By contrast, many states in Africa (26 of 38 countries in the two most heterogeneous categories) reflect little correspondence to cohesive ethnic identities, owing to their artificially contrived boundaries dating from the colonial era (Asiwaju, 1985; Smith, 1983; Snyder, 1984; Young, 1976). In fact, some of the most cohesive African groups (e.g., Mandinge, Fulani, Bakongo, Ewe, Hutu) are spread over two or more current borders, while many other states are made up of numerous sub-national "tribes." This somewhat derogatory term for an ethnic group is sometimes used to indicate a lack of heightened ethnic consciousness and, in many cases, a lack of significant numbers of people too, two concepts important to issues of ethnic politics which will be discussed at greater length below.

In any event, the concept of ethnicity includes some inheritances of birth (such as tribe or nationality) which might be regarded as immutable as compared with the concepts of religion and language which are subject to change by acts of individual will (albeit often with some psychological difficulty). These two factors will be further analyzed next before moving on to a more detailed analysis of the political relevance of ethnicity in 70 selected states.

V4.2b. Religion

Freedom of religion will be covered below in section V4.5b; at this point in this ethnographic survey, it is appropriate to look at the distributions of religions around the globe. There are four main religions in the world: Christianity, with approximately 1.669 billion adherents and 32% of global population; Islam, with about 880 million and 17%; Hinduism, with 663 million and 12.5%; and Buddhism with 312 million and 6%. The number of non-religious (886 million) and atheists (230 million) total more than 20% of the world's 5.3 billion people.

Among the two major religions, Christians can be divided into Roman Catholics (about 960 million and 18.8% of global population) and Protestants (410 million and 7.7%) and various national Orthodox groups (135 million and 2.7%). Moslems are mainly in two camps: Sunnis, with about 700 million and 14.4% of world population; and Shiites with about 140 million and 2.8%.

Among minor religious groups comprising less than 9% of global population in total are Chinese folk religions (172 million), Chondogyo New Religion (112 million), tribal religions (92 million), Jews (18 million), Sikhs (17 million), Shamanists (12 million), Confucians (6.1 million), Bahais (4.7 million), Jains (3.5 million), and Shintoists (3.1 million) (Barrett, 1982; updated in *World Almanac 1990*).

The major religions correspond only approximately to the geographic zones of analysis generally employed in this study. Christianity is the main religion in the European and Latin American zones; Islam in the Islamic zone; and Buddhism and Hinduism in Asia. The traditional religions of Africa are referred to as "animist" because in addition to belief in a supreme being, they attribute conscious life to nature and natural objects. The percentages of Africans associated in the survey below with Christianity (predominant in n=14 states) and Islam (n=6) must be regarded with caution because the variation of the major religion practiced is often syncretic (n=8), or one with heavy mixtures of traditional (i.e., animist, n=10) beliefs. Christianity and Islam have made significant inroads into zones other than the ones with which they are primarily associated. Asia and Africa are particularly penetrated with these two as well as with their own indigenous religions.

Table V4.2b presents a summary of states in order of the percentage of people identified with the predominant religious tradition in that state. Major religions are listed in the following order, roughly reflecting size and geographic distribution, and yielding the eight categories to be used in the later discussion (section V4.5b) on freedom of religion: Christianity, Islam, and their syncretic variations in Africa; animism, Hinduism, Buddhism; non-religious/atheism; and Judaism.

The religious percentages associated with each state are often in dispute and represent the best estimates taken from the data bank associated with this project, averaging out and rounding off a number of often contradictory sources. The major references associated with particular religions (Barrett for Christianity and Weekes for Islam) in particular were compared with more secular sources (Kurian, CIA, etc.).

Among the conclusions which can be drawn from this survey is that Christianity is the majority religion in more than half the world's states (n=85/162), and Islam in about one-fourth (n=38/162). Among Christians, most states are identifiably (i.e., greater than 60%) either Roman Catholic (n=43), Protestant (n=28), or some national form of Orthodoxy (n=5); in 9 countries there is a mixture of Christian types. Using the 60% criterion, most Islamic states (n=34/38) are predominantly Sunni; Shiites are in the majority only in Iran, Iraq, Bahrain, and Lebanon, although they are a troublesome minority in at least seven others.

The percentages of identifiably Christian or Islamic *states* (approximately 53% and 23%, respectively) give these religions a political power base somewhat greater than their raw numbers as a percentage of world population (32% and 17%, respectively, listed at the start of this section, would indicate. Whether this religious presence translates into a benign or repressive political power is analyzed below in section V4.5b.

V4.2c. Language

As the principal means of communicating culture and a people's way of life, language is often a more important political force in a society than religion or ethnicity. Depending on where one draws the line between certain dialects and their "mother tongues," there are an estimated 5000-7000 distinct languages spoken in the world today. Among the 10-16 major linguistic families cited in Voegelin (1977), these 12 (expressed in rough order of the five zones used in this study) are generally cited by most authorities: Indo-European, Ural-Altaic,

Caucasian (Georgian); Hamito-Semitic, Nilotic; Sudanese-Guinean, Bantu, Hottentot-Bushman; Dravidian, Sino-Tibetan, Malayo-Polynesian (Austronesian); and Amerindian.

There are about 70 languages which have the status of "official" state languages, with many states having two, three, or four such country-wide languages for transmission of government business, and several other "national" languages which are recognized in smaller subdivisions of the country. Table V4.2c.i lists 68 official state languages in order of the populations of the countries in which they are the official languages. This display shows the international impact of four European languages (English, French, Spanish, and Portuguese) as well as Arabic. Languages are listed in the zone with which they are most prominently associated.

In addition to official and national languages, Barrett (1982) reports more than 250 languages with more than 1 million native speakers. Tables V4.2c.ii(a) and (b) display 202 of these with more than 1.5 million native speakers, in the zone with which they are most prominently identified. Although the numbers for specific states are somewhat understated, since they reflect 1980 data, these linguistic names are helpful in identifying ethnic groups in the V4.2 data bank. Languages with an * form a subdivision of a larger mother-tongue grouping already listed above it (e.g., *Wu native speakers are also generally Chinese speakers, etc.).

The number of such languages in Asia (n=81) is impressive, reflecting once again the significant amount of people in that zone. Most African languages (50 of 57) have less than 6 million speakers, a fact which helps to explain the inherent weakness of many of that continent's states today. The integrative potential of Arabic in the Islamic world and Spanish in Latin America is also notable when compared with the lack of other significant major languages in these zones (19 and 8, respectively). The potential role of language as an element of cultural imperialism can be appreciated if Table V4.2c.ii is seen in the context of the previous Table V4.2c.i—i.e., although English is the official language of states with 1.4 billion people, it is the native language of only 265.1 million speakers (circa 1980).

V4.2d. Ethnic Categories of Analysis

The numbers used to describe the percentage of population in the most politically significant ethnic group in Table V4.2a will be substantiated in this section by reference to excerpts from the computer data bank associated with this study. Problems with respect to minority rights in matters of social justice, however, are often more related to levels of ethnic awareness than to the size of particular groups or to the total number of such groups in a given country, and the states which undergo further analysis here are not simply those which are least homogeneous in Table V4.2a. For a group to move from ethnic identity to mobilization on behalf of social justice, organization and leadership are needed, two factors which often come into conflict with the power of the state (Nielsson and Jones, 1988; Ross and Cottrell, 1980).

To analyze this phenomenon where it has occurred most prominently in the contemporary era, Table V4.2d identifies 70 states and divides them into four categories based upon increasing levels of problems related to ethnicity (and hence in conformance with the rating system introduced in section V4.1c). First, 21 "ethnically interesting" states are noted in passing (Category 1). Next, Category 2 lists 20 states where the majority ruling group's relationship with some minority of the population is such that the country will be classified here as "ethnically problematic." Category 3 includes 14 states where a *minority group* rules over larger segments of the population, but is apparently accepted to the extent that no insurgency has been provoked. Finally, Category 4 is comprised of 15 cases identified in V1.1b as experiencing an insurgency and whose cause will be noted here as based primarily upon ethnic grievances; it includes five states where an ethnic minority group controls the government, including Guatemala where precise percentages are unclear but the guerillas have been estimated as 80% Amerindian.

As might have been expected, Latin America—where the greatest assimilation of white, black, and Amerindian races has occurred—has the least number of states (only 7 of its 33) experiencing problems based upon ethnicity. But Table V4.2d's analysis yields a few surprising results. The Islamic zone, despite its common religion and Arab ethnicity, has the greatest number of states (21 of 28) with ethnic divisions; whereas Africa, despite having the most ethnic groups and the smallest-sized homogeneous majority groups, is only in the middle range of states with problems of social justice related to ethnicity (15 of its 38). This data reinforces the point that it is levels of consciousness resulting from leadership and organization, not simply numbers of ethnic groups or of people in such groups, which are important in raising political questions related to social justice.

The categories of analysis summarized in Table V4.2d will serve as a guide to the excerpts from the ethnic group data bank which follow. Extensive ethnic information is presented there for the 29 states in Categories 4 and 3, and more limited summaries for the countries in Categories 2 and 1. This material is excerpted from the data bank associated with this study where the ethnic situations are coded according to a format which lists for each state the breakdown, in percentages, of its various (a) ethnic, (b) religious, and (c) linguistic groups; followed by (d) some remarks as to how these differences lead to interesting situations of social justice and politics. These might include demands for autonomy to the point of insurgency (I) (covered in section V1.1b), or human rights violations (HRv) or other special restrictive or protective laws and policies (P) vis-a-vis minority groups (to be discussed in sections V4.3-5 of this chapter). *Ruling minority groups*, whether they have provoked an insurgency (Category 4) or not (Category 3), are italicized in bold print; *troublesome minority groups*—whether they have begun an insurgency (Category 4), are problematic (Category 2), or merely interesting (Category 1)—are simply italicized.

Data Bank Format for V4.2 Ethnicity

States ordered by % of largest .2a ethnic group (or .2b or .2c if more relevant)

.2=Top Line: State-population;   TJ discrimination % and intensity (0 to 4=most) and TJ separatism % and intensity (0 to 4=most); (mrg)=Minority Rights Group report number.

.2a= % ethnic group members, largest to #3 or #4; (#)=other ests. of largest group in parens;

.2b = religion %s (incl. 2 types Moslems, 2 types Christians where relevant);

.2c = language %s, where available and relevant (i.e., aids in "a");

.2d=I=insurgency (V1.1b), HRv=Human rights violations(V4.3); P=special policies (V4.4,.5).

Bold Italics = ruling minority group;

Italics = insurgent or other troublesome ethnic group;

% underlined refers to most relevant ethnic % reflected in Table V4.2d.

Special **African** indicator: .... # of "tribes,"

of which: x:y = x major groups, y subgroups (dialects).

Special Glossary of **Latin American** ethnic/racial types:

mestizo = white + Amerindian; mulatto = white + black;

rando = black + Amerindian; Creole = E.Indian(S.Asia)+black+white.

Though not included in the excerpts presented here, the first line of the format employed in the original data bank includes for many states political discrimination and separatism indexes as computed by Taylor and Jodice (1983), and references to whether a state is the subject of a special report by the Minority Rights Group (London). The first line also lists total population; because of the controversial nature of population counts for subgroups in many countries, a single source for percentages of majority and minority group members cannot always be relied upon, and computations from absolute numbers reported in different sources is necessary. It is generally in states where ethnicity is most controversial that the numbers reported are in greatest dispute. Lebanon has not dared to have a census since 1931, Nigeria since 1961, and it is the numbers for groups such as Tibetans in China, Greeks in Albania, Basques in Spain, and Berbers, Kurds, Palestinians, and Chinese throughout their respective regions which show the greatest variations in reference books.

Not every format-line of entries from the complete data bank is reproduced here. The excerpts presented thus are syntheses of composites based upon many sources (see citations at bottom of Table V4.2a). For the leading group in each state, a best estimate (percentage) is computed, with alternate figures reported by various sources listed in parentheses; for other groups a numerical range of their percentages often appears.

V4.2a - Ethnic Homogeneity (by % of Most Populous Ethnic Group)

Europe	Islamic	Africa	Asia	Latin America

Extremely Homogeneous "Nation-States" (≥90% in largest ethnic group), n=50

Europe	Islamic	Africa	Asia	Latin America
Iceland-100			N.Korea-100	
Malta-100		STP-100	Comoros-100	St.Chris.-100
Italy-99			S.Korea-100	
E.Ger.-99				Grenada-99
Portugal-99	Morocco-99	Zambia-99	Japan-99	Antigua-99
W.Ger.-99			Australia-98	Dominica-98
Nethrlnds-99				
Austria-99				Costa Rica-96
Norway-98				
Poland-98	Libya-97			Haiti-95
Greece-97			Bangladesh-94	
Albania-96	Tunisia-95		Seychelles-94	
Denmark-95			Solomons-93	
Hungary-95		Botswana-94	China-93	Uruguay-92
Ireland-94	N.Yemen-90		W.Samoa-93	El Salvador-91
France-94	Somalia-90		Philipines-92	Argentina-91
	Egypt-90			Honduras-90
Finland-90	Saudi A.-90		Vanuatu-90	St.Lucia-90
n=17	n=7	n=3	n=12	n=11

Relatively Homogenous "State-Nations" (66% to 89% in largest group), n=51

Europe	Islamic	Africa	Asia	Latin America
Romania-88	Syria-89	Rwanda-89	Cambodia-89	Brazil-88
Sweden-88			Vietnam-88	Paraguay-88
	Oman-86	Burundi-86	Mongolia-86.5	
Bulgaria-85	Israel-86	Namibia-86	N.Zealand-86	
		Lesotho-84	Taiwan-84	Bahamas-83
UK-82	Turkey-82			Barbados-80
US-81			Thailand-78	St.Vincent-78
	Cyprus-78	Zimbabwe-77	Maldives-77	Chile-78
Spain-75	Algeria-75		Singapore-75	Jamaica-76
	S.Yemen-75	Eq.Guinea-75	Sri Lanka-74	Dom.Rep.-73
Luxmbrg.-73	Iraq-74	S. Africa-73	Nepal-73	
Switz.-72			India-72	
Canada-70		CapeVerde-70	Myanmar-72	Nicaragua-70
			Brunei-69	Panama-69
		Swaziland-66	Mauritius-68	Venezuela-67
n=9	n=8	n=9	n=14	n=11

252

Table V4.2a (continued)

Relatively Mixed Ethnicity (between 41 and 65% largest ethnic group), n=33

Czech.-65	Pakistan-65			
	Iran-64		Bhutan-62	Colombia-63
	Bahrain-63	Sierra L.-60		Mexico-58
Belgium-57	Sudan-58		PapuaNG-59	Guyana-52
	Chad-55	Niger-55		Belize-51
USSR-52	Jordan-55	Burkina F.-52	Fiji-49	Cuba-51
		Mali-49	Malaysia-49	Guatemala-50
	Afghan.-47		Laos-48	Ecuador-46
		Gambia-44		Peru-45
	Djibouti-44	Malawi-44	Indonesia-45	Trinidad-45
		Congo-43		
n=3	n=8	n=7	n=6	n=9

Extremely Heterogeneous (≤40% in largest ethnic group), n=28

	Mauritania-40	Ethiopia-40		
	Kuwait-39	Angola-37	Madagascar-38	
Yugoslavia-38		Benin-37		
		Mozambique-36		Suriname-37
		Gabon-35		
		Senegal-35		
		Guinea-33		
		C.Af.R.-33		
		Nigeria-32		
	Lebanon-30	Cameroon-31		
		GBissau-30		
		Ghana-29		Bolivia-30
		Togo-24		
		Ivory Coast-21		
	Qatar-20	Kenya-20		
	UAE-19	Tanzania-19		
		Liberia-19		
		Zaire-17		
		Uganda-17		
n=1	n=5	n=19	n=1	n=2
TOT: 30	28	38	33	33 (162)

Source of %s (rounded): V4.2 Ethnicity Data Bank, drawn from Sigler 1983, Weekes 1983, Minority Rights Group (periodic), Nielsson and Jones 1985 (see Chapter 4 Bibliography for complete citations); plus CIA 1989, Dept. of State *Background Notes*, Kurian 1987, Taylor and Jodice 1983 (see Chapter 1 Bibliography); and Clements 1990 (see Chapter 5 Bibliography).

Europe	Islamic	Africa	Asia	Latin America

1. Predominantly Christian States (n=85)
95-100%

Europe	Islamic	Africa	Asia	Latin America
Italy, Malta,Ireld.				Chile,Peru,Paraguay
Spain,Port.,Luxmbg.			Seychelles	Ecuador,Bolivia
Poland,Czech.				Venezuela,Colombia
Switz.				Mexico,Panama
UK*,Iceland*				ElSal.,CRica,Hond.
Denmk*,Sweden*			Vanutau*	Dom.,Dom.Rep.
Norway*,Finland*			W.Samoa*	St.Lucia, Grenada
			Solomons*	St.Chris.,St.V.*
Greece⁰				Antigua*
n=16			n=4	n=19 (39)

Groups of states listed in order of predominant religion: RC, *mixed*, *Protestant, ⁰=ørthodox.

71-94%

Europe	Islamic	Africa	Asia	Latin America
Austria-92			Papua NG-94*	Argentina-92
US-92			Phil. I.-89	Brazil-89
France-92				Nicaragua-87
W.Germany-89				
Canada-88		STP-80	N.Zealand-81*	Barbados-83*
Romania-86⁰			Australia-79*	
Bulgaria-85⁰		Lesotho-75*		Jamaica-80*
Hungary-81		Rwanda-74		Haiti-80
Belgium-75	Cyprus-78⁰	Zaire 73		Bahamas-74*
Netherlands-74		S.Africa-72*		
Yugoslavia-71				
n=11	n=1	n=5	n=4	n=7 (28)

70% or less

Europe	Islamic	Africa	Asia	Latin America
		Burundi-67		Guatemala-70
		Uganda-66		Uruguay-68
E.Germany-53*		Kenya-66*		Belize-61
		Gabon-62		
		Namibia-60*		Guyana-57*
		Swaziland-57		Trinidad-49*
		Ethiopia-47⁰		*Suriname-48*
		Tanzania-43*		Cuba-45
		Ghana-42*	S.Korea 33*	
n=1		n=9	n=1	n=7 (18)

Europe	Islamic	Africa	Asia	Latin America
n=28	n=1	n=14	n=9	n=33 (85)

Most Christian states are identifiably (i.e., >60%) either:
Roman Catholic (RC), n=43; *Protestant (P), n=28; or Orthodox(O), n=5.
Ratios in 9 *mixed* states are:

US 55P,32RC;	W.Germany 45P,44RC;	Switzerland 49P,48RC;
Netherlands 41RC,31P;	Canada 47RC,41P;	Yugoslavia 40Srb.O.,31RC;
Uganda 33RC,33P;	Suriname 25P,23RC;	Swaziland 29P,28RC.

Table V4.2b (continued)

Europe	Islamic	Africa	Asia	Latin America
	2. Predominantly Islamic States (n=38)			
		95-100%		
	Turkey,Iran,Iraq		Maldives	
	Pak.,Afghan.,Saudi A.			
	Kuwait,Bahrain			
	N.Yemen,S.Yemen			
	Libya,Tunisia,Somalia			
	Alger.,Mauritan.,Moroc.			
	n=16		n=1	(17)
		71-94%		
	Djibouti-94			
	Qatar-94			
	Egypt-93			
	Oman-88	Gambia-87	Indonesia-89	
	Jordan-88	Niger-82	Comoros-86	
	Syria-87	Senegal-79	Bangladesh-85	
	UAE-78	Mali-75		
	n=7	n=4	n=3	(14)
		70% or less		
	Sudan-65	Guinea-70	Brunei-62	
	Lebanon-65			
	Chad-51	Nigeria-46	Malaysia-48	
n=0	n=3	n=2	n=2	(7)

Most Islamic states are predominantly Sunni; those with significant %s of Shiites are:
Iran-93%; Bahrain-65%; Iraq-55%; N.Yemen-45%; Lebanon-29(>20% Sunni v. 36% Xtn.); Turkey-25%; Kuwait-24%; Qatar-24%; Afghanistan-18%; Syria-16%; UAE-15%; Pakistan-15%; Saudi Arabia-10%; Oman-10%; S.Yemen-7%.

African and Asian Religions(n=33)

African		Asian	
3.Syncretic(n=8)	4.Animist(n=10 +1As)	5.Hindu(n=4)	6.Buddhist(n=10)
Eq.Guin. 90-100	Burkina Faso-65%	Nepal-90	Thailand-94
Congo-93	Benin 51-70	India-80	Cambodia-91
C.Verde-65	Liberia 35-75		Japan 75-94(Sh)
Angola 54-72	Sierra L. 46-70		Myanmar-85
C.Af.R. 56-59	Malawi-53		Singapore-74
Zambia-60	Togo 25-70		Bhutan-73
Botswana-50	GBissau 45-65		Sri Lanka-72
Zimbabwe-50	Ivory Coast 34-63	Fiji-50	Laos-54
	Mozambique 35-69		Vietnam-50
	Cameroon 47-55	Mauritius-49	Taiwan-47
	+ Madagascar-49		

7. Non-Religious/Atheist(5):
Albania ?100%, China 81%, Mongolia 74%, SU 70%, N.Korea 61%.

8. Other(1): Israel 86% Jewish (63% including Occupied Territories).

Source: V4.2 Data Bank (see Table V4.2a).

V4.2c.i - Official Languages
(in order of populations of countries where this is official language)

Europe	Islamic	Africa	Asia	Latin America
English 1.4 bill.			Chinese 914 mill.	
			Hindi 694	
Russian 268 mill.				Spanish 267
French 207	Arabic 169		Indonesian 154	Portuguese 154
German 103			Japanese 117	
			Bengali 84	
			Urdu 82	
Italian 63	Persian 60		Korean 55	
			Pilipino 52	
	Turkish 46		Thai 49	
			Vietnamese 48	
Polish 35		Swahili 33	Burmese 35	
		Amharic 31		
Dutch 24		Afrikaans 29		
^Serbo-Croatian 22				
^Macedonian 22	Pushtu 22			
^Slovene 22				
Romanian 22			Malay 16	Quechua 17
^Czech 15			Sinhalese 15	
^Slovak 15			Nepali 14	
Swedish 13				
Hungarian 10				
Greek 9.7			Khmer 9.4	
Bulgarian 9.0			Malagasy 9.3	
^Romansh 6.7				
Danish 5.1		Chewa 5.5		
Finnish 4.7		Ruanda 4.9		
Norwegian 4.1	Hebrew 3.8	Rundi 4.2	Lao 3.7	Guarini 3.0
Irish 3.3	Somali 3.6		Tamil 2.4	
Albania 2.8		Sango 2.0	Mongolian 1.9	
		Dzongkha 1.3		
		Sotho 1.3		
Luxembrgian 0.3		Tswana 0.8		
Maltese 0.3		Swazi 0.5	Comorian 0.3	
Icelandic 0.2			Samoan 0.2	
n=26	n=6	n=11	n=21	n=4 (68)

Source: Barrett 1982 for 1980, Global Table 19, where ^ = more than one official language recognized country-wide; supplemented by line V4.2c in Ethnicity Data Bank associated with this project.

V4.2c.ii(a) - Languages with more than 6 Million Native Speakers

Europe	Islamic	Africa	Asia	Latin America
			Chinese 886.4 m.	
English 265.1 m.			Hindi 168.3	Spanish 227.9
Russian 142.6	Arabic 144.3m		Bengali 138.4	Portuguese 135.6
			Japanese 117.4	
German 90.0			Punjabi 80.1	
			*Wu 75.6	
French 67.8			Javanese 65.6	
Italian 63.8			Marathi 62.5	
			*Cantonese 59.5	
			Tamil 58.5	
			Korean 58.2	
			Telegu 55.0	
Ukrainian 44.8	Turkish 43.2		*Hsiang 44.5	
			Vietnamese 42.9	
Polish 39.3			Urdu 38.1	
			Kosali 38.0	
			Kannada 37.5	
			*Hakka 35.8	
			*Min 35.6	
			Gujarati 34.8	
			Rajasthani 32.8	
			Bihari 28.9	
			Oriya 27.8	
			Malayalam 27.2	
			Thai 27.2	
			Burmese 25.3	
			*Minnan 23.1	
			*Kan 22.3	
Dutch 20.9	Pushtu 19.5		Sudanese 21.1	
Romanian 19.1	*Lahnda 19.2		*Bhojpuri 18.2	
SerboCroat 17.2	Persian 17.7		Assamese 18.1	
		Hausa 14.8	*Braj Bhasa 14.7	Quechua 14.8
			Cebuano 14.6	
		Yoruba 13.7	Lao 14.2	
Uzbek 14.0			Malay 14.0	
Hungarian 13.9		Ibo 12.8	*Taiwanese 13.4	
*Provencal 13.6	Sindhi 12.5	Galla 12.7	Tagalog 11.2	
Greek 11.5	Azeri 11.8	Fulani 12.0	Sinhala 11.0	
			Madurese 10.8	
Czech 10.1			Nepali 10.1	
Byelorussian 9.9	Kurdish 9.4		Chuang 9.8	
Tadzhik 9.2			Malagasy 9.2	
Swedish 8.9			Khmer 9.1	
Bulgarian 7.9		Amharic 7.9	*Chhattisgarhi 8.6	
Kazakh 7.7			*Marwari 8.0	
Yiddish 6.5		Sotho,S. 6.5	*Maithili 6.4	
Catalan 6.5			Kashmiri 6.0	
n=22	n=8	n=7	n=47	n=3 (87)

Source: Barrett 1982 for 1980, Global Table 6.

*=subdivision of a larger mother-tongue grouping listing above it.

257

V4.2c.ii(b) - Languages with 1.5 to 6 million Native Speakers

Armenian 5.8	Somali 5.9	Shona 5.8	Santali 5.7		
	Hebrew 5.6	Zulu 5.6	Uighur 5.4		
Danish 5.2		Ruanda 5.4	Hiligaynon 5.4		
Romany 5.1		Xhosa 5.2	Yi 5.3		
Slovak 5.1		Ruadi 4.8	Minangkabau 5.2		
Norwegian 5.0		Kanuri 4.6	Tibetan 4.5		
Finnish 5.0		Mongo 4.5	Batak 4.5	Creole 4.9	
		Shangaan 4.3	Buginese 4.4		
Albanian 4.2		Mole, Gondi-4.2	Bikol 4.1	Nahuatl 4.4	
		Nyamwezi 4.0	Miao 4.0		
Georgian 3.9		Sotho,N. 3.8	Mongolian 3.9		
Galician 3.6	Turkmen 3.5	Efik, Luba-3.4	Karen 3.9		
Lithuanian 3.4		Mandingo 3.3	Manchu 3.6		
		Kongo 3.2	*Magahi 3.6		
		Kikuyu 3.2	Bhili 3.5		
	Baluchi 3.1	Chewa 3.1	Balinese 3.3		
Moldavian 2.9		Tsawana 2.9	Achenese 3.1		
		Swahili 2.9			
		Sidamo 2.8			
		Afrikaans 2.8			
		Luo 2.7	*Pahari, W. 2.6	Aymara 2.7	
		Edo 2.6	Shan 2.6		
		Tiv 2.6	Davyak 2.5		
	Dinka 2.4	Mbundu 2.5	*Nagpuri 2.5		
		Azande 2.3			
		Bambara 2.3	Shila 2.3		
		Ewe 2.3	Banjarese 2.3		
		Sukumu 2.3			
		Senufo 2.2	Yuan 2.2		
		Ganda 2.2			
	Gilaki 2.2	(Wa)Yao 2.2			
		Wolof 2.2	Samareno 2.1		
	Tamazigt 2.1	Pedi 2.1			
Slovenian 2.0	Kabyle 2.0	Luhya 2.1	Otomi 2.0		
Kirghiz 1.9	Chuvash 1.9	Tigrinyan 1.9			
	Mazanderani 1.8	*Wallega 1.9			
		Fon, Ronga-1.8		Guarani 1.8	
		Kru 1.7	Puyi 1.7		
Macedonian 1.7		Kimbundu 1.7	*Dogri 1.7		
		Baya 1.6	Chungchia 1.6	Zapotec 1.6	
		Fang 1.6	Pampango 1.6		
		Kalenjin 1.6	Sasak 1.6		
Alsatian 1.5	Afar 1.5	Ashanti 1.5	*Garhwali 1.6		
		Ijaw 1.5	Manipuri 1.5		
		Nupe 1.5	Pangasinan 1.5		
		Tulu 1.5			
		*Malvi 1.5			
n=15	n=11	n=50	n=34	n=5	(115)
TOT: 37	19	57	81	8	(202)

Source: Barrett 1982 for 1980, Global Table 6.

*=subdivision of a larger mother-tongue grouping listing above it.

258

Europe	Islamic	Africa	Asia	Latin Amer.

Category "1" - Ethnically-Interesting States, n=21

Europe	Islamic	Africa	Asia	Latin Amer.
	UAE-19%	Zaire-17%		
	Qatar-20	Kenya-20		Bolivia-30%
Czech.-65%	Mauritania-40	Togo-24		
US-81	Djibouti-44	Cameroon-31	Thailand-78%	
France-94	Algeria-75	Gabon-35	Vietnam-88	Ecuador-46
Albania-96	Morocco-99	Rwanda-89	Cambodia-89	
n=4	n=6	n=6	n=3	n-2

Category "2" - Ethnically-Problematic States, n=20

Europe	Islamic	Africa	Asia	Latin Amer.
Yugoslavia-38	Kuwait-39		Indonesia-45	Suriname-37
USSR-52	Chad-55	Nigeria-32	Laos-48	
Belgium-57	Iran-64		Malaysia-49	
	Pakistan-65			
Canada-72	S.Yemen-75	Zimbabwe-77	Singapore-75	
Bulgaria-85	Cyprus-78			
Romania-88			China-93	
n=6	n=6	n=2	n=5	n=1

Category "3" - *Minority Rule States*, n=14 + 5 in *Category "4"*

Europe	Islamic	Africa	Asia	Latin Amer.
	Syria-13	Uganda-3	Taiwan-14	
		GBissau-8		
		S. Africa-8		
	Bahrain-35	Burundi-14		
	Iraq-40	Liberia-16	Madagascar-32	Guyana-32
	Jordan-44		Fiji-47	Trinidad-42
n=0	n=4	n=5	n=3	n=2

Category "4" - States with Ethnic Insurgencies, n=15

Europe	Islamic	Africa	Asia	Latin Amer.
	Lebanon-24	Angola-26		
	Sudan-42	Ethiopia-29	Myanmar-72	Guatemala-45
	Afghanistan-47		India-72	Peru-45
Spain-75	Turkey-82		Sri Lanka-74	
UK-82	Israel-86		Phil. I.-92	
n=2	n=5	n=2	n=4	n=2
TOT: 12	21	15	15	7 (70)

Source: V4.2 Data Bank.

Numbers refer to percentage of largest ethnic group from Table V4.2a, or of the *ruling* ethnic group(s) in minority rule states.

Category "1" - Ethnically-Interesting (n=21):

Czechoslovakia - 65% Czech, 30% Slovak; federated now after years of SU-enforced integration.

US - 81% white; 12% *black*, 6% *Hispanic;* "melting pot" ideology finding it difficult to absorb racial and linguistic (affirmative action) policies related to these two groups.

France - separatist incidents by *Bretons & Corsicans;* growing *n.African Moslem* pop. (=5%).

Albania - *Greeks* variously estimated at 2 to 15%. Irridentist claims on Yugoslavia (qv).

UAE, Qatar - *foreign workers* overwhelm native citizen pop., but are transient and have no rights.

Djibouti - 44% *Issa* -Somali and 25% *Afar*-Ethiopian have power-sharing arrangement in govt.

Mauritania,Algeria,Morocco - *Berbers* a significant minority, or inter-married group (approx. 70%, 20%, 35%, respectively); Morocco also having probs. with 150,000 (<1%) *Saharui*.

Zaire - periodic secession attempts by south Shaba province *(Bantu)* tribes.

Kenya - ethnic appeals discouraged via 1-party state of first *non-Kikuyu* president.

Togo - 24% *Ewe* and other southern tribes ruled by military regime of northerners.

Cameroon - highland and Christian tribes seem to dominate others.

Gabon - 35% *Fang* controlled by union of all others in Gab. Dem. Party 1-party state.

Rwanda - see Burundi in Category 3.

Thailand, Vietnam, Cambodia - *Chinese* minority is approx. 15%, 10% (pre- 1975-80 boat people exodus), and 5%, respectively. Cambodia had 10% *Vietnamese* before 1979 invasion.

Bolivia, Ecuador - *Amerindian* populations of 55% and 33% do not threaten mestizo rule because of tribal divisions within the Indian racial group.

Category "2" - Ethnically-Problematic (n=20):

Yugoslavia - 38% Serb; 21% Croat, 9% Bosnian, 8% Slovene, 8% *Albanian*, 6% Macedonian, 3% Montenegrin, 2% Hungarian, 5% other/mixed.

USSR - 52% Russian; 18% Ukrainian, 7% Uzbek; 6% Kazak; 4% Byelorussian; plus 10 others, all with their own republics, *many* desiring more autonomy. Also, *0.7% Jews.*

Belgium - 57% Flemish (Dutch-speaking), 33-41% Walloon (French-sp.). Divided electoral rolls.

Canada - 50% English, 28% French, 20% other Europ. who speak English; 2% indigenous.

Bulgaria - 85% Bulgarian, 8% *Turkish* forced to change names and assimilate.

Romania - 88% Romanian, 8% *Hungarians* (Europe's largest minority); 4% other.

Kuwait - 39% Kuwaiti Arab; 39% other Arab (workers) incl. 21% Palestinian; 22% S. Asian.

Chad - 55% Arabs in north fight *among themselves* for control over 45% black tribes in south.

Iran - 64% Persian; 20% Azerbaijani, 12% Turkic, 5% Baluch, 5% *Kurd*, 2.5% Arab, etc.

Pakistan - 65% Punjabi; 15% Sindhi; 12% Pathan; 3% Baluch; 3% Afghan-Pathan refugees.

S. Yemen - 75% Arab, incl. 22 sheikhdoms and 1400 tribes; 11% S. Asian; 8% Somali.

Cyprus - 78% Greek (Orthodox); 18% Turk (Moslem), 4% Armenian & Maronite Christian.

Nigeria - 32% Hausa-Fulani in north; 22% *Ibo* in s.-east; 18% Yoruba in s.west; 28% others.

Zimbabwe - 77% Shona, 22% *Ndebele* refused for 8 yrs. to become part of dominant party.

Indonesia - 45% Javanese; 14% Sundanese; 8% Madurese; 8% Malay; 25% other incl. *Chinese, Mollucans, Acehenese,* and *E. Timorese.*

Laos - 48% Lao; periodic insurgency against Lao-communist rule involves non-Lao tribes.

Malaysia - 49% Malay incl. 16 sub-groups; 36% *Chinese;* 10% Indian Tamils; 5% other.

Singapore - 75% Chinese; 15% Malay; 6% Indian; 4% other.

China - 93% Han Chinese; + 55 minorities incl. 2% Hui (Moslem), and <1% *Tibetan.*

Suriname - 37% S.Asian (E.Indian), 31% Creole, 15% Javanese, 10% *black*, 7 % other.

V4.2 EXCERPTS (continued)

Category "3" - Minority Group Rule:
(n=14 within zones by order of **%** of most relevant ethnic factor)

Syria - b. 87% Moslem, incl.: 71-73% Sunni, 14-17% **Shia** (incl. **13%** *Alawis*), 10% Other.
    d. HRv due to ethnicity based on religious sectarianism.

Bahrain - a. 63% Bahraini Arab, 13% S.Asian(Pakistani,Indian), 10% other Arab, 8% Iranian.
    b. 60-70% Shia (1/2 Arab & poor; 1/2 Persian & well-off); **30-40%** *Sunni.*
    d. Bahraini Sunnis supported in power by Saudi Arabia; Iran stirs up Shiites. About 300,000 citizens
    100,000 foreign workers.

Iraq - a. 74% Arab(64,71,73,75x3,78x2); 18-21% *Kurd,* 3% Turkic, 2% Persian et. al.
    b. 55% Shi'ite (43,52.5,60), **40%** *Sunni,* 5% Grk.Orth.Xtn.
    d. ruling Sunni Arabs are from one village (Tikrit). The 40% Sunni includes the ~20% Kurds, so country
    is not predominantly "Sunni Arab." HRv due to politics, ethnicity & religion.

Jordan - a. 97% Arab (95,98x2), but 52-60% Palestinian, only **40-48%** *Hashemite* ;
    also: 1% Circassian, 1% Armenian, (12% Bedouin absorbed within ruling Hashemite Arabs).
    d. Politics grounded in ethnicity to ensure Hashemite Arab dynasty continues to rule. Bedouins dominate
    army, (c.Asian) Circassians heavy in domestic security and intelligence.

Uganda - a. 17% (Ba)Ganda; all others (n=40 tribes) < 12% ea. incl.: 55% northern Nilotic-Sudanese (incl.
    2.3% Lango and 1.8% Acholi who dominated army and pre-'86 govts.),
    and 45% southern Bantu (incl. Baganda, **3.3%** *Banyankole,* 1.3% (Ba)Toro, 1.2% Banyero).
    d. HRv & past insurgencies due to ethnicity; largest group (& historic kingdom) of Bagandans has never
    ruled; fellow-Bantu (but minority) group governing for first time after 1986.

Guinea Bissau - a. 30% Balante; 20% Fula(ni), 14% Manjaca, 13% Mandinga, but....
    d. **7%** *Papel,* **<1%** *European/mulatto* dominate government (see V5.4c).

South Africa - a. 73% Bantu (African), incl.: 20% Zulu; 19% Xhosa; 6.5% Pedi; 5.3% Tswana;
    1.8% Shangaan/Tsonga; 1.2% Venda; 1.2% Swazi; 0.56% S.Sothos; 0.56% S.Ndebeles;
    and 17% other African (incl.N.Sothos and N.Ndebeles); plus 9% mixed(coloured); 3% South Asian;
    and, esp. 15% white, of wh: *Afrikaner* = 60% (**8.4%** tot. pop.), English=40%.
    b. Most whites & coloureds(=24%) & 60% blacks = Xtian=67%. The 5% Asians are 60% Hindu, 20%
    Moslem. The 73% black are 60% Xtn. (#1=Dutch Refmd.,#2=Method.,#3=Anglic.)
    d. I & HRv due to ethnicity, esp. race. 10 "homelands" established to divide the 73% blacks into smaller
    groups: KwaZulu, Transkei, Ciskei, Lebowa, Bophuthatswana, Gazankulu, Venda, KaNgwane, Quaqua,
    and KwaNdebele; roughly representing groups named in line "a".

Burundi - a. 86% Hutu(Bantu)(83,84,85,96); **14%** *(Wa)Tutsi* (Hamitic);1% Twa(pygmy).
    d. Ethnicity in politics/army/business/govt. retains minority rule & prevents "Rwanda 1960" (when 89%
    Hutu overthrew 11% Tutsi). HRv incl. 1972 & '88 massacres.

Liberia - a. l9% Kpelle; **16%** *Bassa+Krahn* = '80-'90 govt.-mil. tribe; + Gio, Mano, Kru, Gebo, Mandinge,
    Vai, etc. (250 tribes) incl. 2.5-5% *Americo-Liberians* (ruled 1848-1980).
    d. Ethnic factor in politics, esp.in '80 when Americos were ousted, in '85 coup (Gio+Mano),
    and '90 insurgency (Americo Taylor leading Gios & Manos).

Taiwan - a. 84% Taiwanese (Formosan Han-Jen); **14%** *Mainland Chinese,* 2% aborigine.
    d. Lee Teng-hui is 1st Taiwanese Pres., but ruling KMT party still controlled by mainlanders.

V4.2 EXCERPTS (continued)

Madagascar - a. 38% coastals = mixed African, Arab, Polynesian incl.:10-15% Betsimisarka, 7% Tsimihety, 6% Sakalava, 5% Antandroy, 5% Antaisaka; **26-38%** *Malay-Indonesian* highlanders, incl.:17-26% Merina + 8-12% Betsileo;   plus 45% other tribes (no group >4%).
   d. ethnicity in politics; highland Asian Protestants dominate in govt., business, and professions.

Fiji - a. 49% Indian, **47%** *Fijian;* 3% European, 1% Pacific islanders, Chinese, others.
   b. 50% Hindu; 45% Christian; small Muslim minority.
   d. 90% land held communally by Fijians, only 10% avail. for others to buy "freehold" (P). When Indians finally won a majority in Legislature (> PM) in 5/87, Fijian-dominated army & Head of State engineered 2 coups & new constitution to ensure Fijian (Melanesian) rule.

Guyana - a. 51.5% E.Indian; **31.7%** *African* ; 11% mixed; 5% Amerind; 4% Akawaio Indian.
   d. ethnicity a factor in politics; black party dominates (see V5.3c).

Trinidad-Tobago - a. 45% E.Indian; **41.5%** *African* ; 15% Creole (14-16.3); 3% Other.
   d. 30 yr.-black party rule before multi-racial coalition won in '86 (see V5.3a).

Category "4"- States with Ethnic Insurgencies (n=15):

Spain - a. 75%(Lat.-Medit.) Spanish (73,75,80); 17% Catalan; 8% Galician; 2-5% *Basque.*
   d. I due to ethnicity (~2 million Basques in north east).

United Kingdom - a. 81.5% English, 9.6% Scots, 2-5% Welsh, 2.4% Irish;
   + 1.8% Ulster Scots, 1.1% *Ulster Irish* (mrg 2); + S.Asians and W. Indians.
   b. 76% Anglican, 15% Roman Catholic; in Ulster, 1 mil. Protestants, 0.6 mil. *Catholics.*
   d. I due to religion (Irish Catholics v. Scots Protestants) in N. Ireland(=Ulster).

Lebanon - a. 90% Arab(incl. 11% Palestinians, 1% Syrian); 6% Armenian, 3% Kurd, 1% other.
   b. 62-67% Moslem incl.: 28-30% *Shia*, 19-21% *Sunni* (incl. Pals.) 6-10% *Druse;*
      33-38% Christian, incl.: **24%** *Maronite* , 16-20% other including:
         7% Greek Orthodox, 5% Greek Cath., 4% Armenian, Syrian, Roman,&Melchite Cath.
   d. I & HRv due to ethnicity based upon religion. P=quotas for Cabinet & Assy.; see V5.2.

Sudan - a. 58% *black* (52,64) incl. 11% Dinka , other Nilotics (Nuer, Mundari, Hausa ,etc.);
      42% *Arab* (36,48) incl.: 8% Nuba(5)&Nubian(3), 6% Beja, 6% Darfur, etc.
   b. 66% Sunni Moslem (58,72,78) in north; v. 25% indigenous, 5-18% Christian.
   d. I, HRv, & P due to religion, race & ethnicity; generally northern Arab Moslems vs. southern black Xtns.,animists. SPLA(V1.1b) = Dinka,Nuer,Kakwa; & (sometimes) Toposas & Darfurs.

Afghanistan - a. 47% Pushtun or Pathan in s. & east; 25-30% Tajik; 12% Turkic incl.:
      9% Uzbek, 3% Turkmen; 4.3% Persian (Farsiwan); + tribals & mtn. people incl.:
      6-7% Hazara, 5.7% Aimaq; 1.4% Baluchs in southwest.
   b. 74-87% Sunni, 12-25% Shia, esp. among Hazara & other "underclass"; 1% secular.
   d. I & HRv due to ethnicity & religion; govt. *insufficiently Islamic;* in ruling party, Parcham faction (in since '79) is more Persian, Khalq faction is more Pushtun-tribal (see V5.4c).

Turkey - a. 82% Turk, incl.: 75% Anatolian, 11% Rumelian; 10-17% *Kurd* (~8 m.); 3% other.
   b. 98% Moslem: Sunni=75%, Alawite Shiite=25%.
   c. Turkish official, some Arabic also; but Kurdish outlawed(P)!
   d. Insurgency, HRv, & P (language) due to ethnicity (Kurds); HRv for politics too.
   Re: 20 mil. Kurds: 47.5% are in Turkey, 26.9% in Iran, 20.6% in Iraq, 4.7% in Syria.

V4.2 EXCERPTS (continued)

Israel - a. pre-'67: 86% Jewish (83,85,89);14-17% *Palestinian Arab* (.6-.75 mil.)
with post-'67 Territories: 63% Jewish; 37% *Palestinian Arabs* incl.:
0.9mil. in W.Bank (+58,000 Jews), .6-.65 mil. in Gaza (+2000 Jews).
   d. I & HRv due to ethnicity-religion; Palestinians in post-'67 lands will total 50% by 2000.
Re: Palestine-approx.4.7 mil.(in more than 74 states); 14% of Israel; 37% of Israel + Occupied Territories;
52-60% of Jordan (1.2 mil.); 22% Kuwait (0.3m.); 11% Lebanon (0.36m.).

Angola - a. 37% *Ovimbundu*, 24% *Kimbundu* , 13% Bakongo, 2% *mixed*, 1% Eur., 26% other.
   d. I & HRv due to ethnicity; Govt. MPLA mainly mulatto-Kimbundu, urban & RC-educated; some FNLA
   Bakongo absorbed. Rebel UNITA is Ovimbundu, rural & Protestant-educated.

Ethiopia - a. 40% Oromo(+"Galla")(33+6;50); 26-32% *Amharan* incl. 7-12% *Tigrean*;
+ 9% *Eritrean*, 1-9% Sidamo, 6% Shankella, 6% *Somali*, 5% Afar, 2-7% Gurage.
   b. Moslem(mostly Oromo)=40-45%, Ethiop.Orth.Xtn.(Amharans+)=35-40%; animist=8-20%.
   d. I & HRv due to ethnicity esp. Eritreans, Tigreans, Somalis.

Myanmar - a. 72% Burman; 7-13% *Karen;* + indig.tribes: 6% *Shan*; 2% *(Ka)chin, + Arakan, Mon, Karenni,
Pa-o, Paloung, & Wa* ; + non-indigenous: 6% Indian; 3% Chinese.
   d. I & HRv due to ethnicity & politics; 8+ groups in Natl.Dem.Front w/ 25% pop, 30-50% land. 1982 law
   (P) favors Burmans (incl. their minorities) over Indian and Chinese merchants.

India - a. 72% Indo-Aryan (of which: Bengali=8%, Marathi 8, Gujarati 5, Oriyan 4, Punjabi 4, Bihari 4,
Rajathasthani 3, Assamese 3, Kashmiri 0.3; and 32-36% n. Indian Hindustani;
+ 25% Indo-Dravidian: Telegu=9%, Tamil 7, Kannada 4, Malayalam 4; + Nepali Gurkhas;
+ 6% *n.east tribes*, incl.: Mizos, Tripurans, Nagas; + 2-3% Mongoloid; + Sikkimese, Goans.
   b. 80-83% Hindu, 11% *Moslem*, 2% Xtn.(3:2RC), 2% *Sikh*, <1% Buddhists, Jains, Parsis.
   c. 17 main languages, 1400 dialects, incl. Hindi 30%, Urdu 5% educ. Moslems, English 2.5%, & Sanskrit
   (Brahmin priests); plus those associated with the ethno-linguistic based states (n=19 of 23; = 13 main
   ones in line"a"(9+4); + Mizo, Manipuri, Tripuri, Naga, Khasi(in Meghalaya), Bhutia(Sikkim); (+Hindi
   in 4 states: Haryana; & Him.,Mahd.,& Uttar Pradesh).
   d. I and HRv due to ethnicity. Separatism in: Punjab (*Sikhs*), Kashmir *(Moslems*), Tamil Nadu (*Tamils*),
   W.Bengal(*Nep.Gurkhas*); and Assam, Tripura, Mizoram, Nagaland*(n.east tribes*).

Sri Lanka - a. 74% Sinhalese (Aryan), of wh: 43% lowland, 29% Kandyan hill people;
12% *Jafffna Tamil*, 6% Indian Tamil (fm. 19th century); 7% Moslem Moors; 1% other.
   b. 69-74% Buddhist(off.), 15-18% Hindu, 8% Christian,7.6% Moslem.
   d. I & HRv due to ethnic claims of the (esp. Jaffna) Tamils. 95% of army & gov. bur. is Sinhalese despite
   (questionable) minority affirmative action policies (P) in '78 Constitution.

Philippines - a. 91.5% Christian Malay; 4% Muslim Malay; 1.5% Chinese; 3% other.
   b. 83-85% Roman Catholic, 5% Protestant, 5% *Muslim* , 3% Buddhist.
   d. I & HRv due to politics (communism) and (less severely) religion (Islam).

Guatemala - a. 50% Amerindian (41,46,50,63), Mayan, Quiche, etc.; 45% *mestico*; 5% white .
   c. 56% Spanish (official); but 62.5% speak Indian languages (4 leading= Kanjobal, Mam, Quiche,
   Cakechiqual; 18-23 other major ones; 163 dialects) as primary tongue.
   d. minority rule designation for mestizos & white is tenuous; I & HRv due to politics & ethnicity, esp. if
   US Embassy est. of 80% of guerillas being Amerindian is correct (Laffin, '87:89).

Peru - a. 44% *Amerindian* (Quechua-speak.Amusha, Campa), 38% mestizo, 15% white, 3% other.
   d. I & HRv due to politics and ethnicity (most Shining Path members are Amerindians).

263

V4.3. INTEGRITY OF THE PERSON (HUMAN RIGHTS)

After equality and non-discrimination (V4.2), the next matters enumerated in the International Bill of Human Rights pertain to violations of the integrity of the person. Section V4.3 will deal with various forms of repression and violations of human rights which are harsher than the mere denial of legal protections to be covered in V4.4, or the circumscription of personal freedoms treated in V4.5.

Violations of the integrity of the person involve governmental killings, both legal (.3a) and illegal (.3b); torture (.3c); and the taking of political prisoners (.3d). The distinctions between these four forms of infringement of personal integrity are decreasing in their severity as regards governmental culpability. The first category (a) involves the overt, explicit destruction of "disturbing" citizens—i.e., their official execution by the government; next (b) is the extra-judicial elimination of such persons, either by contracting out (with government deniability) their "disappearance" to unofficial death squads, or by government forces acting beyond explicit policy mandates; third (c) is the torturing of such persons; and fourth (d) is the restriction of their activities by jailing, sometimes in comfortable circumstances (e.g., house arrest), but always with the effect of eliminating them from further political activity.

Most human rights organizations have an ongoing concern about such extreme forms of repressive governmental activity. Their regular reports usually address such issues according to a standard framework used year after year. A methodical reading of any group's survey of all countries covered in a given year, along with the perusal of reports on the same states by other organizations, should enable the astute reader to classify states according to some broad categories of frequency and severity of abuses (Claude, 1976; Schwab and Pollis, 1982; Stohl et al., 1986; Gillies, 1990).

In the cases to be analyzed below, the four regularly appearing global human rights narratives (DOS, AI, FH, HUM)—supplemented by relevant regional or special reports—have been surveyed and rating numbers 1-through-4 (as described above in section V4.1c) have been assigned. The global displays of the resulting state rankings will be substantiated in this section of this chapter by excerpts from the reports for some representative set of countries. These generally include several states drawn from Categories 2, 3, and 4 (for these are the most interesting cases), chosen to provide some geographic representation as well. In this way, the different factors involved in assigning scores in each category will be made known.

The style employed in the excerpts uses codes such as DOS90 to indicate the Department of State's Human Rights Report of February 1990 for the year 1989; AI89 for Amnesty International's 1989 report; FH89 for Freedom House's 1988-89 report of the year 1988; and HUM for the most recent Humana report (1986, covering 1983-85). Special AI reports on particular subjects (e.g., on torture in 1984, political killings in 1983, political prisoners in 1981, and the death penalty in 1979 and 1989) will be indicated by an * after AI plus the year; reports on a specific state will be indicated by AI plus the *month* and year. In many instances phrases in these reports remain unchanged from year to year, so old citations do not necessarily mean outdated judgments. Nevertheless, in order to keep the relevant excerpts substantiating state scores up to date, every effort is made to check the most recent annual reports when they appear, as well as any special-focus regional or state studies as they are published.

As mentioned in section V4.1c, the temporal focus of this study is roughly 1987-90, with the latest global report employed being that of the State Department of February 1990, as updated through events reported on in the *New York Times* through July 1990. The rankings thus reflect the momentous events in eastern Europe of late 1989, which have moved many of its countries up from Categories 3 and 4. Because the ratings are multi-year, however, the lingering effect of those lower scores prevents them from being immediately placed in Category 1. The three-year cumulative time frame has a similar delaying impact on a few other states which have experienced coup d'etats or other significant changes in their political administration or system.

In the interests of space, fewer excerpts will be cited and only summaries will be made of state rankings from a single source for some of the "less important" civil and political rights found in the last two sections of this chapter. In this section involving life-and-death human rights issues affecting the integrity of the person, however, several sources will be used, and narrative excerpts from the data bank will be presented in three of four categories.

V4.3a. Government Killings, Legal: The Death Penalty

Table V4.3a is a global survey of states which resort to the death penalty for common criminals as well as for their political opponents. Statistics on the death penalty are somewhat imprecise, and often reflect discrepancies between announced and actual policy (Hood, 1989; AI89*). For example, many states have not formally ended legal executions, but do not carry out the death penalty in practice. Only 14 European states have signed the Council of Europe's Convention pledging not to use the death penalty in peacetime, but in practice none of its members actually carries it out anymore (except Turkey, which is considered Islamic in this study).

Amnesty International (1990) reports that 38 countries or territories had abolished the death penalty for all offenses, and 17 more for all but "exceptional" offenses such as wartime crimes. Another 30 countries, while retaining the penalty in their laws, had not carried out any executions for ten years. These states are roughly those found in the first three categories of Table V4.3a, which is based upon a more extensive survey (see Source notes at bottom of table).

Nevertheless, the death penalty is still commonly practiced in almost half the world's countries (78 are listed in Category 4, Table V4.3a), with Amnesty International reporting 15,320 executions in 90 countries between 1979 and 1989 (AI89*), during which the leading states were (in approximate order of executions) China, Iran, Afghanistan, Ethiopia, Nigeria, Iraq, Somalia, Saudi Arabia, Pakistan, United States, and the USSR.   Moreover, these are only the documented cases where AI had individual details; actual numbers are probably much higher.   There are only about 11 states in the advanced industrial world still employing the death penalty with any regularity: 7 countries in eastern Europe, 3 states whose executions are largely restricted to members of ethnic minority groups (United States, Israel, South Africa), and Japan. Most other countries exercising this ghoulish method of protecting themselves against the transgressions of their troublesome citizens are in the Islamic world (21 of its 28 states), Africa (30 of 38), and Asia (22 of 33).

Adapting the 1-through-4 ranking system, Table V4.3a presents a classification of states with respect to their policies toward the death penalty as of 1990.

V4.3b. Governmental Killings, Illegal

Because of the moral onus associated with the death penalty, more common in today's world than the *official* killing of political opponents is the "disappearance" (and presumed death) of persons suspected of anti-government behavior. Often these actions are attributed to governments which, rather than accept responsibility for such heavy-handed removal of their political opponents, "contract out" such illegal activities to unofficial death squads (often made up of members of the regular security forces working "after hours") or private armies (paid for by wealthy landlords or businessmen) (Ford, 1985). The phrase "illegal government killings" will also apply to prisoners who die in police custody shortly after capture, to civilian deaths during military or paramilitary "sweeps" of "enemy areas," to "summary executions" by soldiers or by local "people's courts" (or "public tribunals") hastily assembled by security forces for such purposes, and to people killed by police quashing of demonstrations which get out of hand ("riots").

Amnesty International defines such deaths as "political"—"the unlawful and deliberate killing of persons because of their real or imputed political beliefs or activities, religion, other conscientiously held beliefs, ethnic origin, sex, color, or language, carried out by a government or with its complicity" (AI83*). Many such human rights violations occur during times of political unrest and insurgency, and there is often a connection between such deaths and a country's appearance on the list of civil wars and insurgencies in section V1.1b. But whereas that earlier section concentrated on the intensity of conflict and the organizational structure of the insurgents, the focus here will be on the behavior of governments, particularly their actions vis-a-vis civilians (refugees, supporters, ethnic kin of rebel fighters, etc.) (Stohl and Lopez, 1986).

FEDEFAM, the Federation of Families of the Disappeared, an organization of about 20 national groups, has identified an estimated 100,000 people who have disappeared since 1970. Although this phenomenon originated as a significant government policy in Latin America in the 1970s (Chomsky and Herman, 1979; US House of Representatives, 1983), a 1986 report by the diplomatically restrained United Nations Working Group on Enforced or Involuntary Disappearances notes that at least 31 countries around the world are involved in such practices today.

Table V4.3b identifies 38 states as major violators of human rights in this regard, with scores of 3 or 4, using the 1-through-4 categories introduced in this chapter. Another 40 states are placed in Category 2, indicating some involvement in such activity. These 78 states represent almost half the countries in the world today. A page of data bank excerpts for 13 particularly interesting states from a representative sample of zones and ratings follows Table V4.3b; where ethnic groups are notable among the victims (Hannum, 1987), they are italicized.

V4.3c. Torture

Prisons everywhere are notable for their deplorable conditions; what is discussed here are those extreme examples of deprivation and regular instances of beatings and other forms of physical or psychological torture, extending as a practice over long periods of time. According to the special Amnesty International report on torture (AI84*), still one of the best surveys focusing exclusively on this phenomenon, more than one-third of the world's countries engage in such practices. The more comprehensive analysis employed here, based upon several global surveys, yields a figure approaching two-thirds, or more than 110, of the world's 162 states being rated 2, 3, or 4, using the scale employed in the previous section.

In some instances (e.g., Albania, Iran, Uganda, Cambodia, Guatemala), such behavior appears in the data bank over successive governmental administrations going back beyond the most recent three years reported on here, prompting speculation that the practice might be more a cultural tradition than the policy of a specific regime. The mode of torture also varies according to national background: European states are more apt to use psychological means and mental hospitals for pernicious political ends; Islamic societies have public hangings, beheadings, floggings, and bodily amputations; many African states employ caning and beatings; and Asian countries apply coercive forms of group pressure and "re-education." Latin America has less of a record on torture because most political opponents "disappear" before they ever see a jail.

The question of cultural relativism is particularly relevant with respect to those Islamic states which have incorporated Sharia Law into their political structures, and mete out punishments consisting of mutilations of the body. To address this issue, Humana asked two questions in his survey, one pertaining to torture (which is seldom sanctioned in law, let alone admitted by governments), and the other concerning legal court sentences of "corporal punishment."

A more extensive survey of all 162 countries has been developed for this report, supplementing Humana's findings with the three annual major regular human rights reports (DOS, AI, FH), the Amnesty International study on torture (AI84*), and special state reports by regional watch groups. Among the factors taken into consideration when assigning ratings here to countries covered in these studies are whether torture is applied to all criminals, or just to political prisoners; whether it happens immediately after arrest during the initial period of interrogation (quite common), or continues for some period later (which would be significant); whether the families of the imprisoned or others are forced to watch the torture; whether the government has enacted any laws or signed any treaties prohibiting the practice (although a survey of the 65 states which have signed the 1986 convention against torture shows little correlation with the actual behavior as rated here and therefore is not reported upon); whether the government responds to queries about such charges from independent human rights watch groups; whether there is any evidence of punishing the perpetrators of such deeds (a factor which is particularly important in military governments returning to civilian control); and, finally, the ghoulish nature of the alleged ill-treatment. (Prisoners who are tortured in jail to the point of death are included here, as opposed to those summarily executed "in the field" by security forces, which would have been covered in the previous section V4.3b.)

The results of this survey yield the ranking of states found in Table V4.3c. This summary is followed by some phrases, selected to indicate gradations between the categories, excerpted from the data bank associated with this project. Examples are selected only for Categories 3 and 4; the "2" designation generally reflects simply harsh prison conditions. As before, minority groups are highlighted in italics.

V4.3d. Political Prisoners

Being a political prisoner—i.e., jailed for opposition to government policies, often on trumped-up charges of disturbing the peace, incitement to riot, etc.—might be regarded as a final form of violation to one's personal integrity (AI81*). Because the government's objective is simply to remove such politically troublesome people from circulation in society, they are sometimes not tortured or even imprisoned, but merely confined to house arrest, or banned (i.e., forbidden from speaking or appearing in public gatherings). Some of them are sent into internal exile, restricted to the confines of small, rural towns; others are expelled from their homeland and not allowed to return. However, for individuals like Martin Luther King (US), Lech Walesa (Poland), Vaclav Havel (Czechoslovakia), Ahmed Ben Bella (Algeria), the Ayatollah Khomeini (Iran), Nelson Mandela (South Africa), Mahatma Gandhi (India), Zulfikar ali Bhutto (Pakistan), Kim Dae Jung (S. Korea), or Jose Napoleon Duarte (El Salvador)—to name just a few of the more prominent people jailed for their political activities in recent history—being outlawed involves more than the mere curtailment of personal freedom (V4.5); it strikes at the heart of their essential being.

As the above list of prominent former political prisoners indicates, many of these persons would be of the stature of cabinet ministers or government officials under different political circumstances; some actually became prime ministers after their release, and others were their country's leaders before their imprisonment. Unfortunately, most political prisoners are not that well known, and many of the numerical estimates given below must be based upon reports which are often unable to be substantiated; exact figures are often confirmed only after amnesties have been declared, prisoners released, and imprisonments become known in retrospect.

Amnesty International has made one of its priorities the identification of such political prisoners, particularly individuals without much notoriety who languish for years in jails because of their political activity. Because it wants to name names, its standards are high and its estimates low compared to many other sources (e.g., opposition groups in exile) often cited for the numbers in a given country. The State Department's annual report on human rights attempts rough calculations of the number of persons being held for their political beliefs and is the best source in reporting on the claims of rival groups and human rights committees in particular states.

Many reports distinguish between political prisoners and prisoners of conscience, the latter being those who have not committed or planned, or been involved in supporting or advocating, any acts of violence (FH87: 22; AI88: 267). Because most of those in jail are accused of being related *in some way* to some breach of the public order, and because the connection to destructive acts of others is difficult to prove (or disprove), this particular classification is not employed in this study. In some instances (e.g., in Cuba and Northern Ireland (UK)), those who consider themselves political prisoners have refused to wear the jail uniforms of common criminals.

A distinction should be made between long-term political prisoners, many of whom have been convicted in (generally unfair) trials, and that larger class of people who are arbitrarily arrested and detained (not charged) for more limited periods of time. The latter are covered in the next section (V4.4a) where less violent infringements of citizens' rights, generally under some cover of law, are analyzed. However, when the word "detained" is used in the data bank in connection with long-term prisoners covered here, it means they have not been charged.

As with the other categories of human rights violations, in many countries political prisoners are drawn disproportionately from among members of minority (ethnic or religious) groups. When this is the case, in the excerpts to follow the name of the group will be italicized to draw further attention to the points made in the previous section (V4.2).

Finally, some sense of proportion must be maintained. The number of political prisoners—even if in the thousands—is everywhere a small percentage of the general population. In most societies no more than 5 to 10% of the people have any desire to participate in politics (see below, section V5.1a); those courageous enough to do so in a way which challenges the prevailing political orthodoxy make up a minuscule minority. Thus, the total population statistics (found in Table I.2) should be kept in mind, particularly when noting the numbers of prisoners in large states like India, Indonesia, the USSR, and China.

In the global survey of political prisoners which appears in Table V4.3d, the following modification of the 1-to-4 rating system for states is made to accommodate the tentative phraseology of the typical human rights reports.

0 - none or very few (less than 10; few).
1 - less than 100 ("several," "dozens," "scores").
2 - between 100 and 500 ("hundreds").
3 - between 500 and 3000 ("several hundreds," "few thousand").
4 - more than 3000 ("several, many thousands").

In the data bank associated with this project, ranges of numbers are maintained as reports from human rights groups are received throughout the year. Because precise statistics are difficult under any circumstances, the positioning of countries in Table V4.3d is only approximate. Fifty-eight states have been determined to have more than 100 political prisoners each, with the Islamic zone being the worst offender in terms of number of countries noted (16 of its 28). At the other extreme, even the 44 countries coded "0" probably have a few imprisoned dissidents or conscientious objectors who could arguably be called political. The page of data bank excerpts following Table V4.3d indicates the range of prisoners typically cited, as well as the major sources for this data (mainly the annual DOS and AI surveys, supplemented by news reports from credible newspapers and magazines).

V4.3a - Death Penalty

Europe	Islamic	Africa	Asia	Latin America

1-States Without Death Penalty (n=58)

Europe	Islamic	Africa	Asia	Latin America
Ireland			Comoros	Argentina
Romania	Oman		Bhutan	Uruguay
Italy,Greece	Bahrain		Nepal	Brazil
Spain,Portug.	Qatar	CVerde	Madagascar	Venezuela
France,Malta		Togo		Ecuador
UK,Canada		STP	Solomons	Colombia
Iceland,Belgium	Libya	Congo	New Zealand	Dom.Rep.
Norway,Denmk.		Gabon	Papua NG	Grenada
Finland,Sweden	Pakistan	Rwanda	Fiji	Mexico,Belize
Nthrlds.,Luxmbg.				Honduras
W.Ger.,E.Ger.		Lesotho	Cambodia	Costa Rica
Austria,Switzrld.		Namibia		Nicaragua,El Sal.
n=22	n=5	n=8	n=9	n=14

2-States with de jure Death Penalty Rarely Used de facto (n=9)

Europe	Islamic	Africa	Asia	Latin America
		Ivory Coast	Australia	Bolivia
		Niger	Seychelles	Antigua
		C.Af.R.	Maldives,Brunei	

3-Death Penalty Sometimes Used (n=13)

Europe	Islamic	Africa	Asia	Latin America
	Israel, UAE	Senegal	Sri Lanka	Peru, St. Vincent
	Morocco,Algeria	GBissau	Japan,Mauritius	Panama, Guyana

4-Death Penalty Regularly Used (n=78)

Europe	Islamic	Africa	Asia	Latin America
US	Turkey	Kenya,Zaire	China	Cuba
	Iraq, Iran	Uganda	Taiwan	Barbados
USSR	Afghanistan	Ethiopia	S.Korea	Suriname
	Syria	Burundi	N.Korea	Dominica
Hungary	Jordan	Nigeria	Thailand	Haiti
Czech.	N.Yemen	Guinea	Malaysia	Trinidad
Bulgaria	S.Yemen	Liberia	Singapore	Jamaica
Poland	Saudi Arabia	Cameroon	India	Bahamas
Yugoslavia	Kuwait	Burkina F.,Mali	Bangladesh	Guatemala
Albania	Egypt,Sudan	Sierra L.,Gambia	Vietnam	St. Chris.
	Mauritania	Benin,Ghana	Laos	St.Lucia
	Somalia,Chad	Eq.Guinea	Myanmar	Paraguay
	Djibouti	Angola,Malawi	Philippines	Chile
	Tunisia	Zambia,Zimbwe.	W. Samoa	
		Botswana,Swazi.	Indonesia	
		Tanzania		
		Mozambq.,S.Africa		
n=8	n=17	n=25	n=15	n=13

no (or unclear) information (n=4)

Europe	Islamic	Africa	Asia	Latin America
	Cyprus,Lebanon		Vanuatu,Mongolia	
30	28	38	33	33 TOT:162

Source: *AI Annual Reports*, 1980-1990; AI79*; AI89*; Humana 1986, Qu.#11.

V4.3b - Illegal Government Killings

Europe	Islamic	Africa	Asia	Latin America

1 (n=84)

Europe	Islamic	Africa	Asia	Latin America
US,Can.,Ice.,Ire.	Cyprus	Gambia,Ghana	Bhutan,Maldives	Antig.,Bah.,Barb.
Nor.,France	Jordan, Bahrain	STP,CV,Mali	Madagascar	St.K.,St.L.,St.V.
Bel.,Neth.,Lux.	Kuwait, Qatar	GB,IC,Togo	Mauritius	Dominica,Trinidad
Denmk,Swed,Fin.	UAE, Oman	Niger, Sierra L.	Mongolia	Belize,Guyana
WGer.,Austria	Saudi Arabia	Congo, Gabon	Singapore,Malaysia	Grenada
Switz.,Malta	N.Yemen	CAfR,Eq.G.	Solomns,Vanuatu	Costa Rica
Italy,Greece	Tunisia, Morocco	Rwanda	Fiji,WSamoa	Ecuador,Bolivia
Portugal,Spain	Egypt, Djibouti	Zambia	Jap.,Austrl.,NZ	Uruguay
Czech.,Hungary		Swazi.,Botswana	Brunei,Papua	

2 (n=40)

Europe	Islamic	Africa	Asia	Latin America
		Senegal	Seychelles	Dom.Rep.
UK	Pakistan	Benin	Comoros	Jamaica
	Turkey	Cameroon	Nepal	
E.Germany		Nigeria	Bangladesh	Suriname
Poland	Mauritania	Guinea	Thailand	Paraguay
	Chad	Burundi	Taiwan	Chile
Albania		Kenya,Tanz.	S.Korea	Venezuela
	Algeria	Namibia	Vietnam	Argentina
		Zimbabwe	Cambodia	
		Lesotho	Laos	Nicaragua
		Malawi		Honduras

3 (n=23)

Europe	Islamic	Africa	Asia	Latin America
USSR	Israel	Zaire		
	Syria	Liberia	Indonesia	Brazil
	S.Yemen	Burkina Faso		Colombia
Yugoslavia	Somalia	Uganda	N.Korea	Cuba
Bulgaria	Lebanon	Mozambique		Mexico
	Libya	Angola	Phil. I.	Panama

4 (n=15)

Europe	Islamic	Africa	Asia	Latin America
Romania	Iran,Iraq	S.Africa	India	Haiti
	Afghanistan	Ethiopia	Sri Lanka	Guatemala
	Sudan		Myanmar	El Salvador
			China	Peru
n=30	n=28	n=38	n=33	n=33

Source: DOS90, AI90, FH88-89 (and earlier editions); HUM Qu. #8; AI83*, and other special reports as noted in Data Bank excerpts.

2

UK - At least 34 disputed killings at times of (instead of) capture of *IRA* suspects during '82-85 (NYT, 3/17/86). In 1/88 dismissed prosecutions for deaths of 6 unarmed under "shoot-to-kill" policy of '82. Ulster Def. Assoc., violent pro-Govt. paramil. group is legal; IRA is not. 3/88 kill of three "suspected terrorists" in Gibraltar may have been "extrajudicial execution" (AI89,90).

E.Germany - About 200 died trying to escape through Berlin Wall (1961-89) under policy of border guards shooting fleeing refugees.

3

Bulgaria - Up to 1000 *Turks* killed in '85 assimilation campaign (HW 2/87). Whole villages sealed off, women raped, men murdered; as late as 5/89 peaceful demonstrations by ethnic Turks and *Pomaks* (Bulgarian Moslems) led to clashes w/ security forces & deaths (DOS90).

Israel - more than 700 *Palestinians* (at least 260 unarmed civilians including children, AI90) killed by army during 1st 2 yrs. of intifada (uprising) in Gaza and West Bank, 12/87-12/89.

Syria- Since '82 "massacre" of 10,000 at Hama, pol. killings "have subsided", so that only a few unconfirmed reports in '82-85 (DOS86). Killings subside when threats to govt. do (DOS89). Credible reports of those arrested for security reasons, then disappearing, stopped in 1986 (DOS88). "Many disappearances" (AI84), incl. some 500 pol. prisoners killed at Tadmur, mid-1980s.

Phil. I. - Unsupervised paramilitary squads (Alsa Masas) "cleaning up" s.Mindinao, Davao, et al. resp. for 40% of illeg. killings; AI 88 repts. >100 leftists killed by pro-Govt. vigilante groups; *The Economist* 10/7/89 says more left-wing priests and lawyers killed in '86-89 than in '75-86 Marcos era; *The Nation*, 6/19/89 identifies more than 50 political assassinations.

Panama - Although torture was Noriega regime's preferred mode of intimidation, one cause célèbre: opp. leader H. Spadafora found beheaded, 9/85; also several killed, dozens disappeared during 5/89 (annulled) election week, attributed to new paramilitary Dignity Brigade. 10+ summarily executed after 10/89 coup. Hundreds died during change of regime in 12/89.

Mexico - Disapps. follow interrogs., esp.in rural areas where security forces operate v. militant peasants in disputes with landowners (HUM:4). Acc. to Ibarra, opp. Pres. cand. in 9/84: 460 disapp. since '69; about half in '73 sweep. 18 peasant org. leaders killed, Su'84; 21 more in 1985 (DOS86). 123 peasants killed in '87 confrontations (DOS88). 2 top aides to losing Pres. candidate murdered during election week, '88; also opp. cand. for Mayor of Tezonapa (DOS89).

4

Iran - "Conservative" UN HR Cmsn. ests. 7000 executions after '79 revolution, declined to 500 in '84, fewer in '86, but "still continuing." Leaders of respective groups claim: 12,000-50,000 Moslem Socialist Party (Mujahadeen Khalq) and 300 *Bahai.* HUM reports summary executions, even of children, and "virtual genocide" against *Kurds.*

Iraq - entire *Kurdish* villages wiped out with chemical weapons for collaborating with Iran (3/88); mass executions of *Shias* suspected of pro-Iran sympathies, 1980-81; refugee Isl. Cmtee for HR in Iraq claims 300,000 "executions" by 1968-85 regime, (NYT adv.,8/85).

India - 1988 emerg. law to shoot "suspect *Sikh* terrorists"; 100s killed in "staged encounters." Many killings by police "often out of control" in dealing with *Moslem & Sikh* groups (FH87), & other communal unrest. Dozens die after capture and torture (AI8/88). None of 80 officials named by Govt. as instigators of 1984 anti-Sikh massacres (2700 dead) have been punished.

China -Hundreds of demonstrating ("rioting") *Tibetans* killed in 10/87, 3/88, 12/88 (As.W.,2/88; DOS89). In 6/89 suppression of pro-democracy movement, Govt. killed at least 1000 in Beijing (AI90); also 300-400 in Chengdu and other cities (NYT).

El Salvador - more than 40,000 of the 62,000 deaths in the war since '79 involved killings of civilians by govt. forces or their allied "death squads." Drop off in recent years: from 9600/yr most by govt. in 1980-2, to 360/yr, some by rebels in '86 (NYT), to 159 in '87, 261 in '88 (ratio 2:1 pro-Govt: rebels). "Assassinations common, perpetrators not tried" (FH87). Squad of D'Aubuisson, leader of '88 ruling party, implicated in assassinations of Atty.Gen. Zamora 2/80, Abp. Romero 3/80, HR ldr. Anaya '87, Labor Fed. ldr. Velasquez 11/89. Army implicated in killing of 4 US nuns ('83), 6 Jesuits (11/89).

273

V4.3c - Torture

<u>Europe</u>	<u>Islamic</u>	<u>Africa</u>	<u>Asia</u>	<u>Latin America</u>
		1 (n=50)		
US, Canada	Cyprus	Rwanda	Japan	Antigua
Iceland,Ireland	Jordan	Gambia	New Zealand	Barbados
Norway,Finland	Qatar	C.Af.R.	Mongolia	Dominica
Sweden,Denmk.		Cape Verde	Maldives	St.C.,St.L.,St.V.
Belg.,Neth.,Lux.			Comoros	Grenada
France,W.Ger.			Bhutan,Mauritius	
Switzerland			Malaysia,Brunei	Uruguay
Austria,Hungary			Papua NG, Sol.I.	Belize
Portugal,Malta			Vanuatu,W.Sam.	Costa Rica
Italy, Greece				
		2 (n=64)		
Spain	Bahrain,Oman	STP,Ghana	Australia	Argentina
UK	UAE,Kuwait	S.Leone,Mali	Fiji	Venezuela
Poland	Lebanon	Congo,Gabon	Bangladesh	Bolivia
E.Germany	Egypt,Tunisia	Benin,Togo	Seychelles	Bahamas
Czech.	Algeria	Iv.Cst.,Eq.G.	Nepal	Trinidad
Yugoslavia		Niger,Guinea	Phil. I.	Dom. Rep.
Bulgaria		Nigeria,Camrn.	Taiwan	Jamaica
		GBissau,Sengl.	Laos	Guy., Suriname
		Burkina F.	India	Colombia
		Kenya,Tanz.		Peru, Brazil
		Burundi,Malawi		Ecuador
		Swazi.,Leso.		Panama
		Bots.,Namibia		Nicaragua
		3 (n=33)		
USSR	Israel	Liberia	China	
Romania	Djib.,Somalia	Zimbabwe	Vietnam	Haiti
Albania	Chad,Sudan	Zambia	S.Korea	Mexico
	Mauritania	Angola	Indonesia	Honduras
	Morocco	Mozambique	Singapore	Paraguay
	Libya,Turkey		Thailand	Chile
	Saudi Arabia		Myanmar	
	N.Yem.,S.Yem.		Madagascar	
		4 (n=15)		
	Iran, Iraq	S.Africa	Sri Lanka	El Salvador
	Afghanistan	Ethiopia	Cambodia	Guatemala
	Pakistan	Uganda	N. Korea	Cuba
	Syria	Zaire		
n=30	n=28	n=38	n=33	n=33 (162)

Source: DOS90 (and earlier), AI90 (and earlier), FH88-89 (and earlier); HUM Qu. #9 & 12; AI84*; and special reports as noted in Data Bank excerpts.

274

3

USSR - 5 mil. people on "psychiatric register," includes many dissidents; but ˜40% don't belong and are being removed under Gorbachev reforms which incl. removing psychiatric hospitals fm. control of Interior Min. (& KGB) and placing under Min. of Health; but most personnel, policies remain unaffected (DOS88), and DOS90 and AI89,90 report both physical and psychological abuses still occur often; also, allegations of pre-trial beatings (AI90).

Turkey - systematic, and consistent since the early 1970s, esp. of *Kurds* & pol. prisoners (AI89). Electric shocks, rape, beatings "on a large scale" (HW 3/86). System so bad 5 Europ. states had to sue in European HR Court before a pledge of change in 1982-85 torture policy finally extracted, though HW 12/87 says it still continues, and DOS89 says "still widespread." Convention vs. torture finally signed in 1/88, allowing announced visits by outside groups.

Saudi Arabia - unique in Islamic World that beheadings, floggings and amputations ("with anesthetic") are incorporated into Sharia Law (others allow them in practice)—AI84*. Many deaths under torture alleged by Cmtee. for Def. of Pol. Prisoners in Saudi A., (London, 8/86). DOS88 says "some" reports of beatings to elicit confession; AI87 says a "pattern" of it.

China - Law prohibits torture, though public humiliation is often used to deter crime (DOS86). Many local abuses, esp. in *Tibet* where cattle prods are common during interrogation, and of suspected *Taiwan* connections; accepted form of prison punishment for "recalcitrants" (HUM:3)

Chile - Many instances: RC Vicariate of Solidarity reports: 102 cases in '87, 130 in '86, 81 in '85; as % of detainees, 22%, 17%, 15%, respectively. OAS HR Cmsn. reports 850+ in '82-84, and a "continuous, deliberate, systematic policy since '73." Techniques include: electric current to genitals, cigarette burns, suspension by wrists, mock execut. shots fired near heads, threats to female relatives witnessing the torture, etc. "Many hundreds of victims...officially approved" (HUM:4). Also psychiatric treatment used on dissidents acc. to Physicians for HR group. One of six states mentioned by UN Special Rapporteur on Torture, 1/87. But DOS90 reports "large reduction in reported incidents" as Govt. moves from military to civilian rule, 1989.

4

Pakistan - "many" reported torture cases, amputations & floggings (although not for pregnant women "until 2 months after they have given birth" acc. to criminal code). Hair pulled out, eyebrows & pubic hair burned, electric shocks (AI85); many prisoners in leg irons (HUM:4); "physical abuse common...esp. in Class C prisons"(DOS88). Still "routine" even after 1988 change of regime from Zia to Bhutto (DOS90, AI89); "widespread", incl. 2 public lashings (AI90).

Iraq - reliable reports of physical and psychological torture, esp. during periods of interrogation, which can last for months (DOS88); beatings, burns, electric shocks, sexual violations to such an extent must be regarded as condoned by the state (HUM:4). Torture even of children to get information on their parents (AI 2/89); torture of pol. prisoners widespread (AI90).

Iran - torture "widespread" (UN, the mildest HR watchdog, 11/88 and 11/89 Reports), incl. suspensions from ceilings, relatives being forced to watch executions (n=200-300).

S. Africa - Security laws allow police unsupervised discretion in interrogations, exemption from liability for "good faith" acts, resulting in abusive conduct, esp. against *blacks*. Detained Parents Support Cmtee. reports 83% of 500 released('86) showed evidence of physical abuse; Natl. Medical Assoc. reports 50% abused in '87 (DOS88). *Black* detainees, incl. children, often beaten and whipped, incl. with metal whips; more than 200 killed (Lwyrs. Cmtee, 4/86).

Cuba - US claims "systematic," AI says "some" but not systematic & certainly no disappearances. Cuban HR Cmtee. (Madrid, Chm. Armando Villadares) names over 50 prisoners tortured in '87; hours of shivering in refrigerated cells a common technique (DOS88). "Plantados," politicals who refuse uniforms, subjected to particular abuse. Some improper commitments to facilities for the insane. "Systematic abuse, long terms, frequent beatings, long periods confining in solitary or in sun; food & water deprivation; psycholog. & biolog. experiments by E.European technicians" (CHRC Villadares at Paris conf., 4/13/86). "Beatings, broken limbs" (HUM:3).

V4.3d - Political Prisoners

Europe	Islamic	Africa	Asia	Latin America

0 = Probably None, Few (n=44)

Europe	Islamic	Africa	Asia	Latin America
US, Canada	Cyprus	Cape Verde	Mongolia	Venezuela
Ice.,Ire.,Nor.	UAE	Senegal, Gabon	Bhutan,Maurits.	Barbados,Jamaica
Finland	Kuwait	C.Af.R.,Tanzania	Sol.I.,W.Samoa	Bahamas,St. V.
Bel.,Neth.,Lux.	Algeria	Botswana	Papua NG	Antigua,St.Chris.
Aust.,Den.,Swed.		Swaziland	Vanuatu,Fiji	Belize,St. Lucia
			Australia,NZ	Dom.,Dom.Rep.

1 = less than 100 (n=60)

Europe	Islamic	Africa	Asia	Latin America
W.Ger.,Switz.	Lebanon	Ghana,Benin	Comoros	Colombia
Italy,Malta	Jordan	Eq.G.,Burkina F.	Maldives	Uruguay
Portugal	Oman,Qatar	Niger,Congo	Seychelles	Paraguay
E.Ger.,Poland	N.Yemen	Mali,Sierra L.	Singapore	Brazil,Ecuador
Czech.,Hung.	Djibouti	Iv.Coast,Togo	Malaysia	Bolivia
Romania	Egypt,Tunisia	GBissau,Gambia	Brunei	Guy.,Suriname
		STP, Cameroon	Thailand	Panama
		Kenya,Zambia	Taiwan	Costa Rica
		Rwanda,Burundi	Japan	Grenada
		Lesotho,Malawi	Phil. I.	Trinidad

2 = 100 to 500 (n=30)

Europe	Islamic	Africa	Asia	Latin America
USSR	Pakistan	Liberia	Indonesia	Chile, Peru
Bulgaria	Saudi A.,Bahrain	Guinea	Nepal	Argentina
UK	S. Yemen	Zaire	Madagascar	Mexico
France	Somalia	Zimbabwe		Honduras
Spain	Libya,Sudan	Namibia		Guatemala
Greece	Mauritania			Haiti,Nicaragua

3 = 500 to 3000 (n=12)

Europe	Islamic	Africa	Asia	Latin America
	Morocco	Nigeria	Vietnam	Cuba
	Chad	Uganda	Bangladesh	El Salvador
		Ethiopia	Sri Lanka	
		Angola	S. Korea	

4 = 3000+ (n=16)

Europe	Islamic	Africa	Asia	Latin America
Albania	Afghanistan	S.Africa	India	
Yugoslavia	Iran, Iraq	Mozambique	Myanmar	
	Turkey		China	
	Syria		N. Korea	
	Israel		Laos	
			Cambodia	
n=30	n=28	n=38	n=33	n=33

Source: DOS90 (and earlier), AI90 (and earlier), FH88-89 (and earlier); HUM Qu. #13; AI81*; and special reports as noted in Data Bank excerpts.

2: 100-500

Spain - 400 - mainly *Basque* ETA members under anti-terrorists laws.

France - 200 - about 100 *Basque* separatists expelled w/o legal proceedings in 1986 and 1987; similarly, several dozen Moslems suspected of aiding Islamic terrorist groups.

UK - 150 (AI85), among both Protestants and Catholics in *N. Ireland.* Hunger strikes killed several *N. Irish Catholics* in early '80s before status as political prisoners was recognized.

USSR - ~100 - DOS cited 750, AI had 250 in '88; Am.Psychiatric Assoc. says 50-100 in hospitals; UK Keston Coll. says 200 religious prisoners (*Econ.*, 6/4/88). 40% of all are *Ukrainians*; other ethnic dissidents include: *Jews* wishing to emigrate, 1989 *Armenian* Karabakh Cmtee., *Georgians* violating curfew, etc. But since 1989 none serving solely under Articles 190 & 70 (anti-Soviet activity), or under Arts. 142 & 227 (religious activities).

Saudi Arabia - 200 - 700+ acc. to Cmtee. for Def. of Pol.Pris. in Saudi A. (London, 8/86); svl. doz. Shi'a arrested in e.prov. in '86 released in general amnesty of 1/87 (DOS88); "clear pattern" of suspected political opponents arrested without warrant, held long periods (AI, 1/90).

Mexico - 200 - DOS88 says 150, most arrested in disputes over land titles; 100s(AI85). opp.ldr.Rosario Ibarra says Govt. holding 315 Mexicans and 150 *Indians* (DOS84). 800 released at 2/89 inauguration of Pres. Salinas de Gotori.

3: 500 to 3000

S.Korea - 800 - according to DOS90 at end of 1989; Kim Dae Jung claimed hundreds in spring '88, after new (2/88) Roh govt. freed 125 and claimed only 260 left, incl. several dozen "communists & leftists," student leaders and Kim Keun Tae, '87 RFK HR award winner.

Vietnam - low 1000's - after two major amnesties in 1988 released about 5800. Govt. had admitted to 7000-to-10,000 (DOS86), before 8/87 amnesty of 6685 ex-SVN officials, and before release of 1014 on Tet '88; claims only 150 left. After 1975, 90,000 SVNmese US collaborators sent to re-education camps (internal exile) (DOS88). Only about 130 remain today (AI89); plus several 100 others were arrested in later years.

El Salvador - sevl. 100 - about 400 (incl. pro-Govt. death squad mbrs. suspected of killing US nuns) released in 10/87 Esquipulas II amnesty, but many other leftists and FMNLF sympathizers remain (AI89). 100s more leftist labor & political leaders arrested in 5/89, and after 11/89 rebel offensive, some 50 churchworkers, 40 human rights observers.

Cuba - sevl. 100 - once 1000s, but several hundred released in last two years. Am. Watch 1/89 est. "several score to a few hundred;" local HR activists claim many mrore. Govt. 3/88 admitted 455 "for crimes against state." 5/89 Intl. Red Cross visit identified 1257 (DOS90).

4=3000+

Iran - many 1000 - 1000s since '79 (AI,5/87), esp. *Kurds*, and about 750 *Bahais* acc. to R. Reagan, 12/85; hundreds still in '89, despite some releases (AI90) by new 8/89 govt.

Israel - 6000 - at least 4000 *Palestinians* swept up in Gaza/W.Bank uprising, 12/87ff, 500 in admin detention (w/o charges), 4 (only) expelled. Earlier, at least the 400 Palestinians & Lebanese from s. Leb. security zone Islamic Holy War is trying to bargain Isr. kidnappees for.

Syria - thousands (AI 10/87), incl. 2000 *Palestinians* & their Leb. sympathizers acc. to Arafat(4/28/88,IHT). Of Syrians, many under martial law (esp.'82) regs., 260 long-term.

South Africa - sevl. 1000 - Still 3000 after 10/89 release of nine long-term *African* National Congress leaders incl. hundreds in jail since early 1960's (Mandela released 2/90). Since 6/86 state of emergency, about 25,000 arrested, 20,000 released..

India - 10,000 - mostly *Sikhs*, under Terror.Prevention Act of 1987, incl.4000 in Punjab, 2200 in Gujarat, 1400 in Haryana; and 1000 more in Punjab under Natl.Security Act in late 1980s; ~1000 *Kashmiri Moslems* in spring 1990. Several 100 others in various states, especially in northeast tribal areas, under Terrorist and Disruptive Activities Act (AI89).

China - unknown 1000s - Govt. admits to 3586 sentenced for counter-rev. activities after 6/89 democracy demonstrations (NYTimes). Others claim 10,000 in Beijing and more than 100,000 nationwide (AI 8/30/89). Token releases (~600) in late '89. 300-500 *Tibetans* after 3/89 demonstrations. Many still since 1979 Democracy Wall movement (DOS90).

V4.4. THE RULE OF LAW (CIVIL RIGHTS)

The issues analyzed in the next two sections of this chapter—civil rights and personal freedoms—are not quite as urgent in a life-and-death sense as the matters covered under human rights. Therefore, there will be fewer excerpts from multiple sources, and not all of the global surveys used will be cited in every category which follows. Although the data bank associated with this project continues to be maintained, only the summary rankings will be reported, with particular sources cited in cases where they are deemed to have special expertise or methods of estimation (e.g., Humana for due process and judicial independence; Sivard and the Population Crisis Committee for women's rights; Barrett for freedom of religion; Freedom House for freedom of the press). One result is that for certain categories the universe of states reported upon will be less than the 162 countries analyzed in the rest of this study and the results somewhat more dated. As indicated in the introductory chapter, however, the main purpose of this work is more to show sources and means of measurements than to provide complete global scores in every category.

V4.4a. Due Process: Arrest and Detention, Fair Trial

The plight of political prisoners (section V4.3d) called attention to the many more of their supporters often caught up in arbitrary government sweeps of people protesting regime policies. Often, innocent bystanders or people whose sole crime is that they are members of the wrong ethnic group or locality are thrown in jail for (generally) short periods of time while governments attempt to quell situations of unrest. With respect to due process of law for such citizens, two issues will be addressed here: (i.) arbitrary arrest and prolonged periods of "preventive detention"; and (ii.) the fairness of trials to which they might eventually be brought.

Humana asks five questions in this regard: one explicitly highlighting indefinite detention without charge; and four relating to due process in trials. Although Humana's findings reveal a significant distinction in state rankings between arbitrary arrest and detention (which a large number of states engage in when responding to situations of unrest), and attention to due process after the initial sweep has been made (where considerable variation among state practices exists), the two activities will be combined for analysis here. One reason is that Humana's findings are somewhat dated, particularly with respect to eastern Europe; more significantly, it provides a good opportunity to discuss Humana's methodology, especially his practice of giving greater (triple) weight to 7 of his 40 questions (Humana, 1986: 4).

Humana's ratings of "YES, yes, no, NO" for state compliance with human rights standards lends itself readily to transfer to the 1-through-4 system used in this study. When dealing with his questions which are similarly weighted, the results can be added up and states placed in broad categories based upon their totals over several questions. This has been done here in the case of Humana's four questions dealing with fair trials, before they are combined with the more important question on arbitrary arrest and detention.

The most notable cases of arrest and detention are political in nature, and it is often difficult to distinguish between people arrested as a result of their political beliefs for "parading without a permit," "vandalism," or "destruction of property" during strikes, demonstrations, or rallies, and those thrown in jail because they were merely present on such occasions. Some 30,000 Palestinians have been arrested by Israel at some point during the first three years of the uprising in the Occupied Territories which began in December, 1987; more than 10,000 blacks were swept up after the state of emergency announced by South Africa in June, 1986. Only the leaders of these large groups are genuine political prisoners retained in jail over the long term. Most of the followers in such instances are released after short periods of detention, if for no other reason than lack of prison facilities.

Political prisoners were covered in V4.3d; the arrest and detention measure here applies to more ordinary citizens, especially as they might be caught up in states of emergency or declarations of martial law. Humana's Question #13, one of his seven "heavily weighted" questions, asks about such detention without charge. After the initial police sweep, there are a number of stages detainees might go through depending on a state's criminal justice system. Humana addresses at least four of these in his Questions #30-33, for all of which he draws upon either the Civil and Political Rights Convention (Article 9.3) or the Universal Declaration (Articles 10 and 11.1). Chronologically, from the time of arrest, they would include a.) whether the detained person will be brought before a judge and charged with a crime (in Western law, the writ of *habeas corpus*), b.) whether there will be a fair and public trial before an independent tribunal, including c.) a presumption of innocence until proven guilty and d.) legal assistance of one's own choosing, provided free by the government if needed.

Such legal niceties are ignored in many states, and are easily suspended during times of unrest and emergency. Even citizens in the most liberal of societies can be arrested and detained without formal charges for brief periods of time. It is the unreasonable extensions of such governmental action which are addressed in the following survey.

After translating Humana's results into 1-through-4 ratings, the scores for each of the four questions are totaled up, and states given a sum of between 4 and 16. Then the 1-through-4 scores for the more important arrest and detention question are multiplied by three and the resulting numbers (3 through 12) for each state added to the 4-through-16 fair trial scores. The resulting number (between 7 and 28) results in the display of states in four categories (1=7 to 11; 2=12 to 17; 3=18 to 23; 4=24 to 28) presented in Table V4.4a.

V4.4b. Freedom of Movement; Privacy

The next civil rights to be discussed—freedom of movement and privacy—are generally more respected by states than are the considerations of due process in the criminal justice system. They are more closely related to the personal freedoms covered in section V4.5 and for ordinary (i.e., apolitical) citizens during normal times there is usually no problem in having these rights respected. However, for politically active individuals, and during states of emergency when the rule of law is suspended, these rights are frequently breached.

i. Freedom of Movement.   Freedom of movement is a civil right easily restricted with respect to disruptive dissidents and political prisoners (as seen in sections V4.4a and .3d), and during times of unrest (as will be seen in V4.4d). Movement into and out of countries over international borders is everywhere strictly controlled by governments, and is not even recognized as a right by many states (Dowty, 1987). On the other hand, within one's country the freedom to live and work where one wants, and to travel without unreasonable governmental restrictions in search of residence and employment (as well as for pleasure), would seem to be among the most basic of individual rights.

A variation of the 1-through-4 scale used earlier can be employed here so that:

1 = generally **free movement** within and out of a country.
2 = **restrictions** via indirect controls (like currency regulations, permits, etc.), or as related to national security areas during insurgencies, etc.
3 = **more limits,** especially including unfair restrictions on minority ethnic group members.
4 = **intensive controls:** internal passports; permission to change jobs, move residence, etc.; forced movements of large segments of population.

Table V4.4b.i places states in these categories based upon Questions #1 and 2 in Humana (travel within, and travel outside of, one's country, respectively), as updated through mid-1990 in the data bank being maintained for this project. Many of the states in Categories 3 and 4 have tight controls over political dissidents or over certain types of "minority" people (e.g., Jews in USSR, women in Islamic states) irrespective of their political activities. Also with high scores are countries which have engaged in forced movements of large segments of the population, generally during conditions of civil war to remove such "hearts and minds" from areas of rebel control (e.g., Ethiopia, El Salvador, Iraq). Perhaps the most extreme case (even before the onset of insurgency in 1984) is the situation of South Africa's "homelands" policy with its deportations of millions of blacks to "homelands" and the accompanying destruction of their existing homes in townships near South Africa's residentially-white-only cities.

ii. Privacy. Warrantless police searches of the homes of those of dubious political loyalty are addressed by Humana in his Question #34. He also gives state-rankings with respect to censorship of mail and telephone-tapping (Question #18) and the arbitrary seizure of personal property (Question #35). Using the methods employed earlier, the ratings of these three similarly weighted questions were combined to begin the data base for Humana's 88 states in 1986. Since that time, using the annual major human rights reports (DOS, AI, and FH) and other specific studies, these judgments have been updated and expanded to include all 162 countries through mid-1990. In Table V4.4b.ii, countries are ranked with respect to the right of privacy in categories 1 through 4, where:

1 = government **seldom** interferes in private lives of citizens; becomes involved only if suspected wrongdoing, and only within legal guidelines.
2 = **some** reports of government illegal searches and seizures in homes, mail and telephone tampering, etc.
3 = though rights to privacy may exist, government intervenes **frequently** in private lives of citizens and tries to control many aspects of life.
4 = right to privacy **non-existent**; in fact, government **often** acts as if it has right to interfere in citizens' private lives.

For the reasons of space explained earlier, no excerpts are provided from the data bank to substantiate the rankings in Tables V4.4b.i and V4.4b.ii. Except in the case of eastern European states which are now moving into higher categories, however, they have not varied much over the past five years.

(Related to both movement and privacy is the common practice of governments requiring several months (sometimes, years) of military service from every one of its able-bodied male citizens. Table V1.2a.iii in Chapter 1 provided data on states with mandatory conscription as compared with those with provisions for conscientious objection.)

V4.4c. Women's Rights

A civil right which can no longer be ignored in the contemporary era is that of women vis-a-vis men (Iglitzen and Ross, 1985; Seager, 1986). Although women comprise slightly more than one-half of the planet's population, they account for two-thirds of the world's working hours, but receive only one-tenth of global income, and own just one-hundredth of all deeded property (United Nations, 1985a; Fuentes, 1983).

For this measure, a return to the methods of Chapters 1 through 3 is preferable to excerpted narratives because statistics have been collected which actually compare the performance of women vis-a-vis men with respect to certain measurable social activities and achievements. Two studies in the past decade are particularly helpful in producing comparative data on the status of women versus men on a state-by-state basis.

Sivard (1985) provides statistics for women as compared with men relating to literacy, higher education, and employment for some 140 countries. Tables V4.4c.i(a) through (c) reproduce, for the top- and lowest-ranked countries in each zone, the *ratio* between the average percentage of adult women and the comparable percentage for men (=100%) in these three categories.

The Population Crisis Committee (1988) surveyed 98 countries, representing 2.3 billion women (92% of the world's female population) with respect to 20 indicators, four in each of five sectors: health, marriage, education, employment, and social equality. In each area, one measure compared the relative size of the gender gap within countries.

These measures were, respectively, health—the difference in years between female and male life expectancy at birth, 1987; marriage—widowed, divorced, or separated women per 100 widowed, divorced, or separated men, latest data available, 1973-86; education—the difference between literacy rates for men and women aged 25-45 years, 1973-83; employment—the percentage of all salaried employees and wage earners aged 15 years and over who are female, latest available data, 1973-86; and social equity—the absence of discrimination against women in society, 1986-88, representing the total of several variables relating to economics, politics, law, marriage, and the family. (This fifth measure comes closest to the legal theory spirit of the rest of this section on rights.)

For each of the five areas, the gender gap was normalized on a 1-to-5 point scale (5 being the best) and added up, yielding totals between 5 and 25. The results are reproduced here in Table V4.4c.ii.

In both Tables V4.4c.i and ii, the European zone is easily the most advanced as regards gender equality, with even its lowest ranked countries often having higher scores than those in the top ranks of the other zones. The Islamic world generally has the countries with the lowest scores, with Latin America, Asia, and Africa (in about that order) being in the middle.

V4.4d. Constitutions and Courts

If the civil rights of citizens are to be respected, then the state must operate according to some guidelines which define its relationship to the individual. Most countries claim to respect some such set of constitutional rules even if they might be honored in the breach (Ladd, 1985; Falk, 1979). Unfortunately, many governments—most notably those 40 or so described in Chapters 1 and 5 as military coup regimes—have suspended their countries' basic law.

"Martial law" will be defined here as the general exercise of all state powers by *military* governments, and includes putting the entire judicial system under military courts, making it easier to convict and imprison anyone disagreeing with the military seizure of power (including members of the recently replaced government). A "state of emergency" enables even *civilian* administrations to assume special temporary powers which are often used to arrest and detain persons without benefit of trial or other forms of due process, to engage in improper surveillances and other violations of individuals' privacy, and to invoke curfews and other restrictions upon people's movements.

Such states of suspended law are frequently invoked by governments (both military and civilian) when they are challenged by insurgencies or riots, and sometimes even when they are faced with more peaceful general strikes or mass political demonstrations. In these situations, the state of emergency can provide an excuse for the government to crack down on opponents of the regime, and a cover for gross abuses of human rights (Chowdhury, 1989). Even if this does not occur, the mere existence of a state of emergency often becomes an issue between the government and the opposition, as the excerpts relating to Jordan and South Africa in Table V4.4d.i indicate.

This table summarizes a 1990 survey which indicates that 21 countries (in addition to most of Chapter 5's military regimes) were under some form of emergency rule, with special laws suspending normal due process in at least parts of the land. Nine of these states were listed as beset by insurgency or civil war in section V1.1b, a situation that might be deemed a mitigating circumstance behind the decision to invoke such special powers. On the other hand, several countries (e.g., Egypt, Zambia, Indonesia, Brunei, Paraguay) seem to be under a more or less permanent state of siege with no obvious insurgent activity to justify this policy.

The data bank's historic record of countries with recently removed states of emergency (excerpts of which are provided on the bottom of Table V4.4d.i) reveals that Taiwan's had been in effect for some 38 years, and that others (Argentina, Bolivia) are invoked for only brief periods of economic austerity. Whatever the reason and however long the time, the point is that governments can use the state of suspended law to override the civil rights of ordinary citizens.

The rule of law is also significant in defining the relationship between the executive apparatus of the state and its citizenry in normal times. The existence of an independent judiciary sets limits upon the actions a state may legally take vis-a-vis its people. This relationship in turn is determined by the degree of subservience or dominance between the courts (particularly the highest court in the land) and the executive branch of government. This equation is influenced by such factors as how many actors within the political system have control over the appointment and dismissal of judges; the term of office of judicial appointees; and whether the courts have judicial review powers—i.e., can the courts declare actions of the government to be illegal or unconstitutional?

With respect to the appointment of judges to the national court, the best way to ensure judicial independence is to have more than one political actor involved, such as (a) the head of government recommending names for approval by (b) a representative assembly, with final appointment by (c) the head of state. In many countries, only one or two of the above participants are involved; in one-party states, the input of the ruling party may be the only significant factor. (For variations of practice across different cultural traditions, see Butler, annually; Fletcher, 1987; Khadduri, 1984).

Concerning term of office, to be independent, judges should not serve terms concurrent with those of their appointers. Most states ensure judges have fixed terms longer than that of the executive or legislative branch of the government which names them (i.e., generally in the range of 5 to 10 years, often until some fixed age like 65-70, sometimes for life).

Finally, many high courts have powers of review over civil and criminal matters adjudicated in lower courts, and over political matters decided at lower levels of government in federal or decentralized systems. Very few courts have such judicial review power with respect to acts of the national executive or legislative branches of the government (Cappellitti, 1971).

Table V4.4d.ii draws upon Humana (Question #27) to assess the independence of countries' court systems. Although dated and covering only 88 states, the Humana results are instructive. Except for the evolving situation in eastern Europe, this is not a relationship that varies much over time, even as governmental administrations and systems change in most other countries (Berman and Hazard, 1987). The independence of the judiciary must be interpreted relative to each state's political and cultural system and to other sharers of political power as this concept is discussed in section V5.2 (Bassiouni, 1982; Liebesny, 1983; Verner, 1984). It must also reflect the reality of corruption, bribery, and intimidation in each state, as compared with the ideal relationship described in its constitution. Finally, as mentioned at the outset of this section, military coups and states of emergency often suspend the normal functioning of the court system in any case.

V4.4e. Transition: From Civil to Political Rights

In this section on civil rights, the concentration has been on how governments treat their people, with an emphasis on private individuals in essentially apolitical situations. The next section will focus upon the activities of such persons in social groups which have a *potential* political influence. (Chapter 5 on political participation will analyze how citizens can more directly affect their government through societal institutions with an *explicitly* political purpose like political parties and representative assemblies.)

The annual Freedom House survey bridges the gap between these concepts by dividing its central concept of "freedom" into "civil liberties" and "political rights" (roughly equivalent to the way the terms "civil rights" and "personal freedoms" are used in sections 4 and 5 of this chapter). Freedom House has not always been explicit in defining what was included within each of these two phrases in substantiating the 1-through-7 scores given to states in each category. In a recent report (FH87: 9-10), 13 factors were mentioned as entering into the *civil* liberties judgments. About one-half of them relate to human and civil rights already covered here in sections V4.3 and .4 (e.g., freedom from government-organized terror, torture, imprisonment, or exile for reasons of conscience; freedom of movement and privacy; and an independent judiciary). The remaining ones pertain to the activities of organized groups with political potential (such as freedom of assembly and demonstration; freedom for the print and broadcast media; free trade unions, business, professional, and other private organizations; and free religious institutions), and are covered in the next section V4.5. (The 11 factors reflected in Freedom House's *political* rights scores generally include the kinds of issues which will be analyzed in Chapter 5.)

As a transition to these more political concepts, Freedom House's scores for states in civil liberties and political rights for the years 1980-89 will be presented in Tables V4.4e.i and ii. Although Freedom House's global reports go back to 1973, the most recent 10-year period of time is selected for analysis in order to avoid some of the anomalies of the first few years of the Freedom House survey (e.g., dividing South Africa into black and white populations; treating Vietnam as two states, divided Cyprus as one; omitting several countries which were not independent before 1978). A rolling 10-year average, moreover, is easier to update for future years than the cumulative record going back to the start of the survey. It is also more representative of long-term societal behavior than scores from the most recent year only. For all its methodological faults and ideological biases, Freedom House is distinguished for its longevity and regularity of appearance. Its technique has also improved and become more explicit over the years.

V4.4a - Due Process: Arrest and Detention; Fair Trial

Europe	Islamic	Africa	Asia	Latin America
		1		
US, Sweden-7			N. Zealand-7	
Denmk.,Neth.-7			Australia-7	
W.Ger.,Switz.-7				
Finld.,Norway-8				
UK,Ireland,8			Japan=8	
Canada-8				
Austria,Belg.-8				
Greece,Port.-9		Botswana-9	Papua NG-9	Jamaica-10
France-10				Costa Rica-11
	Israel-11			Dom.Rep.-11
				Argentina-11
		2		
Spain-12		Senegal-12		Venezuela-12
				Panama-13
				Trinidad-13
Hungary-14	Algeria-14			Ecuador-14
		Sierra L.-15		
Italy-16				Brazil-17
	Egypt-17		Sri Lanka-17	Bolivia-17
		3		
	Tunisia-18			
Yugoslavia-19	Kuwait-19		India-19	
	Morocco-20	Cameroon-21		Colombia-20
		Benin-21		
		Tanzania-21		Peru-22
	Saudi A.-22	Zambia-21	Singapore-22	Mexico-22
	Turkey-23	Zimbabwe-23	Thailand-23	Paraguay-23
		4		
		Nigeria-24	Taiwan-24	
Czech.-25		Kenya-25	Indonesia-25	Chile-25
Bulgaria-25		Liberia-25	Bangladesh-25	
	Syria-26	Mozambique-25	S. Korea 25	
Poland-26	Pakistan-26	Ghana-26	Malaysia-25	
E.Germany-26	Libya-26	Zaire-26	Phil. I.-26	Cuba-26
		Ethiopia-26	China-26	
USSR-27	Iraq-27	S. Africa-26	N. Korea-27	Haiti-27
Romania-27			Vietnam-28	
n=26	n=12	n=16	n=17	n=17 (88)

Source: Humana, 1986, Question 13 (x weight of 3) plus Questions #30-33 (all with weight of 1 and combined), n=88.

V4.4b.i - Freedom of Movement

Europe	Islamic	Africa	Asia	Latin America

1- Generally Free (n=65)

Europe	Islamic	Africa	Asia	Latin America
US,Canada	Bahrain	Cape Verde	India,Nepal	St.C.,St.L.,St.V.
Belg.,Neth.,Lux.	UAE	Senegal	Mald.,Seych.	Antig.,Bah.,Barb.
UK,Ireland		Nigeria	Comoro,Madagscr.	Dom.,Dom.Rep.
Iceland,France	Djibouti		Mauritius	Trin.,Gren.,Jam.
Norway,Sweden	Algeria	Gabon	Japan	Mexico,Belize
Finlnd,Denmark			Brunei,Fiji	C.Rica, Panama
Austr.,W.Ger.		Namibia	Austral.,N.Zealand	Venezuela
Switz.,Italy		Botswana	PapuaNG,Sol.	Bolivia
Spain,Portugal			Vanuatu,WSam.	Brazil
Greece,Yugo.				

2 - Some Restrictions (n=53)

Europe	Islamic	Africa	Asia	Latin America
Malta	Libya,Tunisia	Ghana,Gambia	Bangla.,Bhutan	Haiti
	Egypt,Sudan	Togo,Iv.Coast	China,Taiwan	Sur.,Guy.
E.Germany	Kuwait,Iran	Benin, Eq.G.	Thailand	Hond., Guat.
Hungary	Lebanon	Guinea,GBiss.	Singapore	Colombia
Poland	Israel	Burkina F.,Mali	S.Korea	Chile, Peru
Czech.	Pakistan	S.Leone,Niger	Sri Lanka	Argentina
		Liberia,C.Af.R.	Malaysia	Ecuador
		Kenya,Burundi	Phil. I.	Uruguay
		Lesotho		Paraguay

3 - More Limits (n=33)

Europe	Islamic	Africa	Asia	Latin America
	Morocco	Zimbabwe	Indonesia	
USSR	Chad,Mauritan.	Zaire,Congo		
Romania	Saudi A.	Cameroon,STP		Cuba
Bulgaria	Qatar,Oman	Tanzania,Rwan.	Nicaragua	
	N.Yem.,S.Yem.	Zambia,Uganda	Vietnam	El Salvador
	Turkey,Cyprus	Malawi,Swazi.		
	Syria,Jordan	Angol.,Mozamb.		

4 - Intensive Controls (n=11)

Europe	Islamic	Africa	Asia	Latin America
	Afghanistan	Ethiopia	N.Korea	
Albania	Iraq		Laos,Cambodia	
	Somalia	S.Africa	Myanmar	
			Mongolia	
n=30	n=28	n=38	n=33	n=33 (162)

Source: Humana, 1986, Qu.#1 -2; supplemented by FH88-90, AI87-90, DOS87-90, and other human rights reports excerpted in V4.4b data bank.

V4.4b.ii - Right to Privacy

Europe	Islamic	Africa	Asia	Latin America

1 - Limited Government Interference with Legal Guidelines (n=51)

Europe	Islamic	Africa	Asia	Latin America
US, Canada			Australia	Argentina,Venez.
UK, Ireland			New Zealand	Boliv.,Uruguay
Iceland,Norway		Senegal	Maldives	Costa Rica
Sweden,Finland			Mauritius	Honduras,Belize
Denmk.,W.Ger.		Sierra L.	W. Samoa	Dom.,Dom.Rep.
France, Luxmbg.			Vanuatu	Bahamas,Barbados
Belgium,Nethrlds.			Papua NG	St.C.,St.L.,St.V.
Austria,Switz.			Solomons I.	Antigua
Port.,Spain		Botswana	Japan	Grenada
Italy,Greece			Thailand	Trinidad
Malta				
n=21	n=0	n=3	n=10	n=17

2 - Some Reports of Government Interference (n=45)

Europe	Islamic	Africa	Asia	Latin America
Poland	Cyprus	CV,Gambia	Sri Lanka	Brazil
Hungary	Israel	Iv.Coast,C.Af.R.	Bangladesh	Colombia
	Kuwait	Ghana,Congo	India,Bhutan	Ecuador
	Jordan	Mali,Cameroon	Seychelles	Peru
	Egypt	Nigeria,Benin	Madagascar	Mexico
	Algeria	Zambia,Bur.	Sing.,Taiwan	Jamaica
	Tunisia	Zimbwe.,Swazi.	Phil.I.,Fiji	Suriname
	Djibouti	Les.,Namibia	Mongolia	Guyana

3 - Government Frequently Intervenes in Citizens' Lives (n=38)

Europe	Islamic	Africa	Asia	Latin America
E.Germany	Pak.,Turkey	GBissau,Niger	S. Korea	Chile
Czech.	Lebanon,Iraq	BF,Togo	Malaysia	Paraguay
	Saudi A.,Oman	Guinea,Eq.G.	Indonesia	
	UAE,Qatar	STP,Liberia	Brunei	Guatemala
	N.Yem.,S.Yem.	Rwanda,Zaire		Panama
	Morocco	Tanzania	Comoros	
	Chad,Bahrain	Ang.,Mozambq.	Nepal	

4 - Right to Privacy Generally Does Not Exist (n=28)

Europe	Islamic	Africa	Asia	Latin America
USSR	Iran	Ethiopia	Vietnam	Nicaragua
Romania	Afghanistan	Kenya	Cambodia	El Salvador
Yugoslavia	Syria,Libya	Uganda	Laos	
Bulgaria	Somalia	Malawi	Myanmar	Haiti
Albania	Sudan	Gabon	China	Cuba
	Mauritania	S. Africa	N. Korea	
n=30	n=28	n=38	n=33	n=33

Source: Humana, 1986, Qu. #18, 34, 35 (similarly weighted); supplemented by FH88-90, AI87-90, DOS87-90, and other human rights reports.

V4.4c.i - Women:Men Ratios in 3 Areas (men=100%)

Europe	Islamic	Africa	Asia	Latin America

(a) - Ratio of Women's to Men's Literacy Rate

Europe	Islamic	Africa	Asia	Latin America
18	Israel 96	Lesotho 136	Australia 100	Jamaica 102
@	Cyprus 93	S.Africa 100	N.Zealand 100	Cuba 100
100%	Lebanon 80	Botswana 96	Japan 100	Nicaragua 100
	Kuwait 77	Swaziland 94	Phil. I. 99	6 @
	Jordan 76	Tanzania 90	Mongolia 95	99
....	....	....	....	....
Spain 95	Saudi A.43	Benin 44	Papua NG 64	El Salvador 92
Malta 95	N.Yemen 42	Burundi 44	India 57	Peru 86
Portugal 91	Somalia 33	Gambia 42	Bangladesh 52	Bolivia 77
Greece 90	Chad 28	Guinea 42	Cambodia 50	Haiti 76
Yugoslavia 87	S.Yemen 11	Burkina F. 29	Nepal 21	Guatemala 75
n=29/30	n=22/28	n=33/38	n=21/33	n=24/33 (129)

(b) - Ratio of Women to Men in Higher Education

Europe	Islamic	Africa	Asia	Latin America
E.Germany 141	Qatar 162	Lesotho 153	Mongolia 142	Panama 120
Poland 123	Kuwait 122	Swaziland 107	Phil. I. 120	Brazil 116
Bulgaria 113	Israel 104	Botswana 86	Brunei 96	Uruguay 113
Hungary 107	UAE 93	Zimbwe. 57	Thailand 85	Guyana 107
Canada 107	Cyprus 80	Mozambq. 44	Australia 84	Argentina 103
....	....	....	....	....
UK 60	Turkey 36	Mali 18	China 36	Peru 54
Iceland 57	Libya 30	Zambia 18	Cambodia 36	Mexico 53
Switzrld. 48	Somalia 20	Congo 18	Nepal 26	Bolivia 50
Luxmbrg. 40	N.Yemen 17	Ghana 17	Papua NG 26	Haiti 43
Malta 25	Chad 14	Eq. Guinea 10	Bangladesh 22	Guatemala 37
n=30	n=23/28	n=32/38	n=23/33	n=24/33 (132)

(c) - Ratio of Women to Men in Labor Force

Europe	Islamic	Africa	Asia	Latin America
USSR 88	Turkey 59	Rwanda 90	Thailand 84	Haiti 79
Poland 83	Cyprus 54	C.Af.R. 88	N.Korea 82	Jamaica 64
Czech. 83	Israel 43	Mali 88	Madagascar 79	Barbados 63
E.Germany 81	Somalia 40	Botswana 87	Laos 79	Trinidad 45
Romania 80	Chad 30	Burkina F. 86	Vietnam 78	Uruguay 42
....	....	....	....	....
Luxmbrg 38	Saudi A. 6	2 @ 45	Singapore 38	El Salvador 26
Nethrlds. 35	S.Yemen 6	Zimbwe. 41	Sri Lanka 35	Mexico 25
Portugal 32	Libya 6	Mozambq. 33	Bangladesh 22	Guatemala 17
Spain 27	Iraq 5	Niger 12	Fiji 15	Honduras 16
Malta 26	N.Yemen 4	Angola 10	Mauritius 6	Dom.Rep. 15
n=30	n=20/28	n=33/38	n=23/33	n=24/33 (130)

Source: Sivard,*Women*, 1985. (*US figures are: 100, 104, and 61.*)

V4.4c.ii - Gender Gaps in 5 Areas*

Europe	Islamic	Africa	Asia	Latin America
Finland 23.5				
USSR,Sweden-23				
US,Norway-22				
E.Germany 21.5				
Canada 21.5				
Denmark 21.5				
Czech. 21.5			Australia 21.5	
Bulgaria 21.5				Jamaica 21
Hungary 21.5				Barbados 20
Austria 21				Uruguay 19.5
Poland 21			New Zealand 20.5	Panama 19
Belgium 20.5				Costa Rica 18.5
France 20.5				Trinidad 18.5
W.Germany 20.5				Cuba 18
Nethrlds. 20.5			Phil. I. 18.5	Argentina 18
UK 20				Mexico 17.5
Switzerland 20			Japan 18	Ecuador 17.5
Portugal 19.5		Botswana 18		El Salvador 17.5
Yugoslavia 19			Thailand 17	Dom.Rep. 17.5
Italy 19	Israel 17.5		Singapore 17	Venezuela 17
Romania 19				Guyana 17
Spain 18				Colombia 16.5
Greece 17.5		Mozambique 16.5		Chile 16.5
Ireland 17			Sri Lanka 16.5	Nicaragua 16.5
			S. Korea 16.5	Paraguay 16
		S. Africa 15.5		Peru 15
	Algeria 14.5	Benin 14.5	Taiwan 16	Brazil 15
		Zambia 14	China 15.5	Honduras 15
		Lesotho 13.5	Malaysia 15.5	Bolivia 14.5
		Zimbabwe 13.5	India 14	Guatemala 14.5
	Turkey 13	Kenya 12.5	Indonesia 13	Haiti 14.5
		Rwanda 12.5	Nepal 12.5	
		Cameroon 12		
	Jordan 11.5	Senegal 12		
	UAE 10.5	Tanzania 12		
	Iraq 10.5	Malawi 11.5		
	Afghanistan 10.5	Liberia 11.5		
	Tunisia 10.5			
	N. Yemen 10			
	Sudan 10			
	Kuwait 10	Mali 10		
	Morocco 9.5			
	Pakistan 9.5			
	Libya 9			
	Syria 8.5	Nigeria 8.5		
	Egypt 7.5			
	Saudi A. 6.5		Bangladesh 5.5	
n=26/30	n=17/28	n=16/38	n=15/33	n=24/33 (98)

Source: Population Crisis Committee, Population Briefing Paper, No. 20, June, 1988; *composite scores (5 through 25) for health, marriage, education, employment and social equality.

V4.4d.i - (Non-military) Regimes under States of Emergency, 1990

(most states designated mil^, mil° in Chapter 5 are under martial law by definition)

	V1.1b
UK — in N.Ireland — via special Prevention of Terrorism acts of 1973, '78, '84, '87.	Yes
USSR — peridocially, since 1986, in response to ethnic unrest in *Armenia, Azerbaijan, Georgia, Uzbekistan,* and other nationality-based republics.	
Israel — some emergency leg. since 1948; St. of Emerg. in Occup.Territories after 12/87.	Yes
Lebanon — since 1975 civil war outbreak.	Yes
Jordan — declared in 6/67, reaffirmed in 1973; all cands. in 11/89 election oppose it.	
Turkey — in 9 of 67 *Kurd* provinces still despite '83 return to civilian rule; martial law lifted, 7/87, in 4 southeast provs., but emerg.regs. allow civ.govts. some mil. powers.	Yes
Egypt — under emerg. laws for much of last 40 years; especially since 10/81 Sadat assassination, renewed ev. 3 yrs. (most recently in 3/88) to control Islamic Funds.	
Senegal — after 2/88 election violence; spring '89 during anti-*Mauritanian* unrest.	
Zambia — since 1964 independence!	
Zimbabwe — almost continuous since 1960 under 3 regimes; until 7/90 removal.	
S. Africa — declared 6/12/86; renewals in 6/87, 6/88; removed in three of four provinces (not Natal), 6/90; as part of ANC conditions for talks.	
India — since '82 v. Punjab *Sikhs*; esp. after 1984 Temple massacre & PM assass.; 1987 Terrorist Prevention Act esp. applied here & vs. *Kashmiri Moslems* in 1989ff.	Yes
Sri Lanka — 7/79-1/89 vs. *Tamils*, under Prevention of Terrorism Act which permits 3 yrs. aa&d, military "disposal of bodies" w/out supervision; 7/89ff vs. *Sinhalese* JVP.	Yes
Malaysia — esp. since 1969 Spec. Powers Act vs. "*Chinese* riots", no rallies, etc. Though Legislature regained its power in 1971, special laws remain on books.	
Singapore — Special Powers Act applied to dissidents in 1988 ended judicial review, etc.	
China — in parts of Beijing, 5/20/89-1/11/90, used to crush 6/89 Tienanminh Square student demonstrations; also in *Tibet*, 3/89-4/90.	
Indonesia — since 1957, and esp. after 1965/66 in *E. Timor, Irian Jaya,* and Lampung.	
Brunei — since 1962, Internal Security Act renewed every 2 yrs. used to keep opp. detained.	
Peru — since 6/84, in about 20%(~40 of 180) provs. in the eastern and mountain regions; in 10/89 pre-local elections in 8 Depts. (of 24) with 60% land, 50% population; in 8/90 in whole country for economic reasons.	Yes
Colombia — periodically since '81 as 220 judges & court employees killed; esp. after 3/84 assass. of Justice Min.; also in '88, and after 8/89 declaration of "war against drugs."	Yes
El Salvador — from 10/79 coup to 1987; again after 11/89 FMNLF offensive.	Yes

Tot.Yes=9/22

(Non-Mil.) Regimes with *Recent* "State of Emergency" Experience

(includes some which may have been designated "mil" regimes during some of this time)

Poland — from 12/81 to 10/85 (designated mil^ in V5.1a then).

Pakistan — from 1965-85, under three regimes; also 8/88-11/88 and 8/90ff transitions.

Gambia — from 9/81 through 2/85.   Sierra Leone — emerg. econ. legislation; ended 1987.

Cameroon — 1984-1989.   Gabon — in Port Gentil, 5/90.

Bangladesh — 3/82-11/86 and 11/87-4/88.   Mauritius — 1968-70; 1971-78.

Thailand — 10/77-8/84.   Phil. I. — under Marcos, 1972-81.

Taiwan — From 1949 to 1987, 38 yrs.!   S. Korea — under "Public Security Law", 1981-88.

Nicaragua — from 2/82 (start of US/contra war) to 1/88 (Arias peace plan ceasefire).

Bolivia — 90 da. in '89, 180 da. in '86 for economic reasons.   Trinidad — abu Bakr coup, 7/90.

Argentina — 30 da. in Su.'89 during govt. transition, for economic reasons.

   Plus: All military regimes coded mil^ or mil° in Chapter 5, Table V5.1a.

Source: DOS86f85 thru 90f89; as updated in *New York Times* through mid-1990.

V4.4d.ii - Independent Court Systems

Europe	Islamic	Africa	Asia	Latin America
		1 (n=32)		
Denmark	Israel		Australia	Costa Rica
Sweden		Senegal	New Zealand	
Finland				
Norway				
Netherlands	Kuwait			Jamaica
Ireland			Japan	Trinidad
Belgium		Botswana		
UK, France			Papua NG	Bolivia
W.Ger.,Switz.				Peru
Spain,Portugal				Argentina
Italy, Greece				Venezuela
US, Canada				
		2 (n=23)		
Austria	Egypt	Benin	India	Dom. Rep.
	Tunisia	Kenya	Bangladesh	Ecuador
	Algeria	Tanzania	Sri Lanka	Panama
	Morocco	Zambia	Thailand	Brazil
	Saudi A.	Zimbabwe	Malaysia	
		S. Africa	Singapore	
			S.Korea	
		3 (n=14)		
Hungary		Sierra Leone	China	Mexico
Czech.		Liberia	Taiwan	Paraguay
Bulgaria		Cameroon	Phil. I.	Chile
		Mozambique	Indonesia	
		4 (n=19)		
Yugoslavia	Turkey	Zaire	Vietnam	Colombia
Romania	Iraq	Nigeria	N. Korea	Haiti
E. Germany	Pakistan	Ghana		Cuba
Poland	Syria	Ethiopia		
USSR	Libya			
n=26	n=12	n=16	n=17	n=17 (88)

Source: Humana, 1986, Question #27; n=88

V4.4e.i - Civil Liberties - 1980-89 10-yr. FH Average

Europe	Islamic	Africa	Asia	Latin America
US,UK-1			Australia 1.0	Costa Rica 1.0
Ire.,Ice.-1			N. Zealand 1.0	Barbados 1.2
Canada,Norway 1			Japan 1.0	
Belg.,Neth.-1				Belize 1.6
Luxembrg. 1			Papua NG 2.0	Trinidad 1.7
Denmk,Swed.-1		Botswana 2.9	Solomons 2.1	Dominica 1.9
Austria,Switz.-1		Namibia 3.0^	Mauritius 2.5	St. Vincent 2.0
	Israel 2.0	Gambia 3.2	Fiji 2.7	St. Chris. 2.0
Italy 1.4	Cyprus 2.0		W.Samoa 2.8	Venezuela 2.1
		Senegal 3.8	India 2.9	St.Lucia 2.2
W.Germany 1.9				Bahamas 2.3
Finland 1.9			Thailand 3.5	Ecuador 2.3
France 2.0			Vanuatu 3.6	
Portugal 2.0		Nigeria 4.1	Phil. I. 3.7	Brazil 2.6
Greece 2.0	Lebanon 4.3		Sri Lanka 3.8	Argentina 2.7
Spain 2.1	Kuwait 4.3			Antigua 2.7
	Turkey 4.3		Nepal 4.1	Jamaica 2.7
Malta 2.9		Uganda 4.6		Dom.Rep.2.8
	Egypt 4.5		Bangladesh 4.4	Honduras 3.0
		Sierra Leone 5.0	Malaysia 4.5	Colombia 3.1
	Morocco 4.7	Kenya 5.0	Taiwan 4.6	Peru 3.2
Hungary 4.6	Pakistan 4.7	Ivory Coast 5.1	S.Korea 4.8	Grenada 3.3
Poland 4.6		Lesotho 5.2	Singapore 4.9	Uruguay 3.4
	Bahrain 4.8	Liberia 5.2	Bhutan 5.0	Bolivia 3.4
Yugoslavia 4.9	Tunisia 4.8	BF,Ghana-5.2		Mexico 3.8
		Zimbabwe 5.2		El Salvador 4.1
	Qatar 5.0	Zambia 5.3	Brunei 5.2	Suriname 4.1
	UAE 5.0	Swaziland 5.5	Comoros 5.2	Panama 4.2
	N.Yemen 5.0		Maldives 5.3	
		C.Af.R. 5.8	Indonesia 5.4	
	Jordan 5.4	Gabon 5.9	Madagascar 5.5	
	Djibouti 5.4	S.Africa 5.9		Guatemala 4.5
	Sudan 5.5	Niger 6.0		Guyana 4.6
		Mali,Rwanda-6.0		Chile 4.7
	Iran 5.8	Togo,Tanzania-6.0		
Czech. 6.0	Algeria 5.8	C.Verde 6.1	Seychelles 5.9	Nicaragua 5.0
	Oman 6.0	Burundi 6.1	China 6.0	Paraguay 5.1
	Mauritania 6.0	Guinea 6.1		Haiti 5.4
	Libya 6.2	Congo,Cameroon 6.2		
E.Germany 6.3		GBissau 6.3		Cuba 6.1
USSR 6.4		Eq.Guin.6.4		
	Chad 6.5	Zaire 6.5	Myanmar 6.6	
Romania 6.6	Saudi A. 6.6	STP 6.5		
	Syria 6.7	Benin 6.6	Vietnam 6.8	
	Iraq 6.9	Malawi 6.9	Laos 6.9	
	Afghanistan 6.9	Mozambique 6.9	Cambodia 7.0	
Bulgaria 7.0	Somalia 7.0	Ethiopia 7.0	N.Korea 7.0	
Albania 7.0	S.Yemen 7.0	Angola 7.0	Mongolia 7.0	
n=30	n=28	n=38	n=33	n=33 (162)

Source: Gastil, 1988-89; plus *Freedom at Issue*, January/February 1990; ^ = 1989 only.

V4.4e.ii - Political Rights - 1980-89 10-yr. FH Average

Europe	Islamic	Africa	Asia	Latin America
US,Canada-1			Australia 1.0	Costa Rica 1.0
Iceld.,Ireld.-1			N.Zealand 1.0	Venezuela 1.0
UK,Norway-1			Japan 1.1	Barbados 1.0
France,WGer-1	Cyprus 1.4			Belize 1.1
BeNeLux-1			Solomons 1.9	Dom.Rep. 1.3
Denmk,Swed-1	Israel 2.0	Botswana 1.9	Mauritius 2.0	Trinidad 1.3
Aust.,Switz.-1		Gambia 2.7	India 2.0	St.C.,St. L.-1.4
Italy 1.1	Turkey 3.2		Papua NG 2.0	Bahamas 1.6
Portugal 1.3		Senegal 3.5	Vanuatu 2.1	St. Vincent 1.7
Spain 1.3				Jamaica 2.0
			Sri Lanka 2.8	Dominica 2.0
		Namibia 4.0^	Thailand 3.0	Antigua 2.0
Greece 1.6	Morocco 3.9	Zimbabwe 4.3	Fiji 3.1	Ecuador 2.0
Finland 1.7				Colombia 2.1
Malta 1.7		Nigeria 4.6	Malaysia 3.3	Peru 2.3
			Nepal 3.3	
		S.Africa 5.0		Honduras 2.8
	Egypt 4.8	SLeone 5.0	Phil. I. 3.8	Brazil 2.9
	Djibouti 4.9	Lesotho 5.1	W.Samoa 3.8	Bolivia 3.1
		Uganda 5.1		Argentina 3.2
	Lebanon 5.0	Swaziland 5.1	S.Korea 4.0	Mexico 3.4
	UAE 5.1	Zambia 5.1	Bangladesh 4.2	Uruguay 3.5
	Sudan 5.1		Singapore 4.2	Grenada 3.7
	Kuwait 5.2			El Salvador 3.7
	Pakistan 5.2	Ghana 5.4	Bhutan 4.9	
	Qatar 5.2	Kenya 5.5	Comoros 5.0	Guatemala 4.1
	Iran 5.3	Liberia 5.5	Taiwan 5.0	
	Tunisia 5.4		Indonesia 5.0	Suriname 4.8
	Bahrain 5.4		Maldives 5.0	Guyana 4.8
	N.Yemen 5.4	Cape Verde 5.8	Madagascar 5.3	Paraguay 5.0
	Jordan 5.5	Ivory Coast 5.8		Panama 5.2
		Gabon,Tanzan.-6.0		Nicaragua 5.2
	Syria 5.8	Rwan.,Camrn.-6.0		
		GBiss.,BFaso-6.1		
Hungary 5.4	Algeria 6.0	Malawi 6.1	Seychelles6.0	Chile 5.7
Poland 5.5	Oman 6.0	Zaire 6.3	Brunei 6.0	
	Saudi A. 6.1	Togo,Mozmbq.-6.4		
Yugoslavia 5.9	Libya 6.1	STP 6.5	China 6.1	Cuba 6.2
	S.Yemen 6.2	C.Af.R. 6.7		
		Mali 6.8		
USSR 6.4		Ethiopia 6.8		Haiti 6.5
	Iraq 6.7	Angola 7.0	Vietnam 6.8	
Czech. 6.9	Chad 6.7	Burundi 7.0	Laos 6.8	
E.Germany 6.9	Mauritania 6.7	Guinea 7.0		
		Benin 7.0	Myanmar 7.0	
Romania 7.0	Afghanistan 6.9	Eq. Guinea 7.0	Cambodia 7.0	
Bulgaria 7.0		Niger 7.0	Mongolia 7.0	
Albania 7.0	Somalia 7.0	Congo 7.0	N.Korea 7.0	
n=30	n=28	n=38	n=33	n=33 (162)

Source: Gastil, 1988-89; plus *Freedom at Issue*, January/February 1990; ^ = 1989 only.

V4.5. PERSONAL FREEDOMS (POTENTIAL POLITICAL RIGHTS)

Whereas section V4.3 covered activities which ought to be prohibited to governments (i.e., violations to the integrity of the person), and V4.4 treated those policies which should be carried on by governments only under legal guidelines (i.e., arrests, detentions, trials, invasions of privacy, restrictions of movement), V4.5 investigates certain personal freedoms of individuals vis-a-vis governments which many states do not even recognize (Bollen, 1986; Lungu, 1986; Beer, 1984). These liberties are often dismissed as "bourgeois freedoms" to be considered expendable when they come into conflict with governmental authority. Nevertheless, they are formally enumerated in the International Bill of Human Rights' conventions which many countries from many cultures have endorsed. Hence, they can be analyzed from a global perspective just as the previous two categories.

V4.5a. Freedom of Expression

Freedom of expression is defined here to cover one's thoughts and opinions, especially as these might be expressed in public speech and associations. A continuum can be elaborated wherein one first has an independent thought ("conscience") about which he or she feels compelled to express an opinion. Such "speech" might be made in private to family or close friends, or in larger groups organized together (in "assembly") for purposes of acting upon the expressed ideas. It is these larger associations which will be analyzed in this section as this narrative moves its focus from individual behavior to wider societal and political group activity.

Personal religious preferences, speech in limited social arenas, and associations of people for artistic, athletic, or cultural endeavors are examples of freedom of expression which are generally not infringed upon by governments. However, such personal freedoms, if developed in the context of certain organized groups, can become highly political. For example, religious freedom expressed as the demands of an organized clerical institution, is an especially potent political force in many Catholic and Islamic countries. Freedom of speech, if carried on with the resources of a newspaper, radio, or television station, moves from the category of personal liberty into more public behavior. Finally, freedom of association translates in the workplace into the forming of labor unions, and in the arena of public policy into the creation of political parties.

Chapter 5 covers *explicit* political participation and adapts a framework in which the political party is the most distinguishing characteristic. This section of this chapter will restrict its analysis to such *potentially* political groups as organized religions (.5b), the press (.5c), and labor unions (.5d). (For economic institutions with obvious political impact (capitalist entrepreneurs, multinational corporations, etc.), see section V2.4c where the percentage of private vs. public consumption is measured, and V5.3e and .4d where the terms left, right, socialist, and capitalist are employed in connection with governmental types and political parties. See also Mower, 1985; Siegel, 1984; and Howard, 1983.)

Before studying the latest global findings with respect to these three specific group-manifestations of freedom of expression and association, a brief reference to Humana's work on the most general forms of peaceful association and assembly will be made. His Question #3 deals with the ability of "ordinary citizens" (i.e., those not permanently organized into parties, unions, or other long-standing pressure groups) to hold mass meetings and public demonstrations. Even in the freest societies a permit is often required, though it is usually granted unless some threat to public safety is anticipated. In other states a great deal more harassment and restriction occur of any group deemed likely to criticize the state, its personnel, ideology, or policies. Because this type of government activity is widespread and difficult to document, especially with respect to peripheral groups, Humana's 1986 results (24 states in Category 1, 16 in 2, 19 in 3, and 29 in 4) are not easily updated and therefore will not be displayed here.

Rather, in the next three sections on specific, more well-established associations, the surveys of group-state relations with respect to freedom of expression will draw upon several sources and return to their global and more current scope. Before leaving this section, however, two other aspects of the general concept of freedom of expression should be addressed: things that cannot be said, and the requirement of official registration with the state.

A complete list of "taboo topics" around the world would be difficult to catalogue. In general, such words or thoughts are those most intimately involved with a country's ideology. For example, in Turkey communism cannot be advocated, and in Pinochet's Chile (1973-89) not even Marxism. In Taiwan, a 10-year jail sentence can result from suggesting the island-state should be independent from China. In many African states advocacy of tribalism or other forms of blatant ethnic appeals are forbidden; in Islamic countries questioning the dominant faith is prohibited; in monarchies the royal family often can't be insulted; and in coup regimes the military cannot be criticized.

Finally, it must be noted that many states require that all explicitly political associations (especially political parties) must be registered with the government before they may legally operate. In some countries (especially one-party communist states), this injunction also applies to associations of cultural, economic, religious, and ethnic groups as well. The reason is to enable the governments to maintain control over them. It is to three such entities—churches, unions, and the mass media—that this study now turns.

V4.5b. Organized Religion

The status of organized religion around the world varies widely, from countries which are openly hostile to religious belief and have outlawed its public practice, to countries which officially embody and promulgate the values of a single state religion. In between these two poles are governments which are avowedly secular and guarantee individuals the freedom to practice whatever religion they prefer.

Two concepts are involved in analyzing this issue: a.) individual freedom of religion (which seldom enters the political arena); and b.) the role of organized religious establishments (which often act politically). Two of this chapter's sources (Barrett, 1982, and Humana, 1986) address these issues in turn. A composite of them both—using the religious sect categories of section V4.2b and the 1-through-4 ranking system, and supplemented by this chapter's other sources—has been developed for use here.

Barrett considers two dimensions—states by religious type, and degree of religious liberty—for the purpose of assessing opportunities for Christianity. First, states are divided into three basic types: atheistic, secular, and religious. In *atheistic* countries (n=29), the state formally promotes irreligion; in *secular* countries (n=53), the state promotes neither religion nor irreligion; in *religious* countries (n=80), the state identifies itself with a particular religion (or religion in general). Among the particular religions with which specific states are identified are Islam (n=25), Roman Catholicism (18), Christianity (4), Lutheranism (4), Buddhism (3), Anglicanism (2), Orthodox Christianity, Hinduism, and Judaism (1 each); 21 states are simply committed to "religion."

Within these three categories, Barrett next ranks states on a scale of 1 through 10 with respect to religious liberty or persecution as concerns Christianity . The criteria—which will be helpful in developing the broader-based scale to be used in this study—are as follows:

1-state propagates Christianity;
2-massive state subsidies to churches;
3-limited state subsidies to churches;
4-state subsidies to church schools only;
5-complete state non-interference;
6-limited restrictions on churches' political activities;
7-state ambivalent toward religion, regulations and subsidies used to control, discrimination against minority religions;
8-state interference and obstruction (including massive subsidies for purposes of surveillance and control);
9-state hostility and prohibition;
10-state suppression or eradication.

The composite summary of state rankings in accordance with Barrett's types and criteria is presented in Table V4.5b.i. Notice that states of all three religious types might rank anywhere along the 1-through-10 degree of freedom scale. Although Barrett is most interested in the status of only one religion (Christianity), his survey is nevertheless most comprehensive (covering 223 states and dependent territories, including all 162 of this study's), and will be used here as a starting point for this work's broader focus upon all the world's religions.

This study next combines Barrett's interest in the status of organized Christian churches with Humana's concern for individual religious freedom, in an effort to develop a measure which adequately conveys freedom from and freedom of religion around the world. Humana asks three questions: a.) whether there is compulsory religious training in schools; b.) whether one has the right to inter-religious or civil (i.e., non-religious) marriage; and c.) whether one has the freedom to practice any religion. His results are incorporated into this project's larger data bank in which countries are divided in the "Christian-Islamic-Other" order of section V4.2b's religious membership data. The typical 1-through-4 scoring framework of this chapter is significantly scrambled here so that *2.5* represents the *preferred mean* of a secular state which guarantees freedom of individual religious belief, and also the right of people to organize themselves into a collective body for religious (but not necessarily political) purposes. The extremes of government favoritism or hostility to religion are coded 1 and 4, respectively. A fuller explanation of the criteria for measuring the status of organized religion in a country is presented in Table V4.5b.ii. Even within this framework there is great difficulty in clearly coding states and a number of them are placed "between categories" in Table V4.5b.iii.

In addition, modifications are needed to adapt this scheme to each major religion, and therefore Table V4.5b.iii superimposes section V4.2b's religious sect divisions over the five geographic zones. A "1" signifying an official state religion in a Christian European state is quite different from a "1" in an Islamic country. In the latter, religion so suffuses daily culture that the "2.5" designation for "secular" is applied to Moslem countries like Turkey and Egypt where, despite the heavy presence of religion in everyday life, there is at least an attempt at separating government from religion (this is even truer in Ba'athist Syria and Iraq).

Within Christian countries, the Protestant tradition is to allow for individual freedom even if there is an official state religion (e.g., the Scandinavian states), whereas in Catholic states there is more merging of church and state, which in some cases (in Latin America and eastern Europe) has led to particularly severe political backlashes against the organized church. Highly organized religious establishments have never been part of African culture, where tolerance for a wide variety of beliefs has been the tradition. The 2.5 preferred mean applies to virtually all of them until some particular religious preferences or persecutions become evident. This is somewhat true also in Asia, more so in the Hindu states than in the Buddhist, but even in the latter, religion has generally been absorbed into wider social codes (note especially China and Japan).

Table V4.5b.iii's two-page spreadsheet adapts these criteria to states within the eight religious traditions and in their various zones, a geographic context which is often important for this measure. Some of the eastern European scores will have to be modified after 1990.

V4.5c. The Press

A step beyond freedom of individual conscience and private speech is the promulgation of one's thoughts through a printed statement, a pamphlet, or (if one is financially well endowed) a regularly appearing newspaper ("the press"), or (if one is extremely wealthy) a radio or television station ("the broadcast media"). Unlike freedom of religion, whose practice often involves masses of people, freedom of the press (as contrasted with freedom of speech) is enjoyed by relatively few. Although significant numbers may read newspapers and even the illiterate may relate to radio and television, the wealth factor in the promulgation of ideas in these ways prompts recall of Benjamin Franklin's remark that freedom of the press is a right reserved for those who own a printing press. In most states, such organs of mass communication as newspapers, magazines, radio, and television are generally under the control of the government and this "bourgeois freedom" is not considered to be one of the rights citizens usually hold vis-a-vis their government (Martin and Chaudhary, 1983; Nimmo and Mansfield, 1982).

Two sources used earlier, Humana and Freedom House, are particularly good at disaggregating and making explicit their measurements when considering categories which fall within the realm of freedom of the press. Although each has an overall Western ideological bias in declaring as "free" media controlled by wealthy entrepreneurs rather than by governments (Smith, 1980), their judgments with respect to the way the term "free" is used in this context are generally sound. The data bank associated with this project (not excerpted here) generally confirms this evaluation, as do other surveys by Curry and Bassin (1982), Merrill (1983), and Boyle (1988).

Humana covers fewer countries (n=88) and is dated, but is better at indicating clearly which of four different factors he is weighing in each instance: is there political censorship of the press, and are there non-governmental (i.e., independent and privately-owned) newspapers, book publishing companies, and radio and television stations. As with his earlier work (on due process and independent judiciaries), the answers to Humana's four questions can be assigned a 1-through-4 rating, which can be added up so that each state has a score between 4 and 16. Table V4.5c.i groups the resulting state clusters into five categories, where 1=4-5-6, 2=7-8-9, 2.5 = 10; 3=11-12-13, and 4=14-15-16.

Freedom House's survey is more recent and includes all 162 states. In the last few years, it has appeared in the form of 1-through-7 scores (paralleling those for civil liberties and political rights) in the January edition of *Freedom at Issue*. Table V4.5c.ii translates these numbers into the 1-through-4 scale of this chapter, with Freedom House's 4—the mid-point between its 1 and 7, being reproduced here as "2.5."

V4.5d. Unions

Trade unions—workers expressing their freedom of association for improvement of their working conditions—can be analyzed with respect to several factors relating to (1) their method of organization, (2) the conditions under which they may strike, and (3) potential involvement in politics (Gladstone et al., 1989; Harper, 1987; Kelly, 1988; Southall, 1987). The 1-to-4 scores applied to each state below reflect a continuum from openness to repression along each of these three dimensions.

With respect to mode of organization, the spectrum varies from unions freely formed by workers not affiliated with the government; to those which are subtly controlled by government via financial subsidies, registration requirements, or other regulations; those which must compete with government-sponsored unions; those which must affiliate with government-sponsored confederations; those which must be approved by the government in order to exist; single national unions which are the monopoly of the government; and the extreme case where all unions are outlawed.

With respect to the right to strike, the ways in which unions are restricted vary from requirements first to go through a "sincere" process of collective bargaining (often as defined by a government ministry); to prohibitions from striking in "essential services" (sometimes defined to include the entire public sector); to the denial of the right to strike at all. In some states the right to strike exists under law, but rarely occurs in reality. In other countries, although strikes are illegal, they do often occur.

Unions might be forbidden to engage in politics at all, be relatively uninvolved in politics and restricted by their own traditions to workplace issues, or be politically powerful with influence over government policies and personnel. General strikes, called for some political (or wider economic policy) purpose, are common in states of the latter group.

Table V4.5d adapts this chapter's 1-through-4 categories to these three criteria so that:

1 = free unions **permitted**; liberal right to strike; politically influential.

2 = government-supported or subsidized (subtly **subverted**, coopted) unions;

some registration requirements; strikes either not allowed or minimally tolerated; unions generally refrain from political activity.

3 = government-approved unions, or mandatory federations; tight registration results in unions being highly **restricted**; strict controls virtually prohibit strikes; unions used as conduit for government policies.

4 = unions and strikes **outlawed**, though the latter may sometimes occur.

There are very few states (n=15) which do not admit at least in theory the right of workers' organizations to exist. Workers' rights are most firmly established in Europe and Latin America where 43 of the 68 countries in Category 1 are found; in some of these places, unions are influential in creating and toppling governments, and the "n=" number found in parentheses after some of the state entries refers to the number of unions (or union confederations) associated with particular political parties.

Table V4.5d lists states within each of the four categories, in order of the percentage of workers in labor unions (where this information is available), and with annotations of the initials of the leading union (or confederation of unions) in countries where such an entity plays a major political role. In the 79 states of Categories 2 and 3, this organization often serves as the government's instrument for coopting or controlling the country's labor movement. In this regard, eight eastern European states have recently been moved in the data bank from Category 3 (indicating they had a single union confederation tied to the ruling party representing almost all workers (Pravda and Ruble, 1986)) to Category 2 (to indicate the continued strength of this entity, initials given in parentheses, plus the existence of new more independent unions).

There are other methods which might be used to measure the status of workers' rights. The International Labour Office (ILO) maintains records on 108 conventions which govern the treatment of workers, and has summarized the number of these signed by some 145 states (ILO, 1984). The results, unfortunately, do not reflect the reality of workers' conditions as much as Table V4.5d's look at actual country behavior does. For example, as of 1984 Cuba led Latin America with 86 international instruments signed, while the United States was last in the European zone with only 7 treaties accepted.

As with the section on human rights (V4.3), data bank excerpts substantiating the rankings of countries in this and the other subsections of V4.4 and V4.5 could be presented, but have been omitted due to space limitations. Production of the complete V4 data bank is planned for a later publication.

V4.5b.i - Freedom for Religion (especially Christianity)

Europe	Islamic	Africa	Asia	Latin America
		atheistic states (n=29)		
		STP -3		
Yugoslavia-6		Benin,Zimb.-6		Gren.^,Nicar.-6
E.Germany^-7		Angol.,Cong.,GB-7	Madagascar-7	
Bulg.,Hung.^-8		Ethiopia-8	Laos,VN-8	Cuba-8
Pol.^,Rom.-8		Guinea,Mozmbq-8		
Czech.^,SU^-9	Afghan.-9		China,Camb.-9	
Albania-10			Mong.,NKorea-10	
n=9	n=1	n=9	n=7	n=3
		secular states (n=53)		
Austria-2			Mauritius-2	St.L.,Suriname-2
Canada-3		Iv.Coast,Bur.-3	N.Zealand-3	Chile,Uruguay-3
Nethrlds.-3		Nigeria-3	Papua NG-3	Jamaica-3
France-4		Sierra L.,Niger-4	Solomons-4	Belize-4
US-4		Senegal,Mali-4	Seychelles-4	St.Chris.-4
	Djibouti-4	CAfR,Camrn.,Ken.-4		St.Vincent-4
		Botswana,Malawi-4	Japan-5	Antigua-5
		Gambia,BF,Tanz.-5	Indon.,Sing.-5	Dominica-5
	Chad-6	Eq.G.,Zamb.,Lesotho-6	Taiwan,SKor.-6	Mexico-6
	Syria-7	CV,Togo,Uganda-7	Comoros-7	
	Turkey-8		Myanmar-8	
n=5	n=4	n=21	n=12	n=11
		®religious states (n=80)		
Belg.,W.Ger.-2			Australia-3	Barbad.,Trinidad-2
Switzrlnd.-2		Gabon,Ghana-4	Indon.,Phil. I.-3	CPeru,Paraguay-2
XFinland-2	IPak*,Jord,Leb-4	Rwanda,Swazi.-4	BThailand-3	CVenez.,Bolivia-2
CSpain,Lux-2	IMauritan.,Tun.-5	XLiberia-4	XVanuatu-3	CCRica,DomRep-2
LIceld,Norway-2	IOman,UAE-6	Fiji-4		Ecuador-3
LSwed.,Denmk-2	JIsrael-6	S.Africa-6	XW.Samoa-4	CGuatemala-3
OGreece-2	Cyprus-7	Zaire-6	IBangladesh-4	ABahamas-4
AUK-3	IBahrain,Iran-7	Namibia-6	IMaldives-5	
CItaly,Malta-3	IIraq,Kuw.,Qat-8		IBrunei-6	Guyana-6
CSpain-3	IN.Yem,S.Yem-8		BSri Lanka-6	CElSalvad.,Hond.-6
CIreland-5	ISudan,Somalia-8			Brazil-7
	IAlgeria,Egypt-8		IMalaysia-8	CArg.,Col.,Pan.-7
	ILibya,Morocco-9		HNepal-8	CHaiti-8
	ISaudi Arabia-9		BBhutan-9	
n=16	n=23	n=8	n=14	n=19
TOT: 30	28	38	33	33 (162)

Source: Barrett, 1982, Global Table 31, columns 21-22.

® = Codes for particular religions: C=Roman Catholic, I=Islam; X=Christianity;
  L-Lutheran; B=Buddhism; A=Anglican; O=Orthodox Christian, H=Hindu, J=Judaism;
  no code signifies a general commitment to "religion".
^ government policy has changed significantly since 1982 publication date.

302

1 = a government-**sponsored** official (state) religion; religious tests for certain political offices (e.g., Head of State); no proselytizing (or conversion) other than to the preferred religion; although free private individual practice generally allowed, often significant state pressure to conform to the majority practice.

2 = churches have significant political influence; government supports or subsidizes (either massively and directly, or in limited or indirect fashion such as tax relief) some religious activities; proselytizing, conversion, and free individual practice allowed; general government **approval** of religion, especially of majority religion, including some favorable laws (divorce, holidays, aid to schools, etc.); minority sects may be banned or harassed, especially if they are perceived to be involved in political activities (e.g., Jehovah's Witnesses' opposition to conscription).

2.5 = strictly **secular** government; neither harrassment of, nor subsidies for, religious activity; government guarantees of **free** practice.

Note: secular states with a "wall of separation" between church and state written into their constitutions (e.g., Indonesia, Turkey, India, US) in practice might grant preferential treatment to religious activities and so in the survey below often rate 2.0 rather than 2.5.

----

3 = general government **disappproval** of religion, even of majority religion especially if it has political potential (e.g., Islamic Brotherhood in Egypt, Turkey, Indonesia; Catholic Church in Mexico, pre-1989 eastern Europe); churches and religious schools exist, but there are many restrictions; religious proselytizing allowed, including religious schools and seminaries, but there are restrictions (e.g., registrations, state approval of hierarchy appointments, subsidies for the purpose of control and surveillance, etc.); a "lack-of-religion" test for some government and (especially, party) positions.

4 = state **hostile** to religion; may tolerate public displays (i.e, churches), but otherwise keeps organized religion under strict governmental control; does not allow widespread or easy proselytizing (e.g., schools, access to electronic media); in extreme cases, organized religion is outlawed and only private (secret) practice exists.

1	2		2.5	3	4	

PREDOMINANTLY CHRISTIAN STATES (n=85)

Europe(+1 Islamic^) (n=29)

1	2		2.5	3	4	
UK	Belgium		Canada	E.Germany		
Denmark	France		Switzrld.	Hungary	Bulgaria	
Finland	Italy	Luxmbrg.	Nethrlds.	Poland	Czech.	
Iceland	Spain	Austria		Malta	Romania	
Norway	Portugal				Yugoslavia	
Sweden	Ireland					
Greece ˍ	US					
Cyprus^	W.Germany					

Latin America (n=33)

1	2		2.5	3	4	
Bahamas	Belize		Antigua			
	Suriname		Barbad.,Dom.			
			Gren.,Guy.			
Haiti			St.L,St.V.			
	Argentina		St.C.,Jam.	Ecuador	Mexico	Cuba
	Peru	Chile	Trinidad	Bolivia	Nicarag.	
		Colombia	Braz.,Ven.	Uruguay		
Paraguay	El Sal.		Pan.,Hond.			
	C.Rica	Guat.	Dom.Rep.			

Christian Africa (n=14)

1	2		2.5	3	4	
		Rwanda	Lesotho	S.Africa		
		Zaire	Namibia		Burundi	
		Gabon	Uganda	Kenya		
		Swaziland	Tanzania		Ethiopia	
		STP	Ghana			

Christian Asia (n=9)

1	2		2.5	3	4	
	Phil. I.	S.Korea	W.Sam.,Van.	Seychelles		
			Solomons			
			Papua NG			
			Australia			
			New Zealand			

Table V4.5b.iii (continued)

1	2	*2.5*	3	4

PREDOMINANTLY ISLAMIC STATES (n=38)

Islamic Zone (n=26)

Saudi A.	Morocco		Turkey	Syria	S.Yemen
N.Yemen	Tunisia		Chad	Iraq	Afghan.
Oman	Somalia	Algeria			
Kuwait	Djibouti	Egypt			
UAE	Mauritania		Lebanon		
Qatar	Jordan				
Sudan	Bahrain				
Iran	Libya				
Pakistan					

African Zone (n=6)

		Gambia	
	Niger	Guinea	Senegal
		Nigeria	Mali

Asian Zone (n=6)

Maldives	Comoros		
	Bangladesh		
	Malaysia	Brunei	Indonesia

OTHER STATES (n=39)

PREDOM. SYNCRETIC/ANIMIST (n=19)

Cameroon	Benin,GB,BF	Angola	Congo
Eq.Guin.,Togo	CV,IC,Liberia	Mozambique	
Malawi,Zamb.	C.Af.R.,Madgscr.		
Sierra L.	Bots.,Zimbwe.		

BUDDHIST (n=10)

Thailand	Taiwan	Myanmar	Cambodia
Bhutan	Japan		Laos	Vietnam
Sri Lanka		Singapore	

HINDU (n=4)

Nepal	Mauritius	Fiji	India

JEWISH (n=1)

Israel

PREDOM. NON-RELIGIOUS (n=5)

	USSR	N.Korea
	China	Albania
	Mongolia	

Source: V4.2b,.5b data bank based upon Barrett, HUM86, DOS90, and FH89.

305

V4.5c.i - Freedom of the Press, Humana (1986)

Europe	Islamic	Africa	Asia	Latin America
1 (n=27)				
US,Can. 4			Japan 4	Costa Rica 4
UK, France-4			Australia 4	
Nor.,Swed.-4			N.Zealand 4	
Denmark-4				Venezuela 6
Aust.,Switz.-4			Papua NG 5	Agentina 6
W.Ger.Neth.,-4				Bolivia 6
Italy, Ire.-5				Ecuador 6
Belgium 5				Peru 6
Finland 6		Senegal 6		Panama 6
2 (n=12)				
	Israel 7	Botswana 7		Dom.Rep. 7
Greece 7				Jamaica 7
Spain 7				Trinidad 7
Portugal 7				Brazil,Mexico 8
			India 9	Colombia 9
2.5 (n=5)				
		Nigeria 10	Phil. I. 10	
	Egypt 10	Liberia 10	S.Korea 10	
3 (n=22)				
		Sierra Leone 11	Malaysia 11	
	Morocco 11	Cameroon 11	Singapore 11	
	Pakistan 11	Kenya 11	Thailand 11	
		Zimbabwe 11	Bangladesh 11	
Yugoslavia 12	Kuwait 12	Ghana 12	Sri Lanka 12	Paraguay 12
	Saudi A. 12	S.Africa 12		
Hungary 13	Tunisia 13		Indonesia 13	
	Turkey 13	Zambia 13		
4 (n=22)				
		Zaire 14	Taiwan 14	Haiti 14
		Tanzania 15		Chile 14
USSR 16				
Czech. 16	Algeria 16	Benin 16	China 16	
Poland 16	Libya 16	Ethiopia 16	N. Korea 16	Cuba 16
E.Germany 16	Syria 16	Mozambique 16	Vietnam 16	
Bulgaria 16	Iraq 16			
Romania 16				
n=26	n=12	n=16	n=17	n=17

Source: Humana, *World Human Rights Guide*, Questions 17, 24, 25, 26, n=88.

V4.5c.ii - Freedom of the Press, Freedom House (1989)

Europe	Islamic	Africa	Asia	Latin America
		1(n=35)		
US, Canada	Cyprus		Japan	Costa Rica
Iceland,Ireland			Australia	St.Chris.
Belgium,Neth.			N.Zealand	Barbados
Luxmbg.,France			Mauritius	Trinidad
Norway,Finland				Venezuela
Sweden,Denmk.				Ecuador
W.Ger.,Austria				Uruguay
Portug.,Spain				Dom.Rep.
Switzerland				St.Lucia
Italy,Malta				
UK,Greece				
		2(n=31)		
	Israel	Nigeria	S.Korea,Taiwan	Guat.,Hond.,El Sal.
		Gambia	India	Mexico,Suriname
		Botswana	Sri Lanka	Bolivia,Peru
			Thailand	Argentina,Brazil
			Phil. I.	Colombia,Belize
			Papua NG	Antigua,Dominica
			Brunei	Jamaica,Grenada
			Fiji,Vanuatu	St.V.,Bahamas
		2.5(n=16)		
Poland	Egypt		Maldives	Chile
Czechoslovakia	Tunisia	Senegal	Bhutan	Nicaragua
Hungary	Algeria	Ivory Coast	Sri Lanka	
E.Germany	Turkey		Nepal	
		3(n=32)		
USSR	Pakistan	Liberia,Togo	Bangladesh	
Yugoslavia	Iran, Iraq	Mali,Sierra L.	Madagascar	Guyana
	Kuwait,Bahrain	Kenya,Uganda		
	Qatar,N.Yemen	Lesotho,Zambia	Singapore	Paraguay
	Jordan,Lebanon	Swaziland	Malaysia	
	Morocco,Sudan	S.Africa,Zimbabwe	Solomons	Haiti
		4(n=43)		
	Afghanistan	CVerde,GBissau	Myanmar	
Bulgaria	Saudi Arabia	Burkina F.,STP	Seychelles	Panama
Romania	S.Yemen	Niger,Cameroon	China	Cuba
Albania	UAE	Eq.Guinea,Gabon	N.Korea	
	Oman	Congo,C.Af.R.	Mongolia	
	Chad	Guinea,Ghana	Vietnam	
	Somalia	Zaire,Ethiopia	Laos	
	Libya	Benin,Burundi	Cambodia	
	Mauritania	Tanzania,Malawi		
	Syria	Angola,Mozambique		
		n.a.(n=5)		
	Djibouti	Rwanda,Namibia	Comoros,WSam.	
n=30	n=28	n= 38	n=33	n=33 (162)

Source: Adapted from *Freedom at Issue*, January-February 1990: 61.

V4.5d - Workers' Unions, Status and % of Labor Force

Europe	Islamic	Africa	Asia	Latin America

Category 1 = Labor Most Free (Unions, Strikes, Politics)

Europe	Islamic	Africa	Asia	Latin America
Denmark-90%(CLU)				
Sweden-85				Urug.80%(PITCNT)
Finland-80 (SAK)	Israel-80+% (Histradut)			
Belgium-75				Brazil-50%(CGT)
Norway-60+(LP)				
Iceland-60(IFL)		Lesotho-60% (NUM;LCFTU)	Papua NG-50%(TUC)	
Austria-60(ATUF)				
Ireland-56(ICTU)				
Malta-51 (GWU/LP;UMH)				Antigua-45(n=2)
Luxembourg-50 (SP;CSP)				
Italy-45(n=3)		Uganda-42(NOTU)	N.Zealand-43	Mexico-35(CT)
			Australia-40	Barbados-32
W.Ger.-41(GTUF)				Argentina-31
UK-37(TUC)	Lebanon-37(CGTL)			Venezuela-28(CTV)
		Sierra L.-35(SLLC)		Bahamas-25
Canada-36				
Greece-35				
Portugal-33 (GGTP-IN, UGT)			SriLanka-33	Jamaica-25 (n=2)
Nethrlds.-30(FNV)		Senegal-30 (CNTS;UDTS)		Dominica-25
			Mauritius-25	Honduras-24
			India 25(ICFTU)	Belize-23
			Fiji-25(FTUC)	Trinidad-22
			Japan-27	St.Lucia-20
France-20(GCL)				Grenada-20
Switzerld-20(STUF)				El Salvador-20
		S.Africa 18(COSATU)		Ecuador -15(n=4)
				Costa Rica-15
Spain-17(ELA;STV)		Ghana-13		
US-14(AFL-CIO)		Namibia-12		Dom.Rep.-13
	Morocco=13(n=3)			St.Vincent-12
		Swaziland-10 (SUFIAW;SFTU)	Thailand-10	Bolivia-10
			Madagascar-4	
			Bangladesh-na	
			Sol. I.-na(NUWA)	St.Chris.-3
			W.Samoa-na	
			Vanuatu-na	
n=21	n=3	n=8	n=14	n=22 (68)

Table V4.5d (continued)

Category 2 = Labor Subverted by Govt. Ties

%=90-100					
USSR (AUCCTU)	Cyprus-75%			Suriname-40%	
Poland (NATU;		C.Verde-33%(UNTC)	S.Kor.-37%(FISTU)	Nicaragua-35	
Solidarity)	Egypt-25(ETUF)			Guyana-34	
Hungary(SZOT)		Gambia-24(n=2)	Taiwan-30(CFL)		
E.Ger.(FDGB)	Tunisia-20(UGTT)			Peru-18	
Bulgaria(CCTU)		Kenya-21(COTU)	Sing.-18(NTUC)	Panama-17	
Czech.(ROH)	Jordan-15(JFTU)	Zimbwe.-17(ZTCU)			
Romania(UGSR)	Turkey-12(IS)	Liberia-15(LFLU)		Chile-12	
	Pakistan 8	Nigeria-10(NLC)	Malaysia-10(TUC)	Colombia-8(CUT)	
Yugoslavia(CTUY)		Zambia-10(ZCTU)		Guat.-8(GCLU)	
	Mauritan.-6(UTM)	C.Af.R.-5+		Paraguay-5	
	Kuwait-4(KFTU)	Malawi <1(TUCM)	Brunei-4		
		BF <1 (BNCFTU)		Haiti <1	
	Djibouti-2(UGDT)	Botswn.-na(BFTU)			
n=8	n=9	n=11	n=5	n=10	(43)

Category 3 = Labor Controlled by Government

		Guinea-100%(CNTG)			
Alban.-100%(UTUA)		Togo-100%(CNTT)	Seych.-100%(NWU)		
		Burundi-100(UTB)	China-90(ACFTU)		
		Benin-75(UNSTB)		Cuba-na(CTC)	
		Tanzania-60(JUNATA)			
		Gabon-50(COSYGA)			
		GBissau-50(UNTG)			
		ICoast-33(UGTCI)			
		Niger 30(USTN)			
	Chad-20(UNST)	Cameroon-30(OCWU)			
	Algeria-18(GUAW)	Mozambiq.-25(OTM)			
		Congo-20(CSC)			
		Angola-16(UNTA)	Philippines-15(n=3)		
		Rwanda-7(CESTRAR)			
	Iraq-10(IGFTU)				
	Syria-5(GFTU)		Indonesia-5(SPSI)		
	Somalia-na	Ethiopia <5(ETU;EPA)			
	Bahrain-na		Nepal-na		
	Afghanistan-na	Zaire-na(UNTZ)	Comoro-na		
	S.Yemen-na(GFTU)	Mali-na(UNTM)	Mongolia-na		
	N.Yemen-na(YTUC)		Cambodia-na		
n=1	n=9	n=17	n=8	n=1	(36)

Category 4 = Virtually No Labor Rights

	Saudi Arabia	STP	Bhutan,N.Korea		
	Oman,UAE	Eq.Guinea	Laos,Vietnam		
	Qatar,Libya		Maldives		
	Iran,Sudan		Myanmar		
n=0	n=7	n=2	n=6	n=0	(15)
TOT: 30	28	38	33	33	(162)

Source: Categories based on narratives in DOS90, and Humana'86, Qu. #28;
%s are estimates derived from DOS90 or earlier, and *CIA World Factbook* 1988 or earlier.
( ) = initials of, or number of, major union confederations with political significance.

BIBLIOGRAPHY

AFRICA/AMERICAS/ASIA/HELSINKI/MIDDLE EAST WATCH (periodic) *Reports*. New York: Human Rights Watch Publications.

AL-FARUQI, I. R. (1986) *The Cultural Atlas of Islam*. New York: Macmillan.

AMNESTY INTERNATIONAL (annual) *Annual Reports*. London: Amnesty International (AI) Publications.

_____. (1979*) *The Death Penalty*. London: AI Publications.

_____. (1981*) *Prisoners of Conscience*. London: AI Publications.

_____. (1983*) *Political Killings by Governments*. London: AI Publications.

_____. (1984*) *Torture in the 1980s*. London: AI Publications.

_____. (1989*) *When the State Kills: The Death Penalty: A Human Rights Issue*. London: AI Publications.

ARONOFF, M. J. (1984) *Religion and Politics*. New Brunswick, N. J.: Transaction Books.

ASIWAJU, A. I. (ed.) (1985) *Partitioned Africans: Ethnic Relations across Africa's International Boundaries 1884-1984*. New York: St. Martin's Press.

BARRETT, D. B. (ed.) (1982) *World Christian Encyclopedia*. Oxford: Oxford University Press.

BASSIOUNI, C. M. (1982) *The Islamic Criminal Justice System*. Dobbs Ferry, N. Y. Oceana Publications.

BEER, L. W. (1984) *Freedom of Expression in Japan: A Study of Comparative Law, Politics and Society*. Tokyo: Kodansha International.

BERMAN, G. A., and J. N. HAZARD (eds.) (1987) *The World's Legal Systems Past and Present*. Dobbs Ferry, N. Y.: The Oceana Group, Condyne Cassettes.

BOFF, L. (1985) *Church, Charisma and Power: Liberation Theology and the Institutional Church*. Crossroads, N. Y.: Crossroads Publishing Co.

BOLLEN, K. A. (1986) "Political Rights and Political Liberties in Nations: An Evaluation of Human Rights Measures, 1950 to 1984," *Human Rights Quarterly* 8: 567-591.

BOYLE, K. (ed.) (1988) *Article 19 World Report 1988: Information, Freedom, and Censorship*. New York: Times Books.

BRASS, P. R. (ed.) (1985) *Ethnic Groups and the State*. New York: Barnes and Noble.

BUTLER, W. E. (ed.) (annual) *Yearbook on Socialist Legal Systems*. Ardsley-on-Hudson, N. Y.: Transnational Publishers Inc.

CAPOTORTI, F. (1979) *Study on the Rights of Persons Belonging to Ethnic and Religious Minorities*. New York: United Nations Publications.

CAPPELLITTI, M. (1971) *Judicial Review in the Contemporary World*. Indianapolis: Bobbs-Merrill.

CARROLL, T. G. (1984) "Secularization and States of Modernity," *World Politics* 36: 362-382.

CHOMSKY, N., and E. S. HERMAN (1979, 1982) *The Political Economy of Human Rights*. Boston: South End Press, 2 vols.

CHOWDHURY, S. R. (1989) *The Rule of Law in a State of Emergency: The Paris Minimum Standards of Human Rights Norms in a State of Emergency*. New York: St. Martin's Press.

CLAUDE, R. P. (1976) *Comparative Human Rights*. Baltimore: Johns Hopkins University Press.

CLAUDE, R. P., and T. B. JABINE (1986) "Symposium: Statistical Issues in the Field of Human Rights. Editors' Introduction," *Human Rights Quarterly* 8: 551-566.

CURRY, J. L., and J. R. BASSIN (eds.) (1982) *Press Control around the World*. New York: Praeger Publishers.

DONNELLY, J. (1984) *The Concept of Human Rights*. New York: St. Martin's Press.

————. (1989) *Universal Human Rights in Theory and Practice*. Ithaca, N. Y. Cornell University Press.

DOWTY, A. (1987) *Closed Borders: The Contemporary Assault on Freedom of Movement*. New Haven: Yale University Press.

DRINAN, R. F. (1988) *Cry of the Oppressed: The History of the Human Rights Revolution*. New York: Harper and Row.

EIDE, A. (1986) "The Human Rights Movement and the Transformation of the International Order," *Alternatives* 11: 367-402.

ENCYCLOPEDIA OF RELIGION (1987) New York: Macmillan.

ENLOE, C. M. (1973) *Ethnic Conflict and Political Development*. Boston: Little, Brown and Co.

EVANS, R., and A. FRAZER (1983) *Human Rights: A Dialogue between the First and Third Worlds*. New York: Orbis Press.

FALK, R. A. (1979) "Comparative Protection of Human Rights in Capitalist and Socialist Third World Countries," *Universal Human Rights* 1(2): 3-29.

FLETCHER, G. P. (1987) *Comparative Jurisprudence*. Dobbs Ferry, N. Y. The Oceana Group, Condyne Cassettes.

FORD, F. L. (1985) *Political Murder: From Tyrannicide to Terrorism*. Cambridge: Harvard University Press.

FORSYTHE, D. P. (1983) *Human Rights and World Politics*. Lincoln: University of Nebraska Press.

FRANCK, T. M. (1982) *Human Rights in Third World Perspective*. Dobbs Ferry, N. Y. Oceana Publications.

FUENTES, A. (1983) *Women in the Global Factory*. Boston: South End Press.

GASTIL, R. (annual) *Freedom in the World: Political Rights and Civil Liberties*. Westport, Conn.: Greenwood Press, for Freedom House.

GELLNER, E. (1983) *Nations and Nationalism*. Ithaca, N. Y.: Cornell University Press.

GILLIES, D. W. (1990) "Evaluating National Human Rights Performance: Priorities for the Developing World," *Bulletin of Peace Proposals* 21(1): 15-27.

GLADSTONE, A., R. LANDSBURY, J. STIEVER, T. TREN, and M. WEISS (eds.) (1989) *Current Issues in Labour Relations: An International Perspective*. Hawthorne, N. Y.: Aldine de Gruyter.

HANNUM, H. (1987) "Ethnic Conflict and Human Rights: A Comparative Perspective," *Bulletin of Peace Proposals* 18: 651-659.

HARPER, F. J. (ed.) (1987) *Trade Unions of the World*. London: Longman.

HENKIN, L. (ed.) (1981) *The International Bill of Human Rights*. New York: Columbia University Press.

HOOD, R. (1989) *Death Penalty: A Worldwide Perspective*. New York: Oxford University Press.

HOWARD, R. (1983) "The Full-Belly Thesis: Should Economic Rights Take Priority over Civil and Political Rights? Evidence from Sub-Saharan Africa," *Human Rights Quarterly* 5: 467-490.

————. (1990) "Monitoring Human Rights: Problems of Consistency," *Ethics and International Affairs* 4: 33-52.

HUMAN RIGHTS INTERNET REPORTER (five times a year) Washington: Human Rights Internet.

HUMAN RIGHTS QUARTERLY (quarterly) College Park: University of Maryland.

HUMANA, C. (1984; 1986) *World Human Rights Guide.* New York: Universe; and London: The Economist Publications.

HUMPHREY, J. P. (1984) *Human Rights and the United Nations: A Great Adventure.* Ardsley-on-the-Hudson, N. Y.: Transnational Publications.

IGLITZEN, L. B., and R. ROSS (1985) *Women in the World, 1975-1985: The Women's Decade.* Santa Barbara: ABC-Clio Publications.

INTERNATIONAL LABOUR OFFICE (ILO) (1984) *World Labour Report.* vol. 1 -*Employment, Income, Social Protection, New Information Technology;* vol. 2 -*Labour Relations, International Labour Standards, Training, Conditions of Work, Women at Work.* Geneva: International Labour Office.

JOHANSEN, R.C. (1983) "Human Rights in the 1980s: Revolutionary Growth or Unanticipated Erosion," *World Politics* 35: 286-314.

KELLY, J. (1988) *Trade Unions and Socialism.* New York: Verso.

KHADDURI, M. (1984) *The Islamic Concept of Justice.* Baltimore: Johns Hopkins University Press.

KOTHARI, R. (1980) "Human Rights as a North-South Issue," *Bulletin of Peace Proposals* 11: 331-338.

LADD, C. S. JR. (1985) "The Evolution of Constitutional Forms of Government: Special Reference to Asian and Third World Countries," paper delivered at International Studies Association meeting, Washington, D. C.

LAWSON, E. H. (ed.) (1989) *Encyclopedia of Human Rights.* New York: Taylor and Francis.

LAWYERS COMMITTEE ON INTERNATIONAL HUMAN RIGHTS (periodic) *Reports.* New York: Lawyers Committee on International Human Rights.

LIEBESNY, H. J. (1983) "Judicial Systems in the Near and Middle East: Economic Development and Islamic Revival," *Middle East Journal* 37: 202-217.

LUNGU, G. F. (1986) "The Church, Labour, and the Press in Zambia: The Role of Critical Observers in a One-Party State," *African Affairs* 84: 385-410.

MARTIN, L. J., and A. G. CHAUDHARY (1983) *Comparative Mass Media Systems.* New York: Longman.

MERKL, P. H., and N. SMART (eds.) (1983) *Religion and Politics in the Modern World.* New York: New York University Press.

MERRILL, J. C. (ed.) (1983) *Global Journalism: A Survey of the World's Mass Media.* New York: Longman.

MINORITY RIGHTS GROUP (periodic) *Reports.* London: Minority Rights Group.

MORRISON, D. G. (1989) *Black Africa Comparative Handbook,* 2d ed. New York: Paragon House.

MOWER, G. A. (1985) *International Cooperation for Social Justice: Global and Regional Protection of Economic and Social Rights.* Westport, Conn. Greenwood Press.

MURDOCK, G. P. (1967) *Ethnographic Atlas.* Pittsburgh: University of Pittsburgh Press.

NANDA, V. P., J. R. SCARITT, and G. W. SHEPHERD, JR. (eds.) (1981) *Global Human Rights: Public Policies, Comparative Measures, and NGO Strategies.* Boulder: Westview Press.

NEVITTE, N., and C. H. KENNEDY (eds.) (1986) *Ethnic Preference and Public Policy in Developing States.* Boulder: Lynne Rienner Publications.

NIELSSON, G. P. (1985) "States and Nation-Groups: A Global Taxonomy," in TIRYAKIAN, E. A., N. NEVITTE, and R. ROGOWSKI (eds.), *New Nationalisms of the Developed West: Toward an Explanation.* Boston: Allen and Unwin.

NIELSSON, G. P., and R. JONES (1988) "From Ethnic Category to Nation: Patterns of Political Modernization," paper delivered at International Studies Association annual convention, St. Louis, Mo.

NIMMO, D., and M. W. MANSFIELD (1982) *Government and the News Media. Comparative Dimensions.* Waco, Tex.: Baylor University Press.

ONUF, N. G., and V. S. PETERSON (1984) "Human Rights from an International Regimes Perspective," *Journal of International Affairs* 37: 329-342.

ORGANIZATION OF AMERICAN STATES. COMMISSION ON HUMAN RIGHTS (periodic) *Reports.* Washington: Organization of American States.

OSMANCZYK, E. (1985) *Encyclopedia of the United Nations.* Philadelphia and New York: Taylor and Francis.

POPULATION CRISIS COMMITTEE (1988) *Country Rankings of the Status of Women: Poor, Powerless and Pregnant.* Washington: Population Crisis Committee, Population Briefing Paper, No. 20, June, 1988.

PRAVDA, A., and B. RUBLE (eds.) (1986) *Trade Unions in Communist States.* Winchester, Mass.: Allen and Unwin.

RENTELN, A. D. (1985) "The Unanswered Challenge of Relativism and the Consequences for Human Rights," *Human Rights Quarterly* 7: 514-540.

ROSS, J. A. and A. B. COTTRELL (1980) *The Mobilization of Collective Identity: Comparative Perspectives.* Lanham, Md.: University Press of America.

ROTHCHILD, J. (1981) *Ethnopolitics: A Conceptual Framework.* New York: Columbia University Press.

SAID, A. A., and L. R. SIMMONS (1976) *Ethnicity in an International Context.* New Brunswick, N. J.: Transaction Books.

SCHWAB, P., and A. POLLIS (eds.) (1982) *Towards A Human Rights Framework.* New York: Praeger.

SEAGER, J. (1986) *Women in the World: An International Atlas.* New York: Simon and Schuster.

SHIELS, F. L. (1984) *Ethnic Separatism and World Politics.* Lanham, Md.: University Press of America.

SIEGEL, R. L. (1984) "Socioeconomic Human Rights: Past and Future," *Human Rights Quarterly* 7: 255-267.

SIGLER, J. A. (1983) *Minority Rights: A Comparative Analysis.* Westport, Conn.: Greenwood Press.

————. (1987) *International Handbook of Race Relations.* Westport, Conn.: Greenwood Press.

SIMPSON, G. E., and J. M. YINGER (1985) *Racial and Cultural Minorities: An Analysis of Prejudice and Discrimination*, 5th ed. New York: Plenum Publishing Corp.

SIVARD, R. L. (1985) *Women: A Global Survey*. Washington: World Priorities.

SMITH, A. (1980) *The Geopolitics of Information: How Western Culture Dominates the World*. New York: Oxford University Press.

SMITH, A. D. (1983) *State and Nation in the Third World*. New York: St. Martin's Press.

SNYDER, L. L. (1982) *Global Mini-Nationalisms: Autonomy or Independence*. Westport, Conn.: Greenwood Press.

_____. (1984) *Macro-Nationalism: A History of the Pan-Movements*. Westport, Conn.: Greenwood Press.

SOUTHALL, R. (ed.) (1987) *Labor and Unions in Asia and Africa*. New York: St. Martin's Press.

STACK, J. F., JR. (1986) *The Primordial Challenge: Ethnicity in the Contemporary World*. Westport, Conn.: Greenwood Press.

STOHL, M., and G. A. LOPEZ (eds.) (1986) *Government Violence and Repression: An Agenda for Research*. Westport, Conn.: Greenwood Press.

STOHL, M., et al. (1986) "State Violation of Human Rights: Issues and Problems of Measurement," *Human Rights Quarterly* 8: 592-605.

TAYLOR, C. L., and D. B. JODICE (1983) *World Handbook of Political and Social Indicators*. vol. 1, *Cross National Attributes and Rates of Change*. New Haven: Yale University Press.

THOMPSON, D. L., and D. RONEN (eds.) (1986) *Ethnicity, Politics and Development*. Boulder: Lynne Rienner Publishers.

TOLLEY, H., JR. (1987) *The United Nations Commission on Human Rights*. Boulder: Westview Press.

UNITED NATIONS (1985a) *Women and Development: Guidelines for Program and Project Planning*. New York: United Nations Publications.

_____. (annual) *Yearbook*. New York: United Nations Publications.

_____. (annual) *Yearbook on Human Rights*. New York: United Nations Publications.

UNITED STATES. DEPARTMENT OF STATE (annual) *Country Reports on Human Rights Practices*. Washington: US Government Printing Office.

UNITED STATES. DEPARTMENT OF STATE. BUREAU OF PUBLIC AFFAIRS (semi-annual) *Implementation of Helsinki Final Act: Reports by the President to the Commission on Security and Cooperation in Europe (CSCE)*. Washington: US Department of State.

UNITED STATES. HOUSE OF REPRESENTATIVES. COMMITTEE ON FOREIGN AFFAIRS. SUBCOMMITTEE ON HUMAN RIGHTS (1983) *Hearings: Political Killings by Governments of Their Citizens*. Washington: US Government Printing Office.

VAN DYKE, V. (1985) *Human Rights, Ethnicity, Discrimination*. Westport, Conn.: Greenwood Press.

VERNER, J. G. (1984) "The Independence of Supreme Courts in Latin America: A Review of the Literature," *Journal of Latin American Studies* 16: 463-506.

VERRSTAPPEN, B. (ed.) (1987) *Human Rights Reports: An Annotated Bibliography of Fact-Finding Missions*. Munich: K. G. Saur Verlag.

VOEGELIN, C. F. and F. M. (1977) *Classifications and Index of the World's Languages.* New York: Elsevier.

WEEKES, R. V. (ed.) (1983) *Muslim Peoples: A World Ethnographic Survey.* Westport, Conn.: Greenwood Press.

WIRSING, R. G. (ed.) (1981) *Protection of Ethnic Minorities: Comparative Perspectives.* New York: Pergamon.

YOUNG, C. (1976) *The Politics of Cultural Pluralism.* Madison: University of Wisconsin Press.

5

Political Participation

Chapter 4 analyzed social justice as it applied to individuals and their involvement in essentially non-political groups; Chapter 5 will focus upon participation in explicitly political associations (i.e., parties) and organs of government. This study, thus, is more restrictive in its interpretation of political participation than Huntington and Nelson (1976:4-7) and Milbraith (1965:1-3), whose more expansive definitions encompass all activity by private citizens ("ordinary people") designed to influence government decision-making and hence would include a lot of what is covered here in section V4.5. See also Nelson in Weiner and Huntington (1987: 104).

V5.1. COMPARING GOVERNMENTAL SYSTEMS

V5.1a. Parties and Polities

The chief unit of participation to be studied here will be the political party. Section V4.5 analyzed social groups which were potentially political, but whose primary orientation was in a different direction (religious, economic, etc.). Political parties, on the other hand, are organized specifically for the purpose of influencing the political system and making government responsive to their ideas (Panebianco, 1988; Wildermann, 1987: vol. 1).

In many societies, to the extent that there is no desire on the part of large numbers of people to participate in the task of governance, policies can be just and individual rights respected under a benign monarch or a "moderately authoritarian" military dictator. Assuming, however, that some active minority of citizens desires influence over the making of public policy, Chapter 5 addresses such questions as what avenues of participation are open to them and, alternatively, what measures are available (or forbidden) to the government in restricting them. In other words, can putative political actors participate in such ways as to get a positive response from society's institutions of governance?

The Comparative Government Spread Sheet (hereafter, CGSS), which appears as Table V5.1a, posits nine polity types arrayed in descending order roughly corresponding to the number and vitality of their political parties. As Chapter 4 adopted a rating system based upon four levels of severity to rank states with respect to social justice, the CGSS and its categories will provide the framework for ranking countries with respect to political participation. By characterizing each state's governmental system in this manner, some preliminary indication is also made of the openness of the ruling administration as well as its degree of legitimacy, power-sharing, and militarization, as these terms will be developed in this chapter (for other typologies, see Baker and Seroka, 1989).

The major divisions of Table V5.1a's Comparative Government Spread Sheet relate to whether a political system is primarily civilian or military, and to whether a country has several, one, or zero parties available to those interested in participating in the political process. The distinction between primarily civilian and predominantly military polities is the more basic of the two divisions in this framework of analysis, and is reflected in the separation of CGSS into two pages. Naturally, even in the most civilian of republics, the military undergirds the system and is the ultimate guarantor of its existence, but as long as this protective power is generally not used in an unduly intrusive way, the states are deemed to be civilian (CGSS-page 1).

In most societies the military maintains law and order and safeguards governmental institutions, but in the context of value V1 and indicator V4.4d, overt military participation in the political process is considered improper. The period of socialization and promotion required in a military establishment before one becomes a significant participant is so great as to render this approach to the political arena off-limits to all but a few members of a rather select caste. Access to political party machinery, on the other hand, for that minority of the population interested in such matters, is somewhat easier in most societies (Day and Degenhardt, 1988; Janda, 1981; Sartori, 1976).

In the global analysis which follows, the political systems of slightly more than half the states (n=85) are characterized as civilian and hence relatively open and responsive to citizen participation. This statement embraces not only the 53 multiparty republics where participation in the political process can even take the form of significant *opposition* to the ruling administration, but also 32 one-party polities where the degree of participation in the single party can be taken as some indication of the legitimacy of the system. (See page 1 of Table V5.1a=CGSS.)

On page 2 of the CGSS are the remaining 75 states, wherein the military (or a monarchy originally based upon military conquest) dominates, and the system is more closed and difficult for ordinary citizens to influence. Among these 75 countries are 22 annotated with an asterisk (*), which will be considered evolving party states, but where the military still retains predominant influence; 41 states which are virtual military dictatorships despite some evidence of party activity in 21 of them (which will be called "moderating military" polities and designated by a caret (^)); and 12 monarchies where little or no civilian participation is allowed. With respect to participation outside civilian, generally democratic, contexts, there has not been much systematic comparative research (Nelson, 1987: 125); one of the contributions of this chapter is that almost as much attention will be given to participation in the various militarized systems (in section V5.4) as in the civilian and democratic ones (in section V5.3).

In this framework for comparative government analysis, there are several areas where the judgment for state placements between civilian and military is problematic. These are generally found on the bottom third of CGSS-page 1, where reliance upon the military to enforce the political or economic orientation of one-party other and one-party communist systems is often high; and on the top quarter of CGSS-page 2 (militarized party systems), where many of the modalities of civilian party-states exist, but where the military still retains the most significant political role.

Just as with the state rankings for indicators in Chapters 1 through 4, the placements of particular countries in the CGSS are not as significant as the development of categories of analysis. Further elaboration of polity definitions as well as discussion of possible mergings of categories, of marginal state members in each classification, and of how each government type relates to political participation, will be provided throughout the rest of this chapter: in sections V5.3ab for multiparty republics; V5.3cde for the three types of one-party systems; V5.4 for militarized party systems and other forms of military governance; and V5.5a for monarchical regimes. Throughout, historical information drawn from the narrative data banks associated with this project, as well as some statistics from the earlier chapters, will be used to substantiate conceptual judgments.

Table V5.1a will be the controlling document for this comparative analysis of 160 states with respect to political participation. Because data in this chapter is up-to-date and not one to three years old as in earlier sections, the analysis reflects the unifications of the two Germanies and the two Yemens, reducing by two the total number of states analyzed in the rest of this book. However, Iraq's annexation of Kuwait is not judged to be permanent at the time of this writing (December, 1990).

The CGSS is a flexible framework which can be used vertically to compare states within common cultural zones, or horizontally to compare countries with similar political systems. Concerning the columns representing the five zones, it is often desirable that states with similar heritage be analyzed together. For example, mpr Venezuela might be more appropriately compared with *mpr Brazil, and mil^ Paraguay, than with other mprs such as Australia, Israel, or Norway. Similarly, it might be more fruitful to consider the 9 entrenched military (mil^o) states of Africa along with the 12 moderating mil^ states and the 9 strict single party (1p-other) polities of that zone, than with other military states in the Middle East, Asia, and Latin America. (Polity type abbreviations used in this section are introduced on the CGSS and explained at greater length throughout the remainder of this chapter.)

Employing the CGSS horizontally to compare states within a single polity type, between two and nine levels of analysis could be chosen. The most basic two-fold division, between civilian and military states, has already been mentioned. But depending on the focus of one's research, it might be more appropriate to divide the world's 160 states into three broad categories based on party: multiparty (n=71: 36 mpr + 17 ~mpr + 18 *mpr), one-party (n=36: 32 1pp + 4 *1pdom), and no (credible) party (n=53: 21 mil^ + 20 mil^o + 12 mon). For other matters, four (mpr, 1pp, militarized (*,^,^{o}), monarchy) or five (mpr, 1pp, militarized party, military, monarchy) gross political types might be employed. For still other issues, all nine sub-types (mpr, ~mpr, 1pdom, 1pcom, 1p-other, *milp, mil^, mil^o, and mon—in rough order of their openness to political participation) might be used.

Obviously, state placements in the CGSS are subject to periodic updating due to changes in the political histories of states, or differences in the way the definitions of polity types might be applied to the factual situation of countries by other analysts. However, after five years of working with this framework, the author has found significant stability in state/polity identifications. The most enduring are in the first and last categories (mpr and mon); among the others, seldom are states reclassified between gross polity types. Most of the movement—involving perhaps not more than 5% of the state placements in a single year—will be within main categories, say from mil^o to mil^, or from mil^ to *ed party (either *mpr or *1pdom); or between related categories, such as from *1pdom to 1pdom, or *mpr to mpr. In short, as a framework of analysis, the CGSS is quite enduring over time for comparing states within macro-polity types; it is also effective in the short term for analyzing states within particular sub-types.

Finally, nine states listed below the main body of the CGSS should be noted because their status as sovereign entities might change over time. They include three nations (Cyprus, China, and Korea) which have long been formally divided (separated here by a slanted line, "/"), and covered in the CGSS as five individual states, each of which has significant legal recognition in the world community, and one anomaly (North Cyprus); and three other colonies or submerged states indicated by #s (Palestine, Western Sahara, and Hong Kong) which are not counted among the states formally recognized in this study, but are treated in sections V1.1b and V5.5b.

V5.1b. Regime Legitimacy/Elections

One issue which must be addressed before beginning this chapter's analyses of power-sharing within governments, among political parties, and between civilians and the military, relates to regime legitimacy—evidence of popular support for the current ruling administration.   Resort to force can bring a government to power and maintain it in place, often for a considerable period of time.   But direct, periodic national elections, however much they might be rigged by regimes to restrict opposition candidates, are also held in 130 of 160 states as a way of displaying their popular acceptance.   Those few states (n=30) which have had no such legitimizing exercises as of December 20, 1990, are limited to 8 of the 12 monarchies, 17 of 20 mil⁰s, 1 of 21 mil^s, and 4 of the 32 one-party polities. (See Table V5.1b: "no elections" and "no *direct* elections.")

The primary electoral point of contact between government and the people varies among countries, falling into three main categories (Lijphart and Grofman, 1984; Lijphart, 1984a; Rose, 1980; Mackie and Rose, 1984).   First (*Electoral Type 1*), 51 states elect a legislature out of which and by which is chosen the head of government (or "**Leg** > **PM**"); these are primarily the governments to be defined in section V5.3a as parliamentary multiparty republics, but also include about half of the one-party dominant polities.

There are separate elections *(Electoral Type 2)* for both a representative assembly and for an executive head of state, or president, in 51 states. Among these states are the 20 "strong presidential" mprs (n=8 + *12)—where the president may sometimes appoint a (distinctly subordinate) prime minister (who need not be selected from the assembly as in parliamentary mprs) to administer the government—as well as about 45% of the one-party polities (n=16/36) and moderating military (n=12/21) regimes.

Finally *(Electoral Type 3)*, 22 states have elections only to a representative assembly, the executive leadership of government being decided mainly by the party, the military, or a monarch, subject in some instances to a rubber-stamp ratification by the assembly.   This type of system generally does not have a direct election for the executive (as in Type 2), and differs from Type 1, Leg > PM, in that the chief political actors are determined more by other structures within the system than by the electoral exercise.

(A minor variation of these main forms of electoral experience (*Electoral Type 1a* in Table V5.1b) occurs in the mixed parliamentary/presidential systems (n=6), with both an elected representative assembly out of which comes the head of government, and a directly elected head of state.)

A distinction should be made between states where elections may result in an actual choice of leadership and a change in the governing regime, and those which are essentially legitimizing exercises (Denitch, 1978; Hermet et al., 1978). Direct popular elections, with a choice of opposition candidates supported by the mobilized resources of an organized political party, are held in all 71 multiparty republics (36 mpr + 17 ˜mpr + 18 *mpr). In the 89 other polities (36 one-party states including 4 *ed, 41 military regimes, and 12 monarchies), elections (if they are held at all) do not signify the *selection* of a government so much as the approval of an administration already chosen by more elite members of the society.

Some would say this is virtually the case in many of the 71 multiparty republics too, for in addition to 17 ˜mprs where the ruling party has seldom lost a national election, incumbent parties are ousted from power only about one-third of the time (in 13 of 36 of the mprs in the most recent V5.1b data bank results). Particularly in the 18 *mprs, elections often result in the selection of military-approved successors to coup regimes (see section V5.4b). In addition, in some mprs, the ruling administration can adjust the electoral machinery in subtle ways which will give it an advantage (e.g., redrawing district boundaries, changing the number of representatives per constituency, varying between the methods of direct and proportionate representation (see section V5.3a)). More heavy-handed techniques often associated with one-party, military, and monarchical governments include controlling access to the media, and tampering with the vote count. Nevertheless, there is at least *some* choice in these mpr regimes, as the regularity of *eventual* change in government leadership following elections would indicate (Jackman, 1986).

In the 36 one-party states, 41 military regimes, and 12 monarchies, assembly elections and referendums on the heads of state and government more obviously serve the *legitimating* function, whereas the true leadership selection comes out of a more restrictive political process which occurs within the party, the military, or the royal family. In these states, however, the turnout of voters, and the contesting of elections by parties or candidates other than those approved by the ruling regime, are evidence of political participation and acquiescence in the legitimacy of the system. In many states a choice of candidates approved by the regime is offered in elections to a representative assembly; in more restrictive countries, only a single list is presented for a yes/no vote. At the executive level, generally no opposition is tolerated, and elections are referendums on the head of state and/or government presented by the regime (Rustow, 1985; Smith, 1986).

Among the 30 states not represented in any of the above forms of direct electoral legitimation are a few (n=9) which allow *indirect* elections for national offices. These occasionally are for the chief executive as part of a referendum on a constitution the regime has written, but more commonly would be to an assembly selected by an "electoral college" of lower-level office-holders and/or national party councils.

Table V5.1b identifies specific states by both their electoral and governmental types.   The next section V5.2 discusses certain common elements of power-sharing in all political systems. Further analysis of regime legitimation and party representation in each of the polity types is provided in the remaining sections of this chapter: mpr-V5.3ab; 1pp-V5.3cde; *milp-V5.4b; mil^-V5.4c; mil$^{\circ}$ -V5.4d; and mon-V5.5a.

Europe	Islamic	Africa	Asia	Latin America	
mpr = multiparty republics (n=36—V5.3a)					
US,Canada,Iceland	Cyprus		Australia	Venezuela	
Ireland,Norway			New Zealand	Ecuador	
Bel.,Neth.,Lux.	Israel			Costa Rica	
UK,France			India	Belize	
Germany				Jamaica	
Dnmk.,Swed.,Finld.				Barbados	
Switz.,Austria				Dom.Rep.	
Spain,Port.,Italy				St.V.,St. L.	
Malta,Greece				Trinidad	
Sbtot: 21	2	0	3	10	(36)
~mpr = **weak multiparty republics** (n=17—V5.3b)					
			Japan	Antigua	
		Gambia	Mauritius	Bahamas	
Hungary			W. Samoa	Dominica	
Czechoslovakia		Botswana	Papua NG	St.Chris.	
Poland			Vanuatu	Grenada	
		S. Africa	Solomon I.		
Sbtot: 3	0	3	6	5	(17)
Tot.mpr: 24	2	3	9	15	(53)

****

Europe	Islamic	Africa	Asia	Latin America	
1pp = One-Party Polities (n=32=13+8+11)					
1pdom = 1-party dominant (n=13—V5.3c)					
Bulgaria	Iran	Senegal,Iv.Coast	Mongolia	Mexico	
Romania		Zimbabwe	Singapore		
	Egypt	Namibia	Malaysia	Guyana	
Sbtot: 2	2	4	3	2	(13)
1pcom = 1-party communist (n=8—V5.3d)					
USSR			China	Cuba	
Yugoslavia			N.Korea		
Albania			Vietnam		
			Laos		
Sbtot: 3	0	0	4	1	(8)
1p-other = 1-party other (n=11—V5.3e)					
	Tunisia	Sierra Leone			
		Gabon,Cameroon			
	Djibouti	C.Verde,STP			
		Kenya,Tanzania			
		Zambia,Malawi			
Sbtot: 0	2	9	0	0	(11)
Tot.1P: 5	4	13	7	3	(32)

****

TOT.CIV.: 29	6	16	16	18	(85)

Table V5.1a (page 2)

V5.1a-COMPARATIVE GOVERNMENT-SPREAD SHEET (page 2)

Eur.=0	Islamic	Africa	Asia	Latin America

militarized party systems = *s: (n=22—V5.4b)

	Islamic	Africa	Asia	Latin America
*milp	Turkey		Madagascar,Sri Lanka	Arg.,Brazil,Chile
n=22			Bangladesh	Urug.,Bol.,Peru
			Thailand	Colombia,Suriname
	Pakistan		S.Korea,Taiwan	Guatemala,Honduras
			Phil. I.,Indonesia	Nicaragua, El Sal.
Sbtot:	2	0	8	12 (22)

----

military regimes (n=41: 21^ + 20ᵉ—V5.4cd)

	Islamic	Africa	Asia	Latin America
mil^	Afghanistan	GB,Benin,Mali	Seychelles	
n=21	Iraq,Syria	CAfR,Togo,Niger		
	Yemen	Congo,Zaire	Cambodia	Paraguay
	Somalia	Rwanda,Ethiopia		
	Algeria	Angola,Mozambique		
Sbtot:	6	12	2	1 (21)

	Islamic	Africa	Asia	Latin America
	Lebanon	Burkina F.,Nigeria	Comoros	
	Sudan,Chad	Ghana,Guinea,Liberia	Maldives	
milᵉ	Libya	Eq.Guinea,Burundi	Myanmar	Haiti
n=20	Mauritania	Uganda,Lesotho	Fiji	Panama
Sbtot:	5	9	4	2 (20)

| Tot. V5.4 | 13 | 21 | 14 | 15 (63) |

****

mon = monarchies (n=12— V5.5a)

	Islamic	Africa	Asia	Latin America
	Morocco		Bhutan	
	Jordan,Saudi A.		Nepal	
	Oman,Bahrain	Swaziland		
	UAE,Kuwait,Qatar		Brunei	
Sbtot:	8	1	3	0 (12)

| TOT:MIL/MON | 21 | 22 | 17 | 15 (75) |

| TOT: 29 | 27 | 38 | 33 | 33 (160) |

XXXXXXXXXXXXXXXXXXXXXXXXXXXXXXXXXXXXXXXXXXXXXXXXXXXXXXXXXXXXXXXXXX

Important Colonies/Divided States (n=9—V5.5bc)

Cyprus/#N.Cyprus		N.Korea/S.Korea
#W.Sahara		China/Taiwan
#Palestine		China/#Hong Kong

Defs/Criteria:

* = party states with heavy military influence (n=22): 18 *mpr plus 4 *1pdom;

^ = moderating mil. regimes where military controls executive branch, but sometimes allows parties
    to run and be represented in a weak assembly (n=21);

ᵉ = entrenched mil. regimes where party activity is minimal/non-existent (n=20);

= colony, possession, submerged nation; not among independent states recognized here.

V5.1b - Summary of States by 3 Electoral and 10 Polity Types

	mpr str-wk~	1p d-c-o	*milp m - 1p	mil - °	mon	TOT.
Electoral Type						
1. Leg>PM	25-15	6-0-0	4 - 0	0 - 1	0	51
1a. Leg>PM,&Pres(mix)	5-0	0-0-0	1 - 0	0 - 0	0	6
2. Assy & Pres	6-2	7-0-7	13-2	12-2	0	51
3. Assy	0-0	0-5-3	0 - 2	8 - 0	4	22
No *direct* elections	0-0	0-3-1	0 - 0	1 - 3	1	9
No elections at all	0-0	0-0-0	0 - 0	0- 14	7	21
Totals	36-17	13-8-11	18-4	21-20	12	160

Europe	Islamic	Africa	Asia	Latin America

.3a=**strong mpr** (n=36)

1. Leg>PM
Ire.,Belg.,Neth.,Lux.
Can.,UK, Nor.,Swed.   Israel   Austrl.,NZ   Belize,Trin.
Switz.,Den.,Ger.,It.   India   St.V.,St.L.
Malta,Spain,Greece   Barbados
                                                     Jamaica   (25)
1a. Leg>PM & dir.el.Pres(mixed)
Ice.,Fin.,Port.
France,Austria   (5)
2. Assy & dir.el.Pres=Hd.Gov
US   Cyprus   Ec.,Ven.,C.Rica
                                                     Dom.Rep.   (6)

.3b=**weak ~mpr** (n=17)

1. Leg>PM: Czechoslovakia   S. Africa   Maurits.,Japan   Antigua,Bahamas
            Hungary   Botswana   Papua,WSam,Sol,Van. Dom.,St.C.,Gren. (15)
2. Assy & dir.el.Pres=Hd.Gov.
            Poland   Gambia   (2)

.3c=**1pdom** (n=13)

1.Leg>PM: Bulgaria   Namibia   Malay.,Sing.,Mong.   Guyana   (6)
2.Assy & dir. el. Pres: Iran   Senegal,Iv.Coast
           Romania   Egypt Zimbabwe   Mexico   (7)

.3d=**1pcom** (n=8)

3.Assembly only
           USSR, Albania   N.Kor.,VN,Laos   (5)
No dir. el. Yugoslavia   China   Cuba   (3)

.3e=**1p-other** (n=11)

2.Assy & dir. el. Pres: Djib.   Gab.,Camr.,Sierra L.   (7)
                                  Kenya,Tanz.,Zambia
3.Assembly only   Tunisia C.Verde, Malawi   (3)
No dir. el: STP   (1)

Table V5.1b (continued)

	Islamic	Africa	Asia	Lat.Am.		

.4b=**milp states** (n=22)   *mpr   *1pd

	Islamic	Africa	Asia	Lat.Am.	*mpr	*1pd
1.Leg>PM (or Pres):	Turk.,Pak.	Thailand	Suriname		(4)	
1a.Leg>PM,&Pres(mix):		Sri Lanka			(1)	
2.Assy & dir.el.Pres:		Phil.I,S.Korea	Arg,Brz,Bol,Col,Peru			
			Chile,Guat,ElSal.,Nic.		(11)	
		Bangldsh.,Madag.				(2)
+ variant (*party* of leading dir.el.Pres.cands.):			Urug.,Honduras		(2)	
3.Assy only:		Taiwan,Indonesia				(2)
					(18)	(4)

.4c=**mil^** (n=21)

	Islamic	Africa	Asia	Lat.Am.	*mpr	*1pd
2.Assy&dir.el.Pres:	Syria,Algeria	CAFR,Mali,Togo,Niger	Seychelles	Paraguay		
	Somalia	Zaire,Congo,Rwanda			(12)	
3. Assy only:	Afghan.,Iq.,Yemen	GBissau,Benin,Ethiop.,Moz.	Cambodia		(8)	
No *dir.* el.:		Angola			(1)	

.4d=**mil°** (n=20)

	Islamic	Africa	Asia	Lat.Am.	*mpr	*1pd
1.Leg>PM:	Lebanon					(1)
2.Assy & dir.el.Pres≈:			Comoros	Haiti	(2)	
No *dir.* el.:	Libya	Eq.Guinea,Uganda			(3)	
No elections:	Chad,Sudan	Ghana,Guinea,BF,Liber.	Maldives			
	Mauritania	Nigeria,Burundi,Lesotho	Myanmar,Fiji	Panama	(14)	

≈ As of 12/90, only presidential elections have been held in Comoros, and Haiti is in transition.

.5a=**monarchy** (n=12)

	Islamic	Africa	Asia	Lat.Am.	*mpr	*1pd
3. Assy only:	Jordan,Morocco		Nepal,Bhutan		(4)	
No *dir.* el:		Swaziland			(1)	
No elections:	Kuwait,SaudiA.,Oman		Brunei		(7)	
	UAE,Bahrain,Qatar					

Summary by 3 Electoral and *4 Gross* Polity Types

Electoral Type	mpr	1pp	*milp	mil/mon	TOT.
1. Leg>PM	40	6	4	1	51
1a. Leg>PM,&Pres(mix)	5	0	1	0	6
2. Assy. & dir. el. Pres	8	14	15	14	51
3. Assy. only	0	8	2	12	22
No *direct* elections	0	4	0	26	30
Totals	53	32	22	53	160

Source: V5.1b Data Bank.

V5.2. POWER-SHARING WITHIN GOVERNMENTS

The main forms of government will be defined and described at greater length in sections V5.3 and .4; regardless of political system, however, there are certain institutions common to almost all regimes, and they will be discussed here. They include a.) the heads of state and government, and of the leading political party, and of the armed forces; b.) representative assemblies; and c.) constitutional or informal "balancing arrangements" for other important societal groups. An analysis of how power is distributed among such structures will set the framework for this chapter's measurements of political participation.

V5.2a. Heads of Major Political Institutions

A fundamental division of power within governning regimes involves the distinction between the head of state and the head of government. The head of *state* represents the nation and possesses control of its most treasured and enduring symbols (the flag, the anthem, etc.); he or she generally holds office for an extended period of time, and is considered to be "above the battle" of partisan skirmishes for power. In contrast, the head of *government* makes day-to-day policy (which often can be controversial and unpopular), and is supposed to be more readily accountable to the citizenry. In some systems there is an executive head of state who performs both the ceremonial functions and is the actual head of government as well, even though sometimes a first (or "prime") minister is appointed from the cabinet to assist in the more mundane matters of daily governance.

At this level of analysis, civilian multiparty republics (n=53) may be either parliamentary (40), presidential (8), or mixed (5). In *parliamentary* mprs, the head of government is the leader of the majority party (or coalition of parties) in the representative assembly, and all (cabinet) ministers of government come out of that body (relationship to be abbreviated here as *Leg>PM*). The prime minister is more important in a daily, political sense than the head of state, whose identity is determined in a number of different ways (constitutional monarch, appointed governor general, indirect election). A minority of mprs have a *strong presidential* system where the head of state is directly elected and the two functions of head of government and head of state are generally combined. Finally, there are a few *mixed* systems, where the head of state and head of government are both selected by the people, at different times (the former in a direct election, the latter via the legislature), and are potential competitors for power. (For examples of each of the above, see Table V5.1b, Electoral Types 1, 1a, and 2; section V5.3ab; and for militarized mprs, V5.4b.)

In one-party states (n=32) where government is considered an instrument of the party's rule, neither the head of government nor the head of state is the most significant position. Rather, the head of *party* (generally called the secretary general) is the most powerful political actor, although the person holding this post might also serve as head of state or (less frequently) head of government. Within the party, the politburo, central committee, and party congress are organs which decrease in importance as the number of their members increases. (See sections V5.3cde.)

In military systems (n=41: 21 mil$^\wedge$ + 20 mil^{o}), the armed forces are a more important institution than either the head of state or head of government, or head of party (if any exists). In fact the military chief often arrogates to himself some or all of these titles. The most important of these offices usually is head of state, for the army typically portrays its intervention into the political process as necessary to save the nation. Its involvement in politics is often accompanied by the abolition (or suspension) of most other governmental and party institutions. (See sections V5.4cd.) Militarized party systems (n=22: 18 *mpr + 4 *1pdom) are a transitional category with elements of all the polity types mentioned so far, and are described at greater length in sections V5.4ab.

Like military dictators, monarchs also often claim to embody the nation ("*L'Etat , c'est moi*," said France's King Louis XIV) and always hold the title of head of state. In about half of the cases they refuse even to delegate more detailed governmental matters to a first minister. In the rest, this head of government function might be carried out by the crown prince or some other trusted member of the royal family. (See V5.5a.)

For analytic purposes here, the number of people (one, two, three, or four) holding these main positions will be taken as evidence as to whether power is being shared at the highest levels of government. It will be deemed a sign of maturity in a political system, and the first indicator of broadness of political participation, if these few positions are separated, and not held by a single individual.

A summary of the information in the V5.2a data bank (excerpts from which are presented at the end of this section) yields the results presented in Table V5.2a for 160 states as regards heads of state and government. States are divided into three gross political types: multiparty, including ¯mpr and *mpr; one-party, including *1pdom; and military/monarchy where if there are civilian parties, they are subordinate to militarized forces in the society.

The head of state and head of government are divided between two persons in 94 states, and are the same person in 66. The general pattern is that these positions are separated in the party states (74/107 for both mprs and 1pps) and centralized in the non-party states (33/53 for the mil/mons). No definitive conclusions should be drawn, however, for there is about a 33% variation in both cases.

V5.2b. Representative Assemblies

A directly elected representative assembly (also called a parliament, congress, legislature, etc.) is a second institution which might share power in a government. The number of these which are truly independent and serving such a function, generally found in the 71 mprs (36 + ˜17 + *18), is only about half of those which exist in the world (n=138). There are 22 states which have no representative assemblies at all as of December 20, 1990.

In non-militarized parliamentary mprs—the most common form of multiparty system (n=40)—the leading ministers of the government (i.e., the cabinet, including its first or prime minister) must be nominated by the legislature, and come from within its membership. The executive thus is in some respects a creature of this strong representative branch. In the mixed presidential/ parliamentary mprs (n=5), a directly elected president chosen separately from the assembly sometimes vies for power with, but is generally less important than, the prime minister who comes out of the relatively strong representative body. In strong presidential mprs (n=8), despite the existence of a moderately strong representative assembly, the executive is not chosen by or responsible to it, but rather is elected directly by the people. (See tables in sections V5.1b and V5.3a.)

The 18 militarized mprs can be divided into 4 in which the prime minister comes out of the legislature (i.e., parliamentary), 1 mixed, and 13 with separate elections for the assembly and president (i.e., presidential). (See tables in sections V5.1b and V5.4b.)

The other 67 representative assemblies are generally weak rubber-stamps for the ruling administration (either party- or military- dominated), ratifying bodies whose purpose is to perform some ceremonial or symbolic measure of representation of the people, and thus legitimation for the regime, but to share little meaningful power (Mezey, 1985; Loewenberg et al., 1985; Loewenberg and Patterson, 1979; Smith and Musolf, 1979). They generally meet only from a few days to a few weeks per year, sometimes deputizing a smaller standing committee to remain in session to "consult" with the government for the rest of the time. This type of assembly is definitely in a subservient position to the executive branch of the government and cannot really be said to share power. This is especially true in those 10 states with mostly indirectly elected or appointed assembly members, or where more than half the assembly is composed of permanent members (coded †, ª, and ´, respectively, and listed between the dashed lines in Table V5.2b.i, which ranks all assemblies in order of the total number of their members).

One final matter of representation in assemblies, summarized in Table V5.2b.ii, is addressed by the device of having more than one chamber of representation. The "lower" house *(LH)* is usually larger and has most of its members directly elected by the people, whereas a more significant percentage of members of the (usually smaller) "upper" house *(UH)* is often appointed, or indirectly elected, in a way which ensures representation of certain interest groups in society. The types of groups which might be represented is covered in section V5.2c; here, Table V5.2b.ii reveals simply that most representative assemblies (n=76/138) are unicameral and directly elected.

Of the 52 states with two chambers with most members directly elected, 19 have upper houses which are totally or predominantly appointed. Of the remaining 33, the method of election is usually structured so that the elected officials represent larger numbers of people (and hence are less directly responsive to "popular passions") than in the lower house, or in some instances is indirect. Finally, in ten states the assemblies (seven unicameral, three bicameral) are primarily indirectly elected, appointed, or made up of permanent members. Twenty-two states have no representative assembly at all at the time of this writing, though the suspended ones in Fiji and Panama might soon be reactivated, and the rare successful elections of presidents in Haiti (in December, 1990) and Comoros (in March, 1990) may presage elections of assemblies there in the near future. (Predominantly appointive, totally advisory "consultative councils" in several of the monarchies (see section V5.5a) are not considered to be representative assemblies for purposes of this analysis.)

V5.2c. Constitutional or Other Balances

Other dimensions of power-sharing within government involve constitutional or other more informal arrangements which provide for the participation in government of important societal groups. These might include provisions for (i) a politburo, central committee, military council, or other elite group of notable persons, including a "college of electors"; (ii) ethnic quotas or other "balancing schemes" for important religious, social, or economic groups; and (iii) federal or autonomous subunits which demarcate geographically decentralized authority. (Courts were covered in section V4.4d; their special role in upholding the law often includes passing judgment as to whether the arrangements discussed here are working properly.)

In one-party states, the party's politburo and central committee produce a general secretary who is more important than the head of state or government (which titles he sometimes also assumes); these two inner party councils are also more significant than the representative assembly whose members they propose to the electorate for endorsement. In military regimes which have not built any other institutional structure, a military council (which often goes by a name such as the "committee of national salvation"; see Burundi, in excerpts at end of this section) initially serves as the junta's cabinet, and often remains in an overseeing capacity during the transition back to civilian rule; first-generation revolutionaries sometimes play a similar role (see Iran's two councils of revolution defenders). (*Advisory*, totally appointive councils with no pretense of being representative, such as are found in some monarchies, are not covered here.)

Electoral colleges (other than those associated with representative assemblies) are not too significant in most states today in choosing the head of government; they are somewhat more in evidence in selecting some heads of state. In Brazil such a body (made up of members of the constituent assembly and state governments) served as the vehicle for the transition back to civilian rule in 1985. In Taiwan, the National Assembly (as opposed to the Legislative Yuan) serves such a function, electing the president but doing little else during its six-year term. In Finland, an electoral college operates only if no candidate receives a majority in the direct presidential election, and then usually (as in 1987) picks the leading candidate anyhow. In the United States the electors representing the 50 states invariably follow the will of the majority popular vote in that state, a device which gives added importance in presidential elections to large states (though actual added weight on a per capita basis to smaller states). (For other examples of electoral colleges, see states with "indirect elections" in Table V5.1b.)

Other bodies with a constitutionally specified role in government might be based upon religion, ethnicity, or race; economic or social prominence also often results in more informal assurance of representation in government. The concept of a niche for aristocratic nobles or wealthy landholders was the historic justification for many of the upper houses found in 55 (33+19+3 in Table V5.2b.ii) of the 138 legislatures, 20 of which remain predominantly appointive today. The Council of Experts in Iran and the rabbinical courts in Israel are examples of religious representation; the V4.5b data bank for states rated 4 has details of others.

With respect to ethnic representation, Lebanon has the most elaborate scheme, setting aside specific seats in the assembly for each of several different religious groups—Maronite Catholic, Greek Orthodox, Protestant, Greek Catholic, Armenian Orthodox, Armenian Catholic, Sunni, Shiite, and Druze—and requiring the heads of state, government, and assembly houses (including a new upper house created by the latest 1989 accord) each to be of specific different faiths. Singapore in 1988 required 13 constituencies to be represented by three-member teams, one of whom had to be non-Chinese. Similar arrangements with lesser impact can be found in the upper chambers where nationalities are represented in Czechoslovakia and Yugoslavia; in Malaysia (to restrict Chinese); and in several Islamic states (to ensure some representation for women and, in Egypt, for Coptic Christians). In South Africa there are three separate houses divided by race (for whites, Asians, and "coloureds" (i.e., mixed races), respectively), although the latter two do not have much credibility.

Even if not formally included in law as in the above examples, the informal but undeniable power in government of the various ethnic, religious, and economic groups covered in sections V4.2 and V4.5 should be noted in passing at this point. Such considerations might include the power of the family of a charismatic leader still commanding political loyalty years after it has lost its official position.

Decentralization of power is not common among the world's 160 states, and the amount of authority passed down to lower levels of government is difficult to calibrate, particularly on a comparative basis. There is even some dispute as to what is meant by the terms "federal" and "autonomous," often used to describe sub-units of government (Brown-John, 1988; Burgess, 1988; Duchacek, 1987). Table V5.2c.i identifies 36 states with special powers reserved in the national assembly and/or over certain local matters for lower-level states, provinces, republics, or regions. As the dates shown after certain of the countries imply, the issue of decentralized power is often one of some tension which has frequently to be renegotiated.

Electoral balancing schemes which are unrelated to any identifiable power centers will be explained at greater length in the analyses of polity types in sections V5.3 and V5.4, especially V5.3a (mprs) where such devices are most in evidence. Table V5.2c.ii outlines the format for four pages of excerpts from the V5.2 data bank which show how some of the matters related to power-sharing discussed in this section are presented for 20 states drawn from a representative sample of zones and polity types.

V5.2a - Head of State/Head of Government Relationship

Europe	Islamic	Africa	Asia	Latin America
States where Hd. of State and Hd. of Govt. are divided (n=94)				
mpr, ~mpr & *mpr				
Can,UK,Nor,BeNeLux	Israel		India,~Maurts.,*Sri L.	Belize,Barb.
Swed.,Den.,Spain	*Turkey		*Phil.I.,*Thailand	St.L., St.V.
Ire.,Ice.,Fr.,Fin.	*Pakistan	~S.Africa	~Japan, *S.Korea	~Jam., ~Gren.
Ger.,Aust.,Port.			~PapuaNG,~Solom.	~St.C., ~Baham.
Italy,Malta,Greece			~WSamoa,~Van.	~Antig., ~Dom.
~Pol.,~Hung., ~Czech.			Australia, NZ	Trinidad
22	3	1	13	11 (50/71)
1p & *1p				
USSR	Iran	C.Verde,Gabon	*Madagascar	Guyana
Yugoslavia	Egypt	Tanzania	Malay.,Singpore	
Albania	Tunisia	Zambia	China,Mong.,NKor.	
Bulg.,Romania	Djibouti	Zimbabwe	VN,Laos,*Taiwan	
5	4	5	9	1 (24/36)
mil/mon				
	Afghan.,Jordan	Niger,Congo	Nepal	
	Syria,Lebanon	Eq.Guinea	Myanmar	
	Kuw.,Bahr.,UAE	Uganda,Lesotho	Cambodia	
	Mor.,Alg.,Libya	Swaziland	Fiji	
	10	6	4	0 (20/53)
(27)	(17)	(12)	(26)	(12) (94/160)
States where Hd. of State = Hd. of Govt.(n=66)				
mpr & *mpr				
US	Cyprus	~Gambia		*Arg.,*Peru,*Chile,*Col.
Switzerland		~Botswana		*Urug.,*Bol.,*Brz.,*Sur.
				*Hond,*ElSal,*Guat,*Nic
				C.Rica,Dom.Rep.,Ven.,Ec.
2	1	2		16 (21/71)
1p & *1p				
		IC,SL,Senegal	*Bangladesh	Mexico
		STP, Camr.,Kenya	*Indonesia	
		Malawi,Namibia		Cuba
	0	8	2	2 (12/36)
mil/mon				
	Yemen,Oman	Liberia,Benin	Comoro	
	Saudi A.,Qatar	BF,Mali,Nigeria	Seychelles	Paraguay
	Mauritania	GB,Guinea,Ghana	Maldives	Haiti
	Chad,Sudan	C.Af.R.,Togo,Zaire	Bhutan	Panama
	Somalia,Iraq	Rw.,Bur.,Ethiopia	Brunei	
		Angola,Mozambique		
	9	16	5	3 (33/53)
(2)	(10)	(26)	(7)	(21) (66/160)
TOT: 29	27	38	33	33 (160)

Source: V5.2a Data Bank.

V5.2b.i - Numbers Elected[^] to Representative Assemblies

Europe	Islamic	Africa	Asia	Latin America
USSR 1500		Ethiopia 835	India 792	Mexico 564
Italy 945			Japan 764	Brazil 559
France 896	Egypt 458	Benin 336		
Germany 656	Turkey 450	Zaire 310	N.Korea 615	
UK 650	Afghan. 334	S.Africa 308		Colombia 313
Poland 560	Pakistan 324	Uganda 298	Indonesia 500	Argentina 300
Spain 558	Yemen 309	Tanzania 244	Vietnam 496	Venezuela 250
US 535	Morocco 306	Mozambique 210		Peru 240
Romania 519	Algeria 295	Kenya 200	Mongolia 430	Chile 158
	Iran 270	Cameroon 180		Bolivia 157
Bulgaria 400	Syria 250	Ivory Coast 175	Thailand 357	Uruguay 130
Belgium 393	Iraq 250	Congo 153	Bangladesh 330	Honduras 128
Hungary 386			S.Korea 299	Dom.Rep.120
	Somalia 177	Zambia 136	Sri Lanka 225	Paraguay 108
		Senegal 120	Phil. I. 224	Guatemala 100
Czech. 350	Tunisia 141	Zimbabwe 120	Australia 224	
Sweden 349	Lebanon 128	Malawi 112		Nicaragua 91
Greece 300	Israel 120	Sierra L.104	Malaysia 180	Ecuador 71
Canada 295		Gabon 120	Bhutan 150	Guyana 65
Portugal 250			Nepal 140	Jamaica 60
Albania 250		Niger 93	Madagascar 137	El Salvador 60
Austria 246		C.Verde 83	Cambodia 117	Costa Rica 57
Switz. 246	Jordan 80	Mali 82	Papua NG 109	Suriname 51
Ireland 226		Togo 77	N.Zealand 95	Bahamas 49
Nethrlds. 225	Djibouti 65	Namibia 72	Singapore 81	Trinidad 36
Finland 200	Cyprus 56	Rwanda 70	Laos 79	Belize 28
Denmark 179			Mauritius 70	Barbados 27
Norway 165		C.Af.R. 52	Maldives 48	Dominica 21
		Gambia 44	W.Samoa 47	St. Lucia 17
Malta 65			Vanuatu 39	Antigua 17
Luxembrg. 64		Botswana 38		Grenada 15
Iceland 63			Solomons 38	St. Vincent 13
			Seychelles 25	St. Chris. 11
n=28	n=17	n=26	n=27	n=30 (128)

Europe	Islamic	Africa	Asia	Latin America
	Libya 618†	Angola 289†	China ~3000†	Cuba 510†
Yugo. 308†		GBissau 150†		
		Swazi. 70[a]	Taiwan 101+189′	
		Eq.Guinea 60†		
		STP 54†		
n=1	n=1	n=5	n=2	n=1 (10)

† indirectly elected;   [a] = predominantly appointed;   ′ = permanent members;

Europe	Islamic	Africa	Asia	Latin America
NONE:	None=9	None=7	None=4	None=2 (22)
	Saudi A.,Bahr.,Kuw.	Nigeria,Liberia,BF	Myanmar	Haiti*
	Qatar,Oman,UAE	Guinea,Ghana	Fiji,Brunei	Panama
	Chad,Sudan,Mauritan.	Lesotho,Burundi	Comoros*	
29	27	38	33	33 (160)

[^]Figures do not include totals in Upper Houses whose members are *predominantly appointed*.
(e.g.,UK,SU,Indon.,many Caribbean); they are included if their number is minimal or token.
*Figures do not reflect changes in assemblies in transition in December, 1990 (Comoros, Haiti).

V5.2b.ii - Houses of Assembly

Europe	Islamic	Africa	Asia	Latin America

Unicameral Assembly, directly elected

Europe	Islamic	Africa	Asia	Latin America
Malta	Israel,Syria	Sen,Gamb,CV,IC,Ben.	Madag.,Mauritius	Ecuador
Portugal	Iran,Iraq	Sierra L.,Mali,Togo	Seychelles,Maldives	C.Rica,Honduras
Greece	Turkey,Cyprus	Niger,C.Af.R.,Gabon	Sri Lanka,Bhutan	El Sal.,Guatemala
Albania	Morocco	Camr.,Congo,Zaire	Nepal,Bangladesh	Nicaragua
Bulgaria	Tunisia	Rwanda,Ethiopia	Mong.,NKor.,SKor.	St.Chris.
Hungary	Djibouti,Somalia	Kenya,Uganda	VN,Laos,Cambodia	Grenada
Finland	Algeria	Mozambq.,Namibia	Singapore,Papua NG	Guyana
Sweden	Egypt	Tanzania,Zambia	Vanuatu, W.Samoa	Suriname
Denmark	Yemen	Zimbwe.,S.Africa[e]	Solomons,N.Zealand	
9	13	24	20	10 (76)

[e] S.Af. has three houses, divided by race; but the Asian and Coloured houses are not credible.

Bicameral Assembly, mostly elected (incl. indir. el=†)

Europe	Islamic	Africa	Asia	Latin America
US,Ire.,Ice.	Pakistan		India	Arg.,Venez.,Col.
Nor.,Belg.,Neth.	Lebanon		Phil.I.	Brazil,Chile
France†,Switz.			Australia	Peru,Bolivia
Ger.,Austria†			Japan	Uruguay,Paraguay
Spain,Italy,Pol.				Dom.Rep.
Czech.,Rom.,USSR†				Mexico
16	2	0	4	11 (33)

Bicameral Assembly, predominantly appointed([a]) Upper House

Europe	Islamic	Africa	Asia	Latin America
Canada	Jordan	Botswana	Thailand	Belize,Antigua
UK	Afghanistan	Malawi	Malaysia	Bahamas,Barbados
Luxmbrg.			Indonesia	Dominca,Jamaica
				St.L.,St.V.,Trinidad
3	2	2	3	9 (19)

NOT Primarily Directly Elected

Europe	Islamic	Africa	Asia	Latin America
		GB†, STP†,Eq.G.†	China†	Cuba†
Yugoslavia††	Libya†	Angola†		
		Swaziland[a]†	Taiwan''	
1	1	5	2	1 (10)

[a]† = Swaziland has **two** houses, one predominantly appointive, one mostly indirectly elected;

†† = Yugoalvia has **two** houses, both indirectly elected ;

'' = Taiwan has **two** houses, *both* predominantly life-long members;

No Representative Assembly

Europe	Islamic	Africa	Asia	Latin America
	Saudi A.,Bahr.,Kuw.	Nigeria,Liberia,BF	Myanmar	Panama
	Qatar,Oman,UAE	Guinea,Ghana	Comoros	
	Chad,Sudan,Mauritan.	Burundi,Lesotho	Fiji,Brunei	Haiti
	9	7	4	2 (22)
29	27	38	33	33 (160)

V5.2c.i - Federal (or Significantly Decentralized) States

Europe	Islamic	Africa	Asia	Latin America
		(a) - Federated States		
US	Pakistan	Botswana	India	Brazil
Canada		Tanzania	Australia	St.Chris.-Nevis
Belgium			Papua NG	Trinidad-Tobago
W.Germany			Solomons	Antigua-Barbuda
Switzerland			Vanuatu	Argentina(?)
Austria				Venezuela(?)
Czechoslovakia		Nigeria		Mexico(?)
Belgium(?)				
		(b)-States with Important Autonomous Units		
Spain	Iraq	Ethiopia ('87)	Comoros	
Yugoslavia ('74)	Lebanon^	S. Africa (h)	Sri Lanka ('88)	
USSR	Cyprus^		China	
			Malaysia	
n=11	n=4	n=5	n=9	n=7 (36)

^ = defacto, by military force of insurgents;   (date)=most recently federalized.
(?)-weakly federal either in fact (Venez.) or in law (Belg.);   (h)=homelands scheme.

V5.2c.ii - Format for V5.2abc-Power Sharing Data Bank EXCERPTS

Name of state - polity type

2a - names of Head of State, Head of Govt., & (if relevant) Head of Party, Army;
  with summary of their relationship (<, >, and = used to describe actual (not formal) power
  relationships; i.e., Queen<PM, exec. Pres.>PM, etc.; if Hd. Party, Army *is* Hd. St. or Govt. this office
  need not be mentioned until .2c, (otherwise, < .2c by exception only).
(Official titles & date of accession & relegitimation, where available.)

.2b - representative assembly: i. tot. # mbrs.: lower + upper houses (LH+UH);
  #elected, #appointed; terms of office for all;
  N.B. tot. # often varies due to ex-officios, appointees, etc., esp. in UH;
    # dir. el. usually fixed, but often increases as population rises.

.2c - constitutional (or other informal) balancing arrangements re .2a & .2b, and as concerns
  other important power centers such as:
    i. dominant party (& its politburo, central committee #s); other revolutionary or military
  councils (=Cabs. in mil.regimes); electoral colleges;
    ii. interest groups (ethnic, religious, economic, etc.) from V4.2, V4.5, V1.1b; also
  charismatic personalities, families;
    iii. decentralized sub-units (federal states; or autonomous regions, provinces,
  republics).

EUROPE

USA - mpr
- a. Pres. G.Bush (1/89) is both Hd. of State & Govt. Dir.elected; two fixed 4-yr.renewable terms.
- b. Congress=535: House (435, el. ev. 2 yrs) + Senate(100, 1/3 el. ev. 6 yrs.). Moderate strength, in strong presidential system.
- c.i) electoral college gives added importance to largest of 50 federal states in selection of President.
- ii) military-industrial complex since Cold War has kept most govts. to center-right. V1.2's mil.exp. 30-50% of natl. budget, 5-10% GNP.

Finland - mpr
- a. Pres. Mauno Kovisto (1/82,1/88) > PM Harri Holkeri (5/87)
- b. Edeskunta = 200 members (unicam.); el., 4 yrs., pop. vote. "Consensual" Leg (>PM) has only moderate strength vs. strong Pres; 2/3 majority needed to pass much legislation for >1 yr.
- c.i) strong Pres., 6 yr. terms, renewable; vetoes; may dissolve Leg. at any time; decides which party to form govt. (brought in Cons. in '87).
- i) Each citizen has 2 votes, 1 for Pres., 1 for mbr. of Electoral College (n=301), which chooses if no Pres. cand. has >50% vote (always).

Czechoslovakia - ˜mpr
- a. Pres. Vaclav Havel (12/89; 6/90) > PM Marian Calfa (12/89; 6/90)
- b. Fedl.Assy n=300: 150 in House of the People (101 fm. Czech. republic, 49 fm. Slovakia) plus 150 in House of Nations (75 fm. each).
- c.i) Communist Party relinquished its monopoly of power in 12/89, and lost in first multiparty elections in 6/90. Soviet troops scheduled to leave by 1991.
- ii) Dubcek's 1968 federalism between 2/3 Czech and 1/3 Slovak population (see V4.2) made more meaningful after 6/90 change to ˜mpr and 12/90 changes to constitution.

USSR - 1pcom
- a. Pres. Mikhail Gorbachev (10/88; 3/90) > PM N.I. Ryzhkov (12/85; 3/90)
- b. new (3/89) Congress of Peoples Deputies (n=2250, in 3 houses: 750 apptd. by CPSU (n=100) and its Fronts, 750 dir. el. fm. Territorial Districts acc. to population, 750 dir.el. fm. National Territorial Districts). Elects State Pres. & Supreme Soviet (n=542), 5 yrs.
- c.i) Communist Party (CPSU) & esp. its Genl. Secy. Gorbachev (3/85) was formerly the most powerful actor, with Politburo n=13, Cent. Cmtee. n=300. New Pres. Gorbachev balances between party forces, new more freely elected assembly, and strengthened republics.
- iii) 15 "union" republics based on nationalities (see V4.2) to be stronger under proposed union treaty; + 20 "autonomous" republics, enclaves within some union republics.

ISLAMIC

Iran - 1pdom
- a. Pres. ali Akbar Hashemi Rafsanjani (8/89; 4 yrs., non-renew.) > PM (abolished 8/89)
- b. Natl. Islamic Consultative Assy n=270; elected (1/2 clerics), 4 yr.terms. Speaker: Mehdi Karrubi (9/89). Spirited debate, some executive-proposed laws voted down. Though parties abolished in 7/87, Govt. has slim majority for economic centralization (> minimalist Islamic-state mullahs who prefer more private (esp. church) property).
- c. i) 1980-88 Iraq war consolidated power of religious mullahs (esp. Ayatollah Khomeini) in:
  - 1. Council of Guardians f. Protection of Constitution (n=12; 6 relig. apptd. by Khomeini, 6 lay nom. by Judic. Council, appvd. by Assy.); ensures Assy. bills iaw Islamic Law & Constitution; also screens candidates for Pres., Assy., & Council of Experts.
  - 2. Council of (Relig.) Experts (n=80), el. in 1982 to choose Khomeini successsor as Velayat Fagih (Supreme Jurist & Revolution Guide); ex-'84-89 Pres. Khamenei chosen (6/89).

V5.2abc EXCERPTS (continued)

Algeria -mil^
- a. Pres. H.E.Chadli Benjedid (2/79; 2/84; 2/89) > PM Mouloud Hamrouche (9/89).
- b. Natl. Pop. Assy.: 295 mbrs; elected by pop. vote ev. 5 yrs. Weak: Pres. may dissolve at any time, rules by decree between sessions. Con. amndmts. for more powers in 11/88.
- c.i) FLN (Natl.Lib.Front) party and military both more impt. than Assy.; all elected officials must be nominated by FLN. Chadli is its head. FLN is dominated by military (Boumedienne, Chadli). This system is under challenge from newly-legalized parties in 1990, esp. at local level.

Jordan - mon
- a. King Hussein (8/52) > PM Mudar Badran (12/89).
- b. Assy = Natl. Consultative Council (House of Deputies), n=80; el.,4 yrs.; + Senate (n=40, apptd. by King, 8-yr. terms). Weak; was dissolved (1967-84 and 7/88-11/89) by King.
- c.i) King (since 1952) is real power. Parties not allowed. In Natl. Assy.,.....
- ii) ..... 18 seats reserved for minority Bedouins, Christians, & Circassians; and
- iii) districts drawn to favor rural villages (> cities which are mainly Palestinian). No West Bank representation since 7/88 renunciation of claim.

AFRICA

South Africa - ˜mpr
- a. Pres. F. W. de Klerk is Hd. of State & Govt. (8/89; 9/89).
- b. House of Assy (whites), n=178, 166 elected, 12 appointed by President.
  8/84 Constitut. Amendmt. created 2 other Houses (tot. strength: 130): House of Reps.(n=45) for Asians, & House of Delegates (n=85) for "coloureds/mixeds". No elected representation for blacks (72% population).
- c.i.a) Electoral college of "Assy+" chooses President. 4/88 proposal to bring in blacks; also to allow appointees to Cabinet from "other than Leg." (i.e., blacks).
- i.b) F.W.deKlerk elected party chm., 3/89, succeeded as state pres. in 8/89.
- ii.a) Apartheid policy separating 4 races (and tribes within the African race) in all areas of life under increasing challenge after 2/90 legalization of ANC and other black political groups.
- ii.b) Even the nominally multiparty white political sector divides along English and Afrikaans lines, enabling the dominant (pro-apartheid) Afrikaans National Party to rule since 1948.

Kenya - 1p-other
- a. Pres. Daniel Arap Moi is Hd. of State & Govt. ('78, '83, 3/88).
- b. Natl.Assy.=200: 188 dir. el., 5 yrs. + 12 apptd. by Pres.; + Spkr. F. Mati & Atty.Genl.
- c.i) Only one legal party (Kenya Afr. Natl. Union) acc. to 6/82 constitution; 2/87 law makes KANU > Assy. Its Pres. < state Pres. arap Moi, however.
- ii) KANU purposely multi-ethnic for though Kikuyu dominated, Pres. arap Moi is Kalenjin unlike predecessor Kenyatta.

Sierra Leone - 1p-other (formerly mil^)
- a. Pres. Maj. Gen. Joseph Saidu Momoh = Hd. State & Govt. (11/85).
  Succeeded retiring Siaka Stevens (civ. Pres. since '67-8); 7 yr. term (2 max.), el. by mbrs. of Natl. Delegates Conf. of the All-Peoples Congress (=party).
- b. House of Reps. n=104, 85 dir. el., 5 yrs., APC mbrs.; + 12 el. by traditional councils, 7 appointed by Pres. (Proposed raise to 127; 105 el. + 12 + 10 apptd.).
- c.i) After 4/68 coup, mil. appointed '67 election winner Stevens Pres. in 10/68. 1978 Constitut. makes 1-party system; opp. SLPP (n=15/89 seats) merged into All-Peop.Cong. (party). But Stevens successor & choice (via party structure) Momoh came out of mil.
- ii) Election slates strive for Temne/Mende (=SLPP/APC) balance; ex-Pres. Stevens still powerful. So are Lebanese merchants in economy. A Council of Elders made up of 147 chiefs.

V5.2abc EXCERPTS (continued)

Ethiopia - mil^
a. Pres.=Lt.Col. Mengistu Haile Mariam (12/77; 9/87) > PM Fikre Selassi Wogderess.
b. Shengo=Natl. Assy., n=835(DOS-HR88). 1st rep. body since Imperial Parl. abolished, 9/74. 1st direct election ever, 6/87, of 1-party assembly, which elected president in 9/87.
c.i) Workers Party of Ethiopia named "guiding force of the state" in constitut. ref. 2/87. But this merely extends 1974-87 system where exec. & leg. power were held by Provisional Military Admin. Council, its Centl. Cmtee.(Mengistu Chm.), & its 1979 Council of State.
ii) Govt. trying to break ethnic secessionist movements (see V1.1b, V4.2) with 1987 constitution of 5 autonomous regions: Eritrea, Tigray, Ogaden, Assab, & Dira Dawa.

Burundi - mil°
a. Maj. Paul Buyoya=Hd. of State Pres.(9/87) > Hd. of Govt. PM A. Sibornana (Hutu, 10/88).
b. Natl. Assy = 65, 52 dir. el, 13 apptd., 5-yrs. Suspended by 9/87 coup.
c.i) Mil. Cmtee for Natl. Salvation (n=31, with Exec.Cmtee. n=10) suspended UPRONA (Union for Natl. Progress) Party (+24 others) activity.
ii) Hutu majority (85% pop.) doesn't rule. Supported by RC Church (67% pop.) whose services were banned, spring '87 (previous Bagaza govt.).

ASIA

India - mpr
a. Pres. Ramaswami Venkataraman (7/87) < PM Chandra Shekar (11/90). Leg.>PM, 5 yr. term; Pres. el. by both houses of Parliament plus 24 state legs., 5 yr. term.
b. Parl.=792: 542 Lok Sabha (House of People), 540 dir. el., 2 apptd., 5 yrs. + 250 Rajya Sabha (Council of States); 232 dir. el., 18 apptd., 6 yrs.
c.ii) Gandhi family has ruled India for 38 of its first 43 years; their Congress Party for 40/43.
iii) 25 federal states (with own Parls. etc.), linguistically based (see V4.2).

Malaysia - 1pdom
a. Paramount Ruler Azlan M. Shah(3/89) < PM Mahathir bin Mohammed ('81,'82,'86, 10/90).
b. Leg.=238: 180 in House (up from 177 in '86, 154 in '82), 5 yr. terms. + 58 in Senate, 32 apptd. by Hd. St., 26 el. by 13 state assys., 6 yr. terms.
c.i.) Paramount Ruler el. by (& rotates among) hereditary rulers of 9 states, 5-yrs.; has broad powers which PM & Leg. tried to restrict in '83, but Prmt. Ruler would not sign.
ii) Dominant UNMO party positions self between Chinese on the left and Fundamentalist Islamics on the right. PM must be Malay (among other restrictions on Chinese-see V4.2d data bank).
iii) Regional Leg. seats (1986): 132 fm peninsula, 25 fm Sarawak, 20 fm Sabah; nine royal states represented in Pres. incl: Jahore, Kedah, Kalantan, Perak, Perlis, Penang, etc.

Indonesia - *1pdom
a. Pres. Suharto is Hd. of State & Govt., el. by Assy. for 5 yr terms ('66;'68;'73;'78;'83;3/88).
b. Peop.Consultative Assy.=1000 mbrs: 500 House of Reps. (400 el., 100 apptd.(see V5.4b)), 5 yrs. (weak; no Leg. init.); + 500 Others (indir. el. representing provinces, parties, military, & govt. appointees) to elect Pres. only (i.e., electoral college).
c.i) military powerful since 1965-takeover. '88 law enshrined its role (dwifungsi) in politics (incl. 230 Assy. seats). Dominant Golkar Party of '65 coup leaders continues to dominate .
ii) Since '68, Party has been Gen. Suharto's vehicle for five 5-yr. terms. 3/88 Vice Pres. Sudharmono, Golkar Chm. & likely next Pres., is more Suharto's than military's man.
ii) '85 law requires all groups to endorse *Pancasila* ideology--1. one God; 2. humanitarianism; 3. national unity; 4. consensus democracy; 5. social justice;—which virtually outlaws sectarian (i.e., Islamic Fundmentalist) politics.

V5.2abc EXCERPTS (continued)

Myanmar - mil²

a. Gen. Saw Maung (9/88), Chm. of State Cmtee for Restoration of Law and Order (SLORC, n=17, mostly military) holds powers of Hd. of State and Govt.

b. Peoples Assembly (n=489) suspended since coup of 9/88. Elections held 5/90, but junta refuses to honor results, saying elections were not for rep. assy. but for constitutional assembly to draft constitution in accordance with junta guidelines.

c.i.) Formerly dominant military party Burma Socialist Program Party, which ruled 1962-88, renamed National Unity Party after 1988 unrest; its chairman General Ne Win (1962 coup-leader) is assumed to be its leading figure still.

iii.) 1974 constitution replaced federal state with unitary one in attempt to stifle demands (incl. periodic armed insurgency since 1948) of several ethnic groups for greater autonomy.

LATIN AMERICA

Cuba - 1pcom

a. Hd. St.,Govt., & Party: Pres. and 1st. Sec. CCP: Fidel Castro (1/59; '76;'81;'86).

b. National Assembly of Peoples Power (n=510); indir. el., 5 yr. terms; 55% fm. municipal assys, 45% nominated by govt. & party; meets briefly; weak.

c. Communist Party (Cent. Cmtee n=146, Politiburo n=24) and Govt.'s Council of Ministers are both dominated by charismatic 1959 revolution leader Castro.

Colombia - *mpr

a. Hd. St. & Govt.: Pres. Cesar Gaviria (5/90).

b. Congress=312: 199 Chamber of Deps. + 113 Senate, elected to concurrent 4-yr. terms with separately elected President.

c.i) 2 parties (Cons. & Libl.) dominate, even alternated 4-yr. Pres. terms under 1958-74 "agreement"; since 1974, they compete, but losing party assured representation in Cabinet & bureaucracy, a system which has discouraged new parties from forming. Attempt to open system to more parties via 12/90 constitutional convention.

ii) many paramilitary groups on right and left; "world's most violent country" (*Econ.,* 8/11/90).

Brazil - *mpr

a. Hd. State & Govt.: Pres. Fernando Collor de Mello (3/90).

b. Natl. Cong.&Constit.Assy. n=559: Chamber of Deputies (n=490: 479 dir. el. + 11 apptd., 4 yrs.) + Senate (69; 3 ea. fm. 23 state assys., 8 yrs.).

c. 3/88 compromise on new constitut. for dir. el. Pres. (over proposed parl. system) in '89, and to reduce VP-accessor Sarney's term to 5 yrs. Referendum on final govt. form deferred to '91.

i) 1964-85 coup-regime followed by mil.-controlled electoral college choice of "acceptable" civilian president in 1985. Only one democratically-elected civilian Pres. has ever served full term (Kubitschek, 1956-60). 1988 constitut. retains military's historic right to intervene in politics. First free pres. el. since 1960 held 11/89.

iii) 23 fedl. states with separately elected governors & power in Upper House. Proportional representation favors small states in assy.

Panama - mil²

a. Pres. Guillermo Endara (12/89) is Hd. of State and Govt.

b. Natl. Leg. Council, n=67, dir.el., 5 yr. terms; suspended after annulled election of 5/89; not revived (as of 12/90) after US invasion and overthrow of govt. in 12/89.

c.i) military has been main power for 22 yrs., since 1968 coup (esp. Gens. Torrijos and Noriega).

ii) US historic power since its crucial role in 1903 secession from Colombia; 10,000 troops permanently there used in 12/89 invasion to install Endara, alleged winner of 5/90 election.

V5.3. PARTICIPATION IN CIVILIAN POLITIES

Eighty-five countries, divided into five polity types, will be analyzed in this section. Two kinds of multiparty systems and three forms of single-party polities will be discussed. The one characteristic they all have in common is that the political process is essentially in civilian hands. As is the case throughout the entire Comparative Government Spread Sheet, arguments could be made for different placements of certain countries; the main point of this analysis is to employ the definitions of the various governing systems, and to test indicators for measuring whether states conform to the categories in which they have been put.

V5.3a. Multiparty Republics

mpr = <u>multiparty republics</u> (n=36—V5.3a)

US,Canada,Iceland	Cyprus	Australia	Venezuela
Ireland,Norway		New Zealand	Ecuador
Bel.,Neth.,Lux.	Israel		Costa Rica
UK,France		India	Belize
Germany			Jamaica
Dnmk.,Swed.,Finld.			Barbados
Switz.,Austria			Dom.Rep.
Spain,Port.,Italy			St.V.,St. L.
Malta,Greece			Trinidad
Sbtot: 21	2	3	10 (36)

Multiparty republics (mpr) are defined in this study as countries with essentially civilian political structures (V5.1a), legitimation from regularly scheduled elections (V5.1b) in which opposition parties have a realistic chance of coming to power, and executive power-sharing with an independent legislature (V5.2b). This definition thus includes as a "republic" constitutional monarchies because the characteristics just mentioned are more important than the functions played by the royal head of state. The presence of such a figure, however, highlights the fact that the political structure of most (40) of the 53 mprs is quite different from that of the United States in that they are parliamentary mprs. In these states, great power is centered in the representative assembly whose members choose the head of government and in many cases a separate head of state as well. Moreover, there are generally more than two viable parties which divide the popular vote in such a way that a single party seldom wins a clear majority of support, necessitating post-election bargaining to create coalition governments. Finally, most mpr governments do not have a fixed term of office and can "fall" if they lose the support of a majority in the legislature.

The above characteristics describe mainly the 36 mprs found in the top tier of the CGSS, and also (in theory) the 17 relatively weak ˜mprs which will be discussed in the next section V5.3b. The remarks which follow immediately below, however, apply to all 53 multiparty republics.

With respect to the divided head of state and head of government, most mprs have devised mechanisms for ensuring that the head of state, who represents the nation and its most cherished symbols, remains above the fray of party politics. Table V5.3a.i analyzes the selection of the head of state in the 53 mprs and shows that among the 40 parliamentary mprs, 10 states have constitutional monarchs who serve for life; 15 are former British colonies which accept a governor general designated by the queen of England; and 15 others elect their head of state indirectly by way of some electoral college such as the national representative assembly (generally both houses), or this body plus certain state officials like governors, mayors, or provincial assemblymen.

In the mixed mprs (n=5) a directly elected president chosen separately from the legislature shares power with a prime minister who comes out of the representative body. Ranked by strength of presidency, these states could be ordered: France, Finland, Portugal, Austria, Iceland. In strong presidential mprs (n=8) the directly elected president is an *executive* head of state (i.e., also the head of government, with an option of appointing a prime minister).

There is no mpr in which the head of state and the head of government are *both* directly elected. In three parliamentary mprs—Switzerland, Botswana, and South Africa—the head of government selected by the assembly is also the head of state, and thus these parliamentary systems can be said to have executive presidents. (The head of Switzerland's collective presidency rotates yearly.)

Throughout the remaining sections of this chapter, excerpts will be presented from the data bank associated with this study to illustrate the type of information stored for states in each of the different types of political systems. Where possible, examples are drawn in rough proportion from the zones in which the particular type of polity is found. The format for excerpts from the data bank for the 53 mprs is found at the bottom of Table V5.3a.ii.

Table V5.3a.iii presents a further breakdown of the 40 parliamentary mprs and 5 mixed mprs, where the composition of the legislature is critical to the formation of a government. For these 45 states, the V5.3ab data banks display by party the numerical composition of seats in the (normally lower) house of the legislature, which determines the prime minister, the more important of the two executive positions.

In about half the cases (23/45), the determinative number is derived from a relatively *simple majority* , as the excerpts from the United Kingdom, Canada, Spain, and Barbados indicate. In the remaining 22 states, a number of parties must combine their votes in order to form *coalition* governments. This is often caused by the fact that these states generally have proportional representation of parties rather than single member districts represented in the assembly. In

Israel, for example, parties winning as little as 1% of the national vote are allotted that percentage of seats in the legislature; in Denmark the cutoff is 2%, and in Germany and Austria it is 5%. In such systems many parties are almost guaranteed some representation, and in closely divided elections, small parties can hold the balance of power when it comes to forming governing coalitions. Unlike the electoral balancing schemes mentioned in section V5.2c, however, proportional representation is not related to any *predetermined* identifiable power centers.

In the 22 parliamentary mprs which have governing coalitions in 1990, the number of additional parties needed to govern varies from one to more than six. In three of these states (designated ^ in Table V5.3a.iii), parties cast their votes to help form governments, but do not join those governments (i.e., do not take cabinet seats), which are thus *minority* regimes. In three others (designated +), non-party independents are needed to form governments. (The excerpted data for Denmark and Ireland, respectively, highlight these phenomena.) A trade-off for this high degree of openness in party participation is the relatively frequent changes in government before legislative terms are completed in mpr-coalition states below the dotted line in Table V5.3a.iii. There is some debate over whether governments' falling and reconstituting themselves (without necessarily calling for new elections) is evidence of instability, or responsiveness to popular will (Lijphart, 1984b; Powell, 1982).

One of the most interesting features of these 45 parliamentary (or mixed parliamentary) mpr systems is the number of competitive parties and the various alliances they must enter in order to create governments. Ideology is often a consideration in the forming of governments in these states. Although this subject is not discussed at length until sections V5.3d and V5.4d, it will be noted here that all 53 mprs are basically capitalist in economic orientation (or in the case of the three eastern European states, in a transition in this direction). Within this paradigm, the political spectrum of viable parties (i.e., ones which normally take seats in governing coalitions) runs from socialist to conservative, as these terms are coded and defined in Table V5.3a.iv. Communist parties (on the far left) and ethnic or theocratic parties (on the far right) are generally beyond the mainstream and not members of ruling coalitions in most multiparty republics.

Where it is deemed to be relevant to the analysis of the distribution of power among parties, the abbreviations relating to left, right, and centrist ideology found in Table V5.3a.iv are used in the data bank. Parties aligning to form governments are indicated by * and annotated with their ideologies in the excerpts for the simple majority and coalitional parliamentary mprs at the end of this section.

In the remaining 13 mpr states with presidents elected independently of the representative assembly, electoral data on both the head of state and the head of government is maintained in the V5.3a data bank. In mixed mprs (n=5) the results of both these elections—percentage of vote for president, number of seats by party in legislature—are relevant to identifying the locus of power. In strong presidential mprs (n=8) the distribution of seats by party in the legislature is less significant than the percentage of vote of the winning presidential candidate, and in some cases (see Venezuela excerpt) is even tied directly to the presidential party vote. Nevertheless, an attempt is made to code both bits of information in the data bank, as is shown in the excerpts for the United States, Finland, and Venezuela.

V5.3b. Weak Multiparty Republics

~mpr = **weak** multiparty republics (n=17—V5.3b)

		Japan	Antigua
	Gambia	Mauritius	Bahamas
Hungary		W. Samoa	Dominica
Czechoslovakia	Botswana	Papua NG	St.Chris.
Poland		Vanuatu	Grenada
	S. Africa	Solomon I.	
Sbtot: 3	3	6	5 (17)

Up to this point, this analysis has covered all 53 mprs, but detailed examples and excerpts were drawn exclusively from the data bank for 36 (regular) mprs. The 17 weak ~mprs also deserve some scrutiny. Weak mprs can be found among all three major mpr types—parliamentary, presidential, and mixed—but are generally notable for the immaturity of their multiparty structure. This can be due to a number of factors, among which are a recent long history of one-party rule (∂); the domination of a single party even though all conditions for multiparty rule are present ($\sim$); a fluidity of movement among parties by major political figures ($\hat{\ }$); and restrictions upon suffrage (Δ). The major factor applicable to each ~mpr, indicated with the abbreviations just noted, can be found annotated on the 17 ~mprs in Table V5.3b. (Other mprs are weak in the sense that they are dominated by the military, but these (*mprs) are not covered until section V5.4 on militarized governance.)

The three eastern European states currently emerging from more than 40 years of one-party communist rule—Hungary, Czechoslovakia, and Poland— are obvious examples of the first category. Since 1989, they have been genuinely multiparty; however, they should not be moved to the higher mpr category until at least one more successful election employing multiparty modalities, preferably one where power passes from one group to another.

With respect to the transfer of administration to an opposition party (or coalition), in 7 of the remaining 14 ~mprs, the ruling party has never lost power despite submitting regularly to open elections—Gambia, Botswana; Vanuatu;

Antigua, Bahamas, Dominica, St. Christopher. These states are generally small and relatively inexperienced in independent government. But even in South Africa and Japan, the major party has ruled for all but two or three years since 1945.

Finally, in three small Asian island states (Mauritius, Solomons, Papua New Guinea), the party structures are so amorphous that governments are often formed by luring winning candidates away from their parties after, or between, elections; and in one (Western Samoa) suffrage is restricted to the heads of extended families. Finally, Grenada is a special case ($\partial^{\wedge}$); after periods of single-party dominance (under Gairy, Bishop, and US occupation forces), the 1990 elections yielded a fluidity of movement between parties reminiscent of the three Asian islands.

Reasons for the various deficiencies in traditional mpr power distributions can be found in the last line of the excerpts for ~mprs following Table V5.3b. In concluding this section, it might be noted that this table is a composite which summarizes many of the concepts discussed in sections V5.3a and .3b—presidential, mixed, and parliamentary mprs; simple majority versus coalitional mprs; and weak mprs, including reasons why. The display also ranks mprs by openness to party participation (a feature which also relates to governmental responsiveness and stability), as measured by the number of parties in ruling coalitions.

(with indication how Hd. of Govt. data is encoded in V5.3ab data bank)

Parliamentary: (n=40; V5.1b Elec.Type 1: Leg>PM)
Head of State for Life (contitutional monarchs):
   UK, Norway, Netherlands, Belgium, Luxembourg;
   Sweden, Denmark; Spain; ~Japan, ~W.Samoa.

                -------Hd.Govt. from # seats in Leg.   (10)

Hd. of State (Governor General) appointed by Head of Commonwealth:
   Canada; ~Mauritius, Australia, New Zealand, ~Papua New Guinea,
   ~Solomons; Belize, ~Antigua, ~Bahamas, Barbados, ~Grenada,
   Jamaica, St. Lucia, ~St. Chris., St. Vincent.

                --------Hd.Govt. from # seats in Leg.   (15)

Hd.St. (indirectly) elected (by rep. assy. or some other electoral college):
   Ireland, Germany, Switzerland, Italy, Malta, Greece,
   ~Hungary, ~Czechoslovakia; Israel; ~Botswana, ~S. Africa;
   India, ~Vanuatu; ~Dominica, Trinidad.

                --------Hd.Govt. from # seats in Leg.   (15)

Mixed (n=5; Elec.Type 1a: Leg>PM and dir. el. Pres.)
Hd.St. directly elected, but is NOT Hd. of Govt. which comes out of Leg.:
   France, Iceland, Finland, Austria, Portugal.

            --------% vote Pres. and # seats Leg. both in data bank   (5)

Strong Pres.(n=8; Elec.Type 2, Assy. & dir. el. Pres.)
(Virtually) directly elected Hd. of State who is also Hd of Govt:
   US; ~Poland; Cyprus; ~Gambia;
   Venezuela, Ecuador, Costa Rica, Dominican Republic.

             ---------%v Pres. more impt. than #Leg.seats in V5.3a data bank   (8)

Head of State and the Head of Government *both* directly elected: NONE
                                                                  (53)

Summary - mpr & ~mpr Hds. of *Govt* (from V5.1b & .2a)
Leg. > PM = 40: 25+15~   Leg. > PM; + dir. elected Pres. = 5
              dir. el. Pres.=Hd. of Govt & Hd. of State; + Assy. = 8: 6+2~

Summary - mpr & ~mpr Hds. of *State* (from V5.2a & .3a):
Hd. of State f.Life = 10:8+2~;   Hd. of State apptd. = 15:8+7~;   Hd. State indir. elected = 15:9+6~;
Hd. State dir. elected, is not Hd. of Govt. = 5;   Hd. of State dir.el.=(or appts.)Hd. of Govt. = 8:6+2~;
             (Indir. el. Hd. Govt. = Hd. State as well = 3: Switz.,Bots.,S.Af.)

Source: V5.1b, .2a, .3ab Data Banks; ~ = weak mprs.

Europe	Islamic	Africa	Asia	Latin America

mpr=multiparty republics (n=36—V5.3a)

Europe	Islamic	Africa	Asia	Latin America
USA,Can.,Iceld.	Cyprus		Australia	Venezuela
Ireland,Norway			New Zealand	Ecuador
UK, France	Israel			Costa Rica
Bel.Neth.Lux.			India	Belize
Dnmk.,Swed.,Finld.				Dom.Rep.
Ger.,Switz.,Austr.				Jamaica,Barb.
Spain,Port.,Italy				Trinidad
Malta,Greece				St.Lucia, St.V.
Sbtot: 21	2	0	3	10 (36)

mpr=*weak* multiparty republics (n=17—V5.3b)

Europe	Islamic	Africa	Asia	Latin America
Poland		Gambia	Mauritius	Bahamas
Czech.			Japan	Dominica
Hungary			Papua NG	St.Christopher
		Botswana	Vanuatu	Grenada
			Solomon I.	Antigua
		S. Africa	W. Samoa	
Sbtot: 3	0	3	6	5 (17)
Tot.mpr: 24	2	3	9	15 (53)

Format for V5.3ab - mpr and ˜mpr Data Bank EXCERPTS

a.) **State** + note whether: PRES., MIXED, or PARL. mpr; if mixed or parl., whether simple majority, coalition, or minority govt.; and # parties.

  n = # of parties or coalitions with seats in the significant (generally, lower) house;

  + = if larger total # of parties, or # parties on ballot, is known

  * = # seats needed to govern (usually LH/2); in a few cases *both* houses, (LH+UH)/2.

b) - party strengths (for latest and, if appropriate, any earlier elections) by seats in significant house, with governing coalition partners *ed.

  # = number of seats won by party, in 41 parl. & 5 mixed systems; and/or,

  % = % popular votes for party's pres. cand., in 5 mixed & 7 pres. systems.

c.) Remarks relevant to the distribution of power such as:

  % required for representation in proportional representation systems;
  turnout; ideological orientation; term of office;
  history of 1-party or military influence.

d.) why "weak" (∂, $\approx$, $\hat{}$, or Δ; see V5.3b), where weak ˜mprs.

V5.3a.iii - # Parties Forming Govts. in 45 mprs & ˜mprs, 1990

(includes 40 parl. and 5 mixed (=†) pres./parl. systems)

Europe	Islamic	Africa	Asia	Latin America
		1 party, simple parl. majority govts. (n=23)		
UK,Canada			Australia,NZealand	Belz., ˜Bah.,Barb.
Malta		˜S.Africa	˜Van., ˜W.Samoa	˜Ant., ˜Dom., ˜Gren.
Spain, Portugal†		˜Botswana	˜Japan	Trinidad,Jamaica
				˜St.C.,St.L.,St.V.
5		2	5	11 (23)

Europe	Islamic	Africa	Asia	Latin America
		multiparty coalition govts. (n=22)		
		2 parties		
Ireland+,Lux.,Nethrlds.				
Greece, Sweden, Austria†				(6)
		3 parties		
France†, Germany			˜Solomons+	
˜Hungary, ˜Czech.				(5)
		4 parties		
Iceland†, Finland†			˜Mauritius	(5)
Switz., Denmark^				
		5 parties		
Italy				(1)
		6 or more parties		
Belgium	Israel		˜Papua NG+	(3)
		1 party minority		
Norway^			India^	(2)
TOTS: 17	1		4	(22)

Legend:
^ = other parties caucus to form govt., but do not hold any Cabinet seats = *minority* govts.
(Norway, Denmk.,India); + = non-party independents needed to form govt. (Ire.,Sol.,Papua).

not applicable (strong pres. mprs & ˜mprs) (n=8):

Europe	Islamic	Africa	Asia	Latin America
USA; ˜Poland		Cyprus;	˜Gambia;	Dom.Rep.,Ven.,Ecuador,C.Rica (8)

V5.3a.iv - Abbreviations and Definitions for Party Ideologies

Abbreviations:
f-l=far left;   l=left;   l-c=left center;   c=centrist;   r-c=right-center;   r=right;   f-r=far right
comm............soc................soc-dem...................libl................cons.............ethnic/theocratic

Short ideological definitions:
comm. = vanguard party controls economics, government, politics, and culture.
soc. = government controls macro-management of the economy; pluralist politics.
soc-dem. = government involved in economic regulation; pluralist politics.
libl. = "free" economy; minimal government protection/interference.
cons. = government protects private power concentrations in economy (incl. church).
ethnic/theocratic = government protects/advances interests of a special group.

Unit.Kingdom n=2 main,11 w/ seats   650/2=325 to *

	6/83	6/87
r:Conservative P. (Thatcher; Major)	397*	375*
l:Labor P. (N.Kinnock)	209	229
c:Liberal P.(18 in '87) + Soc.Dem.P.(4)--Alliance	27	22

Regional Parties (#s fm. 9/83 el.):

N.Ireland: Offic. Unionist (Molyneux,mod.) P. (11);

Dem. Un. P. (Paisley) (3),United Ulster Pop.Un.P.(l),	21	24
Sinn Fein (IRA) (l), Soc.Dem.&Lab P.(mod.RC) (1)		

Scottish Natl. P. (2) + Welsh Natl. P./Plaid Cymru (2)

TOT.------------------------------------- 650 ------------ 650

Canada   n=3   295/2=147 to *

	9/84	11/88
r:Prog. Conservative P. (ldr: Mulroney=PM)	211* (50% v.)	170*(43%v)
l:Liberal P. (ldr: Turner)	41 (31% v.)	82 (32%v)
c-l:New Democratic P. (new,1961; Broadbent)	29 (19% v.)	43 (20%v)
independents	1	0 (5%v)

TOTALS ---------------------------------- 282 --------------- 295

Spain   n=40+, ~10 w/ seats   350/2=175 to *

	12/82	6/86	10/89
c: Socialist Workers P. (PM Gonzales)	202*-48%	184*-44%	175*
r: Pop. Alliance (Franco Min. Fraga; Anzar, Mancha)	106-27%	105-26%	106
(2:1:1 coalit. w/ ex Pop.Dem.P. & Libl.(=Xtn.Dem.)P.			
c-r: Soc. Dem. Center (ex-PM Suarez's old Un.Dem.Ctr.)	12-10%	19-9%	14
l: Communist P. (& United Left; Carillo, Iglesias, Anguita)	4-4%	7-5%	18
Sub-Total major national parties	(324)	(315)	(313)
Regional Parties: (Sub-Total)	(26)	(35)	(37)
Catalan Converg.&Union P./Repub. Lg. of Cat.(1 in ;82)	13-4%	18-5%	18
Basque Natlist. (original, moderate) P.	8-3%	6-3%	5
Herri Batasuna=Rad.Coal.f.Pop.U.(pro-ETA) P.(boycotting)	2	5	4
Basque Left (pacifist)	1	2	?
Galician,Aragonese,Canary I.,Valencian & other parties	2-4%	4-8%	10

Proportional representation to ensure each province has at least 3 seats helps regional parties.
Senate (n=208 (+42 inter-territorial = 250) does not vote to select PM.

Barbados   n=2   27/2=14 to *

	5/86	
c-r: Dem. Labor P. (ruled '61-76; Barrow ('86-7), Sandiford)	24*(59%v)	(-4;'87)
Natl. Dem. P. (1987 split-off from DLP; n= 4 of 20 MPs)	0	(+4;'87)
c-l: Labor P. (ruled '76-86; Adams, St. John)	3 (41%v)	

TOT.--------------------------------------- 27

Ireland n=4+ 166/2=84 to *	10/83	2/87	6/89
r: Fianna Fail/Warriors of Destiny (Haughey)	75	81*	77*
r-c: Prog.Dem.P.(1987 F.F. split-off; O'Malley)	n.a.	14	6*
c-r: Finn Gael/Tribe of Gaels (Fitzgerald)	70*	51	55
l: Labor Party	16*	12	15
f-l: Workers (Dem.Labor) Party	2	4	7
f-l: Dem. Soc. Party	0	1	0
independents & others	3	3*	6(1*)
	166	166	166

*1 independent joined to form 1989 coalition.

Denmark n=10+ 175/2=88 to *	1/84	9/87	5/88	12/90
f-r: Progress P. (anti-:tax,immigrants; Kjaersgaard)	6^	9^	16^	12^
r: Conservative Peop. P. (Schluter, since '82)	42*	38*	35*	30*
r-c: Liberal Dem. P.	22*	19*	22*	29*^
c-r: Center Dem. P.	8*	9*	9^	9^
c-r: Christian Peoples P.	5*	4*	4	4
# in governing coalition^ = *	(77*	70*	67*	59*)
c: Rad.Soc. Libl P. (rgt.on econ, lft on foreign;Peterson)	10^	11^	10*	7^
c-l: Soc.Dem.Party(anti-nuke; Auken);#1% votes, but...	56	54	55	69
l: Socialist Peop. P. (anti-NATO,EEC)	21	27	24	15
Others w/ seats: Common Cause	0	4	0	0
Left Socialists, Communists	5	0	0	0
	175	175	175	175
+Regional Reps: Greenland P. (2), Faeroes (2)	4	4	4	4

^ = caucus to form govts., but don't share in govt.coaliton = *minority* govt.;
minority govts. don't need majority to rule, just no majority against rule.
With 2% vote for a prop.rep. seat, Dnmk. has *never* had a simple majority govt.

Switzerland n=10+, 8+ w/ seats 200/2=101 to *	10/83	10/87
f-r: Swiss Peoples (Volks) P.	23*	26*
r: Christian Dem. Peop. P.	42*	42*
c-r: Radical Dem. P. (cons.; Richter)	54*	50*
c-l: Soc. Dem. P.	47*	40*
# in governing coalition = *	(166*	158*)
8 other parties (a,b='83,'87), incl.: on the left: Libl. P.(8,9),		
Greens (3,9), Prog. Org.(3,4), Workers P.(1,1); on right:		
Evangel.P.(3,3), Automobile P.(0,2), Natl.Action P.(3,5);		
other parties (3,1); & indeps.(8,8).	34	42
TOT. ---	200	200

Grand rotating coaliton has governed since 1959; results from proportional
representation; turnout never >50%, was lowest ever in 10/87.

USA	Pres. system, divided control*	n=2 main parties
	11/88 Pres.	11/90 Leg:(218 to *LH; 51 to * UH)
c-r: Repub.P.: Bush = 54%v, 425 electoral*		167 House + 44 Senate
c-l: Democ.P.: Dukakis = 46%v, 112 electoral		*267 House + *56 Senate
TOTALS -------------------------------------		434+ ----------100

*Strongly presidential; opposition party control of Congress serves only a mild restraining function on otherwise activist executive branch.

Strong 2-party; 3rd parties seldom win seats in Congress (+=1 Soc.P. in '90); 3rd party pres. candidates seldom survive to next 4-year election cycle.

Finland   n=8+ parties; mixed pres./parl. system, with coalition govt.

200/2=101 to *	3/83	3/87	1/88Pres.
l-c:Social Dem. P. (ex-PMSorsa;Pres.Koivisto). 25%v	57*	56*	47.9%*
c-r:Center P.(rural;Varynen)+Libl.P. coalition. 22%v.	38*	40	19.8%
r: Rural P. (populist; replaced Commies as * in '82))	17*	9*	
r: Swedish Peop. P. (Taxell)	11*	13*	
r: Natl. Conservative P. (anti-SU; PM Holkeri)	44	53*	18.3%
l: Peop.Dem.Lg.-Socs. (Euro-communists; Kavisto; 15%v)	26	16	10.4%
l: PDL-"Dem. Alt."(pro-SU communists; Kajanoja)	0	4	1.4%
Others: r:Christian U. Lg. (5), Greens(2), indeps & others etc.	8	9	2.2%
TOT.------------------------------	200	200	100%

Holkeri govt. of 5/87 ended 50-yr. broad center-left coalition (w/o coms. or cons.); conservatives taken in, first time since '67, & given PM, first time since '45.

Re: Pres.: each voter has 2 votes, 1 for cand., 1 for mbrs. of 301-mbr. electoral college used if no cand. gets 50% (none ever has); generally go with popular favorite in 2nd round. Important bec. 6-yr. Pres. > PM in this mixed system. (SDP had 144/301 in electoral college; NCP gave Holkeri 45 of its 63 in 2nd round of electoral college ballotting; Center had 68; Socs. 26.)

Venezuela   n=3+ parties, strong pres. with single-party control

12/83 and 12/88 elections (& Pres. cands):	83LH	83UH	83Pres.	88LH	88UH	88Pres.
c-r: Soc.Xtn.P.(COPEI; Herrera, Fernandez)	61	14	34.5%	67	22	40%
c-l: Democratic Action (AD; Lusinchi, Perez)	112*	28*	56.8%*	97*	23*	53%*
l: Movement to Socialism (MAS; Petkoff)	10	2	4.2%	18	3	3%
Others, incl:	18	5	4.5%	19	1	4%
DRU,NO,CP,RC,RM,NIM,NDG,UNA,etc.;+indeps.						
	201	49	100%	201	49	100%

Strong 2-party system; until AD won last two elections, government had alternated in previous four presidential elections.

Strongly presidential; legislators must be elected on presidential ticket on basis of proportional representation percentage of vote.

Europe	Islamic	Africa	Asia	Latin America
(LEAST STABLE/ /MOST RESPONSIVE)				(LEAST STABLE/ /MOST RESPONSIVE)

multiparty coalition govts.(n=22)

Europe	Islamic	Africa	Asia	Latin America	
Norway			India		
Belgium, Italy	Israel		^Papua NG		
Switz., Denmark					
Finland†, Iceland†			^Mauritius		
Germany, Greece					
∂Hung., ∂Czech.,Swed.			^Solomons		
France†, Austria†					
Lux.,Neth.,Ireland					
17	1	0	4	0	(22)

simple parl. party majority rule(n=23)

Europe	Islamic	Africa	Asia	Latin America	
UK, Malta			Australia	St.L.,St.V.,Trinidad	
Canada			N.Zealand	Belz.,Barb.,~Bahm.	
Spain		~Botswana	~Van., ΔWSam.	~St.C., ~Ant.,~Dom.	
Portugal†		~S. Africa	~Japan	Jamaica, ∂^Grenada	
5	0	2	5	11	(23)

presidential systems (n=8)

Europe	Islamic	Africa	Asia	Latin America	
USA, ∂Poland	Cyprus	~Gambia		Venezuela,Ecuador	
				Costa Rica, Dom.Rep.	
2	1	1	0	4	(8)

Europe				Latin America
(MOST STABLE/ /LEAST RESPONSIVE)				(MOST STABLE/ /LEAST RESPONSIVE)

Why n=17 ˜mprs judged to be "weak" mprs:

∂ = recent 1-party experience (n=3.5);

Δ = limited suffrage (n=1);

^ = major political figures easily transfer party allegiances (n=3.5);

~ = one dominant party has ruled every year since independence (n=7), or almost so (n=2: S.Africa, Japan).

Source: V5.3ab Data Bank.

†=mixed parliamentary/presidential system (n=5)

≈**Bahamas** n=2 parl. simp. maj. mpr	8/82	6/87
Progressive Libl./Labor? P. (Pindling since '67; 55%v.)	32*	31*
Free Natl. (Dem.) Mvmt. (est. '71; K.Isaacs; 45% v.)	11	15
independents+undecided	0	3=2+1
TOT.--------------------	43	49

≈ Same party has ruled since 1973 independence.

≈**Gambia** n=2+ pres. mpr	5/82 parl.	3/87 Pres.	3/87 parl.
Peop. Prog. P.(Jawara=Pres. since indep.)	28*	59% v.*	31*
Natl. Conv. P. (Sherif Mustafa Dibba)	3	28% v.	5
Gamb. Peop. P. (Hussan Musa Camara)	0	13% v.	0
4 other parties	0	n.a.	0
	31	100%	36

≈ 5 minor parties never have received 20% votes need for representation in assembly in this
prop.rep. electoral system. 1987 was first time independence era president was challenged.

≈**Vanuatu** n=2+ parl. simp. maj. mpr	11/83	11/87
Vanua'aku P. of Our Land (Rev. Lini & B. Sope)	24*	26*
Union of Moderates P.	12	19
Others: (Na Griamel, Namake Auti, Fren.Melanes.,etc.) & indeps.	3	1
	39	46

≈Same party has won both elections since 1980 independence.

∂**Hungary** - emerging parl. mpr/transitional coalition
  3/25, 4/8 1990 2-rounds of voting (final results)

	# seats	(% vote)
f-r: Christian Democrats (Keresztes, Giczi; pro-RC Church)	21*	(7%)
r: Independent Smallholders (pre-'48 party, Voros)	43*	(12%)
c-r: Democratic Forum (PM Antall)	165*	(25%)
c: Young Democrats (<35 yrs. old; compete with Free Dems.)	21	(9%)
c-l: Alliance of Free Democrats (old dissidents; Pres. Goncz)	92	(21%)
l: Socialist (reform communists: Nyers,Poszgay,Szuros)	33	(11%)
f-l: Socialist Workers (unreformed communists: Grosz)	0	(3.6%)
Others, including:	11	(11.4%)
Social Democratic P., Entrepreneurs P., Peoples P.		
Patriotic Election Coalition, Agrarian Federation		
	386	100%

∂ = Former 1pcom state from 1946-89; as part of effort to get broadest possible base for
transition from 1pcom system, center-right coalition government tolerates president from
opposition (but second largest) party.

V5.3cde. Single-Party Polities

In addition to the 53 non-militarized multiparty republics, there are some 32 states with civilian rule which either do not allow opposition political parties or restrict them so severely that they have no real chance of coming to power. In such *one-party polities (1pp)*, most meaningful political participation takes place *within* the structure of the ruling party; therefore, the character and size of this single party, and the regularity and openness of legitimizing electoral experiences, need to be assessed if one wishes to measure political participation.

Table V5.3cde displays the 32 states with the three types of civilian one-party systems in the world today. The order in which these one-party polities are arrayed in the CGSS and in which they will be discussed next is:

first, *1pdoms,* for they are most like the mprs just covered in the regularity of their elections and the ability of opposition parties to win some seats in the representative assembly, though seldom any power in the government (covered at greater length in section V5.3c).

second, *1pcoms,* for these are most like the 1pdoms in reliance upon sophisticated (though essentially civilian) party controls to structure the political system so that the single party's rule is not threatened (see V5.3d).

finally, *1p-others* which, while predominantly civilian, are often similar in the authoritarian and restrictive nature of their political systems to the militarized polities of the following section (see V5.3e).

As this text is being written, considerable change is overtaking many of the one-party communist states in eastern Europe, and it remains unclear whether these governments will evolve into multiparty systems (n=3 in the current CGSS) or into one-party dominant with the communist party still the most significant actor (n=3 here, counting Mongolia), or revert to more militarized regimes. This section will be written, however, under the assumption that the Marxist-Leninist model is still viable as a prototype and in existence in a handful of countries.

The characteristic of these 32 states which distinguishes them from the 63 militarized polities to be studied in section V5.4 is their civilian political nature. These countries have less heavy involvement of the military in politics as measured by Chapter 1's indicators, especially V1.1d (wars) and V1.2c (history of military coup regimes). Regardless of the thoroughness or brutality of party control in some of these states (e.g., Albania, Iran, Zambia, North Korea, Cuba), the leadership did not emerge from the narrow base of the country's established military institutions, but rather from a more political process (which could include armed revolution as defined in Chapter 1).

Following the next three sections, excerpts from the data bank associated with this project for sections V5.3cde will be presented. The formats to be followed for the display of this information appear in the bottom half of Table V5.3cde.

V5.3c. One-Party Dominant Polities

lp-dominant (n=13—V5.3c)

Bulgaria	Iran	Senegal,Iv.Coast	Mongolia	Guyana	
Romania		Zimbabwe	Singapore		
	Egypt	Namibia	Malaysia	Mexico	
Sbtot 2	2	4	3	2	(13)

A variation of single party participation with elements of the mpr is the *one-party dominant (lpdom)* polity, where opposition parties are permitted, but there is little realistic chance that they will ever rule because the system is structured so that only the dominant party has a credible chance of prevailing in electoral competition. The origins of these regimes and their broad-based national political movements are varied: seven have emerged from their leadership roles in anti-colonial independence struggles (Senegal, Ivory Coast, Zimbabwe, Namibia; Singapore, Malaysia, Guyana). Two have had indigenous revolutions (Iran and Mexico) and two are evolving from one-party communist systems (Bulgaria and Mongolia), whereas Romania is a combination of both these methods. Finally, Egypt has progressed through time from a modernizing military coup regime up to its present place in the CGSS.

Choices for executive leadership in lpdoms reflect the electoral methods of mprs: six states have parliamentary systems (Electoral Type 1: Leg. > PM): Bulgaria, Namibia, Singapore, Malaysia, Mongolia, Guyana); and seven have presidential systems (Electoral Type 2: Pres. & Assy.: Romania, Iran, Egypt, Senegal, Ivory Coast, Zimbabwe, Mexico). However, as will be made clear, in lpdoms these modalities are tampered with to prevent any but the ruling party from prevailing.   Nevertheless, the other parties serve more than a representational function. In allowing genuine opposition parties to run and win elections for seats in a representative assembly, the lpdom polities reflect some form of legitimation in their system, and provide a safety valve to relieve pressure against the regime (Diamond et al., 1987).

As evidence of political participation, it is instructive to identify the functioning opposition parties, and some measure of their strength. Table V5.3c ranks these 13 states in the order of the percentage of assembly seats won by the opposition in the last election. It also summarizes the percentage of the vote received by the non-dominant party candidates for the assembly (where available), and for the presidency (in the seven cases where there was a direct vote for an executive head of state).

This summary table, along with the excerpts from the lpdom data bank presented for n=4 states on the same page as the table, reveals a number of interesting points relating to tactics used by dominant parties to maintain their monopoly of political control. For example, in many states coalitions of opposition parties are prohibited. The dominant party as a tool of minority ethnic group control is used in Malaysia (against Chinese), Singapore (against non-Chinese), and Guyana (against Asians). The impact of structuring electoral rules so that opposition parties' percentage of seats in the representative assembly is much less than their percentage of votes is especially evident in the case of Singapore (1.2% vs. 37%), Zimbabwe (3.3% vs. 20%), and Bulgaria (47.3% vs. 55%) where the opposition actually got a majority of the votes but not of the seats in the assembly. Saving or allotting a specific number of seats for the opposition—a practice which often condemns opposition forces to fighting amongst themselves—is employed by Mexico and Senegal.

The party as an all-powerful front seems to be the reality in Singapore (where only two opposition members have been elected in 23 years), and in Malaysia (where more than ten ethnically based minor parties are embraced within the ruling coalition). This is also the pattern in Mongolia, Romania, and (with less success) Bulgaria, where the former communist parties seem to have succeeded in hanging on to power with changed names but continued control of new umbrella political organizations, not to mention the military and security services.

Egypt's 13-year-old 1pdom system was dealt an embarrassment in 1990 when opposition parties boycotted an assembly election. In an opposite trend, Ivory Coast moved up from 1-party other when it allowed opposition parties to win assembly seats and contest the presidential election for the first time.

Iran is somewhat of an anomaly. The prevailing Islamic Republican Party was deemed irrelevant and abolished at the request of its secretary general in 1987, but the principles of the 1979 revolution are so dominant within the society that this country will continue to be carried in this category; although there is no party, the governmental leadership (largely religious) is definitely not military.

With respect to future movement of states, Mexico has shown signs of evolving into a weak mpr system; in the other direction, Zimbabwe's leader has taken preliminary steps to outlaw other parties after 1992. Possibly coming up to this category in the future are Yugoslavia and USSR from the 1pcoms, Tunisia from 1p-other, Taiwan from *1pd, and Algeria from mil^.

V5.3d. One-Party Communist Systems

1-party communist (n=8—V5.3d)		
	China	
USSR	N.Korea	
Yugoslavia	Laos	Cuba
Albania	Vietnam	
3	4	1 (8)

As mentioned in the introduction to sections V5.3cde, this study will continue to recognize eight states as *one-party communist (1pcom)* despite the changes occurring in eastern Europe. In this Leninist tradition, the party is an elite vanguard, membership is small, and dissident factions are not tolerated. There is also a historic commitment in the 1pcoms to greater economic and social equality (unlike in the one-party "other" states to follow, where this may or may not be the case).

In addition to control over the government and the economy, the party is constitutionally mandated to play a leading role in society, directing all aspects of the country's cultural life (including ethnic associations, churches, the mass media, workers' unions, and other such V4.5 interest groups). These entities often receive formal representation in the government by virtue of belonging to the party's "front" organization which nominates candidates for the national assembly. In some instances, the party's monopoly of power in society extends to control even over a few token other parties which are represented in the front; these, however, are not significant enough for the system to be considered 1pdom.

In traditional 1p communist states, there is no direct election (or even referendum) for the chief executive officers of the state. The party selects the president (i.e., the chairman of the council of state) and the prime minister (chairman of the council of ministers), and the assembly (also chosen by the party but generally confirmed in a legitimizing election) ratifies these choices. All these governmental positions are considered subservient to parallel bodies in the party, which, according to Leninist theory, has control over the government. Within the party, the secretary general is the most 'important figure; he is selected by the politburo (generally n=10 to 20 members who meet weekly), which is chosen by and from the central committee (n=50 to 200, meeting semi-annually). This body self-selects its own members who are later ratified by larger national party congresses (every four or five years), or the even rarer full party conferences for major changes (e.g., in 1941 and 1988 in the USSR) (Hobday, 1986; Szajkowski, 1981; Fukuyama, 1985).

There are another 11 states which are arguably 1pcom, but which will not be considered such here. The first three (Bulgaria, Romania, Mongolia) have already been discussed as 1pdoms. Seven others have been designated (at the Soviet Union's 1988 party conference) as only "vanguard revolutionary democratic movements," meaning they are "on the verge of evolving into full-fledged communist parties" (Staar, 1988b: 70 and 1989b: 48; other sources refer to them as "socialist-oriented" as opposed to "socialist"). They include South Yemen (before its 1990 unification with the North), Afghanistan; Benin, Congo, Ethiopia, Mozambique, and Angola. This study regards these seven countries as military (mil^) regimes, a category which also includes an eighth state (Cambodia) which the USSR recognizes as fully communist, but which is not considered so here because its government was created and sustained for ten years (until 1989) by the presence of foreign (Vietnamese) troops, and its fate is still ultimately subject to international (perhaps UN) determination.

What these eight states lack to qualify for inclusion in this work as 1pcom is a sufficiently large base of communist party members and institutionalized civilian governmental structures. Table V5.3d.i's statistics on party membership as a percentage of population show the relatively high degree of participation (5.85% of population as party members, on average) in the mature party states (the eight 1pcoms), as compared to the low level of participation (0.6% of population as party members, on average) in the eight regimes designated militarized in this study (Staar,1989b).

A high percentage of the population as members of the party does not necessarily mean liberality of rule. Among other factors which should be considered when analyzing participation in communist regimes are 1.) choice in elections to representative assemblies; 2.) the existence of other parties (or fronts controlled by the vanguard party) which competed in elections; and 3.) whether or not the top three positions (head of state, head of government, head of party) were held by one, two, or three persons.

A summary of this data is displayed in Table V5.3d.ii. In the most liberal states, the three positions are separated, many organizations and possibly even other (subservient) political parties are represented in the front controlled by the party, there is choice in elections, and candidates endorsed by the front do not need to be party members, but only persons approved by the party. Additional evidence of political participation and of regime strength and party character can be garnered by looking at the frequency of party congresses and conferences, and the size of the central committee and politburo at the top of the party structure, some of which information is found in the data bank excerpts for three 1pcom states presented at the end of this section.

With respect to movement in and out of this category, it would seem that Yugoslavia and the USSR would be the next to move up to the 1pdom classification. Already, rivals to the vanguard communist party have been permitted at the local (i.e., republic) level, where they hold seats in assemblies and administrative branches of government; at the time of this writing, however, this is not true at the national level so these two countries will remain in the 1pcom category. Staar (1990b: 77) claims Zimbabwe has a ruling "vanguard revolutionary democratic movement"; but a look at its party membership as a percentage of population (30%) and at its mixed economy argues for the African model (of a 1pdom moving into 1p-other) rather than that of Marxism-Leninism.

V5.3e. One-Party Other States

<pre>
              1-party other (n=11—V5.3e)
     Tunisia   Sierra Leone
                      Gabon,Cameroon
                      STP,C.Verde
     Djibouti   Kenya,Tanzania
                      Zambia,Malawi
         2   9   (11)
</pre>

The 11 one-party other states are problematic to place in the civilian/military framework of analysis. Like the 21 one-party polities already discussed (13 1pdom, 8 1pcom), these countries are essentially governed by civilian political actors. Although there are tight institutional controls which limit the scope of political participation, the structures which exist are legitimate under indigenous historical mores (Kothari, 1984; Thomas, 1985). These norms are not those generally associated with western Europe; in fact, all of the remaining examples to be cited throughout the rest of this chapter are from the Islamic, African, Asian, and Latin American zones (Hudson, 1977; Foltz and Bienen, 1987; Soedjatmoko, 1983; Malloy and Seligson, 1987). Although other parties are sometimes permitted, they do not hold any seats in the representative assembly. However, unlike in the 75 states to follow in sections V5.4 and .5, the military has not intervened to install the government in any of the 11 one-party polities to be covered here.

One-party other (1p-other) polities might have elite parties (like the 1pcoms) or they might have grown out of mass independence movements and embrace various nationalist tendencies (like many 1pdoms). They also might be evolving from military (mil^) regimes, though this normally would take a couple of generations of leadership. Sierra Leone in this category, and Egypt (now among the 1pdoms), followed this pattern, but it is more common for military regimes to evolve into militarized party states (*mpr, *1pdom) and then into mprs or 1pdoms (see section V5.4).

The economic-ideological orientation of these one-party polities is often such that they will not tolerate even token second-party opposition in the political arena. They might be either capitalist *(1pcap)* or socialist *(1psoc)* depending on the party's orientation toward the management of the economy, i.e., respectively, whether the public (government) or private (corporate) sector is the predominant economic actor in the country. (Section V5.4d, below, identifies all states in accordance with their economic ideology and adds a third category of mixed economies as well.)

In general, states identified as 1pcap will be more receptive to Western outside investment (and political influence); those labeled 1psoc will be more rhetorically hostile in accommodating such penetration. Recall, however, from

Chapter 2 that there is often a discrepancy between a state's announced preferred economic orientation and its actual policies. Many developing countries claim to be socialist but in practice they are often very much part of the world capitalist economic system.

In any event, in one-party socialist states the ruling party generally claims to be building a new society after years of exploitative treatment within the world capitalist system (especially as a colony during the era of European imperialism); to the extent that significant segments of society preferred the earlier arrangements, their political participation must be restricted. Similarly, in one-party capitalist states, the ruling party often must limit participation in politics in order to carry out austerity programs dictated by foreign investors and lenders (most notably, the International Monetary Fund), or to enforce other economic arrangements which appear to the domestic public primarily to benefit outsiders.

With respect to political institutions, the 1psoc states tend towards the 1pcom model in their assiduous building of civilian party structures, whereas the 1pcap countries are more like the regimes which follow in section V5.4 in their reliance upon instruments of the traditional military to remain in power. If they can succeed in solving the problem of governmental succession without military intervention, 1pcap states may evolve over time into 1pdom systems along the model of Egypt, Senegal, Ivory Coast, and Singapore, all of which were at one time 1p-other. Notice the use of the phrases "tend toward" and "may evolve." In most instances this is a gradual progress with no inevitability. Since all governments exist in the near term, the world presents at any one time a complicated mosaic of polity and economic types, mostly militarized or (as in the case of the 32 one-party polities) restricted in access to one degree or another, but in various stages of evolution and not poised on the perch of one archetypical model or the other.

Concerning political participation, the restrictiveness of both 1pcap and 1psoc states is comparable and does not seem to relate to ideological coloration in the economic sphere. With respect to choice in the elections for representative assembly, two of the states (Sierra Leone and Tanzania) offer at least two party-approved choices for most seats, and one (Kenya) offers some lesser choice among party candidates. Six regimes (Djibouti, Cape Verde, Cameroon, Sao Tome and Principe (STP), Zambia, and Malawi) present only a single list for approval/disapproval.

Tunisia and Gabon are in transition as of 1990. Tunisia allowed other parties to run for the first time in years in 1989, but none won any assembly seats despite getting about 19% of the popular votes nationwide. In Gabon the opposition won some 40% of the seats in the assembly in October, 1990, but until a contested presidential election is held, this state will be kept in the CGSS as 1p-other.

For legitimation of the executive administration, three 1p polities (STP, Cape

Verde, Malawi) offer no direct elections for head of state or of government, while the remaining eight have a president who periodically stands for endorsement in a referendum and gets more than 95% approval. More details concerning elections and other means by which the ruling party consolidates its control in these one-party states can be found in the excerpts for selected countries drawn from the data bank associated with this project and presented at the end of this section.

What distinguishes these states from the militarized polities to follow is the history of their civilian political institutions, and the lack of involvement by the established military in the transition between ruling administrations. Most (9 of 11) of these states have been led by the same single party since independence; in three cases (Tunisia, Sierra Leone, Cameroon), a "second single party" formed around the personality of the leader who replaced the first (now retired) one. Civilian control of the military, however, is only one of the characteristics of multiparty democracy, and it will probably be some time before most of these countries tolerate other real contenders for political power. In this respect, and since 9 of 11 of the states in this section are African, it might be appropriate to quote General Olusegun Obasanjo, former president of Nigeria (1976-79), and one of the few military coup regime leaders ever to step down voluntarily as head of state and pass the government over to civilian rule.

> (H)aving an institutionalized opposition (is) a concept not only alien but profoundly incongruent with most African political culture and practice, in which government functioned by consensus. In many African languages the word "opposition" is the same as that for "enemy." How can one conceptualize a loyal enemy? (Speech to Council on Foreign Relations (New York),   August 1987; cited in *World Development Forum*, May 31, 1989: 3.)

Among the 11 one-party states in this section, 3 (Tunisia, Zambia, and Kenya) were 1pdom at one time, but at some later point absorbed the other political parties. Two others (Tanzania and Djibouti) maintain fronts which accommodate diverse groups within their ethnically divided states. The other 6 have been single party since inception, although the name and identity of the party has changed in Sierra Leone and Cameroon, and Gabon allowed parties to contest assembly seats in 1990. At the time of this writing, governments have been responding to pressures for the legalization of other parties in Cape Verde, Sao Tome and Principe, Cameroon and Zambia. But until one electoral cycle (both presidential and assembly) is held in which the opposition fields candidates and wins some seats, it would be premature to move these countries up to the 1pdom category.

Historically, five of these governments (Djibouti, Cape Verde, Sao Tome and Principe, Malawi, and Zambia) are successors to departing colonial regimes, and were installed by the legitimate authorities at that time of transition. In five others, the civilian independence leader has been followed by a legitimate successor (in Gabon 1966, Kenya 1976, Cameroon 1982, Tanzania 1985, and Tunisia 1987) without military intervention. Only in Sierra Leone did the military intervene, in 1967, and within one year turned over power to the opposition party leader who had won the previous presidential election. In short, civilian politicians, not the institutional military, are in charge of the political process in the 11 one-party other states. War, coup d'etat, or external armed intervention have not been the primary mode of governmental transition as will be the case in the military regimes to be discussed next in section V5.4.

V5.3cde – Single-Party Polities (n=32=13+8+11)

Europe	Islamic	Africa	Asia	Latin America	
		1pdom = <u>1p-dominant</u> (n=13–V5.3c)			
Bulgaria	Iran	Senegal,Iv.Coast	Mongolia	Guyana	
Romania		Namibia	Singapore		
	Egypt	Zimbabwe	Malaysia	Mexico	
Sbtot: 2	2	4	3	2	(13)
		1pcom = <u>1-party communist</u> (n=8—V5.3d)			
USSR			China	Cuba	
Yugoslavia			N.Korea		
Albania			Vietnam		
			Laos		
Sbtot: 3			4	1	(8)
		<u>1-party other</u> (n=11—V5.3e)			
	Tunisia	Sierra Leone			
		Gabon,Cameroon			
		C.Verde, STP			
	Djibouti	Kenya,Tanzania			
		Zambia,Malawi			
Sbtot:	2	9			(11)
TOT 1P:5	4	13	7	3	(32)

Format for V5.3c – *1pdom* Data Bank EXCERPTS
State – a. name of party
    b. date, level (i.e., Assy. and/or Pres) most recent election (see V5.1b).
    c. % vote and/or # seats of 1pdom party.
    d. # seats, names of *other parties.*

Format for V5.3d – *1pcom* Data Bank EXCERPTS
State – a. name of party (&/or front), & SG   b. *party* membership *% pop.*
    c. date, term most recent election to Assy. *(No exec. refs.)*
    d. degree of choice (v. single list), including status of non-party members.
    e. *other info.*: e.g. # in Politburo and Cent.Cmtee.; other positions & duration of SG;
       date of most recent party congress or conference; explanation of **1pcom** if designation
       in doubt.

Format for V5.3e – *1p-other* Data Bank EXCERPTS
State – a. name of party & SG (=Hd. State often)
    b. date, level most recent election: Pres. &/or Assy.; (% vote, # seats)
    c. choice, incl: if candidates m/b party members vs. m/b party appvd. vs. indeps.; also,
       number of incumbents defeated; etc.
    d. reason for **1p-other** designation in dubious (i.e., 1pdom or mil^) cases.

State	Date	# & % of minority assy.seats	% assy.vote	opp. % Pres.vote
Mexico	7/88	241/500 seats = 48.2%	49%	48% (among two)
Bulgaria	6/90	181/400=47.3%	55%	na: Leg>PM
Namibia	11/89	31/72=43.1%	42.7%	na:Con.Assy.>Pres.
Romania	5/90	116/396LH=41.1%	34%	15%
Mongolia	7/90	21/53LH=39.6%	n.a.	na: Leg>PM
Malaysia	10/90	50/180 = 27.7%	n.a.	na: Leg.>PM
Guyana	12/85	12/65 = 18.5%	20%	na: Leg.>PM
Senegal	2/88	17/120 = 14.1%	20%	26%
Ivory Coast	12/90	10/175 = 5.7%	n.a.	18%
Zimbabwe	4/90	4/120=3.3%	20%	16%
Singapore	9/87	1/81 = 1.2%	37%	na: Leg.>PM
Iran	4/88	No parties	n.a.	8/88: 5.5%
Egypt	11/90	0/458 =0%	opp. boycott	10/87: 3% (reject)

EXCERPTS from V5.3c Data Bank - 1p dom (n=4 of 12)

Ivory Coast - a. Democratic Party; SG = Houphouet-Boigny since 1960 independence.

b,c. 10/90 Pres. el.: F.Houphouet-Boigny 82%, L.Gbagbo 18%.

  11/90 Assy. el.: 490 candidates from about 20 parties for 175 seats. Results:
  Democratic P. 163, Popular Front 9, Workers P. 1, indeps. (pro-govt.) 2.

d. Indep.-era president was elected to 7th 5-yr. term, in first contested election, against opponent who had spent 2 yrs. in jail, 7 yrs. in exile. Opp. parties legalized in 5/90. System further skewed toward ruling party by allowing 3-4 million foreign nationals, dependent on government bureaucracy for their work permits, to vote.

Senegal - a. Socialist Party (PS); mass-based indep. party of L. Senghor; + 16 others today

b,c. 2/88 Pres. - incumbent Pres. Diouf=73% > A. Wade 26%, two others 1%.

  2/88 Assy. - PS=103 seats; SDP (Sen.Dem. P)=17.

d. Fairly open vote, though rioting & unrest at election time resulted in state of emergency and jailing of Wade & many of his SDP supporters. Combination of direct and proportional representation voting systems ensures some, but not 50%, of vote to opposition; opposition "coalitions" declared illegal in 1985.

Singapore - a. Peoples Action Party-mbrshp. is 7.9% pop. but otherwise a "mass" party.

b,c. 9/88 Leg. - 80/81 seats; 63% vote (down from 64% vote in '84, 75% vote in '80).

  156 cands. for 70 contested seats (11 incumbents unopposed), structured as follows:
   13 constituencies w/ slates of 3 cands. w/1 required minority (i.e., non-Chinese; = Indian, or "Malay"=Javanese,Boyanese,Bujis,&Arabs(i.e.Moslems))=39; + 42 single-mbr. districts.

d. Also: WP=Workers Party(1 seat in '81 & '84; then jailed); SDP=Sing.Democ.P.(1 seat in '84 & '88); 7 opposition parties on ballot in '88; up to 20 in earlier years.

Namibia - a. SWAPO = SouthWest African Peoples Organization + ~10 others

		#s	%v
bcd. 11/89 con. assy. el.; 72/2=36 to rule; x 2/3=48 for constitution articles			
c-l:SWAPO-Sam Nujoma-esp. Ovambos		41	57.3%
c-r:DTA=Dem.Turnhalle Alliance-esp. whites & Hereros(Mudge,Chief Kw.)		21	28.6
l: United Dem. Front - ldr. M.Muyongo (ex-SWAPO)		4	5.6
f-r: National Christian Action (whites)-Jaime de Wet,M.Katjoungua		3	3.5
Others: n=8 parties, of wh. 3 got 1 seat each		3	5.0

97% turnout; proportional representation; Ovambos 48% population probably ensures SWAPO domination of otherwise ~mpr system.

V5.3d.i – Party Strength as % of Population, 1pcom and others

Europe	Islamic	Africa	Asia	Latin America
			N.Korea-11.4%	
Yugoslavia-7.9%				
USSR-6.8				
Albania-4.7				Cuba-4.8%
			China - 4.3	
			Vietnam-3.3	
			Laos-1.0	AVG: 5.85%

(+ n=3 designated 1pdom)

| Romania-16.5% | | | | AVG: 10.6% |
| Bulgaria-11.0 | | | Mongolia-4.2 | |

(+ n=8 others designated mil^)

	Afghan.-1.35%			AVG: 0.60%
	S.Yemen-1.24	Mozambique-0.88		
		Angola - 0.53		
		Congo - 0.44		
		Ethiopia-0.14	^Cambodia-0.15	
		Benin - 0.06		

Source: Richard F. Staar, "Checklist of Communist Parties in 1989," *Problems of Communism*, March-April 1990: 77-84.

V5.3d.ii - 1pcom Summary

most open   **most restrictive**

1. Choice in Assembly Elections

some choice	no choice/single list	no direct election
USSR-1500/2895=.518		Yugoslavia
Vietnam-496/829=.598	Albania	China
Laos-79/121=.653	N. Korea	Cuba
3	2	3 (8)

2. Existence of Other Parties

indep.natl.parties	indep.regnl.parties	Front parties(#)	Fronts only	CP only
	USSR	China (8)	Vietnam	Laos
	Yugoslavia	N.Korea(2)	Albania	Cuba
0	2	2	2	2 (8)

3. Top Three Positions (Hd.St,Hd.Govt.,Hd.Party) Held by:

three persons	two persons	one person
USSR	Albania	Cuba
China	Laos	
Vietnam	N.Korea	
Yugoslavia		
4	3	1 (8)

Source: V5.3d data bank based on: Staar, *Yearbook*, annual.

366

USSR — a. Communist Party of SU - SG Gorbachev   b. 6.8% pop.
c,d. 3/89 Congress of Peoples Deputies, n=2250; though competing parties banned and
9/10 cands.party members, considerable choice: 750 chosen by Front Orgs. from 880
cands.; 1500 dir. el., fm. 2895 cands. of which 384 unopposed; 953 districts w/ 2, 163
with 3+ cands.; in all cases, 50% needed to win (some unopposed lost to 50+%
strike-outs); 76 runoffs.
e. 12/89 Assy vote (1139-834) to maintain CPSU's "leading role", though not the
"monopoly" of old, with tolerance of "factions" in CPD; such as:
   Inter-Regional Group (9/89): n=~400, more reformist; ldrs. V. Popov, B. Yeltsin
   more orthodox communists: n=~300 incl. K. Ligachev & many military men.
4/90 constitutional changes strive to make CPD assy. more powerful than party, and
President it elected (Gorbachev, with 59% Yes vote, to 5 yr. term; next election, by
universal adult suffrage) more important than Party SG (also still Gorbachev, but
probably will change after next Party Congress).
1pcom despite introduction of choice in elections since 6/88 Party Conference & allowing
of "factions," no other parties at national level as of 12/90. However, several
independent parties have won office at the republic level (Lithuania, Latvia, Estonia,
Georgia, Armenia, etc.) and independents or ex-CPSU reformers at local level (Moscow,
Leningrad, etc.).

Vietnam — a. VN Communist Party & Fathrlnd.Front, SG Van Linh.   b. 3.3% pop.
c. 4/87 Natl. Assy., 5 yrs. ~800 cands. for 496 seats (v. ~600 for 496 in '81). Lists from
which voters may strike undesirables.
d. Party selects candidates chosen at public village meetings from Front's mass
organizations; all must "accept Communist ideology" (not necessarily be party
members).
e. Politburo n=124 (+49 alternates); C.Cmtee. n=13 (+ 1 alt.); 3/89 = 6th Congress of
strong revolutionary independence 1pcom party.

China - a. Chinese Communist Party (CCP), SG Jiang Zemin; + 9 smaller unimpt. parties
in Front under control of CCP.   b. 4.3% pop.
c,d. 4/88 Natl. Peop. Congress; n=2978, indirectly elected to 5-yr. term (by local assys.
and parties) from approved CCP lists.
e. Politburo (n=17-20) and C.Cmtee. (n=175) dominate all sectors of govt. and army (esp.
through party's Military Commission, 11/89 Chm. Yang Baibing succeeding Deng
Tsiao Ping). 1p com with considerable shared power during apparent time of transition,
esp. in Standing Cmtee. of Politburo (n=6: SG Jiang, Pres. Yang Shangkun, PM Li
Peng, Party Mil. Cmsn. Chm. Yang, VP Wang Zhen, and Natl. Party Cong. Chm. Wan
Li).

Tunisia – a. Constitutional Democratic Rally (RCD) of new Pres. Ben Ali has replaced Destourian Soc. Party (PSD) of independ. Pres.-for-Life Bourguiba (constitutionally removed for senility in 11/87). New Pres. reformed it into RCD (500,000 mbrs.), & legalized some 14 opposition parties.
b. 4/89 Pres. election – sole candidate Ben Ali received 99.3% votes.
4/89 Assy. – RCD party won all 141 seats, 81% vote.
c. Islamic candidates running as independents (their MTI party, and leader Ghannouchi, outlawed) got 14.5% vote (30% in some cities); pro-West Movement for Democ. Socialism (MDS; leader: A. Mestria) got 3.8% vote. Electoral law favors big parties.
1p–other (>1pdom) bec. opp. still wins no seats, despite "reforms," and main threat MTI party still outlawed. RCD won 99% seats in 6/90 local elections.

Cameroon – a. Cameroon Peoples Democratic Movement(CPDM) of Pres. Biya replaced 1960–82 Pres. Ahidjo's CNUP as only legit. party in 1985.
b,c. 4/88 Pres. Biya unopposed for 2nd 5–yr. term;
4/88 Assy (n=180); voters must choose 1 of 2 lists presented by CPDM; all candidates members of CPDM.
1p–other despite CPDM's greater openness vs. ex-CNUP; 5/90 pro-democracy rallies (6 dead) resulted in promises of legalized opp. parties in future.

Kenya – a. Kenya African National Union (KANU); 1982 Constitution decreed 1-party state, absorption of opposition KADU and APP parties.
b,c. 3/88 Pres. el. – President (Arap Moi) unopposed for 3rd 5–yr. term; as has been case in all Pres. elections back to 1964 independence.
2/88 Assy. el. – 1st round primary neeeded if >3 KANU cands., to narrow field for runoff; hence, multiple cands. but 1987 electoral change requires public queueing (no secret ballot) for choice. Result: <20% turnout.
3/88 2nd round, secret ballot returned, 123 of 188 seats contested.
1p–other – former 1pdom under independence leader Kenyatta (1963–78) becoming more restricted since 1982; in 1987 party held superior to parliament, in 1988 to judiciary.

Zambia – a. United Natl. Independ. Party (UNIP) sole legal party from 1972 to 12/90; 10% of pop.; Pres. Kaunda determines mbrship. of its C.Cmtee. (n=68).
b,c.10/88 Pres.– Kaunda re-el. to 6th 5–yr. term; 96% Yes vote, 56% turnout.
10/88 Assy. – 610 UNIP cands. for 125 seats; but ballots numbered and can be cross-checked to voting registration number.
1p–other under strain after pro-democracy rallies and failed coup attempt in spring 1990. First multiparty elections promised for 1991.

V5.4. MILITARIZED GOVERNANCE

In the remaining 75 countries of Table V5.1a's Comparative Government Spread Sheet (CGSS-page 2), armed force replaces civilian institutions as the most significant political variable (Linz and Stepan, 1986; Thomas, 1985; Horowitz, 1982; Perlmutter and Bennet, 1980; Kennedy, 1974). This section will investigate 63 states with such militarized governance (see Table V5.4a.i); section V5.5 will continue the analysis for 12 monarchies. No European states are mentioned in what follows; since the movement to civilian rule in Portugal and Spain in 1974, and the end of martial law in Poland in 1985, this zone seems to have settled the issue of civilian control over the military.

V5.4a. Institution-Building in Militarized Governments

Crow and Thomas (1984: 64) define a military-dominated country as one where one or more of the following exist: (i) key political leaders from the armed forces; (ii) martial law, or a legal system based on military courts; or (iii) significant links between the military and political police. Some of these concepts have been covered earlier, in sections V1.2c on coups and V4.4d on suspension of the rule of law. Governments which are characterized by such activity generally over time rewrite the rules for political participation (i.e., their countries' constitutions) in ways which legitimate (retroactively) their policies (Danopoulas, 1987; Maniruzzaman, 1987; Welch, 1987; and Clapham and George, 1984). This process usually follows a predictable pattern involving several elements. First, some evidence of public electoral approval is sought, even if this is only a plebiscite on a constitution which justifies the coup regime itself (including a referendum on its leader as "president"). Under conditions of martial law, it is fairly easy to compel a significant percentage of the population to participate in such an exercise and give such consent. It is not even necessary to have a political party as a vehicle to execute this initial legitimation, for no organized opposition political forces are allowed to take part.

The longer the coup regime stays in office, however, the more it becomes necessary for it to start acting politically and building a base of support. This usually takes the form of giving "the people" (more precisely, those centers of societal power and interest groups favored by the junta) representation in an elected popular assembly. Oftentimes only independent candidacies are permitted for these are more susceptible to intimidation and control. If the regime is serious about prolonging its rule, it is at this point that a political party composed of its supporters begins to be built. With such machinery, the regime can then seek additional mandates for its policies. A form of referendum, on a single list of candidates, is again the easiest type of electoral exercise to control.

When the regime has a bit more confidence in its support and in its party structures, it can tolerate opposition candidates (though not any significant party organization mobilized behind them), or a choice of candidates all of whom are members of (or approved by) the ruling party. It usually takes some time before the regime's civilian political institutions have matured to the point where other parties organized in support of opposition candidates are permitted, and this only at the representative assembly level, seldom to contest the executive leadership itself.

This pattern can be varied in its particulars as the discussion and data bank excerpts of examples of militarized regimes in sections V5.4bcd will indicate. In general, however, the process can be summarized according to the four steps presented in Table V5.4a.ii. Reversing the order of coverage so that the military regimes with the greatest political sophistication are analyzed first would yield the V5.4bcd order for the remaining sections of this chapter.

In the analyses which follow, each of the military polity categories will be compared with its civilian counterpart on CGSS-page 1, and with one another, for purposes of illustrating their respective definitions and showing how various indicators can be applied to substantiate state placements. For example, most of the 63 states have a history of war (V1.1ab) or military coup rule (V1.2c) which exceeds that of comparable countries on CGSS-page 1. Excerpts at the end of each section following the formats found in Table V5.4a.iii will provide additional information on political institution-building.

V5.4b. Militarized Party Systems

*milp = militarized party systems (n=22—V5.4b)

	Turkey	Thailand	Arg.,Braz.,Chile
*mpr		Phil. I.	Urug.,Bol.,Peru,Col.
n=18	Pakistan	S.Korea	Sur.,Guat.,Hond.
		Sri Lanka	Nicaragua, El Sal.
	2	4	12 (18)

*1pdom		Mdgscr.,Bngldsh.	
n=4		Taiwan,Indonesia	
		4	(4)

The *militarized party (*milp)* category represents a transitional classification between the civilian and military parts of the CGSS and can be divided into two types depending on the number of significant parties—*mprs (n=18) and *1pdoms (n=4). In these 22 states, there is some party activity, but it is not as significant in determining governmental power-sharing as in the 85 civilian party-states covered in section V5.3. Here, instead of being the ultimate guarantor of national institutions, the military is a proximate arbiter of who rules. Although the recent record may reveal genuine efforts at building (or restoring) civilian political institutions, the legacy of military rule looms. The historical record of wars (V1.1ab) and coups (V1.2c) is more important in placing these states here than the evidence of elections, parties, and representative assemblies which, taken alone, might argue for some as having evolved into civilian party states.

As compared with section V5.3's 53 mprs and 13 1pdoms, the 18 *militarized multiparty* states *(*mpr)* and 4 *militarized one-party dominant* countries *(*1pdom)* have a recent, or a long, history of military coup rule, or war, or both.

Table V5.4b ranks these 22 states according to their V1.2c coup regime data and with respect to their involvement in war as measured in section V1.1d. This record shows that 12 of the 22 states have historically been beset by war (more than 20 years of war since 1945 or date of independence), 16 of the 22 countries have spent almost half their measured time under coup regimes ($\geq$ .467 coup years duration), and 17 of 22 have had more than two successful coups or a coup frequency ratio at least .067.

More than half of these states are in Latin America (Lowenthal and Fitch, 1986; Rouquie, 1987), and almost all of them are closely identified with the United States in their foreign policy orientation, raising once again some of the issues mentioned in Chapters 2 and 4 about the necessity of state repression in order to maintain capitalist economic systems in the developing world (Henderson, 1982; Wolpin, 1986; Baxter, 1985; Feith, 1981; Stohl and Lopez, 1984).

At the bottom of Table V5.4b are outlined the formats for the data bank excerpts presented for 3 of the 22 *milp countries at the end of this section.

The 18 *mprs can also be analyzed with respect to the political institutions mentioned in V5.4a: viz., the way in which their chief executive is chosen, the strength of their representative assemblies, and the number and viability of opposition parties. In the relative weakness of their parties and assemblies, many of these *mprs resemble the military regimes to follow, but their institutional forms are those of the multiparty republic.

Ten chief executives are directly elected in strong presidential systems: the Philippines, S.Korea, Argentina, Peru, Colombia, Nicaragua, Brazil, Chile, Guatemala, and El Salvador. (The last four have run-off elections between the top two candidates if no one gets a majority in the first round, which makes for an even stronger presidential system.) In only four of the *mpr states—Turkey, Pakistan, Thailand, Suriname—is the head of government selected by the representative assembly.

The remaining states are more mixed in their operation. In Bolivia, the assembly selects an executive president if no presidential candidate emerges with a popular majority, as has happened in both elections since the return from military rule in 1982. Uruguay and Honduras have a combined primary and general election at the presidential level, where several candidates from the same party may run for the office; the party whose candidates get the most votes wins the office, with the leading candidate in that party becoming president. Sri Lanka has had a checkered constitutional history, especially since 1977 when it changed from a parliamentary to a presidential system and then in 1983 when it suspended elections for six years under the threat of the Tamil insurgency. The result has been to consolidate the power of the ruling party so that this country borders on being a *1pdom state today.

With respect to opposition party strength in the representative assembly in late 1990, the states range from having two main parties (Pakistan, Philippines, S.Korea, Colombia, Honduras), to three (Turkey, Sri Lanka, Uruguay, Chile, El Salvador), four (Argentina, Peru, Suriname, Guatemala), five (Bolivia), six (Brazil) or ten or more (Thailand, Nicaragua). (The +s in the data bank excerpts which follow indicate the presence of parties on the ballot which won no seats, or less than the minimum percentage of the vote required for seats in proportional voting systems.) In virtually all cases, however, because of the legacy of military rule, even the main parties do not have strong roots and are often coalitions formed for electoral convenience which may not hold together until the next election (see especially Pakistan, Turkey, Thailand, Philippines, Nicaragua, and Brazil).

Despite these weak parties and the continuing presence of military influence, the 18 *mprs are in some respects closer to the mprs and more open to political participation than many of the civilian one-party polities. Given the passage of time and the experience of a few more elections—including one in which the ruling party is defeated and the opposition comes to power—some of these *mprs might be moved to the mpr category as was the case in earlier years with Venezuela, Ecuador, and the Dominican Republic.

With respect to the four *1pdom states, an argument could be made to classify some of them with the military regimes. There are, however, political parties (weak) other than the one favored by the military. (There is no category for *1pcom or *1p-other in the CGSS framework; military regimes tending in the direction of the two civilian one-party archetypes move directly into these categories from the strictly military classifications since they never allow other parties even though they may civilianize.)

Using the methodology of previous sections, the *1pdoms can be analyzed with respect to method of executive selection, opposition parties in the representative assembly, and legacy of military rule. In two out of the four states, the governments are still headed (in December, 1990) by the persons who perpetrated the original coups, which in some cases go back many years: Indonesia, Suharto, 1966; and Madagascar, Ratsiraka, 1974. This was also the case in Bangladesh whose leader since 1982 (Ershad) was forced to resign in late 1990. Despite evidence of elections involving opposition parties which win some seats in the representative assembly, the political structure that has been established tends primarily to legitimate the original coup regime. It is difficult to say whether the length of time these coup regimes have lasted is testimony to their success in building support through political institutions, or to the thoroughness of their control over the process of political participation. The answer will have to await the departure of the original coup leader. Many of the mil^ and mil² states at one time had parties and an assembly which did not survive the passing of the junta which presided over them, and the fate of Bangladesh is uncertain at this time.

The one remaining case merits special mention. The Taiwan regime was formed after the retreat to that island by the government of the Republic of China after losing its civil war in 1949. It established for the next 38 years a martial law regime headed by the losing general and his successor (and lineal descendant); only since January, 1988, has a new generation of non-mainland Chinese begun to move into positions of power.

In addition to two original coup leaders as current rulers, all four *1pdom states have a tradition of military rule—average coup frequency ratio of .092 (total of nine coups), percentage of coup regime years of .712. Some measure of the restrictions on participation in the *1pdoms might be gained by an analysis of the way in which opposition parties are treated. Madagascar's opposition parties have traditionally been of little consequence, whether under its independence leader Tsiranana (1960-72), or since 1975 under the National Front, which has 117 of 137 assembly seats. In Bangladesh's 1986 presidential election, the referendum on General/President Ershad was boycotted by all the opposition parties, and the estimated turnout varied from 1% (opposition figure) to 50% (government claim); the 1986 and 1988 assembly elections were also boycotted by the most important parties (one of them in 1986, both in 1988).

Some of the techniques mentioned in section V5.3c concerning civilian 1pdoms whereby only a limited number of seats in the assembly are open to competition are also employed by the states discussed here. In Indonesia, the opposition wins about one-third of the seats contested in the House of Representatives (n=400 in 1987); but another 25% of members (n=100) are appointed to this house, and an additional 500 seats are totally reserved for appointment by the ruling party and the military to the Peoples Consultative Assembly, which (along with the House of Representatives) elects the executive president. In Taiwan, the opposition won 29 of 101 contested seats in the Legislative Yuan (lower house) in 1989; but another 189 seats are reserved for life for the Kuomintang Party members who held these posts when they came to Taiwan from the mainland in 1949. Similarly, 668 of the 752 National Assembly electors who chose Taiwan's president in 1990 were permanent members.

However elaborate or unsophisticated these schemes might be, at least other political parties are legal and have some formal representation in the assemblies of the *1pdoms, unlike in the 41 military regimes to be discussed in the next two sections.

V5.4c. Moderating Military Regimes

mil^ = <u>moderating military regimes</u> (n=21—V5.4c)

Afghanistan	GB,Benin,Mali	Seychelles	
Iraq,Syria	CAfR,Togo,Niger		
Yemen,Somalia	Congo,Zaire	Cambodia	Paraguay
Algeria	Rwanda,Ethiopia		
	Angola,Mozambique		
6	12	2	1 (21)

In the 21 *moderating military* states *(mil^)*, the military is the predominant political actor. Although the junta may have begun to build a political party and allowed a direct national election to a representative assembly, the political history of these states as well as their indicators from V1.1d (war), V1.2c (coups), and V4.4d (states of emergency) are more persuasive than party activity in placing these countries here and not earlier in the CGSS. In short, the mil^ states' efforts at regime legitimation and power-sharing are deemed less convincing than those of the countries covered before this point.

Five of the 21 states are governed by first-generation coup regimes which overthrew their countries' independence governments—Somalia, Guinea Bissau, Zaire, Mali, and Seychelles. (In Seychelles, it was the civilian opposition party vice president who, with the army, ousted the civilian president and political structure left behind by the UK.) Ten others overthrew earlier coup regimes to attain power: Iraq, Syria, Yemen (i.e., both N. Yemen and S. Yemen before their unification), Benin, Togo, Central African Republic, Congo, Ethiopia, Rwanda, and Paraguay. Following the death of the original coup or revolutionary leader, Algeria, Niger, Angola, and Mozambique passed power on to another member of the ruling group using party framework that had been established. External armies were instrumental in bringing to power the governments in Cambodia and Afghanistan.

Table V5.4c.i analyzes these countries with respect to their history of military rule and involvement in war. Because most of these 21 states have had military regimes almost since independence (or since the traditional authoritarian political leader left behind by the departing colonialists was overthrown), the *number* of coups is more interesting than the duration of military rule (which is high in most cases) in assessing which have been the least successful in building civilian political structure (see first two columns in Table V5.4c.i). About half the countries have been at war for significant periods of time (column 3).

The countries at the bottom of the first column in Table V5.4c.i would appear to have made the most progress in building political structure in that they have had fewer violent changes of regime. To ensure that they are not just more successfully repressive, however, all these states should be analyzed with respect to the categories of political institution building. Such scrutiny will reveal distinctions not only among the 21 mil^ governments, but especially as they might be compared with the 20 entrenched military (mil°) states in the next section, with respect to credibility of elections, modes of representation, and use of party machinery.

One of the main distinctions between mil^ and mil° states is the willingness of a regime to allow some form of direct national election. There have been referendums on both a representative assembly and a chief executive officer in 11 of the 21 mil^s—Syria, Somalia, Algeria; Niger, Mali, Togo, Central African Republic, Congo, Zaire, Rwanda; and Seychelles. Nine other mil^s have allowed elections for a representative assembly—Iraq, Afghanistan, Yemen (both North and South, before the unification); Guinea Bissau, Benin, Ethiopia, Angola, Mozambique; and Cambodia. Paraguay's 1989 coup leader ran (unopposed) to finish the unexpired term of the president-general he overthrew; the one-party-dominated assembly remained in place during the change in the executive branch.

Table V5.4c.ii reports on the dimension of choice allowed among candidates for seats in representative assemblies of the 21 mil^s. In a few cases (Paraguay, Syria, and Iraq) other parties are tolerated, but the system is rigged so that the ruling party wins, and hence if it were not for their overwhelming military history, these regimes would approximate the militarized one-party dominant (*1pdom) states. At the other extreme are about eight countries where only a single list of party member (or party approved) candidates is offered the voters. Finally, there is a middle group of ten states where there is choice, within the military's party; selection ratios of candidates-to-seats are indicated in column 3 of Table V5.4c.ii, which draws upon data bank information in a way which enables a rough ranking (from most to least open) of the mil^ states in political participation. More detailed information about specific states can be found in the V5.4c data bank excerpts presented after the table.

Concerning movement out of this category, other legal parties have recently been permitted in Algeria, Benin, and Zaire, and promised in Mozambique. Until they actually run in national elections and win seats in the representative assembly, however, these states must remain designated mil^. Nevertheless, the most significant distinguishing characteristic between these 21 governments and the mil°s to be covered in the next section is that all of the mil^s (as compared with only about half of the 20 mil°s) have a political party which is the government's vehicle for legitimation, and sometimes even opposition parties (see Algeria, Zaire, Congo, and Paraguay in the excerpts at the end of this section). Whether these parties will provide the vehicle over time for the orderly transfer of power even within the ruling group, not to mention to putative opponents, remains to be seen. In all these countries, until there is a transfer of power to personalities not involved in the original coup, these states must remain in the category of military regimes.

V5.4d. Entrenched Military Regimes

mil² = <u>entrenched military regimes</u> (n=20—V5.4d)

Lebanon	BF,Nigeria,Liberia	Comoros	
Chad,Sudan	Ghana,Guinea,Eq.G.	Maldives	Haiti
Libya	Uganda,Burundi	Myanmar	
Mauritania	Lesotho	Fiji	Panama
5	9	4	2 (20)

In the 20 *entrenched military (mil ²)* states, civilian political participation is historically minimal to non-existent. Two states (Comoros and Haiti) have begun the process of institution-building by having direct elections for president in 1990, and three (Libya, Equatorial Guinea, and Uganda) have had indirect elections. But 2 countries (Lebanon and Liberia) are beset by war, and their politics are totally militarized, at the time of this writing; and the remaining 13 are long-standing military dictatorships which have made little progress in establishing broad-based civilian political structure.

Table V5.4d.i shows that most of the 20 mil² countries are African or Islamic and most have had greater frequency of violent regime transitions than the 21 mil^s of the previous section. More than half (13/20) of the entrenched military regimes are successors to juntas (Chad, Mauritania; Nigeria, Burkina Faso, Burundi, Lesotho; Myanmar, Comoros; Panama, Haiti), or emerged from civil wars (Liberia, Uganda, and (in a different way) Sudan). Four of the other seven (Libya, Guinea, Ghana, Equatorial Guinea) overthrew civilian or monarchical regimes which had deteriorated into various forms of authoritarianism before the military moved into power. Only Fiji (before 1987) and Lebanon (until 1974) had histories of multiparty civilian rule. (The Maldives are a special case; there are no parties and a single clan has run the island for centuries, giving it many of the aspects of a monarchy; the sultan was ousted from office in a vote for a republic in 1968, however.)

States under the second or third successive junta give little evidence of success in the building of political institutions. Kennedy (1974: 23-30) says that of all the factors related to the military's coming to power, the most important is simply that the previous regime was also a military government which gained power illegally. Burkina Faso has had violent transitions going back six consecutive administrations. Nine of these states have never had a peaceful change of government: Mauritania, Chad, Libya, Burkina Faso, Uganda, Equatorial Guinea, Guinea, Lesotho, and Comoros. Although Sudan, Ghana, and Nigeria have had intermittent periods of civilian rule, they have experienced four to six coups each in their brief histories. Haiti, at the time of this writing is planning to inaugurate the first freely elected president in its history; it remains to be seen whether the militarized forces in that society will respect his mandate.

The average number of coups since independence (or 1945) in the 20 mil$^{\circ}$ states is 3.2, significantly higher than the 2.5 for the similar measure for the 21 mil$^{\wedge}$ countries. The averages of columns 1 and 2 in Table V5.4d.i, when contrasted with their counterparts in Table V5.4c.i, reveal that high coup frequency is a better indicator of entrenchment than long regime duration for the latter sometimes provides the time and stability to build civilian political institutions. The average number of war years (column 3) is also not higher for the entrenched mil$^{\circ}$s, indicating that the main enemy of the institutionalized armed forces in many of these states is not external or internal armed belligerents, but the prospect of power-sharing with the civilian populace.

In this regard, the mil$^{\circ}$ regimes can be analyzed with respect to the political institutions described earlier: elections, parties, representative assemblies, etc. (See excerpts at end of this section.)   Table V5.4d.ii shows the lack of even rigged electoral exercises in 13 of the 20 states. In fact, the totals in the far-right column show a pattern in electoral modes from the *milp states, which allow elections resulting in a head of government in 20 of 22 cases; to the mil$^{\wedge}$, which has elections for the executive branch 12 of 21 times; to the mil$^{\circ}$, where the number is only 3 out of 20.

Civilian party activity is illegal in eight out of 20 mil$^{\circ}$ countries: Libya, Sudan, Chad, Mauritania; Ghana, Uganda, Lesotho; and Maldives. Three countries have legalized a single party: Burkina Faso, Burundi, and Equatorial Guinea. Two states (Nigeria and Guinea) have recently drafted constitutions permitting multiparty competition (and even specifying the number of parties to be allowed, not a good sign). Comoros had its first multiparty election for president in March, 1990 under the watchful eye of French troops; after they leave whether other civilian political institutions will be built remains to be seen. Of the final six states, three have a multiparty tradition (Lebanon, Fiji, Panama), and three have a history of military-dominated government (Liberia, Myanmar, Haiti).

With respect to economic ideology, 18 of the 20 mil$^{\circ}$ states are solidly capitalist. Table V5.4d.iii puts the issue of right-wing entrenched military states in some perspective by summarizing remarks first made in section V5.3d. Among civilian polity types, at the two extremes, all one-party communist states are socialist in economic orientation, and most multiparty republics are capitalist (50 of 53; all except three $\tilde{\ }$mpr eastern European states which are currently deemed mixed). In the mprs, the power centers created by private capital concentrations are often intimately involved with the identity of parties in the political system. The necessity for wealth in order to participate meaningfully in politics ensures that to be viable in an mpr system a party must be committed to capitalism. The one-party communist states are socialist by definition; according to Marxist-Leninist theory, the vanguard party directs a government which controls the major economic means of production and distribution. Not only are parties opposed to this doctrine not permitted in most 1pcom states, but it is often illegal even to advocate a different system in speech or writing.

The other one-party states present a more mixed record with respect to economic ideology, preferring a combination of public and private sector activity. Of the 13 states designated 1pdom, 5 are capitalist in orientation, 2 are officially committed to socialism, and 6 are difficult to categorize with the government in control of some major resources and significant activity in the private sector too. The 11 "one-party other" polities are comprised of 2 socialist, 6 capitalist, and 3 mixed (or unclear) in economic orientation. Data from Chapter 2 relating to the amount of CGE (V2.2c), outside private investment (V2.3a), and private consumption (V2.4c) has been consulted in making the distinctions between 1psoc and 1pcap states. However, because of the discrepancy between rhetoric and practice, and because getting sufficient reliable data to draw these lines is difficult in any case, the socialist v. capitalist judgments must be regarded as tentative.

Because military regimes generally do not have as coherent an economic or political belief system as party states, there is a shift in terminology to the fuzzier "left" and "right" in the bottom half of Table V5.4d.iii. The *milp states follow the pattern of their civilian counterparts; all 18 *mprs are capitalist, and so too are even the four *1pdoms. The spectrum of opinion as presented for all militarized/monarchical states—60 of 75 on the right side of the display—reinforces Chapter 2's point that most countries are capitalist, and raises again the question of whether these most militarized regimes are "holding operations" for the unpopular workings of the global economic system.

The excerpts at the end of this section show that the mil$^\circ$ countries trail the moderating mil$^\smallfrown$ regimes (more than half of which can be described as center-left) in the building of civilian political institutions. In both their economic and political dimensions, most of the 20 mil$^\circ$ states are more like the 12 monarchies to be discussed in the next section.

Eur.=0	Islamic	Africa	Asia	Latin America
		militarized party systems = *s: (n=22—V5.4b)		
*milp n=22	Turkey		Madagascar,Sri Lanka Bangladesh Thailand	Arg.,Brazil,Chile Urug.,Bol.,Peru Colombia,Suriname
	Pakistan		S.Korea,Taiwan Phil. I.,Indonesia	Guatemala,Honduras Nicaragua, El Sal.
Sbtot.	2	0	8	12 (22)

Eur.=0	Islamic	Africa	Asia	Latin America
		military regimes (n= 41: 21^ + 20º—V5.4cd)		
	Afghanistan	GB, Benin, Mali	Seychelles	
mil^ n=21	Iraq, Syria	CAfR,Togo,Niger		
	Yemen	Congo, Zaire	Cambodia	Paraguay
	Somalia	Rwanda, Ethiopia		
	Algeria	Angola, Mozambique		
	6	12	2	1 (21)

Eur.=0	Islamic	Africa	Asia	Latin America
	Lebanon	Burkina F.,Nigeria	Comoros	
	Sudan,Chad	Ghana, Guinea,Liberia	Maldives	
milº n=20	Libya	Eq.Guinea,Burundi	Myanmar	Haiti
	Mauritania	Uganda,Lesotho	Fiji	Panama
	5	9	4	2 (20)
Tot. V5.4	13	21	14	15 (63)

V5.4a.ii - Institution-Building in Militarized Regimes

0 - None of the following.

1 - referendum on constitution including existing Hd.State/Govt.　　　　V5.4º=d

2 - election for a representative assembly; could be with:

  a. no parties;　　b. one (the govt'.s) party and its single list　　V5.4º=cd

  c. one party with choice of party-mbr. candidates or party-approved candidates　　V5.4^=c

  d. more than one party allowed, but win no seats　　V5.4^=c

3 - other parties allowed and actually win some seats in assy.,

    but system still structured so they have little chance to rule.　　V5.4*1p=b

4 - other parties allowed to run cands. for exec. office,

    but legacy of mil. rule is pervasive.　　V5.4*mp=b

V5.4a.iii - Format for Militarized Polity Data Bank EXCERPTS

(Format to vary from *milp to mil^ to milº)

State — a. info. on political institution building, esp. party

b. data on any elections to rep. assys., exec. branch

c. why state placed here and not higher or lower in CGSS, using V1 historical data (esp. V1.1d, V1.2c).

V5.4b - Legacy of Militarism in *milps (n=22)

V1.2c.i - # coups & freq.			V1.2c.ii - % coup-yrs.		V1.1d -# war yrs.	
Thailand	9	.200	Taiwan	.927	Indonesia	126+
Guatemala	9	.200	El Salvador	.867	Philippines	108+
El Salvador	9	.200	Thailand	.844	Guatemala	64.5+
Bolivia	8	.178	Bangladesh	.778	Colombia	63+
Argentina	7.5	.167	Nicaragua	.756	Pakistan	54
Bangladesh	3	.158	Guatemala	.689	Argentina	40
Honduras	7	.156	S.Korea	.619	Bangladesh	33+
Madagascar	3.5	.117	Madagascar	.600	Sri Lanka	32+
Peru	5	.111	Argentina	.600	Turkey	30+
Brazil	5	.111	Pakistan	.581	El Salvador	24+
Pakistan	3	.070	Indonesia	.571	Peru	22+
Turkey	3	.067	Bolivia	.556	Nicaragua	22
Suriname	1	.067	Brazil	.511	Taiwan	15
Uruguay	2.5	.056	Honduras	.489	Uruguay	4.5
S.Korea	2	.048	Suriname	.467	Bolivia	4
Colombia	2	.044	Peru	.467	S.Korea	3
Nicaragua	2	.044	Chile	.350	Suriname	2
Taiwan	1.5	.037	Philippines	.318	Madagascar	1
Indonesia	1	.024	Uruguay	.266	Chile	1
Philippines	1	.023	Turkey	.244	Honduras	1
Chile	1	.022	Colombia	.089	Thailand	0
Sri Lanka	0	.000	Sri Lanka	.000	Brazil	0

Source: V1.2c and V1.1d data banks (1990).

Format for V5.4b - * mpr Data Bank EXCERPTS
State – a. most recent election data re party distributions (seats in assembly, % vote for presidential candidates, etc.). See V5.3a format, plus...
b. why *mpr and not mpr, using V1 historical data.

Format for V5.4b - *1pdom Data Bank EXCERPTS
State – a. most recent election data, especially regarding seats held by non-dominant parties.
b. why *1pd and not 1pd (higher) or mil^ (lower).

Turkey   n=4+ parties   11/83: 400/2=200 to *   11/87: 450/2=226 to *

	11/83			11/87	
c-r:Motherland Party (Ozal)	53%~	212*	c-r: Motherland (Ozal)	36%	292*
c-l:Populist P. (soc.dem)	29%	117	c-l: Soc. Dem.P (Inonu)	24%	99
r: Natl.Dem.Party (military)	18%	71	r: True Path P.(Demirel)	22%?	59
	100% -------- 400		l: Dem.Left P. (Ecevit)	9%	0
			Others, mainly on right	9%	0
				100%	450

In 1983, ~%v = % of seats, strict proportionate voting, but only three "clean" parties
allowed. 1987 constitut. amend. ref. allowed Ecevit, Inonu, & Demirel back into
politics, raised Assy. to 450, but raised % vote to get seat up to 10%;. Motherland got
65% seats with 36% votes, & Ecevit 0 seats with 9% votes.
*mpr because of military's tradition of aborting elected civilian govts. (1960, '71, '80);
  Gen. Evren's retaining of Hd. of State, 1983-89; and continued periodic Kurdish
  insurgency (V1.1b).

S. Korea   n=4+ parties

	12/87 Pres.	4/88 Assy
Roh Tae Woo (Dem. Justice P.)	36.2%	125 (86 el.+39 apptd.,34%v)
Kim Young Sam (New P.of Reunif.&Dem.)	27.2%	59 (46 + 13, 24%v)
Kim Dae Jung (P. for Peace & Dem.)	26.4%	70 (55 + 16, 19%v)
Kim Jong Pil (New Dem-Repub. P.)	8.0%	35 (27 + 8, 15%v)
Others	2.2%	10 with 8% vote)
	100%	299/2 = 150 to control Assy.
Turnout	89.2%	72.6%

1987 constitution resulted in most democratic and highest turnout Pres. election ever.
Assy.'s new single mbr.district system still favors rural areas; bonus seats ("apptd.", above)
give even close party winners a sizable edge in seats. 1990 merger of DJP, NPRD, &
NDRP into one large Democratic Liberal Party giving system look of *1pdom.
*mpr because of history of military rule (26/26 yrs. after Syngman Rhee independence
  leader installed by US Army); and Pres. Roh was member of last 1981-87 junta.

Taiwan - a. Kuomingtang (Nationalist) P. of China (KMT)
Dominant ethnic-based (mainland Chinese>Taiwan islanders) KMT party usually gets 70% of
  vote in controlled elections for small (but growing) % of Leg. Yuan. Other seats (n=189
  in '89) held by mainland Chinese who won them in 1947.
12/89 Leg.Yuan - KMT = 72/101 contested seats, 58% vote;
  Dem. Prog. Party = 21 seats, 30% vote; independents = 8 seats, 12% vote.
3/90 Pres. - indir. el. by Natl. Assy. electoral college (n=~750), similarly structured with
  about 90% of seats held by mainlanders elected in 1947.
*1pd because "state of emergency" military rule used to preserve power of KMT
  mainlanders for 38 years, 1949-87. Recent liberalization results in islander president
  who, however, appointed mainland General PM, 5/90.

V5.4c.i - Military History of mil^ Regimes

V1.2c.i - # coups & freq.			V1.2c.ii - % coup-yrs.		V1.1d - # war yrs.	
Syria	8	.182	Paraguay	1.000	Iraq	175
Benin	5	.167	Syria	.932	Ethiopia	108+
ΔYemen	4.5	.153	Seychelles	.929	ΔYemen	70.5
Togo	3	.100	Togo	.900	Cambodia	58+
Congo	3	.100	Algeria	.892	Angola	58+
C.Af.R.	3	.100	Zaire	.833	Mozambique	44+
Afghan.	4.5	.100	Benin	.800	Syria	30
Iraq	4.5	.100	C.Af.R.	.800	Algeria	30
Seychelles	1	.071	Rwanda	.750	Afghanistan	12+
Rwanda	2	.071	Congo	.733	GBissau	12+
Paraguay	3	.067	Mali	.733	Rwanda	9
Ethiopia	3	.067	Iraq	.711	Zaire	6
GBissau	1	.059	Somalia	.700	Somalia	2
Cambodia	2	.056	ΔYemen	.690	Paraguay	1
Algeria	1.5	.054	GBissau	.588	Togo	0
Niger	1.5	.050	Niger	.533	Niger	0
Zaire	1	.033	Cambodia	.414	Benin	0
Mali	1	.033	Afghanistan	.378	C.Af.R.	0
Somalia	1	.033	Ethiopia	.356	Congo	0
Angola	0	.000	Angola	.000	Mali	0
Mozambique	0	.000	Mozambique	.000	Seychelles	0
AVG:	2.52	.076	AVG:	.651	AVG:	25.8

Source: V1.2c and V1.1d data banks (1990); Δ=average for N.Yemen and S.Yemen.

V5.4c.ii - Analyses of Political Institutions in mil^ Regimes

State	Date	Assy.Choice	Candidates	Other Remarks
Paraguay	2/88	ex-*1pdom	structured; winning presid.party gets 2/3 seats	
Syria	2/90	contested	1/3 seats resrvd. for indeps.; Ba'ath,allies win rest	
Iraq	4/89	"limited"	Ba'ath allied parties and indeps. win a few seats	
Zaire	9/87	1075:210	party-approved	Other parties legalized, 5/90.
C. Af. R.	7/87	142:52	party-approved	
Togo	3/85	216:77	party-approved	
Algeria	2/87	885:295	party members	Other parties win in '90 local els.
Seychelles	6/87	2-3 :1	party members	
Rwanda	12/88	140:70	party-approved	
Mozambique	1986	252+:210	party-approved	Constitut. requires +20% choice.
Somalia	12/84	171:150	party-approved	
Cambodia	'81 & '86*	148:117	party-approved	*Retroactive referendum in '86
ΔN.Yemen	7/88	1200:128	no parties;	But "factions" & independents OK
ΔS.Yemen	10/86	"controlled"	party-approved	
Niger	12/87	1 list	party members	
Benin	6/84	1 list	party members	Other parties legalized, 2/90.
Mali	6/85	1 list	party members	
Congo	7/89	1 list	party members	
GBissau	5/84	1 list	party members	
Ethiopia	6/87	1 list	party-approved	
Afghanistan	4/88	1 list	party members	
Angola	1986	1 list	party-approved	Electoral college of party mbrs.

Source: V5.4c Data Bank; Δunited Yemen has not had any elections as of December, 1990.

Format for V5.4c - mil^ Data Bank EXCERPTS
a. information on party strength, including time between coup and party(s) legalization.
b. information on representative assembly, including date and degree of choice in elections.
c. information on executive branch referendum (if any).
d. why **mil^** and not 1p civilian (higher) or mil^ⁿᵉ (lower) in CGSS.

Algeria - a. National Liberation Front (NLF) was 1954-62 revolutionary independence party.
b. 2/87 Assy. - choice within party; 885 cands. for 295 seats; 15% ballots spoiled.
c. 12/88 ref. (81% Yes, 89% turnout) approved Pres. Chadli's handling of 10/88 pro-democracy riots, and
  gave him third 5-year term (to 1993).
d. liberalizing **mil^** - 2/89 constitut. change separates Hd. State & Hd. Party, gives more power to assy.,
  allows other parties which run & win 65% vote, 55% seats in 6/90 local elections; but NLF still rules at
  national level. Multiparty natl. assy. elections scheduled for 1991.

Zaire - a. Pop. Mvmt. of Rev.(MPR), estab. in 4/67, is only legal party; SG=Mobuto.
b. 9/87 - Natl.Leg.Coun., 5 yr. term; 1075 cands. approved by MPR for 210 seats; only 68 incumbents
  returned, 142 elected for first-time. (Good turnover).
c. 7/84 el., Pres. of Party and Republic; 99% Yes vote for third 7-year term.
mil^ bec. mil. rule since Mobuto/CIA coup of 1965. Even advocacy of other parties was illegal until 4/90;
  now four new weak ones have formed to contest 1991 presidential. election.

Congo - a. Congolese Workers Party (CTP), SG Sasson-Nguesso; (Cent.Cmtee, n=75).
b. 7/89 - Pres. & Assy: CTP=153 seats; no choice/one list.
mil^ bec. 1968 mil. coup of Ngoubi formed current ruling govt. & party; passed power on to Nguesso, 2/79.
  Insufficient party structure (0.44% pop.=mbrs.) for this to be 1p soc. Opposition parties to be legal in 1991.

Rwanda - a. National Rev. Movement for Development (MRND), formed 2 yrs after 7/73 coup.
b. 12/88 - National Development Council election; 140 MRND-approved candidates for 70 seats; some
  incumbents defeated.
c. 12/88: 99.9% Yes in presidential referendum for third straight 5-yr. term.
mil^ because Gen.Habyarimana is MRND Sec.Gen., chooses its Cent.Cmtee, and party is his (and military's)
  vehicle for legitimation. All citizens must belong and pay two-days wages as dues.

Paraguay	4/89 Pres.	2/88 Pres.	2/88 H+S	2/84 Pres.	2/84 H+S
Colorado(Natl.Repub.) P.	Rod.-74%	Strs.88.5%	48+24	Strs.-90%	40+24
Authentic Rad. Lib. P.	Laino-19%	in jail	illegal	in exile	illegal
others	n=4: 7%				
Radical Lib. P. (Franco)		Vega-?%	17+9	Doldan-6%	13 + 6
Liberal P. (Celauro)		Fer.Ib.-?%	7+3	Fulvio=3%	7 +4
	Totals:-------------------		72+36=108		60 +30=90

Colorado P. factions: 1. "militants" - support militarized party regime since 1954;
  2. "traditionalists" - pre-1954 families; supported Stroessner, but for reforms later;
Others include: Humanist P.; plus other prev. unrecognized ones: Febrerist Rev. P., Xtn. Dem. P., Colorado
  Pop.Mvmt, Communist P. ARLP,FRP,XDP,CPM in Natl.Pact to boycott 2/88 election.
mil^ because Gen. Rodriguez 2/89 coup was supposedly "reformist," leading to mpr in 1993; ran to fill out
  Stroessner term in possible deal with Colorado Party traditionalists which would give them presidency in
  1993. A reform(?) of Gen.Stroessner's *1pdom system structured to legitimize his 1954 coup. (His) party
  with highest % of vote got 2/3 assy. seats; presidential nominees by coalitions forbidden; communists
  "and others with similar aims" banned.

V5.4d.i - Military History of mil° Regimes

V1.2c.i - # coups & freq.			V1.2c.ii - % coup yrs.		V1.1d - # war yrs.	
Comoros	4.5	.300	Comoros	1.000	Myanmar	78+
Burkina Faso	6	.200	Haiti	1.000	Uganda	60
Nigeria	6	.200	Burundi	.857	Lebanon	51+
Haiti	7.5	.167	Lesotho	.833	Sudan	48+
Ghana	5	.152	Burkina Faso	.800	Chad	33+
Sudan	4	.147	Sudan	.765	Libya	3
Uganda	4	.143	Myanmar	.714	Nigeria	3
Chad	3	.133	Nigeria	.633	Liberia	1
Mauritania	3.5	.117	Panama	.622	Burundi	1
Panama	5	.111	Ghana	.576	Panama	1
Burundi	3	.107	Libya	.538	Mauritania	0
Fiji	2	.100	Chad	.500	Burkina Faso	0
Myanmar	4	.095	Uganda	.500	Ghana	0
Lesotho	2	.083	Equat. Guinea	.500	Guinea	0
Eq.Guinea	1	.045	Mauritania	.400	Eq. Guinea	0
Guinea	1	.031	Liberia	.222	Lesotho	0
Libya	1	.026	Guinea	.188	Comoros	0
Liberia	1	.022	Fiji	.150	Maldives	0
Lebanon	0	.000	Lebanon	.000	Fiji	0
Maldives	0	.000	Maldives	.000	Haiti	0
AVG:	3.19	.107		.539		13.8
vs.V5.4c^ AVG:	2.52	.076		.651		25.8

Source: V1.2c and V1.1d data banks (1990).

V5.4d.ii - Recent Electoral Experience of Military Regimes

.4b=*milp (n=22)

1.Leg>PM(or Pres):	Turkey,Pakistan	Thailand	Suriname	(4)
1a.Leg>PM,&Pres(mix):		Sri Lanka		(1)
2.Assy & dir. el. Pres:		Phil.I.,S.Korea	Arg.,Brz.,Chile	
			Bol.,Col.,Peru	
		Bangldsh.,Madag.	Guat.,El Sal.,Nic.	
			Urug.,Honduras	(15)
3.Assy only:		Taiwan,Indonesia		(2)

.4c=mil^ (n=21)

2.Assy & dir.el.Pres:	Syria,Algeria	CAfR,Mali,Togo,Niger	Seychelles	Paraguay	(12)
	Somalia	Zaire,Congo,Rwanda			
3. Assy only:	Afghan.,Iraq,Yemen;	GBissau,Benin,Ethiop.,Moz.;	Cambodia		(8)
No dir.el.:		Angola			(1)

.4d=mil° (n=20)

1.Leg>PM:	Lebanon				(1)
2.Pres & dir.el.Assy≈:			Comoros	Haiti	(2)
3.Assy only:		Liberia			(1)
No dir. el.:	Libya	Eq.Guinea,Uganda			(3)
No election:	Chad,Sudan	Ghana,Guinea,Burkina F.	Maldives		
	Mauritania	Nigeria,Burundi,Lesotho	Myanmar,Fiji	Panama	(13)

≈only presidential elections have been held in Comoros and Haiti as of 12/90.

Source: V5.1b Data Bank.

V5.4d.iii - Economic Orientations of Governments

socialist=all 8 **1pcom**-V5.3d   V5.3ab-**mpr**: 50 of 53 are capitalist

mixed/unclear(n=3)
Hungary,Czech.,Poland

	socialist	mixed/unclear	capitalist	
1pdom n=13--V5.3c	Guyana Mongolia	Bulgaria,Romania Iran,Mexico Namibia,Zimbabwe	Egypt Senegal,Iv.Coast Singapore,Malaysia	
	2	6	5	
1p-other n=11--V5.3e	STP Tanzania	Cape Verde Sierra L. Zambia	Djibouti,Tunisia Gabon,Cameroon Kenya,Malawi	
	2	3	6	
CIVILIAN SUM:	12	12	61	(85)

...........L E F T..R I G H T.................

1pcom	1psoc	mixed/unclear	1pcap	*milp cap.	
		***milp** (n=22--V5.4b)		Turkey,Pakistan,Sri Lanka Thai.,Phil.I.,S.Korea Brazil,Chile,Arg.,Peru Bol.,Urug.,Col.,Suriname Guat.,Hond.,El Sal.,Nic. Madagascar,Bangladesh Taiwan,Indonesia 4 *1p + 18 *mp = (22)	

		mil^(n=21--V5.4c)			
Afghan.	Somalia Syria	Algeria Yemen,Iraq			
Ethiopia	Congo Angola	Benin Mozambique	Mali,GB,CAfR,Niger Togo,Zaire,Rwanda		
Cambodia	Seychelles			Paraguay	
3	5	5	7	1	(21)

		mile (n=20--V5.4d)			
		Libya	Chad,Mauritan.,Sudan Eq.G.,BF,Ghana Guinea,Uganda Burundi,Lesotho	Lebanon Nigeria Liberia	
	Myanmar		Comoro,Maldive	Fiji Haiti,Panama	
0	1	1	12	6	(20)

                                   V5.5a-**mon**: all 12 are capitalist

MIL/MON SUM:	9	6	60	(75)

TOTAL:	21	18	121	(160)

Format for V5.4d - mil° Data Bank EXCERPTS

a. "lack of" party information
b. info. on representative assembly (if any), especially election restrictions
c. info. on executive branch referendum (if any), especially any restrictions
d. military history information from V1.1d, V1.2c data banks.

Mauritania - a. Structure for the Education of the Masses (SEM), is a program, not a party; it mobilizes people, channels grievances.
b. 12/86 elections for local, regional councils. No national elections since '78.
c. Col. Taya, in 12/84 coup, became Chief of State and Chm. of Military Committee for National Salvation (CMSN, n=18-23), the sole government apparatus.
d. mil° bec. third straight change of govt. by coup, assembly has been dissolved since 7/78 coup, 12 yrs. without any national elections.

Sudan - a. Gen. Bashir 7/89 coup has banned all parties (n=30+, 3 main ones) from six 1986-89 govts.; but seems closest to old National Islamic Front.
b,c. - assembly indefinitely suspended; no referendum on executive.
d. mil° because civil war vs. 58% majority black Christians/animists in the south for 24+/34 years, and under military rule for 26/34 years (.765 duration, 5 coups--V1.2c). Most recent coup attempt, 4/90.

Burkina F. - a,b. No parties or assembly since 1980 coup (3 others since then).
c. 10/87 Capt. Campaore overthrow of Pres.(Capt.Sankara, 1983 coup leader). Heads new Coordinating Cmtee. of the Popular Front (=3/88 Revolutionary Cmtee).
d. mil° - most coups (n=6) in Africa, .800 coup years; #1 in west Africa in mil.exp./CGE.

Guinea - a,b. Assembly and 1958-84 Pres. Sekou Toure's PDG (Parti Democratique de Guinee) party dissolved; all political activity banned since 4/84 coup.
c. Pres. = Col./Gen. Lansana Conte; governs through Military Committee for National Recovery (CMRN), headed by 10-man executive board.
d. mil° - even civilian independence president Toure's regime was quite militarized by end of his 26-year rule.

Myanmar- a. Military's Burma Soc.Program Party, formed in '74 constitut. to legitimize '62 coup regime renamed Natl.Unity Party during summer '88 unrest.
b. 5/90 assy - NUP wins only 2 (of 489) seats, with about 30% of vote; vs. National League of Democracy 392 seats, 67% vote, despite its two leaders' detentions.
c. Military refuses to allow newly-elected assy. to sit. After arrests of NLD's acting leaders, parties agree to give army right to draft new constitution.
d. mil° bec. mil. rule since 1962 (.714 coup years, 4 coups), 78+ war years vs. insurgencies; pro-democracy movements violently suppressed in '62,'74,'88.

V5.5. ANACHRONISMS AND CONNECTIONS

This chapter concludes with a look at some waning forms of government in today's world. The first, monarchies, completes the analysis of polity types defined on Table V5.1a's Comparative Government Spread Sheet. The others—colonies, divided states, and governments in transition—provide the occasion for a return to the starting point of this book in Chapter 1.

V5.5a. Monarchies

monarchies/traditional regimes (n=12—V5.5a)		
Morocco		Bhutan
Jordan,Saudi A.		Nepal
Oman,Kuwait	Swaziland	
UAE,Qatar,Bahr.		Brunei
8	1	3 (12)

Table V5.1a's CGSS identifies 12 monarchical (or traditional) regimes, most of them small (9 of 12 with less than 3 million people each) and most in the Islamic zone (7 from the Arabian peninsula alone). Power is only minimally shared in such political systems; the royal family, and the leader it chooses from among its members, dominate these states. Nevertheless, within these systems, some modern political institutions have been introduced, as the following discussion (summarized in Table V5.5a.i) will make clear.

The minimal check upon the power of a royal family is the existence of a written constitution limiting some of its prerogatives. Seven of the 12 monarchical regimes have such a document, even if in most instances it merely codifies traditional practices. In 7 states, the royal head of state delegates some power to a prime minister, usually some other trusted member of the family (e.g., the crown prince, successor to the throne).

Representative assemblies with some (generally minimal) independent powers exist in only 5 of the 12 countries as of 1990, although purely advisory consultative councils are found in a few others. Direct national elections for such bodies have been held in 3 countries (Nepal, Morocco and Jordan) where either tame "loyal-opposition" parties have been allowed to participate, or (as in Nepal) parties have historically operated behind the cover of independent candidacies. In Nepal, these parties may become more significant as a result of the new 1990 constitution permitting them to participate legally in elections for the first time in 1991 (see excerpts at end of this section). Before Kuwait's annexation by Iraq in August, 1990, an election to a consultative council to discuss the return of the assembly suspended in 1986 had been held.

The lack of modern political institutional structure might seem to present a situation ripe for revolution; a closer look at these regimes, however, reveals that most monarchies are rather stable. Their legitimacy stems from the long tradition of many years of rule by a single family or dynasty. Longevity—rather than elections, popular representation in an assembly, or participation in party activity—is the important political component in these regimes. Military might is also critical. In their original foundings, these monarchies (like many other states in their independence struggles) often employed military force; they continue to be supported today by armies loyal to the ruling family.

Table V5.5a summarizes information from the data bank on these traditional regimes. It lists states, first (i) in order (based upon the presence of five possible modern political structures) of those with the greatest institutional possibilities for expanded political participation beyond the royal family; then (ii) in order of dynastic longevity. This section ends with excerpts from the V5.5a data bank for five countries, the format for which is found in Table V5.5a.iii.

V5.5b. Colonies and Possessions

A final form of government in which political participation is minimal is the colony or possession of one state by another. Even more so than monarchies, this polity type is a disappearing phenomenon in the world today. In 1945, 50% of the global population (750 million out of 1.5 billion people) lived in such dependent territories; in 1990 less than 1/2 of 1% did (about 20 million of the world's 5.3 billion).

Table V5.5b.i lists 70 such entities, in columns under the governing power representing, respectively, US, UK, France, South Africa/Turkey, and "Other." Great Britain still has the most colonies (n=17), although after its return of Hong Kong to China (scheduled for 1997), the most *people* subject to foreign rule will be under the United States (especially in its "commonwealth" of Puerto Rico) and South Africa (in its "homelands"). Geographically, most colonies (n=31) are in Asia, where Pacific Ocean islands are especially notable (see Table V5.5b.ii).

The eight *ed "micro-states" are supposedly independent; each, however, is so small that it has to have a supervising power (state at head of column) to which it has transferred its foreign and defense policy, so there are doubts as to genuine sovereignty in these cases. (Kiribati, a former UK possession, is somewhat more self-sufficient in this regard, but has not joined the United Nations and so has not been included among this study's 162 independent countries.)

V5.5c. States in Transition

Selected Colonies/Divided States (n=9)

Cyprus/#N.Cyprus	N.Korea/S.Korea
#W.Sahara	Taiwan/China
#Palestine	#Hong Kong/China
4	5 (9)

Before concluding this chapter, it should be noted once again that the placement of states into polity categories in the Comparative Government Spread Sheet is a tentative undertaking, subject to changing events and refinement of definition. This is especially true for that handful of countries which are at this point in their history divided, or in some form of transition in government type at the time of this writing.

Two classic "divided nations," which trace their origins to the end of World War II, have been treated in this study as the four independent states they have since become: North Korea, South Korea, China, and Taiwan. Unlike the two Germanies, which accepted each other's existence (and membership in the United Nations) in 1971 and were reunited in 1990, the two Koreas and two Chinas each continue to insist on one single state embodying the nation in question. Movement toward reunification of Korea awaits the death of the first-generation independence leaders in the north. In the case of China, some hint as to ultimate resolution of the Taiwan issue may be provided by the way the mainland reabsorbs Hong Kong in 1997; in the meantime this significant political entity of 5.5 million people and $32.2 billion GDP remains classified in the CGSS as a colony of the United Kingdom.

Three political entities not recognized as independent states but each with some significant international legitimacy include Palestine, Western Sahara, and North Cyprus. The Palestine Liberation Organization (PLO) is recognized by the United Nations and by more than 90 countries as the sole, legitimate representative of the Palestinian people; in November, 1988, it formally declared its independence of Israel, though its government is in exile and does not control any of the territory it claims (in the Gaza Strip and the West Bank of the Jordan River). In Western Sahara, POLISARIO forces are recognized by about 70 states, including half the countries in Africa, and the UN is involved in a mediation which could provide for either reconciliation with Morocco or independence. The Republic of North Cyprus (the island's northern quarter) is recognized and defended only by Turkey, but has survived in this rather dependent existence since 1974.

Finally, several of the 13 states listed in Table VI.1b as in the midst of ongoing civil wars are already de facto partitioned as of 1990. Despite the creation of a de jure regime with greater international legitimacy in the 1989 Taif Accords, and the cease-fire in Beirut a year later, the rest of Lebanon is still divided into several warring camps. In Afghanistan, the rebels' interim government in exile is recognized by Pakistan and supported by the United States and much of the Islamic world, but the government in Kabul has survived since early 1989 without its previous Soviet troop support; it is unclear what its ultimate fate will be, but the current CGSS designation of moderating military (mil^) will probably be appropriate for the foreseeable future regardless of which side prevails. In Cambodia, the three-party coalition with the widest international recognition (and United Nations seat) holds virtually no territory; with the departure of Vietnamese troops in September, 1989, the prospects are greater that an international conference might eventually broker some arrangement between these rebel forces and the government which has ruled since 1979.

In Angola and Mozambique none of the parties seems able to prevail in the wars which have been fought almost from the time of the departure of the Portuguese colonialists in 1975; negotiated settlements without partition are probably the most likely outcome. But in the Sudan, Ethiopia, and Myanmar, the central governments seem unable to dominate definitively over ethnic groups which have been fighting for more than a generation; the ultimate resolutions might involve some sort of secession arrangements disguised as autonomy.

Insurgencies and civil wars, perverse forms of political participation (Powell, 1982), are nevertheless an appropriate point on which to end this study, for they were the first matters covered back in Chapter 1. The connection between peace and political participation—Values #1 and #5—is just one of many that can be made within the Framework for Measuring Global Values. A few others will be noted in the brief concluding section.

.i - Summary of Modern Political Institutions

State	Constitut.	Divided Hds.	Assy.	Elections	Parties	Rating
Nepal	Yes	Yes	Yes>PM	Yes	Yes	5.0
Morocco	Yes	Yes	Yes	Yes	Yes	5.0
Jordan	Yes	Yes	Yes	Yes	No	4.0
Kuwait	Yes	Yes	suspended	restricted suff.	No	2.5
Bhutan	Yes	No	Yes	restricted suff.	No	2.5
Swaziland	No('65-73)	Yes	Yes	indirect	No	2.5
Bahrain	Yes	Yes	No	No	No	2.0
Qatar	Yes	No	No	No	No	1.0
UAE	provisional	Yes	No	No	No	1.0
Brunei	No ('59-62)	No	No	No	No	0.0
Oman	No	No	No	No	No	0.0
Saudi A.	No	No	No	No	No	0.0

.ii - Legitimacy Based upon Date of Original Dynastic Accession

Islamic	African	Asian
Jordan (Hashemites)1517		Brunei (Bolkiahs) 1400's
Morocco (Alawites) 1660		
Qatar (Thanis) 1716		
Kuwait (al Sabahs) 1756		
Saudi A. (Sauds)1766		
Oman (Saids)1775		
Bahrain (Khalifas) 1782		Nepal (Shahs) late 1700's
UAE (Nahayans)1790s		
	Swaziland (Swazis)-1899	Bhutan (Wangchuks) 1907

.iii Format for V5.5a - monarchy Data Bank EXCERPTS

State - a. evidence of shared power (constitutionally-mandated?) with a PM or a representative assembly (appointed or elected).

b. distribution of seats in representative assembly (not consultative council), especially where elections and parties are operating.

c. historic legitimacy data, incl. **starting date** and *name* of dynasty.

d. other remarks.

Jordan - a. King Hussein ibn Talal, since 8/52 constitution (> PMs).
  b. 11/89 Assy. el. (first since '67; third in history); 652 cands. for 80 seats (not including 18 reserved for
     minority Bedouins, Christians, Circassians). 62% turnout (=.5m./3.4m.pop.)
     Parties illegal, making seats won unclear, but "tendencies" represented included:
       r: Islam.Fundmtlsts. (incl.Mosl.Brotherhd., registered as a "charity") 20-25 seats (of 26 cands.)
       r: others identified as pro-Islamic state   6-14 (of 15 cands.)
       c: traditionalist independents (pro-monarchy and pro-govt.)   19
       l: Arab nationalists, Baathists, communists   11
     Overlap in 1st 2 groups, which comprise ~1/3 Assy (31-34/80); resulting in King's 12/89 appointment of
     favorable PM Badran, but not allowing them to form govt.; UH (n=40) also appointed.
  c. Hashemite kingdom of Hussein's family ruled in n. Arabia under Ottomans since 1517; placed in
     Transjordan (out of Palestine mandate) by UK in 1921.
  d. Electoral history: '56: free, but then assy. suspended & parties outlawed after '57 coup attempt; '67: rigged,
     many boycott, soon suspended after 6-Day War until 1984; '84 & '85 by-elections to fill 11 of 30 East
     Bank seats only. Claim to represent West Bank Palestinians dropped, 7/88.

Kuwait - a. Sheikh Jaber Al-Ahmad al Sabah, King since 1977. Emir > Crown Prince PM; a sometimes
     functioning Natl. Assy.(1976-81; 1985-86), n=50.
  b. Assy. dir. el. based on electorate restricted to approx. 60,000 male descendants from 1920 Kuwaiti male
     citizens (= ~3.5% of 1.7 mill. population.)
     No parties, but some recognized "factions": in '85 assy: Left Democrats 3 seats; pan-Arab nationalists 5;
     two Islamic Fundamentalist groups, several.
     6/90 shura (Natl.Consult.Counc.) to review recommendations for return to elected assy. by 1994; n=50
     elected (fm. 348 cands.; 60% turnout v. 85% in '85) + 25 appointed by Emir.
     8/90 annexation by Iraq suspended all indigenous political institutions.
  c. In 1711-16, clans of Aniza tribe (Uteiba sect) migrated from Arabia; head of al Sabah family was selected
     Emir in 1756. Senior *al Sabah* family members choose Crown Prince (successor) from either the al-Jaber
     or the al-Salim branch of family.

Saudi A. - a. no constitution; King Fahd ibn Abdal-Aziz al Saud is Hd. St. & Govt. (since 1982).
  b. no assembly or parties.
  c. Dynasty from Mohammed ibn *Saud*, King of Daraiyya (died, 1766); Kingdom of Saudi Arabia proclaimed
     in 1932 by Emir Abdul Aziz II ibn Saud.
  d. legitimacy stems from defense of Islam and protection of its holy places.

Nepal - a. King Birendra bir Bikram *Shah* Dev = Hd. of State since 1972; but PM comes out of Assy.,
     112/140 members of which are directly elected.
  b. 5/86 el. - independent candidates only under '62 constitut.; 5 yrs. to Natl.Panchayat > PM < King.
     2/90 unrest (5 dead, 4000 aa&d) led by Mvmt. for Restoration of Dem. alliance of 8 banned parties resulted
     in 4/90 coalition govt. with 4 Cab.Mins. from Congress P. (Ldr. PM Bhattari), 4 fm. Communist P. (Ldr.
     S. Pradhan), 5 independents; and new 9/90 constitution legalizing parties and calling for 1991 election.
  c. Prithvi Narayan *Shah*, ruler of Gorkha Kingdom, founded dynasty in late 1700s; King Tribhuvan (+ India
     vs. Rana family) established constitutional monarchy in 1951.

Bhutan - a. King Jigma Singhye Wangchuk is Hd. of St. & Govt. since 1972.
  b. 1985 Assy.; 110/150 dir. el., 3 yrs.; 1 vote per *family*; opposition parties illegal.
  c. Sir Ugyen *Wangchuck* started dynasty in 1907. Ruler of one principality asked by others to start rule
     (probably with UK protection).

V5.5b.i - "Possessions": Populations under External Political Rule

US	UK	France	S.Afr./Turkey	Other[a]
Puerto	HongKong-5.7 m.			
Rico-3.3 mil.			Transkei-2.0 m.	SP:Canary I.-1.5m.^
			Bophutswana-1.4m.	ISR:West Bank-900,000
			Ciskei-740,000	INDN: E.Timor-630,000
		Reunion-572,000	Venda-550,000	ISR: Gaza-600,000
		Guadloup.-337,000		PRT:Macao-400,000^
		Martinq.-300,000		PRT:Azores-292,000^
				PRT:Madeira-266,000^
	Channel I.-140,000			AUS:Bismrk-239,000
		Polynesia-189,000		NTH:Antilles-200,000
Guam-130,000		N.Caledon-154,000	N.Cyprus-150,000	MOR:W.Sahara-200,000
n=2	n=2	n=5	n=5	n=10 (24)

--100,000---

US	UK	France		Other
Virgin I.-97,000	*Tonga-95,000			SP: Ceuta-67,000
Micronesia-85,000	(Kiribati-65,000)	Fr.Guiana-73,000		NTH: Aruba-67,000
Marshalls-48,000	I. of Man-64,000	Mahore-67,000		SP: Melilla-63,000
N.Marianas-39,000	Bermuda-57,000	+SP:*Andorra-43,000		DMK: Greenlnd-54,000
Am. Samoa-36,000	Gibraltar-29,000	*Monaco-27,000		DMK: Faeroes-47,000
	Cayman I.-22,000			SW: *Liechtn.-27,000
Belau - 14,000	B.Virgin I.-12,000			IT: *S.Marino-22,000
	Montserrat-12,000	Wallis&Frt.-12,000		NZ:Cook I.-17,000
n=6	n=8	n=5		n=8 (27)

....10,000..

US	UK	France		Other
	*Tuvalu-9200			ANZUK:*Nauru-8000
	Turks&Caicos-7400			AUS: Xmas I.-3000
	Anguilla-6500^	St.Pierre&Mq.-6300		NZ: Niue I. - 2500
	St.Helena-5600			AUS: Norfolk I.-2400
				CHILE: Easter I.-2000
Midway I.-450	Falklands-1900			NZ: Tokelau I.-1700
Wake I.-300	BIOT(DGarcia)-1500			IT: *Vatican-1000
Johnston Atoll-300	Pitcairn-60			NZ: Cocos-600
n=3	n=7	n=1		n=8 (19)

n=11	n=17 w/2*	n=11 w/ 2* (S.AF./Trk:5)		n=26 w/4* (70)

* = nominally independent, n=8; (+ Kiribati, see Text):

Andorra, Monaco, Liechtenstein, San Marino, and Vatican City;   Tonga, Tuvalu, and Nauru.

[a] = Abbreviations & Totals:

ISR=Israel-2; SP=Spain-3; INDN=Indonesia-1;PRT=Portugal-3; AUS=Australia-5;
NTH=Netherlands-2; MOR=Morocco-1; DMK=Denmark-2; SW=Switzerland-1; IT=Italy-1;
CHILE=Chile-1; NZ=New Zealand-4.

Source: *World Eagle,* November, 1989 for mid-1989 populations;
    ^plus Gastil, *Freedom in the World,* Part VI, "Related Territories."

V5.5b.ii - Possessions, Displayed by Zone
(in approximate order of populations in Table V5.5b.i)

Europe	Islamic	Africa	Asia	Latin America	
	W.Bank	Transkei	Hong Kong	Puerto Rico	
	Gaza	Bophutswana			
		Canary I.	E.Timor		
			Reunion	Martinique	
		Ciskei		Guadeloupe	
Azores		Venda		Neth. Antilles	
Madeira			Macao		
			New Caledonia		
Channel I.			Bismarck		
	W.Sahara		Polynesia		
	N.Cyprus		Guam		
n=3	n=4	n=5	n=8	n=4	(24)

--pop. =100,000--

			*Tonga	US Virgin I.	
I. of Man	Ceuta		Micronesia	Fr. Guiana	
Greenland	Melilla		Mahore	Aruba	
Faeroes			Am. Samoa		
			(Kiribati)		
Bermuda			Marshall I.		
*Andorra			N. Marianas	Cayman I.	
Gibraltar			Belau	British Virgin I.	
*Monaco			Cook I.		
*Liechtenstein				Montserrat	
*San Marino			Wallis & Fortuna		
n=9	n=2		n=10	n=6	(27)

--pop. =10,000--

			*Tuvalu		
			*Nauru	Turks&Caicos	
			Nieu I.	Anguilla	
St.Pierre & Miq.		St. Helena	Midway I.		
			Xmas I.		
			Easter I.		
			Wake I.	Falklands/Malvinas	
			Norfolk I.		
			Tokelau I.		
			BIOT(D.Garcia)		
			Cocos		
			Johnston Atoll		
*Vatican			Pitcairn		
n=2		n=1	n=13	n=3	(19)

| TOTS: 14 | 6 | 6 | 31 | 13 | (70) |

Source: Table V5.5b.i

* = nominally independent microstates, not recognized in this study, n=8; (+ Kiribati; see Text)

BIBLIOGRAPHY

ALEXANDER, R. J. (ed.) (1982) *Political Parties of the Americas: Canada, Latin America, and the West Indies*. Westport, Conn.: Greenwood Press.

ANDRIOLE, S. J., and G. W. HOPPLE (1986) "The Process, Outcomes, and Impact of Regime Change in the Third World, 1959-1981," *International Interactions* 12: 363-392.

BAKER, A., and J. SEROKA (eds.) (1989) *Contemporary Political Systems: Classifications and Typologies*. Boulder: Lynne Rienner Publications.

BANKS, A. S. (annual) *Political Handbook of the World*. New York: McGraw-Hill.

BAXTER, C. (1985) "Democracy and Authoritarianism in South Asia," *Journal of International Affairs*, 38: 307-319.

BETTS, R. K., and S. P. HUNTINGTON (1985-86) "Dead Dictators and Rioting Mobs: Does the Demise of Authoritarian Rulers Lead to Political Instability?" *International Security* 10:112-146.

BLONDEL, J. (1973) *Comparative Legislatures*. Englewood Cliffs, N. J.: Prentice-Hall Co.

BROWN-JOHN, C. L. (1988) *Centralizing and Decentralizing Trends in Federal States*. Lanham, Md.: University Press of America.

BURGESS, M. (1988) "Can Comparative Federalism Really Be Comparative?" in BROWN-JOHN (1988): 11-22.

CHIH-YUAN, C. (1985) *Communist Parties in the World*. Taipei: World Anti-Communist League, China Chapter.

CLAPHAM, C., and P. GEORGE (1984) *The Political Dilemmas of Military Regimes*. Totowa, N.J.: Rowman and Allenheld.

CLARK, R. P. (1986) *Power and Policy in the Third World*. New York: Wiley.

CLEMENTS ENCYCLOPEDIA OF WORLD GOVERNMENTS (1990) Dallas: Political Research Inc.

COLLIER, R. B. (1978) "Parties, Coups, and Authoritarian Rule: Political Change in Tropical Africa," *Comparative Political Studies* 11: 62-93.

COUNCIL ON FOREIGN RELATIONS (annual) "Chronology of Year," in *Foreign Affairs: America & the World*. New York: Council on Foreign Relations.

CROW, B., and A. THOMAS (1984) *Third World Atlas*. Philadelphia: Taylor and Francis.

DAHL, R. A. (1971) *Polyarchy: Participation and Opposition*. New Haven: Yale University Press.

DANOPOULOS, C. P. (ed.) (1987) *Military Dictatorship in Retreat: Comparative Perspectives on Post-Military Regimes*. Boulder: Westview Press.

DAY, A. J., and H. W. DEGENHARDT (1988 and 1984) *Political Parties of the World*. New York: Keesings Reference Company.

DECALO, S. (1973) "Military Coups and Military Regimes in Africa," *Journal of Modern African Studies*, 11: 105-127.

DELURY, G. (1987 and 1983) *World Encyclopedia of Political Systems and Parties*. New York: Facts on File.

DENITCH, B. (1978) *Legitimation of Regimes: International Framework for Analysis*. Beverly Hills: Sage Studies in International Sociology.

DIAMOND, L., J. LINZ, and S. M. LIPSET (eds.) (1987ff) *Democracy in Developing*

Countries series. vol. 1-*Persistence, Failure, and Renewal;* vol. 2-*Africa;* vol. 3-*Asia;* vol. 4-*Latin America.* Boulder: Lynne Rienner Publishers.

DILEMMA OF DEMOCRACY (1985) *Journal of International Affairs,* Special Number, 38: entire issue.

DUCHACEK, I. D. (1987) *Comparative Federalism: The Territorial Dimension of Politics.* Lanham, Md.: University Press of America

FALK, R. A. (1982) "The Global Setting and Transition to Democracy: Preliminary Conjectures," *Alternatives* 8:193-208.

FEITH, H. (1982) "Repressive-Developmentalist Regimes in Asia," *Alternatives* 7: 491-506.

FOLTZ, W. J., and H. S. BIENEN (eds.) (1987) *Arms and the African.* New Haven: Yale University Press.

FUKUI, H. (ed.) (1985) *Political Parties of Asia and the Pacific.* Westport, Conn.: Greenwood Press.

FUKUYAMA, F. (1985) "The Rise and Fall of the Marxist-Leninist Vanguard Party," *Survey* 29: 116-135.

GREENWOOD HISTORICAL ENCYCLOPEDIA OF THE WORLD'S POLITICAL PARTIES. (1982, 1983, 1985) Westport, Conn.: Greenwood Press, 3 vols. (see Alexander, Fukui, and McHale citations in this bibliography).

HALPERN, M. (1987) "Choosing between Ways of Life and Death and between Forms of Democracy: An Archetypal Analysis," *Alternatives* 12: 5-35.

HENDERSON, C. (1982) "Military Regimes and Rights in Developing Countries: A Comparative Perspective," *Human Rights Quarterly* 4: 110-123.

HERMET, G., A. ROUQUIE, and R. ROSE (eds.) (1978) *Elections without Choice.* London: Macmillan.

HOBDAY, C. (1986) *Communist and Marxist Parties of the World.* Santa Barbara: ABC-Clio Publications.

HOROWITZ, I. L. (1982) *Beyond Empire and Revolution: Militarization and Consolidation in the Third World.* New York: Oxford University Press.

HREBANAN, R. J. (1986) *The Japanese Party System: From One-Party Rule to Coalition Government.* Boulder: Westview Press.

HUDSON, M. C. (1977) *Arab Politics: The Search for Legitimacy.* New Haven: Yale University Press.

————. (1985) "The Breakdown of Democracy in Lebanon," *Journal of International Affairs* 38: 277-292.

HUNTINGTON, S. P., and J. M. NELSON (1976) *No Easy Choice: Political Participation in Developing Countries.* Cambridge: Harvard University Press.

INTERNATIONAL INSTITUTE FOR STRATEGIC STUDIES (annual) "Annual Chronology," in *Strategic Survey 19xx/xx.* London: International Institute of Strategic Studies.

INTERNATIONAL PARLIAMENTARY UNION (annual) *Chronicle of Parliamentary Elections and Developments, 198x/198x.* Geneva: International Centre for Parliamentary Documentation.

JACKMAN, R. W. (1986) "Elections and the Democratic Class Struggle," *World Politics* 39: 123-146.

JACKSON, R. H., and C. G. ROSBERG (1985) "Democracy in Tropical Africa: Democracy versus Autocracy in African Politics," *Journal of International Affairs* 38: 293-305.

JANDA, K. (1981) *Political Parties: A Cross-National Survey.* New York: Free Press.

KENNEDY, G. (1974) *The Military in the Third World.* New York: Scribners.

KOTHARI, R. (1984) "Party and State in our Times: The Rise of Non-Party Political Formations," *Alternatives* 9: 541-564.

LAMBERT'S WORLDWIDE GOVERNMENT DIRECTORY (annual) Washington: Lambert.

LAUNDY, P. (1989) *Parliaments in the Modern World.* Brookfield, Vt.: Dartmouth Publishing Co., in association with Inter-Parliamentary Union.

LIJPHART, A. (1984a) "Advances in the Comparative Study of Electoral Systems," *World Politics* 36: 424-436.

_____. (1984b) *Democracies: Patterns of Majoritarian and Consensus Government in Twenty-One Countries.* New Haven: Yale University Press.

LIJPHART, A., and B. GROFMAN (eds.) (1984) *Choosing an Electoral System: Issues and Alternatives.* New York: Praeger Publishers.

LINZ, J. J., and A. STEPAN (eds.) (1986) *The Breakdown of Democratic Regimes: Crisis, Breakdown, and Reequilibration.* Baltimore: Johns Hopkins University Press.

LOEWENBERG, G., and S. C. PATTERSON (1979) *Comparing Legislatures.* Boston: Little, Brown and Co.

LOEWENBERG, G., S. C. PATTERSON, and M. E. JEWELL (eds.) (1985) *Handbook of Legislative Research.* Cambridge: Harvard University Press.

LOWENTHAL, A. F. (1974) "Armies and Politics in Latin America," *World Politics* 27: 107-130.

LOWENTHAL, A. F., and S. FITCH (eds.) (1986) *Armies and Politics in Latin America.* New York: Holmes and Meier.

MACKIE, T., and R. ROSE (1984) *The International Almanac of Electoral History.* New York: Facts on File.

MALLOY, J. M., and M. A. SELIGSON (eds.) (1987) *Authoritarians and Democrats: Regime Transition in Latin America.* Pittsburgh: University of Pittsburgh Press.

MANIRUZZAMAN, T. (1987) *Military Withdrawal from Politics: A Comparative Study.* Cambridge: Ballinger Publishing Co.

MCHALE, V. (ed.) (1983) *Political Parties of Europe.* Westport, Conn.: Greenwood Press.

MCKINLAY, R. D., and A. S. COHAN (1976) "Performance and Instability in Military and Nonmilitary Regime Systems," *American Political Science Review* 70: 850-864.

MEZEY, M. L. (1985) *Comparative Legislatures.* Durham, N. C.: Duke University Press.

MILBRAITH, L. W. (1965) *Political Participation: How and Why Do People Get Involved in Politics.* Chicago: Rand-McNally.

NELSON, J. M. (1987) "Political Participation," in WEINER and HUNTINGTON (1987):103-159.

O'DONNELL, G. A., P. C. SCHMITTER, and L. WHITEHEAD (eds.) (1986) *Prospects for Democracy* series. vol. 1-*Southern Europe;* vol. 2-*Latin America;* vol. 3-*Comparative Perspectives;* vol. 4-*Tentative Conclusions about Uncertain Democracies.* Baltimore: Johns Hopkins University Press.

PANEBIANCO, A. (1988) *Political Parties: Organization and Power.* Cambridge: Cambridge University Press.

PERLMUTTER, A. (1981) *Modern Authoritarianism: A Comparative Institutional Analysis.* New Haven: Yale University Press.

PERLMUTTER, A., and V. P. BENNETT (eds.) (1980) *The Political Influence of the Military: A Comparative Reader.* New Haven: Yale University Press.

POWELL, G. B. (1982) *Contemporary Democracies: Participation, Stability, and Violence in 29 Countries.* Cambridge: Harvard University Press.

PROBLEMS OF COMMUNISM (bimonthly) Washington: United States Information Agency.

PROSTERMAN, R., and J. REIDINGER (1982) "Toward an Index of Democratic Development," in GASTIL (see Chapter 4 Bibliography).

RADU, M. (1982) "Ideology, Parties, and Foreign Policy in Sub-Saharan Africa," *Orbis* 25: 967-992.

RANDALL, V. (ed.) (1988) *Political Parties in the Third World.* Beverly Hills, Calif.: Sage Publications.

ROSE, R. (1980) *Electoral Participation: A Comparative Analysis.* Beverly Hills: Sage Publications.

ROUQUIE, A. (1986) "Demilitarization and the Institutionalization of Military-dominated Polities in Latin America," in O'DONNELL et al., vol. 2: 108-136.

_____. (1987) *The Military and the State in Latin America.* Berkeley: University of California Press.

RUSTOW, D. A. (1985) "Elections and Legislatures in the Middle East," *Annals of the American Academy of Political and Social Science* 482: 122-146.

SALLNOW, J., and A. JOHN (1982) *An Electoral Atlas of Europe 1968-1981.* London: Butterworth Scientific.

SARTORI, G. (1976) *Parties and Party Systems: Framework for Analysis.* London: Cambridge University Press.

SMITH, J., and L. D. MUSOLF (eds.) (1979) *Legislatures and Development.* Durham, N. C.: Duke University Press.

SMITH, T. B. (1986) "Referendum Politics in Asia," *Asian Survey* 26: 793-814.

SOEDJATMOKO (1983) "Political Systems and Development in the Third World: New Directions for Social Science Research in Asia," *Alternatives* 8: 483-499.

STAAR, R. (annual, a) *Yearbook on International Communist Affairs.* Stanford, Calif.: Hoover Institution Press.

_____. (annual, b) "Checklist of Communist Parties in 198x," *Problems of Communism* , annual issue.

STAMMEN, T. (1980) *Political Parties of Europe.* London: John Master.

STOHL, M., and G. LOPEZ (1984) *The State as Terrorist: The Dynamics of Governmental Violence and Repression.* Westport, Conn.: Greenwood Press.

STUDIES IN COMPARATIVE COMMUNISM (3 times a year) Stoneham, Mass.: Butterworths.

SZAJKOWSKI, B. (1981) *Marxist Government: A World Survey.* New York: St. Martin's Press.

THOMAS, C. Y. (1985) *The Rise of the Authoritarian State in Peripheral Societies.* New York: Monthly Review Press.

UNITED STATES. DEPARTMENT OF STATE (1985) *Atlas of United States Foreign Relations.* Washington: Department of State Publication 9350.

_____. (various) *Countries of the World and Their Leaders: Background Notes.* Detroit: Gale Research Company.

VANHANEN, T. (1984) *The Emergence of Democracy: A Comparative Study of 119 States, 1850-1979.* Helsinki: The Finnish Society of Sciences and Letters.

VON BEYME, K. (1985) *Political Parties in Western Democracies.* New York: St. Martin's Press.

WEINER, M., and S. P. HUNTINGTON (eds.) (1987) *Understanding Political Development.* Boston: Little, Brown and Co.

WELCH, C. E. (1987) *No Farewell to Arms? Military Disengagement from Politics in Africa and Latin America.* Boulder: Westview Press.

WESSON, R. (ed.) (annual) *Democracy: World Survey, 198x.* Boulder: Lynne Rienner Publications.

WILDERMANN, R. (ed.) (1987) *The Future of Party Government.* vol. 1 - *Visions and Realities of Party Government,* by F. G. Castles and R. Wildermann (eds.); vol. 2 - *Party Governments: European and American Experiences,* by Richard Katz (ed.); vols. 3-8 in preparation. Hawthorne, N.Y.: Aldine de Bruyter.

WOLPIN, M. D. (1986) *Militarization, Internal Repression, and Social Welfare in the Third World.* New York: St. Martin's Press.

WORLD DEVELOPMENT FORUM (semimonthly) San Francisco, Calif.: The Hunger Project.

Conclusion

The final display in this book, Figure C.1, presents a composite summary of the Framework for Measuring Global Values. As the foregoing narrative makes clear, some of the data needed to activate the indicators in this framework are more readily available and subject to quantification than other types of desired information. In addition, the usual warnings about drawing unwarranted comparisons from aggregate data naturally apply to this study. Nevertheless, if a start is to be made in measuring global progress toward the achievement of these five values, it is hoped that the work presented here is a helpful first step.

As indicated in the introduction, for many inquiries associated with global values, much of the relevant data is inherently "soft." On the other hand, where the data is more concrete, it does not seem to vary widely from year to year. In testing this model over several years, it has been found that *rankings of states* within world order value categories and within smaller geographic regions do not differ significantly over short periods of time. In fact, for certain categories decades might be a more appropriate time frame than years in assessing longitudinal progress for specific countries. If this model were used for regular global surveys of a specific value, or for states in a particular region with respect to all five values, the general conclusions would probably not vary much from year to year.

The data displayed by way of examples in this book is also useful in a more general sense. When data is applied in other contexts, questions can be asked and rankings and other uses made of it in ways which are typically not the concern of the original gatherers of the information. For example:

a.) is Country X moving closer to or further away from a particular world order value compared to some previous time of measurement;

b.) does this country more nearly approximate the ideal represented by this value than its neighbors;

c.) is it closer than some other group of cohort states (e.g., allies, regimes of similar governmental or social structure).

The Framework for Measuring Global Values can also be used to analyze connections between value indicators both within and among states. The interrelationship between militarized governance (V5.4) and several of the indicators relating to war under Value #1 was noted in the last chapter. Other links that were mentioned in the text and which can be appreciated at a glance in Figure C.1 include:

V2.1 (economic productivity) and V1.2ab (defense budgets);
V2.1a (economic growth) and V3.1a (population growth);
V2.2b (unemployment) and V4.5d (unions);
V2.4 (distribution of economic benefits) and V4.2 (equality);
V3.1a (population growth), V4.4c (women's rights), and V2.4b (literacy);
V3.3bc (fuel and mineral resources) and V2.3d (trade dependencies);
V4.2a (ethnicity), V4.3 (human rights), and V1.1b (insurgencies);
V4.2a (ethnic differences) and V5.2c (power-sharing arrangements);
V4.3 (human rights violations) and V5.4 (militarized governance);
V4.4 (rule of law, respect for civil rights) and V5.3 (civilian polities);
V4.4b (forced movement) and V1.1c (refugees); and
V4.5a (freedom of expression) and V5.1ab (political parties and elections).

Although there has not been the space to develop these potential points of contact at greater length in this work, it is hoped that the preliminary work which has been done here will be of service to others who may wish to further elaborate upon these connections.

The conceptual framework developed here also provided a number of places where the concept of interdependency among nations might be measured. Most notable were sections V1.1b (support for insurgencies); V1.3a and .3b (overseas forces and weapons transfers); V2.2d (international debt); V2.3abc (foreign aid, trade, and investment); V3.3bcd (natural resources); V4.2 (ethnicity and expatriate minorities); and V5.5bc (colonies, possessions, and divided nations). In all these cases only the briefest of starts has been made in developing measures which might reveal skewed power relations between pairs of states.

Finally, the values which form the focus of this study correspond to subjects at the heart of five major divisions of the field of international studies in American universities today:

V1 - war and peace studies/world politics;
V2 - international political economy;
V3 - global ecology;
V4 - international law; and
V5 - comparative government.

The framework proposed in each of this book's major chapters thus could be used as a method of organization and a basis for further research for students in any of these areas.

Scholars are urged to apply the indicators described here to regions of their particular expertise. Contemporary measures with respect to groups of states, or time-series studies of individual countries, are among the exercises that might be attempted. Additions and deletions to the concepts and categories of analysis suggested here are encouraged in the hope of further refinement of this global framework for measuring world order values. The development of data-gathering procedures and techniques might thus progress at a pace commensurate with normative theory in the five identified fields. In this manner, the model may continue to evolve in ways which keep pace with the world that both scholars and policy-makers would like more properly to "order."

Figure C.1 — Framework for Measuring Global Values

V1-Peace

.1—war

a. wars by type,severity,duration
i.intl; ii.anti-colonial; iii.civil
b. civil wars & insurgencies
i. % land,# groups vs. govt.
ii. group name,leader,ideology
iii. armed strength, supporters
EXCERPTS fm. V1.1b Data Bank
c. "refugees from war
d. state experience in wars: i. number
i. their yrs.; iii. total duration

.2—domestic impact: budgets & coups
a. armed personnel
i. absolute #; ii. relative measures
per 1000 pop., per 1000 sq.km.
iii. conscription v. CO
b. military expenditures
i absolute $s
ii. relative measures
(a) mil.exp/cap.; (b) mil.exp/GNP
(c) mil.exp/CGE (Cent.Govt.Exp.)
(d) mil.exp/soldier
iii. relative "burden" composite
c. revs. & mil. coup-regimes
i. coup freq. ratios
ii. % coup regime years
EXCERPT from V1.2c Data Bank

.3—external manifestations
a force projections
i. deployed overseas:
troops: #, names states where
ii. "hosted" on home soil:
troops: #, names states present
b. weapons transfers
i. arms X; arms X/total X
ii. arms M; arms M/total M
iii. arms M dependencies
iv. 3rd World arms producers
c. arms issues of global concern
i. ABC wpns; ii. arms control treaties

.4—summary and transition

V2-Economic Well-Being

.1—inherent economic strength
a. productivity - i. GNP; ii. GNP/cap.
iii. multi-yr. growths of i.ii
b. investment & saving
i. GDI as % GDP; ii. GDS/GDP
c. reserves ($, M months)
d. positive account balances
e. ideology of development
LDCs, LLDCs, MSAs, & CMEA

.2—economic weaknesses
a. inflation, multi & recent yr.
b. unemployment
c. consumption: i. CGE &/cap.
ii. GNP/GNP; iii. GGC/GDP
d. i. Govt.Budget Deficit as % GNP
ii. Debt: Ext. Extd.: (b)Exd.Pub. as
% GNP; (c) service ratio(% of X)

.3—international capital transfers
a. i. Net "Direct" Investment
ii. workers remittances
b. Econ. Aid- i. tot, per cap. % GNP
ii. US,OECD DAC, & OPEC donors
c. Trade: i. X+M; ii. X+M as % GNP
iii. terms of trade
d. Dependencies - i. on aid (n=5)
ii. trade commodity Cls (n=3)
iii. trade partner Cls (n=2)

.4—distribution of benefits
a. amenities: i. electricity;
ii. tels./100; iii. cars/1000
b. education: i. literacy;
ii.(a) % CGE educ.; (b) educ. $/cap.
iii. school population/teacher
c. health: i. % CGE; $/cap.; % GNP;
ii. pop/phys; pop/nurse; pop/hosp. bed
d. soc.welfare & other consumption:
i. % CGE HEWelfare;
ii.private:Govt. cons./GDP
iii. consumer expend. $/cap.
iv. Gross Natl. Income per capita
v. real GDP/capita

V3-Ecological Balance

.1—population
a. size; growth rates, incl.
i. natural incr. rate (>ZPG,NRR yrs.)
ii.% in age cohort 0-15
b. methods of control, incl.
i.Natl. Fam. Planning: state ratings
ii.% BC users; iii.abortion #s,policies
c. women's fertility rate
d. hunger(food)-i.Inf.Mort.Rate>50
ii. child death rate per 1000
iii.(a)da.protein/cap;(b)da.cals./cap

.2—environment
a. land: i. area;
ii.(a) pop.density; (b)dus./agric.land;
iii. % arable, % meadows & pastures
b. water: i. landlocked & island states
ii. coastline; iii.inland; iv. rivers,lakes
c. cities: i.(a) slum pop.; (b)densest;
ii.# cities > 1/2 mil., names > 2 mil.;
iii.% urban(>urban pop.growth rate)
d. pollution- i. air: (a)% SO2; (b)SPM
(c) CO2; (d) greenhouse gas additions
ii.water: (a)susp.sediment; (b)diss.mins.
iii.% pop.(a)safe water; (b)sanitation

.3—resource consumption
a. i. energy: tot. & per cap. consumption
ii. nuclear power: (a) # reactors;
(b) power capac. & % electricity
b. fossil fuels-production & reserves
i. oil; ii. gas; iii. coal
c. minerals & metals-reserves & prod.
d.i.forests: % tot & % removed ea. yr;
ii. fisheries: sea, freshwater catches

.4—international & composite measures
a. exports
i.% FMM exports; ii.>30% X-CI
b. global coop.- i.protected areas:
(a)land; (b)heritage sites;
(c)wetlands; (d)biosphere reserves
ii. intl. environmental treaties
c. composite quality of life rankings
i. life expectancy; ii Sivard ECOSOC;
iii. PQLI; iv.ISP, v.UN HDI

V4-Social Justice

.1—Intl.Bill of Human Rights
a. articles vs. MGV text
b. CP,ESC,ICJ signatories
c. Reporting Agencies &
Rating Scale 1-2-3-4 (=S)

.2—equality
a. ethnic homogeneity %s
b. religious %s; by type, state
c. language groups
d. ethnic categories of analysis:
i. interesting; ii. problematic
iii.minority rule; iv.ethnic insurgency
EXCERPTS from V4.2 Data Bank

.3—integrity of the person(human rights)
a. legal killings: death penalty (S)
b. illegal: disappearances, deaths (S)
c. torture (S)
d. political prisoners (S)
EXCERPTS from V4.3 Data Bank

.4—the rule of law (civil rights)
a. i. arb.arr. & det.; ii. fair trial (S)
b. i.free movement(S); ii.privacy(S)
c. women's rights: i.ratios v.men(n=3)
ii. gender gaps v. men (n=5)
d. constitutionalism:
i. states of emergency
ii independent courts (S)
e. transition: civil/political rights
i. FH civil liberties10-yr. avg.
ii. FH political rights10-yr. avg.

.5—personal freedoms (political rights)
a. expression, gen.: assy. & assoc.
b. religion:
i. freedom of
ii. criteria
iii. status of organized religion
c. freedom of press, Human a.FH (S)
d. labor: unions & % workforce

V5-Political Participation

.1—Comparing Govt. Systems:
a. CGSS, 10 polity types, 5 zones
b. regime legitimacy/elections, by:
i. 3° electoral types; ii. 10 polity types

.2—power sharing within govts.
a. Hds. State, Govt. relationship
b. rep.assy. i. # mbrs.; ii.# chambers;
(#elected, apptd.; terms in both)
c. constitut. & other balances
i.dom.parties, councils, colleges
ii. int.groups from V4; iii. federalism
EXCERPTS from V5.2etc Data Bank

.3—civilian polity participation
ab. multi-party republics (n=53)
i. Hd. State types (40+5+8)
ii. assy. distrib. types (23+22+8)
EXCERPTS fm. mpr:
SIMP., COALIT., PRES.:
(a) parties in Leg.: (b) strengths (#s; %v)
(c) ideologies & °partners; incl. mpr
cde. single-party polities (n=32)
i. name; ii. date most recent elec.
iii. % votes and/or #seats
iv. degree of choice; v. other info:
EXCERPTS fm. 1pp Data Banks

.4—militarized governance (n=63)
a.i. political institution-building factors
(exec.ref.; assy.el.choice; party roles)
ii. V1.1d &.2c - war and coup data;
iii. econ. orientation; applied to:
b. *milp systems (n=22) EXCERPTS
c. moderating mil (n=21) EXCERPTS
d. entrenched milp (n=20) EXCERPTS

.5—anachronisms & connections
a.monarchies (n=12) EXCERPTS
i. mod.pol.institutions; ii. dynasty date
b. colonies & possessions (n=70)
i. by ruler; ii. by zone
c.states in Xition/divided nations(10)

Index of Geographic Names

References to states in tables based upon narratives from data bank EXCERPTS are indicated in **bold type**, with an "X-" before the V-designation of the table.

General Index

References to Tables are indicated by their V-designations in **boldface type**; EXCERPT–Tables are indicated by an "X–" before the V-designation of the table.

abortion, 10, 164-65, **V3.1b.iii**

ACDA. *See* United States Arms Control and Disarmament Agency

account balances, 99

advanced industrial states, 99-100, 166, 182, 200, 202, 205, 216, 266. *See also* North(ern core), rich states advisory councils, 332, 387

age cohort: 0 to 15, 162, 163, **V3.1a.ii**; 15 to 18, 111

agriculture, 178, 204, 217

aid, 99, 126-27, 402; donors of, **V2.3b.ii**; for economic development (Official Development Assistance, ODA), 10, 94, 125-27, 129, **V2.3d.i**; recipients of, **V2.3b.i**. *See also* military aid

air pollution. *See* pollution

alliances, 67, 72

amenities (economic), 142

American Association for the Advancement of Science, 235

American Indians, 246, 250, 251; Amerindian language, 249

American Statistical Association, 235

Amnesty International (AI), 2, 11, 12, 14, 239, 264-70

anachronisms (political), 387-390

animism, 247-48; **V4.2b.4**

Arab League, 5, 26

Arab OPEC (states), 129, **V2.3d.i(c)**

arable land, 11, 178, **V3.2a.iii(a)**

Arad, Ruth W. and Uzi B., 203

area. *See* land

armaments: industry, 69-72; issues of global concern, 47, 73-74; producers, **V1.3b.iv**

armed personnel, 9, 47-49, **V1.2a.i,ii**

arms control, 74; treaties accepted, **V1.3c.ii**

arrest (and detention), 12, 237, 240, **V4.4a**, 269-70, 278-79

arms trade, 9, 67; exports, 52, 71, **V1.3b.i**; imports, 71-72, 74, **V1.3b.ii**. *See also* weapons transfers

assembly, freedom of, 285, 295-96. *See also* representative assembly

association, freedom of, 237-38, 295-96

atheism, 247-48; **V4.2b.7**

atmosphere, pollution in, 11. *See also* pollution

automobiles, 10, 142, **V2.4a.iii**, 182

autonomy, political, 114, 115, 250; autonomous political units, 331, 333, **V5.2c.i**

Bakongo tribe, 246

balance of trade, 99, 128

balancing power in constitutions, 331-33

ballistic missiles, 74, **V1.3c.i(c)**

About the Author

MICHAEL J. SULLIVAN III is Professor of Political Science at Drexel University. The author of several articles on international arms control in various scholarly journals, Dr. Sullivan has spent the past 8 years measuring global values using data-based management software systems and micro-computer technology.